T0351781

Controlling Crime

A National Bureau of
Economic Research
Conference Report

Controlling Crime
Strategies and Tradeoffs

Edited by **Philip J. Cook, Jens Ludwig, and Justin McCrary**

The University of Chicago Press

Chicago and London

PHILIP J. COOK is the ITT/Terry Sanford Professor of Public Policy and professor of economics and sociology at Duke University, where he is also senior associate dean for faculty and research. He is a research associate of the NBER. JENS LUDWIG is the McCormick Foundation Professor of Social Service Administration, Law, and Public Policy at the University of Chicago, director of the University of Chicago Crime Lab, and a research associate of the NBER. JUSTIN MCCRARY is professor of law at the University of California, Berkeley, and a faculty research fellow of the NBER. All three editors codirect the Working Group on the Economics of Crime at the NBER.

The University of Chicago Press, Chicago 60637
The University of Chicago Press, Ltd., London
© 2011 by the National Bureau of Economic Research
All rights reserved. Published 2011.
Printed in the United States of America

20 19 18 17 16 15 14 13 12 11   1 2 3 4 5
ISBN-13: 978-0-226-11512-2 (cloth)
ISBN-10: 0-226-11512-7 (cloth)

Library of Congress Cataloging-in-Publication Data

Controlling crime : strategies and tradeoffs / edited by Philip J. Cook, Jens Ludwig, Justin McCrary.
    p. cm.—(National Bureau of Economic Research conference report)
    Papers of the NBER conference hosted by the Berkeley Law School on January 15–16, 2010.
    Includes bibliographical references and index.
    ISBN-13: 978-0-226-11512-2 (cloth : alkaline paper)
    ISBN-10: 0-226-11512-7 (cloth : alkaline paper) 1. Crime prevention—Economic aspects—United States—Congresses. 2. Crime prevention—United States—Cost control—Congresses. I. Cook, Philip J., 1946– editor. II. Ludwig, Jens, editor. III. McCrary, Justin, editor. IV. Series: National Bureau of Economic Research conference report.
    HV7432.C66 2012
    364.40973–dc22
                                                                        2011004667

♾ This paper meets the requirements of ANSI/NISO Z39.48-1992 (Permanence of Paper).

Relation of the Directors to the
Work and Publications of the
National Bureau of Economic Research

1. The object of the NBER is to ascertain and present to the economics profession, and to the public more generally, important economic facts and their interpretation in a scientific manner without policy recommendations. The Board of Directors is charged with the responsibility of ensuring that the work of the NBER is carried on in strict conformity with this object.

2. The President shall establish an internal review process to ensure that book manuscripts proposed for publication DO NOT contain policy recommendations. This shall apply both to the proceedings of conferences and to manuscripts by a single author or by one or more coauthors but shall not apply to authors of comments at NBER conferences who are not NBER affiliates.

3. No book manuscript reporting research shall be published by the NBER until the President has sent to each member of the Board a notice that a manuscript is recommended for publication and that in the President's opinion it is suitable for publication in accordance with the above principles of the NBER. Such notification will include a table of contents and an abstract or summary of the manuscript's content, a list of contributors if applicable, and a response form for use by Directors who desire a copy of the manuscript for review. Each manuscript shall contain a summary drawing attention to the nature and treatment of the problem studied and the main conclusions reached.

4. No volume shall be published until forty-five days have elapsed from the above notification of intention to publish it. During this period a copy shall be sent to any Director requesting it, and if any Director objects to publication on the grounds that the manuscript contains policy recommendations, the objection will be presented to the author(s) or editor(s). In case of dispute, all members of the Board shall be notified, and the President shall appoint an ad hoc committee of the Board to decide the matter; thirty days additional shall be granted for this purpose.

5. The President shall present annually to the Board a report describing the internal manuscript review process, any objections made by Directors before publication or by anyone after publication, any disputes about such matters, and how they were handled.

6. Publications of the NBER issued for informational purposes concerning the work of the Bureau, or issued to inform the public of the activities at the Bureau, including but not limited to the NBER Digest and Reporter, shall be consistent with the object stated in paragraph 1. They shall contain a specific disclaimer noting that they have not passed through the review procedures required in this resolution. The Executive Committee of the Board is charged with the review of all such publications from time to time.

7. NBER working papers and manuscripts distributed on the Bureau's web site are not deemed to be publications for the purpose of this resolution, but they shall be consistent with the object stated in paragraph 1. Working papers shall contain a specific disclaimer noting that they have not passed through the review procedures required in this resolution. The NBER's web site shall contain a similar disclaimer. The President shall establish an internal review process to ensure that the working papers and the web site do not contain policy recommendations, and shall report annually to the Board on this process and any concerns raised in connection with it.

8. Unless otherwise determined by the Board or exempted by the terms of paragraphs 6 and 7, a copy of this resolution shall be printed in each NBER publication as described in paragraph 2 above.

Contents

Acknowledgments

The papers in this volume were presented and discussed at an NBER conference hosted by the Berkeley Law School on January 15–16, 2010. The conference, and the preparation and publication of the papers, have been supported by grants by the Public Welfare Foundation and the MacArthur Foundation to the National Bureau of Economic Research and by a visiting scholar award by the Russell Sage Foundation to Jens Ludwig. We thank Christopher Edley, Debby Leff, Jim Poterba, and Michael Stegman for making the conference and the book itself possible.

Acknowledgments

Economical Crime Control

Philip J. Cook and Jens Ludwig

Introduction

During the early 1990s, Americans reported to pollsters that crime was far and away the number one problem facing the country.[1] The remarkable drop in crime that we have experienced since then has substantially improved our standard of living. It has allowed residents to reclaim public spaces, helped reverse the long-term loss of population in many central cities, and enhanced property values and the tax base available to address other public problems. The reduction in robbery, rape, assault, and murder has generated social benefits valued in the tens of billions of dollars. Because crime, particularly violent crime, disproportionately victimizes residents of disadvantaged communities, the drop in violence has been progressive in its effects, and has helped remediate this source of disparity in health and longevity. (Homicide remains the leading cause of death for black males twenty to thirty-four, with a victimization rate fifteen times as high as for white males in this age

Philip J. Cook is the ITT/Terry Sanford Professor of Public Policy and professor of economics and sociology at Duke University, where he is also senior associate dean for faculty and research. He is a research associate of the NBER and a codirector of the NBER Working Group on the Economics of Crime. Jens Ludwig is the McCormick Foundation Professor of Social Service Administration, Law, and Public Policy at the University of Chicago, director of the University of Chicago Crime Lab, a research associate of the NBER, and a codirector of the NBER Working Group on the Economics of Crime.

We thank Jonathan Caulkins, John Donohue, and two anonymous referees for valuable comments on an earlier draft and Clive Belfield and Henry Levin for their assistance with calculating the social benefits of dropout prevention. Erin Hye-Won Kim and Laura Brinkman prepared the figures. Comments can be addressed to either author, at pcook@duke.edu or jludwig@uchicago.edu. All opinions and any errors are our own.

1. In a 1994 Times Mirror survey, 32 percent of the public reported that crime was the "top problem facing the nation;" the next two most frequently mentioned problems were health care (14 percent) and unemployment (13 percent). See Kohut et al. (1994).

group.)[2] Looking to the future, the challenge is to preserve and extend these gains. Crime deserves priority among the litany of social ills, both for the magnitude and the distribution of its costly impact.

So saying, it is also true that crime *control* is a costly enterprise. Criminal justice expenditures more than doubled since the early 1980s, even after adjusting for population growth and inflation. The growth in the prison and jail population has been particularly costly. The United States currently incarcerates about 2.3 million individuals, 1 percent of all adults. The *per capita* incarceration rate has increased by a factor of five since the early 1970s, and has reached levels that have no precedent in American history. In his seminal article on crime and punishment, Gary Becker (1968) observed that the social cost of crime is the sum of the direct costs of victimization and the costs of control. By that definition, the crime "problem" may have been growing despite the crime drop of the last two decades. The costs of control include not just the public expenditures, but also the pains of imprisonment to the prisoners themselves. The preponderance of the incarcerated population consists of youthful minority males from disadvantaged neighborhoods.

The Great Recession has led to cuts in criminal justice expenditures, and the trend in imprisonment appears to have finally turned the corner. That raises the question of whether the crime drop can be sustained. State and local revenue shortfalls have engendered intense interest in cost-cutting measures that do not sacrifice public safety.[3] We believe there is reason for optimism, simply because current criminal justice allocations and policies appear to be inefficient—more crime control could be accomplished with fewer resources. Of course, efficiency is not the only goal of public policy, and other values also play a role. For example, public support for long prison sentences may stem in part from a willingness to pay for retribution against those who have violated society's norms, regardless of the effect on crime (if any). But it is important to at least understand the tradeoff between retribution and crime prevention. In any event, one way to reduce the demand for retribution is to reduce the amount of crime.

What would a more efficient crime-control strategy look like? The crime problem is often framed as a debate between those who favor a "tough" punitive approach, versus those who favor a "soft" approach that focuses on prevention or remediation programs to improve legitimate opportunities

2. Because homicide victims tend to be young, nearly as many years of potential life are lost among black males from murder as from the nation's leading killer, heart disease.
3. The Center on Budget and Policy Priorities projects the cumulative shortfall for 2011 in state budgets nationwide to be on the order of $140 billion (Williams et al. 2010). The Pew Center on the States, working with the Council of State Governments Justice Center and Vera Institute of Justice has, since 2006, consulted with a number of state governments to find ways to reduce incarceration rates while preserving public safety.

for those at risk. But the canonical economic model of crime from Becker (1968) suggests that the decision to commit crime involves a weighing of both benefits and costs. This model suggests the logical possibility that both tough and soft approaches might be useful in reducing crime. It is ultimately an empirical question about where the marginal dollar can be spent most effectively. The goal is to find the diverse "golden portfolio" that is broadly responsive to the multifaceted nature of crime, and which takes account of the likelihood of diminishing returns to any one approach.

Rather than thinking in terms of tough versus soft, we find it more useful to categorize crime-control strategies by whether they seek to change the environment that determines the opportunities for crime (whether crime "pays"), or instead try to change individual propensities toward criminal behavior through investments in education, child development, drug treatment, and so forth. This distinction between criminal opportunity and criminal propensity helps move us toward a more pragmatic rather than ideological discussion about how best to control crime, and also makes clear that tough and soft approaches may sometimes be complementary. For example, in the 1990s, Boston's Operation Ceasefire combined a tough deterrence strategy directed at gang members with church-based community programs to help gang members who wanted to reform. The combination of enhancing both the threat of punishment and legitimate opportunities helped strengthen the deterrent effect, while also helping garner valuable community support for the program (Kennedy, Piehl, and Braga 1996). Similarly, some soft social programs can involve elements of coercion, like compulsory schooling laws or higher alcohol taxes.

The quest for a golden portfolio of crime-control measures reflects the economics orientation of the majority of the book's authors. This perspective represents one contribution of our volume to crime policy analysis. For example, much of the academic and public debate has been about whether America's prison boom has reduced crime. But within an economics framework, the question of whether (and by how much) imprisonment reduces crime is not well specified. Since prison consumes resources that could have been spent on other activities, a better question is whether imprisonment reduces crime by *more than* it would have been reduced by alternative crime-control uses of the same resources.

This attention to clearly specified counterfactuals—"compared to what?"—is also characteristic of this volume's approach to empirical evidence as well. Popular discussions of the value of different crime control strategies often focus on whether crime rates are higher or lower this year compared to the previous year, even though crime rates change over time for a large number of reasons—only some of which are understood, much less under the control of government officials. Analysts have difficulty identifying the causal effects of government interventions on crime, in part because crime is both cause and consequence of criminal justice policies and budgets. Police are concentrated in areas with high crime rates for the same reason that people in doctor's offices are more likely to be sick compared to the general population. Economists have been among the most enthusiastic converts to the design-based approach to empirical research, which focuses on the use of randomized and natural experiments to overcome challenges to causal inference (see, for example, Angrist and Pischke 2009, 2010).

In terms of substantive conclusions, the findings summarized here suggest that the push for longer prison sentences over the last three decades is likely to have sharply diminishing returns. More cost-effective uses of those resources are readily identifiable, even within the criminal justice system: for example, by putting more police on the street, or improving the capacity of the courts to deliver swift, certain, and mild punishments for drug use by convicts on supervised release. The implication is that the inefficiency with our current criminal justice system arises not necessarily because the system is too punitive, but rather because it focuses too much on meting out severe rather than certain punishments.

The private sector also has an underappreciated role to play in reducing crime. Much of the stunning decline in motor vehicle thefts and burglaries since the 1980s is due to changes in private precautions, enhanced by technological improvements in vehicle locks, electronic tracking devices, alarm systems, and means of payment. The number of private security employees exceeds the number of public law enforcement officers and has been growing faster, trends that are surely relevant to the crime drop. Private security protects whole neighborhoods in business improvement districts, and in that arena generates benefits to society far in excess of costs. Private actions could be encouraged through changes in insurance regulation and other reforms. Regulation of private consumption of intoxicants is also relevant. While the net effects of changing regulations of illegal drugs are difficult to predict, we are confident in predicting that increases in the price of alcohol (such as through taxation) would reduce crime.

The chapters in this volume also dispel some of the pessimism that lingers from the 1960s and 1970s about the ability of social policy to prevent or remediate criminality. The available evidence suggests that giving people money and jobs is not as cost-effective in reducing crime as investing in human capital. Our improved understanding of human development suggests academic and mental health interventions may be most productive when delivered relatively earlier in life, while "social-cognitive skills" (in Ken Dodge's terms) are amenable to intervention even among the highest-risk, criminally involved adolescents and adults. Most of the social programs that help prevent criminal behavior are carried out by agencies outside of criminal justice, and so controlling crime is incidental to their main purpose. But ignoring effects on crime may lead to substantial underinvestment in these programs.

The next section documents the growth in America's incarceration rate and overall criminal justice expenditures, which provides the context for the remainder of this chapter (and the volume as a whole). The third section then sketches a conceptual framework for understanding crime in terms of criminal opportunity and the distribution of criminal propensities. The following sections discuss the evidence on how to change the environment to make criminal opportunities less attractive, and then how to change individual propensities toward antisocial or criminal behavior. The final section provides a summary list of noteworthy interventions, and concludes with a thought experiment about reallocating resources currently expended on imprisonment.

The Growth in Incarceration and Criminal Justice Expenditures

For half a century, from the 1920s through the 1970s, the state and federal prison population hovered around 110 per 100,000 with little variation despite the very large swings in crime rates (see figure I.1). The upward trend in the rate of imprisonment began in the mid 1970s. The number in local jails also increased dramatically during this period, and by 2008 the overall incarceration rate was equal to 753 per 100,000, a total of 2.3 million people. That rate, equal to 1 percent of all adults, is a multiple of the

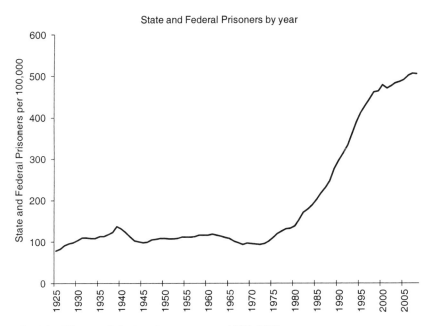

Fig. I.1   History of the imprisonment rate, 1925–2008

Source: www.albany.edu/sourcebook/tost_6/html.

Criminal Justice Spending by year

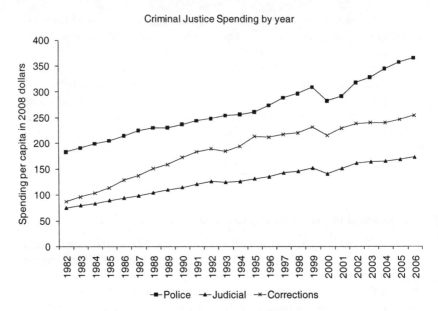

Fig. I.2   Combined local, state, and federal spending per capita in 2008 dollars by area
Source: bjs.ojp.usdoj.gov/content/glance/tables/exptyptab.cfm.

incarceration rates found in other Organization for Economic Co-operation and Development (OECD) nations, and even exceeds the rates found in repressive regimes found in Russia, Cuba, China, and Iran. The direct costs to American taxpayers of locking up so many, and supervising millions of others on conditional release, amounted to $70 billion in 2006—about $230 per capita. The increase in spending on corrections has been proportionally larger than police or the courts (figure I.2), although there has been impressive growth in all three areas.

A notable share of the growth in imprisonment, but by no means all, was associated with the war on drugs. The number of state prisoners locked up for drug offenses has increased from 19,000 to over 250,000 since 1980, while the number in federal prisons increased by over 70,000 during this period. (See figures I.3 and I.4.) But the data in figure I.3 make clear that most of the increase in state prisoners comes from greater use of prison for violent crimes.

An interesting decomposition of the growth in the state prison population from 1984 to 2002 was computed by Raphael and Stoll (2009). During this period the prison population almost tripled. Something like 20 percent of this increase derived from a large increase in the parole failure rate (from 13 percent annually in 1980 to 29 percent in 2003), which was apparently due to increasingly punitive policy, rather than a change in behavior of the

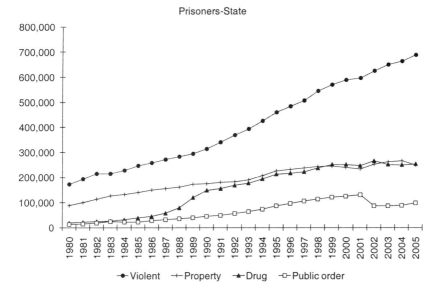

Fig. I.3   History of state prisoners by offense type, 1980–2005

Source: hjs.ojp.usdoj.gov/content/glance/tables/corrtyptab.cfm.

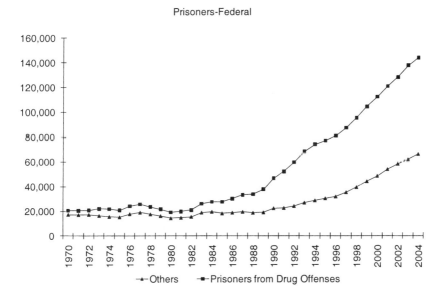

Fig. I.4   History of federal prison population, 1970–2004

Source: www.albany.edu/sourcebook/tost_6/html.

parolees. With respect to the growth in the prison population that was not due to parolee recidivism, 48 percent was due to an increase in the likelihood of imprisonment given crime, and 35 percent to longer time served for a given type of crime. The latter trend is associated with legislated sentence enhancements (including the three strikes laws) and truth in sentencing laws. Interestingly, this increase in prison sentence lengths would be almost invisible if one were to simply compare the average prison sentence length for people incarcerated today versus, say, a quarter century ago—the share of people in prison for relatively minor offenses has been increasing over time, diluting the average sentence length.

Why did America increase its prison population so much over the past three decades? William Spelman (2009) argues that the growth in state budgets is the most important driver of growth in state prison populations. From 1977 to 2005, "prison populations grew at roughly the same rate and during the same periods as spending on education, welfare, health and hospitals, highways, parks, and natural resources" (29). His analysis accurately predicts what we have actually seen, the drop in the prison population during 2009, evidently resulting from the advent of declining state budgets. Yet it is important to note that growth in government revenues is only a proximate explanation, and one that did not apply prior to the 1970s (Raphael 2009). The US incarceration rate held steady from the 1920s to the 1970s, even during large swings in gross domestic product (GDP) and government revenues.

So what exactly is it about the political environment in America during the last generation that has linked increased government revenues to expanded imprisonment? Whatever the underlying political dynamic pushing prison construction and tougher sentencing, it is surely relevant that most of the prisoners are from politically marginal groups (Alexander 2010; Loury 2010). At present around one out of every nine black men ages twenty to thirty-four is in prison (Pew 2008), and high school dropouts in this group are more likely to be in prison than employed (Raphael and Sills 2008). Bruce Western traces imprisonment rates across decades, finding that the percentage of black male dropouts who had served time in prison by age thirty-five increased from 17 percent for those born in the late 1940s, to 59 percent for the late 1960s cohorts and around 70 percent in the late 1970s cohorts (figure I.5). Both the levels and changes over time in lifetime imprisonment risk are much lower for whites.

The vastly disproportionate racial impact of the incarceration surge is one of its most problematic features, but leaves open the question of the overall balance between costs and benefits. How much of the crime drop (which disproportionately benefits minority neighborhoods) is due to the surge in imprisonment?

The evidence on which to reach a conclusion on this vital issue is not as strong as we would like. Widespread skepticism about the benefits of

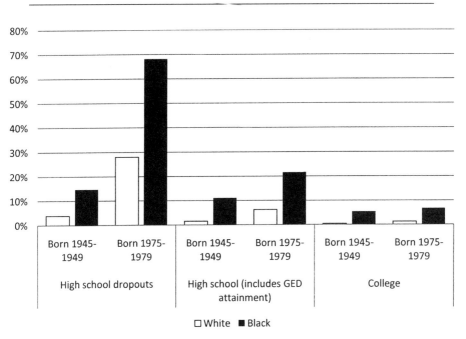

Fig. I.5   Risk of Imprisonment by Education Level and Race
Source: Western (2006, 27).

mass incarceration stems from the fact that the growth in imprisonment has spanned both periods when crime rates were increasing and declining. But this sort of simple time-series association is a weak basis for drawing inferences about policy impacts. Imagine the plight of governors or mayors who had the misfortune of being in office in the late 1980s, subject to criticism as violence surged in their particular jurisdictions—even though crime rates were increasing almost everywhere in the United States, probably due to the epidemic of crack cocaine.[4] On the other hand any governor or mayor lucky enough to be in office during the 1990s, when crime rates were dropping almost everywhere across the country, looked like a genius (and indeed many have developed lucrative consulting practices dispensing their own magic potion for crime control).

A more scientific approach to the study of imprisonment and crime still leaves us short of a confident conclusion. There is some persuasive evidence, summarized in the chapter in this volume by Steven Durlauf and Daniel Nagin, that crime choices are sensitive to the probability of punishment. Since the fraction of crimes that resulted in a prison term increased

4. The dominant view among scholars is that the massive surge in youthful homicide and robbery rates that began in the United States in the mid-1980s was due to the invention and spread of crack cocaine (Blumstein 1995; Levitt 2004).

between 1984 and 2002, it is reasonable to conclude that the increased use of imprisonment does get part of the credit for the crime drop—a conclusion supported by the assumption that imprisonment also prevents crime through the incapacitation effect. But what is the counterfactual? If the vast increase in prison expenditures came at the cost of better educational programs, treatment for mental illness or drug abuse, and improvements in policing, then the net effect of the imprisonment boom is not so clear, even qualitatively.

Conceptualizing Crime and Crime Control

Our vision for this volume begins with the view that crime is a complex, multifaceted phenomenon for which the most productive portfolio of responses is likely to be quite diverse. Guidance in imagining that portfolio comes from thinking of observed crime rates as the outcomes of an interaction between potential criminals (which is to say, most everyone), and the environment of opportunities, licit and illicit, for achieving individual goals (Cook 1986). In this account the promising crime-reducing interventions include both those that focus on changing the structure of opportunities, and those that invest in individuals to improve their access to licit opportunities while strengthening their resistance to criminal enticements.

Much of the public conversation about crime often focuses on just one aspect of this framework, the character of the youths. In the simplistic version, the population consists of good guys and bad guys. The bad guys commit crimes and the good guys do not. The crime rate is proportional to the number of bad guys who are at large. Crime control then is a matter of locking up as many bad guys as possible (or, when the bad guys are immigrants, deporting them). Public opinion polls suggest that much of the public believes that offenders are made, not born, and so the number of bad guys can also be reduced through better parenting. In any event, the natural tendency is to seek explanations for crime increases in the character of the youths, and some version of the old refrain of "What's the matter with kids today?" (Cook 1985; Cook and Laub 1998). This sort of explanation, in more nuanced form, has also been prominent in analyzing the crime drop, where the legalization of abortion in the early 1970s (Donohue and Levitt 2001; Joyce 2009) and the reduction in lead ingestion since it was removed from gasoline (Reyes 2007) are offered as mechanisms that helped produce cohorts of children with lower criminal propensity.

An extreme version of this view had considerable influence during the great epidemic of youth violence that began in 1984 and crested in the early 1990s. The most prominent commentators at the time were William Bennett, John DiIulio, and John Walters (1996), who attributed the extraordinary surge of youth violence to the increase in the number of "superpredators"— youths who had grown up in chaotic neighborhoods with little adult guidance ("moral poverty") and became remorselessly violent and incorrigible criminals. The Bennett-DiIulio-Walters explanation for the tripling of youth homicide rates was simply that there were that many more killers in our midst: more criminals, more crime. That account helped persuade legislatures in most states to facilitate waiver of juveniles to adult court, and provided support for tougher sentencing across the board.

The superpredator explanation was plausible, but wrong. A careful study of homicide patterns during that period has documented that a ten-year span of birth cohorts were caught up in the epidemic simultaneously, and that their involvement also subsided together—demonstrating that the dominant effect of the era was not the deteriorating character of the youths who were coming of age during that period, but rather the changing circumstances in which at-risk youths found themselves (Cook and Laub 1998, 2002).

A number of commentators have since documented the likely source of those changing circumstances—the advent of the crack cocaine era, which engendered gang violence in contests for control of street markets, and recruited many minority teens into drug dealing while arming them with guns. The resulting violence may have overwhelmed the resources of the police and courts in many cities, further aggravating the problem. Crime rates among groups who were on the front lines of the epidemic were extraordinarily volatile—young black men in the District of Columbia experienced a ten-fold increase in their homicide victimization rate during the epidemic increase, and a few years after the peak the rate was back near the pre-epidemic level (Cook and Laub 1998). We can only conclude that the particular mix of youths in a community does not come close to determining the crime rate.

What is missing from the "good guys, bad guys" account of crime is that crime is a choice, and as such is influenced by incentives as well as character. Indeed, the theory of crime developed by economists begins where the character analysis leaves off, and focuses on how incentives influence crime-related choices for someone of given character (or, as economists would say, preferences). The simplistic notion that crime is proportional to the number of criminals provides no more illumination than asserting that farm output is proportional to the number of farmers. Just how many farmers are active, and how much they produce, depends on incentives mediated by the relevant input and product markets. Similarly, the incentives to engage in crime relate to the perceived payoff to crime, the opportunity cost of time spent doing crime, and the risks associated with crime—including inherent risks (gang warfare, victim retaliation) and the risk of punishment. Those incentives depend on individual circumstances and are subject to change with changes in criminal and licit opportunities.

The idea that potential criminals respond to incentives has been met with some skepticism by criminologists, who point out that potential criminals are rarely well informed about the prevailing penalties for different crimes, and that many crimes are committed by people who are not thinking clearly because they are (for example) surrounded by their peers, drunk, high, or sexually aroused. But the fact that a large number of individual crimes are committed without much regard for the consequences does not invalidate the idea that the total number of criminal acts varies with respect to the benefits and costs of crime. Many people seem to pay little attention or have limited information about the sales tax on consumer goods (for example, see Chetty, Looney, and Kroft 2009), yet typically an increase in the tax rate for some good tends to depress the quantity of the good that is purchased. In order for a change in incentives to change the aggregate level of some behavior, it is enough for just a subset of the population to pay attention and adapt their behavior.

In short, by focusing on crimes as choices made in response to the available options and individual circumstances, the economists' framework provides guidance in understanding trends and patterns, and also in identifying some of the interventions that are likely to be effective in reducing crime. The relevant interventions go well beyond expanding enforcement efforts, although law enforcement is a vital part of the mix. The proximate goal can be loosely expressed as taking the profit out of crime, which invites discussions on such topics as how to incentivize installation and use of better locks and alarms, how to shrink illicit markets for drugs or stolen property, and how best to provide at-risk youths with attractive licit opportunities. A variety of actors play a role in influencing opportunities for crime. Indeed, much of the relevant action is private, as exemplified by the story of motor vehicle theft, as told in the chapter by Philip Cook and John MacDonald. The fact that fewer vehicles were stolen in 2008 than 1980, despite the doubling in the number of vehicles on the road, is at least partly the result of the great improvement in locking devices built into modern vehicles—a car equipped with an electronic immobilizer, which most new cars are, is essentially impossible to steal without either the key or a tow truck. And owners who choose to equip their vehicles with an electronic tracking device like LoJack or OnStar greatly enhance the ability of the police to track them if stolen and arrest the thief or a chop shop owner.

For violent crime it is useful to understand that criminal opportunity is influenced by social context. Youths typically commit their crimes in groups, and organized criminal gangs are contributors to crime and violence in some cities. Addressing the interactions and social consequences that induce criminal violence provides a richer menu of possible interventions. For example, Boston's Operation Ceasefire of the 1990s sought to create a group deterrent to gun misuse by threatening the entire gang with negative consequences for gun misuse by any member (Kennedy, Piehl, and Braga 1996; Kennedy 2009). Street mediation of violent conflicts has been an important element of a number of interventions, including the Crisis Intervention Network implemented in Philadelphia in the 1970s, the Chicago Crisis Intervention Services Project that Irving Spergel implemented in the 1980s, and the more recent Chicago Ceasefire project developed by Gary Slutkin (Spergel 1986; Skogan et al. 2009).

Curtailing criminal opportunity is an important goal for much of the crime-control portfolio of interventions, but not the whole story. The choice to commit crimes also reflects the opportunity cost of crime involvement, which is to say the quality of licit opportunities, as well as personal qualities encapsulated in the term "personality." The notion that some youths enter adolescence with a greater propensity to crime than others takes us back to the focus on character, but with this proviso—in the economists' account, character is not destiny, and does not in itself determine crime involvement. In any event, making well-directed investments in child development, and in skill building at all ages, can shape character and be part of the crime-control portfolio. There are a variety of interventions that may help direct individuals away from a crime trajectory, starting at birth or even before. A common feature of these efforts is that to a greater or lesser extent, these programs supplement and support the traditional role of the family in providing for children and instilling human and social capital. And the possibility of preempting or derailing criminal careers through investing in individuals at risk does not end with childhood. Intervention opportunities continue for adults who are deemed likely to be attracted to crime due to mental illness, drug dependence, lack of marketable skills, criminal associates, or other reasons.

In sum, given our understanding of crime as a choice that reflects both individual propensities and incentives—both of which are malleable—there is a broad spectrum of policies and programs that can contribute to the goal of reducing crime rates without expanding the prison population. The list of alternatives begins with more effective allocation of prison (as both a threat and an incapacitation device), and goes on to include alternative punishments; situational crime prevention and better mobilization of private inputs; stronger regulation of criminogenic commodities, especially alcohol and guns; more investment in treatment for drug addiction, mental illness, and conduct disordered youths; programs intended to improve job opportunities for released offenders; family, education, housing, and income maintenance programs intended to assist parents in the task of raising children who are productive members of the community. This rich menu of possibilities needs to be evaluated carefully. Viewed from the perspective of cost-effective crime control, some of these options are more promising than others.

Changing the Offending Environment

The most obvious way policymakers can change the incentives people face for criminal behavior is by changing the way that the criminal justice system works. But this is not the only way. Policymakers can also change the social environment, for example, by changing the opportunities that people have to get income by legal means or the control of illicit drugs.

Efficient Sanctioning

From the crime-control viewpoint, the most important role of the criminal justice system (CJS) is to deter criminal activity by generating a credible threat of punishment contingent on crime commission. Since for serious crimes the punishment usually takes the form of incarceration (jail or prison time), the CJS also reduces crime through incapacitation of those who have a relatively high criminal propensity.

As described previously, there has been considerable growth in the resources allocated to police, courts, and corrections at the local, state, and federal levels. There is good reason to believe that the CJS is effective in reducing crime, and also that it is inefficient, in the sense that the same crime-reduction effect could be accomplished with fewer resources if appropriate reforms were adopted. Of particular interest here is the possibility of economizing on the use of prison and jail.

The usual economic model of criminal choice, such as the one proposed by Steven Durlauf and Daniel Nagin in their chapter, concludes that the crime rate is inversely related both to the probability and the severity of punishment. Various refinements of the theory, in addition to a good deal of empirical evidence, suggest that the deterrent effect with respect to a unit increase in severity declines as severity increases, but not so with respect to probability. Moreover, if there is a fixed cost to arrest and conviction (possibly including pretrial jail time or bail payments, legal costs, as well as damage to reputation), then the formal sentence following conviction is only one component of the overall negative consequence of arrest. For that reason we would expect some deterrent even if the formal punishment were zero.

The threat of a prison term deters crime, but time served in prison further reduces crime through the incapacitation effect. The simple notion here is that offenders who are locked up or otherwise incapacitated are unable to commit crimes—at least crimes against victims on the "outside." The size of the incapacitation effect depends on how criminally active the offender would have been if left at large. Here too there is reason to believe that the marginal effect declines with longer prison terms, since criminal careers tend to be quite short. It is likely that many prisoners serving long terms have reached what Alfred Blumstein has called the point of redemption, when their crime rate if free would be no higher than age peers who had never been convicted (Blumstein and Nakamura 2009).

While the incapacitation effect is easy to grasp, it is not the same as the net reduction in crime stemming from locking up a particular individual. If the offender is a drug dealer, it is quite possible that another will step in to take his place, with little net effect on drug related crime. Replacement may also be found in other gang- and group-oriented crimes. It is also true that most prisoners are released eventually, and the net effect of the prison term on the crime rate depends on the effect of the prison experience and its consequences for the postrelease behavior of the offender. The evidence on this issue is mixed at best.

These ideas suggest a number of ways in which the criminal justice system might be made more efficient.

Focus on Punishment Certainty, Not Severity

The relevance of the declining returns to punishment severity to the use of prison and jail is clear. Consider two sentencing regimes. In regime A, there is a 1 percent chance of a ten-year sentence for robbery, while in regime B there is a 10 percent chance of a one-year sentence. If there are the same number of robberies in the two regimes, then in a steady state there will end up being the same number of robbers in prison. But the theory and evidence both suggest that regime B will have a greater deterrent than regime A. The result: more robberies in regime A, and paradoxically, a larger prison population.

A confirmation of this view in one arena comes from the evidence on coerced abstinence. A randomized field trial in Honolulu, Hawaii's Opportunity Probation with Enforcement (HOPE), reported very strong results from subjecting felony probationers to frequent random drug tests with an immediate (but brief) jail term in the case of failure (Kleiman 2009; Hawken and Kleiman 2009). This experimental group had a far lower arrest rate and revocation rate than the control group, who were less likely to be caught using drugs, but with the possibility of a more severe penalty (probation revocation). The experimental group ended up committing less crime and receiving less total days of incarceration.

Much of the increase in the prison population since 1980 has come from longer sentences, including life sentences with no possibility of parole. For offenders with short time horizons, the deterrent effect from extending prison sentences into old age is likely to be very small, but the cost to the state or federal government is substantial. Durlauf and Nagin suggest the payoff from CJS activities that increase the probability of punishment are likely to have a greater benefit-cost ratio than lengthening already long prison sentences.

The Value of Stepped-Up Policing

Criminologists have long been skeptical about the value of simply putting more police on the street to carry out standard reactive policing practices like random preventative patrol and responding to 911 calls for service. To support this view, criminologists point to the fact that places with relatively more police do not reliably have lower rates of crime (Sherman 2002). Yet the challenge to drawing valid inferences from this sort of correlational evidence was noted earlier—more crime may lead to more police on the street, potentially masking any crime-reducing benefits from increased police resources.

While the 2004 report of a National Research Council committee on policing was agnostic about whether there is a link between police strength and crime (Skogan and Frydl 2004, 224–5), in our view more recent research provides stronger evidence for a causal connection. Evans and Owens (2007) examine what happened to crime when the US Department of Justice under the Clinton Administration distributed Community Oriented Policing Services (COPS) hiring grants to local police departments, a convincing "natural experiment" that helps overcome the omitted variables concerns that plague most previous studies.[5] Their results suggest that each additional dollar devoted to police hiring may generate from four dollars to eight dollars in benefits to society (Donohue and Ludwig 2007). *Why* police reduce crime is not entirely clear—whether police deter crime by reducing the availability of attractive criminal opportunities, or simply incapacitate more criminals by making more arrests. Regardless of the underlying mechanism, these findings are important in part because of the feasibility of implementation—it is relatively easy to increase police department budgets and hire more officers. An increased role for federal support for police hiring may be particularly valuable. The federal government (unlike state or local governments) can engage in countercyclical deficit spending to help increase police resources during recessions, when robberies and burglaries tend to increase.

The efficiency of police spending could be enhanced further by changing what police do. Despite the widely perceived success of New York City's "broken windows" policing efforts, there is no evidence that having police spend more of their time issuing citations or making misdemeanor arrests for minor offenses is an effective way to reduce the prevalence of more serious offenses (Levitt 2004; Harcourt and Ludwig 2006, 2007). On the other hand, a variety of high-quality randomized experiments find that crime can be reduced in targeted areas by explicitly shifting police time and attention from reactive to proactive policing strategies focused on identifying and solving the local crime problems that are of primary policy concern. Focusing police resources on high-crime "hot spots" also has a firm basis in

---

5. The size of these COPS hiring grants varied across areas in a way that was systematically related to the level of crime in each jurisdiction, but was apparently unrelated to preexisting crime trends. A difference-in-difference comparison finds that increased police hiring (even absent any changes in police practices) causes sizable reductions in crime, with an elasticity of crime with respect to police officers per capita of −.26 for property crimes and −.99 for violent crimes (see also Levitt 2002). What police actually do to reduce crime remains something of a mystery, since the elasticity of crime with respect to the clearance rate (the ratio of arrests to crimes committed) seems to be relatively low. Thanks to Steve Levitt for helpful conversations on this point.

the evidence (Skogan and Frydl 2004; Braga and Weisburd 2010). Whether these strategies simply displace crime to other areas is more difficult to determine, because policing experiments usually have better statistical power to detect effects on the targeted areas than on the much larger set of areas to which crime might be displaced.[6] Still, it appears that positive spillovers from focused policing are as likely as negative. But there is also a relevant implementation challenge associated with getting police to change what they do—after all, there is presumably a reason why more police departments are not implementing these strategies more widely or intensively.

Changing law enforcement practices appears to be a particularly promising avenue for reducing one of the most socially costly aspects of America's crime problem—gun violence. Guns greatly increase the lethality of violent crime (Zimring 1968; Cook 1991). The prevalence of guns in the US helps explain why our homicide rate is a multiple of other developed countries, even those that have similar levels of overall violent crime (Zimring and Hawkins 1997). For better or worse, the US Supreme Court has recently struck down local handgun bans and may be moving in the direction of preempting other sorts of local gun regulations, and the national political scene is such that any change in federal gun laws seems unlikely for the foreseeable future.

Against this backdrop, it is encouraging that stepped-up police efforts to get guns off the street seems to generate sizable declines in different measures of illegal gun use (Cohen and Ludwig 2003), although the challenge is to implement these types of "stop-and-frisk" activities in ways that do not exacerbate police-community tensions. Other research has found that the underground gun market seems to have more frictions than commonly thought (Cook et al. 2007). These findings indicate the potential value of enforcement activities like buy-and-bust operations, efforts to debrief arrestees about where they obtained their guns, and rewards for information about illegal gun possession, although good evaluation evidence confirming the value of such strategies is currently lacking (Cook and Ludwig 2006).

Encouraging Private Cooperation with the Criminal Justice System

In their chapter, Cook and MacDonald point out that the effectiveness of police depends very much on the voluntary cooperation of citizens, and encouraging productive cooperation is a key part of the portfolio of crime control. Voluntary cooperation starts with reporting crimes to the police and includes the provision of useful reports and tips during the investigation and, in some cases, testimony at trial. Since these private inputs are typically costly and uncompensated, they are likely to be undersupplied. Cooperation can be encouraged through more generous victim compensation payments (which are contingent on cooperation) and stepped-up efforts to protect

6. Thanks to Justin McCrary for highlighting this point.

witnesses. Also of fundamental importance is to establish a trusting relationship between the police and the community.

Two specific mechanisms to improve cooperation have been carefully evaluated. Ayres and Levitt (1998) found that jurisdictions that were organized to take advantage of LoJack (transmitting devices installed in vehicles that could be switched on remotely if the vehicle was stolen) enjoyed a substantially lower vehicle-theft rate as a result, with a benefit-cost ratio of about twenty. The authors suggest since thieves cannot tell which vehicles have LoJack installed, it has a general deterrent effect—and it helps identify and shut down the chop shops. The second example is Cook and MacDonald's evaluation of crime prevention efforts organized by business improvement districts in Los Angeles. There too the benefit-cost ratio is about twenty. These districts hired private security guards and enjoyed reduced crime rates, presumably because offenders perceived an increased probability of arrest and less attractive criminal opportunities. The crime reduction was coupled with a reduction in the number of arrests, so there were savings to the CJS.

Alternatives to Incarceration

Reducing crime through incapacitation does not require prison and can be accomplished to some extent by restrictions on behavior, perhaps enforced through electronic monitoring and regular check-ins with an agent. Such approaches are far less costly than prison itself and can be coupled with a fine if deterrence is the issue.

The chapter by Anne Piehl and Geoffrey Williams explores the mystery of why courts in fact make so little use of financial penalties for crimes more serious than traffic violations. One problem is that it is difficult to collect a fine from a defendant who has little or no assets. Garnishing their wages may weaken whatever incentive they have to work. More importantly, perhaps, is that courts are typically not well organized to serve as collection agencies, and have been reluctant to do what is necessary in this area. The high costs of collection documented in several studies may reflect inefficient practice or lack of commitment on the part of the courts. A robust program of fine collection requires a real threat of a jail term for failure to pay. It remains an open question whether there is an opportunity to replace some jail terms with fines (as in the traditional sentence of "30 days or 30 dollars") so as to reduce social costs while preserving the deterrent. In his comment, David Sklansky endorses the Piehl-Williams conclusion that fines should be evaluated relative to the alternative means of punishment, rather than on the basis of whether the revenues exceed the costs of collection. He encourages a broader discussion that brings in other intermediate sanctions, such as those conveyed by the term "restorative justice."

Jobs and Income Supports

A long-established belief is that crime rates are exacerbated by declines in economic conditions, such as the deindustrialization that occurred in cities like Chicago starting in the mid-1980s, or more recently the Great Recession that has increased unemployment rates nationwide. The best available empirical evidence suggests that recessions do result in modest increases in burglary and robbery, but homicide appears immune to the business cycle and motor vehicle theft is actually procyclical, presumably because stolen vehicles are worth more during good times than bad (Cook and Zarkin 1985; Raphael and Winter-Ebmer 2001; Bushway, Cook, and Phillips 2010).[7] In any event, other things being equal (which they are decidedly not during the business cycle) our theory predicts that an improvement in licit opportunities will make crime a less attractive choice.

In practice, efforts to improve the employment prospects of released offenders have met with limited success. Prisoners typically have little work experience or education, and many employers refuse to hire ex-cons or are actually barred from doing so for sensitive positions. A number of programs intended to improve employment opportunities have been evaluated. According to Steven Raphael's review, the results have not been particularly encouraging, either in improving employment over the long term, or in reducing criminal involvement. There have been a few highlights, including the residential program for high-risk youths called Job Corps, but a number of programs delivering training or other employment services have failed to reduce recidivism over the long run (Redcross et al. 2009, 2010).

Raphael argues in his chapter that the least encouraging evidence is with respect to the value of straight income supports. In their chapter, Sara Heller, Brian Jacob, and Jens Ludwig find that while there is some evidence that changes in family poverty status may reduce rates of criminal involvement by disadvantaged youth, the effects appear to be small. Of course, these programs may be justified by other goals. If the public supports funding programs to, say, improve the housing conditions of poor families without consideration of the potential effects on delinquency, evidence of crime reduction is a bonus that supports an already desirable program.

Heller, Jacob, and Ludwig note that social policies designed to reduce the concentration of poverty by helping poor families move to lower-poverty areas may also help reduce their criminal involvement, but the scope for achieving large-scale reductions in crime through that sort of strategy is limited by the great difficulty of getting families to move to different types of

---

7. We note that the treatment induced by changes in economic conditions operates through mechanisms other than the proportion of the population out of work—for example, the income that people have available to spend on criminogenic commodities like alcohol, or government revenues available for crime prevention activities such as corrections or police. Grogger (2000) argues for a focus on the relationship between wages and crime, rather than unemployment and crime, noting that individual decisions about both legal employment and criminal behavior will be driven by market wages. Grogger shows that in the National Longitudinal Survey of Youth, employment rates were quite similar for the 24 percent of youth who reported receiving some income from crime during the past year compared to the 76 percent who did not engage in crime, while wages and annual hours of work were quite different for the two groups ($4.34 vs. $497, and 1,500 vs. 1,755 hours per year of work).

neighborhoods. While families living in public housing (a small fraction of the total poverty population) can be induced to move to less distressed areas by offering them a housing voucher, providing housing-voucher subsidies to families already living in private-market housing rarely leads to relocation to a more prosperous neighborhood. Furthermore, if substantial numbers of poor households did relocate, their new neighborhoods might experience some increase in crime as a result of the actions or the influence of the teenage children of these households. That outcome has not been measured in the experimental studies. There is some suggestive evidence from studies of court-ordered school desegregation that the net system-wide effect of resorting disadvantaged youth across social settings is to reduce violent crime (Weiner, Lutz, and Ludwig 2009). Deconcentrating poverty is a long-term project that has much to recommend it, but the potential effects on crime are not well understood.

Drug Policy

The government's influence on crime rates is not confined to the criminal justice system. The uses of government authority to regulate, tax, and prohibit various commodities and activities may influence crime rates by creating or curtailing criminal opportunities. Most notable is the prohibition of transactions in and possession of cocaine, heroin, methamphetamine, and various other recreational drugs that are much in demand. The prohibition reduces use, which may in turn curtail some criminal activity associated with the intoxicating effects of these drugs. But it also creates crime, by defining as criminal anyone who uses or supplies them, and, more importantly, by creating underground markets that engender violence. (Another potential mechanism is that the high prices of illicit drugs may induce users to commit crime to support their habits.) Of course, crime and the costs of crime control are not the only considerations in regulating alluring and potentially damaging intoxicants. In an earlier era the United States repealed alcohol prohibition in part because of the crime and corruption it induced (Cook 2007).

The chapter by John J. Donohue III, Ben Ewing, and David Peloquin provides a thorough analysis of the dilemmas associated with regulating illicit drugs, focusing on marijuana and cocaine. The stakes are very high—currently 500,000 people are incarcerated for drug offenses, including over half of federal prisoners and one-fifth of state prisoners. The enormous growth in the prison population since 1980 is costly and its effectiveness remains unclear—most of the drug-crime prisoners are there for selling, yet during this period the average street price of illicit drugs has actually declined (Reuter 2001; Caulkins et al. 2004; Fries et al. 2008).[8] Prohibition has also

8. As noted earlier, one challenge with drawing inferences about policy impacts from simple time-series evidence is the possibility of changes in other factors over time—which in the

induced a high level of systemic violence, with notable surges of murder and robbery associated with the growth in heroin markets during the Vietnam era, and then with the subsequent epidemics of powder cocaine, crack, and methamphetamine.[9] The market for drugs in the United States has also had devastating effects in inducing violence and corruption in source and trans-shipment countries, notably Mexico and Colombia, which also attempt to prohibit commerce in these drugs.

The high costs of prohibition motivate a close look at the alternatives. In Europe and Latin America there has been a recent trend to "depenalize" drug possession while preserving the criminal prohibition on manufacture and sale. The more radical alternative is to repeal one or more of the drug prohibitions and replace them with a system of taxes and regulations. It is possible that high taxes could have the effect of preempting a surge in use while still shutting down much of the underground market. But Donohue and coauthors emphasize that the actual consequences are unknown, given the lack of experience with legalization. They offer reason to believe that if legalization does result in increased use, it would be more criminogenic in the case of cocaine than marijuana.

In his comment, Robert MacCoun applauds the authors' recognition that there is great uncertainty about the long-term effects of a major regime change in drug regulation, and provides as an example the differing judgments by experts concerning the potential of marijuana legalization in California. MacCoun suggests that an intermediate policy of legalizing home cultivation would be less risky.

Reducing Criminal Opportunity

While underground markets create lucrative opportunities for crime, most property crime is an effort to steal legal commodities or money from their owners. The chapter by Cook and MacDonald observes that property crime rates and patterns are influenced by the availability of attractive opportunities, and that owners respond by investing in protection against theft.

---

present case could include changes over time in the nature of drug production or distribution. Kuziemko and Levitt (2004) try to overcome this problem by comparing trends in drug prices over time across states that have different trends in incarceration of drug offenders over time, which allows them to control for common period effects. They find some evidence that locking up drug offenders does reduce crime and increase cocaine prices, although as the authors note, this analysis is also primarily correlational.

9. The minimum drinking age provides an interesting counter example about the link between prohibition and crime. Those under twenty-one are prohibited from purchasing and possessing alcohol, and while this partial prohibition does have some effect on consumption and abuse, it is very widely violated. For example, about 80 percent of college-aged youths drink. However, unlike the prohibition of cocaine or heroin, or of alcohol in the 1920s, this partial prohibition causes few systemic problems. Most underage drinkers get their beverages from social connections—family or friends—or patronize a legal outlet that is willing to serve them. The result is that there is no profitable niche for illicit suppliers, and no bloody contests between underground dealers.

That investment is influenced by law and policy. For example, motor vehicle theft has been combated through manufacturer-installed locks of increasing sophistication, and the current immobilizers are so effective that stealing a new car requires a thief to have either the key or a tow truck. Motor vehicle theft prevention has been promoted through federal regulation and in some cases through the structure of insurance premiums, although there may still be a moral hazard problem given theft insurance and the fact that the police do not charge for their service of recovering stolen vehicles. In any event, the fact that there are fewer thefts now than in 1980 despite doubling the number of vehicles on the road—as well as the sharp reduction in joyriding—has much to do with improved locking devices. Private action enhanced by significant technological change has also been paramount in defending against credit card theft, shoplifting, and a variety of other potentially lucrative crimes.

Thus the first line of defense in property crime is private protection efforts, which do a great deal of the work in taking the profit out of crime. For various reasons the private incentive may be out of line with the public interest, in either direction. Cook and MacDonald discuss circumstances in which private incentives may induce an inefficiently high level of private action, for example, in the case of buying handguns for self-protection, or of avoiding public places that are deemed dangerous and become more so when abandoned by the public.

Finally, we note that juvenile curfew laws provide yet another avenue to limiting criminal opportunities. In effect they seek to incapacitate large numbers of underage youth during late evening hours, when the temptations for criminal activity (often fueled by intoxication) are high. Kline (2010) finds that juvenile curfew laws reduce violent and property crimes by around 8 percent the first year, with sustained declines in violent crimes that may be as large as 30 percent of previous levels. The overall scope for juvenile curfew laws to reduce crime is more limited than these large effects would suggest, since they apply to youth just below the curfew age, a group that accounts for an important but relatively modest share of all criminal behavior.

Changing Individual Propensities Toward Crime

The hope that social policy might be able to improve people's life chances, and reduce their propensity toward crime, was dimmed during the 1960s and 1970s. First, the distinguished sociologist James Coleman issued a landmark report in 1966, *Equality of Educational Opportunity,* which led many people to conclude that there was little that schools could do to improve children's schooling outcomes. Eight years later Robert Martinson published an essay in the *Public Interest* that reviewed the research on rehabilitation programs and came to the memorable (and influential) conclusion that "nothing works." The legacy of these gloomy reports is still in evidence. For example, a 2002 poll by Peter D. Hart Associates asking the public about the most promising ways to prevent crime found that just 15 percent of respondents endorsed "improving public education for poor children."[10]

More recent research, however, has identified interventions that do work. For example, schooling attainment has a powerful protective effect against criminal involvement, and a number of educational interventions can improve schooling attainment and related outcomes. While most of the educational interventions that have been targeted at disadvantaged adolescents or young adults have had disappointing results, there is at least one exception that is remarkable for its conceptual simplicity—extending mandatory school attendance to age eighteen. Other interventions that address social-cognitive skill deficits are promising—even (or perhaps, especially) for the highest-risk teens and adults. An important feature of programs to reduce criminal propensities is that they are also likely to have positive effects in a number of other domains. That is clearly true for education and early childhood programs, which influence prospects for success as a parent, a worker, and a citizen.

Schooling

In the standard Becker (1968) model of criminal behavior, schooling interventions may reduce crime by improving labor market prospects, thereby increasing the opportunity costs of crime or incarceration, or by changing "tastes" for the outcomes offered by criminal opportunities.

The ability of education policy to improve children's schooling outcomes was called into question by the Coleman Report in 1966. Among its findings, the Coleman report noted that disparities across schools in measurable inputs were less pronounced than many people had believed, that most of the variation in children's achievement test scores was within rather than between schools, that measurable school inputs were only weakly correlated with children's test scores, and that actually the strongest predictors of children's test scores were family background and the social composition of the child's school (Coleman 1968). Decades of subsequent nonexperimental studies seemed to confirm this general picture (Hanushek and Lindseth 2009). The Coleman Report also showed that disparities in children's school performance were already apparent during the preschool years, suggesting another possible target for educational interventions. But the possibility of "fade out" in the benefits of Head Start, the federal government's main early childhood program became evident within a year of the program's launch as part of the War on Poverty.

More recent studies that use stronger research designs show that selected interventions can improve children's achievement test scores, although this is an outcome that is somewhat remote from either high school graduation or

10. Peter D. Hart Research Associates (2002).

criminal involvement.[11] One common denominator for many of these interventions is that they seek to increase the time that children spend interacting in developmentally enriching ways with teachers. Examples of interventions that seem to improve achievement test scores include early childhood education (which substitutes time with teachers for time with parents or other caregivers); reductions in class size in the early elementary grades (which may reduce classroom disruptions and so increase time-on-task, and also facilitate more individualized teacher instruction); selected comprehensive school reform models like Success for All (which includes increased instructional time and an emphasis on reading); Accelerated Middle Schools (which allow students behind in grade level to advance more than one grade during an academic year), and to some extent school accountability reforms as well, which increase time on academic subject areas and are also intended to improve the quality of instruction (and sometimes student effort) (see Jacob and Ludwig 2009). Another common denominator is that most of the interventions that have been found to be successful so far tend to target relatively young children.

In terms of the implications for criminal behavior, there is both bad news and good. The bad news is that in many cases, short-term gains in achievement test scores are not sustained; the good news is that some programs nonetheless seem to have positive effects on graduation or other outcomes many years later. These possibilities are illustrated by research on early childhood educational interventions. Most of these programs have test score gains that disappear after a few years, yet some interventions—including Head Start—appear to increase long-term schooling attainment (Garces, Thomas, and Currie 2002; Ludwig and Miller 2007; Deming 2009). As Lance Lochner notes in his chapter, direct evidence for impacts on crime is mixed across different early childhood programs. But given the generally encouraging impacts on schooling attainment, and evidence that schooling attainment has a causal effect on crime (Lochner and Moretti 2004),[12] our best guess is that later criminal involvement is likely reduced by preschool

11. Using test scores as a short-term outcome measure is akin to what medical researchers call a "surrogate clinical endpoint," such as blood pressure. The real interest is in the longer-term outcomes we care about (schooling attainment and crime, as well as lifetime earnings), which may or may not be predicted by the near-term effect on test scores.

12. The chapter by Lance Lochner argues that raising the compulsory schooling age reduces criminal involvement by increasing schooling attainment, and in particular the likelihood of graduation from high school. Less certain is whether *any* intervention that raises graduation rates would reduce criminal behavior. If there are heterogeneous effects of school attainment on crime, it is possible that different educational interventions may act on different subpopulations and so differ in their impacts on crime. Some indirect evidence on this point comes from Oreopoulos (2004), who finds that the effect on earnings from compulsory schooling laws in the United States, which affect a relatively modest share of the population, are not so different from the effect of such laws in the United Kingdom that increased schooling for nearly half the population. Put differently, the local average treatment effect (LATE) does not appear to differ substantially from the average treatment effect (ATE), at least for earnings—an outcome not entirely unrelated to criminal behavior.

programs that are effective in improving education outcomes. Impacts on criminal behavior can lead early childhood programs to have very large benefit-cost ratios—for example, up to 13:1 for the Perry Preschool model program, with nearly 70 percent of the program's benefits coming from reduced criminal behavior (Belfield et al. 2006).

Lochner's chapter notes that one of the few educational interventions that has been shown to improve schooling outcomes for adolescents (as opposed to young children) is increasing the compulsory schooling age. This finding speaks to the possibility of motivation as being a key factor in the success of educational interventions, an idea that receives some additional support from considering the short list of other programs that the US Department of Education's What Works Clearinghouse[13] considers at least promising in this regard: High School Redirection, which emphasizes basic skills development and small school environments to improve connections between students and staff, and encouragement to teachers to also act as mentors; Check & Connect, which involves mentoring relationships and ongoing monitoring and supports for school attendance; and financial incentives for teen parents to stay in school, including Wisconsin's Learnfare program (Dee 2009).[14] In his chapter, Steven Raphael notes that the interventions shown to improve schooling attainment for at-risk youth, such as the Job Training Partnership Act (JTPA), Job Corps, and JOB START, all have a vocational orientation, which further speaks to the possible importance of attending to motivation for educational programs for older youth.

Social-Cognitive Skill Interventions

The evidence that early childhood interventions increase schooling attainment despite test score fadeout highlights the potential importance of socioemotional and behavioral skills—what economists like to call "noncognitive outcomes"—as key mediating mechanisms for long-term behavioral impacts (Heckman et al. 2010). The chapters by Patrick Hill, Brent Roberts, and colleagues, by Seth Sanders, and by Richard Frank and Thomas McGuire highlight the evidence on psychological interventions that directly seek to build what Ken Dodge calls social-cognitive skills. The underlying logic of these interventions is fairly compelling, given descriptive evidence that many disadvantaged children have social-cognitive skill deficits that may stem in part from harsh and inconsistent parenting, as well as a large body of evidence that a variety of social-cognitive skill measures are strongly

---

13. See http://ies.ed.gov/ncee/wwc.

14. MDRC's randomized experimental evaluation of Career Academies, which use small-school environments, vocationally oriented curricular materials and internships to help increase the relevance of school for high school-age students, seems to improve earnings prospects even without affecting schooling attainment. The intervention does not have any detectable effect on self-reported criminal behavior, although whether that is simply an artifact of respondent unwillingness to report criminal involvement is unclear. See Kemple (2008).

correlated with future risk of criminality, schooling attainment, earnings, and other key outcomes (Heckman 2008; Heckman, Stixrud, and Urzua 2006; Heckman and Rubinstein 2001). Terrie Moffitt and Stephen Ross, in their comment for this volume, provide a striking demonstration of the importance of one such skill—self-control. Based on their analysis of two large extended cohort studies, they demonstrate that self-control measured in childhood strongly predicts subsequent criminal activity as well as a variety of other problem behaviors.

The review by Brent Hill and colleagues notes that encouraging evidence is available from randomized controlled trials for interventions that try to work with youth and their families, such as Functional Family Therapy, Multisystemic Therapy, and Multidimensional Foster Care. The goal is to change the social-cognitive skills of youth and to modify the social systems that may contribute to or reinforce the youth's delinquency. For interventions that try to work just with the at-risk youth themselves, such as cognitive behavioral therapy, the quality of evaluations is more mixed, with few randomized experiments. But those experiments and the larger set of observational studies point in the same general encouraging direction.

The existing evaluation evidence on skill-building interventions, if taken at face value, suggests benefit-cost ratios of up to 15:1 or 20:1, at least as large as those for the most promising early childhood interventions (Greenwood 2008; Drake, Aos, and Miller 2009). One possible reason these programs have such high benefit-cost ratios is that they focus on working with justice system-involved populations whose baseline crime rates are high. If the effects of these skill-building interventions fade out (decline in magnitude) over time, then there may be value in targeting these interventions toward the highest-risk people during the highest-risk life stages (adolescence and early adulthood) rather than at younger children who have many years to go before their key high-risk period.

How do we reconcile this cautiously optimistic take on the efficacy of social-cognitive skill development in reducing crime, including among justice-involved populations, with the gloomy assessment of rehabilitation programs from Martinson back in 1974? We do not question his judgments about the evidence available to him.[15] The more optimistic conclusion stems

15. Martinson's (1974) original conclusion was: "With few and isolated exceptions, the rehabilitative efforts that have been reported so far have had no appreciable effect on recidivism" (25). In his 1979 essay he notes that on the basis of including nonexperimental studies in his review, "I withdraw this conclusion . . . treatments will be found to be 'impotent' under certain conditions, beneficial under others, and detrimental under still others." The new evidence "warns against confining juvenile offenders without some kind of treatment. The pattern of effects does not indicate that any treatment will work (for example, job placement and benign custody are questionable). But most treatments for incarcerated juveniles have negative effect sizes and one suspects that a common process may be at work" (Martinson 1979, 252, 256–7). It is possible that Martinson recanted for the wrong reasons, since the large number of nonexperimental studies that he added to his literature review were plagued by selection bias (Miller 1989).

from evidence on efficacy of new developments in the field, and new evidence on long-standing programs (such as compulsory school attendance).

Mental Illness and Drug Abuse

Drug Courts

Harold Pollack, Peter Reuter, and Eric Sevigny analyze the capacity of drug courts to address the problem of drug-involved offenders. A casual look at the data suggests that drug courts, with their focus on diversion and treatment, should be well positioned to make a large dent in both incarceration and crime. The authors note that there were upward of half a million inmates convicted of drug-related offenses in 2002, and that something like half of all adult arrestees test positive for some drug other than marijuana. The HOPE experiment described earlier, along with other evidence, demonstrates that interventions that reduce offenders' drug use also reduce their rate of crime commission. Yet, conclude Pollack and his coauthors, the fact is that the typical scope of drug courts is so narrow that they have little effect on the rate of prison admissions. The aging cohorts of drug-involved offenders left behind by the heroin and cocaine epidemics have long criminal records and are not eligible for diversion—even though their risk of committing a violent crime may be lower than that of younger offenders with shorter records. In fact, the authors find that even if drug courts were available in every jurisdiction, it would make very little difference in the rate of new prison sentences, given the stringent eligibility criteria for diversion to drug court. Younger defendants picked up for possession, who are eligible for diversion to a drug court, would not be sentenced to prison in any case.

In his comment on Pollack, Reuter, and Sevigny, Jonathan Caulkins expands on the notion of an epidemic cycle in drug initiation and abuse. He documents the remarkable similarity in the temporal pattern across ten types of drugs, and concludes that the appropriate response requires an understanding of how the characteristics of the typical user changes over time for each type of drug.

Alcohol Control

Alcohol is the main intoxicant that has not been subject to prohibition in recent history. Alcohol use and abuse is widespread, and an important ingredient in domestic violence, violent crime (both perpetration and victimization), reckless driving, and a variety of problems in noncriminal domains. Since repeal in 1933, alcohol has been subject to a variety of taxes and regulations—these days much laxer than a generation or two ago, but still somewhat effective in limiting abuse. The chapter by Christopher Carpenter and Carlos Dobkin reviews the evidence on the causal role of alcohol in crime, and then provides an assessment of the various regulatory approaches. The most compelling evidence is in support of the crime prevention effects of raising prices through higher excise taxes. The minimum legal drinking age also is effective in this respect, but in that case there is nowhere to go—every state sets twenty-one as the minimum age and has no appetite for raising it to, say, twenty-five. There is some evidence that outlet density (which can be controlled through licensing) has an effect on abuse and its consequences. In terms of a cost-benefit analysis, raising excise taxes scores well since it is readily justified as a Pigovian correction for the negative externalities of drinking—and surprisingly well targeted (Cook 2008).

Mental Health Treatment

Richard Frank and Thomas McGuire provide an analysis of mental health courts. They note that about one-quarter of inmates of both jails and state prisons have had a diagnosis of mental illness other than drug dependence, and that the rates are still higher for adjudicated delinquents. A clear causal link between psychosis and violence exists, a link that is exacerbated by substance abuse, which often co-occurs. Yet there is scant evidence that getting mentally ill offenders into treatment rather than prison will reduce their subsequent criminal behavior. One problem that Frank and McGuire mention is that mental health disorders contribute to a constellation of other life problems that create a legacy of elevated risk for criminal involvement, even if the mental health disorder itself is eventually treated. With some exceptions, the authors conclude that the treatment-oriented approaches offered by the 150 mental health courts currently operating would have to be justified by goals other than crime reduction.

In his comment, Jeffrey Swanson extends the discussion of the causal pathways that link mental illness and crime, noting that both constructs are complex and that they interact and overlap in a variety of ways. The inherent complexity in these domains should be considered in developing worthwhile interventions.

Conclusion

The chapters in this volume provide assessments of a variety of approaches to controlling crime. All of these approaches can be understood within a simple framework, which specifies that observed crime rates are the result of individual choices of whether to exploit available opportunities for crime. The characteristics of criminal opportunities available to any one individual—characteristics such as the likelihood of success and payoff if successful, likelihood of arrest and severity of punishment—are determined by private actions (including the general level of precaution and expenditures on private security) as well as public law enforcement. How individuals evaluate a criminal opportunity will depend in part on their preferences, their ability to achieve their goals by alternative licit means, and their self-management skills.

In this introductory chapter, we organized our summary of findings into two large and somewhat overlapping bins, which we labeled "changing the offending environment" and "changing individual propensities toward crime." Each bin includes promising, well-documented approaches to controlling crime, and also includes examples of what might be termed negative knowledge—negative assessments of common practices. Unfortunately, we usually do not have enough information about a promising intervention to do a complete assessment, which would include, at a minimum, good information on the benefits and costs, the potential scope (that is, what portion of the crime problem does it address), and the ease of implementation. The information needed for a complete assessment is especially great in the case of programs that do not have crime control as the primary goal, such as schooling, income maintenance, and alcohol taxation. Also relevant to judging which types of interventions should be the focus of policymaker attention is ease of implementation. For example, proactive and antigun policing strategies have the potential to exacerbate police-community tensions if not implemented well. The dramatic success of Hawaii's HOPE program, which provides swift, certain sanctions to drug-involved probationers, has been possible in part because of a truly exceptional local judge (and perhaps a general Aloha spirit), and may prove difficult to export.

Here we recap the list of topics and identify some of the programs that appear particularly promising based on current assessments of costs and benefits, together with a few cases where assessments are negative or indeterminate. We conclude with a back-of-the-envelope exercise that helps highlight the potential magnitude of the inefficiency within our current policy approach—that is, how much extra crime prevention could be achieved by simply reallocating resources from less efficient to more efficient uses.

Changing the Offending Environment

Efficient Sanctioning of Crime

Coerced abstinence for convicted criminals. The experimental evaluation of HOPE in Honolulu provides strong evidence that criminal activity by felony probationers is closely linked to their drug use, and that the drug use can be controlled through a regime of frequent drug tests and sure but mild penalties for failure. Benefits greatly exceed costs (which on balance are negligible or even negative), and the potential scope is broad. The key challenge is implementation within the existing system of courts and corrections.

Police resources. Evaluation of the federal COPS program indicates that providing police departments with more funding has benefits (in terms of crime control) that are a multiple of costs. In some departments, still further gains may be possible through focusing on the most socially costly aspects of the crime problem—such as gun violence.

Private coproduction. State and local governments can encourage private action that makes law enforcement more productive. Two examples for which the benefits exceed costs by an order of magnitude are creation of the police-tracking infrastructure for LoJack, and creation of the legal framework that facilitates successful business improvement districts.

Jobs and Income Supports

Jobs. There is an oft-repeated saying in Chicago and many cities around the country: "Nothing stops a bullet like a job." Yet the evidence on job training and placement for offenders is mixed at best.

Transfer programs to alleviate poverty. The evidence on crime-reducing effects is even more discouraging for income support programs for ex-offenders than for job programs. On the other hand, income support programs for poor families, which are not usually justified by their effects on crime, have some beneficial side effects in reducing criminal behavior by youth in participating families.

Regulation of Drugs and Alcohol

Drug policy reform. While underground markets for some prohibited drugs engender crime and violence, the United States has no contemporary experience with a more liberal regime and there remains considerable uncertainty about the potential effects of liberalization on crime, arrests, and imprisonment.

Reducing Criminal Opportunity

Regulations to reduce motor vehicle theft. Immobilizers are installed in 85 percent of new vehicles in the United States. It is plausible that an increase in that prevalence would be cost-beneficial, and could be achieved either through direct regulation or a requirement for an insurance premium surcharge on new vehicles that lack this protection.

Changing Individual Propensities Toward Crime

Schooling Interventions

Intensive preschool programs. Current funding levels for Head Start are sufficient to enroll only around half of the nation's three- and four-year-old children in poverty (Haskins and Barnett 2010). Moreover, even those children who do get to participate in Head Start receive services that are much less intensive than those provided through model programs like the widely cited Perry Preschool intervention. While the evidence for the effects of early childhood interventions on criminal behavior itself is mixed, the strong evidence for beneficial effects on schooling attainment leads us to conclude that effects on crime are quite likely even if they are difficult to measure directly.

Compulsory schooling age. There is strong quasi-experimental evidence from both the United States and Great Britain that cohorts exposed to an increased compulsory schooling age have reduced crime involvement. That benefit augments the usual list of benefits associated with more schooling.

Social-Cognitive Skill Interventions

Skill-building interventions with adolescents and their families. A cluster of programs that take this approach seek to change the social-cognitive skills of youths and to modify the social systems that may contribute to or reinforce delinquency. Included here are Functional Family Therapy, Multisystemic Therapy, and Multidimensional Foster Care. Strong evidence suggests benefits are a multiple of costs for high-quality programs in this area.

Mental Illness and Drug Abuse

Mental health and drug treatment. Crime has considerable overlap with both drug abuse and mental illness. Specialized courts designed to get defendants into treatment have value, but their domain is quite limited in practice to lesser offenders.

Alcohol excise tax rates. The federal and state excise tax rates on beer and liquor have declined markedly (in real terms) during the post–World War II period. These rates are considerably below the marginal external social cost, even if effects on crime are not considered. The evidence that raising taxes and prices would reduce some types of crime is very strong.

Note that the previous list is far from exhaustive, but sufficient to provide a sense of the diverse menu of possibly effective interventions, drawing on a wide variety of domains. And it bears repeating that the goal is not to identify the best option, but rather the best portfolio of options.

Potential Efficiency Gains From Reallocating Resources

Our review of the chapters in this volume suggests that America's current approach to crime control is inefficient—more crime control could be accomplished with the same level of resources. To help illustrate the potential gains from improving the efficiency of the current system, consider the following hypothetical policy experiment.

Imagine that we changed sentencing policies and practices in the United States so that average prison sentence lengths reverted back to the levels of 1984—that is, midway through the Reagan presidency. We estimate that this policy change would reduce the size of our current prison population by around 400,000 people and reduce total prison spending (currently equal to $70 billion annually)[16] by about $12 billion per year.[17]

16. http://www.albany.edu/sourcebook/pdf/t122006.pdf.
17. Our $12 billion estimate is derived as follows. Raphael and Stoll (2009) present results suggesting that 35 percent of the increase in state prison populations from 1984 to 2002 was the result of increased prison sentence length. We extend this estimate and assume that 35 percent of the total increase in federal plus prison populations from 1984 through 2009 is due to increased sentence lengths (but that changes in sentence lengths over time have no effect on the

What would we give up by reducing average sentence lengths back to 1984 levels? In terms of crime control, the chapter by Steve Durlauf and Daniel Nagin in this volume suggests the answer may be: not all that much. The $12 billion we spend per year to have average sentence lengths at 2009 rather than 1984 levels must presumably produce some crime reduction, although Durlauf and Nagin's chapter suggests the impact might be fairly modest. For the sake of argument, we assume that society breaks even on that expenditure, although more pessimistic assumptions are also warranted.

What could we do instead with this $12 billion in freed-up prison spending? One possibility would be to put more police on the streets. Currently, the United States spends around $100 billion per year on police protection,[18] so this hypothetical policy switch would increase the police budget by 12 percent and put perhaps as many as 100,000 more police officers on the streets.[19] The estimated elasticity of crime with respect to police is far larger (in absolute value) than even the most optimistic assessment of what the elasticity of crime would be with respect to increased sentence lengths. This resource reallocation would lead to a decline of hundreds of thousands of violent and property crime victimizations each year.[20] A different way to

---

size of the jail population, which may or may not be true). Data from the Bureau of Justice Statistics indicate there were 462,000 people in state and federal prisons in 1984, and 1,613,656 people in 2009 (see http://bjs.ojp.usdoj.gov/content/dtdata.cfm#corrections and http://bjs.ojp .usdoj.gov/index.cfm?ty=pbdetail&iid=2272). Scaling back average sentence lengths to 1984 levels under our assumptions would have reduced the size of this increase by 35 percent, so that current prison populations would be 403,000 lower than actual levels. We assume that the costs to the government per prisoner are on the order of $30,000 per year, which is consistent with the figures reported in Donohue (2009). Reducing average sentence lengths to 1984 levels would then free up 403,000 × $30,000 ~ $12 billion in government resources, ignoring for the moment any secondary effects on other government activities.

18. http://www.albany.edu/sourcebook/pdf/t122006.pdf.

19. The total number of police employees in the United States is currently around 1 million, about 70 percent of which are sworn police officers. http://www.albany.edu/ sourcebook/pdf/t1682009.pdf.

20. John Donohue (2009) provides a best guess for the elasticity of crime with respect to imprisonment (at present incarceration levels) of between −.1 and −.15 (283), although this estimate mixes together the effects of punishment certainty with punishment severity and so is almost surely an upper bound for the elasticity of crime with respect to extended sentence lengths. If we conservatively assume an elasticity of −.1 (which is probably too large in absolute value), and assume that our hypothetical change in sentence lengths reduces the size of the prison population by around 20 percent, and if we focus just on Uniform Crime Reports (UCR) part 1 index offenses known to the police, the result of the smaller prison population absent any other policy change would be around 26,000 more part 1 violent crimes and 186,000 more part 1 property offenses (see www.albany.edu/sourcebook/pdf/t31062009.pdf for 2009 FBI figures for part 1 crimes). Evans and Owens (2007) estimate that the elasticity of crime with respect to police is around −.26 for property crimes and −.99 for violent crimes. So all else equal, the 12 percent increase in police spending would lead to around 290,000 fewer UCR part 1 property crimes and around 156,000 fewer part 1 violent crimes. Our estimated net change in UCR part 1 offenses from switching $12 billion from the prison system to police hiring would then be (156,000 − 26,000) = 130,000 fewer part 1 violent crimes, and (290,000 − 186,000) = 104,000 fewer part 1 property crimes. This calculation is subject to two sources of potential error that work in opposite directions. On the one hand, if increased policing reduces crime through incapacitation as well as deterrence, then putting more police on the streets will lead to more

think about the potential size of the efficiency gain here is to note that the benefit-cost ratio for increased spending on police may be on the order of 4:1 or 8:1 (Donohue and Ludwig 2007). If the benefit-cost ratio for marginal spending on long prison sentences is no more than 1:1, then reducing average sentence lengths to 1984 levels in order to increase spending on police could generate net benefits to society on the order of $36 billion to $90 billion per year.

Suppose instead that we devoted the resources freed up from a $12 billion cut in prison spending toward Head Start. This 17 percent cut in the prison budget would support a 150 percent increase in the annual Head Start budget (currently around $8 billion per year). Current Head Start funding levels are enough to enroll only around one-half of poor three- and four-year-olds in the United States, and provide them with early childhood education services that are far less intensive than widely cited and well-regarded model programs like Perry Preschool and Abecedarian in terms of the number of years of program participation (usually one for Head Start versus two to five for the others) and the quality (schooling attainment) of teachers. A 150 percent increase in Head Start's budget could dramatically expand the program on both the extensive and intensive margins. No one really knows what would be accomplished by an increase in Head Start funding that is so much larger than anything in our historical experience, but our best guess is that the benefit-cost ratio might be from 2:1 to 6:1.[21] A defensible guess is that reallocating resources from long prison sentences to early childhood education might generate from $12 billion to $60 billion in net benefits to society.

If crime reduction is a key goal then we might do even better still by focusing on human capital investments in the highest-risk subset of the pop-

arrests and prison spells, which will offset part of the gains from reducing average sentence lengths. On the other hand, our calculation focuses just on crimes reported to the police, while data from the National Crime Victimization Survey suggests that only around half of violent crimes and 40 percent of property crimes are reported to the police.

21. Ludwig and Miller's (2007) study of the launch of Head Start suggests that a 50 to 100 percent increase in Head Start funding at the county level increases a county's high school completion rate by 3 to 4 percentage points (about 5 percent of the control mean). Suppose that a 150 percent increase in Head Start funding to expand enrollments and make the program look more like, say, Perry Preschool increased the overall high school graduation rate by 4 to 9 percentage points. The US statistical abstracts show that in recent years, birth cohorts have averaged around four million people. The estimates from Belfield and Levin (2007) (http://www.cbcse.org/media/download_gallery/AGGREGATE_REPORT_v7.pdf) suggest that the benefits to society for each extra high school graduate are (conservatively) around $250,000 from increased present value of lifetime earnings, $40,000 in present value from health improvements, and $27,000 in reductions in criminal behavior, for a total of around $317,000. If we discount this back to age four from age eighteen using a 3.5 percent rate, the present value would be around $196,000. We can then think of a $12 billion per cohort increase in early childhood spending to expand and intensify Head Start as leading to an aggregate benefit per cohort in present value terms ranging from $(.04) \times 4,000,000 \times \$196,000 = \$31$ billion up to $(.09) \times 4,000,000 \times \$196,000 = \$70$ billion, for a B/C ratio ranging from $(31/12) = 2.6$ up to $(70/12) = 5.8$.

ulation—namely, trying to address social-cognitive skill deficits of young people already involved in the criminal justice system. Research going back to Marvin Wolfgang's seminal study of a Philadelphia birth cohort from the 1950s has found that a small fraction of each cohort commits the bulk of all crime. While early childhood interventions have the benefit of targeting people during the time of life in which they may be most developmentally "plastic" (see Shonkoff and Phillips 2000; Knudsen et al. 2006), interventions directed at adolescents and young adults enables us to more tightly target those who have emerged as the most likely members of that high-offending subset through their arrest histories. Another relative benefit of targeting criminally active teens and adults is the immediate (rather than long-delayed) payoff from reductions in crime.

What sort of social-cognitive skill development could we provide to high-risk young people with $12 billion per year? With around $1 billion annually, we could provide functional family therapy (FFT) to each of the roughly 300,000 youths on juvenile probation each year.[22] Drake, Aos, and Miller (2009, 186) report that FFT costs something on the order of $2,500 per youth, with a benefit-cost ratio that may be as high as 25:1 from crime reductions alone. With the remaining $11 billion we could provide multisystemic therapy (MST) to almost every person aged nineteen and under who is arrested each year.[23] Drake and colleagues estimate the cost of MST is around $4,500 per year, with a benefit-cost ratio of around 5:1. These estimates, if taken at face value, indicate that diverting $12 billion from long prison sentences to addressing social-cognitive skill deficits among high-risk youth could generate net social benefits on the order of $70 billion per year. Even if FFT and MST were only half as effective as previous experiments suggest when implemented at large scale, this resource switch would still generate perhaps on the order of $30 billion in net benefits to society.

Our calculations are intended to be illustrative rather than comprehensive benefit-cost analyses. The estimates are self-evidently subject to a great deal of uncertainty. But they provide a suggestion of the efficiency gains that could result from reallocating resources from prison to other uses that will, among other outcomes, reduce crime.

Efficiency is by no means the sole criterion by which government programs are (or should be) evaluated. But we tend to doubt that apparently large deviations from efficient policy reflect other normative standards. More likely it reflects the intrinsic difficulty of rationalizing policies across domains, agencies, and levels of government. The result is that in the quest for effective crime control, it appears possible that we could have more for less.

22. See http://www.ojjdp.gov/ojstatbb/probation/qa07104.asp?qaDate=2007.
23. FBI data suggest that around 2.6 million people aged nineteen and under were arrested; http://www.albany.edu/sourcebook/pdf/t442009.pdf. There will be a smaller number of unique individuals who are arrested in this age range because a given adolescent could be arrested more than once per year.

References

Alexander, Michelle. 2010. *The New Jim Crow: Mass Incarceration in the Age of Colorblindness.* New York: New Press.

Angrist, Joshua, and Jorn-Steffen Pischke. 2009. *Mostly Harmless Econometrics: An Empiricist's Companion.* Princeton: Princeton University Press.

———. 2010. "The Credibility Revolution in Empirical Economics: How Better Research Design is Taking the Con Out of Econometrics." *Journal of Economic Perspectives* 24 (2): 3–30.

Ayres, I., and S. Levitt. 1998. "Measuring Positive Externalities From Unobservable Victim Precaution: An Empirical Analysis of LoJack." *Quarterly Journal of Economics* 113 (1): 43–77.

Becker, Gary S. 1968. "Crime and Punishment: An Economic Approach." *Journal of Political Economy* 76 (2): 169–217.

Belfield, Clive R., and Henry Levin. 2007. *The Price We Pay: Economic and Social Consequences for Inadequate Education.* Washington, DC: Brookings Institution Press.

Belfield, Clive R., Milagros Nores, Steve Barnett, and Lawrence Schweinhart. 2006. "The High/Scope Perry Preschool Program: Cost-benefit Analysis Using Data from the Age–40 Followup." *Journal of Human Resources* 41 (1): 162–90.

Bennett, William J., John DiIulio, and John P. Walters. 1996. *Body Count: Moral Poverty—and How to Win America's War Against Crime and Drugs.* New York: Simon and Schuster.

Blumstein, Alfred. 1995. "Youth Violence, Guns, and the Illicit-Drug Industry." *Journal of Criminal Law and Criminology* 86 (1): 10–36.

Blumstein, Alfred, and Kiminori Nakamura. 2009. "Redemption in the Presence of Widespread Criminal Background Checks." *Criminology* 47 (2): 327–59.

Braga, Anthony A., and David Weisburd. 2010. *Policing Problem Places: Crime Hot Spots and Effective Prevention.* New York: Oxford University Press.

Bushway, Shawn, Philip J. Cook, and Matthew Phillips. 2010. "The Net Effect of the Business Cycle on Crime and Violence." Duke University, Sanford School of Public Policy. Working Paper.

Caulkins, Jonathan P., Rosalie Liccardo Pacula, Jeremy Arkes, Peter Reuter, Susan Paddock, Martin Iguchi, and Jack Riley. 2004. *The Price and Purity of Illicit Drugs: 1981 Through the Second Quarter of 2003.* Report prepared by RAND. NCJ 207768, November. Washington, DC: Office of National Drug Control Policy.

Chetty, Raj, Adam Looney, and Kory Kroft. 2009. "Salience and Taxation: Theory and Evidence." *American Economic Review* 99 (4): 1145–77.

Cohen, Jacqueline, and Jens Ludwig. 2003. "Policing Crime Guns." In *Evaluating Gun Policy: Effects on Crime and Violence,* edited by Jens Ludwig and Philip J. Cook, 217–39. Washington, DC: Brookings Institution Press.

Coleman, James S. 1968. *Equality of Educational Opportunity.* Washington, DC: Superintendent of Documents, GPO.

Cook, Philip J. 1985. "Is Robbery Becoming More Violent? An Analysis of Robbery Murder Trends Since 1968." *Journal of Criminal Law and Criminology* 76 (2): 480–89.

———. 1986. "The Demand and Supply of Criminal Opportunities." In *Crime and Justice: An Annual Review of Research,* Vol. 7, edited by Michael Tonry and Norval Morris, 1–28. Chicago: University of Chicago Press.

———. 1991. "The Technology of Personal Violence." In *Crime and Justice: An Annual Review of Research,* edited by Michael Tonry, 1–71. Chicago: University of Chicago Press.

————. 2007. *Paying the Tab: The Economics of Alcohol Policy.* Princeton: Princeton University Press.

————. 2008. "A Free Lunch." *Journal of Drug Policy Analysis* 1 (1): article 2. http://www.bepress.com/jdpa/vol1/iss1/art2.

Cook, Philip J., and John H. Laub. 1998. "The Unprecedented Epidemic in Youth Violence." In *Youth Violence,* edited by Michael Tonry and Mark H. Moore, 101–38. Chicago: University of Chicago Press.

————. 2002. "After the Epidemic: Recent Trends in Youth Violence in the United States." In *Crime and Justice: A Review of Research,* edited by Michael Tonry, 117–53. Chicago: University of Chicago Press.

Cook, Philip J., and Jens Ludwig. 2006. "Aiming for Evidence-based Gun Policy." *Journal of Policy Analysis and Management* 25 (3): 691–735.

Cook, Philip J., Jens Ludwig, Sudhir Venkatesh, and Anthony Braga. 2007. "Underground Gun Markets." *Economic Journal* 117 (524): F588–F618.

Cook, Philip J., and Gary Zarkin. 1985. "Crime and the Business Cycle." *Journal of Legal Studies* 14 (1): 115–28.

Dee, Thomas. 2009. "Conditional Cash Penalties in Education: Evidence from the Learnfare Experiment." NBER Working Paper no. 15126. Cambridge, MA: National Bureau of Economic Research, July.

Deming, David. 2009. "Early Childhood Intervention and Lifecycle Skill Development: Evidence from Head Start." *American Economic Journal: Applied Economics* 1 (3): 111–34.

Donohue, John J. III. 2009. "Assessing the Relative Benefits of Incarceration: Overall Changes and the Benefits on the Margin." In *Do Prisons Make Us Safer? The Benefits and Costs of the Prison Boom,* edited by Steven Raphael and Michael A. Stoll, 269–342. New York: Russell Sage Foundation Press.

Donohue, John J. III, and Stephen D. Levitt. 2001. "The Impact of Legalized Abortion on Crime." *Quarterly Journal of Economics* 116 (2): 379–420.

Donohue, John J. III, and Jens Ludwig. 2007. "More COPS." Brookings Policy Brief 158. Washington, DC: Brookings Institution.

Drake, Elizabeth K., Steve Aos, and Marna G. Miller. 2009. "Evidence-based Public Policy Options to Reduce Crime and Criminal Justice Costs: Implications in Washington State." *Victims and Offenders* 4 (2): 170–96.

Evans, William N., and Emily G. Owens. 2007. "COPS and Crime." *Journal of Public Economics* 91 (1–2): 181–201.

Fries, Arthur, Robert W. Anthony, Andrew Cseko Jr., Carl C. Gaither, and Eric Schulman. 2008. *The Price and Purity of Illicit Drugs: 1981–2007.* Alexandria, VA: Institute for Defense Analysis.

Garces, Eliana, Duncan Thomas, and Janet Currie. 2002. "The Long-Term Effects of Head Start." *American Economic Review* 92 (4): 99–1012.

Greenwood, Peter. 2008. "Prevention and Intervention Programs for Juvenile Offenders." *The Future of Children* 18 (2): 185–210.

Grogger, Jeff. 2000. "An Economic Model of Recent Trends in Violence." In *The Crime Drop in America,* edited by Alfred Blumstein and Joel Wallman, 266–87. New York: Cambridge University Press.

Hanushek, Erik, and Alfred Lindseth. 2009. *Schoolhouses, Courthouses and Statehouses.* Princeton, NJ: Princeton University Press.

Harcourt, Bernard, and Jens Ludwig. 2006. "Broken Windows: New Evidence from New York City and a Five-City Social Experiment." *University of Chicago Law Review* 73 (1): 271–320.

————. 2007. "Reefer Madness: Broken Windows Policing and Misdemeanor Marijuana Arrests in New York City, 1989–2000." *Criminology and Public Policy* 6 (1): 165–81.

Haskins, Ron, and W. Steven Barnett. 2010. "New Directions for America's Early Childhood Policies." In *Investing in Young Children: New Directions in Federal Preschool and Early Childhood Policy,* edited by Ron Haskins and W. Steven Barnett. Washington, DC: Brookings Institution and National Institute for Early Education Research. http://www.brookings.edu/~/media/Files/rc/reports/2010/1013_investing_in_young_children_haskins/1013_investing_in_young_children_haskins.pdf.

Hawken, Angela, and Mark Kleiman. 2009. *Managing Drug Involved Probationers with Swift and Certain Sanctions: Evaluating Hawaii's HOPE: Executive Summary.* Report submitted to the National Institute of Justice. http://www.ncjrs.gov/pdffiles1/nij/grants/229023.pdf.

Heckman, James J. 2008. "Schools, Skills, and Synapses." *Economic Inquiry* 46 (3): 289–324.

Heckman, James J., Lena Malofeeva, Rodrigo Pinto, and Peter Savelyev. 2010. "Understanding the Mechanisms Through Which an Influential Early Childhood Program Boosted Adult Outcomes." University of Chicago, Department of Economics. Working Paper.

Heckman, James J., and Yona Rubinstein. 2001. "The Importance of Noncognitive Skills: Lessons From the GED Testing Program." *American Economic Review* 91 (2): 145–9.

Heckman, James J., J. Stixrud, and S. Urzua. 2006. "The Effects of Cognitive and Noncognitive Abilities on Labor Market Outcomes and Social Behavior." *Journal of Labor Economics* 24 (3): 411–82.

Jacob, Brian A., and Jens Ludwig. 2009. "Improving Educational Outcomes for Poor Children." In *Changing Poverty, Changing Policies,* edited by Maria Cancian and Sheldon Danziger, 266–300. New York: Russell Sage Foundation.

Joyce, Theodore J. 2009. "Abortion and Crime: A Review." NBER Working Paper no. 15098. Cambridge, MA: National Bureau of Economic Research, June.

Kemple, James J. 2008. *Career Academies: Long-Term Impacts on Labor Market Outcomes, Educational Attainment, and Transitions to Adulthood.* Accessed June 2008. http://www.mdrc.org/publications/482/full.pdf.

Kennedy, David. 2009. *Deterrence and Crime Prevention: Reconsidering the Prospect of Sanction.* New York: Routledge.

Kennedy, David, Anne Piehl, and Anthony Braga. 1996. "Youth Violence in Boston: Gun Markets, Serious Youth Offenders, and a Use-Reduction Strategy." *Law and Contemporary Problems* 59 (1): 147–83.

Kleiman, Mark. 2009. *When Brute Force Fails: How to Have Less Crime and Less Punishment.* Princeton: Princeton University Press.

Kline, Patrick. 2010. "The Impact of Juvenile Curfew Laws." University of California, Berkeley, Department of Economics. Working Paper.

Knudsen, Eric I., James J. Heckman, Judy L. Cameron, and Jack P. Shonkoff. 2006. "Economic, Neurobiological, and Behavioral Perspectives on Building America's Future Workforce." *Proceedings of the National Academy of Sciences* 103 (27): 10155–62.

Kohut, Andrew, Larry Hugick, Robert C. Toth, and Carol Bowman. 1994. "Economic Recovery Has Little Impact on the American Mood." Times Mirror Center for the People and the Press. April, 6. http://people-press.org/reports/pdf/19940406.pdf.

Kuziemko, Ilyana, and Steven Levitt. 2004. "An Empirical Analysis of Imprisoning Drug Offenders." *Journal of Public Economics* 88 (9–10): 2043–66.

Levitt, Steven D. 2002. "Using Electoral Cycles in Police Hiring to Estimate the Effects of Police on Crime: Reply." *American Economic Review* 92 (4): 1244–50.

———. 2004. "Understanding Why Crime Fell in the 1990s: Four Factors That

Explain the Decline and Six That Do Not." *Journal of Economic Perspectives* 18 (1): 163–90.

Lochner, Lance, and Enrico Moretti. 2004. "The Effect of Education on Crime: Evidence from Prison Inmates, Arrests, and Self-Reports." *American Economic Review* 94 (1): 155–89.

Loury, Glenn. 2010. "Crime, Inequality, and Social Justice." *Daedalus* 139 (3): 134–40.

Ludwig, Jens, and Douglas L. Miller. 2007. "Does Head Start Improve Children's Life Chances? Evidence from a Regression Discontinuity Design." *Quarterly Journal of Economics* 122 (1): 159–208.

Martinson, Robert. 1974. "What Works? Questions and Answers about Prison Reform." *The Public Interest* 35:22–54.

———. 1979. "New Findings, New Views: A Note of Caution Regarding Sentencing Reform." *Hofstra Law Review* 7 (2): 243–58.

Miller, Jerome G. 1989. "The Debate on Rehabilitating Criminals: Is It True that Nothing Works?" *Washington Post,* March. http://www.prisonpolicy.org/scans/rehab.html.

Oreopoulos, Philip. 2004. "Estimating Average and Local Average Treatment Effects of Education When Compulsory School Laws Really Matter." *American Economic Review* 96 (1): 152–75.

Peter D. Hart Research Associates. 2002. "Changing Public Attitudes Toward the Criminal Justice System: Summary of Findings." http://www.soros.org/initiatives/usprograms/focus/justice/articles_publications/publications/hartpoll_20020201.

Pew Center on the States. 2008. *One in 100: Behind Bars in America 2008.* Accessed February 22, 2011. http://pewcenteronthestates.org.

Raphael, Steven. 2009. "Explaining the Rise in U.S. Incarceration Rates." *Criminology & Public Policy* 9 (1): 87–95.

Raphael, Steven, and Melissa Sills. 2008. "Urban Crime, Race, and the Criminal Justice System in the United States." In *Companion to Urban Economics,* edited by Daniel P. McMillen and Richard Arnott, 515–35. New York: Blackwell Publishing.

Raphael, Steven, and Michael Stoll. 2009. "Why Are So Many Americans in Prison?" In *Do Prisons Make Us Safer? The Benefits and Costs of the Prison Boom,* edited by Steven Raphael and Michael Stoll, 27–72. New York: Russell Sage Foundation.

Raphael, Steven, and Rudolf Winter-Ebmer. 2001. "Identifying the Effect of Unemployment on Crime." *Journal of Law and Economics* 44 (1): 259–83.

Redcross, Cindy, Dan Bloom, Gilda Azurdia, Janine Zweig, and Nancy Pindus. 2009. *Transitional Jobs for Ex-Prisoners: Implementation, Two-Year Impacts, and Costs of the Center for Employment Opportunities (CEO) Prisoner Re-Entry Program.* New York: MDRC.

Redcross, Cindy, Dan Bloom, Erin Jacobs, Michelle Manno, Sara Muller-Ravett, Kristin Seefeldt, Jennifer Yahner, Alford A. Young, and Janine Zweig. 2010. *Work After Prison: One-Year Findings from the Transitional Jobs Re-Entry Demonstration.* New York: MDRC.

Reuter, Peter. 2001. "The Limits of Supply-side Drug Control." *Milken Institute Review* 1:14–23.

Reyes, Jessica Wolpaw. 2007. "Environmental Policy as Social Policy? The Impact of Childhood Lead Exposure on Crime." NBER Working Paper no. 13097. Cambridge, MA: National Bureau of Economic Research, May.

Sherman, Lawrence W. 2002. "Fair and Effective Policing." In *Crime: Public Policies for Crime Control,* edited by James Q. Wilson and Joan Petersilia, 383–412. Oakland, CA: Institute for Contemporary Studies Press.

Shonkoff, Jack, and Deborah A. Phillips. 2000. *From Neurons to Neighborhoods*. Washington, DC: National Academies Press.

Skogan, Wesley G., and Kathleen Frydl, eds. 2004. *Fairness and Effectiveness in Policing: The Evidence*. Washington, DC: National Academies Press.

Skogan, Wesley G., Susan M. Hartnett, Natalie Bump, and Jill Dubois. 2009. *Evaluation of Cease-Fire Chicago*. Evanston, IL: Northwestern University.

Spelman, William. 2009. "Crime, Cash, and Limited Options: Explaining the Prison Boom." *Criminology & Public Policy* 8 (1): 29–77.

Spergel, Irving A. 1986. "The Violent Gang Problem in Chicago: A Local Community Approach." *The Social Service Review* 60 (1): 94–131.

Weiner, David, Byron F. Lutz, and Jens Ludwig. 2009. "The Effects of School Desegregation on Crime." NBER Working Paper no. 15380. Cambridge, MA: National Bureau of Economic Research, September.

Western, Bruce. 2006. *Punishment and Inequality in America*. New York: Russell Sage.

Williams, Erica, Phil Oliff, Ashali Singham, and Nicholas Johnson. 2010. *New Fiscal Year Brings More Grief for State Budgets, Putting Economic Recovery at Risk*. Center on Budget and Policy Priorities. Washington, DC.

Zimring, Franklin E. 1968. "Is Gun Control Likely to Reduce Violent Killings?" *University of Chicago Law Review* 35 (4): 721–37.

Zimring, Franklin E., and Gordon Hawkins. 1997. *Crime Is Not the Problem: Lethal Violence in America*. New York: Oxford University Press.

I

Criminal Justice Reform

1

The Deterrent Effect
of Imprisonment

Steven N. Durlauf and Daniel S. Nagin

1.1 Introduction

This chapter is designed to provide an overview of the state of knowledge on the deterrent effects of imprisonment. Much of what we say constitutes a selective summary of existing research. At the same time, we provide some general critiques of the state of knowledge on imprisonment and deterrence and identify some implications for policy.

Our reading of the current empirical literature is that there is overwhelming evidence of substantial deterrent effects across a range of contexts. Therefore, a well-balanced crime-control portfolio must necessarily include deterrence-based policies. Yet the magnitude of deterrent effects depends critically on the specific form of the sanction policy. In particular, there is little evidence that increases in the severity of punishment yield strong marginal deterrent effects; further, credible arguments can be advanced that current levels of severity cannot be justified by their social and economic costs and benefits. By contrast there is very substantial evidence that increases in the certainty of punishment produce substantial deterrent effects. In this regard the most important set of actors are the police since, in the absence of detection and apprehension, there is of course no possibility of conviction

Steven N. Durlauf is the Kenneth J. Arrow Professor of Economics at University of Wisconsin-Madison, and a research associate of the National Bureau of Economic Research. Daniel S. Nagin is associate dean of faculty and the Teresa and H. John Heinz III University Professor of Public Policy and Statistics at the Heinz College, Carnegie Mellon University.

We thank Philip Cook, John Donohue, Mark Kleiman, Justin McCrary, Thomas Miles, Daniel Quint, and Richard Rosenfeld for valuable comments and suggestions on an earlier version of this chapter and Amanda Agan, Hon Ho Kwok, and Xiangrong Yu for excellent research assistance. Durlauf thanks the Wisconsin Graduate School and the Laurits R. Christensen Chair in Economics for financial support.

or punishment. Many studies show that the police, if mobilized in ways that materially heighten the risk of apprehension, can exert a substantial deterrent effect. There is also evidence that if the parole and probation systems are similarly deployed they too can exert a substantial deterrent effect. Thus, one policy relevant implication of our conclusions is that lengthy prison sentences, particularly in the form of mandatory minimum type statutes such as California's Three Strikes Law cannot be justified based on their deterrent effect on crime. In fact, our review suggests a stronger implication: it is possible that crime rates can be reduced without an increase in the resource commitment to crime control; such a reduction may be achieved by shifting resources from incarceration via reducing sentence severity and shifting these resources to policing and parole and probation monitoring systems. These conclusions, to be clear, are tentative and we will discuss why firm claims of this form are difficult.

Our review also has suggestions for the importance of generalizing the economic model of crime in a number of directions; in particular, we address psychological and sociological aspects of criminal behavior whose integration into the standard economic crime model would, in our view, enhance its explanatory power. We take the perspective that the "economic way of looking at behavior" (Becker 1993) has much to commend it for the study of crime and for interpreting psychological and sociological ideas in ways to enhance the perspective.

The chapter is organized as follows. We begin by laying out what we refer to as the "baseline" economic model of crime due to Gary Becker. The Beckerian model provides a framework for our discussion of empirics. We then turn to a review of the literature and our interpretation of implications. Our discussion closes with an assessment of policy implications and directions for future research including expansion of the baseline model.

1.2   The Economic Model of Crime

In order to provide a conceptual framework for our discussion, we employ a version of the economic model of crime pioneered by Gary Becker (1968). Becker's analysis of crime, particularly at the time of its publication, is a fundamental theoretical contribution because it conceptualizes the commission of a crime as a purposeful choice, one that reflects a comparison of costs and benefits. While Becker's formulation, as well as subsequent "rational choice" crime models, describe individual choices by way of particular formulations of a potential criminal's beliefs, preferences, and constraints, it is the notion of crime as a choice that is an irreducible requirement of the approach. Much of the criticism of Becker's model, especially by noneconomists, amounts to criticisms of the ways in which the crime choice is delineated. In fact we will argue that what might, given the existing deterrence and imprisonment literature, appear to be empirical limitations of the economic approach to crime are remedied in a straightforward fashion by alternative formulations of the same choice-based logic that is the basis of Becker's model.

A very simple variant of the Becker model may be constructed as follows. In formulating this baseline model we think of a single cross section of choices made across a population at a fixed point in time; the fact that sentences are served over time and crime/no crime choices are made throughout the life course will be ignored. We will discuss the implications of dynamic versions of the model later. Denote individuals by i and distinguish heterogeneity across them by the vector Z_i. Each individual faces a binary choice as to whether or not commit a crime; that is, a choice between C and NC.[1] If the criminal commits a crime, there is a probability p of being caught and punished. This means that a potential criminal will, depending on his choice, experience one of three utility levels: the utility of not committing a crime, $U_{NC}(Z_i)$, the utility of committing a crime and being punished, $U_{C,P}(Z_i)$, and the utility of committing a crime and not being punished, $U_{C,NP}(Z_i)$. Individual i chooses to commit a crime if the expected utility from commission of a crime exceeds the utility from not committing a crime. A crime is therefore committed if

(1) $$pU_{C,P}(Z_i) + (1 - p)U_{C,NP}(Z_i) > U_{NC}(Z_i).$$

From the perspective of criminal sanctions, this elementary calculation highlights the two distinct aspects of crime sanction policy that are the appropriate focus of scholarly research on deterrence: p, the probability of being punished, and $U_{C,P}(Z_i) - U_{C,NP}(Z_i)$, which will depend upon (among other factors) the nature of the punishment. Suppose that the nature of the punishment is summarized by length of imprisonment; assuming this is the only source of the utility loss in being caught, one can simplify the analysis by treating the utility of crime as $U_c(Z_i, L)$ where L denotes the length of the sentence served having committed the crime; we treat the sentence length as a sufficient statistic for the penalty associated with conviction and do not explicitly account for the fact that a sentence is served over time. We return to this issue later. This allows us to rewrite the condition for commission of a crime as

(2) $$p(U_C(Z_i, L) - U_{NC}(Z_i)) + (1 - p)(U_C(Z_i, 0) - U_{NC}(Z_i)) > 0.$$

From this perspective, commission of a crime is analogous to the purchase of a lottery ticket. The distribution of the heterogeneity Z_i induces an equilibrium aggregate crime rate. We can think of individual crime choices as binary functions $\omega(Z_i, p, L)$, with 1 denoting crime and 0 no crime such that

---

1. We abstract away from richer descriptions of the crime decision such as Becker's original (1968) formulation, which considers the number of offenses a potential criminal will commit in a time period, and Ehrlich (1973) who explicitly considers the allocation of available time between criminal and noncriminal activity.

(3) $\omega(Z_i, p, L) = 1$ if equation (2) holds; 0 otherwise.

Letting dF_z denote the cross-population probability density of the heterogeneity measure Z, the aggregate crime rate $\Pr(C|p, L)$ is characterized by

(4) $\Pr(C|p, L) = \int\omega(Z, p, L)dF_Z.$

For this simple specification, the decision problem facing a policymaker is the choice of a sanction regime, which is described by the pair (p, L). Formally, a policymaker assesses the benefits of a given policy via some function of the crime rate

(5) $\phi(\Pr(C|p, L)).$

In turn, the cost of the policy pair may be represented as a function

(6) $\lambda(p) + \mu(I)$

where the variable I, defined as

(7) $I = \Pr(C|p, L)pL$

is the expected per capita imprisonment rate in the population. In equation (6), the overall cost of the sanction regime, $\lambda(p)$ captures the cost of law enforcement needed to achieve a particular apprehension rate for crimes while $\mu(I)$ captures costs of incarceration. Additivity of the two types of costs seems a natural first-order approximation since it distinguishes between police activity and imprisonment.

How should a policymaker choose among possible (p, L) pairs? Rather than solve for the optimal pair that requires consideration of a budget constraint for total law enforcement expenditure, it is more insightful to solve for the conditionally optimal levels of p and L under the constraint that the product pL is constant. Since pL equals the expected sentence length for a criminal who is caught, conditioning on this value provides a clean way of interpreting the respective roles of certainty of punishment and severity of punishment in influencing the individual crime decisions and hence the aggregate crime rate when the expected sentence length is fixed. Suppose that $U_C(Z_i, L)$ is a concave function of L; that is, the marginal disutility of a marginal change in sentence length is increasing in the level of the sentence. This increasing marginal disutility of sentence length is equivalent to assuming that a potential criminal is risk averse with respect to the sentence "lottery." An agent who chooses to commit a crime faces an expected sentence length pL and will prefer to trade p against L when the marginal disutility of sentence length is increasing in the level of the length. Further, since a lower p reduces policing costs $\lambda(p)$ and must also reduce prison costs as it minimizes $\Pr(C|p, L)$ given constant pL, it hence minimizes $\mu(I)$. This is the basis of Becker's conclusion that efficient sanction policy leads to relatively low punishment probabilities and long sentences. In terms of interpreting the relationship between sentence policy and deterrence, Becker's analysis concludes that, for a locus defined by $pL = K$, deterrence effects are greater, ceteris paribus, for higher L values *so long as criminals are risk averse along this locus.*

Becker's conclusion about optimal sanction policy should not be interpreted as meaning that severity is more important than certainty in deterrence; it is obvious from the structure of the decision problem that the two interact nonlinearly. When we evaluate evidence on the effects of marginal changes in severity and certainty, it is important to keep these interactions in mind. In particular, differences in estimated magnitudes of marginal deterrence effects from severity may be explained by differences in the background certainty levels; the converse may also hold.

In referring to this model as a baseline, we do Becker a partial injustice in that there are dimensions along which one can alter the structure we have described, while at the same time fully preserving the choice-based logic that underlie Becker's analysis. A simple example is the concavity of $U_C(Z_i, L)$; this assumption has no bearing on the interpretation of crime choices as determined by expected utility maximization.[2] While alterations in various assumptions in the baseline may change conclusions concerning the relationship between certainty, severity, and efficient punishment regimes, they do so via the same reasoning pioneered by Becker.

1.3   Empirics

There have been three distinct waves of studies of the deterrent effect of imprisonment. The first wave was conducted in the 1960s and 1970s. The best known study, conducted by Ehrlich (1973), examined the relationship of statewide crime rates to the certainty of punishment, measured by the ratio of prison admissions to reported crimes, and the severity of punishment as measured by median time served. Ehrlich, however, was not alone in employing this or closely related methods for measuring the certainty and severity of punishment (cf. Gibbs 1968; Tittle 1969; Sjoquist 1973; Forst 1976). These studies consistently found that certainty was inversely related to crime rate, which was interpreted as a deterrent effect. By contrast, the severity measure was generally not systematically related to crime rate, which was interpreted as indicating that severity was not an effective deterrent.

These studies suffered from a number of serious statistical flaws that are detailed in Blumstein, Cohen, and Nagin (1978), Nagin (1978), and Fisher and Nagin (1978). The two most important problems involved endogeneity and measurement error. This generation of studies typically failed to account for the endogenous relationship between crime rates and sanction

---

2. Polinsky and Shavell (1999) provide a comprehensive analysis of how optimal sanction policy changes according to whether $U_C(Z_i, L)$ is concave, linear, or convex.

levels predicted by Becker's model. Alternatively, those that attempted to account for endogeneity used implausible identification restrictions to parse out the deterrent effect of sanction levels on crime rates from the effect of crime rates on sanction levels. Papers in this first generation literature, for example, assumed that demographic or socioeconomic characteristics such as percentage of males aged fourteen to twenty-four or mean years of schooling of persons over twenty-five or per capita public safety expenditures lagged one year causally affected sanction levels but did not causally affect crime rates. Studies that fall under this criticism include Avio and Clarke (1976), Carr-Hill and Stern (1973), and Ehrlich (1973). The examples we have listed are examples of what Sims (1980) dubbed "incredible" identifying assumptions and are now recognized as an inadequate basis for making causal claims in social science. The second problem arose from measurement error in crime counts, of which there are many sources. It can be shown that these errors can artificially induce a negative correlation between the crime rate and the certainty of punishment because the measured level of crimes form the numerator of crime rate, that is, crimes per capita, and the denominator of the measure of certainty of punishment, that is, prison admissions per crime (Nagin 1978).

In response to these deficiencies, two subsequent waves of crime/deterrence research emerged, each of which is an ongoing literature. First, starting in the 1990s a number of authors began to use time series methods developed in the econometrics literature to understand the temporal relationship between imprisonment and crime. This new group of studies continued to use states as the unit of observation but unlike the first generation studies that primarily involved cross-sectional analyses of states, this second generation of studies had a longitudinal component. The panel structure of these studies allowed for the introduction of state and time specific fixed effects and the use of various differencing strategies to control for some forms of unobserved heterogeneity. Another important difference is that this wave of studies did not attempt to estimate certainty and severity effects separately. Instead they examined the relationship between the crime rate and rate of imprisonment as measured by prisoners per capita. Another distinct modern research program also emerged that focuses on the effect of police resources on crime rates, particular statutory changes in criminal penalties (severity) or abrupt changes in the level of police presence arising from events such as terror alerts (certainty). Some of these studies may also be distinguished from the first generation by their use of quasi-or natural experiments to uncover deterrence effects. In organizing our survey of the state of the literature, we review these two modern literatures separately by first considering studies that have attempted to link aggregate crime and imprisonment rates, and second, considering studies that have considered the effects of criminal sanction policy on crime.

1.3.1   Aggregate Studies Relating Imprisonment Rate to the Crime Rate

An important recent review by Donohue (2009, table 9.1) identifies six published articles that examine the relationship between aggregate crime rates and imprisonment rates. Each of these studies finds a statistically significant negative association between imprisonment rates and crime rates, and each has been interpreted as implying a crime prevention effect of imprisonment. However, the magnitude of estimates of the parameter varied widely—from nil at current levels of incarceration (Liedka, Piehl, and Useem 2006),[3] to an elasticity of –0.4 (Spelman 2000). It is important to note that these studies are actually measuring a combination of deterrent and incapacitation effects. Thus, it is impossible to decipher the degree to which crime prevention is occurring because of a behavioral response by the population at large or because of the physical isolation of crime-prone people.

Donohue (2009), in the context of generating a cost-benefit analysis of imprisonment, discusses the heterogeneity of elasticity estimates. He argues that values in the lower range of the estimates, –.15 to –.20, are most plausible, but concedes that this judgment is highly uncertain. He favors the lower range estimates on two grounds. First, while the majority of prisoners are confined in state prisons, it is only a near majority. In 2004, for example, 42 percent of the incarcerated population was confined in federal prisons and local jails. If, as one would expect, federal and jail inmate populations are negatively correlated with crime rates and positively correlated with state prison populations, the exclusion of the federal and jail imprisonment rates from the regression will cause an overstatement of the magnitude of the crime prevention effect of the state level imprisonment rate. Second, Donohue is sympathetic with the arguments of Liedka, Piehl, and Useem (2006) that the parameter relating the imprisonment rate to the crime rate is not constant but instead declines in absolute magnitude with the scale of imprisonment. As an empirical matter, he points out that this conclusion is not only consistent with the findings of Liedka, Piehl, and Useem, but is also mirrored in parameter estimates based on constant coefficient models in which the absolute magnitude of parameter estimates decline as data from more recent years are added to the analysis; these more recent data involve higher imprisonment rates and so implicitly (if parameters are not constant) would intuitively suggest the reduction of the estimated parameter that is observed.

While the literature relating crime rates to imprisonment rates has served

---

3. Liedka, Piehl, and Useem (2006) explicitly allow for the marginal effect of imprisonment on the crime rate to depend upon the scale of imprisonment. They do this by regressing crime rate on quadratic and spline functions of the lagged imprisonment rate. Their analysis implies that by the 1990s the preventive effect of imprisonment in some states (e.g., California) had diminished to a negligible level and perhaps was even criminogenic.

the valuable purpose of resuscitating interest in the crime prevention effects of imprisonment, we are less sanguine about the usefulness of this body of literature than Donohue. Our more critical stance stems from both statistical and theoretical considerations. Four of the six analyses are based on the application of time series analyses that in essence look for contemporaneous and dynamic correlations between the levels of crime rates and imprisonment rates (or on changes in the two series). Unfortunately, any claims that these correlations imply a counterfactual-based causal relationship between imprisonment rates and crime rates are, in our judgment, not valid.

To see why these studies are not informative about the presence (or absence) of a causal mechanism that links imprisonment policy to crime, we focus on Marvell and Moody (1994); we single out this study because it has been quite influential and arguably launched the literature on which we focus.[4] Marvell and Moody in essence establish two facts about the time series for imprisonment and crime. First, they establish that imprisonment levels Granger-cause crime levels. This finding has no logical bearing on whether changes in imprisonment policies will alter crime rates. The term causality has a different meaning in the phrase Granger causality than does the word causality as understood in microeconometrics and elsewhere in economics and criminology. Granger causality simply means that lagged imprisonment levels help forecast current crime levels, even when lagged crime rates have been accounted for. This marginal utility in forecasting has no counterfactual implications, which is the definition of causality that is relevant to understanding policy effects.[5] Second, moving from levels to first differences, Marvell and Moody, for a panel of states, regress changes in crime rates against changes in the contemporary imprisonment rate and some additional controls. This regression does not, under any interpretation of causality of which we are aware, provide a policy relevant measure of the effects of imprisonment. Here the problem is simply that changes in contemporary imprisonment and crime rates are simultaneously determined,

4. In terms of delineating the joint time series properties of crime and imprisonment, Spelman (2008) is state of the art, using the data series studied by Marvell and Moody and subjecting them to a wide range of time series analyses. That said, the Spelman paper follows the tradition established in Marvell and Moody in terms of focusing on the joint stochastic process of crime and imprisonment and from this drawing conclusions about policy.

5. Marvell and Moody recognize that there are interpretation issues regarding Granger causality. They argue that their results can be interpreted in the sense of counterfactuals. However, their arguments in this regard are informal and mathematically incorrect. For example, they remark on "the possibility that omitted variables could create a spurious regression, but the presence of lagged values of the dependent variable presumably controls for such variables" (122–3). This claim is incorrect except for the nongeneric case where the omitted variables are linearly dependent on the lagged dependent variables; in general, all lagged variables can be useful in constructing empirical proxies for the omitted variables and hence both sets of lags will have nonzero coefficients in the bivariate VAR. It is straightforward to construct examples where this occurs.

and so the Marvell and Moody finding makes no advance over the first generation of studies in terms of dealing with endogeneity. This type of criticism, in fact, applies to any of the time series studies as the presence of correlated unobservables that simultaneously affect crime and imprisonment will lead to spurious dynamic correlations, a problem that is exacerbated by the fact that the criminal justice system creates simultaneity between the two series.

As we have said, these criticisms do not uniquely apply to Marvell and Moody (1994). Becsi (1999) runs panel regressions of state level crime indices normalized by the national US level against a set of controls including a one year lagged measure of the state population share of convicts relative to the national level.[6] Spelman's (2000) analysis employs Granger causality ideas, arguing two things. First, Spelman (2000, 456) states that "Because the Granger test is explicitly a test of causality, it is critical that exogenous variables be somehow controlled for" and subsequently produces results (458) titled "Controls Improve Interpretability of Granger Test Results." Second, he argues that the differencing to address trends (Spelman 2000, 456) "Although . . . not a perfect solution . . . is probably sufficient to clarify the general direction of causality." Neither proposal addresses the distinction between Granger causality and causality that is understood in policy counterfactuals. Liedka, Piehl, and Useem (2006) employ Granger tests to justify causal interpretations of regressions of crime rates against lagged imprisonment rates and controls; while they make a valuable contribution in assessing the constancy of parameters in these regressions, they follow the same approach to causality as Marvell and Moody.

Even when the limitations of nonstructural time series methods are explicitly acknowledged, the proposed solutions are inadequate. Spelman (2005) attempts a different strategy for using aggregate regressions to study crime by focusing on counties in Texas. In this analysis, changes in county-specific crime rates are regressed against changes in public order arrest and incarceration rates and some set of controls. The arrest and incarceration rates are then instrumented using lagged values of variables such as police resources, republican voting, and jail capacity. No explanation is given as to why these are valid instruments; that is, why they should not appear in the original crime regression. We will address this issue in more detail later.

Levitt (1996) is the single aggregate study reviewed by Donohue that constructively addresses the simultaneous interdependences between crime

6. Becsi (1999) acknowledges that his analysis suffers from interpretation problems. His footnote 17 states "Using lagged variables is perhaps the simplest way of dealing with the simultaneity bias inherent in empirical time series analysis." Yet he follows this with, "One problem with this method is that it may not adequately represent dynamic interrelationships in the data and may in particular miss serial correlation effects." But these remarks ignore the post hoc ergo propter hoc problem associated with nonstructural time series regressions of the type he employs.

and imprisonment rates through a principled argument on instrumental variable validity. Levitt employs court orders requiring reductions in prison populations as an instrument, reasoning that such orders will cause a reduction in the imprisonment rate that is unrelated to the endogeneity of the imprisonment rate. He goes on to argue that crime rates will only be affected through the court order's effect on imprisonment rates. Even here one can question instrument validity. Liedka, Piehl, and Useem (2006) challenge Levitt's identification on the grounds that the court orders themselves are endogenous because prison overcrowding is itself a function of the crime rate. A natural response to this criticism is that Levitt's analysis includes tests that bear on instrument validity. Levitt's analysis is based on multiple forms of the overcrowding instrument that reflect the stage to which the overcrowding litigation had progressed, which allows for tests of over identifying restrictions. These tests support Levitt's contention that the overcrowding litigation has no direct effect on crime rate but only work through the level of imprisonment. Klick and Tabarrok (2010) assert that Levitt's tests of over identifying restrictions have low power, so that the validity of his instruments can only be assessed on a priori grounds. However, in fairness to Levitt, Klick and Tabarrok do not empirically demonstrate any lack of power in Levitt's analysis; in our view a priori arguments on instrument validity tend to be stronger than a priori arguments about test power, as power depends on details of the data generating process whereas instrument validity often involves economic or other social science theory.

In our view, the primary concern with the Levitt analysis involves the question of what the findings tell us about the ability of sanction policies to affect crime rates. There is an important distinction between a policy that forces the release of a set of current prisoners as opposed to one that alters the composition of the prison and civilian populations via a change in sanction regime (Nagin 1998). What Levitt establishes, in our view persuasively, is that exogenous court orders to reduce imprisonment levels appear to lead to short-term increases in crime rates. This is not equivalent to establishing that changes in p or L will affect crime rates, let alone establish the mechanism by which the reduction occurred from the policy that was in fact implemented. For example, it is reasonable to believe that criminals responded directly to the litigation as signaling a reduction in either the certainty or severity of punishment or both; without knowing how beliefs changed, it is difficult to assess exactly what is learned from Levitt's exercise relative to the question of deterrence versus incapacitation.[7]

---

7. Even if one interprets Levitt's findings exclusively in terms of incapacitation, extrapolation of his findings is difficult. It may be the case that the imprisonment reductions induced by court orders were not rationally responded to by the freeing of those prisoners whose recidivism probabilities were especially low. This possibility is plausible. It is very difficult to parole old prisoners who have committed very serious crimes because of objections by the victim or the victim's family and the public in general.

Beyond the specific issue of the handling of endogeneity, a number of fundamental criticisms may be raised concerning the literature relating aggregate crime rates to imprisonment rates. In our judgment, this style of research suffers from two important conceptual flaws that limit its usefulness in devising crime-control policy.

First, this literature generally ignores the fact that prison population is not a policy variable, but rather is an outcome of the interplay of sanction policies dictating who goes to prison and for how long with all other determinants of the crime/no crime decision. Changes in the size of prison populations can only be achieved by changing policies affecting the imprisonment/no imprisonment outcome or the length of incarcerations for those sent to prison. As discussed in section 1.2, all incentive-based theories of criminal behavior, including most importantly Becker's model, are posed in terms of the certainty (p) and the severity (L) of punishment not in terms of the imprisonment rate, I. The policy relevant variables p and L are not the control variables that are directly employed in the crime and imprisonment studies. Put generally, the imprisonment regression literature are not grounded in microeconomic theory in the way that makes clear the distinction between exogenous and endogenous variables; by implication, the way in which endogenous and exogenous variables are interrelated is not specified. As a result, the statistical crime/imprisonment models that are typically estimated are not amenable to counterfactual analysis of the type needed for policy comparison since they do not represent instantiations of the aggregate consequences of individual decisions. This is not a minor conceptual quibble; it lies at the heart of the modern approach to policy evaluation. Heckman (2000, 2005), for example, has famously (and we believe correctly) remarked that "causality is a property of a model of hypotheticals . . . A model is a set of counterfactuals defined under the same rules" (2005, 2).[8] For us, "the same rules" constitute a description of individual decisionmaking and the counterfactuals refer to fully delineated punishment regimes.[9]

This problem is evident when one specifically considers the limits of the informational content in I with respect to the policy choices p and L. Given that p and L may be thought of as distinct aspects of the lottery associated with commission of a crime, one obvious problem is even efforts to use

8. This issue is well understood by philosophers and is known as the Duhem-Quine thesis; see Quine (1951) for the classic formulation. Judgment is intrinsic to the scientific enterprise, and for our purposes judgments about how to model criminal decision making are necessary to make claims about the effects of alternative policies.

9. A deterrence skeptic might counter that our criticisms do not apply if the estimates are interpreted as solely measuring incapacitation effects. This argument cannot be sustained. The point that Granger causality tests do not have a counterfactual interpretation still applies. Further, the magnitude of the incapacitation effect depends upon the mean rate of offending of the incarcerated population, which in turn depends on the types of criminals a policy regime incarcerates. For example, policies resulting in the incarceration of aged criminals likely have small incapacitation effects.

instruments to account for the endogeneity of I cannot uncover the respective roles of the policy variables. Further, there is no guarantee that there exists a monotonic relationship between I and the policy choices. The lack of such a unique relationship, which was first demonstrated in Blumstein and Nagin (1978), extends to the theoretical indeterminacy of the sign of the derivative of I with respect to a change in either p or L. If the elasticity of $\Pr(C|p, L)$ with respect to p or L is greater than -1, an increase in either of these variables will result in an increase in prison population, whereas if the elasticity is less than -1, an increase will result in a reduced prison population. The indeterminacy in the sign of the relationship between p, L, and I implies the possibility of a Laffer curve-style relationship between a given sanction variable and the imprisonment rate. If there were no sanction threat there would be no one in prison even though crime rates would be very high. Alternatively, if sanctions could in practice be made sufficiently severe and certain, there would again be nobody in prison because everyone would be deterred. We return to the policy implications of the possibly "inverted U" relationship between imprisonment rate and crime rate in the discussion of policy implications and future research.

Second, we observe that all of the statistical models of crime we have discussed suffer from the problem of ad hoc model specifications. Focusing again on Marvell and Moody to provide a concrete example but not to single them out, their crime rate/imprisonment rate regression includes variables for the proportions of the population in different age groups, year fixed effects, and the first lagged value of the crime rate. No principled basis is given for this particular choice of variables. For example, indicators of state level economic conditions were not included, yet these are natural proxies for an individual's opportunities if he chooses not to commit a crime. To be clear, Marvell and Moody are not alone in making arbitrary variable choices on what to include and not include in the model. The basic problem is what Brock and Durlauf (2001b) have called theory openendedness. In the imprisonment case, theory openendedness means that the prediction that criminal sanctions affect crime rates is consistent with many theories of criminality, so that empirical evidence of the importance of one explanation can only be assessed against the full background of competing explanations. For our context, some of these explanations have to do with the opportunity cost of crime; one example is the state of the economy in which a potential criminal resides, which naturally is informative about his individual prospects in the (legal) labor market. Others involve the composition of the population in a locality; while Marvell and Moody focus on age, one could just have easily focused on more subtle descriptions of the characteristics of the population in a state or other locality that account for gender as well as age shares. We emphasize that this is not a cynical suggestion in the sense that we are arguing that an empirical finding must be evaluated against every variable that enters a researcher's imagination. Judgments are inevitable in empirical work, including judgments on the plausibility of various controls. Rather our claim is that because there is no settled theory on the causes of crime let alone the appropriate way to quantify these causes, choices about control variables in the deterrence literature are necessarily ad hoc to some degree and so the influence of such judgments needs to be assessed.

Ad hocness occurs for reasons beyond questions of control variables. A second problem concerns the nature of the time series under study. This is evident, at one level, in the choice of the form of time trend made in various empirical studies. According to which paper one reads, one finds the use of linear trends, quadratic trends, or perhaps more sophisticated spline approaches. The choice of time trend has been shown to matter in the shall issue concealed weapons context in that Black and Nagin's (1998) use of quadratic trends reduced the evidence of a crime effect from shall issue laws versus the use of a linear trend by Lott and Mustard (1997). As far as we know, there does not exist *any* theory as to the appropriate formulation of trends in crime regressions.[10] The trend variables employed in crime regressions trends are not formulated as ways to capture population growth or technological change (goals which for theoretical and empirical reasons motivate the use of linear deterministic trends or unit roots in macroeconomics), but rather are included because of the presence of persistence in the model's residuals; that is, the presence of some set of temporally dependent unobservables that the regressions under study cannot explain and for which there is no behavioral theory that provides implications for the form of the dependence. Further, conditional on the choice of trend, the data are typically assumed to be stationary in either levels or first differences. We do not see how assumptions of stationarity from trend can be justified when there is no theoretical basis for the modeling of crime trends. Further, there can be substantive prior information that implies that stationarity is violated. To give a concrete example, the Mariel boatlift is known to have induced first order changes in the crime and imprisonment rates for Florida (Black and Nagin 1998). Such an event presumably affects the dynamic correlation structure between crime rates and other variables beyond simply introducing a correlated unobservable. Yet another source of ad hocness concerns the use of linear regressions to model discrete decisions; Durlauf, Navarro, and Rivers (2010) discuss how the aggregation of individual crime decisions into linear regressions that are used to explain crime rates requires strong assumptions on the details underlying individual decision problems. Aggregation issues further turn out to call into question the interpretation of instrumental variables for aggregate crime regressions, an issue we do not pursue here.

10. This claim is distinct from the question of cycles in crime rates; Philipson and Posner (1996) is an example of a model that produces equilibrium crime rate cycles. Our argument concerns time-varying deterministic components.

A final source of ad hocness concerns parameter heterogeneity. It is typical in crime imprisonment studies to assume constant coefficients across states; parameter heterogeneity may be allowed via state-specific fixed effects, but other parameters, most importantly those linking imprisonment to crime, are assumed to be homogeneous across states. This assumption strikes us as problematic, and is indeed rejected by Spelman (2005) for his joint time series analysis of crime and prison rates. Further, it is known, for example, that measures of the deterrent effect of capital punishment sensitively depend on whether Texas and California are treated as having the same parameters as the rest of the United States (Dezhbakhsh, Rubin, and Shepherd [2003] versus Donohue and Wolfers [2005]) and that inclusion of the state of Florida affects conclusions about shall issue concealed weapons laws (Lott and Mustard [1997] versus Black and Nagin [1998]).[11] These examples call into question the validity of cross-state studies of imprisonment. Conceptually, the problem is that states represent complex heterogeneous objects whose associated data do not naturally lend themselves to interpretations as draws from a common data generating process. One can make parallel arguments concerning the assumption of parameter constancy; that is, nonlinearities are rarely systematically examined, with Liedka, Piehl, and Useem (2006) representing an important exception. The importance of nonlinearities for deterrence is also suggested by Shepherd (2005) who found that the signs of state level estimates of capital punishment effects depended on the level of executions that are carried out.

One response to the ad hocness of model specifications is that criminal sanction policies can only be understood via quasi-randomized experiments. This is the position taken in Horowitz (2004); while his focus is on shall issue concealed weapons laws, his logic applies to crime policy in general and imprisonment policy in particular. Our view is that the randomized experiments approach is valuable, but is best treated as complementary to other studies. One reason why we see value to regression studies using observational data is that the sensitivity of statistical studies to model specification can be assessed both through sensitivity analyses and through model averaging methods (e.g., Raftery, Madigan, and Hoeting 1997) that can provide ways to evaluate the robustness of a given empirical finding. Put differently, we concur with Horowitz that regression studies of criminal policy effects should be viewed with skepticism because of the many auxiliary assumptions made in formulating estimates of policy effects; in contrast, we believe the appropriate response to this problem is to explore policy effects across model spaces that are rich enough to span those assumptions the analyst deems reasonable. See Durlauf, Navarro, and Rivers (2008) for conceptual

11. It is also now well understood that the failure to account for parameter heterogeneity can lead to misleading conclusions in cross-country growth studies; see Durlauf, Johnson, and Temple (2005) for an overview.

discussion of the role of assumptions in crime regressions and Cohen-Cole et al. (2009) for an example of how one can constructively proceed. We believe the sensitivity and model averaging methods can move criminological research beyond the often vituperative debates one sees. For example, Lott's (1998) response to Black and Nagin (1998) and Dezhbakhsh and Rubin's (2007) response to Donohue and Wolfers (2005), in which resolution is not achieved because of the failure to employ methods that integrate the model uncertainty implied by differences in assumptions across studies. At the same time, we are sympathetic to concerns that the virtues of randomized experiments have been exaggerated. One limitation of many randomized experiments concerns general equilibrium effects. An example of this arises in the Klick and Tabarrok (2005) finding that increased police presence during terror alerts is associated with lower crime. Their finding cannot be extrapolated to a claim about the effects of a constant increase in police presence since one does not know to what extent criminals are merely adjusting the timing of activity. Further, even setting aside ethical considerations, some policies may not be amenable to experimental analysis; capital punishment is an example as it is already sufficiently freakish that any effort to randomize its use would make firm inferences impossible.[12]

Our discussion of obstacles to making valid causal inferences about the effects of sanctions on crime from panel data on heterogeneous geographic units should not be interpreted to mean that we view such studies as having no value. To the contrary, as we indicated earlier, the studies relating imprisonment rates to crimes have served the extremely valuable purpose of reopening research on the deterrent effect of imprisonment. We do, however, hold the position that the uncertainties that are inherent in most inferences based on panel data across heterogeneous geographic units such as states are sufficiently large that conclusions from such studies should be treated with great caution until they are confirmed by alternative study designs that are less subject to the inferential challenges inherent to panel studies of aggregate-level crime data.

Studies of the effects of imprisonment exist against a background of large sustained increases in imprisonment. Blumstein and Beck (1999) and Raphael and Stoll (2009) have closely scrutinized the primary sources of the increases in imprisonment over the past four decades. Both reviews conclude that the primary reason for the growth in prison populations during this period has been increased punitiveness. For the last twenty-five years, Raphael and Stoll conclude that only 15 percent to 20 percent of the increase in the overall US incarceration rate is due to increased crime rates. Blumstein and Beck (1999) who focus on state imprisonment rates from 1980 to 1996 conclude that none of the increase in state level incarceration rates for nondrug-related

---

12. A distinct question is whether capital punishment is sufficiently freakish to render regression analysis useless as well; see Donohue and Wolfers (2005) for arguments along this line.

offenses during this period is due to increased crime rates. Both papers find that increased certainty and severity each played a major role in the rise in incarceration. We therefore turn to studies that examine particular mechanisms by which the criminal sanction regime affects crime rates.

1.3.2   Studies of the Effects of Severity of Punishment

The literature on the deterrent effect of the obvious form of severity, prison sentence length, is surprisingly small. However, these studies are of great value because of their focus on the effects of individual policies. Studies based on individual policies do not require that policy effects are constant across locations and, depending on the nature of the policy change, provide evidence that is more likely to be uncontaminated by the presence of unobserved heterogeneity. We note that for the case of severity, aggregate crime regressions are infeasible for the simple reason that aggregate data on the severity of punishment is unavailable.

The earliest post-1970s attempts to measure severity effects analyzed the deterrent impact of sentence enhancement for gun crimes. A series of studies conducted by Loftin, McDowall, and colleagues (Loftin and McDowall 1981; Loftin, Heumann, and McDowall 1983; Loftin and McDowall 1984) examine whether sentence enhancements for gun use in committing another type of crime such as robbery deter gun use in the commission of crime. While their findings are mixed, they generally fail to uncover evidence of a deterrent effect (but see McDowall, Loftin, and Wiersema 1992).[13] The generally null findings may reflect that gun-using criminals did not respond to the incremental increase in severity. However, Loftin, McDowall, and colleagues also found that these laws were not effective in increasing the sentences actually received in gun-related crime prosecutions. Thus, gun-using criminals may not have responded because the real incentives were not actually changed.

A large number of studies have examined the deterrent effect of California's Three Strikes and You're Out law, which mandated a minimum sentence of twenty-five years upon conviction for a third strikeable offense. Zimring, Hawkins, and Kamin (2001) conclude that the law at most reduced the felony crime rate by 2 percent. Only those individuals with two strikeable offenses showed any indication of reduced offending. The analysis was based on a variety of empirical comparisons designed to detect whether

13. McDowall, Loftin, and Wiersema (1992) combine data from the different locations they had previously studied for evidence of a deterrent effect of sentence enhancements. While none of the individual site analyses produced evidence of a deterrent effect, the combined analysis did. For several reasons we are skeptical of the combined analysis. First, it is vulnerable to many of the criticisms we have leveled at aggregate regression analyses. Second, their finding that at the individual sites the laws were ineffective in increasing sentence length suggests that the null findings at the individual sites were not a result of a lack of statistical power that might be remedied by combining data across sites. Third, the combination of results from different studies involves ad hoc statistical assumptions that are a separate source of possible nonrobustness.

there was any evidence of a discontinuous decline in offending following the effective date of the statute (March 1994) or whether there was a reduction in the proportion of crimes committed by the targeted groups, individuals with convictions for strikeable offenses. They found no indication of a drop in crime rate following enactment that could be attributable to the statute, but did find some indication in reduced offending among individuals with two strikeable offenses. Other studies by Stolzenberg and D'Alessio (1997) and Greenwood and Hawken (2002) also examine before and after trends and find similarly small crime prevention effects.

The Zimring, Hawkins, and Kamin (2001) finding of a potential deterrent effect among individuals with two strikeable offenses accords with the results of Helland and Tabarrok (2007), a study that we regard as particularly well crafted. This analysis focuses exclusively on whether the law deterred offending among individuals previously convicted of strike-eligible offenses. Helland and Tabarrok compare the future offending of individuals convicted of two previous strikeable offenses with that of individuals who had been convicted of only one strikeable offense but who, in addition, had been tried for a second strikeable offense but were ultimately convicted of a nonstrikeable offense. The study demonstrates that these two groups of individuals were comparable on many characteristics such as age, race, and time in prison. Even so, it finds that arrest rates were about 20 percent lower for the group with convictions for two strikeable offenses. The authors attribute this reduction to the greatly enhanced sentence that would have accompanied conviction for a third strikeable offense.

As is standard in studies of this type, the interpretation of the findings in terms of the marginal deterrence effects of the three strikes law is contingent on the comparability of the two groups under study. There are reasons why unobserved heterogeneity may be present; for example, those individuals who were convicted of a second nonstrikeable offense may have had better legal representation than those that were convicted of a second strikeable offense. In such a case, the incentives for further crime commission may differ for reasons outside the penalty differential.[14] Another reason for non-comparability may be that those convicted of a nonstrikeable offense are simply better criminals than those convicted of strikeable offenses in the sense that they are better able to generate alibis, avoid leaving evidence, and so forth, and so were convicted of lesser offenses than those of which they were, in fact, guilty. Our own view is that the concerns raised by these possible sources of heterogeneity are sufficiently speculative that we find the Helland and Tabarrok results to still be persuasive. Helland and Tabarrok also conduct a cost-benefit analysis and conclude that the crime reduction benefits likely fall far short of the cost of the prison enhancement, twenty years or more. They go on to point out that a comparable investment in

---

14. We thank Philip Cook for this observation.

policing that primarily affects the certainty of punishment are likely to yield far larger crime reduction benefits. We return to this observation later.[15]

Kessler and Levitt (1999) examine the deterrent impact of another California sentence enhancement law, Proposition 8 passed in 1982. Proposition 8 anticipates the three strikes–type laws passed by many states in the 1990s. Their aim was to distinguish deterrent effects from incapacitation effects. Most state criminal statutes provide for a sentence enhancement for repeat offenders. Proposition 8 increased the severity of those enhancements and mandated their application. Kessler and Levitt argue that prior to enactment of Proposition 8 repeat offenders covered by the proposition were still sentenced to prison, just not for as long. Thus, any short-term drop in crime rate should be attributed to deterrence rather than incapacitation. They estimate a 4 percent decline in crime attributable to deterrence in the first year after enactment. Within five to seven years the effect grows to a 20 percent reduction. The longer term estimate includes incapacitation effects. Indeed, Kessler and Levitt acknowledge that the incapacitation effect may dominate the deterrent effect.

Webster, Doob, and Zimring (2006) challenge the basic finding of any preventive effects. Kessler and Levitt examine only data from every other year. When all annual data are used, Webster, Doob, and Zimring (2006) find that the decline in crime rates in the effected categories begins before Proposition 8's enactment, and the slope of this trend remains constant through implementation. This critique has not been resolved: see Levitt (2006) for a response, and further commentary supportive of aspects of Webster, Doob, and Zimring by Raphael (2006). In our view, the strongest critique of the Kessler and Levitt analysis concerns the assumption that the time series properties of either crime rates unaffected by Proposition 8 in California or the equivalent Proposition 8 crime rates for other states can, via comparison with the crime rates in California for crimes affected by Proposition 8, be used to uncover the effect of Proposition 8. To be fair, both Kessler and Levitt and Levitt are very clear that comparability is a judgment call. Our judgment is that Raphael, in particular, makes a strong argument against comparability.[16]

---

15. Shepherd (2002) also found crime prevention effects of California's Three Strikes Law, mostly from a reduction in burglaries. The aim of the analysis was to estimate the total deterrent effect of the law as reflected in the article's title "Fear of the First Strike . . ." The validity of the findings are difficult to judge because the statistical analysis rests on many fragile assumptions; for example, that police and court expenditures are independent of the crime rate.

16. We also come to this conclusion because Kessler and Levitt do not provide a clear conceptualization of what is meant by a comparable data series. It appears that they are assuming that if a group of states follow a similar crime trend to California pre-Proposition 8 they are comparable. Variance, however, may be just as important as trend. Suppose that both series are white noise, but that shocks to the California series are two times the value of shocks to the other states. If Proposition 8 had no real effect; that is, the reduction in California's crime rate was a function of a series of draws of shocks; then under the assumptions of this example, the reductions would be twice the other states. One can construct similar examples if the degree of dependence in the series is different.

For most crimes, the certainty and severity of punishment increases discontinuously upon reaching the age of majority, when jurisdiction for criminal wrongdoing shifts from the juvenile to the adult court. In an extraordinarily careful analysis of individual-level crime histories from Florida, Lee and McCrary (2009) attempt to identify a discontinuous decline in the hazard of offending at age eighteen, the age of majority in Florida. Their point estimate of the discontinuous change is negative as predicted, but minute in magnitude and not even remotely close to achieving statistical significance.

An earlier analysis by Levitt (1998) finds a large drop in the offending of young adults upon their reaching the age of jurisdiction for the adult courts. For several reasons we judge the null effect finding of Lee and McCrary more persuasive. First, Levitt (1998) focuses on differences in age measured at annual frequencies, whereas Lee and McCrary measure age in days or weeks. At annual frequencies, the estimated effect is more likely to reflect both deterrence and incapacitation, something that Lee and McCrary note. Second, the Lee and McCrary analysis is based on individual level data and so avoids interpretation problems that can arise from aggregation (Durlauf, Navarro, and Rivers 2010). Further, the individual-level data employed by Lee and McCrary are of particular interest because of the common discontinuity in severity faced by all individuals at age eighteen and the fact that the exact ages of arrested individuals are identified, allowing one to pinpoint very short-term effects of the discontinuity on criminal behavior.

The literature on whether increases in prison sentence length serve as a deterrent is not large but there are several persuasive studies. These studies suggest that increases in the severity of punishment have at best only a modest deterrent effect. We emphasize, however, that this conclusion concerns changes in severity at margin. For deterrence to be effective there must be negative consequences. Much research in the perceptual deterrence literature, which surveys individuals on their sanction risk perceptions and intentions to offend, finds that perceived severity of sanction consequences are inversely related to self-reported offending or behavioral intentions to offend (Nagin 1998). This research, however, also makes clear that perceptions of severity are tied in complex ways to attachments to family, friends, and the legal labor market (Nagin and Paternoster 1991, 1993). It also finds that unlike perceptions of the risk of apprehension, perceptions of sentence length are generally not associated with self-reported offending.

It is important to note that most research on sentence length involves increases in already long sentences. There is some evidence that Massachusetts' Bartley-Fox gun law mandating a one year prison sentence for unlawful carrying of a gun may have been a deterrent (Wellford, Pepper, and Petrie 2005). Further, we will discuss experiments that show short but certain incarceration deters. We thus see a need for research on the likely nonlinear relationship between deterrence and severity.

1.3.3   Studies of the Effect of Certainty of Punishment

Severity alone, of course, cannot deter. There must also be some possibility that the sanction will be incurred if the crime is committed. For that to happen, the offender must be apprehended, usually by the police. He must next be charged and successfully prosecuted, and finally sentenced by the judiciary. None of these successive stages in processing through the criminal justice system is certain. Thus, another key concept in deterrence theory is the certainty of punishment. For two reasons the discussion that follows on evidence pertaining to the certainty of punishment focuses mainly upon the deterrent effect of the police. First, the police are the most important actors in generating certainty—absent detection and apprehension, there is no possibility of conviction or punishment. Second, there is little research on the deterrent effect stemming from the certainty of prosecution or sentencing to prison conditional on apprehension.[17]

The police may prevent crime through many possible mechanisms. Apprehension of active offenders is a necessary first step for their conviction and punishment. If the sanction involves imprisonment, crime may be prevented by the incapacitation of the apprehended offender. The apprehension of active offenders may also deter would-be criminals by increasing their perception of the risk of apprehension and, thereby, the certainty of punishment. Many police tactics such as rapid response to calls for service at crime scenes or postcrime investigation are intended not only to capture the offender, but to deter others by projecting a tangible threat of apprehension. Police may, however, deter without actually apprehending criminals because their very presence projects a threat of apprehension if a crime were to be committed. Indeed, some of the most compelling evidence of deterrence involves instances where there is complete or near complete collapse of police presence. In September 1944, German soldiers occupying Denmark arrested the entire Danish police force. According to an account by Andenaes (1974), crime rates rose immediately but not uniformly. The frequency of street crimes like robbery, whose control depends heavily upon visible police presence, rose sharply. By contrast, crimes such as fraud were less affected. See Sherman and Eck (2002) for other examples of crime increases following a collapse of police presence.

Research on the marginal deterrent effect of police has evolved in three distinct literatures. One set of studies has focused on the deterrent effect of the aggregate police presence measured, for example, by the relationship between police per capita and crime rates. A second body of work, based on regression discontinuity designs, examines the effects of abrupt changes

---

17. Several studies conducted in the 1970s examined the deterrent effect of conviction risk, usually measured by the ration of convictions to changes (Avio and Clark 1976; Carr-Hill and Stern 1973; Sjoquist 1973). These studies suffered from a number of important methodological limitations including, most importantly, their treating conviction risk as exogenous.

in police presence. A third research program has focused on the crime prevention effectiveness of different strategies for deploying police. We review these literatures separately.

Studies of police hiring and crime rates have been plagued by a number of impediments to causal inference. Among these are cross-jurisdictional differences in the recording of crime, feedback effects from crime rates to police hiring, the confounding of deterrence with incapacitation, and aggregation of police manpower effects across heterogeneous units, among others (see Nagin 1978, 1998). Of these problems, the challenge that has received the most attention in empirical applications is the endogeneity problem, namely the feedback from crime rates to police hiring.

Two studies of police manpower by Marvell and Moody (1996) and Levitt (1997) are notable for their identification strategies as well as for the consistency of their findings. The Marvell and Moody (1996) study is based on an analysis of two panel data sets, one composed of forty-nine states for the years 1968 to 1993 and the other of fifty-six large cities for the years 1971 to 1992. To untangle the causality problem they regress the current crime rate on lags of the crime rate, as well as lags of police manpower. The strongest evidence for an impact of police hiring on total crime rates comes from the city-level analysis, with an estimated elasticity of –0.3. In the spirit of Marvell and Moody's multiple time series analysis, Corman and Mocan (2000) conduct tests of Granger causality using a single, high-frequency (monthly) time series of crime in New York City (January 1970 to December 1996). They find that the number of police officers is negatively correlated with some crimes (robbery, burglary) but not with others. In addition, the number of felony arrests is a robust predictor of several kinds of crime (murder, robbery, burglary, vehicle theft). They conclude that policymakers can deter serious crimes by adding more police officers, and also by allocating existing police resources to aggressive felony enforcement (see also Corman and Mocan 2005).

Levitt (1997) performs an instrumental variable analysis from a panel of fifty-nine large cities for the years 1970 to 1992. Reasoning that political incumbents have incentives to devote resources to increasing the size of the police force in anticipation of upcoming elections, he uses election cycles to help untangle the cause-effect relationship between crime rates and police manpower and finds large preventive effects of police on violent crime and smaller, but still significant, effects on property crime. However, in a reanalysis of Levitt's data, McCrary (2002) corrects technical problems in Levitt's analysis and finds no significant preventive effect of police on crime. In a reply and new analysis, Levitt (2002) uses an alternative identification strategy based on the number of firefighters and civil service workers and obtains similar elasticity estimates to his original analysis. More recently, Evans and Owens (2007) examine the crime prevention effects of police by analyzing hiring and crime reduction effects associated with federal subsidies disbursed through the Office of Community Oriented Policing Services for the hiring of new police officers. Their elasticity estimates of the crime rate to police expenditures per capita are −0.99 for violent crime and −0.26 for property crime.

To summarize, aggregate studies of police presence conducted since the mid-1990s consistently find that putting more police officers on the street— either by hiring new officers or by allocating existing officers in ways that put them on the street in larger numbers or for longer periods of time—is associated with reductions in crime. This negative association is interpreted as reflecting the deterrent effect of police presence. There is also consistency with respect to the size of the effect. Most estimates reveal that a 10 percent increase in police presence yields a reduction in total crime in the neighborhood of 3 percent.

How should these aggregate police/crime regressions be evaluated in light of our criticisms of the aggregate crime and imprisonment regressions? On some dimensions, the police/crime regressions are clearly more persuasive. Unlike the imprisonment regressions, all of the studies we cite that employ aggregate police regressions ask a meaningful policy question; changes in policing are subject to policy choice in a way that the imprisonment rate is not. Further, there is less emphasis on Granger causality in the police regressions literature than the imprisonment literature; so while Marvell and Moody (1994) explicitly use Granger causality notions and Corman and Mocan (2000) do so implicitly, neither Levitt (1997, 2002) nor Evans and Owens (2007) fall into the misinterpretation of marginal time series predictive power as evidence of causality in a counterfactual sense. It is true that the studies we have cited suffer from issues of theory openendedness and lack of attention to robustness with respect to the way variables are measured, the possibility of parameter heterogeneity across geographic units, theory, and the difficulties of distinguishing between deterrence and incapacitation. Still, it is noteworthy that with the important exception of McCrary's reanalysis of the data used in Levitt (1997), panel-based studies fairly consistently find evidence of a preventive effect of the police. So, read in isolation, the evidentiary strength of the studies is limited by inadequate attention to model uncertainty.

On the other hand, the findings of aggregate police regressions are consistently replicated in a number of tests of police effects of crime via particular policy changes. This is not true for imprisonment/crime studies in the sense that the time series evidence is not systematically matched by evidence that particular penalty enhancements are efficacious. As in the case of targeted studies of severity, we are well disposed to these targeted studies of police, in this case because they provide a more transparent test of the effect of police presence on crime, are less subject to biases that may attend analyzing data across a highly heterogeneous set of cities, and are less likely to measure incapacitation effects.

Several of these targeted studies investigate the impact on the crime rate of reductions in police presence and productivity as a result of massive budget cuts or lawsuits following racial profiling scandals. Such studies have examined the Cincinnati Police Department (Shi 2009), the New Jersey State Police (Heaton 2010), and the Oregon State Police (DeAngelo and Hansen 2008). Each of these studies concludes that increases (decreases) in police presence and activity substantially decrease (increase) crime. By way of example, Shi (2009) studies the fallout from an incident in Cincinnati in which a white police officer shot and killed an unarmed African American suspect. The incident was followed by three days of rioting, heavy media attention, the filing of a class action lawsuit, a federal civil rights investigation, and the indictment of the officer in question. These events created an unofficial incentive for officers from the Cincinnati Police Department to curtail their use of arrest for misdemeanor crimes, especially in communities with higher proportional representation of African Americans out of concern for allegations of racial profiling. Shi demonstrates measurable declines in police productivity in the aftermath of the riot and also documents a substantial increase in criminal activity. The estimated elasticities of crime to policing based on her approach were -0.5 for violent crime and -0.3 for property crime.

The ongoing threat of terrorism has also provided a number of unique opportunities to study the impact of police resource allocation in cities around the world, including the District of Columbia (Klick and Tabarrok 2005), Buenos Aires (Di Tella and Schargrodsky 2004), Stockholm (Poutvaara and Priks 2006), and London (Draca, Machin, and Witt 2008). The Klick and Tabarrok (2005) study examines the effect on crime of the color-coded alert system devised by the US Department of Homeland Security in the aftermath of the September 11, 2001, terrorist attack to denote the terrorism threat level. Its alert system's purpose was to signal federal, state, and local law enforcement agencies to occasions when it might be prudent to divert resources to sensitive locations. Klick and Tabarrok (2005) is especially interesting because of its use of daily police reports of crime (collected by the District's Metropolitan Police Department) for the period March 2002 to July 2003, during which time the terrorism alert level rose from "elevated" (yellow) to "high" (orange) and back down to "elevated" on four occasions. During high alerts, anecdotal evidence suggested that police presence increased by 50 percent. Their estimate of the elasticity of total crime to changes in police presence as the alert level rose and fell was -0.3. One limitation of their finding concerns general equilibrium effects, which we raised in the context of experiments. Their evidence of lower crime during higher police presence cannot be extrapolated to a claim about the effects of a constant increase in police presence since one does not know to what extent criminals are merely adjusting the timing of activity.

Cohen and Ludwig (2003) take a third approach by studying the outcomes of policies by the Pittsburgh Police Department, which assigned additional police resources to selected high-crime communities within the city. These patrols were relieved from responding to citizen requests for service (911 calls) to work proactively to search for illegally carried guns. Police contacts were initiated mainly through traffic stops and "stop-and-talk" activities with pedestrians in public areas. Carrying open alcohol containers in public and traffic violations were frequent reasons for initiating contact. These targeted patrols were directed to two of Pittsburgh's five police zones that had unusually high crime rates. Based on a difference-in-difference-in-differences type analysis they found that this heightened enforcement activity was associated with significant declines in shots fired and assault-related gunshot injuries. The conclusion of the Cohen and Ludwig study nicely accords with the conclusions of hot spots policing literature discussed later.

These police manpower studies mainly speak only to the number and allocation of police officers and not to what police officers actually do on the street beyond making arrests. So in this sense, they are something of a black box. We now turn to the question of how police are used. Much research has examined the crime prevention effectiveness of alternative strategies for deploying police resources. This research has largely been conducted by criminologists and sociologists. Among this group of researchers, the preferred research designs are quasi-experiments involving before-and-after studies of the effect of targeted interventions as well as true randomized experiments. The discussion that follows draws heavily upon two excellent reviews of this research by Weisburd and Eck (2004) and Braga (2008). As a preface to this summary, we draw the theoretical link between police deployment and the certainty and severity of punishment. For the most part, deployment strategies affect the certainty of punishment through its impact on the probability of apprehension. There are, however, notable examples where severity may also be affected.

In considering the effect of police on apprehension risk, it is important to recognize that there is heterogeneity in the effects of alternative police deployment tactics on apprehension risk. As will be discussed, some tactics appear to be very effective whereas others seemingly have no effect. Even more important, apprehension risk itself is a heterogeneous quantity. A given police deployment strategy may differentially affect offender types (e.g., gang members versus nongang members) or crime types (drug dealing versus robbery).

One class of strategies for affecting apprehension risk involves the way the police are mobilized once a crime is reported. Studies of the effect of rapid response to calls for service (Kansas City Police Department 1977; Spelman and Brown 1981) find no evidence of a crime prevention effect, but this may be because most calls for service occur well after the crime event with the result that the perpetrator has fled the scene. Thus, it is doubtful that rapid response materially affects apprehension risk. Similarly, because most arrests result from the presence of witnesses or physical evidence, improved investigations are not likely to yield material deterrent effects because, again, apprehension risk is not likely to be affected.

Another strategy in this class involves the implementation of mandatory actions when the police are called onto the scene of a crime. A series of randomized experiments were conducted to test the deterrent effect of mandatory arrest for domestic violence. The initial experiment conducted in Minneapolis by Sherman and Berk (1984) found that mandatory arrest was effective in reducing domestic violence reoffending. Findings from follow-up replication studies (as part of the so-called Spouse Assault Replication Program, or SARP) were inconsistent. Experiments in two cities found a deterrent effect, but no such effect was found in three other cities (Maxwell, Garner, and Fagan 2002). Berk et al. (1992) found that the response to arrest in the SARP data depended upon social background. Higher status individuals seemed to be deterred by arrest whereas the assaultive behavior of lower status individuals seemed to be aggravated. The heterogeneity in response is important because it illustrates a more general point—the response to sanction threats need not be uniform in the population. Sherman, Schmidt, and Rogan (1992) and Sherman et al. (1992) propose a theoretical explanation called defiance theory to explain the status-based heterogeneity in response to mandatory arrest.

A second class of strategies involves the deployment of police resources in a city. We distinguish this class of policies from the first class as the latter involves the way the police respond to a reported crime, whereas this strategy is one that establishes police locations and procedures in light of the characteristics of crime in the area under consideration. If an occupied police car is parked outside a liquor store, a would-be robber of the store will likely be deterred because apprehension is all but certain.[18] Two examples of police deployment strategies that have been shown to be effective in averting crime in the first place are "hot spots" policing and problem-oriented policing. Weisburd and Eck (2004) propose a two-dimensional taxonomy of policing strategies. One dimension is "level of focus" and the other is "diversity of locus." Level of focus represents the degree to which police activities are targeted. Targeting can occur in a variety of ways, but Weisburd and Eck give special attention to policing strategies that target police resources in small geographic areas (e.g., blocks or specific addresses) that have very high levels of criminal activity, so-called crime hot spots.

The idea of hot spots policing stems from a striking empirical regularity uncovered by Sherman and colleagues. Sherman, Gartin, and Buerger

---

18. An implication of this type of strategy is that measures of apprehension risk based only on enforcement actions and crimes that actually occur, such as arrests per reported crime, are seriously incomplete because such measures do not capture the apprehension risk that attends criminal opportunities that were not acted upon by potential offenders because the risk was deemed too high (see Cook 1979 for more discussion).

(1989) found that only 3 percent of addresses and intersections ("places," as they were called) in Minneapolis produced 50 percent of all calls to the police. Weisburd and Green (1995) found that 20 percent of all disorder crime and 14 percent of crimes against persons in Jersey City, New Jersey, arose from 56 drug crime hot spots. In a later study in Seattle, Washington, Weisburd et al. (2006) report that between 4 and 5 percent of street segments in the city accounted for 50 percent of crime incidents for each year over a fourteen-year period. Other more recent studies finding comparable crime concentrations include Brantingham and Brantingham (1999), Eck, Gersh, and Taylor (2000), and Roncek (2000). As in the liquor store example, the rationale for concentrating police in crime hot spots is to create a prohibitively high risk of apprehension and thereby to deter crime at the hot spot in the first place.[19]

The first test of the efficacy of concentrating police resources on crime hot spots was conducted by Sherman and Weisburd (1995). In this randomized experiment, hot spots in the experimental group were subjected to, on average, a doubling of police patrol intensity compared to hot spots in the control group. Declines in total crime calls ranged from 6 to 13 percent. In another randomized experiment, Weisburd and Green (1995) found that hot spots policing was similarly effective in suppressing drug markets and Weisburd et al. (2006) found no evidence that hot spots policing simply displaced crime to nearby locations. It is important, however, to note that these experiments do not test long-term effectiveness. Even if in the short term there is no displacement, over the long-term new hot spots may emerge in response to the suppression of prior hot spots.

Braga's (2008) informative review of hot spots policing summarizes the findings from nine experimental or quasi-experimental evaluations. The studies were conducted in five large US cities and one suburb of Australia. Crime incident reports and citizen calls for service were used to evaluate impacts in and around the geographic area of the crime hot spot. The targets of the police actions varied. Some hot spots were generally high-crime locations, whereas others were characterized by specific crime problems like drug trafficking. All but two of the studies found evidence of significant reductions in crime. Further, no evidence was found of material crime displacement to immediately surrounding locations. On the contrary, some studies found evidence of crime reductions, not increases, in the surrounding locations—a "diffusion of crime-control benefits" to nontargeted locales. We also note that the findings from the previously described econometric studies of focused police actions, for example in response to terror alert

---

19. Zenou (2003) provides a theoretical analysis that explains the spatial concentration of crime via the interplay of social interactions and economic opportunities and provides corroborating empirical evidence.

level, buttress the conclusion from the hot spots literature that the strategic targeting of police resources can be very effective in reducing crime. The second dimension of the Weisburd and Eck taxonomy is diversity of approaches. This dimension concerns the variety of approaches that police use to impact public safety. Low diversity is associated with reliance on time-honored law enforcement strategies for affecting the threat of apprehension, for example, by dramatically increasing police presence. High diversity involves expanding beyond conventional practice to prevent crime. One example of a high-diversity approach is problem-oriented policing (POP). Problem-oriented policing comes in so many different forms that (like pornography) it is regrettably hard to define, but the essence of POP is devising strategies for increasing apprehension risk or reducing criminal opportunities (see Cook and MacDonald, chapter 7, this volume) that are tailored to address the crime problem at a specific location or involving a specific type of activity (examples include targeting open air drug markets or focusing on the protection of adolescents being victimized going to and coming from school).

Weisburd et al. (2010) conduct a review of the POP evaluations and report overwhelming support for its effectiveness. While the great majority of evaluations are of very low quality—little more than before and after studies—they identified ten studies with credible designs (i.e., randomized experiments or quasi-experiments with credible control comparisons). Eight of the ten studies report statistically significant reductions in crime. For several reasons the findings are notable for our purposes here. First, effect sizes vary considerably across interventions, a finding that reinforces our argument that police-related deterrent effects are heterogeneous—they depend on how the police are used and the circumstances in which they are used. A second and related point is that two of the interventions involved monitoring of probationers to avert probation revocation due to reoffending or violation of conditions of parole. This highlights the point that police can be effectively used to deter crime not only at high-risk locations but also among high-risk individuals.

Taken as whole, the literature on the preventive effect of policing provides a compelling scientific case that police prevent crime. It also makes clear that the effects of police on crime are heterogeneous—not all methods for deploying police are comparably effective in reducing crime; indeed, some deployment strategies seem to be completely ineffective. Thus, policy recommendations for increasing police resources to prevent crime are incomplete without further elaboration on how they should be used. We are thus very sympathetic with the intellectual tradition in the police deployment literature of testing the effectiveness of alternative strategies for using police resources. We return to this observation in the conclusions.

The observation that police can be used to affect the criminality of high-risk individuals brings us to another relevant literature—field interventions in which sanctions are specifically focused on high-risk groups. Like POP tactics, all of the interventions are multifaceted but deterrence-based tactics are a core feature of each. In all cases the deterrence component of the intervention involved an attempt to make sanction risk certain and salient to a selected high-risk group. In our judgment these interventions deserve special attention because they provide a useful perspective on the promise and uncertainties of such focused deterrence-based interventions.

We begin by summarizing the findings of an underappreciated randomized experiment by Weisburd, Einat, and Kowalski (2008) that tests alternative strategies for incentivizing the payment of court-ordered fines. The most salient finding involves the "miracle of the cells," namely, that the imminent threat of incarceration is a powerful incentive for paying delinquent fines. The common feature of treatment conditions involving incarceration was a high certainty of imprisonment for failure to pay the fine. However, the fact that Weisburd, Einat, and Kowalski label the response the "miracle of the cells" and not the "miracle of certainty" is telling. Their choice of label is a reminder that certainty must result in a distasteful consequence, namely incarceration in this experiment, in order for it to be a deterrent. The consequences need not be draconian, just sufficiently costly to deter proscribed behavior.

The deterrence strategy of certain but nondraconian sanctions has been applied with apparently great success in Project Hope, an intervention heralded in Mark Kleiman's (2009) highly visible book *When Brute Force Fails*. Project Hope is a Hawaii-based probation enforcement process. In a randomized experiment probationers assigned to Project Hope had much lower rates of positive drug tests, missed appointments, and, most importantly, were significantly less likely to be arrested and imprisoned. The cornerstone of the HOPE intervention was regular drug testing, including random tests, and certain but short punishment periods of confinement (i.e., one to two days) for positive drug tests or other violations of conditions of probation. Thus, both the Weisburd, Einat, and Kowalski (2008) fine experiment and Project Hope show that highly certain punishment can be an effective deterrent to those for whom deterrence has previously been ineffective in averting crime.

The strategy of certain punishment is also a centerpiece of field interventions in Boston, Richmond, and Chicago that are specifically aimed at reducing gun violence. However, unlike Project Hope and the fine-paying experiment, the certain punishment is far more draconian—a very lengthy prison sentence. For descriptions of a Boston intervention called Operation Ceasefire see Kennedy et al. (2001), for the Richmond intervention called Project Exile see Raphael and Ludwig (2003), and for the Chicago-based intervention see Papachristos, Meares, and Fagan (2007). A common feature of each intervention was commitment to federal prosecution for gun crimes which, upon conviction, allowed for very lengthy prison sentences. Notably, there were also concerted efforts to communicate the threat of certain and severe punishment to selected high-risk groups (e.g., members of violent gangs). All interventions claimed to have substantial success in reducing gun crime but at least in the cases of Boston and Richmond questions have been raised about whether the declines preceded the intervention or were no different than other comparable urban centers (Cook and Ludwig 2006; Raphael and Ludwig 2003). These concerns notwithstanding, each of these interventions illustrate the potential for combining elements of both certainty and severity enhancement to generate a targeted deterrent effect. Further evaluations of the efficacy of this strategy should be a high priority.

1.4   Interpretations: Certainty, Severity, and the Economic Model of Crime

In this section, we discuss how our conclusions about certainty versus severity relate to the baseline model of crime. These findings do not argue against the value of the economic approach, but rather suggests dimensions along which the modeling of beliefs and preferences should be generalized relative to standard formulations.

In understanding why certainty might trump severity in criminal decision making, we first return to the fact that the implications of our formulation of the Becker crime model concerning the relative efficacy of certainty and severity depended on assumptions about the concavity of $U_C(Z_i, L)$. For several reasons, this assumption may be challenged. One reason is that the baseline model neglects the intertemporal dimensions of the payoffs under the different crime/no crime and punished/not punished scenarios. The role of the timing of benefits and punishments to crime was recognized early in Cook (1980). Polinsky and Shavell (1999) provide a formal and very complete demonstration of the importance of timing in understanding certainty/severity tradeoffs; here we provide the basic intuition underlying the ideas in these papers. In thinking about the effects of penalties on individuals, it is necessary to consider the commission of a particular crime at a particular date in the context of an individual's lifetime utility. In other words, the choice to commit a crime at time t is one element of the many decisions an individual makes over time. What this means is that the payoffs embedded in each of the terms in equation (2) are in fact a sequence of expected discounted utilities over the future, in which the commission of a crime (or lack thereof) represents one element of a dynamic choice problem. This dynamic choice problem calls into question the assumption that $U_C(Z_i, L)$ is concave since the function is appropriately understood as depending on the degree to which future utility is discounted. A marginal increase in sentence length affects utilities starting at time $t + L$. If utility between times t and $t + 1$ is discounted by β, then it is evident that for initially long sentences, the effects on crime decisions may have relatively little effect, especially if potential criminals have high discount rates. Thus, there is no logical reason why concavity should hold for $U_C(Z_i, L)$. Put differently, if one considers the different certainty/severity values that lead to a given value of pL, this expected value masks the time of life where changes in L become operational. Hence it is possible that the disutility effects of longer sentences are simply not that important in the calculation of lifetime utility.

It is beyond the scope of this chapter to analyze a lifetime utility model in which agents consider a sequence of crime/no crime decisions. Models of this type are developed in Imai and Krishna (2004) and Lee and McCrary (2005, 2009).[20] Imai and Krishna study an environment in which sentence length is constrained to be one time unit, which allows them to estimate the model in absence of sentencing data. The sentence length assumption means that issues of severity certainty tradeoffs cannot be addressed; on the other hand, this paper is of particular interest in terms of understanding how individual heterogeneity affects crime decisions. Lee and McCrary allow for variable sentence length and study the effects of certainty and severity via calibration of parameters to match various aggregate crime statistics. The additional theoretical richness of Lee and McCrary comes at the expense of a less rich version of individual heterogeneity. These important papers illustrate the possibility that dynamic structural analyses of crime can play a valuable role in the study of sanctions policies. The differences in the modeling assumptions between the papers also illustrate some of the defects of the current crime statistics, an issue we address later.

The embedding of our initial model into a dynamic framework is fully consistent with the view of economic actors as rational, purposeful decision makers who follow consistent discounting procedures when weighing the present and future and whose subjective beliefs about probabilities correspond to the objective probabilities for the phenomena under question, most notably the probability of punishment if a crime is committed. Beyond the implications of the effects of increased severity in the context of a lifetime utility model, there may be reasons to believe that deviations from the baseline rational crime model provide additional explanatory power if one backs awway from the particular rationality assumptions with which we have so far worked. An example of why this may be needed is the finding in Lee and McCrary (2009) that the shift from juvenile to adult penalties has little deterrent effect; this is not explainable by the fact that the additional penalty occurs later in life, but speaks to something about the way that future consequences are considered. To formalize this intuition, we distinguish between deviations our original rationality postulates based on the ways in

20. Earlier examples of dynamic crime choice models include Polinsky and Shavell (1998) who show how, in a two-period version of Becker's model, optimal sanction policy may imply that the severity of a penalty depends on previous convictions. Polinsky and Shavell's finding reinforces the idea that sanction severity should not be reduced to a scalar in considering alternative punishment regimes.

which individuals discount the future versus deviations based on the way probabilities are formulated in assessing uncertain outcomes.

There is a growing body of research from psychology and criminology linking criminal and delinquent behavior in adolescence and beyond to problem behaviors and cognitive deficits measured in childhood (Jolliffe and Farrington 2009; Moffitt 1993; White et al. 1994). One of the most prominent findings in this literature is the linkage between crime and impulsive behavior in noncriminal settings. Impulsivity is measured in many different ways in psychology. In part, the differences in measurement reflect different theoretical conceptions of what constitutes impulsivity. Some traditions conceive of impulsivity as a cognitive deficit in executive functions such as abstract reasoning, self-monitoring, and self-control. All of these cognitive functions are associated with the functioning of the frotal lobes of the brain. This conception of impulsivity is at the core of a theory of criminal behavior, posited by Wilson and Herrnstein (1985), that persons who are "present oriented," individuals who attend mainly to incentives and disincentives over a short rather than long time horizon, are more prone to crime. Psychologists working in this theoretical tradition have devised many tests of impulsivity that primarily focus on measuring the capacity for focused attention. Another tradition conceives of impulsivity as a personality characteristic. In this tradition impulsivity is measured by scales designed to capture the degree to which an individual acts without forethought or planning.

Within the economics literature, ideas of impulsivity are paralleled in the development of models of hyperbolic discounting. Hyperbolic discounting is designed to explain behaviors where the temptation of the moment appears to lead to a failure to consistently evaluate future consequences. Models of this type can explain forms of regret on the part of decision makers that do not naturally arise on standard geometric discounting. Lee and McCrary (2005) provide a formal analysis of the effects of hyperbolic discounting on crime choices; see the discussion in Utset (2007). As shown by Lee and McCrary, hyperbolic discounting can produce behaviors that seem analogous to those associated with impulsivity. To be clear though, hyperbolic discounting does not directly translate into claims about the roles of strong emotions in decision making.

Questions of discounting are logically distinct from those concerning the formation of beliefs about the future and the ways in which these beliefs affect decisions; in our context, the key variable being the probability of punishment p. Our baseline formulation assumed that expected utility calculations are linear in these objective probabilities. There are a number of reasons to question this assumption. One reason may have to do with bounded rationality. While there is a growing body of evidence that individuals update their sanction risk perceptions based on past experiences in successfully and unsuccessfully avoiding apprehension in a fashion that at least crudely approximates Bayesian updating (Lochner 2007; Hjalmarsson 2008; Anwar and Loughran 2009), there is also a large body of evidence that perceptions of risk diverge substantially from actual risk with most people overestimating the actual risk.[21] This constitutes one reason why the way in which p appears in equation (2) may be empirically inadequate. In such contexts, it might make sense to work with subjective probabilities $p^i(p)$ that depend on the objective probabilities but do not equal them.

Further, in the modern decision theory literature, many arguments have been made that expected utility calculations should be replaced with nonexpected utility alternatives in order to better describe actual decision making. A number of these alternatives involve replacing p in equation (2) with a probability weighting function $\pi(p)$,[22] which means that the choice to commit a crime requires

(8) $\pi_i(p)(U_C(Z_i, L) - U_{NC}(Z_i)) + (1 - \pi_i(p))(U_C(Z_i, 0) - U_{NC}(Z_i)) > 0.$

We will focus on the implications of the use of probability weighting functions for crime decisions. While the replacement of objective with subjective probabilities can be mathematically equivalent to the use of probability weighting functions (as occurs when subjective probabilities follow $p^i(p)$), the interpretation of the two approaches is quite different.[23]

With respect to assessing the effects of sanction policy changes, the key difference between equation (8) and the baseline model equation (2) is that the marginal effect on the payoff to criminality with respect to changes in certainty of punishment is changed to

(9) $\dfrac{d\pi_i(p)}{dp} (U_C(Z_i, 0) - U_C(Z_i, L)).$

While an increase in p still makes crime less attractive, the magnitude of this increase on the expected utility from crime commission will now vary according to $d\pi_i(p)/dp$; in the baseline model this term always equals one. Hence, evaluating a sanctions policy should perhaps include consideration of how changes in objective probabilities affect choices via the probability weighting function. Evaluating a sanctions policy under both expected and nonexpected utility approaches to decision making can provide a check

---

21. See Apel and Nagin (2010) for a summary of evidence on sanction risk perceptions.

22. Starmer (2000) provides a very clear discussion of nonexpected utility theories that lead to the use of probability weighting functions; see also Machina (1987) for a very accessible overview of modern approaches to decision theory.

23. The nonexpected utility literature focuses on formulations of individual preferences that do not lead to equation (2) as the description of decision making under uncertainty. One example is rank-dependent expected utility thory (Quiggin 1982), in which the payoff to a particular outcome is affected by its relative ranking compared to other possible outcomes. Nonexpected utility models do not require that individuals fail to assess the consequences of actions using objectively correct probabilities. Rather, they lead to formulations of the effects of these probabilities that differ from equation (2).

on the robustness of the effects of the sanctions to uncertainty about the decision-making process.

Unsurprisingly, there is a large empirical literature that has studied the properties of $d\pi_i(p)/dp$ in a range of experimental contexts.[24] At the risk of oversimplifying a complex body of work, considerable evidence exists that many individuals tend to overweight small probabilities and underweight large probabilities, relative to standard expected utility calculations. More specifically, there appears to be good evidence that the probability weighting function follows an inverse S-shape, which means that

(10) $\dfrac{d\pi_i(p)}{dp}$ is large if p near 0 or 1.

In words, the effects of an increase in the certainty of punishment are strongest, given a fixed value of $U_C(Z_i, 0) - U_C(Z_i, L)$, when the punishment probabilities are relatively large or small to begin with. This suggests that an additional candidate explanation for the relatively robust evidence that increases in certainty of punishment lower crime in contexts such as hot spot policing is that such policing tactics are being implemented in a circumstance where standard policing practice projects only a small probability of apprehension. We note that Berns et al. (2007) find an inverse S-shape is common in an experiment where the rewards were electric shocks, which suggests that the inverse S-shape is relevant for adverse outcomes; that is, being punished for a crime. However, as far as we know, there does not exist a body of research that focuses on the properties of probability weighting functions among that part of the population in which the decision to commit a crime is close to marginal. This strikes us as a valuable area for future work.[25] And of course, if the appropriate deviation from equation (2) is bounded rationality rather than nonexpected utility, one needs to know the functional form that relates subjective beliefs to objective probabilities for those whose decisions on criminality are near the margin in order to draw conclusions about the effects of changes in certainty.

While impulsivity, discounting, and generalizations of the role of probabilities in determining individual decisions all revolve around efforts to relax our initial assumptions about the cognition process of potential criminals, we close this discussion by considering a different dimension along which the baseline model can, we believe, be fruitfully extended. We are motivated by a consideration that, at first blush, might appear to be inconsistent with the

---

24. Starmer (2000) reviews the experimental evidence.

25. There are findings in the behavioral economics literature that would suggest modifications of the baseline Beckerian model beyond discounting and the probability weighting functions. For example, Post et al. (2008) find, for a high-stakes television game show, risk aversion decreases across rounds of play. This perhaps speaks to a channel by which the fact of arrest and imprisonment might affect preferences. To push this line of argument further would require more expertise in behavioral economics that we possess.

Beckerian model of crime—namely, the possibility that the imposition of sanction may be criminogenic even as it is preventive. A key conclusion of a review by Nagin, Cullen, and Jonson (2009) of the effect of the experience of imprisonment on recidivism is that the great majority of studies point to a criminogenic effect of the prison experience on subsequent offending. While this literature suffers from many statistical shortcomings that make this conclusion far from definitive, serious attention should be committed to extending the economic model of crime to account for the possibly criminogenic effect of the experience of punishment. Criminogenic effects may stem from either the crime-inducing effects of the *experience* of punishment and/or stigma. As a prelude to discussing the types of model generalizations that might be used to account for potentially criminogenic effects of heightened sanctions, we summarize the state of relevant literature and we then consider modifications of the Beckerian model.

Much data documents that most crime is attributable to a small proportion of the population who repeatedly recidivate. In their seminal study of the criminal activity of a birth cohort of 9,945 males born in Philadelphia in 1945, Wolfgang, Figlio, and Sellin (1972) find that through age eighteen, 6 percent of the cohort accounted for over half of the cohort's total arrests. Also, rates of recidivism of former prisoners are very high. The latest available analysis for the United States as a whole is based on 272,111 individuals released from the prisons of fifteen states in 1993. Langan and Levin (2002) find that within three years 68 percent had been arrested, 46.9 percent had been convicted, and 25.4 percent had been reimprisoned. Thus, as an empirical matter it is not surprising that most people who have contact with the criminal justice system are not novices. According to a 2006 Bureau of Justice Statistic study of felony defendants in the seventy-five largest cities, at the time of arrest 32 percent of defendants had an active criminal justice status, such as probation (15 percent), release pending disposition of a prior case (10 percent), or parole (5 percent). Further, 76 percent of all defendants had been arrested previously, with 50 percent having at least five prior arrest charges.

There are two very different interpretations of these statistics. One is that the high concentration of recidivists in the criminal justice system represents the ongoing failure of deterrence to suppress the criminal behavior of a small minority of the population. The other is that the experience of contact with the criminal justice system, most specifically in the form of imprisonment, is criminogenic. These two diametrically opposing interpretations of the data lay at the core of much academic and public policy debate about the role of imprisonment in crime control. The difficulties in disentangling them may be seen in a recent study by Drago, Galbiati, and Vertova (2009) of Italy's Collective Clemency Bill. In May of 2006, this bill resulted in the release of more than 20,000 inmates from Italian prisons. The release came with the condition that individuals convicted of another crime within five years of their release would have to serve the residual of the sentence that was suspended in addition to the sentence for the new crime. The residual sentence length varied between one and thirty-six months. Drago, Galbiati, and Vertova (2009) find that each month of residual sentence was associated with 1.2 percent reduction in the propensity to recommit crime. The authors interpret this finding as a deterrent, but an alternative and equally valid interpretation is that each additional month of imprisonment increases the propensity to offend by 1.2 percent.[26] The respective roles of these distinct explanations cannot be identified.

Moving beyond interpretation problems for a particular study, there are good reasons to think that the severity of a punishment does a poor job of summarizing the effects of incarceration on an individual. In the economic model of crime, deterrence is the behavioral response to the threat of crime. In criminology the term "specific deterrence" is used to describe the behavioral response to the experience of punishment. The logic of specific deterrence is grounded in the idea that if the experience of imprisonment is sufficiently distasteful some of the punished may conclude that it is an experience not to be repeated. The structure of the law itself may also cause previously convicted individuals to revise upward their estimates of the likelihood and/or severity of punishment for future lawbreaking. Criminal law commonly prescribes more severe penalties for recidivists. For example, sentencing guidelines routinely dictate longer prison sentences for individuals with prior convictions. Prosecutors may also be more likely to prosecute individuals with criminal histories. The experience of punishment may affect the likelihood of future crime by decreasing the attractiveness of crime itself or by expanding alternatives to crime. While imprisoned the individual may benefit from educational or vocational training that increases postrelease, noncriminal income earning opportunities (Layton MacKenzie 2002). Other types of rehabilitation are designed to increase the capacity for self-restraint in the presence of situations such as a confrontation that might provoke a criminal act such as violence (Cullen 2002).

There are, however, a number of reasons for theorizing that the experience of punishment might increase an individual's future proclivity for crime. One argument relates to the effect of the experience of crime on expectations about the prison experience. While some individuals might conclude imprisonment is not an experience to be repeated, others might conclude that the experience was not as adverse as anticipated. Other reasons have to do with the social interactions induced by imprisonment. Prisons might be "schools for crime" where inmates learn new crime skills even as their noncrime human capital depreciates. Associating with other more experienced inmates could lead new inmates to adopt the older inmate's deviant

---

26. We thank Philip Cook for this important insight on the alternative interpretation of the Drago, Galbiati, and Vertova (2009) study.

value systems or enable them to learn the tricks of the trade (Hawkins 1976; Steffensmeier and Ulmer 2005). Being punished may also elevate an offender's feelings of resentment against society (Sherman, Schmidt, and Rogan 1992) or strengthen the offender's deviant identity (Matsueda 1992).

The experience of imprisonment may also increase future criminality by stigmatizing the individual socially and economically. There is much evidence showing that an important part of the deterrent effect of legal sanctions stems from the expected societal reactions set off by the imposition of legal sanctions (Williams and Hawkins 1986; Nagin and Pogarsky 2003; Nagin and Paternoster 1994). Prior research has found that individuals who have higher stakes in conformity are more reluctant to offend when they risk being publicly exposed (Klepper and Nagin (1989a, 1989b)). While the fear of arrest and stigmatization may deter potential offenders from breaking the law, those that have suffered legal sanctions may find that conventional developmental routes are blocked. In their work on the 500 Boston delinquents initially studied by Glueck and Glueck (1950), Sampson and Laub (1993) have called attention to the role of legal sanctions in what they call the process of cumulative disadvantage. Official labeling through legal sanctions may cause an offender to become marginalized from conventionally structured opportunities, which in turn increases the likelihood of their subsequent offending (Bernburg and Krohn 2003; Pager 2003). Sampson and Laub (1993) propose that legal sanctions may amplify a snowball effect that increasingly mortgages the offender's future by reducing conventional opportunities. Several empirical studies support the theory that legal sanctions downgrade conventional attainment (Freeman 1996; Nagin and Waldfogel 1995, 1998; Sampson and Laub 1993; Waldfogel 1994; Western 2002; Western, Kling, and Weiman 2001) and increase future offending (Bernburg and Krohn 2003; Hagan and Palloni 1990).

Moving from this review of empirical work to the economic model of crime, our two channels for criminogenic effects imply somewhat different modeling strategies. The possibility that the experience of punishment affects proclivity for crime creates an important additional source of heterogeneity in the population at a given point in time. To see this, let CR_i denote the criminal record of the individual. Crime commission now requires that

(11) $p(U_C(Z_i, CR_i, L) - U_{NC}(Z_i, CR_i))$
$$+ (1 - p)(U_C(Z_i, CR_i, 0) - U_{NC}(Z_i, CR_i)) > 0,$$

which is an algebraically trivial extension of our baseline model but in fact gives a very different view of the determination of the aggregate crime rate. To see this, consider a generalization of equation (3)

(12) $\omega(Z_i, CR_i, p, L) = 1$ if equation (11) holds; 0 otherwise.

The equilibrium crime rate will now equal

(13) $\qquad \Pr(C|p,L) = \int\omega(Z,CR,p,L)dF_{Z,CR} =$

$$\iint\omega(Z,CR,p,L)dF_{Z|CR}dF_{CR}.$$

The double integral in equation (13) is a mixture density and represents averages (based on population weights) across the crime probabilities at each level of prior criminal record in the population; that is, probability weighted averages of the criminal record-specific crime rates $\int\omega(Z,CR,p,L)dF_{Z|CR}$.[27] By allowing the expected utility of a crime choice to depend on an individual's criminal record, it is evident that a criminal record can increase the probability of crime commission. Experience of punishment effects, whether generated by the learning of crime-related skills in prison or by the diminution of labor market opportunities after prison introduce additional heterogeneity in the population that can raise the probability of crime on the part of an individual.

Of course, one would expect that the lowered utility for an agent after imprisonment would work to reduce the incentive to commit a crime at t, especially among those who have never committed a crime. This possibility is masked in the formulation because we have not written an explicit intertemporal decision problem; rather, the possibility is implicitly embedded in $\omega(Z,0,p,L)$. Therefore, the presence of experience of punishment effects does not provide an a priori implication for the aggregate crime rate; it could be either increased or decreased. Notwithstanding, these effects can help explain why criminal behavior is concentrated in a small fraction of the total population who repeatedly recidivate. Among those relatively few individuals who initially commit crimes, recidivism rates are high because of the changes induced in the relative costs and benefits of crime.

One way to model stigma effects is to modify the various utility functions so that the imprisonment rate I is an additional argument in the utility functions when a crime is committed. This assumption (at least for previous offenders) is in the spirit of Sirakaya (2006) who found that the time recidivism for individuals is associated with the mean time for recidivism in their communities, even controlling for a host of observed and unobserved community effects.[28] The condition under which a crime is chosen is in this case

(14) $\quad p(U_C(Z_i,L,I) - U_{NC}(Z_i)) + (1 - p)(U_C(Z_i,0,I) - U_{NC}(Z_i)) > 0.$

27. Notice that the distribution of Z will typically differ between subpopulations with different criminal records. Any causal argument that a criminal record is criminogenic needs to account for this heterogeneity, which may not be observable to the analyst.

28. In addition to Sirakaya (2006), which is noteworthy for its econometric sophistication, a number of papers have suggested the presence of social interactions in crime in which the criminal choice of one person depends on the criminal behavior of others within one's community; Glaeser, Sacerdote, and Scheinkman (1996) is an early eample while Bayer, Hjalmarsson, and Pozen (2009) is a recent analysis based on an unusually detailed data set. This type of interaction may involve stigma as well. In terms of formal modeling, one way to model this

If stigma means that $U_C(Z_i, L, I)$ is decreasing in I, then it is trivial to see that expected utility to commission of a crime will be higher when stigma is lower. Since $I = P(C|p,L)pL$, a stigma effect means that the probability that an individual commits a crime is an increasing function of the average probability in the population. Under this modeling assumption, stigma is an example of a social interactions effect, (see Brock and Durlauf [2001c] and Durlauf and Ioannides [2010] for surveys), one consequence of which is the possibility of multiple equilibrium crime rates under a given sanction regime. This possibility is demonstrated theoretically in Rasmusen (1996), which provides microfoundations to a stigma effect in terms of the signal a criminal record gives about an individual's underlying type.

While experience of punishment and stigma effects can explain why increased sanctions can be criminogenic, it is less obvious that they can explain relative efficacy of certainty versus severity. That said, we believe there is good intuition why experience of imprisonment should exhibit the certainty severity differential. Long sentences, we suspect, are very damaging because of the brutality of prison and so render released prisoners especially unlikely to prosper in the noncriminal world. But to be fair, this is no more than an intuition.

It seems less clear why stigma would imply that certainty is more effective in deterring crime than severity. One reason why there may be a differential effect is that our index for stigma, $I = P(C|p,L)pL$ is a nonlinear function of p and L, a differential may simply follow from this. Another reason why stigma leads to this differential effect may occur when one decomposes stigma into different types. One type of stigma may be purely psychological, so that the shame or embarrassment of punishment is lower when a higher fraction of the population has experienced imprisonment at any time.[29] This would create a complicated relationship between stigma, p and L because the relevant variable would be the stock of current and former prisoners. To be clear, neither of these arguments implies that the differential effect should be that certainty is more efficacious than severity, but these mechanisms at least allow the possibility.

A second possibility derives from a conception of stigma that is more in line with the analysis of Rasmusen (1996). Following Rasmusen, one can think of stigma as involving the inference that employers and others make

---

type of interaction, following Brock and Durlaf (2001a), would simply involve replacing I with p in the utility functions associated with commission of a crime. One can also imagine more elaborate network structures for social interactions in determining interdependences in crime choices. See Calvó-Armengol, Verdier, and Zenou (2007) and Ballester, Calvó-Armengol, and Zenou (2010) for theoretical analyses of how network structure can affect aggregate crime and Patacchini and Zenou (2009) for empirical evidence that network structure matters.

29. See Posner (2000) for a discussion of stigma that links the concept to that of shaming. It seems reasonable to think that shaming effects depend on the criminal history of the population as a whole. Of course, one can easily imagine a range of additional factors; Posner, for example, emphasizes the importance of informal sanctions.

about an individual given his criminal record. Suppose that there are two types of offenders, one able to function in a regular job, and one not. If both serve long prison sentences, then the fact of a criminal record does not distinguish between the two types of individuals. In other words, harsh sentencing policies may coarsen the information set by which individuals are differentiated. The net effect on the crime rate will depend on the net effects on the beneficiaries of the coarsening (the bad types) versus those who are harmed (the good types). One cannot give an a priori sign to the net effect, but its presence could produce the certainty severity distinction we have emphasized.

1.5   Policy Implications and Future Research

The key empirical conclusion of our literature review is that there is relatively little reliable evidence of variation in the severity of punishment, L, having a substantial deterrent effect but that there is relatively strong evidence that variation in the certainty of punishment, p, has a large deterrent effect. We have further argued that these findings are consistent with the economic model of crime, so long as one distinguishes between the key behavior logic of the model as opposed to auxiliary assumptions of various types. In this section we discuss the translation of this general reading of the evidence into policy implications.

One specific policy-relevant implication of this general conclusion is that lengthy prison sentences, particularly those that take the form of mandatory minimum-type statutes such as California's Three Strikes Law, are difficult to justify on a deterrence-based crime prevention basis. They must be justified based on either incapacitation benefits or along retributive lines. While we have not surveyed the evidence on incapacitation, we are skeptical of the incapacitative efficiency of incarcerating aged criminals. For their incarceration to be socially efficient it must have a deterrent effect on other presumably younger criminals. There is no reliable evidence of such an effect.

If one takes the total resources devoted to crime prevention as fixed, then another natural implication of our evidentiary conclusion is that crime prevention would be enhanced by shifting resources from imprisonment to policing and also probation and parole monitoring systems designed along the lines of Project Hope. However, even such an apparently self-evident conclusion may be difficult to translate into a defensible operational plan beyond strongly recommending against any further escalation of sentence length. We say this because it leaves open many questions about the way the resources should be used—more police, better logistics, more nonhuman capital, better training, and so forth. The econometrics literature on police resources and crime rates provides very little guidance on how those resources should be utilized. Likewise, there has yet to be a demonstration that probation and parole monitoring systems designed along the lines of

Project Hope can be replicated with comparable results. The success of the monitoring system clearly depends upon the enthusiastic support and coordinated efforts of judges, parole/probation officers, and the police. The question of the mechanism by which the resources would be transferred has also not been addressed. Corrections are, by and large, a state and federal function whereas policing is, by and large, a local function.

Put differently, the details of the policy for cutting back on sentences and shifting the resources to policing and probation and parole supervision are critical to their efficacy in reducing crime without increasing resources committed to crime control. The literature on the crime prevention effects of different strategies for mobilizing the police makes clear that the way police resources are used matters greatly. This literature has assembled an impressive body of evidence that the so-called standard model of policing that involves the nonstrategic use of preventive patrols, rapid response to calls for service, and improved investigation methods is not effective in deterring crime (National Research Council 2004; Weisburd and Eck 2004).

However, more strategic use of police—hot spot policing for example, have been shown to be effective. Also, certain forms of so-called problem oriented policing have shown promise. This research, however, does not form the basis for devising a policy for shifting resources from corrections to policing that we can state with confidence will reduce crime without increasing the overall resource commitment to crime prevention. We thus close with a discussion of the type of research that in our judgment will be most effective in delineating the details of a policy that will achieve this objective.

One area that warrants more research concerns the explicit analysis of the costs and benefits of different combinations of certainty and severity. As noted earlier, if the elasticity of the crime rate with respect to either certainty or severity is less than -1, then one can simultaneously reduce both crime and imprisonment by increasing the policy variable. Additional routes emerge when the policies are considered together. Recall from equation (7) that the elasticity of I, the imprisonment rate, with respect to p is

$$
(15) \qquad \frac{d \log I}{d \log p} = \frac{d \log C \cdot p \cdot L}{d \log p}
$$

$$
= \frac{d \log C}{d \log p} + \frac{d \log p}{d \log p} + \frac{d \log L}{d \log p} = \frac{d \log C}{d \log p} + 1,
$$

and that elasticity of the imprisonment rate with respect to L is

$$
(16) \qquad \frac{d \log I}{d \log L} = \frac{d \log C \cdot p \cdot L}{d \log L}
$$

$$
= \frac{d \log C}{d \log L} + \frac{d \log p}{d \log L} + \frac{d \log L}{d \log L} = \frac{d \log C}{d \log L} + 1.
$$

Suppose that one increases L by 1 percent and increases p by 1 percent. Equations (15) and (16) imply that crime rate and the imprisonment rate change by the same amount:

$$(17) \qquad \frac{d \log C}{d \log p} - \frac{d \log C}{d \log L}.$$

But this means that so long as the elasticity of the crime rate with respect to certainty is smaller than the elasticity of the crime rate with respect to severity, the crime and imprisonment rates will *both* decrease under this policy change. Now, this calculation does not account for the relative costs of this shift from certainty to severity and so does not answer the question of whether this shift from severity to certainty is overall efficient. But the example illustrates how differential crime elasticities may be exploited to reduce both crime and imprisonment rates.

What types of deployment strategies are good candidates for reducing both crime and imprisonment? In terms of increases in certainty, we speculate that strategies that result in large and visible shifts in apprehension risk are most likely to have deterrent effects that are large enough to reduce not only crime but also apprehensions. Hot spots policing may have this characteristic. More generally, the types of problem-oriented policing described and championed in Kennedy (2009) and Kleiman (2009) have the common feature of targeting enforcement resources on selected places or people. While the effectiveness of these strategies for focusing police and other criminal justice resources has yet to be demonstrated, priority attention should be given to their continued evaluation.

We also note that while there is good evidence that severity is not an effective deterrent, the literature is small and mostly focused on severity increments to already lengthy sentences. It is thus important to better understand the circumstances where severity can be an effective deterrent. As we have already noted, the fine payment experiment conducted by Weisburd, Einat, and Kowalski (2008) and the Project Hope experiment make clear that the imminent threat of incarceration is a powerful incentive for paying delinquent fines and for conforming with conditions of probation. These experiments suggest that sanction need not be draconian to deter proscribed behavior. As we noted earlier, there may be a nonlinear relationship between the magnitude of deterrent effects and sentence lengths. Sentence lengths in Western European countries tend to be far shorter than in the United States. For example, over 90 percent of sentences in the Netherlands are less than one year (Nieuwbeerta, Nagin, and Blokland 2009). Research based in European data on the deterrent effect of shorter sentence length should be a priority.

These speculations indicate the importance of additional research on the crime rate elasticities for different policies. In addition, the costs of tradeoffs between various policies are very much underresearched.

Our review made brief references to a large literature on sanction risk perceptions. Most of this literature is outside of economics (but see Lochner 2007; Hjalmarsson 2008). Economic research on crime would benefit from giving closer attention to the origins and development of sanction risk perceptions as they relate to experience with committing crime, frequency of contact with the criminal justice system, the objective characteristics of the quality of a criminal opportunity (e.g., proximity of the police), and the punishments prescribed by criminal statutes. Returning to a distinction we drew earlier between this probability and $p^i(p)$, the subjective probability of potential criminal i of imprisonment, one can imagine that different policies that have equivalent effects on p inducing different deterrent effects. For example, raising the speed of responses to 911 calls may have a lower effect on subjective probabilities than greater street presence even if each has the same effect on p. In cases where changes in p are not accompanied by effects on $p^i(p)$, crime may be reduced by the apprehension and the ultimate incapacitation of active offenders. However, the reduction in crime will necessarily be accompanied by an increase in imprisonment.

As emphasized in Nagin (1998) deterrent effects are ultimately determined by perceptions of sanction risk and severity. We have already shown how allowing for a divergence between perceived and actual probability of punishment in the economic model of crime provides an interesting theoretical explanation for why the deterrent effects of certainty changes might be larger than in the standard model. The noneconomic literature on sanction risk perceptions shows that there is little correspondence between perceptions and reality. This is not surprising for at least two reasons. First, for most people knowledge of actual sanctions is not relevant because for moral, social, and/or economic reasons they are not even remotely close to the margin of committing crime. Second, sanction risks and severity are not posted like most market prices. Instead, for the criminally inclined, they must be learned from experience or word of mouth. This is why the work of Lochner (2007), Hjalmarsson (2008), and Anwar and Loughran (2009) on Bayesian updating of sanction risk perceptions is so important and should be extended. There is also a small body of research which examines how the characteristics of criminal opportunities affect sanction risk perceptions (Klepper and Nagin 1989a, 1989b). More work of this type would also be desirable particularly as it relates to how police deployment affects perceptions of apprehension risk.

Research on the deterrent effect of sentence length and more generally about the effects of changes in sentencing statutes on crime rates and imprisonment rates is seriously hampered by the lack of data on the distribution of sentences lengths and time served by different types of offenders across states. Without such evidence, it is impossible to assess the effects of features of the punishment regime, for reasons we have discussed and that flow immediately from the Beckerian crime model.[30] Such data can be assembled for selected states from prison census data. Prison census data should be expanded to include all fifty states and should be made available in an easily accessible and manipulable format.

Finally we emphasize the importance of recognizing the limits to knowledge faced by policymakers. To some degree, gaps in empirical knowledge can be filled by more complete theory. Thus, we recommend that extending the baseline Beckerian model of crime along the lines we outline in our review be a high priority. However, even with better theory, substantial and irreducible empirical uncertainties will remain. In our judgment, far too many proposals for crime amelioration take as their basis a single study or a subset of studies from a broader literature. Perhaps the best example of this is in the literature on capital punishment. In our view, there is no reasonable basis for concluding *anything* about the magnitude of the deterrent effect of capital punishment. As shown in Cohen-Cole et al. (2009), the distribution of deterrent effects across a space of seemingly second-order changes in regression specification can lead to estimates of net lives saved per execution that vary between –100 and 300, so that model uncertainty is sufficient to prevent one from even identifying the sign of the effect. The appropriate conclusion from the capital punishment literature is not that there is no deterrent effect to capital punishment, but rather that the historical data are uninformative. In terms of decision theory, this is equivalent to saying that a policymaker's prior and posterior beliefs about the deterrent effect of capital punishment ought to coincide. Hence, without a principled basis for having a priori beliefs for a deterrence effect or without a retributive justification, it is difficult to imagine a strong defense of capital punishment as a deterrent strategy. We believe this sort of skeptical perspective is also appropriate for imprisonment policies. At the same time, we see a number of fruitful directions for imprisonment policy analysis.

First, we believe that policy recommendations should place particular value on evidence of the effectiveness of specific crime control treatments. In our view, this emphasis has a strong analogy to the medical literature, where evidence of the efficacy of a particular drug regimen or specific preventive measure is of the highest value. We would also conjecture that more attention should be paid to the effects of policies on particular types of crimes. Again, in the spirit of our medical analogy, policies that are effective for one type of crime may have little effect on others. For example, hot spots policing is unlikely to be effective in reducing crimes such as domestic violence or homicide that generally occur in nonpublic places. Our point is that just

---

30. It is also remarkable that aggregate studies of the deterrent effect of capital punishment are conducted without data on the sentences served by those convicted of a potential capital offense but who are not sentenced to death.

as in medicine where a portfolio of treatments is required to address heterogeneous diseases, a well-designed crime-control policy requires a portfolio of crime-control treatments to address diversity in type of crimes and the people who commit them.

Second, we believe that stricter evidentiary thresholds for aggregate studies need to be established: thresholds that respect the deep limitations such studies face in terms of problems of model specification, exchangeability of data across localities, and the like. As we have indicated earlier, we do not believe such studies are valueless. They clearly can help buttress qualitative conclusions about certainty versus severity. But for aggregate studies to provide firm guidance on policy, much more attention to issues of robustness needs to be paid than has been the norm in the crime literature. Following our medical analogy, John Snow's classic demonstration that the spread of cholera in London in 1854 (enjoyably described in Johnson 2006) was due to transmission via the water supply did not require any experiments, but rather the careful and systematic elimination of alternative explanations.[31] We do not raise Snow for reasons of pedantry; his work is a lasting example of how careful nonexperimental data analysis can produce successful policy interventions and is a useful standard against which to think about regression studies of crime.

Third, we conjecture that serious thought should be given to diversified treatment regimes, in which policies are varied across time and place. We advocate this both as it will enhance learning about effective policies, but also because it provides a form of diversification against the efficacy uncertainty associated with various policies. Manski (2009) provides a framework for optimal policy diversification in contexts where policymakers cannot assign probabilities to the possible effects of a policy; his work is an example of the analysis of decision making under ambiguity. But independent of this, the uncertainty about particular policies does not exist in a vacuum; in particular, uncertainty about particular policies is a manifestation of uncertainty about the decision processes of criminals. So, our final conclusion really brings us back to our initial discussion of the economic model of crime. The economic model of crime, by identifying which aspects of individual decision making matter for the determination of crime rates, also provides a template for understanding how uncertainty about these aspects induces uncertainty in the effectiveness of policies. Standard portfolio diversification arguments, as well as new thinking about decision making under ambiguity suggest that heterogeneity in anticrime policies will reduce the degree of ignorance associated with the effects of policy choices. But as always, the devil is in the details. Hence we see much need for new research.

---

31. David Freedman, a deep and often harsh critic of contemporary empirical practice in social science, regarded Snow's work as an exemplar of good research; see Freedman (1991).

References

Andenaes, J. 1974. *Punishment and Deterrence.* Ann Arbor: University of Michigan Press.

Anwar, S., and T. A. Loughran. 2009. "Testing a Bayesian Learning Theory of Deterrence among Serious Juvenile Offenders." Carnegie Mellon University, School of Public Policy and Management. Unpublished Manuscript.

Apel, R., and D. Nagin. 2010. "Deterrence." In *Crime,* 4th ed., edited by J. Q. Wilson and J. Petersilia, 411–36. Oxford: Oxford University Press.

Avio, K., and S. Clark. 1976. *Property Crime in Canada: An Econometric Study.* Ontario Economic Council. Toronto: University of Toronto Press.

Ballester, C., A. Calvó-Armengol, and Y. Zenou. 2010. "Delinquent Networks." *Journal of the European Economic Association* 8 (1): 34–61.

Bayer, P., R. Hjalmarsson, and D. Pozen. 2009. "Building Criminal Capital behind Bars: Peer Effects in Juvenile Corrections." *Quarterly Journal of Economics* 124 (1): 105–47.

Becker, G. 1968. "Crime and Punishment: An Economic Approach." *Journal of Political Economy* 76 (2): 169–217.

———. 1993. "Nobel Lecture: The Economic Way of Looking at Behavior." *Journal of Political Economy* 101 (3): 385–409.

Becsi, Z. 1999. "Economics and Crime in the States." *Federal Reserve Bank of Atlanta Economic Review* Q1:38–56.

Berk, R., A. Campbell, R. Klap, and B. Western. 1992. "The Deterrent Effect of Arrest in Incidents of Domestic Violence: A Bayesian Analysis of Four Field Experiments." *American Sociological Review* 57 (5): 698–708.

Bernburg, J., and M. Krohn. 2003. "Labeling, Life Chances, and Adult Crime: The Direct and Indirect Effects of Official Intervention in Adolescence on Crime in Early Adulthood." *Criminology* 41 (4): 1287–1318.

Berns, G., C. Capra, S. Moore, and C. Noussair. 2007. "A Shocking Experiment: New Evidence on Probability Weighting and Common Ratio Valuations." *Judgment and Decisionmaking* 2 (4): 234–42.

Black, D., and D. Nagin. 1998. "Do Right-to-Carry Laws Deter Violent Crimes?" *Journal of Legal Studies* 27 (1): 209–19.

Blumstein, A., and A. Beck. 1999. "Population Growth in U.S. Prisons, 1980–1996." In *Prisons* (*Crime and Justice: A Review of Research*), vol. 26, edited by M. Tonry and J. Petersilia, 17–62. Chicago: University of Chicago Press.

Blumstein, A., J. Cohen, and D. Nagin. 1978. *Deterrence and Incapacitation: Estimating the Effects of Criminal Sanctions on Crime Rates.* Washington, DC: National Academies Press.

Blumstein, A., and D. Nagin. 1978. "On the Optimum Use of Incarceration for Crime Control." *Operations Research* 26 (3): 381–405.

Braga, A. 2008. *Crime Prevention Research Review No. 2: Police Enforcement Strategies to Prevent Crime in Hot Spot Areas.* Washington, DC: US Department of Justice Office of Community Oriented Policing Services.

Brantingham, P., and P. Brantingham. 1999. "A Theoretical Model of Crime and Hot Spot Generation." *Studies on Crime and Crime Prevention* 8 (1): 7–26.

Brock, W., and S. Durlauf. 2001a. "Discrete Choice with Social Interactions." *Review of Economic Studies* 68 (2): 235–60.

———. 2001b. "Growth Empirics and Reality." *World Bank Economic Review* 15 (2): 229–72.

———. 2001c. "Interactions-Based Models." In *Handbook of Econometrics,* vol. 5, edited by J. Heckman and E. Learner, 3297–3371. Amsterdam: North-Holland.

Calvó-Armengol, A., T. Verdier, and Y. Zenou. 2007. "Strong and Weak Ties in Employment and Crime." *Journal of Public Economics* 91 (1–2): 203–33.

Carr-Hill, R., and H. Stern. 1973. "An Econometric Model of the Supply and Control of Recorded Offenses in England and Wales." *Journal of Public Economics* 2 (4): 289–318.

Cohen-Cole, E., S. Durlauf, J. Fagan, and D. Nagin. 2009. "Model Uncertainty and the Deterrent Effect of Capital Punishment." *American Law and Economics Review* 11 (2): 335–69.

Cohen, J., and J. Ludwig. 2003. "Policing Crime Guns." In *Evaluating Gun Policy,* edited by J. Ludwig and P. Cook, 217–250. Washington DC: Brookings Institution Press.

Cook, P. 1979. "The Clearance Rate as a Measure of Criminal Justice System Effectiveness." *Journal of Public Economics* 11 (1): 135–42.

———. 1980. "Research in Criminal Deterrence: Laying the Groundwork for the Second Decade." *Crime and Justice* 2 (1): 211–68.

Cook, P., and J. Ludwig. 2006. "Aiming for Evidenced-Based Gun Policy." *Journal of Policy Analysis and Management* 25 (3): 691–735.

Corman, H., and N. Mocan. 2000. "A Time-Series Analysis of Crime, Deterrence, and Drug Abuse in New York City." *American Economic Review* 90 (3): 584–604.

———. 2005. "Carrots, Sticks, and Broken Windows." *Journal of Law and Economics* 48 (1): 235–66.

Cullen, F. 2002. "Rehabilitation and Treatment Programs." In *Crime: Public Policies for Crime Control,* edited by J. Q. Wilson and J. Petersilia, 253–290. Oakland: ICS Press.

DeAngelo, G., and B. Hansen. 2008. "Life and Death in the Fast Lane: Police Enforcement and Roadway Safety." University of California Santa Barbara, Department of Economics. Unpublished Manuscript.

Dezhbakhsh, H., and P. Rubin. 2007. "From the 'Econometrics of Capital Punishment' to the 'Capital Punishment' of Econometrics: On the Use and Abuse of Sensitivity Analysis." University of Georgia, Department of Economics. Unpublished Manuscript.

Dezhbakhsh, H., P. Rubin, and J. Shepherd. 2003. "Does Capital Punishment Have a Deterrent Effect? New Evidence from Post-Moratorium Panel Data." *American Law and Economics Review* 5 (2): 344–76.

Di Tella, R., and E. Schargrodsky. 2004. "Do Police Reduce Crime? Estimates Using the Allocation of Police Forces after a Terrorist Attack." *American Economic Review* 94 (1): 115–33.

Donohue, J. 2009. "Assessing the Relative Benefits of Incarceration: The Overall Change Over the Previous Decades and the Benefits on the Margin." In *Do Prisons Make Us Safer? The Benefits and Costs of the Prison Boom,* edited by S. Raphael and M. Stoll, 269–342. New York: Russell Sage Foundation Publications.

Donohue, J., and J. Wolfers. 2005. "Uses and Abuses of Empirical Evidence in the Death Penalty Debate." *Stanford Law Review* 58 (3): 791–846.

Draca, M., S. Machin, and R. Witt. 2008. "Panic on the Streets of London: Police, Crime and the July 2005 Terror Attacks." IZA Discussion Paper no. 3410. Bonn: Institute for the Study of Labor.

Drago, F., R. Galbiati, and P. Vertova. 2009. "The Deterrent Effects of Prison: Evidence from a Natural Experiment." *Journal of Political Economy* 117 (2): 257–80.

Durlauf, S., and Y. Ioannides. 2010. "Social Interactions." *Annual Review of Economics* 2:451–478.

Durlauf, S., P. Johnson, and J. Temple. 2005. "Growth Econometrics." In *Handbook of Economic Growth,* edited by P. Aghion and S. Durlauf, 555–663. Amsterdam: North Holland.

Durlauf, S., S. Navarro, and D. Rivers. 2008. "On the Use of Aggregate Crime Regressions in Policy Evaluation. In *Understanding Crime Trends: Workshop Report,* edited by A. Goldberger and R. Rosenfeld, 210–42. Washington DC: National Academy of Sciences Press.

————. 2010. "Understanding Aggregate Crime Regressions." *Journal of Econometrics* 158 (2): 306–17.

Eck, J., J. Gersh, and C. Taylor. 2000. "Finding Crime Hot Spots Through Repeat Address Mapping." In *Analyzing Crime Patterns: Frontiers of Practice,* edited by V. Goldsmith, P. McGuire, J. Mollenkopf, and T. Ross, 49–64. Thousand Oaks: Sage Publications.

Ehrlich, I. 1973. "Participation in Illegitimate Activities: A Theoretical and Empirical Investigation." *Journal of Political Economy* 81 (3): 521–65.

Evans, W., and E. Owens. 2007. "COPS and Crime." *Journal of Public Economics* 91 (1–2): 181–201.

Fisher, F., and D. Nagin. 1978. "On the Feasibility of Identifying the Crime Function in a Simultaneous Model of Crime Rates and Sanction Levels." In *Deterrence and Incapacitation: Estimating the Effects of Criminal Sanctions on Crime Rates,* edited by A. Blumstein, J. Cohen, and D. Nagin, 361–99. Washington DC: National Academies Press.

Forst, B. 1976. "Participation in Illegitimate Activities: Further Empirical Findings." *Policy Analysis* 2 (3): 477–92.

Freedman, D. 1991. "Statistical Models and Shoe Leather." *Sociological Methodology* 21:291–313.

Freeman, R. 1996. "Why Do So Many Young American Men Commit Crimes and What Might We Do About It?" *Journal of Economic Perspectives* 10 (1): 25–42.

Gibbs, J. 1968. "Crime, Punishment and Deterrence." *Southwestern Social Science Quarterly* 48:515–30.

Glaeser, E., B. Sacerdote, and J. Scheinkman. 1996. "Crime and Social Interactions." *Quarterly Journal of Economics* 111 (2): 507–48.

Glueck, S., and E. Glueck. 1950. *Unraveling Delinquency.* New York: The Commonwealth Fund.

Greenwood, P., and A. Hawken. 2002. "An Assessment of the Effect of California's Three-Strikes Law." Greenwood Associates. Working Paper.

Hagan, J., and A. Palloni. 1990. "The Social Reproduction of a Criminal Class in Working-Class London, Circa 1950–1980." *American Journal of Sociology* 96 (2): 265–99.

Hawkins, G. 1976. *The Prison: Policy and Practice.* Chicago: University of Chicago Press.

Heaton, P. 2010. "Understanding the Effects of Anti-Profiling Policies." *Journal of Law and Economics* 53 (1): 29–64.

Heckman, J. 2000. "Causal Parameters and Policy Analysis in Economics: A Twentieth Century Retrospective." *Quarterly Journal of Economics* 115 (1): 45–97.

————. 2005. "The Scientific Model of Causality." *Sociological Methodology* 35 (1): 1–98.

Helland, E. and A. Tabarrok. 2007. "Does Three Strikes Deter? A Nonparametric Estimation." *Journal of Human Resources* 42 (2): 309–30.

Hjalmarsson, R. 2008. "Crime and Expected Punishment: Changes in Perceptions at the Age of Criminal Majority." University of Maryland, School of Public Policy. Unpublished Manuscript.

Horowitz, J. 2004. "Statistical Issues in the Evaluation of Right-to-Carry Laws." In *Firearms and Violence*, edited by C. Wellford, J. Pepper, and C. Petrie, 299–308. Washington DC: National Academy Press.

Imai, S., and K. Krishna. 2004. "Employment, Deterrence, and Crime in a Dynamic Model." *International Economic Review* 45 (3): 845–72.

Johnson, S. 2006. *The Ghost Map.* New York: Riverhead Books.

Jolliffe, D., and D. Farrington. 2009. "A Systematic Review of the Relationship Between Childhood Impulsiveness and Later Violence." In *Personality, Personality Disorder, and Violence*, edited by M. McMurran and R. Howard, 41–62. New York: John Wiley and Sons.

Kansas City Police Department. 1977. *Response Time Analysis.* Kansas City: Kansas City Police Department.

Kennedy, D. 2009. *Deterrence and Crime Prevention Reconsidering the Prospect of Sanction.* New York: Routledge.

Kennedy, D., A. Braga, A. Piehl, and E. Waring. 2001. *Reducing Gun Violence: The Boston Gun Project's Operation Ceasefire.* Washington DC: National Institute of Justice.

Kessler, D., and S. Levitt. 1999. "Using Sentence Enhancements to Distinguish between Deterrence and Incapacitation." *Journal of Law and Economics* 42 (S1): 343–63.

Kleiman, M. 2009. *When Brute Force Fails: How to Have Less Crime and Less Punishment.* Princeton: Princeton University Press.

Klepper, S., and D. Nagin. 1989a. "The Anatomy of Tax Evasion." *Journal of Law, Economics and Organization* 5 (1): 1–24.

———. 1989b. "The Deterrent Effect of Perceived Certainty and Severity of Punishment Revisited." *Criminology* 27 (4): 721–46.

Klick, J., and A. Tabarrok. 2005. "Using Terror Alert Levels to Estimate the Effect of Police on Crime." *Journal of Law and Economics* 48 (1): 267–79.

———. 2010. "Police, Prisons, and Punishment: The Empirical Evidence on Crime Deterrence." In *Handbook on the Economics of Crime*, edited by B. Benson and P. Zimmerman, 127–43. London: Edward Elgar.

Langan, P., and D. Levin. 2002. *Recidivism of Prisoners Released in 1994.* Washington, DC: Bureau of Justice Statistics, US Department of Justice.

Layton MacKenzie, D. 2002. "Reducing the Criminal Activities of Known Offenders and Delinquents: Crime Prevention in the Courts and Corrections." In *Evidence-Based Crime Prevention*, edited by L. Sherman, D. Farrington, B. Welsh, and D. Layton MacKenzie, 330–404. London: Routledge.

Lee, D., and J. McCrary. 2005. "Crime, Punishment and Myopia," NBER Working Paper no. 11491. Cambridge, MA: National Bureau of Economic Research, July.

———. 2009. "The Deterrent Effect of Prison: Dynamic Theory and Evidence." Princeton University, Department of Economics. Unpublished Manuscript.

Levitt, S. 1996. "The Effect of Prison Population Size on Crime Rates: Evidence from Prison Overcrowding Litigation." *Quarterly Journal of Economics* 111 (2): 319–52.

———. 1997. "Using Electoral Cycles in Police Hiring to Estimate the Effect of Police on Crime." *American Economic Review* 87 (3): 270–90.

———. 1998. "Juvenile Crime and Punishment." *Journal of Political Economy* 106 (6): 1156–85.

———. 2002. "Using Electoral Cycles in Police Hiring to Estimate the Effect of Police on Crime: Reply." *American Economic Review* 92 (4): 1244–50.

———. 2006. "The Case of the Critics Who Missed the Point: A Reply to Webster et al." *Criminology and Public Policy* 5 (3): 449–60.

Liedka, R., A. Piehl, and B. Useem. 2006. "The Crime-Control Effect of Incarceration: Does Scale Matter?" *Criminology and Public Policy* 5 (2): 245–76.

Lochner, L. 2007. "Individual Perceptions of the Criminal Justice System." *American Economic Review* 97 (1): 444–60.

Loftin, C., M. Heumann, and D. McDowall. 1983. "Mandatory Sentencing and Firearms Violence: Evaluating an Alternative to Gun Control." *Law and Society Review* 17 (2): 287–318.

Loftin, C., and D. McDowall. 1981. "'One with a Gun Gets You Two': Mandatory Sentencing and Firearms Violence in Detroit." *Annals of the American Academy of Political and Social Science* 455 (1): 150–67.

———. 1984. "The Deterrent Effects of the Florida Felony Firearm Law." *Journal of Criminal Law and Criminology* 75 (1): 250–59.

Lott, J. 1998. "The Concealed-Handgun Debate." *Journal of Legal Studies* 27 (1): 221–91.

Lott, J., and D. Mustard. 1997. "Crime, Deterrence, and Right-to-Carry Concealed Handguns." *Journal of Legal Studies* 26 (1): 1–68.

Machina, M. 1987. "Choice Under Uncertainty: Problems Solved and Unsolved." *Journal of Economic Perspectives* 1 (1): 121–54.

Manski, C. 2009. "Diversified Treatment Under Ambiguity." *International Economic Review* 50 (4): 1013–41.

Marvell, T., and C. Moody. 1994. "Prison Population Growth and Crime Reduction." *Journal of Quantitative Criminology* 10 (2): 109–40.

———. 1996. "Specification Problems, Police Levels, and Crime Rates." *Criminology* 34 (4): 609–46.

Matsueda, R. 1992. "Reflected Appraisals, Parental Labeling, and Delinquency: Specifying a Symbolic Interactionist Theory." *American Journal of Sociology* 97 (6): 1577–1611.

Maxwell, C., J. Garner, and J. Fagan. 2002. "The Preventive Effects of Arrest on Intimate Partner Violence: Research, Policy and Theory." *Criminology and Public Policy* 2 (1): 51–80.

McCrary, J. 2002. "Using Electoral Cycles in Police Hiring to Estimate the Effect of Police on Crime: Comment." *American Economic Review* 92 (4): 1236–43.

McDowall, D., C. Loftin, and B. Wiersema. 1992. "A Comparative Study of the Preventive Effects of Mandatory Sentencing Laws for Gun Crimes." *Journal of Criminal Law and Criminology* 83 (2): 378–94.

Moffitt, T. 1993. "Adolescence-limited and Life-Course Persistent Antisocial Behavior: A Developmental Taxonomy." *Psychological Review* 100 (4): 674–701.

Nagin, D. 1978. "General Deterrence: A Review of the Empirical Evidence." In *Deterrence and Incapacitation: Estimating the Effects of Criminal Sanctions on Crime Rates*, edited by A. Blumstein, J. Cohen, and D. Nagin, 95–139. Washington, DC: National Academies Press.

———. 1998. "Criminal Deterrence Research at the Outset of the Twenty-First Century." In *Crime and Justice: A Review of Research*, vol. 23, edited by M. Tonry, 1–42. Chicago: University of Chicago Press.

Nagin, D., F. Cullen, and C. Jonson. 2009. "Imprisonment and Re-Offending." In *Crime and Justice: A Review of Research*, vol. 38, edited by M. Tonry, 115–200. Chicago: University of Chicago Press.

Nagin, D., and R. Paternoster. 1991. "The Preventive Effects of the Perceived Risk of Arrest: Testing an Expanded Conception of Deterrence." *Criminology* 29 (4): 561–86.

———. 1993. "Enduring Individual Differences and Rational Choice Theories of Crime." *Law and Society Review* 27 (3): 467–98.

————. 1994. "Personal Capital and Social Control: The Deterrence Implications of a Theory of Individual Differences in Criminal Offending." *Criminology* 32 (4): 581–606.

Nagin, D., and G. Pogarsky. 2003. "Cheating as Crime: An Experimental Investigation of Deterrence." *Criminology* 41 (1): 167–94.

Nagin, D., and J. Waldfogel. 1995. "The Effects of Criminality and Conviction on the Labor Market Status of Young British Offenders." *International Review of Law and Economics* 15 (1): 109–26.

————. 1998. "The Effect of Conviction on Income Through the Life Cycle." *International Review of Law and Economics* 18 (1): 25–40.

National Research Council. 2004. *Fairness and Effectiveness in Policing The Evidence.* Washington, DC: National Academies Press.

Nieuwbeerta, P., D. Nagin, and A. Blokland. 2009. "Assessing the Impact of First-Time Imprisonment on Offenders' Subsequent Criminal Career Development: A Matched Samples Comparison." *Journal of Quantitative Criminology* 25 (3): 227–57.

Pager, D. 2003. "The Mark of a Criminal Record." *American Journal of Sociology* 108 (5): 937–75.

Papachristos, A., T. Meares, and J. Fagan. 2007. "Attention Felons: Evaluating Project Safe Neighborhoods in Chicago." *Journal of Empirical Legal Studies* 4 (2): 223–72.

Patacchini, E., and Y. Zenou. 2009. "Juvenile Delinquency and Conformism." *Journal of the Law, Economics, and Organization* 26 (3). doi:10.1093/jleo/ewp038.

Philipson, T., and R. Posner. 1996. "The Economic Epidemiology of Crime." *Journal of Law and Economics* 39 (2): 405–33.

Polinsky, A. M., and S. Shavell. 1998. "On Offense History and the Theory of Deterrence." *International Review of Law and Economics* 18 (3): 305–24.

————. 1999. "On the Disutility and Discounting of Imprisonment and the Theory of Deterrence." *Journal of Legal Studies* 28 (1): 1–16.

Posner, E. 2000. *Law and Social Norms.* Cambridge: Harvard University Press.

Post, T., M. van der Assem, G. Balthussen, and R. Thaler. 2008. "Deal or No Deal? Decision Making Under Risk in a Large-Payoff Game Show." *American Economic Review* 98 (1): 38–71.

Poutvaara, P., and M. Priks. 2006. "Hooliganism in the Shadow of a Terrorist Attack and the Tsunami: Do Police Reduce Group Violence?" University of Helsinki, Department of Economics. Unpublished Manuscript.

Quiggin, J. 1982. "A Theory of Anticipated Utility." *Journal of Economic Behavior and Organization* 3 (4): 323–43.

Quine, W. V. O. 1951. "Two Dogmas of Empiricism." *Philosophical Review* 60 (1): 20–43.

Raftery, A., D. Madigan, and J. Hoeting. 1997. "Bayesian Model Averaging for Linear Regression Models." *Journal of the American Statistical Association* 92 (437): 179–91.

Raphael, S. 2006. "The Deterrent Effects of California's Proposition 8: Weighing the Evidence." *Criminology and Public Policy* 5 (3): 471–8.

Raphael, S., and J. Ludwig. 2003. "Prison Sentence Enhancements: The Case of Project Exile." In *Evaluating Gun Policy: Effects on Crime and Violence,* edited by J. Ludwig and P. Cook, 251–286. Washington DC: Brookings Institution Press.

Raphael, S., and M. Stoll. 2009. "Why Are So Many Americans in Prison?" In *Do Prisons Make Us Safer? The Benefits and Costs of the Prison Boom,* edited by S. Raphael and M. Stoll, 27–72. New York: Russell Sage Foundation Publications.

Rasmusen, E. 1996. "Stigma and Self-Fulfilling Expectations of Criminality." *Journal of Law and Economics* 39 (2): 519–44.

Roncek, D. 2000. "Schools and Crime." In *Analyzing Crime Patterns: Frontiers of Practice,* edited by V. Goldsmith, P. McGuire, J. Mollenkopf, and T. Ross, 153–65. Thousand Oaks: Sage Publications.

Sampson, Robert J., and J. H. Laub. 1993. *Crime in the Making: Pathways and Turning Points Through Life.* Cambridge: Harvard University Press.

Shepherd, J. 2002. "Fear of the First Strike: The Full Deterrent Effect of California's Two- and Three-Strikes Legislation." *Journal of Legal Studies* 31 (1): 159–201.

———. 2005. "Deterrence Versus Brutalization: Capital Punishment's Differing Impacts among States." *Michigan Law Review* 104 (2): 203–55.

Sherman, L., and R. Berk. 1984. "The Specific Deterrent Effects of Arrest for Domestic Assault." *American Sociological Review* 49 (2): 261–72.

Sherman, L., and J. Eck. 2002. "Policing for Crime Prevention." In *Evidence Based Crime Prevention,* edited by L. Sherman, D. Farrington, and B. Welsh, 295–329. New York: Routledge.

Sherman, L., P. Gartin, and M. Buerger. 1989. "Hot Spots of Predatory Crime: Routine Activities and the Criminology of Place." *Criminology* 27 (1): 27–55.

Sherman, L. W., J. Schmidt, and D. P. Rogan. 1992. *Policing and Domestic Violence: Experiments and Dilemmas.* New York: Free Press.

Sherman, L., D. Smith, J. Schmidt, and D. Rogan. 1992. "Crime, Punishment, and Stake in Conformity: Legal and Informal Control of Domestic Violence." *American Sociological Review* 57 (5): 680–90.

Sherman, L., and D. Weisburd. 1995. "General Deterrent Effects of Police Patrol in Crime 'Hot Spots': A Randomized Controlled Trial." *Justice Quarterly* 12 (4): 625–48.

Shi, L. 2009. "The Limit of Oversight in Policing: Evidence from the 2001 Cincinnati Riot." *Journal of Public Economics* 93 (1–2): 99–113.

Sims, C. 1980. "Macroeconomics and Reality." *Econometrica* 48 (1): 1–48.

Sirakaya, S. 2006. "Recidivism and Social Interactions." *Journal of the American Statistical Association* 101 (475): 863–77.

Sjoquist, D. 1973. "Property Crime and Economic Behavior: Some Empirical Results." *American Economic Review* 63 (3): 439–46.

Spelman, W. 2000. "What Recent Studies Do (and Don't) Tell Us about Imprisonment and Crime." In *Crime and Justice: A Review of Research,* vol. 27, edited by Michael Tonry, 419–94. Chicago: University of Chicago Press.

———. 2005. "Jobs or Jails? The Crime Drop in Texas." *Journal of Policy Analysis and Management* 24 (1): 133–65.

———. 2008. "Specifying the Relationship Between Crime and Prisons." *Journal of Quantitative Criminology* 24 (2): 149–78.

Spelman, W., and D. Brown. 1981. *Calling the Police: A Replication of the Citizen Reporting Component of the Kansas City Response Time Analysis.* Washington, DC: Police Executive Research Forum.

Starmer, C. 2000. "Developments in Non-Expected Utility Theory: The Hunt for a Descriptive Theory of Choice Under Risk." *Journal of Economic Literature* 38 (2): 332–82.

Steffensmeier, D., and J. Ulmer. 2005. *Confessions of a Dying Thief.* New Brunswick, NJ: Aldine/Transaction Publishers.

Stolzenberg, L., and S. D'Alessio. 1997. "'Three Strikes and You're Out': The Impact of California's New Mandatory Sentencing Law on Serious Crime Rates." *Crime and Delinquency* 43 (4): 457–69.

Tittle, C. 1969. "Crime Rates and Legal Sanctions." *Social Problems* 16 (4): 409–23.

Utset, M. 2007. "Hyperbolic Criminals and Repeated Time-Inconsistent Misconduct." *Houston Law Review* 44 (3): 609–77.

Waldfogel, J. 1994. "The Effect of Criminal Conviction on Income and the Trust 'Reposed in the Workmen'." *Journal of Human Resources* 29 (1): 62–81.

Webster, C., A. Doob, and F. Zimring. 2006. "Proposition 8 and Crime Rates in California: The Case of the Disappearing Deterrent." *Criminology and Public Policy* 5 (3): 417–48.

Weisburd, D., S. Bushway, C. Lum, and S.-M. Yang. 2004. "Trajectories of Crime at Places: A Longitudinal Study of Street Segments in the City of Seattle." *Criminology* 42 (2): 283–320.

Weisburd, D., and J. Eck. 2004. "What Can Police Do to Reduce Crime, Disorder, and Fear?" *Annals of the American Academy of Political and Social Science* 593 (1): 42–65.

Weisburd, D., T. Einat, and M. Kowalski. 2008. "The Miracle of the Cells: An Experimental Study of Interventions to Increase Payment of Court-Ordered Financial Obligations." *Criminology and Public Policy* 7 (1): 9–36.

Weisburd, D., and L. Green. 1995. "Policing Drug Hot Spots: The Jersey City Drug Market Analysis Experiment." *Justice Quarterly* 12 (4): 711–35.

Weisburd, D., C. Telep, J. Hinkle, and J. Eck. 2010. "Is Problem-Oriented Policing Effective in Reducing Crime and Disorder? Findings from a Campbell Systematic Review." *Criminology and Public Policy* 9 (1): 139–72.

Weisburd, D., L. Wyckoff, J. Ready, J. Eck, J. Hinkle, and F. Gajewski. 2006. "Does Crime Just Move Around the Corner? A Controlled Study of Spatial Displacement and Diffusion of Crime Control Benefits." *Criminology* 44 (3): 549–91.

Wellford, C., J. Pepper, and C. Petrie. 2005. *Firearms and Violence: A Critical Review.* Washington, DC: National Academy Press.

Western, B. 2002. "The Impact of Incarceration on Wage Mobility and Inequality." *American Sociological Review* 67 (4): 526–46.

Western, B., J. Kling, and D. Weiman. 2001. "The Labor Market Consequences of Incarceration." *Crime and Delinquency* 47 (3): 410–27.

White, J., T. Moffitt, A. Caspi, D. Bartusch, D. Needles, and M. Stoutheimer-Loeber. 1994. "Measuring Impulsivity and Examining Its Relationship to Delinquency." *Journal of Abnormal Psychology* 103 (2): 192–205.

Williams, K., and R. Hawkins. 1986. "Perceptual Research on General Deterrence: A Critical Review." *Law and Society Review* 20 (4): 545–72.

Wilson, J. Q., and R. Herrnstein. 1985. *Crime and Human Nature: The Definitive Study of Causes of Crime.* New York: Simon and Schuster.

Wolfgang, M., R. Figlio, and T. Sellin. 1972. *Delinquency in a Birth Cohort.* Chicago: University of Chicago Press.

Zenou, Y. 2003. "The Spatial Aspects of Crime." *Journal of the European Economic Association* 1 (2–3): 459–67.

Zimring, F., G. Hawkins, and S. Kamin. 2001. *Punishment and Democracy: Three Strikes and You're Out in California.* New York: Oxford University Press.

Institutional Requirements for Effective Imposition of Fines

Anne Morrison Piehl and Geoffrey Williams

2.1 Introduction

More than at any other time over the past thirty years, state and local governments are interested in reducing the burden of the criminal justice system. While some reform proposals are aimed at reducing the intrusion of the system, current interest in reform is largely motivated by fiscal concerns (Scott-Hayward 2009). To the extent that fines can replace more socially costly sanctions such as incarceration without adverse consequences on crime rates and other goals of the criminal justice system, increasing their use is a move toward "economical crime control."

Limited data suggest that in the early years of the United States, fines were more frequently used than today, and that they were generally an alternative, not a supplement, to confinement.[1] Goebel and Naughton (1970) found that fines were common in the colonial era, based on data from New York courts.

Anne Morrison Piehl is associate professor of economics and director of the program in criminal justice at Rutgers University, and a research associate of the National Bureau of Economic Research. Geoffrey Williams is a doctoral student in economics at Rutgers University.

This chapter was prepared for the National Bureau of Economic Research conference "Economical Crime Control" in Berkeley, California, January 15–16, 2010. For helpful comments, thanks to Philip Cook, Colin Campbell, the University of Michigan law and economics workshop, and conference participants. We also thank members of the National Center for State Courts' COURT2COURT listserv. Any errors are our own.

1. Some of the earliest uses of fines, such as the "wergeld" in Anglo-Saxon law, seem to be essentially negotiated blood money truces between warring clans. Before the technology of incarceration was fully developed, it seems that the average state or ruler could choose from a criminal punishment menu limited to fines, corporal punishment, or capital punishment. It was fairly common for a punishment for a major crime to be "fine if you can pay it, death if you can't," or for a single polity to switch freely between the use of the punishment of a fine and the punishment of a death sentence for the same crime (Zamist and Sichel 1982). Rusche, Kirchheimer, and Melossi (2003) suggest that a growing population of poor in Europe in the

In the more recent period, there was a surge of interest in fines as an alternative sanction in the 1980s, when prison populations were rapidly expanding. Beginning in Sweden, the system of "day fines" was developed in the 1970s and used successfully, spreading to several other European countries. In part inspired by this, a series of articles from the Vera Institute of Justice and the RAND Corporation made the case for fines as a sanction, described and assessed court practices, and evaluated demonstration projects.[2]

Before that point, theoretical analyses of fines were concerned with how to impose fines that did not unfairly discriminate against the poor, but could still be collected and not manipulated by defendants.[3] In the background research on existing practice and field demonstrations evaluated by Vera and RAND, very few of the problems brought up in more theoretical analyses seemed to apply. Fines were used for a significant minority of offenses (perhaps a quarter of offenses); where fines were assessed as a function of income, courts were usually able to get a good sense of the income of the perpetrator quickly, and collection rates were decent, if imperfect. And, once fines are nontrivial, they become more attractive to judges, making them a viable alternative to incarceration (Hillsman and Greene 1988).

Despite these fairly positive findings, fines have not gained much traction as an alternative criminal sanction in the United States. Under Tony Blair, the United Kingdom greatly expanded the use of fines for minor offenses, and many countries in continental Europe seem to be content with day fines.[4] But in the American criminal justice system, outside of automobile offenses and white-collar crime, fines are something of an afterthought. While they seem to be imposed quite frequently as part of a package of sanctions, both across the United States and within specific jurisdictions, fines do not seem to be prioritized, and little thought or planning seems to go into setting up systems to design fines, track them, and enforce collection.

In this chapter, we undertake an analysis of the role of fines as a criminal sanction in the United States today and the potential for fines to play a larger role in crime control. The literature is generally divided into two conceptual strands: one that considers issues such as the setting of fines within a menu

---

Middle Ages and early modern era led to the use of prison as a deterrent. In their view, industrialization and the increased prevalence of money and market relations up to 1850 then made the fine a more practical option in Europe, and it was brought back.

2. The most complete reference on the project, including background on day fines, is Hillsman, Sichel, and Mahoney (1984), but see also Greene (1988), Hillsman (1990, 1988), and Hillsman and Greene (1988). For evaluation results for the demonstration projects, see Turner and Petersilia (1996).

3. See the Equal Protection Clause arguments in Williams v. Illinois (1970) and Tate v. Short (1971), heavily cited Supreme Court cases that established rights of indigent defendants not to face long terms of incarceration for inability to pay criminal fines.

4. The motivation for the expanded use of fines was to reduce pressure on the courts so that major cases would receive more attention and could be resolved more quickly. Some have criticized the lack of due process. Others have argued that fines were more of a tax on behavior than a punishment, suggesting that fines did not communicate sufficiently a sense that the behavior was socially unacceptable.

of criminal sanctions, how fines do or do not fulfill the purposes of punishment, and the deterrent and other impacts of fines on choices of potential offenders; and second, a more descriptive strand that considers mechanisms for increasing collection rates and the perspectives of judges and others on the appropriate utilization of fines and other sanctions. We consider both the policies regarding fines as criminal sanctions and the organizational and ecological issues surrounding their collection in order to assess the practical relevance of an increasing reliance on fines.

A quick summary of our conclusions is that first, fines are economical *only* in relation to other forms of punishment, second, that for many crimes fines will work well for the majority of offenders but fail miserably for a significant minority, third, that they present a number of very significant administrative challenges, and fourth, that the political economy of fine imposition and collection is complex. With the caveats that jurisdictions vary tremendously and that there are large gaps in our knowledge about them, we build a model showing that it is possible to expand the use of fines as a criminal sanction if institutional structures are developed with these concerns in mind.

2.2   Fines as Punishment

Courts have a set of sanctions that can be applied as punishment for criminal offenses, and the very language "alternative sanctions" reflects the central role of secure confinement as a sanction. This chapter generally considers probation, jail, prison, and postincarceration supervision as the main sanctions in order to discuss other options as alternatives. But frequently, these sanctions are not distinct. Probation is backed with the threat of incarceration, as are parole and mandatory postincarceration supervision. Therefore, a given offender may transition through several of these sanction types under a single sentence.

As we begin, it is important to bear in mind that the variation across criminal justice jurisdictions is tremendous—size, rules, allocation of responsibilities, funding, and so forth. As a result, generalizations are necessary. In our discussion, we treat various sanctioning schemes in their narrowest form in order to highlight distinctions across the canonical forms of the sanction types. But we recognize that jurisdictions combine and adjust sanctions so that the distinctions we draw in prose are not nearly so clean in practice.

Alternative sanctions are those forms of punishment other than conventional probation or parole supervision and jail or prison confinement. This category includes intermediate sanctions designed to fall somewhere between probation and incarceration as well as monetary penalties (such as fines, victim compensation, and court and other fees). In practice, monetary penalties are frequently assigned along with probation or incarceration, so in some cases they may not serve as alternatives but as complements. And specialized courts (such as drug courts, mental health courts, and the like) have introduced an alternative way of supervising and punishing, one that is not necessarily intermediate to probation and prison. We return to these more comprehensive sanctioning programs later in the chapter. To begin with, we concentrate on fines as a distinct sanction.

2.2.1   Estimates of the Imposition and Collection of Fines

Many minor infractions are routinely punished with monetary sanctions. A small fine resolves many driving violations, including ones that put people and property at risk. Monetary sanctions are generally considered effective and appropriate for minor infractions.

But for more serious offenses, fines are infrequently applied as the primary punishment. In 2004, there were 2.2 million arrests for serious violent or property crimes. Of these, 68 percent were convicted and 9 percent diverted to another disposition. Of those convicted of a felony, 32 percent were sentenced to prison, 40 percent to jail, 25 percent to probation, and 3 percent to other sanctions (Useem and Piehl 2008, 10). From this accounting, clearly sanctions explicitly labeled as diversion or alternatives, including fines, represent a minority of outcomes. But, as noted earlier, monetary penalties including fines or court costs may be part of a criminal sentence to confinement or probation.

Table 2.1 reports data from federal courts in 2006, showing that 76 percent of convictions have no fine or restitution imposed. Despite the fact that fines are imposed in a minority of cases, the total obligation is substantial: nearly $5 billion. Few offenders had both restitution and fine orders, and, in the federal courts at least, financial obligations vary greatly by offense type. The table reports some of the most common offenses. Immigration offenses are unlikely to have financial penalties, while fraud convictions frequently require restitution. In contrast, drug possession cases frequently result in a fine. Seventy percent of the total payment ordered comes from fraud cases, which represent fewer than 10 percent of the offenses.

For state and local jurisdictions, lack of data on fines and other alternative sanctions seems to be a nearly universal problem—a consequence of the lack of priority placed on these sanctions. Vera researchers made heroic efforts to assemble information, and the reports by Vera represent the high-water mark for concrete data about fines and their implementation in the United States, a level that has never been approximated before or since.[5] So, in spite of the age of the information, we report a few of their findings.

---

5. A sense of the general lack of real numbers comes through in the story of a statistic on the extent of fine use, as reported by Hillsman, Sichel, and Mahoney (1984). Apparently born in 1932, the modal figure in the literature for over forty years was that 75 percent of cases involved fines. A figure of 75 percent was published in 1953 by the University of Pennsylvania Law Review and was passed along by Rubin in 1963 and again in 1973, Davidson in 1966, and the Rutgers Law Review in 1975. Miller used a very similar figure in 1956 without noting a source. It is fascinating that the University of Pennsylvania cites a 1932 article for this figure, and researchers desperate for some measurement have kept this 75 percent alive for over forty years, apparently without confirmation that it reflects current fines use (Zamist and Sichel 1982).

Table 2.1 Monetary penalties in federal cases, 2006: Overall and selected common offense types

Primary offense	Total	No fine or restitution		Restitution ordered/no fine		Fine ordered/ no restitution		Both fine and restitution ordered		Amount of payment ordered			
		Number	Percent	Number	Percent	Number	Percent	Number	Percent	Total	Mean	Median	Sum
Total	72,112	54,974	76.2	8,717	12.1	7,569	10.5	852	1.2	17,126	291,699	4,453	4,995,631,047
Drugs—trafficking	25,035	22,252	88.9	444	1.8	2,267	9.1	72	0.3	2,779	21,013	1,500	58,396,502
Drugs—simple possession	754	283	37.5	4	0.5	461	61.1	6	0.8	471	1,018	1,000	479,486
Firearms	8,354	6,903	82.6	497	5.9	914	10.9	40	0.5	1,450	98,578	2,000	142,938,157
Fraud	6,820	1,935	28.4	3,881	56.9	708	10.4	296	4.3	4,883	729,525	39,532	3,562,271,537
Immigration	17,527	17,058	97.3	46	0.3	418	2.4	5	0.0	469	12,341	1,000	5,787,957

Source: Table 15, US Sentencing Commission, 2006 Datafile, USSCFY06. http://www.ussc.gov/ANNRPT/2006/table15.pdf.

Table 2.2 reports results of a telephone survey of court administrators during the 1980s, showing that the use of fines declines as the seriousness of the offense increases. Our own informal survey of court administrators found a great deal of variation in the role of fines and also in the ability of courts to report on the extent of their use. In fact, most of the information they could provide had to do with the collection more than with the imposition of fines. For example, one county jurisdiction we contacted could easily provide information on active fines outstanding, but could not provide any numbers to put this in context.

The focus of court administrators is generally on the collection of fines. And the general impression in the field is that collection rates are low. Langan (1994) reports that half of probationers had not complied with their conditions of probation, including financial penalties, by the time they were discharged from probation and that noncompliance was infrequently punished. Table 2.3 reports on collection of fines in misdemeanor courts across New York City in 1979. While the sample sizes are small (researchers took a one-week sample from each court), the results show variation in success, both across offense and across court, and generally indicate that fine collections are not uniformly low (Hillsman, Sichel, and Mahoney 1984). McLean and Thompson (2007) report more recent data showing great variation across states in imposition of monetary sanctions and low levels of collection. But this does not mean that collection rates must necessarily be low.

Data from Twin Falls, Idaho, in figure 2.1 show that collection rates for fines in misdemeanor cases and infractions were high in 2001, whereas collection rates were low for felonies and victim restitution. In 2004 the jurisdiction began using a collection agency. Since that time, collections in the lagging categories increased substantially. This is evidence that collection is, at least in part, a function of attention.

One perspective on the potential for fine collection comes from the costs

Table 2.2   Use of fines for cases other than parking or routine traffic (phone survey of select courts around the United States)

Type of court	All or virtually all cases	Most cases	About half	Seldom	Never	Total
Limited jurisdiction						
Misdemeanor and ordinance violation	19	38	10	7	0	74
General jurisdiction						
Felony, misdemeanor and ordinance violation	1	15	7	5	0	28
Felony only	0	5	4	13	2	24
Total	20	58	21	25	2	126

Source: Hillsman, Sichel, and Mahoney (1984) Table II–1, p. 30.

Table 2.3   **Fined offenders who paid in full (New York counties, 1979)**

Conviction charge type	New York No.	%	Bronx No.	%	Kings No.	%	Queens No.	%	Citywide No.	%
Theft-related	17	41.5	4	80	3	42.9	4	50	29	46
Assault	6	85.7	2	66.7	1	100	3	100	12	85.7
Prostitution-related	13	35.1	4	30.8	4	28.6	0	0	21	32.8
Gambling	24	72.7	10	100	9	90	0	0	45	81.8
Disorderly conduct, loitering	24	82.8	26	57.8	33	82.5	48	68.6	143	71.5
Trespass	2	100	2	33.3	6	60	4	100	14	58.3
Drugs	12	52.2	6	50	4	57.1	14	87.5	36	62.1
Motor vehicle	9	75	13	92.2	20	69	27	87.1	75	81.5
Other	7	77.8	6	46.2	5	100	4	100	22	71
Total paid in full	114	59.1	73	60.3	85	69.1	104	76.4	397	66.1
Total fined offenders	193		121		123		136		601	

Source: Hillsman, Sichel, and Mahoney (1984), Table D-4, p. 313

of collection itself. A review of the British experience is that it costs £91 to collect an £80 fine (United Kingdom 2006). An Orange County, California, official reported that its collection costs were an order of magnitude greater than revenues. For an agency charged with collecting fines, such as a county court, this is a large negative return. But for the jurisdiction imposing fines as an alternative to incarceration, including the avoided costs of incarceration would yield a very high financial return. To paraphrase Winston Churchill, fines are the least economical form of punishment, except for all others that have been tried.

This point is best illustrated by results from a felony-collections program implemented by Snohomish County in Washington state. In 2003, the state Department of Corrections (DOC) entered into agreement with local county clerks' offices to assume collection of financial penalties owed to the state by felony offenders. The county reports that the results of its program showed that "collection efforts in felony cases *can* be highly successful" (Snohomish County, Washington 2009, personal communication). And from the county's perspective, it was. From an expenditure of $85,000, the program produced $146,000 for the county. This latter figure was comprised of a $61,000 grant from the state and $85,000 in collection recovery fees ($100 per account). Note that the program would have simply broken even for the county without the state grant. The benefit touted by the county was due to the transfer from the state to encourage counties to participate.

The intervention was relatively simple. Monthly statements were issued and administrative hearings held to monitor these accounts. Only after months of delinquency and repeated administrative intervention is the case referred for formal court hearings. In a sample of 100 cases in the county

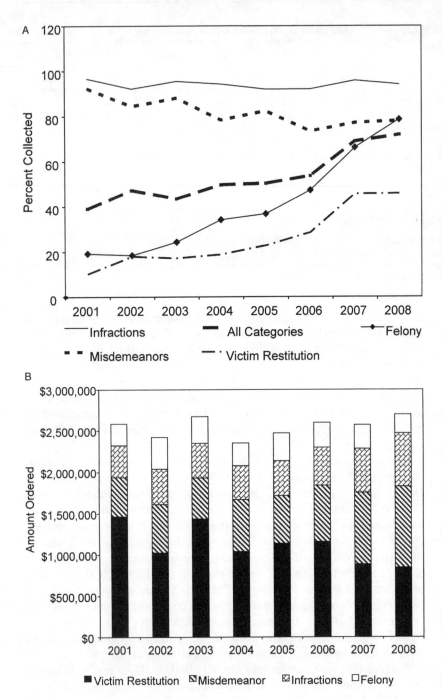

Fig. 2.1   Twin Falls, Idaho: *A*, Percent collected by category; *B*, Amounts ordered by category

Source: Twin Falls County, Idaho. Personal correspondence with the authors.

clerk's program, 16 percent paid in full (three times the rate in a similar group of cases managed by the DOC) and 38 percent of the balance was collected (compared to 6 percent in the DOC sample). The average payment collected was on the order of $100.

As in the earlier cases cited, attention to collection can raise rates of collection substantially, but the return is positive only if the fines have punishment value. From the state's perspective, the program was costly, as the incentives to counties were not covered by the increase in collections. If the fines are alternatives to other more costly punishments, paying more than is recovered *is* economical.

The collection of fines, even when the fine is an alternative to incarceration, is frequently backed up by the threat of incarceration if payment is not made. Nagin (2008) discusses that fine collection requires the "commitment of real resources" including systems to track payment and implement followup punishments, such as incarceration, in the case of failure to pay. He cites Moxon and Whittacker (1996) that roughly 25 percent of persons fined in England and Wales were imprisoned for some period as punishment for nonpayment.

In a finding known as "the miracle of the cells," those with credible threats of sanctioning for nonpayment of monetary penalties had significantly greater compliance. In an experimental design, Weisburd, Einat, and Kowalski (2008) found that 35 to 40 percent of those facing the threat of incarceration paid 100 percent of their obligation compared to just 13 percent of controls. (The addition of other conditions did not increase compliance over and above the threat of incarceration.) Together, with the results of the Snohomish County pilot project, these results show that agencies that make collection a priority can achieve much improved, if still imperfect, compliance rates.

However, a brief look at data from the collection industry suggests that there are serious limitations. Data from ACA International, which describes itself as the Association of Credit and Collection Professionals, suggests that of the total credit granted in the United States in any particular year, as much as 8 percent is written off by the creditor at some point.[6] Collection agencies seem to be able to collect less than 20 percent of debts that go into delinquency.[7] Because the recovery rate tends to vary greatly by type of account, it is hard to make a clear comparison between bad debt in a private transactional setting and bad debt from fines, but the fact that companies that are able to preselect who they lend to have an overall recovery rate that is possibly as low as 92 percent is sobering for agencies trying to collect from individuals who are selected on the basis of noncompliance with criminal law.

6. The authors use Federal Reserve Bank data showing $2,550 billion of outstanding consumer credit in early 2008 and IRS data estimates of $152 billion of bad debt write-offs on consumer debt for the year (PriceWaterhouseCoopers 2008).
7. ACA International (2005) finds a rate of 16.2 percent across the industry.

In figure 2.2 we reproduce a number of data points from diverse agencies in different regions and different time periods, focusing on collecting from very different populations. It should be noted that two courts, Maricopa County Superior and Pima County Superior, that did not deal with traffic cases had total court expenditures thirty-three and eighty-nine times total collections, respectively, and would thus be impossible to include in the graph.

A few patterns seem to come through. First, looking at the different categories, it is clear that collecting on traffic and parking offenses is highly efficient, with low costs per dollar collected and fairly high collection rates (although these are simply guesses by previous researchers in several cases). Second, there is something of a negative relationship between rate of collection and efficiency of collection. Private collection agencies have an extremely high efficiency, paying about $0.20 to collect each dollar, but their recovery rate is under 20 percent. Public agencies are lower in efficiency, but show significantly higher recovery rates. Third, even the highest recovery rates don't get close to 100 percent—all available data suggest that collection rates in the

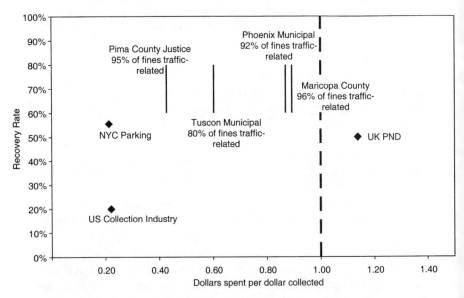

Fig. 2.2   Recovery rates versus costs in fine collection: An efficient frontier?

Source: PricewaterhouseCoopers (2008), ACA International (2005), Sichel (1982), Zamist (1982), UK Home Office (2005).

Notes: Recovery rate ranges for Pima County, Phoenix Municipal, Tucson Municipal, and Maricopa County are from Sichel (1982) but are only speculative. It is important to note that two Arizona courts, Maricopa County Superior and Pima County Superior, both of which deal exclusively with felonies (no traffic offenses) have expenditures thirty-three and eighty-nine times total fine collections, respectively.

70 to 80 percent range are better than average. With more and better data, it should be possible to sketch out an efficient frontier of fine collection.

We draw several conclusions from this review of available evidence on collection practices and success. High rates of collection are possible, as indicated by results from traffic courts and from pilot projects to increase collection. But many jurisdictions appear not to emphasize collection. This may be due to general inattention in light of other workload demands. But it also in part reflects the high costs of collection generally and from the population of convicted offenders in particular. An agency charged with collection will not be motivated to attain high collection rates simply by the financial returns to doing so.

2.2.2   Fines and the Purposes of Punishment

The earlier discussion suggests that fines and other monetary penalties play multiple roles in the criminal justice system. The traditional theoretical purposes of punishment are incapacitation, deterrence, rehabilitation, and retribution. Relative to incarceration, fines (and other alternative sanctions) offer less in terms of incapacitation, but can potentially fulfill the other purposes. But in practice, a particular sanction for a particular offense must fulfill multiple purposes. At the same time, different agents of the system may conceive of the same sanction differently. As an example, the view by court administrators of fines as a potential revenue stream to be balanced against the costs of collection is very different from the view of a fine as a punishment, perhaps to be compared in terms of efficiency to other sanction alternatives.

Economists tend to emphasize the deterrent effect of criminal sanctions. But other justice system participants have other priorities. The victims' rights movement of the 1980s and 1990s led to the increasing imposition of financial penalties in order to provide some compensation to victims and to fund offices to support crime victims. In addition, many states routinely impose a wide range of fees on criminal defendants. Reynolds et al. (2009) report a hypothetical (presented as representative) case of a person convicted of possession of a controlled substance in Texas, facing a prison sentence of five years (expected time served behind bars is two years of these five), a fine of $1500, and court costs of $362, including clerk's fee, records management fee, and court security fee, among others. Some government agencies rely heavily on revenue streams resulting from criminal sentences. McLean and Thompson (2007, 3) report that "administrative assessments on citations fund nearly all of the Administrative Office of the Court's budget in Nevada . . . and [i]n Texas, probation fees made up 46 percent of the Travis County Probation Department's $18.3 million budget."

Another view of the appropriateness of particular sanction options comes from a consideration of the expressive quality of punishment. Many authors express concern that fines do not carry sufficient expressive condemnation of conduct, and thus become more like a "price" of conduct, a licensing fee, or a cost of doing business. To the extent that it is the moral expressiveness of punishment that leads to deterrence, increasing reliance on fines instead of sanctions that restrict liberty may become a false economy.[8] Yet, concerns that fines lack sufficient expression of public scorn often omit consideration of the ways that fines are imposed. As Feeley (1979) and others have described, navigating one's way through the courts, even if one's case ends in charges being dropped or the imposition of a fine, will be experienced by many as punishing. And, as the outcome of criminal conviction is frequently a suspended sentence, an imposed fine could be experienced as a more onerous punishment.

One metric of appropriateness of fines as punishment for particular conduct is judges' willingness to impose them. A 1987 survey of judges found that 53 percent to 64 percent expressed a willingness to punish the sale of one ounce of cocaine with a fine and 27 percent to 46 percent expressed a willingness to punish daytime residential burglaries with a fine. Nagin (2008) interprets these findings as indicating willingness to use fines for fairly serious offenses. He observes "My hunch is that the major barrier to a large increase in the use of fines for nonviolent crimes would not involve adverse public reaction about being soft on crime. Rather, it would involve justifiable concerns about the effectiveness of fine enforcement and the possibility that offenders would pay the fine by committing more crimes" (Nagin 2008, 39).

In contrast, those particularly concerned with rehabilitation, including agencies and organizations focused on the challenges facing prisoners after release, often view monetary sanctions as a barrier to rehabilitation and a driver of recidivism (Mclean and Thompson 2007). Offenders are likely to face a variety of financial obligations, including court costs, victim restitution awards, and other debts (notably child support payments). The marginal tax rates for paying these debts can become extremely high, providing strong disincentive to working in the legal labor market. As noted by McLean and Thompson (2007, 4–5), "Federal law provides that a child support enforcement officer can garnish up to 65 percent of an individual's wages for child support. At the same time, a probation officer in most states can require that an individual dedicate 35 percent of his or her income toward the combined payment of fines, fees, surcharges, and restitution."

Reynolds et al. (2009) report data from an Office of Court Administration study in Texas that shows for the population that have both criminal justice debt and owe child support (which may be 20 to 25 percent of the offenders,

---

8. Zamist and Sichel's (1982) review summarizes the literature on expressive role of sanctions. Gneezy and Rustichini (2000) argue that fines can increase problem behavior under certain circumstances. Their analysis of fines for late arrival at a day care center found that parents were more likely to be late after the fines were imposed. It is unclear whether these findings are relevant to the context of criminal fines, as the day care fines were very small.

or more), offense debt is dwarfed by child support obligations. Perhaps in recognition of the financial demands, the repayment time horizon for the offense debt is long—roughly five years assuming no gaps in payment. Reynolds et al. (2009) recommend, based on these data, providing judges better training on the financial circumstances of the offenders so that they will impose fines that are collectable. The view that sentences do not reflect the practical issues of the collection of monetary penalties was echoed by court administrators with whom we communicated.

McLean and Thompson (2007) make a somewhat different policy recommendation, based on essentially the same findings and with a similar set of concerns. Monetary fines, including court costs and victim restitution, can be effectively collected if caseworkers coordinate debt collection across sources, facilitate the logistics of collection across agencies, and keep the repayment rate practical. Under this approach, the enforcement of the fee requirements will be individualized (as a function of wealth, earnings capacity, and other debt obligations) even if the imposition of the fees is not.

Under both of these recommendations, fines (or their partial forgiveness) may become individualized to an offender's ability to pay. In the process, the link between the fine as a distinct punishment and the particular conviction that lead to it may well become diffuse in the offender's and in the state's perspective (if it wasn't already). There are two main arguments in these policy proposals—that it is not practical to fully collect imposed fines in many cases given the low ability to pay and high debt loads and, furthermore, it may not be in society's interest to push too hard to collect, as it may on the margin drive more out of legitimate labor market activity. These are important constraints to be incorporated into any serious proposal regarding expanded use of fines as an alternative criminal punishment.

2.2.3   Jurisdictional Issues

One institutional matter of particular practical concern is that of jurisdiction. While criminal justice is frequently referred to as a system, it is anything but. There are multiple layers of legal jurisdiction (from local to state to federal), and sometimes overlapping jurisdictions of agencies (such as lower and upper courts, probation, city police, county jails, and state prisons, among many others).

As has been implicit in the earlier discussion, different sanctions are implemented by different authorities, meaning that individuals may transfer from one agency to another within the criminal justice system to fulfill the conditions of a single conviction. These transfers may be transfers of authority or legal responsibility, physical custody, or both.

For violations of state criminal law, a sentence to prison means that the state correctional agency has responsibility for the details of the incarceration experience, subject to the time established by the court and the many restrictions of federal and state laws and regulations. Other sanctions may be carried out by corrections agencies, probation, or the courts. In about two-thirds of states probation is in the judicial branch and in the other one-third it is an executive agency (Piehl and LoBuglio 2005). Therefore, a system of fines collected by the courts with jail time as punishment for noncompliance may require repeated handovers across jurisdiction, as an individual passes from the courts to the county sheriff and back again.

Handovers across these agency boundaries can be clunky, and the time and administrative work involved can undermine efficiency and rehabilitation. In addition, we argued earlier that different agencies may have different goals for the same activities. If a county clerk (or a collection agency operating under contract) sees revenue as the highest priority, fine collection might be treated quite differently than by a probation officer working to attain compliance across a wide range of conditions. As a result, jurisdictional boundaries not only lead to administrative costs, but may by their very existence fundamentally alter the form the imposed punishment takes as it is executed in practice.

A number of alternative sanctions programs have faced this same issue. For example, programs that employ a strategy of quickly administered, minor sanctions for rule infractions have shown a lot of promise for modifying criminal behavior (for examples, see Kleiman 2009; Piehl 2009). But, just as in the fines example, such strategies run counter to traditional jurisdictional boundaries. In order to be successfully implemented, such programs require either the development of new agency relationships or new capacities within agencies.

One approach is to contract out with private (usually nonprofit) entities to manage, as is often done with halfway houses prior to prison release. Another approach has been for agencies to develop new capacities and manage the punishment for rule violations "in house." For example, parole in New Jersey has developed a "halfway back" program to reduce its reliance on county and state prison cells for punishment of violations of parole conditions. To do this, the parole agency now has several facilities with secure cells, located in cities with large numbers of parolees. Parolees in violation are taken to the halfway back facility where they may serve a few days, be held for as long as thirty days to be assessed for appropriate disposition, or transferred to a county or state cell. The new program was promoted as a way to both save resources and improve outcomes.[9]

Yet another solution to jurisdictional conflicts in imposing and carrying out alternative punishments is a relatively new institutional form known

---

9. The added capacity for parole allows more flexibility that can speed resolution, allow punishment with minimum disruption to an offender's productive activities (for example, by allowing him to continue any paid employment), and to individualize parole requirements. It is projected to save money by reducing transfers to physically remote locations and reducing disruption to those facilities. If outcomes improve, then downstream savings will accrue to the system.

as the specialized court. Drug courts, mental health courts, reentry courts, and the like have been promoted to provide more appropriate and flexible supervision and sanctioning. In these courts, a judge (along with a group of law enforcement and social service practitioners) aims to construct a punishment that both sanctions the criminal behavior and facilitates rehabilitation. Because of the individualized program, fines and other monetary obligations of the offender are prioritized and managed against issues such as work disincentives. In these courts, the details of the sanction are organized around the particular circumstances of the offender, and these details can be, and are, modified over time. By including participants from multiple criminal justice and social service agencies, any conflicts can be managed within the team, with the leadership of the judge.

In all of these alternative sanctions models, the punishment is oriented around the *offender* rather than the *offense.* Choices about priorities for expectations of the offender and sanctions for noncompliance are made with the offender as the audience, with the goal of modifying behavior to improve his or her functioning in society in the future. Advocates of such an approach to punishment tend not to be terribly concerned about the impact of these choices on other audiences, such as deterrent impact.

We attempt to accommodate concerns with both the offender and with wider audiences in the theoretical model following. The model explores the possibility of sorting offenders in a way that efficiently deters and at the same time is realistic in its imposition of penalties. Certain offenders are likely to be deterrable by fines or other sanctions, while others may be incapable of being deterred (because unstable income and minimum allowable consumption levels make it impossible to collect sanctions from them or because of low levels of social skills).

2.3 Modeling Offender Choice under Fines

A long theoretical literature in economics addresses the heavy reliance of the criminal justice system on very expensive forms of punishment—prison—when cheaper alternatives—such as fines and other sanctions—are available. Becker's (1968) well-known result that the most efficient way to achieve deterrence is with a maximal fine has been analyzed or extended in a large number of papers, many of which analyze the conditions under which a maximal penalty may not be optimal.[10] (See Durlauf and Nagin, chapter 1, this volume, for more on modeling deterrence.)

But the tradeoff among types of punishment has received somewhat less attention. The essential dimension for present purposes is the tradeoff between fines and incarceration, maximal or not. Incarceration is socially costly, and growing literatures in sociology, criminology, economics, and

---

10. See references in recent reviews by Polinsky and Shavell (2000) and Garoupa (1997).

policy document the various types of social costs involved in the use of incarceration (fiscal costs of provision of secure confinement, labor market impacts, costs imposed on community due to disruption of removal and return of residents, impact on family members, etc.) If the same level of crime could be achieved at lower social cost using alternative punishments, the social cost savings could be substantial. As Polinsky and Shavell (2000, 51) state it, "different types of sanctions should be employed in the order of their costs (per unit of deterrence)." And these sanctions should be imposed so that marginal deterrence is maintained. (We discussed earlier that in practice sanctions are frequently combined. To keep the model tractable, we treat fines and prison as distinct alternative punishments.)

The current literature reports heterogeneity in how people respond to various sanctions and threat of sanctions (Hillsman, Sichel, and Mahoney 1984; Kleiman 2009; Moxon and Whittaker 1996). For example, when given the option, many inmates often prefer incarceration to terms of supervision "on the street" (Piehl 2002). But there is very little empirical data on deterrent impacts of the sanctions much less heterogeneity in the effects. Therefore, the literature does not currently allow for calculations of the cost-effectiveness per unit of deterrence.

One potential limitation on fines is the low level of income and assets of the majority of criminal offenders (James 2004; Tyler and Kling 2007). The deterrent value of fines may be high enough to justify an important role in punishment for richer defendants, but for poor offenders there may be a low deterrent effect. Garoupa (2001) presents a model in which it is optimal for law enforcement to increase both the probability of apprehension and the penalty against richer defendants, as the return to prosecution of poor defendants is so low (yet still somewhat costly).

2.3.1 Fine Structure and Deterrence

We begin with a benchmark model of the deterrent power of fines, where the potential offender has a full-time, stable job. He (without loss of generality, we stick to the male pronoun) receives a fixed wage w every period. If he commits a crime he receives a benefit b. The probability of being caught, convicted and sentenced is p. If honest, his payoff is w. If dishonest, his payoff is $-pf + w + b$.

In this benchmark model, fines can successfully deter crime when our "taxpayer" finds that honesty is a better policy than dishonesty, which under our assumptions reduces to:

$$f > b/p.$$

The interpretation of this is fairly simple: in order to make it advantageous for the average law-abiding citizen to stay law abiding, all that is required in the benchmark model is a simple fine structure, based on an estimate of the upper-bound of the benefit the citizen might gain from breaking a specific law, b and the odds of successfully catching him and convicting him if he does, p. We simply set a fine equal to the first value divided by the second. If it is believed that the citizen would at most gain \$10 from jaywalking, and the state would have a 50/50 chance of catching him, the appropriate fine would be set at or slightly above \$20.[11]

The model assumes that the disutility of the fine is purely the loss of money. There is substantial evidence that many, if not most, fines impose additional disutility on offenders beyond the simple out-of-pocket cost (Feeley 1979 is the classic statement of this). The nonfinancial disutility is even more difficult to measure than financial disutility, and subject to remarkable variance. Various situational issues, such as whether or not there is an actual arrest or simply a ticket or penalty notice for disorder, whether the offender is detained for several hours or days before the fine is imposed, whether the police, court officials, and judge who impose the fine are professional or gratuitously hostile can all play a role here. Additionally, the personality and social disposition of the offender may lead him to see the fine as alternatively a minor nuisance, or a substantial imposition.[12]

To take this into account, we add a variable d_i for the individual i's expected disutility from the procedure itself. For each individual, the nonfinancial disutility is assumed to a random finite positive value that only he knows, updating the equation to:

$$d_i + f > b/p.$$

A few comments are in order. Here fines, wages, and benefits are measured in comparable units. If fines are considered to be relative to wage levels, as a day fine would be, this would require that benefits also be parameterized relative to wages. If utility scales perfectly with earnings, then the results are unchanged by this reparameterization.

Note also that we have assumed the offender can pay the fine from his wage this period. However, the model is effectively identical if the offender is capable of paying from some store of wealth. Thus, for offenders who have either high income or high wealth, deterrent fine size and structure are straightforward.

If the taxpayer has a low income, we will need to make some adjustments to the model. We begin by adding the assumption that consumption is a function of the wage, $c(w)$ and cannot drop below a threshold, $\underline{c}$. Define $c(w)$ as:

11. Note that in Becker (1968) a single variable, f, stands in for a generic form of punishment. It might reasonably be summarized as "total pain," "total disutility," or "total loss of utility" from punishment. While Becker's article discusses the cost to society of inflicting this disutility on individuals, there is no discussion of the issues of uncertainty, income, wealth and so forth. There are numerous papers that incorporate one or more of these additional considerations. See Polinsky and Shavell (2000) for a review of this literature.

12. Under certain circumstances an offender may see a punishment as a badge of honor. We believe these circumstances are unusual, so set this case aside.

$$c(w) = w \text{ if } w \geq \underline{c},$$

$$c(w) = \underline{c} \text{ otherwise.}$$

In the case where consumption hits the lower bar, the fine cannot be levied. This corresponds to a range of real-life scenarios, where convicted offenders are so poor that they have neither income nor assets from which a fine can be collected. In the context of this chapter, if the offender was truly incapable of paying out any money in the near future, the case would no longer be handled by a fine and would instead have to be handled by some combination of incarceration, probation, and so forth. Such cases of completely indigent offenders appear to be a very minor part of overall criminal activity. A system of fines that cannot handle such cases directly can still be effective.

A much more common case is where $w > \underline{c}$, but only by a relatively small amount. That is to say, the offender does have a steady wage, but it is relatively small, and the amount that can be taken by fine is similarly small. Thus, for every period, there is some amount $\xi = w - \underline{c} > 0$ that can be taken from the offender without being excessive punishment. If we assume that this amount is taken regularly every period for a set number of periods, and that the offender discounts the future utility by β (which is both a rate of time preference and a sense of the probability of continued fines), then the expected impact in period 0 of a fine exacted over T periods would be:

$$F_T = \sum_{t=0}^{T} (\beta^t \xi).$$

For a fine to be successfully exacted against a low income offender, it is necessary to find a T, such that

$$F_T + d_i = \sum_{t=0}^{T} (\beta^t \xi) + d_i > \frac{b}{p}.$$

We see that

$$F_T = \sum_{t=0}^{\infty} (\beta^t \xi) - \sum_{t=T+1}^{\infty} (\beta^t \xi) = (1 - \beta^T) \sum_{t=0}^{\infty} (\beta^t \xi) = (1 - \beta^T) \frac{\xi}{(1 - \beta)}$$

and solve for

$$T = \frac{\ln\{1 - [(b/p) - d_i](1 - \beta)/\xi\}}{\ln(\beta)}.$$

Several comments are in order: First, T can only be found if $1 - [(b/p) - d_i](1 - \beta)/\xi$ is positive, which is only true when $[(b/p) - d_i] < \xi/(1 - \beta)$. Since the figure on the right is the net present value of all future payments of ξ, this makes sense; if the inequality did not hold, the net value of all payments would never exceed the b/p value.

Second, the higher ξ, β, d_i and p are, the lower T is. Likewise, the lower b

is, the lower T is. All of which stands to reason—an increase in the steepness of the fine, the greater the "slap in the face" an offender feels from receiving *any* fine, or the certainty of the fine process (both β and p) would lower the number of periods we would need to impose fine payments, while the greater the benefit to the potential offender, the more periods we would need to impose fine payments.

Third, for valid Ts, both the numerator and the denominator are logarithms of numbers between 0 and 1, which means both have negative values (making T positive). If either value approaches zero, then the logarithm of that value will asymptotically approach $-\infty$. This is most critical if $\xi/(1-\beta)$ is only slightly greater than $(b/p) - d_i$, the situation of an agent who will only barely pay off (over an infinite number of periods) a fine equal to the expected benefit. As the net present value of his total fine payments approaches the gain from the crime, the value of the numerator approaches $-\infty$, and the value of the overall expression approaches ∞.

Fourth, we should assume that there is some $\overline{T}$, a maximum number of periods that a system can expect to collect period payments (∞ is a helpful idea for modeling purposes but not susceptible to implementation). We can effectively use fines to deter even very poor individuals from a wide variety of crimes, so long as they have a predictable wage, place a high value on the future, and are unlikely to move around.

The potential criminal we envision in this adjustment, while not indigent, has an uncertain honest wage w, which is a simple Bernoulli variable with a sample space $\{\underline{w}, \overline{w}\}$. The higher wage, $\overline{w}$, allows the agent to pay ξ in each period, while the lower wage draw $\underline{w} \leq \underline{c}$, does not allow the agent to pay anything. The probability of drawing $\overline{w}$ in a given period is ρ, and the probability of drawing $\underline{w}$ is $1 - \rho$.

Because the expected payment any single period is $E(f_i) = \xi \times \rho + 0 \times (1 - \rho) = \xi\rho$, we can very simply adjust the earlier equation to get

$$T = \frac{\ln\{1 - [(b/p) - d_i](1-\beta)/\xi\rho\}}{\ln(\beta)}.$$

The change is simple, but significant: for a given b, p, d_i, β and given time limit $\overline{T}$, a drop in the certainty of employment per period will require a matching increase in ξ; a 1/10th drop in ρ will require a $0.\overline{1}$ increase in ξ; a 50 percent drop in ρ will require ξ to double.

In summary, fines can be powerfully deterrent for a wide range of possible crimes and potential offender situations. However, for every crime there will be some potential offenders for whom the threat of a fine will simply not be credible or threatening. Potential offenders who are indigent, who have highly unstable situations, who discount the future heavily, or who are confident in their ability to outwit the system in the long run will not be deterred by fines in their pure form. Instead, fines will need to be integrated with other forms of punishment.

2.3.2   Fines as the First Line of Defense

Thomas Schelling (quoting Walter Lippman) spoke of the plate glass window as a model deterrent mechanism—once you go too far, it breaks and an uproar ensues (Schelling 1956). Our vision of a fine is close to that, but not quite as binary—something like a thicket. Once you cross the line it marks out, you get immediately stuck by the branches, which will deter most people. However, a minority are so willful or heedless that they will keep on going. To deal with them you need a second, much more powerful, system that they *cannot* ignore. That does not mean the thicket does not play an important role, or that it is not a good investment. By cheaply deterring the hoi polloi, it allows you to focus on the real troublemakers.

Similarly, fines may do an efficient job of deterring the majority of potential offenders, but a significant minority (25 percent, as a rough guess) may crash right through any fine system, accumulating a huge number of fines, failing to pay, and so forth. This is in keeping with a common pattern in criminal justice, and in management and administration generally. DiIulio and Piehl (1991) provide evidence of the high variation in offender patterns, showing that focusing punishment on the minority with the highest rates of offense yields the biggest benefits. Models of offending trajectories likewise show variation in offending that falls into identifiable clusters (Nagin, Farrington, and Moffitt 1995). More generally, a commonplace of management lore is the "80/20 Rule" or "Pareto Principle," the general idea that 80 percent of activity can be traced to 20 percent of individuals (i.e., 80 percent of sales are due to 20 percent of customers, 80 percent of complaints due to a presumably different 20 percent of customers, etc.).[13] This general idea seems to be very clearly borne out in all the available data on fine use and administration. For a wide range of nuisance crimes, misdemeanors, and even some basic felonies, efficient crime control will require a system that effectively sorts offenders.

For the appropriate crimes, fines will represent the first line of defense. An offender who is caught and convicted can be fined using a flat penalty or one scaled according to his wage or expected wage. The research by Vera suggests that this latter method can be trusted to assess a fine that is both payable but onerous. An effective administrative system needs to be in place to follow up (see Turner and Petersilia 1996 for a summary of some of the issues involved).

It is possible to further improve on this by linking fines directly with community service punishments. For some offenders, especially those with limited means and uncertain income, being able to work off the fine will give them a valuable option. Obviously, the administrative costs of linking

13. It appears that Joseph Juran was responsible for the popularization of this idea (Wood and Wood 2005).

offenders with needed service work, perhaps through community organizations will be higher than the cost of processing a one-off payment. However, we believe that this upfront administrative cost will be solidly compensated by allowing more offenders a straightforward way to exit the thicket, saving both them and the system from the costs of harassment and further follow up.

After a certain amount of follow up, triage becomes possible—one group of offenders pay quickly and fully, a second pays slowly and only after harassment, and a third group will completely fail to pay. If the administrative system is well run, the first two groups will have been punished at only minor net cost to the system.

The third group, those who have failed to pay, will have crashed through the fine system into the next level. Most likely a court will need to tailor a solution for them, depending on the pattern of crimes. The development of the solution could draw on the experiences of the miracle of the cells (Weisburd, Einat, and Kowalski 2008) or programs with a more graduated set of sanctions that can be more narrowly tailored, such as those frequently used in specialized courts (Kleiman 2009) or those used to encourage labor force attachment in corrections programs to prepare inmates for release (Piehl 2009).

2.3.3   Using Fines in a System that is Both Fair and Efficient

For this proposed system to work fairly and efficiently for a particular class of crimes, it must do a good job of allocating fines to those for whom they will be effective and retaining the thicket only for the others. Equilibrium is attained when those who never offend are happy to stay that way; those who offend once, in a weak moment, are glad it was not more than that, and wish it had never happened; and those who are undeterred wish they had better control of themselves.

What precepts can we employ to maintain this balance? First, the system should be, on net, forgiving. For offenders with limited or unreliable means, this means always providing a realistic and humane way for them to pay or work off their fine. For all offenders, it means not overreacting to temporary failings. Even the most organized and conscientious citizens occasionally miss a payment deadline; it is easy for a poor but hardworking offender to miss one payment of an overall payment regimen, or to show up late for a community service work session. Carelessly treating them as if they were undeterrable may create needless misery for them, and unnecessary waste for the system. The simple economics of an efficient criminal justice system are that deterrence should not be maximal (Becker 1968). The system proposed here should be evaluated as a whole, not on an incident-by-incident basis.

Second, whatever tailored program is developed for those who are not deterred by the sanctioning scheme must not be compelling to somebody behaving according to the benchmark model, a "taxpayer." This seems easy to achieve. The tailored program should ensure that noncompliance with the sanction produces further obligations to government (such as garnished wages or additional appointments to keep) that the taxpayer will find much more noxious than a simple fine. (For example, someone with regular wages or a hope of regular wages will not want to lose them.) This condition provides a constraint on how generous the tailored program can be in terms of writing down the financial obligations for those who cannot pay (Levitt 1997).

Third, while it is not clear that fines have any less deterrent power than other punishments, we are certain that first, there are some people who will not be deterred by fines, and second, that fines are likely to *look* softer to voters than some other choices available (especially ex post). It is therefore vitally important that fines not be used as punishments in cases where a single failure of deterrence is catastrophic: any crime that directly causes serious pain or anguish to another person would be very inappropriate for punishment *solely* by fines. Obvious examples would be murder, rape, or assault. Built into our model of fines is the certainty that they will fail to deter for a substantial minority of potential offenders.

Finally, the fine system will need to be sensitive both to offenders who fail to pay, and offenders who pay and then commit the same crime again. The second offense should cost more than the first, and the third should cost more than the second. It is important, but perhaps expensive, for the system to prevent the sanction from becoming a cost of doing business or an indulgence for wealthy offenders.[14]

Fines can be an efficient sanction, in equilibrium, where it is possible for the system to sort offenders into different eventual punishments. Note that the imposed sanction is the same for all offenders convicted of the same offense, but the behavioral response to the sanction will vary by offender. After a certain record of failure, courts will tailor a solution. In order to maintain this as an equilibrium, the system must be keep people from "gaming" it—strategically appearing undeterrable to the court in order to have the obligation reduced.

2.4   Discussion

Fines potentially provide a low-cost sanction for criminal activity. Yet fines are infrequently imposed, and when imposed, often not collected. Is there a reasonable scope for increasing reliance on fines to improve the efficiency of the criminal justice system?

In theory, increasing the use of fines could have several benefits. It could provide punishment for criminal offenses that are currently not punished

---

14. Note that Polinsky and Shavell (1984) assume that the fine (net of collection costs) represents the true social cost, and hence is indifferent to repeat offenses.

severely, either because cases are not pursued or because sentences are suspended or otherwise not enforced. At the other margin, fines could also provide a mechanism of punishing at lower social cost than short terms of jail or prison confinement.

The early part of the article described several practical reasons for the limited use of fines currently in the American criminal justice system. Three of these seem of particular importance. One real limitation on the use of fines is the financial position of many offenders: low earnings, no or minimal assets, and high debts, frequently to other government agencies. The high marginal tax rates that would be required to add further fines to such an offender would work against their rehabilitation into work in the legitimate labor market and eventual payments of any of these obligations.

Another constraint is that agencies or units responsible for fine collection frequently view active pursuit of the debts as not worth it due to the high costs of collection. Criminal justice writ large will never be revenue producing for government, as producing order and enforcing laws are expensive. Fines will not be imposed more broadly unless judges and the public see them as real punishments, and this requires that effort be expected to collect the judgments. Even if it costs more to collect a fine than the amount of the fine, doing so is likely to be cheaper at achieving expressive or deterrent purposes of punishment than any alternative method. This issue of organizational perspective is compounded by the many jurisdictional boundaries that may exist in a given criminal case. The overlapping responsibilities of the many agencies that operate within criminal justice mean that any given offender may be transferred (physically or in terms of legal authority) across agencies multiple times during the course of a single term of punishment. These handovers provide repeated opportunities for administrative failures or for priorities to shift. Thus, a fine imposed by a judge to affect deterrence and express social outrage may be forgiven by another agency either due to lack of resources for collection or because it is now viewed as an impediment to rehabilitation.

The model in the previous suggestion proposes to use fines as a first line of defense with another system as backup. In equilibrium, if the system can sort offenders into different eventual punishments, the fine can be an important part of an efficient sanctioning system. Fines may deter and punish many offenders. But the model takes seriously those offenders for whom the first line of defense is insufficient. After a certain record of failure, courts will tailor a solution.[15]

In order to maintain this equilibrium, the system must keep people from strategically appearing undeterrable to the court in order to have the obli-

---

15. Note that the tailored solution is not terribly different from how the current system works in the cases in which the sanction is not simply ignored. Many prisoner reentry programs are designed to work out individualized solutions to accumulated fines and debts. In the model, this tailored solution is purposeful and is designed to maintain the equilibrium.

gation reduced. This means that whatever tailored program is developed for those who are not deterred by the sanctioning scheme must produce further obligations to government (such as garnished wages or additional appointments to keep) that those who are deterrable will find much more noxious than simply paying the fine. This condition requires that the tailored program cannot be overly generous in terms of writing down the financial obligations for those who cannot pay without adding other requirements of participants. Specialized courts, day reporting centers, and comprehensive prerelease programs provide examples of how these programs can be structured.

One negative possibility is that the thicket entered after nonpayment of a fine could be more costly to society than the system it replaces. For example, if incarceration is used as a threat to collect fines, then the use of incarceration could logically increase. Murphy (2009) describes how punishment for process crimes—offenses "against the machinery of justice itself"—can result in substantial criminal penalties that in some cases are more serious than the initial conduct under investigation. This is an important caution. At the same time, for many, the thicket need not be complicated or extensive. As the Snohomish County experience demonstrates, regular follow up can do a lot to support collection, suggesting that many offenders are simply disorganized.

What are the primary threats to the equilibrium envisioned in the model? The single most important requirement to achieve expanded use of fines is that voters, judges, and court administrators believe that fines are efficient, that fines have a punitive and deterrent impact, that fines are regularly collected, and that people who do not pay fines face very serious consequences. Only if voters, judges, and court administrators believe all these things will fines be used on a regular basis, and resources allocated to developing them further. Of these beliefs, the most complicated is the belief in efficiency. Fines have been badly overpromised, suggesting that they are almost perfectly efficient (Becker 1968), while the data suggest that at best, the net loss in fine enforcement (ignoring the economic cost of the crime) is, in the absolute best case, on the order of at least 20 percent.

Combined with the overpromising is the fact that many people think that fines are only efficient if fine collection covers its own cost, narrowly defined. Those who think about efficiency without considering opportunity cost will only want to impose fines on wealthy, white-collar defendants and traffic violators. Court administrators will enthusiastically fight off any attempt to broaden the use of fines when expanding the usage is likely to radically reduce efficiency rates (defined from their perspective) and the overall statistics for their court.

Finally, fines will not work as standalone mechanisms. The substantial majority of those punished with fines will pay them or work them off but a significant minority will crash through the system and enter the thicket.

Fines cannot be successfully implemented without some acknowledgment of this, and a well-developed backup system. For the lowest level offenses, the backup can be largely administrative (at least until several repeat offenses ensue or compliance is unacceptably low). This could involve adopting a traffic offense-like system for nuisance offenses. For more serious offending, the backup could involve incarceration (the miracle of the cells) or some set of tailored and/or graduated consequences sufficient to maintain the equilibrium.

At this time, the research literature does not provide sufficient guidance to allow for detailed consideration of institutional design. The single most important gap in our knowledge about fines is an understanding of their real deterrent power. A stronger empirical base is necessary for informing judgments about the efficiency of fines for particular offenders and particular offenses. Because of the expected heterogeneity, identifying the views at the policy-relevant margins for different offenses and different offender types is the particular research challenge. In light of the potential gains from getting the institutional design right, this is a high priority.

References

ACA International. 2005. "2005 Benchmarking/Agency Operations Survey." Accessed April 6, 2010. http://www.acainternational.org/files.aspx?p=/images/12980/sample_2005benchmarkingsurvey.pdf.

Becker, Gary. 1968. "Crime and Punishment: An Economic Approach." *Journal of Political Economy* 76 (2): 169–217.

DiIulio, John J., Jr. and Anne Morrison Piehl. 1991. "Does Prison Pay? The Stormy National Debate over the Cost-Effectiveness of Imprisonment." *The Brookings Review* 9 (4): 28–35.

Durlauf, Steven N., and Daniel S. Nagin. 2011. "The Deterrent Effect of Imprisonment." In *Controlling Crime: Strategies and Tradeoffs*, edited by Philip J. Cook, Jens Ludwig, and Justin McCrary, 43–94. Chicago: University of Chicago Press.

Feeley, Malcolm. 1979. *The Process is the Punishment: Handling Cases in a Lower Criminal Court.* New York: Russell Sage Foundation.

Garoupa, Nuno. 1997. "The Theory of Optimal Law Enforcement." *Journal of Economic Surveys* 11 (3): 267–95.

———. 2001. "Optimal Magnitude and Probability of Fines." *European Economic Review* 45 (9): 1765–71.

Gneezy, Uri, and Aldo Rustichini. 2000. "A Fine is a Price." *The Journal of Legal Studies* 29 (1): 1–17.

Goebel, Julius, and T. Raymond Naughton. 1970. *Law Enforcement in Colonial New York: A Study in Criminal Procedure (1664–1776).* Montclair, NJ: Patterson Smith.

Greene, Judith A. 1988. "Structuring Criminal Fines: Making an 'Intermediate Penalty' More Useful and Equitable." *The Justice System Journal* 13 (1): 37–50.

Hillsman, Sally T. 1988. "The Growing Challenge of Fine Administration to Court Managers." *The Justice System Journal* 13 (1): 5–16.

————. 1990. "Fines and Day Fines." In *Crime and Justice: A Review of Research,* Vol. 12, edited by Michael Tonry and Norval Morris, 49–98. Chicago, IL: The University of Chicago Press.

Hillsman, Sally T., and Judith A. Greene. 1988. "Tailoring Criminal Fines to the Financial Means of the Offender." *Judicature* 72 (1): 38–45.

Hillsman, Sally, Joyce Sichel, and Barry Mahoney. 1984. *Fines in Sentencing: A Study of the Use of the Fine as a Criminal Sanction: Executive Summary.* Washington, DC: National Institute of Justice, US Department of Justice.

James, Doris J. 2004. *Profile of Jail Inmates, 2002.* NCJ 201932. Washington, DC: Bureau of Justice Statistics, US Department of Justice.

Kleiman, Mark. 2009. *When Brute Force Fails.* Princeton, NJ: Princeton University Press.

Langan, Patrick. 1994. "Between Prison and Probation: Intermediate Sanctions." *Science* 264 (5160): 791–3.

Levitt, Steven D. 1997. "Incentive Compatibility Constraints as an Explanation for the Use of Prison Sentences Instead of Fines." *International Review of Law Economics* 17 (2): 179–92.

McLean, Rachel L., and Michael D. Thompson. 2007. *Summary Reports: Repaying Debts.* New York: Council of State Governments Justice Center.

Moxon, David, and Claire Whittaker. 1996. *Imprisonment for Fine Default.* Research Findings No. 36. London, England: Great Britain Home Office Research Development and Statistics Directorate.

Murphy, Erin. 2009. "Manufacturing Crime: Process, Pretext, and Criminal Justice." *The Georgetown Law Journal* 97 (6): 1435–1507.

Nagin, Daniel S. 2008. "Thoughts on the Broader Implications of the 'Miracle of the Cells.'" *Criminology & Public Policy* 7 (1): 37–42.

Nagin, Daniel S., David P. Farrington, and Terrie E. Moffitt. 1995. "Life-course Trajectories of Different Types of Offenders." *Criminology* 33 (1): 111–39.

Piehl, Anne Morrison. 2002. *From Cell to Street: A Plan to Supervise Inmates after Release.* Boston: Massachusetts Institute for a New Commonwealth.

————. 2009. *Preparing Prisoners for Employment: The Power of Small Rewards.* Civic Report no. 57. New York: Manhattan Institute for Policy Research.

Piehl, Anne Morrison, and Stefan F. LoBuglio. 2005. "Does Supervision Matter?" In *Prisoner Reentry and Crime in America,* edited by Jeremy Travis and Christy Visher, 105–38. Cambridge, England: Cambridge University Press.

Polinsky, A. Mitchell, and Steven Shavell. 1984. "The Optimal Use of Fines and Imprisonment." *Journal of Public Economics* 24 (1): 89–99.

————. 2000. "The Economic Theory of Public Enforcement of Law." *Journal of Economic Literature* 38 (1): 45–76.

PricewaterhouseCoopers. 2008. *Value of Third-Party Debt Collection to the U.S. Economy in 2007: Survey and Analysis.* Accessed April 5, 2010. http://www.acainternational.org/publications-value-of-third_party-debt-collection-to-the-us-economy-in-2007-survey-and-analysis-12983.aspx.

Reynolds, Carl, Mary Cowherd, Andy Barbee, Tony Fabelo, Ted Wood, and Jamie Yoon. 2009. *A Framework to Improve How Fines, Fees, Restitution, and Child Support are Assessed and Collected from People Convicted of Crimes Interim Report.* Austin, TX: Counsel of State Governments Justice Center and the Texas Office of Court Administration.

Rusche, George, Otto Kirchheimer, and Dario Melossi. 2003. *Punishment and Social Structure.* Edison, NJ: Transaction Publishers.

Schelling, Thomas C. 1956. "An Essay on Bargaining." *American Economic Review* 46 (3): 281–306.

Scott-Hayward, Christine S. 2009. *The Fiscal Crisis in Corrections: Rethinking Policies and Practices.* New York: Vera Institute of Justice.

Sichel, Joyce. 1982. *Report on Visits to Selected State and Local Courts.* Fines in sentencing Working Paper no. 8. New York: Vera Institute of Justice.

Snohomish County, Washington. 2009. "A Successful Felony Collections Program." Unpublished Report.

Turner, Susan, and Joan Petersilia. 1996. *Day Fines in Four U.S. Jurisdictions.* Santa Monica, CA: Rand Corporation.

Tyler, John H., and Jeffrey R. Kling. 2007. "Prison-Based Education and Re-Entry into the Mainstream Labor Market." In *Barriers to Reentry? The Labor Market for Released Prisoners in Post-Industrial America,* edited by Shawn Bushway, Michael Stoll, and David Weiman, 227–56. New York: Russell Sage Foundation.

United Kingdom Home Office. 2006. "Strengthening Powers to Tackle Anti-social Behaviour." Consultation paper, ref no.: 278202. London, England: Home Office.

US Sentencing Commission. 2006. "United States Sentencing Commission Year in Review—Fiscal Year 2006." Accessed January 10, 2010. http://www.ussc.gov/ANNRPT/2006.

Useem, Bert, and Anne Morrison Piehl. 2008. *Prison State: The Challenge of Mass Incarceration.* New York: Cambridge University Press.

Weisburd, David, Tomer Einat, and Matt Kowalski. 2008. "The 'Miracle of the Cells': An Experimental Study of Interventions to Increase Payment of Court-ordered Financial Obligations." *Criminology and Public Policy* 7 (1): 9–36.

Wood, John C., and Michael C. Wood. 2005. *Joseph M. Juran: Critical Evaluations in Business and Management.* Abingdon, England: Routledge Taylor & Francis Group.

Zamist, Ida. 1982. *A Report on an Empirical Study of Fine Use, Collection and Enforcement in New York City Courts.* Fines in sentencing Working Paper no. 7. New York: Vera Institute of Justice.

Zamist, Ida, and Joyce Sichel. 1982. *Review of United States Fines Literature.* Fines in sentencing Working Paper no. 5. New York: Vera Institute of Justice.

Comment   David Alan Sklansky

When economists turn their attention to the legal system, the result is often an effort—sometimes successful, sometimes not—to demonstrate that something that on its face has little to do with anything tangible can nonetheless be understood, assessed, and improved by thinking in terms of prices and utility maximization. The insightful chapter that Anne Morrison Piehl and Geoffrey Williams have written about fines is different. Its pleasure and its great value lie in the opportunity to watch two first-rate economists explore how something that seems to lend itself to analysis in the simplest terms of monetized costs and benefits is actually a good deal

David Alan Sklansky is the Yosef Osheawich Professor of Law at the University of California, Berkeley.

more complicated, in ways that present both challenges and opportunities for institutional design.

It can be awkward to think about prison or parole as a "price" that people weigh in deciding to commit a crime, but it seems straightforward to think in that manner about fines. But Piehl and Williams show that two kinds of variability can bedevil efforts to use fines as a means of crime control: variability in individuals, and variability in institutions.

Regarding variability of individuals, Piehl and Williams point out that the problem is not just, as might be supposed, that people vary in their *sensitivity* to fines. Even worse, people vary in their *ability* to be fined. There are defendants who are effectively "fine proof," in a way somewhat analogous to that category of potential civil defendants that have long been the bane of tort plaintiffs' lawyers, the "judgment proof." Lawyers call a tortfeasor judgment proof when her assets, her income stream, and most importantly her liability coverage are, taken all together, just not enough to provide for a meaningful recovery. Piehl and Williams show that a similar problem can occur with fines. There are individuals, for example, whose wages are so unpredictable, and who rely so extensively on forms of consumption beyond the reach of the state, that fines cannot impose a meaningful drop in their overall welfare.

Nor is that the end of it. Piehl and Williams point out that these fine proof defendants are merely a subset of a larger category of offenders whom fines will not deter. There are people who are simply irrational, for example, and individuals whose principal sources of income are themselves criminal. The bottom line is that people vary widely, in ways that present serious challenges when trying to use fines to control crime.

Even more daunting, perhaps, are the challenges posed by variations in institutions. A range of institutions are involved in any effort to impose fines and criminal penalties: police, courts, parole and probation authorities, the agency charged with collecting the fines, and, if another sanction, like imprisonment, is to be used as a backup, then whatever agency administers *that* sanction. The problem is not just that these various agencies may pursue their goals in *different ways*. As Piehl and Williams make clear, the agencies often pursue completely *different goals*. That is true with any form of criminal punishment, because of the familiar range of goals that punishment may be thought to serve: deterrence, incapacitation, rehabilitation, retribution, and expression. But there is a special problem with fines, as Piehl and Williams point out: the tension between viewing fines as a means of revenue collection and viewing them as a way of purchasing a public good, punishment, in a manner that happens to trigger a partial rebate. This is a problem that fines share with any use of monetary sanctions or prices as a means of social control; the same problem is faced, for example, in cap-and-trade systems of emissions control.

Among the many useful lessons that Piehl and Williams draw from all of this, the two that strike me as most important are, first, not to assume that a system of fines needs to pay its way in order to represent an attractive alternative to incarceration, and, second, that there are advantages to a tiered system of penalties, where offenders who somehow pass through the thicket of fines face incarceration or some other form of backup penalty.

It seems both churlish and dispiriting to suggest that efforts to use fines for criminal punishment face additional complexities and difficulties, beyond what Piehl and Williams describe. But I will do so anyway. The three additional challenges I want to flag might be called the problem of unequal justice, the problem of alternative alternatives, and the problem of the cookie jar.

Piehl and Williams themselves flag the problem of unequal justice early in their chapter, when they refer to the challenge of imposing fines in a manner that does not unfairly discriminate against the poor. The challenge is knottier and more pervasive than one might think. As Piehl and Williams make clear, any system of fines, to be effective, needs a set of backup penalties for offenders who fail to pay the fines, and the backup penalties, to be effective, need to be even less pleasant than the fines. So the offenders who wind up saddled with the backup penalties are, of necessity, more sorely imposed on than the offenders who pay the fines. The trouble is that the failure to pay a fine does not always make an offender more blameworthy. All kinds of morally neutral circumstances, including but not limited to poverty, can make it harder for an offender to pay a fine. It turns out to be quite difficult to devise a thicket of fines that sorts offenders based on blameworthiness—and it seems wrong to impose harsher penalties on a group of offenders who are *not* more blameworthy.

Unlike the problem of unequal justice, the problem of alternative alternatives has to do not with the *design* of a system of fines but with its *assessment*. Much of what drives the chapter by Piehl and Williams is the comparison of fines, sometimes explicitly and sometimes implicitly, with incarceration. That makes sense: incarceration is our default form of punishment, and it is scandalously expensive. The problem is that the comparison is almost too easy. Compared to imprisonment, almost everything looks good. Before ramping up our use of fines, we might want to know not just how they compare with prison cells, but how they compare—and how compatible they are—with other alternatives to incarceration.

There are interesting questions to be asked, in particular, about comparing fines with restorative justice, and with combinations of the two kinds of sanctions. John Braithwaite and other proponents of restorative justice have called explicitly for a tiered set of responses very much like what Piehl and Williams advocate, but with the first line of response being efforts at restoration of social peace and reintegration of offenders, rather than fines. Of course, fines can themselves be part of an effort at repairing the social fabric, particularly when they are framed as restitution—or when they enlist relatives, friends, and community members in the sanctioning and reintegration of offenders. The latter approach has deep roots in English legal history, running back to the Saxon system of tything and the Norman frankpledge. We do something similar today (or purport to do so) with bail bonds. All of these mechanisms, though, threaten to produce inquality and unfairness— not just the unfairness of burdening the innocent, but the unfairness of selectively punishing the friendless. For it is precisely the friendless—the socially isolated—who are most likely to slip through this kind of a thicket.

The last problem I want to warn about is the problem of the cookie jar— or, put differently, the problem of institutional dynamics. The range of institutions that Piehl and Williams discuss, and the range of perspectives these institutions have toward fines, will not remain static when a system of fines is introduced or greatly expanded. Two dynamics can be expected. One is an ongoing shift in the back-and-forth between thinking of fines as a source of revenue and thinking of fines as a public good to be purchased. There is a tendency for any social institution that happens to raise revenue to be seen, more and more, as first and foremost a *means* of raising revenue, even if that is not what it was originally designed to be. This was very much the story of frankpledge, for example; it may also be the story of parking tickets. The second kind of institutional dynamic worth worrying about is net widening: the tendency of sanctions initially proposed as a *substitute* for a more onerous or intrusive form of control, such as imprisonment, to morph into a *supplement*—with the result that the use of imprisonment stays constant, but the overall level of punishment increases, because more offenders are being sanctioned. What is more, these two dynamics can interact: once a system of fines becomes viewed as a means of raising revenue, there is a financial incentive to impose the fines on as many people as possible. Designing a system of fines requires attention not just to the existing variation in organizational goals, but to the ways those goals can themselves begin to alter once a system of fines is implemented or expanded.

None of this is to deny that we could use fines more widely, and more productively, than we now do. It is just to underscore and extend the central lesson of Piehl and Williams's chapter: for a system of fines to be fair and effective, it must take account of the complexities both of individuals and of institutions.

3

If Drug Treatment Works
So Well, Why Are So Many
Drug Users in Prison?

Harold Pollack, Peter Reuter, and Eric Sevigny

Drug use and drug sales play central roles in the history of American crime. One cannot discuss crime in America in the 1970s without reference to the heroin epidemic nor in the 1980s and early 1990s without reference to powder and crack cocaine. The highly punitive regime in place now for drug offenders is largely a response to the association of these epidemics with crime waves.

Yet these drug epidemics unfolded a long time ago, with apparently low rates of initiation into drug dependence in recent years. From the vantage point of 2011, one might think that these drugs no longer matter much, and that dependent drug use plays a smaller role in crime and criminal justice policy than it did ten or twenty years ago. In fact, however, data from many sources (some described later) indicate that those arrested or incarcerated within the American criminal justice system remain heavily involved in the consumption of illicit drugs.

There is abundant evidence that inducing criminal offenders to halt or reduce their substance use would reduce crime. Policymakers, researchers, and advocates have long argued that broader provision of substance abuse treatment could reduce the number of Americans behind bars.

In fact, however, a major component of the relentless growth in the US incarcerated population over the last thirty-five years has been the rising

Harold Pollack is the Helen Ross Professor at the School of Social Service Administration and faculty chair of the Center for Health Administration Studies at the University of Chicago. Peter Reuter is a professor in the School of Public Policy and in the Department of Criminology at the University of Maryland. Eric Sevigny is an assistant professor in the Department of Criminology and Criminal Justice at the University of South Carolina.

We thank Holly Nguyen for capable research assistance. We thank Jonathan Caulkins, Steven Raphael, and the conference organizers for excellent comments.

number of people imprisoned for drug offenses, (Blumstein and Beck 1999) a figure that rose from 42,000 in 1980 to 481,000 in 2002 (Caulkins and Chandler 2006). Most of this incarceration burden falls on people who were involved in supplying drugs, albeit sometimes in minor roles (Sevigny and Caulkins 2004). In addition, a large number of those incarcerated for both drug and nondrug offenses appear to satisfy screening criteria for drug use disorders. Many are dependent on cocaine, heroin, or methamphetamine; there is reasonable evidence that their drug use has a causal role in their criminality (MacCoun, Kilmer, and Ritter 2003).

Substance abuse treatment provides a highly imperfect response to these problems. During any given treatment episode, the typical client is likely to continue some level of substance use. Relapse is the norm rather than the exception as a treatment outcome. Even so, at the individual level, there is compelling evidence that treatment markedly reduces both drug use and related criminal offending. Imperfect treatment works. This is just as well, since this describes the treatment we have.

An array of programs have developed over the last twenty years based on this evidence, and more broadly on the well-documented premise that reducing drug use leads to large reductions in the individual offender's crime rate. The list of programs includes drug courts, other forms of diversion from the criminal justice system into treatment (e.g., Proposition 36 in California), intensive supervision probation, and in-prison treatment. All these aim to reduce the extent of criminality among those who have already developed drug abuse or dependency by encouraging/coercing offenders into treatment. A substantial research literature shows that treatment does reduce both drug use and associated criminal activity. In addition to such programs, there is growing recent interest in "coerced abstinence" or "mandated desistance" interventions, whereby drug-involved offenders under criminal justice supervision in noncustodial settings (parole, probation, and pretrial supervision) are subject to short, immediate, and graduated penalties for detected drug use (Kleiman 2009).

Despite this array of efforts, there has been no decline in the incarceration of drug users for either drug offenses or for other criminal activities. The number incarcerated for drug offenses has increased every year since 1980 (Caulkins and Chandler 2006). We show later in this chapter that the number of state prisoners with drug problems also increased substantially from 1986 to 2004, extending analyses of The National Center on Addiction and Drug Abuse at Columbia University (CASA) (Belenko et al. 2002) and Mumola and Karberg (2006). We find strikingly similar patterns within the increasingly important population incarcerated in local jails.

Both of these findings are rather surprising, since the number of individuals with expensive illegal drug habits who are not incarcerated was estimated to have declined in the period 1988 to 2000, the most recent years for which a published estimate is available, (Office of National Drug Control Policy

2001) and there are some indicators that the decline may have continued. This would suggest that there are fewer sellers as well as fewer users to lock up.

Why has the United States achieved such limited success in getting criminal offenders to curtail their drug use? Put slightly differently, why is it so difficult to replicate at the population level the substantial reductions in drug use and criminal offending that treatment appears capable of achieving for individual offenders? Why aren't more offenders in treatment? And why have diversion programs such as California's Proposition 36 and drug courts proved relatively disappointing in achieving their stated goals?

We hypothesize that there are two main reasons for the continued large numbers of drug users flowing into, and remaining within, the correctional system:

First, eligibility criteria for diversion programs, particularly for drug courts, are restrictive. Although the various programs are effective and even cost-effective in serving the specific clients they recruit, they make only a small contribution at the population level. The diverted offenders are at low risk of going to prison or even jail (following sentencing, as opposed to pretrial) in the absence of the drug court intervention. Given limited capacity and the relatively low-risk populations actually served, the currently deployed model of drug courts is unlikely to notably reduce prison populations.

A second, related pattern also hinders the effectiveness of these interventions. There is a systematic mismatch between sentencing practices and actual criminal careers among drug-involved offenders. As individual criminally active drug users get older, the system increasingly treats them harshly for each successive offense. They have longer criminal histories, longer records of unsuccessful treatment, and worse employment histories. Thus, not only are they less eligible for diversion programs, these offenders also receive longer sentences, increasing the share of the incarcerated population with drug problems.

The empirical contribution of this chapter primarily concerns the first of these conjectures. In particular, we examine what share of those currently incarcerated would have been eligible for drug courts with the least restrictive entry criteria. We have not been able to find data that allows testing of the effect of the potentially lengthening criminal careers of dependent drug users.

To test the hypothesis about the ineffectiveness of drug courts to reduce the size of the incarcerated drug-offending population, we make use of the Survey of Inmates in State Correctional Facilities (SISCF) and the Survey of Inmates in Local Jails (SILJ), two Bureau of Justice Statistics (BJS) occasional surveys. Both provide self-reports on, *inter alia*, criminal activity and substance use from nationally representative samples of inmates; the Prison survey has been conducted six times between 1974 and 2004 (with federal inmates surveyed only in the 1997 and 2004 studies), while the Jail survey has been conducted six times between 1972 and 2002. We find that, indeed, very few of those entering state prison in 2004 or jail in 2002 would have been eligible for diversion through state courts. That this is true for local jails is much more surprising than the prison finding. This pattern provides a reminder that, even late in the incarceration boom, it is not so easy to get incarcerated, conditional on arrest.

There are two reasons for the findings about drug courts. First, many entering prison and jail (whether drug users or not) were on supervised release (parole or probation) at the time of their latest arrest, which automatically made them ineligible for most drug court interventions. Second, and more interestingly, most of those who were arrested de novo and who had drug use patterns making them potential clients for drug court, had long, relatively serious criminal records that would have made them ineligible under current conditions. Drug use itself may lead to more intense or longer criminal careers. Moreover, many of those dependent on expensive drugs (cocaine, crack, heroin, and methamphetamine) became drug users a long time ago. These populations are aging, which is not true of nondrug-using criminal offenders. In effect, what we are seeing is two distinct trends in the incarcerated population, separated by drug use.

We also present three other policy-relevant descriptive findings:

First, it is useful to compare the number of dependent drug users entering treatment with the number entering prison. Both in 1986 and 2004, these figures are approximately comparable; the United States is locking up about as many drug addicts as it is treating, a troubling observation about the nation's drug policies.

Second, there are indications that drug dependence is less prevalent among younger offenders than in cohorts that are twenty years older. Absent a new drug epidemic or a newly invigorated drug war, there is a predictable end in sight to the growth of drug-related prisoners.

Third, for drug using prisoners, the probability of a violent offense declines sharply with age after thirty-five.

This last observation leads us to our principal policy suggestion, which needs further investigation. Diversion programs of all kinds require substantial redesign if they are to contribute to a reduction in the incarcerated population. Experienced drug users, who account for an increasing share of drug-related crime, are not attractive (or eligible) candidates for many current efforts. However, if one is willing to take a very long-term social welfare perspective, it may be worth introducing courts specifically designed for the long-term user. Our finding that aging drug users commit relatively few violent crimes is helpful here. The risks associated with treatment-oriented community supervision of older offenders are therefore less than one likely encounters in younger drug-using cohorts.

The chapter begins with three review sections. Section 3.1 describes the changing patterns of drug misuse in the United States over the last forty years, which is necessary to understand the challenge now facing the criminal justice system. Section 3.2 follows with a review of what is known about the effectiveness of drug treatment in reducing crime at the individual level. Section 3.3 briefly discusses interventions aimed at diverting drug-involved offenders from incarceration, such as drug courts, Proposition 36 (the largest diversion program in operation, even though it is restricted to California alone), and coerced abstinence/mandated desistence in Hawaii. Section 3.4 presents our empirical analysis of the surveys of jail and state prison inmates, showing the limited potential impact of drug courts under current eligibility rules. Section 3.5 presents our conclusions.

3.1   Background: The Changing Demography of Drug Misuse

The dynamics of drug-related incarceration in the United States should be examined in light of broader societal trends in drug use and dependence over the last forty years. The characteristics of the drug using population, particularly those dependent on expensive drugs, has changed in ways that complicate the task of keeping criminally active drug users out of prison.

3.1.1   Drug Epidemics

The nation has experienced four major drug-specific epidemics in that period; heroin (ca. 1968 to 1973), cocaine powder (ca. 1975 to 1985), crack cocaine (ca. 1982 to 1988), and methamphetamine (ca. 1990 to 2000). In an epidemic process, rates of initiation rise sharply as new and socially contagious users of a drug initiate friends and peers, a model first well developed by Hunt and Chambers (1976).

In the case of heroin, there is much evidence of a sudden elevation of initiation rates during the late 1960s and early 1970s, followed by a rapid incidence decline over the 1970s and 1980s (Kozel and Adams 1986; Rocheleau and Boyum 1994). A study of an early 1990s sample of street heroin users also found evidence of sharply peaked initiation rates in the late 1960s and early 1970s. For cocaine powder the rise was similarly rapid, but decline was not so pronounced as with heroin (Everingham and Rydell 1994). For crack cocaine the epidemic was still later, starting between about 1982 and 1986, depending on the city (Cork 1999). Caulkins et al. (2004) reported estimates of annual cocaine initiation using the National Household Survey on Drug Abuse (NHSDA) and a variety of methods; all show a peak in 1980 followed by a decline of two-thirds in the next five years.

A new class of epidemiologic models has been developed by Caulkins and collaborators (Caulkins et al. 2004; Caulkins 2007), which use diverse data to document the long trajectory of drug epidemics. After the peak, the initiation rate does not return to its original zero level but falls to a rate well below the peak. Under reasonable assumptions, the result is a flow of new users who do not fully replace those lost through desistance, death, or incarceration. Thus, the number of active users declines gradually over time. Moreover, the drug-using population ages with corresponding changes in the health, employment, and crime consequences of substance use.

Some evidence for this characterization can be seen in the changing characteristics of drug users in TEDS (the Treatment Episode Data System) that includes data on admissions to treatment programs that receive federal funds. We do not report changes in the National Household Survey on Drug Abuse/National Survey on Drug Use and Health (NHSDA/NSDUH) because these include so few dependent users.[1]

For TEDS we are able to compare the admission cohort of 1992 with that of 2006; these two years are the earliest and latest for which detailed data are available. By 1992 all but the methamphetamine epidemics had run their courses but the cocaine and crack epidemics were relatively recent. So many of the users showing up for treatment were still young adults. Figure 3.1, computed using 1992 and 2006 TEDS data, displays changes in the age distribution of adult clients admitted into substance abuse treatment who reported cocaine-related disorders.

In the 1992 data, 40 percent of clients were under the age of thirty. By 2006, that figure had dropped to 26 percent. The fraction of clients over the age of forty rose from 15 percent to 47 percent over the same period. This was not the consequence of an epidemic of new use among older individuals; rather, it represented the aging of those who were caught in the earlier epidemics.

We observed a more complex pattern within the population of admitted heroin users. As shown in figure 3.2, the over-forty-five population displayed a similar pattern to that found in the population of cocaine users. Yet there was also a substantial population of admitted heroin users below the age of thirty.

The Drug Abuse Warning Network (DAWN) shows similar patterns of the aging of cocaine and heroin users appearing in emergency departments or as overdoses examined by medical examiners through 2002.

The result of this epidemiology is that the demography of drug misuse changed substantially between the early 1990s and the 2000s. The average age of drug users increased markedly, with a more diverse set of primary drugs of abuse.

These data suggest that current service utilization reflects the long-term reverberation of specific epidemics of cocaine and heroin use in the United States. They also matter for the criminal justice system.

1. For example, in 2000, self-reported prevalences among NHSDA respondents imply that 1.2 million individuals had used cocaine in the previous month. By comparison, more broad-based estimates that included ADAM estimated a total of approximately two million that met the more stringent requirement of having used the drug more than eight times in the thirty days prior to the interview. The differential for heroin was similar (Boyum and Reuter 2005, 18).

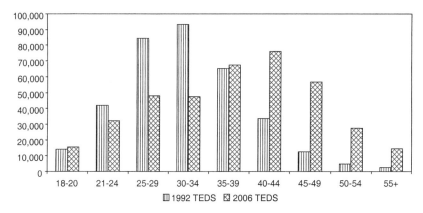

Fig. 3.1   Age distribution of TEDS cocaine admissions, 1992 and 2006

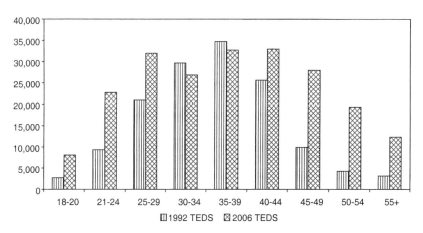

Fig. 3.2   Age distribution of TEDS heroin admissions, 1992 and 2006

The only published estimates, distributed by the Office of National Drug Control Policy in 2001, of the numbers of dependent cocaine and heroin users cover the period 1988 to 2000 (Office of National Drug Control Policy 2001). Figure 3.3 presents these figures, which rely heavily on Arrestee Drug Abuse Monitoring (ADAM), showing a substantial decline, about one-third for each drug, over these twelve years. Both the data and the estimation methodology are weak, as indicated by the frequent adjustment in single year estimates in successive series published by the same research group over the period 1995 to 2000. For example, ONDCP's immediate preceding version of the estimates had shown an increase in heroin use in the early 1990s, followed by a rapid decline (Office of National Drug Control Policy 2000).

Some of the decline in these estimates may represent the consequence of increased incarceration, since those in prison are not eligible for the ADAM

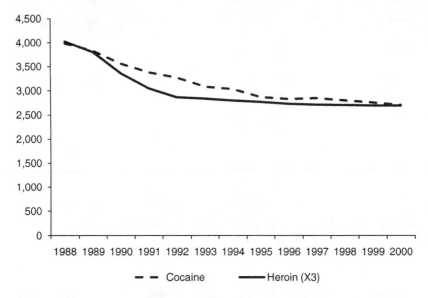

Fig. 3.3   Number of chronic cocaine and heroin users (in thousands), 1988–2000
Source: What America's Users Spend on Illicit Drugs 1988–2000 (ONDCP 2001).

sampling frame. Assume for the purposes of a rough calculation that the share of state prison inmates who would be classified as cocaine- or heroin-dependent prior to entering prison rose from 40 percent of the 557,000 in 1988 to 50 percent of the 1,182,000 in 2000.[2] That would have removed roughly 300,000 dependent cocaine and heroin users from the pool on which these estimates are based. Other trends may also account for some of the observed decline. For example, almost 200,000 injection drug users have died of HIV/AIDS.

Although these trends are important for many reasons, they account for less than one-third of the total decline (from 5.2 million in 1988 to 3.3 million in 2000). The best interpretation of the available data is that the number of individuals dependent on or abusing expensive drugs has been declining for a long period for a variety of reasons. The population of such users has aged, presumably reducing their involvement in violent crime.

3.2   Drug Treatment

Though the research has been critiqued by the National Research Council, (Manski, Pepper, and Petrie 2001), a substantial body of evidence indi-

---

2. The calculation is done only for state prisoners because (a) jail inmates serve short terms on average and are eligible within the year for rearrest and ADAM inclusion, and (b) federal inmates include a large fraction of nonresident offenders.

cates that substance abuse treatment is associated with large reductions in drug use and crime, especially during the period in which the individual drug user is in treatment. United States and British observational cohort studies document the strong association between treatment receipt and increased employment, improved health outcomes, and reduced criminal offending.

For example, Godfrey, Stewart, and Gossop (2004) reported two-year outcome data for 549 drug users enrolled in the British National Treatment Outcome Research Study (NTORS). Expenditures on substance abuse treatment for these individuals totaled 7.3 million British pounds. Economic valuation of treatment-associated crime reduction totaled 27.4 million pounds for the same group. A four- to five-year follow-up indicated reductions in the frequency of heroin, street methadone, and benzodiazepines (Gossop et al. 2003). Crack cocaine and alcohol use were not significantly different after four- to five-years from the corresponding values at intake. Analyzing the same data, Gossop et al. (2005) found substantial reductions in acquisitive, drug selling, and violent crimes. Crime reductions were associated with reduced regular heroin use, simple aging, and living in stable housing.

Similar results were observed with US data collected by the Drug Abuse Treatment Outcome Study (DATOS). Hubbard et al. (1997) reported that clients able to remain in long-term residential treatment for at least six months exhibited a 50 percent reduction in illegal activity and a 10 percent increase in full-time employment. Koenig et al. (2005) and Ettner et al. (2006) observed similar patterns among treatment clients in Cuyahoga County, Ohio, and California, respectively. Both of the latter papers reported strongly positive net benefits from treatment, with reductions in criminal offending accounting for the majority of the observed economic benefit associated with treatment intervention.

Prendergast and colleagues provide one widely cited meta-analysis of these effects (Prendergast et al. 2002). These authors examined results from seventy-eight studies completed between 1965 and 1996. Twenty five of these analyses also examined crime outcomes; forty-six featured randomized study designs. These authors found that treatment was associated with reduced drug use (effect size = 0.30) and reduced crime (effect size = 0.13).

In examining the impact of treatment on crime, reduced substance use appeared to be the critical mediating variable, with reduced substance use inducing lower rates of acquisitive crime. The average age of participating drug users was the only significant predictor of effect size, with treatment having a larger absolute impact in reducing crime among young adults (who are the most criminally active) than among older drug users.

Some of the strongest findings for outpatient treatment arise in the arena of methadone maintenance therapy. For example, Amato et al. (2005) found that methadone maintenance therapy reduces criminality by as much as

60 percent. The findings from a long-term cohort study of heroin users by Hser and colleagues finds similar results for a particularly recalcitrant heroin-using population (Hser et al. 2001).

Retention and treatment outcomes among opiate users appear sensitive to specific quality measures (D'Aunno and Pollack 2002). For example, methadone maintenance clients were markedly more likely to remain in treatment (AOR = 1.72) when methadone doses exceeded sixty mg/day (Bao et al. 2009).

Many studies of opiate substitution therapy (OST) indicate a strong negative correlation between treatment engagement and retention on the one hand, and criminal offending on the other. Campbell, Deck, and Krupski (2007) examined arrest rates among Washington state opiate users. These authors found significantly reduced probability of arrest among treatment participants. Burdon, Messina, and Prendergast (2004) found quite similar results among California offenders participating in prison aftercare.

Given these strong relationships, both state and federal prisons sought to increase treatment provision to drug-involved offenders (Grella et al. 2007; Taxman, Perdoni, and Harrison 2007). Most such services are low-intensity education and counseling services, which probably have a limited impact on criminal offending or drug use. More intensive residential modalities have also been implemented in prison, with greater evidence that treatment participants achieved better outcomes than comparison group members (Prendergast et al. 2004). However, because motivated individuals are more likely to enter and remain in treatment, many of the observed differences between treatment and comparison groups probably reflect favorable selection into treatment.

Given the possibility—indeed the reality—of strong selection effects, randomized trials are especially important in evaluating the causal impact of treatment interventions. In one recent Australian study, Dolan et al. (2005) compared reincarceration, treatment mortality, and hepatitis C infection rates among opiate-dependent prison inmates randomly assigned to methadone maintenance and to a control group. Members of the treatment group displayed lower incidence of hepatitis C. Yet assignment to the treatment group appeared to provide little benefit in terms of long-term treatment retention.

In several recent papers, Gordon et al. (2008) and Kinlock and colleagues examined drug and crime outcomes of 211 heroin-dependent Baltimore prisoners who were randomly assigned to methadone maintenance or a control-group counseling intervention (Kinlock et al. 2007; Kinlock et al. 2008; Kinlock et al. 2009). Offenders offered methadone maintenance shortly after release were significantly less likely to use heroin/cocaine or engage in criminal activity compared to those assigned to the control group.

A randomized trial by McMillan et al. (2008) yielded less favorable findings. Offering opiate-dependent inmates methadone maintenance within the jail setting appeared to confer little benefit absent an effective postrelease intervention.

Outside the arena of opiate substitution therapy, the strongest evaluation results arise in establishing the benefits of therapeutic communities. For example, McCollister et al. (2004) conducted a five-year follow-up study examining the Amity in-prison therapeutic community and an accompanying Vista aftercare program for criminal offenders in southern California.

The average cost of addiction treatment over the baseline and five-year follow-up period was $7,041 for the intervention group and $1,731 for the control group. However, the treatment group experienced eighty-one fewer incarceration days than was observed within the control group. This 13 percent reduction in incarceration more than offset the additional costs of the relatively intensive intervention.[3]

Evaluations of outpatient drug-free interventions yield more mixed results. In the case of cocaine, a meta-analysis of research on interventions aimed at dependent users of a variety of drugs, few of whom were in methadone maintenance, found that those in treatment were about 20 percent more likely to have positive outcomes with respect to criminality than those who did not enter treatment (Prendergast and Burdon 2002). Even though most who enter treatment will relapse to drug use and/or fail to complete their treatment, it is still true that treatment can make a large difference in the lifetime drug use and criminality of a dependent user.

These large differences in criminal offending lead to correspondingly large impacts in cost-benefit analyses of substance abuse treatment. Substance abuse treatment is associated with many economic benefits. Yet crime reduction is consistently the largest single component of the economic benefit of treatment (Dismuke et al. 2004; Sindelar et al. 2004; French et al. 2002; McCollister and French 2003). Indeed, the economic benefits of treatment-associated crime reductions are often larger than all other estimated benefits combined.

The economic valuation of treatment-related crime reduction frequently exceeds, by itself, the entire cost of providing substance abuse treatment. In one prominent analysis of cocaine-dependent clients, Flynn et al. (1999) examined treatment clients' self-reported crime before and after treatment, finding that the economic value of an associated reduction in crime far exceeded the associated treatment costs.

Such findings are doubly striking because most studies in the empirical treatment literature understate the true social benefits associated with reduced crime. Most studies consider the tangible costs of crime—its direct costs to victims and to the health care and the criminal justice systems. The tangible cost approach provides a valuable lower bound to the benefits of

---

3. Analysis that accounted for the social benefits of averted crime would likely find even more striking benefits of substance abuse treatment.

Table 3.1   Treatment admissions for cocaine, heroin, marijuana, and
            methamphetamine, TEDS 1997 and 2006

	1997 (*N*)	1997 (%)	2006 (*N*)	2006 (%)
Cocaine	236,770	15	250,135	14
Heroin	235,143	15	245,984	14
Marijuana	197,840	12	289,988	16
Methamphetamine	53,694	3	149,415	8

Note: Each admission is classified according to primary drug of abuse but may involve poly-drug abuse. Reported percentages are based on treatment admissions for all substances, including alcohol.

crime reduction. However, such costs are a small fraction of the overall social costs of crime (Rajkumar and French 1997). Flynn et al. (1999) cite tangible costs of $1,304 per burglary. By contrast, Cohen et al. (2004) obtain a per burglary cost estimate of $31,000 using contingent valuation methodologies that capture a broader range of crime consequences and societal preferences (Cohen et al. 2004).

Basu, Paltiel, and Pollack (2008) perform a (nonexperimental) prepost analysis of US treatment data from the National Treatment Improvement and Evaluation Study (NTIES) that illustrates the importance of these valuation measures. Using conservative econometric specifications that were biased against a finding of treatment effectiveness, these authors show that the monetized value of treatment-related reductions in armed robbery more than offset the cost of the entire treatment intervention. This finding is especially striking when one considers that less than 7 percent of NTIES respondents reported committing an armed robbery in the year before treatment admission. Moreover, only 32 percent of these robbery offenders reported ever being arrested for using a weapon or force to steal from a victim.

In terms of absolute numbers, substance abuse treatment providers serve a large and diverse population of substance users. As shown in table 3.1, the number of individuals in drug treatment for cocaine or heroin abuse has risen slightly since 1997; for example, TEDS data indicate admissions of 235,000 in 1997 for heroin, compared to 246,000 in 2005. Given that the estimated size of the population of dependent users has, if anything, shrunk, this indicates that the treatment fraction has increased. The figure for methamphetamine admissions almost tripled during the same period.

3.3 Drug Use and Crime

The criminally active population continues to show high rates of drug misuse, another indication that treatment has, at the population level, failed to reduce the connection between crime and drug use.

For this population, ADAM provides the major source for insights into the connection between crime and drug use. The ADAM survey includes data on drug use, both through interview and urinalysis, from a sample of arrestees in a number of counties around the country. Prior to 1998 we must rely on the Drug Use Forecasting system (DUF), a statistically more primitive version of ADAM but one that turns out to provide data of comparable quality. When ADAM was operating most broadly, from 1998 to 2003, the data were collected in thirty-five counties. Data were not collected from 2003 to 2006, and since 2007 have been collected in only ten counties (Office of National Drug Control Policy 2009). Thus, ADAM provides an incomplete depiction of drug use among the arrested population nationally, particularly since 2003; city-level comparisons are more appropriate for comparing trends over time.

The most recent ADAM results (for 2008) show that use of cocaine, heroin, and methamphetamine continues to be common among arrestees in most cities. The percentage testing positive for cocaine varied between a high of 44 percent and a low of 17 percent. Figures for heroin were lower, but were still as high as 29 percent for Chicago, twice as much as the next highest city.

For our purposes the more relevant comparisons are between 1986 and 2004, the era covered by the two inmate surveys we analyzed. The DUF system started collecting data in 1987 in just twenty-one cities (Wish and Gropper 1991). More complete and consistent data are available from Washington, DC, which has collected urinalysis on all adult arrestees since 1984 and on all juvenile arrestees since 1988. The adult data (figure 3.4) show that the percentage of all arrestees testing positive for any drug excluding

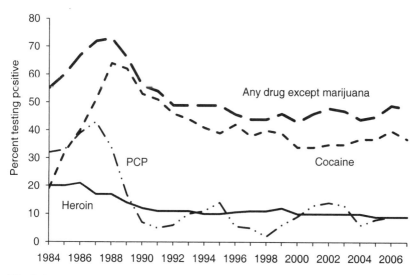

Fig. 3.4 **Arrestees testing positive for various drugs in the District of Columbia, 1984–2007**

Source: Pretrial Services Agency.

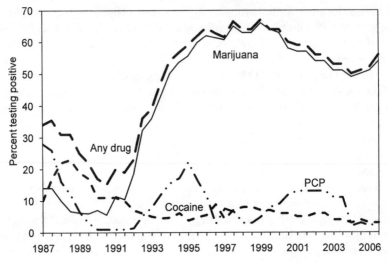

Fig. 3.5   Drug use among arrestees under age 18, the District of Columbia, 1987–2007
Source: Pretrial Services Agency.

marijuana declined from 73 percent in 1987 to 49 percent in 1991, with a stable trend over the following fifteen years.[4]

For juvenile arrestees (figure 3.5) what is striking is how few have tested positive for any drug other than marijuana and PCP since the early 1990s; whereas, in 1987, 23 percent tested positive for cocaine, that figure has hovered around 7 percent since 1993.

3.3.1   Getting Offenders into Treatment

As already noted, the insight that drug treatment could reduce both crime and the demands on the criminal justice system has animated policy for a long time, not just in the United States but in other countries. For example, the United Kingdom saw a near doubling of the population in treatment between 1998 and 2006, largely as a consequence of a large variety of criminal justice diversion programs (Reuter and Stevens 2007). We identify here just the major interventions.

Drug courts aim to use the coercive power of the criminal justice system, particularly the authority of a judge, to persuade drug-involved offenders to cease their drug use rather than face penalties for violating the terms of their release. Drug court clients are encouraged to seek treatment, and

---

4. Most of the late 1980s decline was the result of an abrupt reduction in the percentage testing positive for phencyclidine (PCP), a drug that has been much more prevalent in Washington than any other city, even after the decline.

continued participation in treatment may be a condition for staying out of jail. The evaluation literature, though not technically strong, has generally found positive effects on recidivism, the usual outcome measure (Belenko and Peugh 2005; Wilson, Mitchell, and MacKenzie 2006).

Even though the drug court movement is almost twenty years old and over 2,300 separate programs have been created, (BJA Drug Court Clearinghouse Project 2009), a 2008 study estimated that only 55,000 drug-involved defendants were processed in such courts in the middle of this decade; the same study estimated that over one million such defendants entered the criminal justice system each year (Bhati, Roman, and Chalfin 2008). Despite the rapid expansion of drug courts, the number of defendants who pass through such programs remain relatively low.

This small number of enrollees arises from several factors. Many jurisdictions lack administrative capacity to implement drug courts at-scale. Fifty-two percent of adult drug courts responding to one survey reported they cannot accept some eligible clients due to capacity constraints (Bhati, Roman, and Chalfin 2008). Bhati and colleagues estimate the current number of drug court "slots" at approximately 55,000. Given this constraint, there are strong administrative and political incentives for drug courts to cream-skim by serving relatively low-risk populations most likely to achieve successful outcomes rather than high-risk populations that would experience the greatest net reduction in criminal offending from drug court interventions.

Even if such administrative capacity were available, enrollment would remain sharply constrained by current eligibility restrictions. Despite the pervasiveness of the drug treatment court model, drug courts routinely exclude most of the drug-using offenders. A 2005 survey of adult drug courts (Rossman, Zweig, and Roman 2008) found that "only 12% of drug courts accept clients with any prior violent convictions. Individuals facing a drug charge, even if the seller is drug dependent, are excluded in 70% of courts for misdemeanor sales and 53% of courts for felony sales. Other charges that routinely lead to exclusion include property crimes commonly associated with drug use (theft, fraud, prostitution), and current domestic violence cases (only 20% accept domestic violence cases)" (Bhati, Roman, and Chalfin 2008, 29). An earlier study conducted by the Government Accountability Office (1997) found that only 6 percent of drug courts accept offenders whose current conviction included a violent offense.

A study of drug courts in six Washington state counties found substantial variation in eligibility requirements (Cox et al. 2001). In King County, for example, only defendants facing drug possession charges were eligible; whereas in Pierce County a long list of property crimes charges were also eligible. Similarly, Florida's Dade County accepts offenders with mainly possession or purchase of a controlled substance charges. Marion County stipulates that eligible offenders must be charged with nonviolent drug offenses, with some drug sale and domestic violence cases considered (Florida Supreme Court Task Force on Treatment-Based Drug Courts 2004). Among the seven drug courts in New York City, three accept offenders facing drug sales charges, four do not. Only one court of the seven accepts defendants with nondrug felony charges.

Drug courts originally targeted first-time offenders who were arrested for possession or selling to support their habit. Some programs, however, are expanding to include repeat offenders and a few are accepting violent offenders (Porter 2001). Nevertheless, programs with flexible eligibility criteria are rare. Table 3.2 presents eligibility criteria for four drug courts in major jurisdictions.

More difficult to determine are the eligibility rules with respect to substance abuse. Bhati, Roman, and Chalfin (2008) report that "eligibility based on drug use severity is applied inconsistently–16% of drug courts exclude those with a drug problem that is deemed too serious, while 48% reject arrestees whose problems are not severe enough. Almost 69% exclude those with co-occurring disorders. Even among eligible participants, more than half of drug courts (52%) report they cannot accept some clients who are eligible for participation due to capacity constraints" (8).

These eligibility rules seem likely to exclude most experienced users of cocaine, heroin, and methamphetamine. The few cohort studies of cocaine and heroin users (e.g., by Hser and colleagues) show that long-term users have accumulated long histories of convictions for property and violent crimes and that many—perhaps most—have co-occurring disorders or are polydrug users (Hser et al. 2001; Hser 2007; Hser et al. 2007).

Table 3.2   Eligibility requirements for four major drug courts

County	Program type	Capacity	Eligibility
Dade County, FL	Adult pretrial	1,450	No history of violent crime No arrest for drug sale or trafficking No more than two previous felony convictions
Brooklyn, NY	Postplea	NA	No prior felony conviction No charges involving drug sale near school No prior felony convictions
San Francisco, CA	Preplea	440	No drug court failures in previous five years No convictions for sales in previous eight years No current conviction for violent or serious felony
Broward, FL	Pretrial and postconviction	2,649	No prior felony or conviction No current sales/trafficking conviction

Estimating the potential effect of relaxing eligibility requirements is a major research challenge. Existing effectiveness findings reflect these tight eligibility requirements. Drug courts choose certain clients, and exclude more serious offenders, in the belief that defendants with longer and more serious criminal histories are more likely to have poor outcomes in drug courts. They may be correct; without evaluations of the effects with these other client groups, the research strategies for making projections are inherently speculative. We take this up in more detail in the chapter's conclusion.

California's Proposition 36 provides the largest instance of diversion from the criminal justice system. Under Prop 36 (formally the Substance Abuse and Crime Prevention Act (SACPA)), first- or second-time drug possession arrestees with no record of violent offenses are subject to a drug abuse assessment to determine appropriate referral to a drug treatment program. Parolees or probationers who violate the drug conditions of their release or are arrested for drug possession are also eligible for Prop 36 sentencing to treatment or counseling. Participation in Prop 36 is contingent on pleading guilty to the possession charge. The majority of those arrested for simple possession of marijuana had more attractive legal options, which did not involve pleading guilty and thus did not enter Prop 36. Passed in 2000 by popular referendum, in its fifth year of operation (July 1, 2005 to June 30, 2006) it processed 52,000 individuals, (Urada et al. 2008) almost as many as the national drug court movement.

Given that Prop 36 is focused on individuals early in their criminal careers, it would appear to have little prospect of reducing prison populations. Yet it appears to have had a sizable effect. For example, Ehlers and Ziedenberg (2006) argue that Prop 36 accounted for a decline in the projected California prison population. Whereas the population had been projected to increase from 162,000 to 180,000 between 2000 and 2005, the actual figure ended at only 164,000. Moreover, the rate of prison commitments for drug possession offenses in California fell from 80 per 100,000 on June 1, 2001 (date of implementation) to 57 per 100,000 four years later.

The state has funded a series of detailed evaluations of the effects of Prop 36 (Urada et al. 2008; University of California, Los Angeles Integrated Substance Abuse Programs 2007). A forty-two-month follow-up of the first wave of Prop 36 arrestees found that the measure substantially reduced the levels of jail and prison incarceration of eligible Prop 36 offenders. The comparison was made between those deemed eligible for Prop 36 in the year before enactment and those who were eligible under Prop 36 in its first year. For state prisons, it appears that offenders who would have been eligible for sentencing under Prop 36 prior to its passage spent 100 days in state prison, whereas those who were sentenced under Prop 36 terms spent only about sixty days in prison.[5] For county jails, the figures were similar; the average length of

---

5. This is based on dividing the estimated state prison costs provided in the report by the reported daily cost of a prison stay.

time in jail over forty-two months fell from approximately ninety-five days to sixty-five days.[6] The evaluations do not provide information on how much of that difference was accounted for by the initial incarceration spell, and how much was due to subsequences differences in reincarceration.

Almost three quarters of those who were processed under SACPA entered treatment. Substantial fractions dropped out at various points in the process. The end result is that only one-third (one quarter of the initial intake) were discharged as having completed treatment. That figure is consistent with other studies of outcomes of treatment episodes resulting from criminal justice referrals. Given that Prop 36 clients are under much less threat of rein-carceration than those entering through drug court referrals, for example, this is a surprising and encouraging finding, though it underscores the challenge of retaining criminally active populations in treatment interventions.

The Prop 36 population has some unexpected characteristics. For example, though this option is only available for first or second convictions on drug possession charges, it is a relatively old population with an average age of 34.8 years. Half have never entered treatment before. A substantial percentage have lengthy criminal records, even though this cannot include conviction for a violent offense.

Perhaps the inclusion of parolees among Prop 36 eligibles is an important source of the reduction in the prison and jail populations. However, only 13 percent of the clients in the most recent year of the evaluation entered from parole, and that figure had been as low as 8 percent in the first year of the program.

Over half of those sentenced under Prop 36 were charged with possession of methamphetamine, a drug associated with high levels of criminality. However, ADAM data show a low prevalence of methamphetamine in most US cities (Office of National Drug Control Policy 2009), so the California reductions in incarceration may not generalize to other states.

On their face, the Proposition 36 findings are more encouraging than drug courts as a method for reducing drug-related incarceration at the population level. The California assessments consistently suggest that the use of noncriminal penalties has not produced increases in crime rates, either as a result of higher recidivism or of reduced deterrence. Though high-risk arrestees, primarily those with many prior arrests, fare less well than others, treatment-oriented diversion aimed at nonmarijuana possession arrestees may generate a meaningful reduction in total incarceration. There are, however, some concerns that the state-sponsored evaluation, which is complex and not always clear, does not capture all the problems of implementation. For example, Hawken presents an analysis that finds that at the thirty-

6. The report does not offer a figure for the cost of a day in jail; these calculations assume that it is $62.50, a figure cited by Ehlers and Zeidenberg (2006). Ehlers and Zeidenberg estimate the number of jail days saved per client per year to be approximately twelve, which is roughly consistent with the thirty days estimated in the above calculation.

month mark, arrests for all groups of Prop 36 arrestees (treatment completers, treatment dropouts, and treatment refusers) are higher than for the control group (Hawken 2009).

Coerced abstinence/mandatory desistence, a twenty-year crusade by UCLA's Mark Kleiman (Kleiman 2009; Kleiman 1997; Kleiman and Hawken 2008), is a program that takes advantage of simple findings from behavioral economics, psychology, and public policy. A large number of offenders are under community supervision at any one time, whether it be pretrial release, probation, or parole. Because they have been arrested or convicted, the government can subject these individuals to random drug tests and indeed does from time to time.

Coerced abstinence involves making sanctions certain, immediate, and relatively mild rather than (as is normally the case) random, delayed, and severe. Such interventions have not received widespread evaluation. The small number of existing studies have found that such programs have the predicted effects on recidivism (Harrell, Cavanagh, and Roman 1998). So far, there have been no efforts to implement them on a large scale.

Recently, Hawaii's Opportunity Probation with Enforcement (HOPE) program has implemented the approach for the entire probation population. The results of a random assignment evaluation (Kleiman and Hawken 2008; Hawken and Kleiman 2009) have been very promising. Very few of those enrolled in the program fail more than twice and the recidivism rates have been dramatically lower than for the probation population previously. For example, only 21 percent of HOPE subjects were rearrested in the twelve-month evaluation window, compared to 46 percent among those on routine probation conditions (Hawken and Kleiman 2009).

These results and a clear articulation of the theory underlying the model by Mark Kleiman and others have given this intervention a great deal of political and professional prominence. HOPE-like experiments are being launched in a number of states. It offers the prospect of a large-scale intervention that could be implemented relatively rapidly and without requiring the development of a new expertise in the probation community.

However, for those interested in promoting drug treatment as a major intervention to reduce the incarcerated population, it is striking that coerced abstinence does not necessarily involve treatment. Probation officers want their clients to desist from drug use, and this program gives them the tools to motivate and monitor abstinence. Many drug-involved offenders do not satisfy screening criteria for actual dependence. It is unclear that many of the successful clients entered drug treatment programs or that these individuals needed such services. The adverse consequences of a failed urine test may have been enough to generate abstinence. Whether abstinence will continue postsupervision is an open question but in making a judgment about the utility of coerced abstinence, it is important to note that relapse is the common experience posttreatment.

Table 3.3   Results for the HOPE evaluation involving offenders at risk of jail or prison

	HOPE (%)	Control (%)
No-shows for probation appointments (average of appointments per probationer)	9	23
Positive urine tests (average of tests per probationer)	13	46
New arrest rate (probationers rearrested)	21	47
Revocation rate (probationers revoked)	7	15
Incarceration (days sentenced)	138 days	267 days

The HOPE evaluation involved experienced offenders at risk of jail or prison. Probationers assigned to HOPE were significantly less likely to produce positive drug tests or to be arrested over a twelve-month study period. These offenders spent about one-half as many days in prison on revocations or new convictions. (See table 3.3, reproduced from Hawken and Kleiman 2009.)

If HOPE were implemented on a wide scale, it might cut prison time substantially.

3.4   Incarceration and Drug Courts

This section presents a new analysis of data on the incarcerated population, including both state prisons and local jails. First, we show that offenders with drug use problems continue to be a large share of those in jail and prison, and that recent entering cohorts of drug-using inmates are considerably older on average than late-1980s cohorts. Second, we assess whether under the usual eligibility rules, an expansion of drug courts could substantially reduce the numbers of drug users locked up.

3.4.1   Data and Analytic Framework

We analyzed two waves of data each from the Survey of Inmates in State Correctional Facilities (SISCF) and the Survey of Inmates in Local Jails (SILJ), comparing changes in the standing local jail and state prison populations from the latter part of the 1980s to the early part of the 2000s. Specifically, the prison data are drawn from the 1986 and 2004 waves of the SISCF, and the jail data are drawn from the 1989 and 2002 waves of the SILJ. For the prison population, our analyses focus only on state inmates since the federal inmate survey was only added in 1997. Moreover, federal prisons account for fewer than 10 percent of all those incarcerated on any given day.

In both surveys, all data, including key indicators on prior offenses and on substance use, are based on inmate self-report. There is a substantial literature on such self-reporting in correctional settings both for criminal

Table 3.4   Sample sizes and reference populations for the four inmate surveys

	Late 1980s		Early 2000s	
	1986 prison survey	1989 jail survey	2004 prison survey	2002 jail survey
Stock inmate population				
Sample n	13,711	5,675	14,499	6,982
Population N	450,416	395,554	1,226,171	631,241
Newly incarcerated inmates				
Sample n	5,270	2,656	5,033	4,582
Population N	161,597	180,022	395,865	415,354

involvement (Horney and Marshall 1992) and substance use (Farabee and Fredlund 1996); this research suggests that the self-report methodology is a valuable data collection approach that provides an acceptable level of accuracy for both domains.

The nationally representative inmate surveys employ a stratified two-stage sampling design, first selecting facilities and then inmates within the selected facilities. Total response rates across the four surveys ranged between 84 percent and 92 percent. As shown in table 3.4, the late 1980s prison and jail surveys completed interviews with more than 19,000 inmates, generalizing to a standing incarcerated population of roughly 846,000. In comparison, the early 2000s prison and jail surveys completed interviews with more than 21,000 inmates, generalizing to a standing incarcerated population of about 1.86 million.

For purposes of our analyses, we focus on the past-year admission cohort of convicted inmates. Prior cross-period analyses of the inmate surveys (Mumola and Karberg 2006; Belenko et al. 2002) have made comparisons for the entire incarcerated populations. Since many inmates at each survey were incarcerated long before the survey itself, indeed were potential participants in an earlier wave, comparisons of the total stock population do not describe well the changing dynamics of incarceration. Thus we identify in each case an admission cohort of newly incarcerated offenders consisting of those inmates who entered prison or jail in the twelve months preceding the date of their interview.[7] The resulting sample sizes and reference populations used for the present study are also presented in table 3.4. All analyses were performed using Stata 11.0, with reported estimates weighted to account for the complex survey design.

---

7. Because the SILJ does not ask unconvicted jail detainees pertinent questions on offender substance use and other key indicators, our analyses are by necessity restricted to convicted inmates.

3.4.2 Measuring Drug Misuse

We examined changes among inmate populations in the problematic use of heroin, cocaine, and methamphetamine. For each substance, we operationalized drug abuse as self-reported *daily or near-daily use in the month prior to arrest*. We also defined cocaine to include both powder and crack cocaine, and methamphetamine to include the more general class of amphetamines.[8] Other possible indicators were less valid measures of drug abuse (e.g., *any* drug use in the month prior to arrest, intoxication at the time of the offense) or were entirely incommensurate across survey years (e.g., substance abuse and/or dependence).

3.4.3 Results

Drug Misuse Among the Newly Incarcerated

Our first finding is that frequent drug use continues to be prevalent among recent entering inmate cohorts. Indeed, the percentage of newly incarcerated prison and jail inmates who reported daily or near-daily use of any of the three drugs increased by one quarter and one-fifth, respectively, between the 1980s and the 2000s (see table 3.5). In absolute numbers, this amounts to an overall increase of roughly 129,000 convicted, drug-using offenders entering prison or jail. Of note, this increase appears to be exclusively driven by the rise in methamphetamine use, as the share of heroin and cocaine users declined slightly to moderately across the two periods.

The Changing Age-by-Drug Distributions of the Newly Incarcerated

To capture the changing age profiles of drug-involved offenders, we compared the age distributions of newly incarcerated drug-using inmates for the 1986 and 2004 prison surveys and the 1989 and 2002 jail surveys. Again, by newly incarcerated, we mean admitted to prison within the past year; and by drug abuse, we mean daily or near-daily use in the month prior to arrest. Figures 3.6, 3.7, and 3.8 compare the age group distributions (in five-year increments) for cocaine, heroin, and methamphetamine, respectively.

As shown in figure 3.6, the cocaine-using cohorts aged considerably between the 1980s and 2000s. Reflecting a seven-year increase in the median age from twenty-seven to thirty-four, just 12.1 percent of newly incarcerated cocaine-abusing prison inmates were thirty-five or older in 1986 compared to 47.3 percent in 2004. Among entering jail inmates, similar increases in the

---

8. We note, however, that the 1986 SISCF and 1989 SILJ collected data only on the use of amphetamine, whereas the 2004 SISCF and 2002 SILJ asked separate questions about amphetamine and methamphetamine. Similarly, the 1986 SISCF employed a single measure of cocaine, the 1989 SILJ a single measure of cocaine or crack, and the 2004 SISCF and 2002 SILJ separate measures of crack and cocaine other than crack. Accordingly, the earlier surveys likely provide more conservative estimates of cocaine and methamphetamine use as we have defined it.

median age (twenty-seven to thirty-six) and proportion of those thirty-five or older (17.0 percent to 56.4 percent) were found between 1989 and 2002.

As shown in figure 3.7, we found sizable but relatively smaller increases in population aging across the heroin-using cohorts, with equivalent four-year increases in the median ages of both newly incarcerated prison (thirty to thirty-four) and jail (thirty-two to thirty-six) inmates. Examining the age distributions, we found that the percentage of newly incarcerated heroin-abusing prison inmates who were thirty-five or older increased from roughly one quarter to one-half (25.6 percent to 48.7 percent) between 1986 and 2004. A comparable percentage point increase (from 38.6 percent to 57.2 percent) in those thirty-five or older occurred among the heroin-abusing jail cohort. Of note, however, there was considerable parity across all survey years in the proportion of young (i.e., under twenty-five) heroin abusers.

Table 3.5	Percentage of newly incarcerated convicted inmates reporting daily or near-daily substance use, by drug type and survey year			
Drug Type[a]	1986 state prison inmates (%)	1989 local jail inmates (%)	2004 state prison inmates (%)	2002 local jail inmates (%)
Heroin	7.5	5.1	5.3	4.5
Cocaine	13.7	13.7	13.4	12.0
Methamphetamine	5.1	2.8	11.8	7.7
Any of the three	21.5	17.8	27.0	21.4
N	161,597	180,022	395,865	415,354

[a]Percentage calculations are based on nonmissing data, the amount of which varies by indicator.

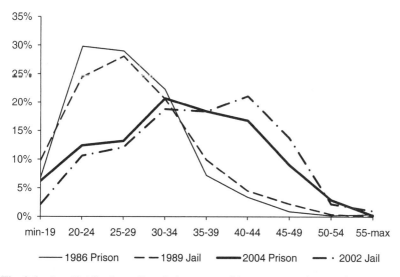

Fig. 3.6   **Age distributions of newly incarcerated inmates reporting cocaine abuse**

For methamphetamine abusers, the median age rose from twenty-six to thirty among entering prison inmates and from twenty-eight to thirty-one among entering jail inmates. In the late 1980s, just 8.0 percent and 11.0 percent of newly incarcerated methamphetamine-abusing prison and jail inmates, respectively, were thirty-five or older (see figure 3.8). By the 2000s,

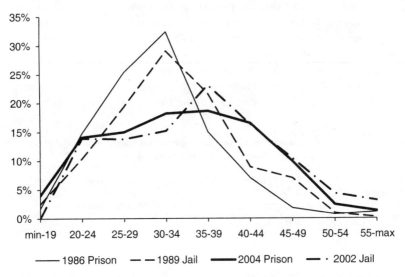

Fig. 3.7   Age distributions of newly incarcerated inmates reporting heroin abuse

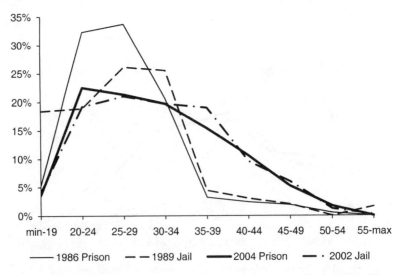

Fig. 3.8   Age distributions of newly incarcerated inmates reporting methamphetamine abuse

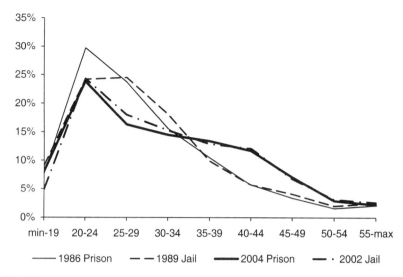

Fig. 3.9   **Age distributions of newly incarcerated inmates reporting no drug abuse**

one-third or more of incoming methamphetamine-abusing prison (32.9 percent) and jail (36.0 percent) inmates exceeded this age.

The remainder of the inmate cohorts—that is, new entrants who did not report daily or near-daily use of any of the three expensive drugs in the month before arrest—showed much smaller aging patterns across survey years (see figure 3.9). Median ages for entering cohorts of prison and jail inmates rose three and two years, respectively. In addition, unlike the drug-abusing inmates, the age distributions of the two nondrug-abusing cohorts were virtually similar across time.

The shifting age distribution of drug-involved offenders is especially important given the declining age profile of violent offenses in this population. The probability that offenders will satisfy criteria that disqualify them from diversion programs increases with age, even as the probability of violent offending declines.

The implications of these age patterns are shown below in figure 3.10. Roughly one in four entering inmates below the age of twenty-five were sentenced for a violent offense, a percentage that steadily declined with age. Yet older offenders were markedly more likely to be labeled habitual offenders or to face sentencing enhancements that would exclude them from typical drug diversion programs.[9]

9. Current violent offense measures any current conviction offense, not just a controlling violent offense. Habitual offender enhancement is defined as receiving a sentence enhancement for a second- or third-strike offense.

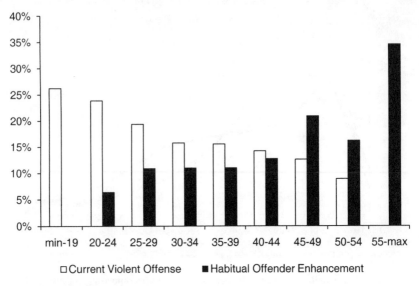

Fig. 3.10   Violent and habitual offending by age group, newly incarcerated drug-abusing inmates, 2002/4

Drug Court Calculations

In addition to examining age distributions, we examined the proportion of incoming prisoners with problematic drug use who would be eligible for drug court diversion.

We classified inmates—first with the entering cohort and then with the entire incarcerated population—by characteristics that affect eligibility for drug courts. In table 3.6, those characteristics that frequently disqualify the individual for drug court are italicized; those that make individuals likely candidates are in plain text.

As shown in table 3.6, virtually all newly incarcerated inmates are likely to be deemed ineligible for drug court intervention. Results are even sharper within the entire (not just the newly incarcerated) population of drug-involved state prison inmates, as shown in table 3.7. Authors' calculations indicate that more than 85 percent have current or past sentences for a serious felony or a gun violation. Nonincident inmates are twice as likely as incident inmates to be serving current sentences for violent offenses.

This pattern illustrates a point that arises in many contexts from unemployment to welfare reform. The stock population of incarcerated offenders are a "length-biased" sample. Compared with new entrants to prison in a given year, incarcerated offenders are more likely to be long-term offenders in the midst of long incarceration spells, and are more likely to satisfy other criteria of serious offending. As in the case of welfare cash assistance (Ellwood 1989), new entrants to prison/temporary assistance for needy

Table 3.6   **Drug court screening and exclusion criteria** *among newly incarcerated* *convicted inmates* **by reported abuse of heroin, cocaine, or methamphetamine, 2002 jail and 2004 prison surveys**

	Reported daily or near-daily use in month prior to arrest			
	2002 entering jail cohort		2004 entering prison cohort	
Drug court criteria[a]	Yes (%)	No (%)	Yes (%)	No (%)
Screening/eligibility criteria				
Current drug conviction	48.2	26.5	46.6	29.8
Drug-related revocation[b]	13.8	7.9	16.3	7.0
Positive drug test after arrest[c]	16.4	6.6	18.2	7.9
Screened for drug abuse[d]	92.0	43.8	92.2	42.6
Screened for drug dependence[e]	85.9	24.5	83.7	24.4
Met any screening/eligibility criteria	97.1	58.5	97.7	60.4
Exclusion criteria				
Current trafficking conviction	*17.9*	*9.6*	*22.4*	*14.8*
Current violent conviction	*17.2*	*28.1*	*17.2*	*30.7*
Current weapon involvement[f]	*7.7*	*7.5*	*10.5*	*11.3*
Habitual offender enhancement[g]	*5.4*	*6.3*	*16.2*	*13.2*
Prior incarceration sentence	*77.2*	*60.6*	*62.5*	*46.3*
Prior violent conviction	*27.8*	*27.6*	*27.4*	*23.8*
Criminal justice status at arrest[h]	*77.5*	*67.7*	*59.0*	*48.2*
Current or prior violent conviction	*32.6*	*39.1*	*36.6*	*45.1*
Met any exclusion criteria	*96.2*	*91.3*	*93.0*	*88.4*
Mean age in years	32.9	31.7	34.0	32.1
N	87,174	328,180	104,005	291,860

[a]Percentage calculations are based on nonmissing data, the amount of which varies by indicator.

[b]Revoked or facing revocation for a positive drug test, possessing drugs, or missing a drug test.

[c]Received positive drug test at booking or shortly after admission to prison or jail.

[d]Met the survey's criteria based on the Diagnostic and Statistical Manual of Mental Disorders (DSM-IV) for drug abuse in past year prior to arrest.

[e]Met the survey's criteria based on DSM-IV for drug dependence in past year prior to arrest.

[f]Revocation for possessing gun, receiving firearm sentence enhancement, having any current weapon conviction, or having gun seized by police at arrest.

[g]Habitual offender enhancement is defined as receiving a sentence enhancement for a second- or third-strike offense.

[h]On probation, parole, or escape.

families (TANF) are a distinct population from those who are long-term prisoners/welfare recipients. Thus, programs that significantly affect the *flow* of new prison entrants may have a much more modest impact on the *stock* of incarcerated prisoners. We return to this point in the Conclusions section.

The patterns in table 3.7 illustrate the central challenge in reducing the

Table 3.7   Drug court screening and exclusion criteria *among all convicted inmates* by reported abuse of heroin, cocaine, or methamphetamine, 2002 jail and 2004 prison surveys

| | Reported daily or near-daily use in month prior to arrest | | | |
| | 2002 jail inmates | | 2004 prison inmates | |
Drug court criteria[a]	Yes (%)	No (%)	Yes (%)	No (%)
Screening/eligibility criteria				
Current drug conviction	47.3	27.1	37.0	20.2
Drug-related revocation[b]	13.6	7.6	11.2	4.6
Positive drug test after arrest[c]	16.4	6.9	22.9	10.8
Screened for drug abuse[d]	92.5	43.6	91.2	40.2
Screened for drug dependence[e]	85.9	24.5	83.1	22.1
Met any screening/eligibility criteria	97.3	58.8	97.0	54.6
Exclusion criteria				
Current trafficking conviction	*18.0*	*10.4*	*19.5*	*11.1*
Current violent conviction	*18.7*	*29.2*	*34.5*	*55.0*
Current weapon involvement[f]	*7.6*	*7.5*	*16.5*	*17.7*
Habitual offender enhancement[g]	*5.7*	*6.7*	*24.8*	*17.4*
Prior incarceration sentence	*77.0*	*60.2*	*65.4*	*46.8*
Prior violent conviction	*28.3*	*27.8*	*31.4*	*25.7*
Criminal justice status at arrest[h]	*75.7*	*66.4*	*50.9*	*40.8*
Current or prior violent conviction	*33.5*	*40.1*	*51.8*	*64.7*
Met any exclusion criteria	*96.1*	*91.3*	*95.2*	*93.1*
Mean age in years	33.0	31.8	35.7	35.2
N	94,017	354,219	278,374	947,797

[a]Percentage calculations are based on nonmissing data, the amount of which varies by indicator.
[b]Revoked or facing revocation for a positive drug test, possessing drugs, or missing a drug test.
[c]Received positive drug test at booking or shortly after admission to prison or jail.
[d]Met the survey's criteria based on DSM-IV for drug abuse in past year prior to arrest.
[e]Met the survey's criteria based on DSM-IV for drug dependence in past year prior to arrest.
[f]Revocation for possessing gun, receiving firearm sentence enhancement, having any current weapon conviction, or having gun seized by police at arrest.
[g]Habitual offender enhancement is defined as receiving a sentence enhancement for a second- or third-strike offense.
[h]On probation, parole, or escape.

prison population through drug courts and other diversion programs. Problematic drug use was common among state prison inmates. The 2004 prison sample included almost 300,000 convicted prison inmates who had used cocaine, heroin, or amphetamine in the month prior to their admission to prison. More than 90 percent of these drug-involved inmates satisfied screening criteria for abuse or dependence. For the 2002 jail inmates, about 94,000 (of the 448,000 convicted inmates) used heroin, cocaine, or methamphetamine in the month prior to their admission. Similarly, more than 90 percent met criteria for substance abuse or dependence in the year prior to arrest. Thus, a rough estimate is that in 2004 (projecting no change in the jail figure between 2002 and 2004) the number of drug dependent individuals entering jail and prison as convicted offenders was approximately 400,000.

To put these numbers into perspective, we compared our descriptive statistics with the 2005 Treatment Episode Data System (TEDS), an administrative data set that captures at least 80 percent of all known treatment admissions in the United States in 2004. The TEDS data yield 680,775 treatment admissions for which cocaine, amphetamine, or heroin was the primary substance of misuse. The incarcerated drug-dependent populations in prisons and jails rival the substance abuse treatment system in the size of the drug-using population receiving services on any given day.

Yet only a small minority of inmates are likely to be eligible for drug courts or similar interventions. Among newly incarcerated inmates, approximately one-fifth were under a current sentence for minor (that is, nontrafficking) drug offenses—the archetypal offense promoted as suitable for drug court intervention. An even smaller fraction were incarcerated for such crimes and had no current or prior record for disqualifying offenses. Minor drug offenders account for an even smaller fraction of the overall state prison population.

If one broadens the universe from minor drug crimes to include other offenses, diversion programs would have a slightly larger population to draw from. Approximately one-fifth of inmates reported no history or current sentences for serious felonies.[10]

Perhaps our most surprising descriptive findings concerned inmates in local jails. Based on our 2002 data, a very small fraction of sentenced jail inmates would be eligible for drug courts based on the eligibility criteria cited previously.

Prior criminal history factors exclude the largest share of offenders with current drug problems from drug court eligibility. More than 70 percent of heroin, cocaine, and methamphetamine users would be drug court ineligible on the basis of being under criminal justice supervision at the time of arrest or of being a habitual offender. Virtually none of these inmates would be eligible for drug courts that applied every common exclusionary criterion. Setting aside important considerations of program capacity, this suggests that relaxing eligibility criteria, especially for offenders with active or long criminal histories, would expand the pool of criminal offenders eligible for drug court and related interventions.

---

10. Homicide, manslaughter, kidnapping, armed robbery, unarmed robbery, burglary, aggravated assault, assault on a police officer, arson, blackmail, extortion, sex crimes, drug trafficking, other violent crimes.

3.5   Conclusion

We began this chapter by noting that diverting drug-involved offenders from the criminal justice system, in particular getting them into treatment rather than jail or prison, has long been a major concern of the criminal justice system. The drug court movement has been a prominent and important innovation, almost universally praised by policymakers at every level of the criminal justice system. Other innovations, such as Proposition 36 in California and intensive supervision probation in various jurisdictions have pursued the same goal.

Notwithstanding that, we have documented that the numbers of drug-involved individuals in the US state prison and local jail systems have risen substantially in the last twenty years, both in absolute numbers and as a percentage of the total. When we confine comparisons to those entering the prison system or jails de novo (our incident cohort) during the 1980s and after the year 2000, we see evidence that the entering drug-involved inmates are aging for the three drugs (cocaine, heroin, and methamphetamine) in contrast to a much slighter increase in the age of those not involved with drugs.

Prior studies, in particular Bhati, Roman, and Chalfin (2008), have shown that drug courts have made little difference to the criminal justice system because they handle such small numbers of criminal defendants. Our chapter adds to these findings with the observation that drug courts, as currently structured, have little potential to make a difference to incarceration totals because so few of those entering jail or prison would meet the eligibility requirements of the current courts.

This importantly reflects the observed aging of the populations involved with the three drugs we examined. A large share of drug-involved offenders entering correctional facilities have accumulated long criminal careers that make them unattractive clients for the drug court movement. It is especially discouraging that this statement applies to inmates in local jails, as well as state prisons.

Ironically, the aging of the drug-using offenders has another consequence. They are now much less likely to be convicted of a new violent offense, the principal public concern about criminal offenders under community supervision. There has been growing interest in the time to "redemption" for those with a criminal history, that is, the number of years after an arrest or conviction at which an individual is no longer much more likely to commit a new offense than someone who has never been arrested/convicted (Blumstein and Nakamura 2009). A more careful analysis of the criminal careers of long-term drug users may allow the selection of some candidates for diversion programs with acceptable risks of committing a serious crime while under the supervision of a drug court or intensive probation.

Our results suggest other potential insights for policy. Reducing prison populations by diverting drug-involved offenders before incarceration seems more difficult than one might suspect. If diversion is unexpectedly difficult at the front end, other strategies may prove more effective. Greater attention and focus on the drug problems of recently released offenders, parolees, and probationers seems especially fruitful.

The results of Proposition 36 are intriguing. Though it is a well-known innovation, we are unaware of any study that has examined its potential to reduce prison and jail populations if taken up nationally.

Mandated desistence programs such as the Hawaii HOPE program yield impressive early results. These seem especially promising for individuals who abuse alcohol or illicit substances, but who may not be dependent or who use substances for which available substance abuse treatment appears relatively ineffective.

For opiate-dependent offenders, strengthening the immediate linkages into postrelease opioid maintenance treatment also appears promising. Similar linkages of drug-involved offenders into long-term residential treatment and therapeutic communities also appear to be associated with reduced rates of subsequent reoffending.

Finally, more effective treatment interventions for young drug users who are not under criminal justice supervision appears especially promising. Young men receiving substance abuse treatment services display strikingly higher rates of criminal offending, particularly violent offending, than do others involved in the treatment system. Some of these young men present to the treatment system under implicit or explicit pressure from the criminal justice system. Others seek services for other reasons.

Although young adults are often more difficult treatment clients and may display poor outcomes by traditional clinical criteria, focusing resources on this key population is likely to yield high dividends for crime control and prevention policy.

References

Amato, Laura, Marina Davoli, Carlo A. Perucci, Marica Ferri, Fabrizio Faggiano, and Richard P. Mattick. 2005. "An Overview of Systematic Reviews of the Effectiveness of Opiate Maintenance Therapies: Available Evidence to Inform Clinical Practice and Research." *Journal of Substance Abuse Treatment* 28 (4): 321–9.

Bao, Yan-ping, Zhi-min Liu, David Epstein, Cun Du, Jie Shi, and Lin Lu. 2009. "A Meta-Analysis of Retention in Methadone Maintenance by Dose and Dosing Strategy." *American Journal of Drug and Alcohol Abuse* 35 (1): 28–33.

Basu, Anirban, A. David Paltiel, and Harold A. Pollack. 2008. "Social Costs of Robbery and the Cost-effectiveness of Substance Abuse Treatment." *Health Economics* 17 (8): 927–46.

Belenko, Steven, and Jordon Peugh. 2005. "Estimating Drug Treatment Needs among State Prison Inmates." *Drug and Alcohol Dependence* 77 (3): 269–81.

Belenko, Steven, Jordan Peugh, Daniel Mendez, Courtney Petersen, Jeffrey Lin, and Jennie Hauser. 2002. *Trends in Substance Abuse and Treatment Needs Among Inmates.* National Criminal Justice Reference Service. New York: National Center on Addiction and Substance Abuse at Columbia University.

Bhati, Avinash Singh, John K. Roman, and Aaron Chalfin. 2008. *To Treat or Not to Treat: Evidence on the Prospects of Expanding Treatment to Drug-Involved Offenders.* Washington, DC: Urban Institute.

Blumstein, Alfred, and Allen J. Beck. 1999. "Population Growth in U.S. Prisons, 1980–1996." In *Prisons (Crime and Justice: A Review of the Research, vol. 26),* edited by Michael Tonry and Joan Petersilia, 17–61. Chicago: University of Chicago Press.

Blumstein, Alfred, and Kiminori Nakamura. 2009. "Redemption in the Presence of Widespread Criminal Background Checks." *Criminology* 47 (2): 327–59.

Boyum, David, and Peter Reuter. 2005. *An Analytic Assessment of U.S. Drug Policy.* Washington, DC: AEI Press.

Burdon, William M., Nena P. Messina, and Michael L. Prendergast. 2004. "The California Treatment Expansion Initiative: Aftercare Participation, Recidivism, and Predictors of Outcomes." *Prison Journal* 84 (1): 61–80.

Bureau of Justice Assistance (BJA) Drug Court Clearinghouse Project. 2009. *Summary of Drug Court Activity by State and County, July 14, 2009.* Washington, DC: BJA Drug Court Clearinghouse Project at American University.

Campbell, Kevin M., Dennis Deck, and Antoinette Krupski. 2007. "Impact of Substance Abuse Treatment on Arrests among Opiate Users in Washington State." *American Journal on Addictions* 16 (6): 510–20.

Caulkins, Jonathan P. 2007. "The Need for Dynamic Drug Policy." *Addiction* 102 (1): 4–7.

Caulkins, Jonathan P., Doris A. Behrens, Claudia Knoll, Gernot Tragler, and Doris Zuba. 2004. "Markov Chain Modeling of Initiation and Demand: The Case of the U.S. Cocaine Epidemic." *Health Care Management Science* 7 (4): 319–29.

Caulkins, Jonathan P., and Sara Chandler. 2006. "Long-Run Trends in Incarceration of Drug Offenders in the United States." *Crime and Delinquency* 52 (4): 619–41.

Cohen, Mark A., Roland T. Rust, Sara Steen, and Simon T. Tidd. 2004. "Willingness-to-Pay for Crime Control Programs." *Criminology* 42 (1): 89–110.

Cork, Daniel. 1999. "Examining Space-time Interaction in City-level Homicide Data: Crack Markets and the Diffusion of Guns among Youth." *Journal of Quantitative Criminology* 15 (4): 379–406.

Cox, Gary, Linda Brown, Charles Morgan, and Michelle Hansten. 2001. *NW HIDTA/DASA Washington State Drug Court Evaluation Project: Final Report.* July 13. Seattle: Alcohol and Drug Abuse Institute, University of Washington.

D'Aunno, Thomas, and Harold A. Pollack. 2002. "Changes in Methadone Treatment Practices: Results from a National Panel Study, 1988–2000." *Journal of the American Medical Association* 288 (7): 850–6.

Dismuke, Clara E., Michael T. French, Helena J. Salomé, Mark A. Foss, Chris K. Scott, and Michael L. Dennis. 2004. "Out of Touch or On the Money: Do the Clinical Objectives of Addiction Treatment Coincide with Economic Evaluation Results?" *Journal of Substance Abuse Treatment* 27 (3): 253–63.

Dolan, Kate A., James Shearer, Bethany White, Jialun Zhou, John Kaldor, and Alex D. Wodak. 2005. "Four-Year Follow-Up of Imprisoned Male Heroin Users and Methadone Treatment: Mortality, Re-incarceration and Hepatitis C Infection." *Addiction* 100 (6): 820–8.

Ehlers, Scott, and Jason Ziedenberg. 2006. *Proposition 36: Five Years Later.* Washington, DC: Justice Policy Institute.

Ellwood, David T. 1989. *Poor Support: Poverty in the American Family.* New York: Basic Books.

Ettner, Susan L., David Huang, Elizabeth Evans, Danielle Rose Ash, Mary Hardy, Mickel Jourabchi, and Yih-Ing Hser. 2006. "Benefit-Cost in the California Treatment Outcome Project: Does Substance Abuse Treatment 'Pay for Itself'?" *Health Services Research* 41 (1): 192–213.

Everingham, Susan S., and C. Peter Rydell. 1994. *Modeling the Demand for Cocaine.* Santa Monica, CA: RAND Corporation.

Farabee, David, and Eric Fredlund. 1996. "Self-reported Drug Use among Recently Admitted Jail Inmates: Estimating Prevalence and Treatment Needs." *Substance Use & Misuse* 31 (4): 423–35.

Florida Supreme Court Task Force on Treatment-Based Drug Courts. 2004. *Florida's Adult Drug Court: Recommended Practice.* Tallahassee, FL: Florida Supreme Court Task Force. http://www.flcourts.org/gen_public/family/bin/dcreport.pdf.

Flynn, Patrick M., Patricia L. Kristiansen, James V. Porto, and Robert L. Hubbard. 1999. "Costs and Benefits of Treatment for Cocaine Addiction in DATOS." *Drug and Alcohol Dependence* 57 (2): 167–74.

French, Michael T., Helena J. Salomé, Jody L. Sindelar, and A. Thomas McLellan. 2002. "Benefit-cost Analysis of Addiction Treatment: Methodological Guidelines and Empirical Application using the DATCAP and ASI." *Health Services Research* 37 (2): 433–55.

Godfrey, Christine, Duncan Stewart, and Michael Gossop. 2004. "Economic Analysis of Costs and Consequences of the Treatment of Drug Misuse: 2-year Outcome Data from the National Treatment Outcome Research Study (NTORS)." *Addiction* 99 (6). 697–707.

Gordon, Michael S., Timothy W. Kinlock, Robert P. Schwartz, and Kevin E. O'Grady. 2008. "A Randomized Clinical Trial of Methadone Maintenance for Prisoners: Findings at 6 Months Post-release." *Addiction* 103 (8): 1333–42.

Gossop, Michael, John Marsden, Duncan Stewart, and Tara Kidd. 2003. "The National Treatment Outcome Research Study (NTORS): 4–5 Year Follow-up Results." *Addiction* 98 (3): 291–303.

Gossop, Michael, Katia Trakada, Duncan Stewart, and John Witton. 2005. "Reductions in Criminal Convictions after Addiction Treatment: 5-year Follow-up." *Drug and Alcohol Dependence* 79 (3): 295–302.

Grella, Christine E., Lisa Greenwell, Michael Prendergast, David Farabee, Elizabeth Hall, Jerome Cartier, and William Burdon. 2007. "Organizational Characteristics of Drug Abuse Treatment Programs for Offenders." *Journal of Substance Abuse Treatment* 32 (3): 291–300.

Harrell, Adele, Shannon Cavanagh, and John Roman. 1998. *Findings from the Evaluation of the D.C. Superior Court Drug Intervention Program.* Final Report. Washington, DC: Urban Institute.

Hawken, A. 2009. "Managing Drug-involved Offenders: Comparing Diversion Programs and Hawaii's HOPE Probation." June 15. Washington DC: Office of National Drug Control Policy.

Hawken, Angela, and Mark Kleiman. 2009. "Managing Drug Involved Probationers with Swift and Certain Sanctions: Evaluating Hawaii's HOPE." Washington, DC: National Institute of Justice.

Horney, Julie, and Ineke Haen Marshall. 1992. "An Experimental Comparison of Two Self-Report Methods for Measuring Lambda." *Journal of Research in Crime and Delinquency* 29 (1): 102–21.

Hser, Yih-Ing. 2007. "Predicting Long-term Stable Recovery from Heroin Addiction: Findings from a 33-year Follow-up Study." *Journal of Addictive Diseases* 26 (1): 51–60.

Hser, Yih-Ing, Valerie Hoffman, Christine E. Grella, and M. Douglas Anglin. 2001. "A 33-year Follow-up of Narcotics Addicts." *Archives of General Psychiatry* 58 (5): 503–8.

Hser, Yih-Ing, David Huang, Chih-Ping Chou, and M. Douglas Anglin. 2007. "Trajectories of Heroin Addiction: Growth Mixture Modeling Results Based on a 33-year Follow-up Study." *Evaluation Review* 31 (6): 548–63.

Hubbard, Robert L., S. Gail Craddock, Patrick M. Flynn, Jill Anderson, and Rose M. Etheridge. 1997. "Overview of 1-year Follow-up Outcomes in the Drug Abuse Treatment Outcome Study (DATOS)." *Psychology of Addictive Behaviors* 11 (4): 261–78.

Hunt, L. G., and C. D. Chambers. 1976. *The Heroin Epidemic: A Study of Heroin Use in the U.S., 1965–1975 (Part II).* New York: Spectrum.

Kinlock, Timothy W., Michael S. Gordon, Robert P. Schwartz, Terrence T. Fitzgerald, and Kevin E. O'Grady. 2009. "A Randomized Clinical Trial of Methadone Maintenance for Prisoners: Results at 12 months Postrelease." *Journal of Substance Abuse Treatment* 37 (3): 277–85.

Kinlock, Timothy W., Michael S. Gordon, Robert P. Schwartz, and Kevin O'Grady. 2008. "A Study of Methadone Maintenance for Male Prisoners: 3-month Postrelease Outcomes." *Criminal Justice and Behavior* 35 (1): 34–47.

Kinlock, Timothy W., Michael S. Gordon, Robert P. Schwartz, Kevin O'Grady, Terrence T. Fitzgerald, and Monique Wilson. 2007. "A Randomized Clinical Trial of Methadone Maintenance for Prisoners: Results at 1-month Post-release." *Drug and Alcohol Dependence* 91 (2–3): 220–7.

Kleiman, Mark A. R. 1997. "Coerced Abstinence: A Neopaternalistic Drug Policy Initiative." In *The New Paternalism: Supervisory Approaches to Poverty,* edited by Lawrence M. Mead, 182–218. Washington, DC: Brookings Institution Press.

———. 2009. *When Brute Force Fails: How to Have Less Crime and Less Punishment.* Princeton, NJ: Princeton University Press.

Kleiman, Mark A. R., and Angela Hawken. 2008. "Fixing the Parole System." *Issues in Science and Technology* 24 (4): 45–52.

Koenig, Lane, Jonathan M. Siegel, Henrick Harwood, Jawaria Gilani, Ying-Jun Chen, Peter Leahy, and Richard Stephens. 2005. "Economic Benefits of Substance Abuse Treatment: Findings from Cuyahoga County, Ohio." *Journal of Substance Abuse Treatment* 28 (2) supp. 1: S41–S50.

Kozel, N. J., and E. H. Adams. 1986. "Epidemiology of Drug Abuse: An Overview." *Science* 234 (4779): 970–4.

MacCoun, Robert, Beau Kilmer, and Peter Reuter. 2003. "Research on Drugs-Crime Linkages: The Next Generation." In *Toward a Drugs and Crime Research Agenda for the 21st Century,* edited by Henry H. Brownstein and Christine Crossland, 65–95. Washington, DC: National Institute of Justice.

Manski, Charles F., John V. Pepper, and Carol V. Petrie, eds. 2001. *Informing America's Policy on Illegal Drugs: What We Don't Know Keeps Hurting Us.* Washington, DC: National Academy Press.

McCollister, Kathryn E., and Michael T. French. 2003. "The Relative Contribution of Outcome Domains in the Total Economic Benefit of Addiction Interventions: A Review of First Findings." *Addiction* 98 (12): 1647–59.

McCollister, Kathryn E., Michael T. French, Michael L. Prendergast, Elizabeth Hall, and Stan Sacks. 2004. "Long-term Cost Effectiveness of Addiction Treatment for Criminal Offenders." *Justice Quarterly* 21 (3): 659–79.

McMillan, G. P., Sandra Lapham, and Michael Lackey. 2008. "The Effect of a Jail Methadone Maintenance Therapy (MMT) Program on Inmate Recidivism." *Addiction* 103 (12): 2017–2023.

Mumola, Christopher J., and Jennifer C. Karberg. 2006. "Drug Use and Dependence: State and Federal Prisoners, 2004." Special Report, NCJ 213530. Washington, DC: Bureau of Justice Statistics.

Office of National Drug Control Policy. 2000. "What America's Users Spend on Illicit Drugs 1988–1998." Washington, DC: White House Office of National Drug Control Policy.

———. 2001. "What America's Users Spend on Illicit Drugs 1988–2000." Washington, DC: White House Office of National Drug Control Policy.

———. 2009. *ADAM II: 2008 Annual Report.* Washington, DC: White House Office of National Drug Control Policy.

Porter, Rachel. 2001. *Treatment Alternatives in the Criminal Court: A Process Evaluation of the Bronx County Drug Court.* New York: Vera Institute of Justice.

Prendergast, Michael L., and William M. Burdon. 2002. "Integrated Systems of Care for Substance-Abusing Offenders." In *Treatment of Drug Offenders: Policies and Issues,* edited by Carl G. Leukefeld, Frank Tims, and David Farabee, 111–26. New York: Springer.

Prendergast, Michael L., Elizabeth A. Hall, Harry K. Wexler, Gerald Melnick, and Yan Cao. 2004. "Amity Prison-based Therapeutic Community: 5-year Outcomes." *Prison Journal* 84 (1): 36–60.

Prendergast, Michael L., Deborah Podus, Eunice Chang, and Darren Urada. 2002. "The Effectiveness of Drug Abuse Treatment: A Meta-analysis of Comparison Group Studies." *Drug and Alcohol Dependence* 67 (1): 53–72.

Rajkumar, Andrew S., and Michael T. French. 1997. "Drug Abuse, Crime Costs, and the Economic Benefits of Treatment." *Journal of Quantitative Criminology* 13 (3): 291–322.

Reuter, Peter, and Alex Stevens. 2007. *An Analysis of UK Drug Policy A Monograph Prepared for the UK Drug Policy Commission.* London: UK Drug Policy Commission.

Rocheleau, Ann Marie, and David Boyum. 1994. *Heroin Users in New York, Chicago, and San Diego.* Washington, DC: White House Office of National Drug Control Policy.

Rossman, S. B., J. Zweig, and J. Roman. 2008. *A Portrait of Adult Drug Courts.* Washington, DC: Urban Institute.

Sevigny, Eric L., and Jonathan P. Caulkins. 2004. "Kingpins or Mules: An Analysis of Drug Offenders Incarcerated in Federal and State Prisons." *Criminology and Public Policy* 3 (3): 401–34.

Sindelar, Jody L., Mireia Jofre-Bonet, Michael T. French, and A. Thomas McLellan. 2004. "Cost-effectiveness Analysis of Addiction Treatment: Paradoxes of Multiple Outcomes." *Drug and Alcohol Dependence* 73 (1): 41–50.

Taxman, Faye S., Matthew L. Perdoni, and Lana D. Harrison. 2007. "Drug Treatment Services for Adult Offenders: The State of the State." *Journal of Substance Abuse Treatment* 32 (3): 239–54.

UCLA Integrated Substance Abuse Programs. 2007. *Evaluation of the Substance Abuse and Crime Prevention Act: Final Report.* Los Angeles: UCLA Integrated Substance Abuse Programs.

Urada, Darren, Angela Hawken, Bradley T. Conner, Elizabeth Evans, M. Douglas Anglin, Joy Yang, Cheryl Teruya, et al. 2008. *Evaluation of Proposition 36: The Substance Abuse and Crime Prevention Act of 2000, 2008 Report.* Los Angeles: Department of Alcohol and Drug Programs California Health and Human Services Agency.

Wilson, David B., Ojmarrh Mitchell, and Doris L. MacKenzie. 2006. "A Systematic Review of Drug Court Effects on Recidivism." *Journal of Experimental Criminology* 2 (4): 459–87.

Wish, Eric D., and Bernard A. Gropper. 1991. "Drug Testing by the Criminal Justice System." In *Crime and Justice: Drugs and Crime, vol. 13,* edited by Michael J. Tonry and James Q. Wilson, 109–58. Chicago: University of Chicago Press.

Comment: Can We Treat Our Way Out of Incarcerating Drug-Involved Offenders?   Jonathan P. Caulkins

Introduction

A conventional wisdom in the drug policy literature is that "treatment works" (e.g., Bhati, Roman, and Chalfin 2008). This leads Pollack, Reuter, and Sevigny to ask, "If treatment works so well, why are so many drug users in prison?"

Their answer addresses most directly drug courts and other diversion programs that target people who have relatively short criminal records (e.g., nonviolent first time offenders). They observe that drug problems evolve over an epidemic cycle, and the United States is now in the mature or endemic stage. There are some new initiates each year, but today, unlike a generation ago, most criminally involved drug offenders have been offending for more than a decade and so have accumulated records that disqualify them from the typical diversion program. This is ironic inasmuch as violence has a sharper age-crime peak than does property offending, so releasing these older offenders under community supervision may be less risky now than in the past.

Figure 3C.1 captures the basic insight. Classic diversion programs affect the flow of first-time offenders into the traditional system for controlling and punishing offenders (prison, probation, and parole), but today the biggest flow of drug-involved offenders into prison comes from people who already had a prior felony conviction. They come mostly from the pool of people on probation or parole (the notorious "revolving door"); others are ex-offenders who had already completed their terms of probation or parole (not shown in the figure because it is a smaller flow).

Cutting the inflow of new people will empty the system eventually, but not quickly. Even in the United States, prison time served (as opposed to sentenced) per offense is usually less than five years, so one might think cutting the inflow would quickly reduce prison populations. However, even though a particular spell of imprisonment may not be terribly long, the typical "career criminal" strings together a long series of such stays. So emptying the system is more like waiting for the current generation of drug-involved offenders to die or age out of drug use than merely waiting for their current sentences to expire.

Jonathan P. Caulkins is the Stever Professor of Operations Research and Public Policy at the Heinz College and the Doha, Qatar, campus of Carnegie Mellon University.

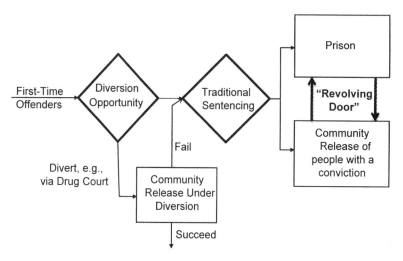

Fig. 3C.1   **Traditional diversion programs address the "front-end flow" but in endemic stage of a drug problem the "revolving door" of repeat offenders generates the larger flow into prison**

Indeed, more formal analysis of "stocks and flows" or differential equation models that embody the architecture of figure 3C.1 shows that changing recidivism rates can be a more powerful way to reduce prison populations than are comparable reductions in the original inflow (Weatherburn et al. 2009). Unfortunately, intervening with first-time offenders is often perceived to be easier both politically and practically.

One interpretation of Pollack, Reuter, and Sevigny's message to policymakers is, "Drug courts are all well and good, perhaps with some tweaking to admission criteria, but do not think they obviate the need for interventions that target the revolving door." This gets back to the question in their title: "If drug treatment works so well . . ." why can we not just use treatment to deal with these recidivists? The answer, in a nutshell, is that treatment can look wonderful in terms of social cost averted per million taxpayer dollars while simultaneously looking awful in terms of recidivism rates (Caulkins and Kleiman, forthcoming).

Most people admitted to treatment relapse. Indeed, many of those diverted into treatment by programs like California's Proposition 36 never even show up for treatment (Urada et al. 2008). One response to this is that people who have been cycling in and out of the criminal justice system need a lot more than basic drug treatment; for example, they may benefit from job training and placement (Raphael, chapter 11, this volume). Another is that even if evidence concerning long prison sentences' ability to deter efficiently is underwhelming (Durlauf and Nagin, chapter 1, this volume), sticks may still usefully complement or even supplant the carrot of treatment for drug-involved offenders if frequent drug tests are combined with immediate, brief (flash) incarceration. This coerced or mandated abstinence model has been advocated by Kleiman (2001, 2009), among others.

Evidence of the Epidemic Cycle

Pollack, Reuter, and Sevigny's analysis leverages the idea that waves of drug initiation create a bolus of dependent users who then gradually age. Even though initiation does not subsequently drop to zero, the average age of problem drug users still increases for a decade or two after the drug burst onto the scene. Aging has implications for how policy ought to evolve, including eligibility requirements for prison diversion programs. Inasmuch as Pollack, Reuter, and Sevigny's conclusions flow from this premise, it is worth looking further into the premise. Two simple pictures are instructive.

The first question is whether there is any consistent pattern to how a drug spreads. Immersing oneself in details uncovers myriad ways in which each drug and associated epidemic is different. Different drugs affect different neuroreceptors (e.g., dopamine vs. serotonin), appeal to different groups (meth is rarely used by African Americans; crack dependence is more common), and so on.

However, stepping back, initiating use of a drug is just an example of "new product adoption," and there are standard models governing how new products such as HDTV and i-Phones diffuse through a population (Bass 1969). The typical result is an S-shaped initial adoption profile driven by viral or word-of-mouth spread. Some people adopt in response to general availability (so-called "innovators"), but most ("imitators") do so through contact with another person who has already adopted the product. Is there evidence that such diffusion models apply to illegal drug adoption?

The short answer is yes. Figure 3C.2 updates Caulkins' (2008) plot of numbers of first time users of a drug in the United States (i.e., initiation) for ten diverse illegal drugs based on self-reports to the 1999 to 2008 National Surveys on Drug Use and Health (a total of 555,070 respondents).[1] The initiation series by drug and year are adjusted in two ways to highlight the commonality: (a) height is normalized since some drugs (e.g., marijuana) are more popular than others (e.g., heroin), and (b) curves are shifted left or right to line up the initial growth phase because some drugs (e.g., marijuana and heroin) became available earlier than others (e.g., cocaine and crack). The key observation is that the adjusted initiation curves for ten quite different chemicals are strikingly similar throughout their initial spread, and are all followed by a subsequent trough. Subsequent patterns are more diverse, but the modal outcome seems to be more or less stable ongoing initiation at rates below the initial peak.

If initiation stabilized at a constant rate per year and remained—as is usual—concentrated among young people, then eventually the age distri-

---

1. Author's analysis using online data sets available at http://www.icpsr.umich.edu/SAMHDA/using-data/sda.html.

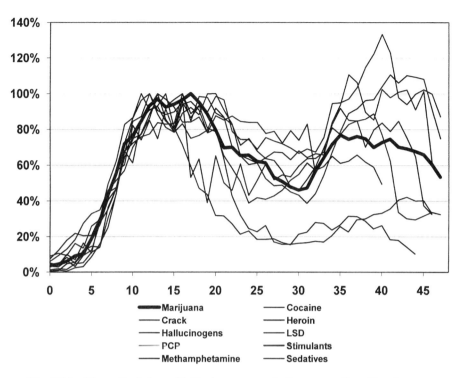

Fig. 3C.2   **Normalized plots of initiation are very similar across all ten illegal drugs, with marijuana in bold**

bution of dependent users would stabilize. However, that takes time, and we have not yet reached that stable pattern. Figures 3C.3 and 3C.4 show how the generational composition of treated cocaine and heroin users, respectively, evolved between 1992 to 2007, as reflected in data from the Treatment Episode Data Set (TEDS-A).[2] Subsequent generations do not always generate as much use; neither early nor late Gen-Xers ever generated as many treatment admissions as did Baby Boomers. And older generations persist in the data. Over the sixteen-year span covered by the graph, roughly two of these groups comprised of nine birth cohorts should have turned over if the system had already been in steady state; instead, the older generations hang on, being added to rather than replaced by the younger generations. So the average age grows over time, as Pollack, Reuter, and Sevigny document in detail.

Conclusion

In closing it is worth stepping back to note two implications Pollack, Reuter, and Sevigny's analysis has for the study of drug-related crime more

2. Ibid.

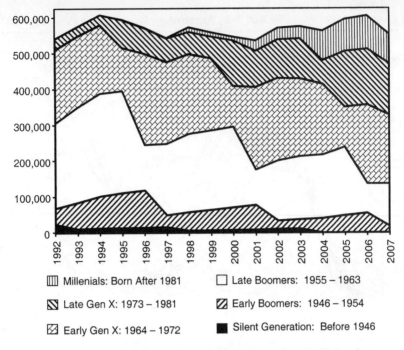

Fig. 3C.3   U.S. cocaine treatment client admissions over time, by birth cohort

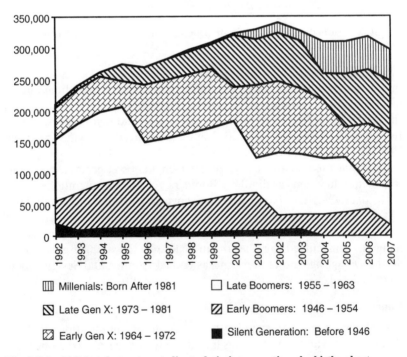

Fig. 3C.4   U.S. heroin treatment client admissions over time, by birth cohort

generally. First, it is important to break analyses down by drug, epidemic stage, and intensity of use. Trends for total prevalence of use of a drug that has recently become available can be entirely different than trends in dependent use of another drug that has been around for many years. That is not a new idea, but it bears repeating because dabblers doing analysis without deep domain expertise can go astray. Second, analysis needs to pay attention to age-period-cohort effects not just age or time or cohort. In the language of systems analysis, one needs distributed parameter or partial differential equation models that track the state as a vector—with components reflecting different intensities of use—that depends on both age and time, that is, $X(a,t)$, not only time, $X(t)$. An interesting question is the extent to which the substantial ebb and flow in juvenile offense rates implies that the same insight holds with respect to analysis of street crime more generally, as opposed to drug-related crime in particular.

References

Bass, Frank M. 1969. "A New Product Growth Model for Consumer Durables." *Management Science* 15 (5): 215–27.

Bhati, A., J. Roman, and A. Chalfin. 2008. *To Treat or Not to Treat: Evidence on the Effects of Expanding Treatment to Drug-Involved Offenders.* Washington, DC: The Urban Institute.

Caulkins, Jonathan P. 2008. "Implications of Inertia for Assessing Drug Control Policy: Why Upstream Interventions May not Receive Due Credit." *Contemporary Drug Problems* 35 (2–3): 347–69.

Caulkins, Jonathan P., and Mark A. R. Kleiman. Forthcoming. "Drugs and Crime." In *Oxford Handbook of Crime and Criminal Justice,* edited by Michael Tonry. New York: Oxford University Press.

Kleiman, M. A. R. 2001. "Controlling Drug Use and Crime with Testing, Sanctions, and Treatment." In *Drug Addiction and Drug Policy,* edited by P. B. Heymann and W. N. Brownsberger, 168–92. Cambridge, MA: Harvard University Press.

———. 2009. *When Brute Force Fails: How to Have Less Crime and Less Punishment.* Princeton, NJ: Princeton University Press.

Urada, Darren, Andrea Hawken, Bradley Conner, Elizabeth Evans, M. Douglas Anglin, Joy Yang, Cheryl Teruya, et al. 2008. *Evaluation of Proposition 36: The Substance Abuse and Crime Prevention Act of 2000.* Los Angeles, CA: University of California, Los Angeles.

Weatherburn, Don, Gary Froyland, Steve Moffatt, and Simon Corben. 2009. *Prison Populations and Correctional Outlays: The Effect of Reducing Re-imprisonment.* Crime and Justice Bulletin Number 138. Sydney: New South Wales Bureau of Crime and Justice Research.

4

Mental Health Treatment and Criminal Justice Outcomes

Richard G. Frank and Thomas G. McGuire

4.1 Introduction

Tragic data relate mental illness and crime. The Los Angeles County Jail, Cook County Jail, and Riker's Island in New York each house more persons with mental illness (about 1,400 in Los Angeles, alone) than any psychiatric institution in the country (Treatment Advocacy Center 2009). Two-thirds of the nation's juvenile inmates have at least one mental illness (Moore 2009). By Skeem, Manchak, and Peterson's (2009) calculations, on a typical day, over one million people with mental illnesses are in jail, in prison, on probation, or on parole. These figures raise natural questions: Are many prisoners in jail or prison *because* of their mental illness? And if so, is mental health treatment a cost-effective way to reduce crime and lower criminal justice costs? The main goal of this chapter is to review and evaluate the evidence assessing the potential of expansion of mental health services for reducing crime. We also undertake two empirical studies to augment the empirical research base relating mental illness to crime.

Richard G. Frank is the Margaret T. Morris Professor of Health Care Policy at the Harvard Medical School and a research associate of the National Bureau of Economic Research. Thomas G. McGuire is professor of health economics in the Department of Health Care Policy at the Harvard Medical School.

This chapter was prepared for presentation at the NBER conference on the Costs and Benefits of Crime Control and Prevention, January 15 and 16, Berkeley, California. The authors are grateful to the MacArthur Foundation for research support and to Pasha Hamed, Tisa Sherry, and Zach Yoneda for excellent research assistance. We are grateful to Harold Pollack and participants at an earlier NBER workshop for comments on an earlier draft, and to Phil Cook for encouragement and ideas. Ellen Meara, Jens Ludwig, John Monahan, Jennifer Skeem, and Hank Steadman commented on an earlier draft. We are particularly grateful to Jeff Swanson for helpful guidance. Colleagues from the MacArthur Foundation Mandated Community Treatment Network, chaired by John Monahan, did much of the research on the relation between mental health and crime.

A simple logic offers a starting point for analysis. If (a) mental illness causes crime, and (b) mental health treatment reduces mental illness, then (c) increasing mental health treatment can reduce mental illness and crime. National efforts based on this reasoning, some led by the Council of State Governments (2009), have been underway for some time, targeting expansion of access to community-based mental health care to the criminally involved.

A good deal of research evaluates premises (a) and (b). The social science literature bearing on the link of mental illness to crime (premise a) is the main focus of this chapter, whereas the clinical literature regarding the effectiveness of mental health treatment (premise b) is also relevant. As we will see later on, the connection between mental illness and crime is predominantly among persons with severe mental illness such as psychosis and major depression. These illnesses are serious and persistent in about 2 percent of the adult population. Development of and evaluation of the effects and costs of treatments for people with these conditions has long been a focus of public and private research. In the cases of both illnesses, effective treatments, largely drug treatments with appropriate monitoring and supportive psychosocial services, have been known for some time.[1] Major advances in the treatment of schizophrenia with psychoactive drugs date from the early 1950s and the marketing of chlorpromazine. Many other antipsychotics are now available, most with comparable effectiveness and side effect profiles (clozapine, introduced in 1989 in the United States, may be particularly helpful for patients who fail on other drugs). A large number of these drugs are now available as generics. The unresolved problems with treatment for schizophrenia is that while many drug treatments have some effectiveness, it is rare for full function to be restored, adjunctive treatments such as vocational rehabilitation and family counseling are expensive and themselves of modest effectiveness, and, unpleasant side effects of drugs lead many patients to discontinue therapy. Less than half of patients with schizophrenia are on a treatment likely to be effective.

Depression is an episodic illness for which there are also many effective drug treatments (which have a major effect on symptoms). Tricyclic antidepressants have been available since the early 1960s, and the selective serotonin uptake inhibitors (the first and most famous of which is Prozac) since 1988. Many effective drugs for depression are available as low-cost generics and are frequently prescribed by nonpsychiatrists. While overtreatment or inappropriate treatment is a concern for people with mild symptoms, a positive trend in the past several decades has been the large increases in share of people with serious depression who are taking medications likely

1. This discussion is based on material in Frank and Glied (2006). For a series of articles on the cost-effectiveness and policy implications of treatment for schizophrenia, see the May 2008 issue of *Psychiatric Services.*

to help them, with recent estimates of over 80 percent (Frank and Glied 2006, 116).

Two difficulties encountered by researchers in assessing the causal link between mental illness and crime are worth calling attention to at the outset. First, mental illness is correlated with many factors (e.g., criminal attitudes) that cause crime and may be difficult to measure. In community and survey data, indicators of mental illness might be picking up effects of other criminogenic factors correlated with mental illness (being raised in a family where there is violence). Related to this common problem of "unobservables" in social science research is a second issue. Mental illness may affect crime directly and indirectly, mediated by other factors, and this process may occur over an extended period of time. Mental illness may have a contemporaneous effect on crime, and in addition, mental illness in the past may have an indirect effect on current crime working through the role of mental illness in elevating other risk factors contributing to current crime (e.g., growing up in bad neighborhoods, substance abuse). These complications are depicted in figure 4.1. Past problems with mental illness, going back to childhood, are tied up with personal and social factors, and are a potential cause of current mental illness and other personal and social factors (some of which are unobserved) causing crime. The link to childhood raises similar issues and possibilities discussed by Heckman and Masterov (2004) related to workplace outcomes. The direct effect of current mental illness on crime (arrow [a]) is the limited sense in which it is usually meant by the question "does mental illness cause crime?" but the full effect of mental illness on crime goes beyond a contemporaneous causal relation.

To preview one conclusion from the literature: a small fraction (Skeem,

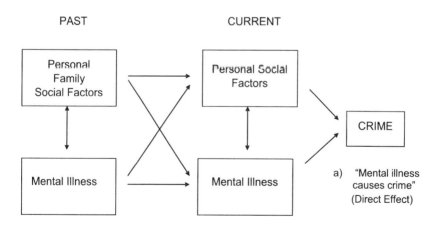

Fig. 4.1   **Past (indirect) and current (direct) effects of mental illness on crime**

Manchak, and Peterson 2009 judge it to be one in ten) of criminals with mental illness commit crimes because of their current illness, but the elevated risk is small. Current treatment can ameliorate current illness and symptoms, but cannot reverse the past effects of illness on the accumulation of other risk factors over a person's lifetime. In light of this, we pay attention in our review to the role of the past on current illness and on other social factors leading to crime. Although the research base is less developed, the effects of childhood mental illness and treatments for children are an important consideration for the intersection of mental health and criminal justice policy.

We also note that our syllogism is a sufficient, but not a necessary, condition for improved mental health treatment to reduce crime and criminal justice costs. Policies that link people at risk for committing crimes to community mental health treatment comprise more than simple mental health care interventions, and their route of cause might be by some mechanism other than improving mental health. Some treatments, like hospitalization or outpatient case management, may keep potential offenders out of trouble simply by keeping them off the streets and providing supervision. A "mental health court," to take another example discussed in more detail later, is a package of interventions that includes an active judge, frequent court monitoring, as well as mandated mental health care. In evaluating the role of mental health interventions in reducing crime, we will comment on whether the mechanism seems to be through improved mental health.

The chapter is organized as follows. In section 4.2 we review research on the association and causal relationship between mental illness and crime. If mental health treatment is to be cost-effective in terms of criminal justice outcomes, it helps to target high-risk populations. The next two sections study mental health treatment in two high-risk groups who are candidates for mental health interventions targeted to reduce crime: children with serious behavioral problems, and adult criminals. Section 4.3 is concerned with the effect of past illness and treatment on subsequent criminal justice contact in the case of children with conduct disorder. Section 4.4 is concerned with current mental health interventions targeted to criminals who are also mentally ill. A large range of programs are designed for this second population—mental health courts, specialty probation programs, forensic-oriented community treatments, among others. We focus on mental health courts. We also consider mandatory outpatient treatment, a widely applied policy with implications for criminal justice. We return, in section 4.5, to the question of the cost-effectiveness of expanding various forms of mental health treatment based on favorable effects on crime and criminal justice costs.

4.2   Mental Illness and Crime

The association between mental illness and crime, with a special focus on whether mental illness causes crime, has attracted a great deal of interest among social scientists. The literature features some excellent analytic reviews.[2] We begin with a review of the association between mental illness and crime.

4.2.1   Mental Illness and Crime in Community Samples

The "dangerousness" of people with mental illnesses emerged as a social concern as state mental hospitals closed beds during the 1960s and 1970s and patients with serious mental illness found themselves in the community, often struggling to maintain stable living arrangements, social support, and basic services. Former mental patients, or those who formally would have been hospitalized for long periods of time, were largely without jobs and visible on city streets. Advocates for the mentally ill claimed that people with mental illness "pose no more of a crime threat than do other members of the general population" (National Mental Health Association 1987), but this conclusion was premature because data to that point were not well-suited to test the relationship (Monahan and Steadman 1983). For example, with data from a psychiatric epidemiologic survey, Swanson et al. (1990) found that violence (self-reported hitting, fighting, or weapon use) was five times higher among persons meeting diagnostic criteria for mental illness than community residents without illness, even after adjusting for demographic and socioeconomic factors, and the presence of a substance abuse diagnosis.[3] This partial association is not necessarily casual.[4]

The conclusions of a community-based study around this time by Link, Andrews, and Cullen (1992), based on comparison of former patients and community residents in one neighborhood in New York City, remain a good summary of the literature. Mental patients had elevated rates of self-reported violence. Substance abuse, correlated with mental illness, also elevates violence but does not account for the full effect of mental illness. Notably, the

---

2. Skeem, Manchak, and Peterson (2009) review a wider literature than is covered here in section 4.4, and their views will be highlighted later. Marcotte and Markowitz (2009) contain a nice review from an economic perspective. See also Monahan and Steadman (1983, 2010), and Fisher, Silver, and Wolff (2006).

3. See also Harry and Steadman (1988). Data on the association of mental illness and crime has been found in other countries. In Australia patients with schizophrenia are more likely to have been convicted of a violent offense than matched controls without schizophrenia (8.2 percent versus 1.8 percent) (Wallace, Mullen, and Burgess 2004). In Sweden men with major mental disorders are four times more likely than men without a mental disorder to be registered for a violent offense; women with major mental disorders twenty-seven times more likely to be registered for a violent offense than women with no disorder (Hodgins 1992). In Switzerland men with schizophrenia were five times more likely to commit violent crimes than matched controls without schizophrenia (Modestin and Ammann 1996). Stueve and Link (1997) found elevated rates of violence and weapon use among persons diagnosed with psychosis or bipolar disorder in Israel. The evidence for the association of mental illness and crime is not uniform, however. A meta-analysis of fifty-eight studies found clinical variables (e.g., diagnosis, treatment history) did not predict criminal recidivism (Bonta, Law, and Hanson 1998).

4. Causality is irrelevant for many purposes. Community residents do not care why someone might be more dangerous.

presence of psychotic symptoms mediates the effect of mental illness.[5] In other words, the elevated violence is found among the patients with more severe and current illness. Other studies come to similar conclusions about the role of substance abuse and mental illness. One review (Friedman 2006) concluded that substance abuse alone dramatically increases the lifetime prevalence of violent behavior, and among people with serious mental disorders, the effects were almost additive.

We add to this literature and characterize the association between crime and mental illness with recent data from the Collaborative Psychiatric Epidemiological Surveys (CPES), designed to capture the prevalence of psychiatric illness and service use with a national sample including an oversampling of minority groups. The CPES combines three surveys conducted with a unified approach during 2002 to 2004, allowing for integration of design-based weights to combine the data as if they were a single, nationally representative study (National Institutes of Mental Health 2007).[6] These data accurately identify recent (twelve month) and lifetime presence of psychiatric disorder. We focus on the effects of serious mental illness, defined to include bipolar disorder or schizophrenia, and substance abuse, defined as abuse of alcohol or illicit drugs.[7] Respondents answered a single question about their arrest history ("have you ever been arrested"), which we use as a dependent variable in our models. After excluding some cases because of missing data, we analyzed a sample of 10,686 individuals.

Figure 4.2 shows both the unadjusted and adjusted association between serious mental illness (SMI) and arrest. The left-hand section of the figure shows the unadjusted rates of arrest at any time during a respondent's lifetime according to whether the respondent reported having an SMI in the past twelve months.[8] Not surprisingly, those with an SMI are at an elevated risk of having been arrested, though in these data the arrest could have pre-

5. One notable study, Applebaum, Robbins, and Monahan (2000), however, did not find this relationship.

6. The University of Michigan Survey Research Center (SRC) collected data for the CPES, combining data from the National Latino and Asian American Study (NLAAS) (Alegría et al. 2004), the National Comorbidity Survey Replication (NCS-R) (Kessler and Merikangas 2004), and the National Survey of African American Life (NSAL) (Jackson et al. 2004). Design and methodological information can be found at the CPES website (https://www.icpsr.umich .edu/CPES/index.html).

7. Bipolar disorder was present in the past twelve months if the respondent met DSM-IV criteria for either Bipolar I or Bipolar II Disorder in the past twelve months. A designation of substance abuse was present if the respondent met DSM-IV criteria for Alcohol or Drug Abuse or Dependence. Psychosis was designated differently on the basis of symptom report and is therefore less reliable. The respondent, were regarded as having psychosis if they reported experiencing at least one of a set of symptoms associated with psychosis in the past twelve months, such as (when not dreaming/sleeping/using substances): If they ever saw visions others could not see, ever felt their mind was being controlled, ever experienced communication attempts from strange forces, and three others.

8. The CPES also collected information about lifetime rates of SMI. The unadjusted rate of arrest is about 40 percent for this group.

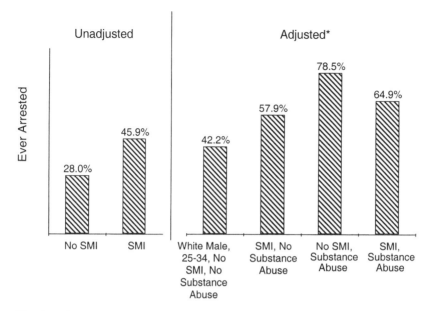

Fig. 4.2   Serious mental illness, substance abuse, and arrest rates
Source: Collaborative Psychiatric Epidemiology Surveys. Rates of arrest are lifetime rates. Illness and substance abuse are rates for past twelve months.
*Linear model adjusted for gender, age categories, and race/ethnicity.

dated illness. The adjusted bars on the right-hand side of the figure report results from a linear model of arrest rates on age categories, gender, race, and having an SMI and abusing substances in the past twelve months. For presentation, rates are compared against a "base case" rate of 42.2 percent for white males aged twenty-five to thirty-four with neither SMI nor substance abuse. Presence of an SMI alone elevates the rate of lifetime risk of arrest to 57.9 percent, and substance abuse alone is much higher. As shown by a negative and significant interaction term for substance abuse and serious mental illness, a person reporting both SMI and substance abuse has adjusted arrest rates more like someone with SMI alone than with substance abuse alone. We added an indicator of "other mental illness" into the model, and the estimated coefficient for this variable was not significant at conventional levels, implying that elevated rates of arrest are concentrated among those with serious mental illness or substance abuse.[9] (Regression results from the basic model are included in appendix A.) From these data, we

9. We have estimated models separately for males and females, and adjusting also for income and education. The results are similar. Having SMI raises risk of arrest, but not as much as substance abuse. The interaction effect between the two conditions is negative. The CPES contains an alternative arrest variable but it is only reported for about half the sample used here.

would conclude that both serious mental illness and substance abuse have an independent effect on arrest rates.

4.2.2   Overlap in Criminal Justice and Patient Samples

Community samples exclude individuals that are institutionalized, those in hospitals, jails and prisons, and may undercount people that are homeless and others without established community ties. A powerful impression of the association of mental illness and criminal involvement emerges from studies of jail and patient samples.

Mental illness and symptoms of mental illness are highly prevalent among adult and child criminal justice populations. In 2002, 25 percent of inmates in local jails had at least one previous diagnosis of a mental illness; in 2004, 25.5 percent of inmates in state prisons and 14.8 percent of inmates in federal prisons had at least one previous diagnosis of a mental illness (Wilper et al. 2009). The prevalence of mental disorders among inmates of the Cook County Department of Corrections was significantly higher than that of the general population, including major depression (3.9 percent versus 1.1 percent), bipolar disorder (1.4 percent versus 0.1 percent), and schizophrenia (2.7 percent versus 0.9 percent); overall, the rate of any severe mental disorder among inmates was elevated more than threefold (6.4 percent versus 1.8 percent) in comparison to the general population (Teplin 1990). Inmates with major psychiatric disorders, particularly bipolar disorder, are more likely to return to jail (Baillargeon et al. 2009). Among inmates, prisoners with any psychiatric disorder were more likely to have committed violent crimes than prisoners with no psychiatric disorder—this rate was further elevated among prisoners with schizophrenia or another psychotic disorder (Baillargeon et al. 2009). The association between serious mental illness and violence and arrest is particularly strong among individuals who are psychotic and do not adhere to medication (Ascher-Svanum et al. 2006).

4.2.3   Criminal Opportunities and Victimization

Before considering the causal connection between mental illness and committing a crime, it is worth mentioning another link between crime and mental illness through the elevated rates of victimization *experienced by* persons with severe mental illness. Issues of reverse causality may confound associations in this literature as in connections already discussed. Teplin et al. (2005) matched a sample of 936 patients with severe mental illness to a much larger comparison group from the National Crime Victimization Survey and found dramatically elevated rates for the mentally ill. Persons with mental illness were eight times more likely to be robbed, fifteen times more likely to be assaulted, and twenty-three times more likely to be raped than the general population. Vulnerability of community-based mentally ill makes them easy marks and creates criminal opportunities contributing to overall criminal activity.[10] Vulnerability of persons with mental illness is exacerbated in prisons. Wolff, Blitz, and Shi (2007) found male prisoners in New Jersey who were mentally ill were three times more likely to be raped that those without mental illness.

4.2.4   Does Mental Illness Cause Crime?

Are people more likely to commit crimes due to having a mental illness? There are many routes by which mental illness may make it more likely for an individual to engage in criminal activity.[11] Mental illness disrupts lives and may put people at higher risk for committing crimes or being victimized. Mental illness interferes with human capital accumulation and wealth building generally. Some psychotic symptoms, such as feeling threatened, may lead directly to criminal conduct. Cognitive distortions associated with mental illness may erode interpersonal relationships and lead individuals to approach situations in a maladaptive fashion. Finally, mental illness can make it more likely that individuals abuse drugs and alcohol, both of which also contribute to crime.

Monahan and Steadman (1983) observe that some mental illnesses (such as bipolar disorder) may predispose individuals to crime whereas others (such as catatonia) may inhibit many activities including crime. Swanson et al. (2008) find a complex mix of effects of correlates and symptoms of schizophrenia on violence. In particular, negative psychiatric symptoms (such as social withdrawal) predicted less violence.[12] Most of the empirical research investigating the causal effect of mental illness on crime has concentrated on serious mental illnesses that blend conditions that may have a positive and negative effect.

As Link, Andrews, and Cullen (1992), Skeem, Manchak, and Peterson (2009) and others have emphasized, interpreting correlations in community-based studies of illness and self-reported violence and crime is problematic because mental illness and crime are both associated in complicated causal webs with disadvantaged social backgrounds. poverty, bad housing, unsafe neighborhoods, among other factors (Swanson et al. 2002). The poor and disadvantaged are both more likely to commit crimes and more likely to be in the hands of the state mental health system. Without being able to control for all of these factors it is difficult to attribute causality to mental illness using data from a community sample.

To what degree is the observed correlation between mental illness and crime due to unmeasured third factors? Skeem et al. (2008) studied 112 parolees with mental illness matched to an otherwise similar group of parolees

10. See Cook, chapter 7, this volume.
11. We are grateful to Harold Pollack for discussion of some of these points.
12. See also Swanson et al. (2006).

without mental illness. The parolees with mental illness had more antisocial personality patterns, earlier and more diverse criminal histories, more criminal attitudes and a pattern of generalized trouble in comparison to the non-ill parolees. These variables, linked to crime, are often unmeasured in empirical investigations and could account for the observed association between mental illness and criminal behavior.

It is useful to place our discussion in the context of more general theories of criminal behavior. Bonta, Law, and Hanson (1998) regard crime as partly a learned behavior ("crime pays") reinforced by environments that tolerate crime and criminals, and personality traits, such as impulsivity or antisocial attitudes. Mental illness has a role within this framework as it may have a direct affect on personality traits, and an indirect effect on the environments a person spends time in. Such a more general theory also, however, points to the possibility that causes of crime, like neighborhood characteristics or even personality, are simply correlates of mental illness. Perspectives from criminology develop broad-based theories of criminal behavior that can accommodate mental illness, but emphasize other more general factors, such as a life-course developmental perspective, or a local life circumstances perspective (Fisher, Silver, and Wolff 2006). The life-course perspective, for example, stresses early parenting styles. These theories are an alternative to conceptualizing crime by persons with mental illness within theories of mental illness, and tend to deemphasize the salience of the illness as a cause of crime.

Interpretation of a correlation as causation is subject to other hazards. Teplin (1983, 1984) and others refer to the "criminalization of mental illness." Fisher, Silver, and Wolff (2006), in their review of the conceptual connections between mental illness and crime, see criminalization as in reaction to the stricter requirements for involuntary inpatient psychiatric treatment imposed in the 1970s. The burden of "social control" of persons with serious mental illness shifted from the mental health to the criminal justice system. On a day-to-day basis, criminalization implies that a person with mental illness committing offenses is more likely to be arrested even when the offending behavior is similar. Higher arrest rates under this explanation can be accounted for by police reaction to disturbed behavior, not a causal effect of mental illness. Presumably this explanation is more relevant to less serious and nonviolent crimes, and the data supporting this contention are equivocal (Fisher, Silver, and Wolff 2006). Conversely, crime and mental illness could be correlated due to the "psychiatrization of criminal behavior" noted by Monahan (1973). Aggression, violence, abuse of substances, among other behaviors, has increasingly fallen within the domain of psychiatry. Those who at one time had been simply called "bad," are now instead or in addition labeled "ill." If we, by definition label criminal behavior to be mental illness, the positive link is not so much causal as definitional. Some mental illnesses, like conduct disorder in adolescents, include criminal behavior as symptoms of the illness itself. This explanation is likely to be more relevant to more serious offenses.

Studies of the clinical situation and criminal behavior of persons with serious mental illness have assessed the degree to which offenses are related to the immediate effects of the symptoms of mental illness. Junginger et al. (2006) and Petersen et al. (2009) both find some, but a small part, of the criminal behavior of offenders with mental illness is due to their immediate symptoms; in Junginger et al. (2006), for example, it is only 8 percent. (The percentage was higher, 26 percent, for substance abuse effects on arrests.) The immediate effect of symptoms means that a person may have reacted violently if, by disordered reasoning, he thought he was being threatened. Serious mental illness can put persons in positions of being likely to commit crimes (e.g., by causing them to be homeless), which would not be accounted for in the methods in these papers.

If current illness causes crime, effective treatment for the illness ought to reduce rates of criminal activity. Another way to test for a causal relationship between serious mental illness and crime is to see, in a treatment study, if randomization to treatment reduces crime. In effect, treatment assignment becomes a kind of instrument for illness, avoiding endogeneity of illness and other social factors. A "no treatment" group for schizophrenia may make such studies hard to find, however.[13]

Marcotte and Markowitz (2009) call attention to the contemporaneous drop in violent crime during the 1990s, and the rapid growth in treatment for mental disorders, particularly drug treatment that occurred during the same period. Large national surveys estimate that between the early 1990s and early 2000s the percent of those with a mental disorder being treated rose from 20.3 percent to 32.9 percent (Kessler, Demler et al. 2005). In an analysis of a panel of US states from 1997 to 2004, they find that violent crime is negatively correlated with rates of prescriptions for some antidepressants, antipsychotics, and stimulants for Attention Deficit Hyperactivity Disorder (ADHD) (in separate models) after adjusting for some other variables likely to affect crime. If those results were interpreted as causal, the observed growth of medication treatment over their time period would account for 12 percent of the crime reduction.

Another perspective on the relationship of mental illness and crime derives from longitudinal data, permitting the study of childhood mental health problems on adult criminal behavior. Attention Deficit Hyperactivity Disorder (ADHD) and conduct disorder are both prevalent illnesses whose consequences for many adult outcomes have been subject to study.

---

13. Reporting results from a prominent trial of treatment for schizophrenia Swanson, Swartz, et al. (2008) report that violence declined by around 15 percent after treatment with antipsychotic medication. The violence reports in this study are pre-post. Randomization in this study was among alternative drug treatments for schizophrenia, and no differences were found in violence reduction by initial drug assignment.

Attention Deficit Hyperactivity Disorder has been linked to risky behaviors, lower academic performance, and poor adult human capital outcomes (see, e.g., Currie and Stabile 2006). A recent paper by Fletcher and Wolfe (2009) uses the large sample from the National Longitudinal Study of Adolescent Health (Add Health) to examine the association between ADHD symptoms and crime in young adulthood. They find that ADHD is positively associated with a range of criminal outcomes. For example, ADHD increases the likelihood of being arrested (by a mean age of twenty-two) by four percentage points (on a sample average of about 12 percent) in a regression with extensive controls for individual, family, and neighborhood characteristics. A significant positive estimated effect of ADHD is maintained in a smaller sample identifying the effect of sibling differences within families.

This strong research design, extensive controls including family fixed effects in a large longitudinal data set, is applied in the next section to the study of conduct disorder.

4.3   Prevention and Treatment of Mental Disorders to Reduce Crime: The Case of Conduct Disorder

Conduct disorder is characterized by aggression toward people or animals, property destruction, deceit or theft, and serious rule violation, and is one of the most prevalent of childhood mental disorders, with estimated lifetime prevalence rates of about 10 percent for males and 7 percent for females (Kessler, Berglund et al. 2005; Nock et al. 2006). The median age of onset is eleven years. Childhood onset of conduct disorder, defined as occurring prior to age ten, is regarded as distinct from adolescent onset at ages ten and above (Kazdin 2002). Childhood onset is more likely to be severe and persistent (Nock et al. 2006). Untreated childhood onset is associated with poor long-term development and poor social and economic outcomes in adulthood (Moffit 1993). Many behaviors associated with the disorder are indeed criminal, and moderation of the symptoms of conduct disorder, by definition, reduces criminal activity. No definitional relationship connects childhood conduct disorder to adult crime. We focus on conduct disorder in children, and its links to adult criminal activity.

Children with conduct disorder are at elevated risk to develop adult mental disorders, drop out of school, abuse substances, and become pregnant as teenagers (Nock et al. 2006; Department of Health and Human Services 1999). Conduct disorder has also been associated with adult crime, whereas the association between crime and other childhood mental disorders is generally weaker. We discuss this evidence later. Prevention and treatment programs aimed at conduct disorder have been found to be effective in controlled evaluations (Kazdin 2002; Farmer et al. 2002). Investment in treatment and prevention of conduct disorder is a candidate policy for an efficient way to reduce criminal activity, the issue we investigate in this section.

4.3.1   General Framework

Cunha and Heckman (2007) regard the social and economic capabilities of adults as being produced by a developmental process that starts in early childhood. Inputs into a child's development include parental capabilities, the household and community environment in which the child grows up, and the investments made in the child and young adult by parents and others (including the child). Research in psychiatric epidemiology and developmental neuroscience calls attention to what might be called "toxic inputs" (our term) into the production of mental health. Adversity early in life can literally damage the structure of a child's brain in a way that increases the likelihood of subsequent mental health problems (National Scientific Council on the Developing Child 2008). Toxic inputs include persistent poverty, abuse, neglect, witnessing domestic violence, and maternal depression (Nock et al. 2006; Rubin et al. 2003; Institute of Medicine 2009). Social programs may be able to counteract some of these negative effects. Investment in prevention and early treatment of conduct disorders include teaching parenting skills, treatment of parental substance abuse and depression, early recognition and treatment of disruptive behavior, and training teachers in the management of disruptive behavior (Kazdin 2002; IOM 2009).

4.3.2   Childhood Conduct Disorder and Adult Crime

We next consider the connection between childhood conduct disorder and adult crime, with a focus on the question of whether conduct disorder in childhood can be considered a cause of adult crime. The causal path could be from early to late mental illness, or from early illness to a personally and socially disadvantaged young adulthood. We know children with conduct disorder are less likely to do well in school and otherwise have a troubled adolescence. How much of this carries over into young adulthood showing up in higher rates of criminal activity?

Swanson, Van Dorn, et al. (2008) used data from a large clinical trial on treatment for schizophrenia to compare rates of violence in adults in patients who did and did not have conduct disorders as children. Rates of violence were significantly higher among patients who had had conduct disorder problems, and the rate of elevation varied uniformly with the number of conduct problems, even in the presence of extensive controls, including substance use. The investigators also found that medication adherence was associated with lower violence only among adults with schizophrenia who did not have a history of antisocial conduct as children.

Large longitudinal data sets enable the study of the relationship between childhood conduct disorders and consequences in later life. The United Kingdom collects data on birth cohorts enabling longitudinal analyses of birth cohorts from 1946, 1958, and 1970 (Sainsbury Center for Mental Health 2009). The 1946 cohort of 5,362 people was followed until age 53.

The 1958 cohort included 17,416 people followed up first at age 7 and until age 45. The 1970 cohort consisted of 16,571 subjects with the first follow-up at age 5, continuing until age 34. In each cohort questions were asked of each child's parents and teachers that enable conduct and other emotional problems to be identified. The 1958 and 1970 cohorts used the Rutter A scale and the 1946 cohort used a prequel to the scale (Rutter, Tizard, and Whitmore 1970).

Recent analyses of the 1958 and 1970 cohorts examine the relationship between childhood and adolescent conduct problems and adult criminal activity (Sainsbury Center for Mental Health 2009). Analysis of the 1958 cohort estimated the relation between the presence of either a severe or mild conduct problem during the teenage years on adult offending between ages thirty-two and forty-two. Analysis of the 1970 cohort estimated the relation between severe and mild conduct problems and lifetime offending up to age thirty-four. Logit models stratified by gender and controlling for IQ and father's occupation revealed elevated rates of adult offending (arrested, convicted of a crime) for people with severe conduct problems as teenagers in the 1958 cohort. The estimated relative odds for men were between 1.1 and 1.9 compared to otherwise similar people without conduct disorder. Analysis of the 1970 cohort linked severe conduct problems at age five and offending between the ages of sixteen and thirty-four. The estimated logit models showed the relative odds of being arrested for men were 3.4 fold and twofold for women, and the relative odds of being convicted of a crime for men was 1.4 times that for men without childhood conduct problems of any kind. The corresponding estimate for women was 1.5. Analyses of severe conduct problems during early adolescence and lifetime offending between sixteen and thirty-four years of age showed relative odds of being arrested for men was about four times that for people with no history of conduct problems. Women with severe conduct problems in adolescence had relative odds that were five times those for women with no history of conduct problems. These estimates are consistent with but do not establish causality because there are a variety of unobserved factors that might affect both the development of conduct problems and criminal behavior later in life.

Nagin and Tremblay (1999) followed a cohort of 1,037 boys in Montreal, Canada, to investigate the effects of externalizing disorders, including indicators of conduct disorder, to juvenile delinquency. Aggression and oppositional behavior persisted from childhood into adolescence. Fergusson, Horwood, and Ridder (2005) studied a twenty-five-year cohort of 973 children beginning at age seven to nine in New Zealand. Conduct problems were identified through teacher and parent interviews. A variety of educations and economic and social outcomes were measured at age twenty-five, including criminal and antisocial behavior. The authors controlled for a variety of individual and family covariates including child and family adversity, family socioeconomic status, parent educational background, family stability (divorce, single motherhood, domestic violence), demographics (ethnicity, age of parents), and child cognitive ability. The analysis compared children with rates of conduct problems in the top 5 percent at ages seven to nine with those below the median. Multivariate analysis showed that those in the top 5 percent of the distribution of conduct problems had rates of property offenses that were three times those below the median (15.3 percent versus 4.8 percent), rates of violent offenses that were roughly four times those below the median (15.9 percent versus 3.9 percent), and rates of arrest/conviction nearly five times higher (19.5 percent versus 4.2 percent).

Currie and Stabile (2007) use the US National Longitudinal Study of Youth (NLSY) and the Canadian National Longitudinal Survey of Children and Youth (NLSCY) to study the effect of mental and emotional problems in children on educational and behavioral outcomes. They measure behavior for the Canadian children aged four to eleven years in 1994, and observe outcomes for the same children in 2002. For the NLSY they examine children aged four to eleven in 1994, and outcomes measured in 1998 to 2004. To address the problem of unobserved factors in an analysis seeking a causal relationship, they examine households with multiple children and including a household fixed effect. Thus, estimates of the impact of early life behavior problems on subsequent delinquency in young adults are identified based on differences between siblings growing up in the same household. Children with higher levels of antisocial and aggressive behavior at ages four to eleven are more likely to display delinquency as young adults. The results were similar for both the US and Canadian cohorts.

We pursue a similar analysis of the NLSY as that conducted by Currie and Stabile (2007), but focus on behavior problems at the most serious end of the spectrum for children aged six to nine years. Specifically, we create an indicator for a child with behavioral problems that are in the top decile of the age-specific population. We also construct an indicator of whether the symptom scale is between the fiftieth and eighty-ninth percentile of the age-specific population. Like Currie and Stabile (2007), we estimate the impact of conduct problems on expulsion/suspension from school and the likelihood of having been arrested/convicted by age sixteen using household (mother) fixed effects, thereby basing identification on sibling differences.

We identified 6,329 children living in multiple-child households where at least two children had reached age fifteen in 2008. Item nonresponse reduced the sample size for the suspended/expelled and arrested/convicted regressions.[14] Descriptive statistics from the estimation samples are included in table 4.1. Note that the percentage of children in our sample who exceed the ninetieth percentile on the Basic Personality Inventory (BPI) antisocial scale is about 24 percent for each outcome, indicating that the children in

---

14. A delinquency scale was asked only in 1994, 1996, and 1998, and led to a smaller sample size.

Table 4.1   Estimation samples from NLSY

	Suspended/ expelled		Convicted/ probation	
Model N	6,329		5,421	
Dependent variable				
No	4,978	78.65%	4,828	89.06%
Yes	1,351	21.35%	593	10.94%
BPI antisocial score (percentile) at age 8 group				
Below 50th percentile	2,155	34.05%	1,787	32.96%
50th to 89th percentile	2,696	42.60%	2,353	43.41%
90th percentile and above	1,478	23.35%	1,281	23.63%
Sex				
Male	3,253	51.40%	2,777	51.23%
Female	3,076	48.60%	2,644	48.77%
Race				
Hispanic	1,420	22.44%	1,258	23.21%
Black	2,020	31.92%	1,833	33.81%
White	2,889	45.65%	2,330	42.98%
First born				
No	4,190	66.20%	3,493	64.43%
Yes	2,139	33.80%	1,928	35.57%
Teen mom				
No	5,191	82.02%	4,426	81.65%
Yes	1,138	17.98%	995	18.35%
Mom divorced in last year				
No	5,928	93.66%	5,088	93.86%
Yes	401	6.34%	333	6.14%
Mom widowed in last year				
No	6,318	99.83%	5,412	99.83%
Yes	11	0.17%	9	0.17%

Notes: The sample is drawn from the children of women in the NLSY 1979 cohort. It is limited to children from households in which at least two children had reached age 15 by 2008 (i.e., born in 1993 or earlier). Dependent variables are "ever" up to age 17. Suspended/Expelled: Respondent (mother) answered yes to "Has child ever been suspended or expelled from school?" or "Suspended/expelled" given as reason child had left school for some period of time. Convicted/ Probation: Respondent (young adult) answered yes to any of the following questions:
"Ever been convicted of charges other than minor traffic violation?"
"Ever been on probation?"
"Ever been sentenced to a corrections institution/jail/reform school?"
"Ever been convicted of anything in adult court?" (1994 to 1998 surveys)
"Ever been referred to court-related counseling by police/courts/school?" (1994 to 1998 surveys)

this sample are considerably more disturbed than a nationally representative sample. The NLSY data guide acknowledges that the BPI distribution was above national values in the early rounds of the NLSY, possibly due to oversampling children born to younger and less-educated women.

Table 4.2 contains the results from three models, one with no controls, one with controls listed in the table, and one adding family fixed effects to

Table 4.2   **Suspension or expulsion by age 17, NSLY regression results**

	No controls	With controls	Controls & fixed effects
BPI 90th	0.269**	0.206**	0.143**
	(0.013)	(0.012)	(0.017)
BPI 50–89	0.090**	0.058**	0.027*
	(0.010)	(0.010)	(0.012)
Male		0.102**	0.116**
		(0.009)	(0.010)
Latino		0.053**	0.620
		(0.015)	(1.095)
Black		0.240**	0.383
		(0.011)	(1.176)
First born		–0.012	0.015
		(0.010)	(0.010)
Teen mom		0.066**	0.006
		(0.014)	(0.018)
Divorce last year		0.019	0.004
		(0.018)	(0.022)
Widow last year		0.018	0.137
		(0.095)	(0.114)
Intercept	0.081**	–0.003*	–0.269
	(0.007)	(0.009)	(0.332)
R^2	0.068	0.151	0.559
N	6329	6329	6329
Fixed effects	No	No	Yes

Notes: Used GLM (generalized linear models) procedure. Observations weighted by custom longitudinal weights created by NLSY: http://www.nlsinfo.org/pub/usersvc/CustomWeight/ CustomWeightingProgramDocumentation.htm.
**$p < 0.01$
*$p < 0.05$

the analysis. The dependent variable is the 0–1 suspension/expulsion by age seventeen. All models are estimated with linear probability models by a generalized linear model (GLM). Key regressors are indicators of externalizing disorder symptoms (measured at the fifty to eighty-ninth percentile and the ninety-plus percentile) and the household fixed effects.

The estimated coefficient for the ninetieth percentile for the externalizing disorder score is positive and significant for being suspended/expelled in all specifications, though the estimated magnitude drops as controls and then fixed effects are added. Having a high level of symptoms of externalizing disorder increases the likelihood of being suspended or expelled by age seventeen by 14.3 percentage points in the model with fixed effects. The sample mean for suspended/expelled is about 21 percent, so this estimate implies a large elevation in the risk.

Table 4.3 contains the results bearing directly on criminal activity, with

Table 4.3   Convicted or probation by age 17, NSLY regression results

	No controls	With controls	Controls & fixed effects
BPI 90th	0.122**	0.108**	0.050**
	(0.011)	(0.011)	(0.016)
BPI 50–89	0.039**	0.036**	0.013
	(0.009)	(0.009)	(0.012)
Male		0.054**	0.068**
		(0.008)	(0.010)
Latino		0.017	0.023
		(0.014)	(0.953)
Black		0.007	0.037
		(0.010)	(1.029)
First born		−0.031**	−0.011
		(0.009)	(0.010)
Teen mom		0.007	−0.036*
		(0.013)	(0.017)
Divorce last year		0.047**	0.004
		(0.017)	(0.022)
Widow last year		0.133	0.165
		(0.097)	(0.123)
Intercept	0.061**	0.041**	−0.078
	(0.007)	(0.009)	(0.173)
R^2	0.022	0.033	0.470
N	5421	5421	5421
Fixed effects	No	No	Yes

Notes: Used GLM (generalized linear models) procedure. Observations weighted by custom longitudinal weights created by NLSY: http://www.nlsinfo.org/pub/usersvc/CustomWeight/CustomWeightingProgramDocumentation.htm.
**$p < 0.01$
*$p < 0.05$

specifications and analysis identical to those described for table 4.2. The estimated impact of high levels of externalizing disorder symptoms on probability of being arrested/convicted prior to age sixteen and on the delinquency score are positive and significant in all models, including with family fixed effects where the point estimate indicates a 5 percentage point elevation on a base of about 4.6 percent, another large increase. To argue that the estimated effects in tables 4.2 and 4.3 are causal, we need to rely on the longitudinal research design with family fixed effects to control for pervasive unobserved factors that might lead to both conduct disorder problems and later behavioral problems. Overall, our findings are consistent with early conduct disorder causing later criminal involvement. Of course, if delinquency in teen years is seen simply as a continuation of externalizing disorder in younger children, identifying this "cause" does not help much in understanding the developmental process behind the later criminal behavior.

4.3.3 Cost-Effectiveness of Prevention of Conduct Disorder

Another way to approach the question of whether extension of mental health treatment to a high-risk group reduces criminal behavior is to examine the results of social programs changing access to, in this case, children with conduct disorder. A variety of prevention and treatment programs aim to reduce the individual and social impacts of conduct disorder. Effective prevention of conduct disorders requires identification of at-risk populations and interventions in place early in a child's life (Conduct Problems Prevention Research Group 1992; IOM 2009). While a number of prevention interventions have been shown to be effective, we focus on prevention interventions where cost-effectiveness has also been assessed.[15]

A pair of meta-analyses identifies prevention programs for which measured benefits, including in terms of crime reduction, exceed costs (Aos et al. 2001, 2004). These are Nurse-Home visitation programs targeted at low income single mothers; Parent Child Interaction Therapy; Home Visiting Programs for At-Risk Mothers, and the Good Behavior Game (delivered in school). Overall, the early childhood home visitation programs reviewed by Aos and colleagues (2004) yielded net social benefits of about $6,000 per child in 2003 dollars. The Good Behavior Game, which uses behavioral techniques in the classroom to prevent conduct problems from developing, yielded small positive benefits of less than $200 per child.

More recently, Foster and colleagues (2005) conducted a cost-effectiveness study of the Fast Track program that focuses specifically on prevention of conduct disorder and violence. The program was likely to be cost effective (70 percent) when targeted at high-risk children but had a less than 1 percent chance of being cost-effective when applied to the general population in high-risk communities.

4.3.4 Cost-Effectiveness of Treatment for Conduct Disorder

Kazdin (2002) identifies 550 psychosocial treatments for conduct disorder in children and youth, noting paradoxically that treatments with the strongest evidence base are those less frequently applied in practice.[16] The treatments most frequently used to treat conduct disorder are psychodynamic psychotherapy, eclectic psychotherapies, and family therapy. Few of these are supported by evidence of effectiveness.[17] Kazdin (2002) identified five main classes of evidence-based treatments for conduct disorder. They

15. Only a small portion of all the interventions that have been shown to be effective have been subjected to economic evaluations (IOM 2009, 254). Furthermore, where economic evaluations have been done, the report notes that the findings are subject to considerable uncertainty from low statistical power, short follow-up periods, and generalizability outside of research contexts.

16. Psychosocial treatments are emphasized because existing research suggests that pharmacotherapies are not effective in treatment of conduct disorder.

17. An exception is Brief Strategic Family Therapy (BSFT), discussed later.

are Parent Management Training (PMT), Multisystemic Therapy (MST), Problem Solving Skills Training (PSST), Functional Family Therapy (FFT) and Brief Strategic Family Therapy (BSFT). Recently, the National Institute for Clinical Excellence (NICE) in the United Kingdom issued a technology appraisal guideline indicating that parent training programs were cost-effective in treating conduct disorder (NICE 2006).

The PMT, MST, FFT, and a program that combines several of these elements known as the Incredible Years program, have been subject to economic evaluations. Parent Management Training (PMT) trains parents to modify their child's behavior at home and in the context of their family. Parent Management Training (PMT) is based on the theory that poor parenting is a source of conduct disorder. Parents are trained to identify problem behaviors and to intervene in ways that do not reinforce bad behavior. The National Institute for Clinical Excellence (2006) concluded that PMT was cost-effective in relation to usual care of conduct disorder due to savings from the health and education sectors. Some evidence of reduced crime-related activity has been reported in outcome studies, but the net economic consequences for criminal activity have not been established (Brestan and Eyberg 1998).

Multisystemic Therapy extends PMT by adding other types of skills and treatment including family communication skills, marital therapy, and problem-solving therapy, among others. Aos and Barnoski (1998) estimated significant net cost savings for MST, on the order of $13,000, in 1997. Aos et al. (2004) conducted a later review of MST on the application of the technology to violent offending youth aged twelve to seventeen years. The assessment was based on three evaluations of MST targeted at offending youth. Multisystemic Therapy incurred direct costs of $4,473 on average in year 2000 dollars, whereas the savings to the criminal justice system were estimated at $31,661. The large benefits in this study appear to stem from the highly targeted nature of the populations treated with MST.

Functional Family Therapy (FFT) was evaluated in Washington state (Washington State Institute for Public Policy 2004) by randomly assigning youth offenders to FFT, MST, Aggression Replacement Training (ART), or a waiting list (with usual care).[18] The FFT focuses on teaching families to change problematic family behaviors through the development of problem-solving skills. Families participate in twelve therapy visits over a ninety-day period. Aggression Replacement Therapy is a group therapy method administered to youth offenders for thirty hours over a ten-week period. It focuses on teaching youth to control impulses and anger. Therapists running the groups received intensive training and their adherence to the ART model was measured. The ART has been widely adopted by juvenile courts

---

18. Implementation problems for MST limited the ability to evaluate the MST intervention.

in Washington state. The meta-analysis by Aos et al. (2004) estimated savings, based on four controlled evaluations, of $10 to $30 in criminal justice spending for each dollar of direct program spending.

The Washington state evaluation found no significant differences between rates of overall recidivism or felony recidivism between FFT, ART, and the controls. However, for therapists that adhere to the treatment, the two experimental programs yielded savings of between $10 and $12 for each dollar of program spending. This analysis, however, sacrifices the virtues of randomization since adherence rates may be associated with a variety of unmeasured characteristics of the youths assigned to different therapists. Furthermore, fidelity to program design is higher in experimental than real-world settings, implying that the overall results might be more of what we could expect in nonexperimental settings rather than results for the therapists with the greatest fidelity.

4.3.5   Summary Comment

Evidence from longitudinal surveys in New Zealand, the United Kingdom, Canada, and the United States, imply that the association between early life conduct problems and later criminal activity is partly causal. Prevention and treatment programs have potential to reduce the economic and social costs of crime stemming from conduct disorder to a degree that may more than pay for treatment. Some studies yield very favorable payoffs in terms of lowering criminal justice costs from investment in treatment and prevention. However, this potential has not been clearly established in the real world of the constrained, poorly coordinated, unevenly staffed social service, education, and criminal justice sectors.

4.4   Mental Health Treatment for Offenders

An obvious high-risk candidate group for enhanced investment in mental health treatment is those who have already offended and are at some stage in the criminal justice system. The left-hand side of figure 4.3 depicts a typical sequence of events for an offender. After a police encounter, arrest and arraignment, the accused proceeds to trial, and if found guilty, is sentenced to prison or jail. Eventually the offender would be released to the community and may be put on probation, remaining for some period under the supervision of the criminal justice system.

Movement down the left-hand side is slow, expensive, and may not be effective in forestalling future problems, especially for people with serious mental illnesses. At virtually every step in the process, interventions addressing the role of mental illness have been devised to divert the offender from the criminal justice system; some of these are indicated in figure 4.3. Some police officers have special training in mental health issues and are trained to handle mentally ill offenders with recognition of the role of symptoms and illness in

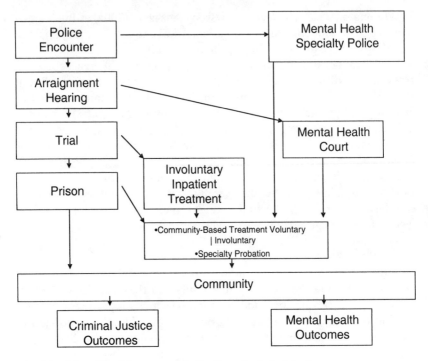

Fig. 4.3   **Mental health treatment in the flow of criminal justice**

behavior. Mental health courts, reviewed in detail later, are an alternative to regular court trials. Judges in these courts work with mental health system professionals, more actively supervise progress, and employ jail-prison as a backup for lapses in progress. Mental health courts are one, but not the only, way that offenders, upon release, can be referred and in many cases forced to receive community treatment (such as medication and counseling). During the probation period, some jurisdictions use probation officers with special training and who specialize in persons with mental illness.

Criminal justice system involvement identifies good targets for intervention, and, furthermore, enforces a link between offenders and mental health treatment. One would expect that closely targeted mental health treatment, with sanctions of the criminal justice system backing up adherence, would have a good chance of being cost-effective. We review here the evidence for mental health interventions associated with mental health courts and mandated community treatment, two prominent policies diverting offenders from the left-hand side of figure 4.3.[19]

19. See Skeem, Manchak, and Peterson (2009) and Monahan and Steadman (2010) for related reviews.

4.4.1   Mental Health Courts

Mental Health Courts (MHCs) are alternatives to regular courts for offenders whose mental illness may have contributed to their criminality, and employ resources of both the criminal justice and the mental health system within a framework of therapeutic jurisprudence (Wexler and Winick 1991). Therapeutic jurisprudence is based on the principle that punishment should not be the sole concern of the courts, but rather the well-being of the accused as well as the potential mitigating circumstances regarding mental health that are required for a more complete sense of justice (Rottman and Casey 1999). The MHCs were modeled on drug courts established earlier (Steadman, Davidson, and Brown 2001), with the important distinction that while drug possession and use are crimes, having a mental illness is not. The monitoring-sanctioning function of MHCs thus works differently than in drug courts, and the enforced treatment handed down by MHCs is also more controversial than treatment mandates set for drug offenders (Slate and Johnson 2008).

Broward County, Florida, established the first MHC in 1997, one county north from the nation's first drug court in Dade (Poythress et al. 2002). Broward's MHC was established with the goals of making sure mentally ill patients were released from jail in a timely fashion, got connected with both legal representation and mental health resources, and were oriented well in a return to the community (Christy et al. 2005). The MHCs have proliferated, mainly in southern and western states (Slate and Johnson 2008). By December, 2005, the National Alliance for the Mentally Ill (2005) counted 113 courts; Steadman recently estimated that there are about 150 courts in operation (Slate and Johnson 2008).[20] The Mentally Ill Offender Treatment and Crime Reduction Act of 2003 awards grants to counties for mental health courts or other court-based programs fueling growth of MHCs. Research on MHCs must contend with local idiosyncrasies (Steadman et al. 2001), and the malleable nature of court administration (Bernstein and Seltzer 2003).

Mental Health Courts are usually defined as courts with a separate docket for mentally ill patients with specialized personnel to handle the cases. Courts set criminal and mental health criteria for selecting candidates (Redlich et al. 2005).[21] To establish leverage, some MHCs require that the defendant enter

20. There is no clear consensus on the definition of a MHC (Christy et al. 2005).
21. Some courts test potential clients after the initial arrest, and some require confirmed diagnosis before considering the candidate eligible for treatment. Referrals to MHCs come from law enforcement personnel, court personnel, district attorneys, public defenders, or patient families. In an early study of twenty MHCs, Bernstein and Seltzer (2003) report that four courts excluded offenders with any history of violent behavior. Ten courts accepted offenders with felony charges, and ten were restricted to those with misdemeanor only charges. In Broward County, referrals to the MHC *must* come post-arrest and may only come from other judges, district attorneys, or lawyers for the defense (Christy et al. 2005). Redlich et al. (2005) distinguish

a guilty plea (Bernstein and Seltzer 2003). Discharge from a MHC may take months or years, and may extend well beyond the time a defendant would have spent in jail had he followed the normal route of criminal justice. Although mental health courts may help mentally ill offenders avoid jail time, they are designed to incur additional costs in terms of MHC supervision and contacts, and in the mental health treatment system.

Mental Health Courts have been studied from several perspectives. Legal scholars question the concept of therapeutic jurisprudence and whether offenders with mental illness are competent to abdicate their rights to regular judicial processing, including jury trial (Slobogin 1995; Allen and Smith; 2001). Others question whether clients in MHCs should be coerced or "leveraged" into treatment (Griffin, Steadman, and Petrila 2002).[22] The MHCs mandate the mental health system to treat court-supervised clients at a high priority and in a setting with limited community-based resources; some other clients, possibly with greater need from a clinical perspective, will be crowded out (Clark 2004; Goldkamp and Irons-Guynn 2000; Steadman, Davidson, and Brown 2001; Watson et al. 2001).[23] Discretion in application of who is appropriate for access to mental health courts may not be fair, in the sense of leading to systematic discriminating on the basis of gender or race.[24]

Our main interest is evaluation of MHCs from the standpoint of their impact on criminal justice and mental health system outcomes and costs.

---

between what they refer to as first and second generation MHCs. Those following the Broward County model, accepting only misdemeanor patients, are termed first generation courts. Second generation courts modify the Broward County model on four dimensions: "(a) type of charges the court accepts (felony vs. misdemeanor), (b) type of adjudicative model the courts follow (pre- vs. postadjudication), (c) sanctions used in the court (specifically the expressed willingness to use jail as a sanction), and (d) supervision of MHC participants (mental health vs. criminal justice professionals)" (Redlich et al. 2005, 528).

22. See Monahan et al. (2005) for an empirical review of the application of "leverage" in mental health courts.

23. In principle, any impact of "queue-jumping" on the mental health system should be taken into account in evaluating the impact of MHCs; this is very difficult to do in practice (Wolff 2002; Petrila, Ridgely, and Borum 2003). In resource constrained mental health systems, persons with mental illness have incentives to offend in order to access treatment, an unintended consequence referred to by a number of observers (Sinaiko and McGuire 2006; Wolff 2002).

24. The MHC clientele differ systematically from traditional criminal caseloads. Referring agents may select for "good" risks based upon personal characteristics. Steadman et al. (2005) studied selection in seven MHCs concluding that older, white females tend to be preferentially referred to MHCs. Naples, Morris, and Steadman (2007) confirmed the Steadman finding in that older, white women without felony or violent charges (even among courts that accept felony cases) appear to be preferentially selected for entry into mental health court. The other way to state these results is that young black males are less likely to be referred to MHCs. Whether this represents unfair discrimination or decisions based on application of reasonable criteria for likely success in MHCs has not been established. Fairness is an issue in other applications of mental health treatments for criminal justice populations, though the treatment is not always regarded as a positive as in the case of MHCs. Blacks are more, not less likely, to be referred to mandated outpatient treatment, though in the case of New York State at least, this is due to blacks' overrepresentation in the denominator population of those at risk for crime with extensive contact with the public mental health system rather than any race-based discrimination by referring agents. See Swanson et al. (2009).

Table 4.4 summarizes the findings of eight case studies of particular courts. The reports are generally positive, but study designs are not uniformly strong.[25]

Cosden et al. (2003) investigated the Santa Barbara MHC/Assertive Community Treatment (ACT) system for clients that received MHC treatment compared to treatment as usual (TAU) using a randomized design. Clients in the MHC system reported marginally better quality of life increases, but similar criminal outcomes in terms of number of times arrested and time in jail. Cosden notes, however, that MHC patients had less intensive jail stays and were more frequently released with no charge.

Ridgely et al. (2007) studied the Allegheny County (Pittsburgh, PA) MHC, oriented to nonviolent offenders (though some aggravated assault cases are admitted). The court accepts only those individuals with a documented diagnosis of mental illness and requires a guilty plea be entered before beginning the MHC intervention. Like most MHCs, the intervention is a form of monitored probation with integrated community treatment and reinforcement hearings in the MHC. Participants are discharged as having completed the program, potentially earlier than a normal sentence, after the MHC team rules treatment to have been effective. The pre-post component of the study yielded savings after one year and even larger savings, more than $9,000, over two years. The savings were largely in the form of reduced jail days, set against estimated MHC and mental health system costs. Investigators attempted to compensate for weaknesses of the pre-post design by construction of a hypothetical counterfactual group. With the assumptions behind this hypothetical group, Ridgely et al. (2007) believed there would be a net savings from MHCs if subjects were followed for at least two years.

The evidence is highly uneven on the effectiveness and cost-effectiveness of MHCs. Some, but not all, of the evaluations of MHCs point to a reduction in criminal activity associated with participation in the court. Little evidence connects the mental treatment component of the mental health

25. Herinckx et al. (2005) studied the MHC in Clark County, Nevada, using a twelve-month pre-post time comparison. Crime dropped after MHC participation, and dropped most for those completing court participation. Boothroyd et al. (2005) and Christy et al. (2005) studied mental health and criminal justice outcomes, respectively, for the Broward court, comparing trends for MHC participants from a matched group of misdemeanants from Hillsborough County. Although the MHC participants were more likely to be linked to treatment, this did not improve mental health outcomes. Christy reported mainly favorable criminal justice outcomes. Compared to offenders handled in regular court, Moore and Aldigé (2006) find reduced recidivism in a MHC in the southeastern United States, particularly for those completing MHC. Trupin and Richards (2003) investigated the effect of MHCs in Seattle on recidivism, clinical outcome measures, and severity. In a pre-post comparison, recidivism dropped. Notably, offenders were in jail longer prebooking with MHCs, offsetting any savings in reduced recidivism. McNiel and Binder (2007) examined the San Francisco County MHC that included violent offenders. Compared to a matched sample, recidivism fell 55 percent, but McNiel cautioned that the propensity matching may not be picking up unobservable characteristics related to being "most likely to violently reoffend," biasing findings in favor of the MHC, a problem plaguing the nonexperimental studies.

Table 4.4   **Summary of mental health court evaluations**

Setting	Court and study population	Comparison population	Notable outcomes	Notes
		Herinckx et al. (2005) Psychiatric Services vol. 56		
Clark County, NV: 2000–2003	**Court:** Diagnosis near time of arrest. In 2001, switched from preplea to postplea. **Study:** Misdemeanor only; Axis I disorder. Majority of court cases, but not all.	Pre-post	**Criminal Justice:** 400% overall crime reduction rate one year after enrollment. 62% reduction in probation violations. MH treatment had no effect on CJ outcomes, court completion associated with less crime. **Mental Health:** Used as covariate, not outcome.	Favorable effects were concentrated among those completing MHC; noncompleters showed little benefit.
		Moore and Aldigé (2006) Law and Human Behavior vol. 30		
Southeastern MHC (Unspecified): 2001–2002	**Court:** Subjective "not a threat to the community." Integrated with drug court. Mental illness evaluated and confirmed after MHC screening for "inappropriate behavior" or prior diagnosis. Subjective evaluation made by MHC. **Study:** White or African American.	Nonequivalent comparison group. Used chief district court judge to identify traditional court participants from the prior year who would have been eligible for the MHC had it been in existance; that is, court defendants with a history of mental illness that did not pose a public safety risk. Comparison group is nonequivalent as it is both time mismatched, and diagnostic criterion mismatched, as diagnosis is not confirmed as it is for MHC patients. Statistical controls for age, race, gender, prior criminal history, prior jail time and severity of current charge.	**Criminal Justice:** MHC reports an order as a six-month treatment window. Negative binomial regressions report that after using prior offense severity, the incident rate ratio for MHC presence at recidivism was −.62, significant at $p < .01$. On average MHC completers were rearrested .58 times, a significant at $p < .001$ chi-squared difference between noncompleters average of 2.03. **Mental Health:** None.	Similar to Herinckx result.

Trupin and Richards (2003) International Journal of Law and Psychiatry vol. 26

Location/Dates	Court/Study	Design	Results	Evaluation
King County, WA/ Seattle, WA: (1999– 2001)	**Court:** Misdemeanor only. Psych evaluation at entry into court. Plea-bargain integrated court process. **Study:** No exclusions, followed sample for nine-month follow-up following MHC enrollment.	Pre-post analysis of MHC sample, along with comparison of MHC sample and those that opted out.	**Criminal Justice:** Post enrollment booking decreased to a $p < .05$ significant level. Cohen d's were reported .587 and .617 for Seattle and King County respectively. Annualized jail length of stay (LOS) decreased for Seattle $p < .01$, $d = .779$. Opt outs in Seattle also appeared to decrease annualized LOS, but not as much, $p < .05$, $d = .442$. **Mental Health:** 95.4% linkage to services in Seattle reported, 84% reported in King County. King County reported an increase in global assessment of functioning, $p < .05$, but the effect is weak, $d = .257$.	Qualitative evaluation of the courts gives a more complete picture than quantitative data. Quantitative results are of weak and mixed effect. Though results are generally strong for treatment access, the selective nature of the opt-in/opt-out process makes the effects on criminal justice uncertain.
Allegheny County, PA: 2001–2006	**Court:** Nonviolent instigating arrests with documented diagnosis of mental illness, felonies and misdemeanors included. **Study:** All participants from inception 2001 through end of Sept. 2004.	Pre-post analaysis and counterfactual hypothetical population.	**Cost:** One year follow-up pre-post overall $1,804 savings per person in MHC, two year $9,584. Against hypothetical, increase in cost of $2,656. In both cases, reduction in jail costs offset by increase in mental health costs.	A cost study of MHC effectiveness. While results are compelling in favor of MHC use, especially from pre-post analysis, the sensitivity of the returns to investment from the counterfactual make positive/negative value largely dependant upon sensitivity assumptions.

Ridgely (2007) RAND Technical Reports TR-439

(continued)

Table 4.4 (continued)

Setting	Court and study population	Comparison population	Notable outcomes	Notes
Santa Barbara, CA	**Court:** Voluntary participation of nonviolent (no longer posed a danger to others), could be either pre- or postplea. Court is integrated with ACT team. **Study:** Stratified random sample from those that were deemed to have met the criterion above. Due to desire to add more to MHC population, randomization occured two-to-one in favor of the MHC at the onset of the study.	Random sample. It should be noted that demographics of the randomization are not perfect, suggesting incomplete randomization, at least on some grounds, though reported chi square values are insignificant.	*Cosden (2003) Behavioral Sciences and the Law vol. 23* **Criminal Justice:** Rearrests, convictions, incarceration days all report no significant effect of the MHC. If the top percent of offenders from both categories are removed, a moderate effect of the MHC appears. The success seems to be determined by "serious substance abuse problems at intake." **Mental Health:** MHC patients received many more treatment hours and moderately better on global assessment of functioning (GAF), Lehman quality of life (QOL), BASIS and addiction severity index (ASI) scores compared to TAU. Partial support for MHC positive treatment on mental health functioning.	True experiment gives a more compelling design, though demographic differences within the normal jail population and those selected for the study call into question the generalizability of the model. Both samples exhibit significant reversion to the mean (both TAU and MHC patients fare better over time). Cosden concludes that MHC is not useful for all offenders, but may be helpful for the majority of moderate cases. Reversion to mean is contrary to behavior exhibited in the Trupin study.

	Boothroyd (2005) Psychiatric Services 56; Christy (2005) Behavioral Sciences and the Law vol. 23		
Broward County, FL: 1999–2003	**Court:** Nonviolent misdemeanors, no formal diagnostic criteria, referred by magistrates. Mental health screening conducted by students after referral. **Study:** English speaking MHC patients, whose initial court date came between Dec. 1999 and April 2001.	Matched sample of misdemeanor defendants from Hillsborough county due to similar demographics and census variables. Matching was done on a one-to-one basis, two month lagged, looking for defendants in other counties exhibiting signs of mental illness.	**Criminal Justice (Christy):** Recidivism and time to rearrest were measured in both groups. Recidivism was lower for the MHC population, but not significantly so. Time to rearrest was longer for MHC patients. Felony vs. nonfelony rearrest rates were not significantly different. Index jail time was significantly reduced. **Mental Health Measures (Boothroyd):** Brief Psychiatric Rating Scale (BPRS) reports no better outcome from MHC patients compared to matched TAU patients in other counties. While MHC patients may be matched more successfully to treatment, "receipt of treatment alone is not sufficient to effect positive changes in clinical status."	MHC does not show significant improvement over base treatment condition; however, it does no worse. As the Broward county mission was to reduce jail time without harming public safety, authors conclude the MHC has succeeded. Study only found a difference in rate patients were matched with services not in outcomes. Study interprets this as MHC working properly, mental health systems in county as deficient. Contrary to the Cosden study, all defendants showed worsening severity over time.
	McNiel and Binder (2007) American Journal of Psychiatry vol. 164		
San Francisco, CA: 2003–2004	**Court:** Diagnosed Axis I mental disorder or developmental disabilities and amenable to community treatment. Does not preclude felonies. **Study:** All participants in the court from inception through November 2004 for whom complete six month follow-up was available.	Used propensity weighting scores to construct a TAU group out of diagnosed mentally ill patients in the San Francisco county jail system. Controlled for nonramdom assignment using observables.	**Criminal Justice Measures:** Reported the effect of the MHC on probability of new charge and probability of new violent charge. The MHC appeared to reduce recidivism by 26% total and violent recidivism by 55% at the 18-month mark. Graduate effect was more striking. **Mental Health Measures:** None.	Study notes that while propensity weighting scores can construct an approximately equal sample in both cases, it can only do so on observables. Unobservables (willingness to accept treatment) may still cause selection bias. Study reinforces the idea that MHC benefit is more easily recognized after both completion of the MHC and longer time frames.

court to these positive outcomes. In some studies mental health outcomes were not evaluated. In others there was a weak or no effect, even when the criminal justice outcomes were affected (as in the Broward evaluations). Good cost data to evaluate the cost-effectiveness of this set of interventions is essentially absent.

4.4.2   Voluntary and Involuntary Community Treatment

By voluntary treatment we have in mind the typical client-provider relationship in which treatment is sought freely by the client, who may terminate treatment at any time, and symmetrically, the provider is under no obligation other than due to normal professional responsibility, to treat the client. Access to public and private mental health care is restricted by nonprice rationing, such as capacity constraints. Relaxation of these constraints will lead to more use, and possibly reduction in criminal justice costs. Expansion of access to voluntary treatment for mental health care is generally not done for the purpose of affecting the criminal justice system. Any such offset would be a kind of bonus over and above the main purpose of providing good mental health care to those who need it.

Two studies of the introduction of managed mental health care in King County (Seattle), Washington, investigate how an exogenous shift in the availability of community-based mental health services affects jail use.[26] For Medicaid enrollees in 1995, a prospective payment system replaced a fee-for-service payment system to community-based mental health care providers in Seattle, giving them new incentives to manage care. Managed care introduces an incentive to providers to reduce costs and even to "cost shift" care of persons with mental illness to other sectors, such as jails. The authors posit this incentive may affect jail use: "If managed care worsens access to adequate mental health treatment and resulting worsened mental health status leads to more criminal offenses, then jail detentions should increase" (Norton et al. 2006, 720).

Outpatient mental health costs fell after the introduction of managed care, and according to the analysis in Domino et al. (2004) of about 40,000 Medicaid enrollees, in which non-Medicaid enrollees were used as a control group, managed mental health care resulted in a 5 percent increase in the likelihood of jail for a typical Medicaid enrollee (on a base rate of about 3 percentage points). In a subsequent analysis of a subset of 6,800 persons who were likely to be severely mentally ill, however, the authors found no effect of managed care on the likelihood of jail (Norton et al. 2006).[27]

Involuntary outpatient commitment, sometimes euphemistically referred to as "assisted outpatient commitment" is a form of civil commitment for

---

26. Domino et al. (2004) and Norton et al. (2006) are essentially the same research team.
27. The statistical methods of the two studies are quite different (two-part model versus Markov model), leaving it unclear how to understand the different findings of the two studies.

persons with mental illness modeled on earlier civil commitment to inpatient care. Under involuntary outpatient commitment laws, a court determines that a person is remanded to care of the mental health system. The subject is obliged to get care and the system is obliged to give it to him.[28] Patient noncompliance can result in transport to an inpatient facility to be evaluated for an involuntary inpatient admission. The impression patients have that they are required to comply with treatment is probably more powerful than any actual legal sanction (Borum et al. 1999). Maximum available sanctions are not always employed. More than forty states have some provision for outpatient commitment, and although the primary legislative intention behind assisted commitment is to convince noncompliant but needy patients to get treatment, outpatient commitment is probably the most prevalent policy with the potential for using the mental health system to avoid crime and criminal justice costs. Outpatient commitment can be evaluated from numerous perspectives, its ethical principles, the experience of coercion, improvements in mental health, as well as its impact on criminal justice (Monahan 2008; Swartz et al. 2002).

The Duke Mental Health Study (Swartz et al. 2001) recruited 331 persons committed by a court in North Carolina to community treatment, and randomly assigned about half of these to be released from the orders. Both groups had access to enhanced mental health care, so the randomization is associated with mandating, not the availability of services. A reduction in arrests was associated with more seriously ill among those whose commitment was extended compared to those whose original commitment was not extended (Swanson et al. 2001). The experimental versus control group found no significant differences in arrests.

New York State (NYS) established an outpatient commitment law (Chapter 408 of the Laws of 1999) known as Kendra's Law, named after a young woman pushed in front of a subway train in New York City by a man with serious mental illness. New York State evaluated the law itself (New York State Office of Mental Health 2005), and commissioned an independent evaluation (Swartz et al. 2009). In addition, researchers have studied the law's impact (Phelan et al. 2010).

New York State created strict criteria for a person to be eligible for assisted outpatient treatment (AOT) including illness, dangerousness, noncompliance history, and likelihood of benefiting from AOT (Swanson et al. 2009). By December 2004, 3,493 had received court-ordered treatment through AOT. New York State's evaluation used a pre-post design and showed very large favorable changes comparing the six-month period prior to AOT assignment to the months afterward. Rates of incarceration fell from 23 percent before to 3 percent during AOT (New York State Office of Mental

---

28. Mandated or involuntary treatment can commit the client to go to care, the provider to supply care, or both. See Sinaiko and McGuire (2006) for discussion and classification.

Health 2005, 18). Arrests fell from 30 percent to 5 percent; psychiatric hospitalization from 97 to 22 percent; homelessness from 19 percent to 5 percent. In the NYS evaluation, AOT assignment is catching individuals at a time of crisis, and they are likely to have improved in any case without AOT.

Phelan et al. (2010) compared 76 individuals assigned to AOT with 108 patients recently discharged from a psychiatric hospital. Matching via propensity scores he found the AOT group had significantly lower rates of suicide risk, serious violent behavior, and better illness-related social functioning. Interestingly, the AOT group reported less subjective coercion associated with treatment compared to the non-AOT group. This matched, cross-sectional, post design relies heavily on the ability to find comparable patients to those assigned to AOT.

Involuntary outpatient commitment shows some promise in improving both mental health and reducing crime. Costs, however, have not yet been systematically studied, and the key question of how the costs of enhanced outpatient treatment stack up against any savings in criminal justice has not yet been answered.[29]

4.5 Conclusion

As others have argued, persons who are severely mentally ill should be offered treatment, independently of any social externalities that might flow to others (Monahan and Appelbaum 2000). This chapter bears on whether extra priority ought to be put on services for persons with mental illness who also commit crimes, in terms of providing these individuals better access, more extensive treatment, or even in terms of imposing sanctions against not adhering to treatment. The potential spillover benefits—less crime, lower criminal justice costs—are experienced by others, not the patient, implying the patient would put little weight on them in deciding about treatment, and creating the classic externality rationale for special subsidy or quantity targets.

The correlation between serious mental illness and crime, especially based on criminal justice-involved samples, lends curb appeal to the case for special priority. Time-series data are also highly suggestive of a close connection between mental illness and the way we manage it and crime. Frank and Glied (2006) tracked the living arrangements of persons with serious and persistent mental illness (SPMI) over the fifty years between 1950 and 2000. Deinstitutionalization reduced the percent of persons with SPMI in

29. Ongoing research on Kendra's Law will address this issue. The costs of enhanced services for criminal offenders through involuntary treatment generally fall on the public mental health system. If this system is capacity constrained, the cost will be manifest as other patients not getting treatment. See Sinaiko and McGuire (2006) for discussion, and Swanson, Van Dorn, Swartz et al. (2010) for evidence that in the early phase of the implementation of Kendra's Law, there was some "crowd-out" effect.

psychiatric hospitals from 23 percent to 7 percent over this period; during the same period, the percent of persons with SPMI residing in jails and prisons went from 1 percent to 5 percent.[30] These associations do not, of course, amount to a sound case for elevated priority.

Researchers do find some convincing causal connection between mental illness and crime, but it is not large, and it is specific to certain groups of patients at certain stages of their illness. The case for broad-based expansion of mental health prevention or treatment would need to rest on grounds other than crime reduction. We identified some potential areas for effective care targeted to high-risk groups, youth offenders with conduct disorders, and adults with serious mental illness. Some criminal justice offsets seem to follow enhanced mental health services for these groups.

The strength of the evidence for positive spillover is not overwhelming. Two recent reviews came to similar conclusions about the limited role of crime-related arguments for putting more resources into mental health care. Skeem, Manchak, and Peterson (2009) conclude that while "theoretically, effective psychiatric treatment would reduce recidivism for the subgroup of offenders for whom mental illness has a direct effect on criminal behavior," there is no evidence to date "that insufficient psychiatric treatment causes criminal justice involvement for this population" (16). Fisher, Silver, and Wolff (2006), referring to the high prevalence of persons with mental illness in the criminal justice system: ". . . targeting mental health treatment services as 'the' problem and 'the' solution is . . . likely ineffective as a means of addressing this issue" (548).

The evidence on criminal justice impacts needs to be understood within the context of the package of social needs and deficits bearing on this group. Among disadvantaged populations with elevated rates of crime, homelessness, welfare, and poverty, effective mental health care produces joint products, better mental health, and better social functioning, including less crime and its associated costs. To judge the value in relation to cost of mental health care, it is insufficient to track just one of the potential joint products and compare value in this one sphere to the costs. Although the interventions reviewed here have in common that they seek to improve mental health and functioning as well as impact criminal justice, the scope of each type of program, and the need to take into account a range of factors, differs across intervention types.

The most focused intervention we covered is the mental health court. These courts are adjuncts to the criminal justice system, and their costs and benefits are directed primarily to criminal justice considerations. Rigorous evaluation of mental health courts are lacking, in spite of the years of experience in many jurisdictions with the courts. Cost data are particularly needed.

---

30. As Frank and Glied point out, the increasing incarceration rates in the 1980s and 1990s swept up larger portions of criminals in the net, including those with mental illness.

Comparison of the full social cost of crime, criminal justice, court operation, and the mental health system will lead to an accounting of a sufficient
set of effects to make a determination of the net value of this policy. Based
on the evidence available to date, it seems unlikely that any effect of mental
health courts is mediated through improvement in the mental health of the
offenders under supervision. If this turns out to be correct, it may suggest
ways to economize on mental health treatment per se, and make an effort to
identify the active ingredient in the mental health court.

Involuntary outpatient treatment is more complex for purposes of evaluation than mental health courts. Involuntary treatment can be targeted to
the set of patients/offenders who are most likely to benefit from treatment
both from a clinical as well as a criminal justice standpoint. The criminal
justice/mental health cost-effectiveness of this policy is important, but it is
only one piece of the set of information needed to conduct a social evaluation. Cost-effectiveness is ill suited to valuing the subjective and ethical
social costs of coercion associated with involuntary treatment. In practice,
those committed to involuntary treatment seem only mildly bothered by the
coercion, but this finding does not fully answer the ethical question about
whether society should be forcing mental health care.

Appendix

Table 4A.1   Basic model estimates from CPES analysis

Ever arrested	Coef.	t	$|p|$
Male	.265	18.10	0.000
Age < 25	.043	1.87	0.064
Age 25–24	.095	3.79	0.000
Age 35–44	.089	4.61	0.000
Age 45–54	.045	2.15	0.034
ASIAN	−.093	−1.52	0.133
AFR	.139	10.45	0.000
HISP	.104	4.49	0.000
RACEOTHER	.083	2.03	0.045
Severe MI	.155	4.74	0.000
SA	.362	8.96	0.000
SevereMI*SA	−.291	−2.48	0.015
Constant	.063	4.22	0.000

Note: Omitted categories: female, age 55+, white race.
Number of obs = 10686; F (12, 85) = 115.68; Prob > F = 0.0000; R^2 = 0.1387

References

Alegría, M., D. Takeuchi, G. Canino, N. Duan, P. Shrout, X. L. Meng, W. Vega, et al. 2004. "Considering Context, Place and Culture: the National Latino and Asian American Study." *International Journal of Methods in Psychiatric Research* 13 (4): 208–20.

Allen, M., and V. F. Smith. 2001. "Opening Pandora's Box: the Practical and Legal Dangers of Involuntary Outpatient Commitment." *Psychiatric Services* 52 (3): 342–46.

Aos, S., and R. Barnoski. 1998. *Watching the Bottom Line: Cost Effective Interventions for Reducing Crime in Washington.* Report (January). Olympia, WA: Washington State Institute for Public Policy. http://www.wsipp.wa.gov/rptfiles/98-01 -1201.pdf.

Aos, S., R. Lieb, J. Mayfield, M. Miller, and A. Pennucci. 2004. *Benefits and Costs of Prevention and Early Intervention Programs for Youth.* Report (July). Olympia, WA: Washington State Institute for Public Policy. http://www.wsipp.wa.gov/ rptfiles/04-07-3901.pdf.

Aos, S., P. Phipps, R. Barnoski, and R. Lieb. 2001. *The Comparative Costs and Benefits of Programs to Reduce Crime.* Report (May). Olympia, WA: Washington State Institute for Public Policy. http://www.wsipp.wa.gov/rptfiles/costbenefit.pdf.

Applebaum, P. S., P. C. Robbins, and J. Monahan. 2000. "Violence and Delusions: Data from the MacArthur Violence Risk Assessment Study." *American Journal of Psychiatry* 157 (4): 566–72.

Ascher-Svanum, H., D. E. Faries, B. Zhu, F. R. Ernst, M. S. Swartz, and J. W. Swanson. 2006. "Medication Adherence and Long-Term Functional Outcomes in the Treatment of Schizophrenia in Usual Care." *Journal of Clinical Psychiatry* 67 (3): 453–60.

Baillargeon, J., I. A. Binswanger, J. V. Penn, B. A. Williams, and O. J. Murray. 2009. "Psychiatric Disorders and Repeat Incarcerations: The Revolving Prison Door." *American Journal of Psychiatry* 166 (1): 103–09.

Bernstein, R., and T. Seltzer. 2003. "Criminalization of People With Mental Illness: the Role of Mental Health Courts in System Reform." University of the District of Columbia Law Review http://www.bazelon.org/LinkClick.aspx?fileticket =QlgULLAWqBY%3d&tabid=222.

Bonta, J., M. Law, and C. Hanson. 1998. "The Prediction of Criminal and Violent Recidivism Among Mentally Disordered Offenders: A Meta Analysis." *Psychological Bulletin* 123 (2): 123–42.

Boothroyd, R. A., C. C. Mercado, N. G. Poythress, A. Christy, and J. Petrila. 2005. "Clinical Outcomes of Defendants in Mental Health Court." *Psychiatric Services* 56 (7): 829–34.

Borum, R., M. S. Swartz, S. R. Riley, and J. W. Swanson. 1999. "Consumer Perceptions of Involuntary Outpatient Commitment." *Psychiatric Services* 50 (11): 1489–91.

Brestan, E. V., and S. M. Eyberg. 1998. "Effective Psychosocial Treatment of Conduct Disordered Children and Adolescents: 29 years 82 studies and 5,272 kids." *Journal of Clinical Child Psychology* 27 (2): 180–9.

Christy, A., N. G. Poythress, R. A. Boothroyd, J. Petrila, and S. Mehra. 2005. "Evaluating the Efficiency and Community Safety Goals of the Broward County Mental Health Court." *Behavioral Sciences and the Law* 23 (2): 227–43.

Clark, J. 2004. *Non-Specialty First Appearance Court Models for Diverting Persons with Mental Illness: Alternatives to Mental Health Courts.* Report from National

GAINS Center, U.S. Department of Health and Human Services. Delmar, NY: Technical Assistance and Policy Analysis Center for Jail Diversion.

Conduct Problems Prevention Research Group. 1992. "A Developmental and Clinical Model for the Prevention of Conduct Disorders: The FAST Track Program." *Development and Psychopathology* 4 (4): 509–27.

Cosden, M., J. K. Ellens, J. L. Schnell, Y. Yamini-Diouf, and M. M. Wolfe. 2003. "Evaluation of a Mental Health Treatment Court with Assertive Community Treatment." *Behavioral Sciences and the Law* 21 (4): 415–27.

Council of State Governments. 2009. *Criminal Justice/Mental Health Consensus Project.* http://consensusproject.org/.

Cunha, F., and J. J. Heckman. 2007. "Technology and Skill Formation." *American Economic Review* 97 (2): 31–47.

Currie, J., and M. Stabile. 2006. "Child Mental Health and Human Capital Accumulation: The Case of ADHD." *Journal of Health Economics* 25 (6): 1094–118.

———. 2007. "Mental Health in Childhood and Human Capital." NBER Working Paper no. 13217. Cambridge, MA: National Bureau of Economic Research, July.

Department of Health and Human Services (DHHS). 1999. "Children and Mental Health." In *Mental Health: A Report of the Surgeon General.* Washington, DC: U.S. Government Printing Office. http://www.surgeongeneral.gov/library/mentalhealth/toc.html#chapter3.

Domino, M. E., E. C. Norton, J. P. Morrissey, and N. Thakur. 2004. "Cost Shifting to Jails After a Change to Managed Mental Health Care." *Health Services Research* 39 (5): 1379–401.

Farmer, E. M., S. N. Compton, B. J. Burns, and E. Robertson. 2002. "Review of Evidence Base for Treatment of Childhood Psychopathology: Externalizing Disorders." *Journal of Consulting and Clinical Psychology* 70 (6): 1267–302.

Fergusson, D. M., L. J. Horwood, and E. M. Ridder. 2005. "Show Me the Child at Seven: The Consequences of Conduct Problems in Childhood for Psychosocial Functioning in Adulthood." *Journal of Child Psychology and Psychiatry* 46 (8): 837–49.

Fisher, W., E. Silver, and N. Wolff. 2006. "Beyond Criminalization: Toward a Criminologically Informed Framework for Mental Health Policy and Services Research." *Administration and Policy in Mental Health* 33 (5): 544–57.

Fletcher, J., and B. Wolfe. 2009. "Long-Term Consequences of Childhood ADHD on Criminal Activities." *The Journal of Mental Health Policy and Economics* 12 (3): 119–38.

Foster, E. M., D. E. Jones, and the Conduct Problems Prevention Research Group. 2005. "The Economic Analysis of Prevention: An Illustration Involving the Fast Track Project." Pennsylvania State University, The Methodology Center. Working Paper.

Frank, R. G., and S. Glied. 2006. *Better But Not Well: Mental Health Policy in the United States Since 1950.* Baltimore, MD: Johns Hopkins University Press.

Friedman, R. A. 2006. "Violence and Mental Illness—How strong is the link?" *New England Journal of Medicine* 355 (20): 2064–6.

Goldkamp, J. S., and C. Irons-Guynn. 2000. *Emerging Judicial Strategies for the Mentally Ill in the Criminal Caseload: Mental Health Courts in Ft. Lauderdale, Seattle, San Bernardino, and Anchorage.* Bureau of Justice Assistance Monograph NCJ 182504. Washington, DC: Office of Justice Programs, US Department of Justice.

Griffin, P. A., H. J. Steadman, and J. Petrila. 2002. "The Use of Criminal Charges and Sanctions in Mental Health Courts." *Psychiatric Services* 53 (10): 1285–89.

Harry, B., and H. J. Steadman. 1988. "Arrest Rates of Patients Treated at a Community Mental Health Center." *Hospital Community Psychiatry* 39 (8): 862–6.

Heckman, J. J., and D. V. Masterov. 2004. "The Productivity Argument for Investing in Young Children." Technical Report Working Paper no. 5. Washington, DC: Committee on Economic Development.

Herinckx, H. A., S. C. Swart, S. M. Ama, C. D. Dolezal, and S. King. 2005. "Rearrest and Linkage to Mental Health Services Among Clients of the Clark County Mental Health Court Program." *Psychiatric Services* 56 (7): 853–58.

Hodgins, S. 1992. "Mental Disorder, Intellectual Deficiency and Crime." *Archives of General Psychiatry* 49 (6): 476–83.

Institute of Medicine (IOM). 2009. *Preventing Mental, Emotional and Behavioral Disorders Among Young People.* Washington, DC: National Academies Press.

Jackson, J., M. Torres, C. Caldwell, H. W. Neighbors, R. M. Nesse, R. J. Taylor, S. J. Trierweiler, and D. R. Williams. 2004. "The National Survey of American Life: A Study of Racial, Ethnic and Cultural Influences on Mental Disorders and Mental Health." *International Journal of Methods in Psychiatric Research* 13 (4): 196–207.

Junginger, J., K. Claypoole, R. Larygo, and A. Cristiani. 2006. "Effects of Serious Mental Illness and Substance Abuse on Criminal Offenses." *Psychiatric Services* 57 (6): 879–82.

Kazdin, A. E. 2002. "Psychosocial Treatments for Conduct Disorder in Children and Adolescents." In *A Guide to Treatments That Work,* 2nd ed. Edited by P. E. Nathan and J. M. Gorman, 57–86. New York: Oxford University Press.

Kessler, R. C., P. Berglund, O. Demler, R. Jin, K. R. Merikangas, and E. E. Walters. 2005. "Lifetime Prevalence and Age of Onset Distributions of *DSM IV* Disorders in the National Comorbidity Survey Replication." *Archives of General Psychiatry* 62 (6): 593–602.

Kessler, R. C., O. Demler, R. G. Frank, M. Olfson, A. Pincus, E. Walters, P. Wang, K. B. Wells, and A. Zaslavsky. 2005. "Prevalence and Treatment of Mental Disorders: 1990 to 2003." *New England Journal of Medicine* 352 (24): 2515–23.

Kessler, R., and K. Merikangas. 2004. "The National Comorbidity Survey Replication (NCS-R)." *International Journal of Methods in Psychiatric Research* 13 (2): 60–8.

Link, B. G., H. Andrews, and F. T. Cullen. 1992. "The Violent and Illegal Behavior of Mental Patients Reconsidered." *American Sociological Review* 57 (3): 275–92.

Marcotte, D. E., and S. Markowitz. 2009. "A Cure for Crime? Psycho-Pharmaceuticals and Crime Trends." NBER Working Paper no. 15354. Cambridge, MA: National Bureau of Economic Research, September.

McNiel, D. E., and R. J. Binder. 2007. "Effectiveness of a Mental Health Court in Reducing Criminal Recidivism and Violence." *American Journal of Psychiatry* 164 (9): 1395–403.

Modestin, J., and R. Ammann. 1996. "Mental Disorder and Criminality: Male Schizophrenia." *Schizophrenia Bulletin* 22 (1): 69–82.

Moffit, T. E. 1993. "Adolescent Limited Life Course Persistent Anti-social Behavior: A Developmental Taxonomy." *Psychological Review* 100 (4): 674–701.

Monahan, J. 1973. "The Psychiatrization of Criminal Behavior: A Reply." *Hospital and Community Psychiatry* 24 (2): 105–7.

———. 2008. "Mandated Community Treatment: Applying Leverage to Achieve Adherence." *Journal of the American Academy of Psychiatry and Law* 36 (3): 282–5.

Monahan, J., and P. Appelbaum. 2000. "Reducing Violence Risk: Diagnostically Based Clues from the MacArthur Violence Risk Assessment Study." In *Effective*

Prevention of Crime and Violence Among the Mentally Ill, edited by S. Hodgins, 19–34. Dordrecht, The Netherlands: Kluwer Academic Publishers.

Monahan, J., A. D. Redlich, J. Swanson, P. C. Robbins, P. S. Appelbaum, J. Petrila, H. J. Steadman, M. Swartz, B. Angell, and D. E. McNiel. 2005. "Use of Leverage to Improve Adherence to Psychiatric Treatment in the Community." *Psychiatric Services* 56 (1): 37–44.

Monahan, J., and H. Steadman. 1983. "Crime and Mental Disorder: An Epidemiological Approach." In *Crime and Justice: An Annual Review of Research,* edited by M. Tonry and N. Morris, 145–89. Chicago: University of Chicago Press.

Monahan, J., and H. J. Steadman. 2010. "Extending Violence Reduction Principles to Justice-Involved Persons with Mental Illness." In *Applying Social Science to Reduce Violent Offending,* edited by J. Dvoskin, J. Skeem, R. Novaco, and K. Douglas. New York: Oxford University Press.

Moore, M. E., and V. Aldigé. 2006. "Mental Health Court Outcomes: A Comparison of Re-Arrest and Re-Arrest Severity Between Mental Health Court and Traditional Court Participants." *Law and Human Behavior* 30 (6): 659–74.

Moore, S. 2009. "Mentally Ill Offenders Strain Juvenile System." *The New York Times,* August 10.

Nagin, D. and R. E. Tremblay. 1999. "Trajectories of Boys' Physical Aggression, Opposition and Hyperactivity on the Path to Physically Violent and Non-Violent Juvenile Delinquency." *Child Development* 70 (5): 1181–96.

Naples, M., L. S. Morris, and H. J. Steadman. 2007. "Factors in Disproportionate Representation Among Persons Recommended by Programs and Accepted by Courts for Jail Diversion." *Psychiatric Services* 58 (8): 1095–101.

National Alliance for the Mentally Ill. 2005. "Survey of Mental Health Courts." http://www.mentalhealthcourtsurvey.com/pdfs/Mental_Health_Courts.pdf.

National Institute for Clinical Excellence (NICE). 2006. *Parent Training/Education Programmes in the Management of Children with Conduct Disorder,* TA102 Guidance. London: National Institute for Health and Clinical Excellence.

National Institutes of Mental Health (NIMH) Data Set: Collaborative Psychiatric Epidemiology Survey Program (CPES): Integrated Weights and Sampling Error Codes for Design-based Analysis, 2007.

National Mental Health Association. 1987. *Stigma: A Lack of Awareness and Understanding.* Alexandria, VA: National Mental Health Association.

National Scientific Council on the Developing Child. 2008. "Mental Health Problems in Early Childhood Can Impair Learning and Behavior for Life." Harvard University. Working Paper no. 6. http://www.developingchild.net.

New York State Office of Mental Health (NYSOMH). 2005. *Kendra's Law: Final Report on the Status of Assisted Outpatient Treatment.* http://www.omh.state.ny.us/omhweb/kendra_web/finalreport.

Nock, M. K., A. E. Kazdin, E. Hiripi, and R. C. Kessler. 2006. "Prevalence, Subtypes and Correlates of DSM-IV Conduct Disorder in the National Comorbidity Survey Replication." *Psychological Medicine* 36 (5): 699–710.

Norton, E. C., J. Yoon, M. E. Domino, and J. P. Morrissey. 2006. "Transitions Between the Public Mental Health System and Jail for Persons with Severe Mental Illness: A Markov Analysis." *Health Economics* 15 (7): 719–33.

Petersen, J., J. Skeem, E. Hart, S. Vidal, and F. Keith. 2009. "Typology of Offenders with Mental Disorder: Exploring the Criminalization Hypothesis." Research Presentation, University of California, Irvine. https://webfiles.uci.edu:443/skeem/Downloads.html.

Petrila, J., M. S. Ridgely, and R. Borum. 2003. "Debating Outpatient Commitment: Controversy, Trends and Empirical Data." *Crime and Delinquency* 49 (1): 157–72.

Phelan, J. C., M. Sinkewicz, D. Castille, S. Huz, and B. G. Link. 2010. "Effectiveness and Outcomes of Assisted Outpatient Treatment in New York State." *Psychiatric Services* 61 (2): 137–43.

Poythress, N. G., J. Petrila, A. McGaha, and R. Boothryod. 2002. "Perceived Coercion and Procedural Justice in the Broward Mental Health Court." *International Journal of Law and Psychiatry* 25 (2): 517–33.

Redlich, A. D., H. J. Steadman, J. Monahan, J. Petrila, and P. A. Griffin. 2005. "The Second Generation of Mental Health Courts." *Psychology, Public Policy and Law* 11 (4): 527–38.

Ridgely, M. S., J. Engberg, M. D. Greenberg, S. Turner, C. DeMartini, and J. W. Dembosky. 2007. "Justice, Treatment and Cost: An Evaluation of the Fiscal Impact of the Allegheny County Mental Health Court." *Rand Technical Reports* TR-439. Santa Monica, CA: RAND Corporation.

Rottman, D., and P. Casey. 1999. "Therapeutic Jurisprudence and the Emergence of Problem-solving Courts." *National Institute of Justice Journal* July: 12–9.

Rubin, K., K. Burgess, K. Dwyer, and P. Hastings. 2003. "Predicting Preschoolers' Externalizing Behaviors from Toddler Temperament, Conflict and Maternal Negativity." *Developmental Psychology* 39 (1): 164–76.

Rutter, M., J. Tizard, and K. Whitmore. 1970. *Education, Health and Behavior.* London: Longmans.

Sainsbury Center for Mental Health. 2009. *Childhood Mental Health and Life Chances in Post-war Britain.* London: The Sainsbury Center for Mental Health.

Sinaiko, A. D., and T. G. McGuire. 2006. "Patient Inducement, Provider Priorities, and Resource Allocation in Public Mental Health Systems." *Journal of Health Politics, Policy and Law* 31 (6): 1075 1105.

Skeem, J., S. Manchak, T. Johnson, and B. Gillig. 2008. "Comparing Specialty and Traditional Supervision for Probationers with Mental Illness." University of California, Irvine. https://webfiles.uci.edu:443/skeem/Downloads.html.

Skeem, J. L., S. Manchak, and J. K. Peterson. 2009. "Correctional Policy for Offenders with Mental Illness: Moving Beyond the One-Dimensional focus to Reduce Recidivism." Unpublished manuscript.

Slate, R. N., and W. W. Johnson. 2008. *The Criminalization of Mental Illness: Crisis and Opportunity for the Justice System.* Durham, NC: Carolina Academic Press.

Slobogin, C. 1995. "Therapeutic Jurisprudence: Five Dilemmas to Ponder." *Psychology, Public Policy, and Law* 1 (1): 193–219.

Steadman, H. J., S. Davidson, and C. Brown. 2001. "Mental Health Courts: Their Promise and Unanswered Questions." *Psychiatric Services* 52 (4): 457–58.

Steadman, H. J., A. D. Redlich, P. Griffin, J. Petrila, and J. Monahan. 2005. "From Referral to Disposition: Case Processing in Seven Mental Health Courts." *Behavioral Sciences and the Law* 23 (2): 215–26.

Stueve, A., and B. Link. 1997. "Violence and Psychiatric Disorders: Results from an Epidemiological Study of Young Adults in Israel." *Psychiatric Quarterly* 68 (4): 327–42.

Swanson, J. W., R. Borum, M. S. Wsartz, V. A. Hiday, H. R. Wagner, and B. J. Burns. 2001. "Can Involuntary Outpatient Commitment Reduce Crime Among Persons with Severe Mental Illness?" *Criminal Justice and Behavior* 28 (2): 156–89.

Swanson, J. W., C. E. Holzer III, V. K. Ganju, and R. T. Jono. 1990. "Violence and Psychiatric Disorder in the Community: Evidence from the Epidemiologic Catchment Area Surveys." *Hospital and Community Psychiatry* 41 (7): 761–70.

Swanson, J. W., M. S. Swartz, S. M. Essock, F. C. Osher, H. R. Wagner, L. A. Goodman, S. D. Rosenberg, and K. G. Meador. 2002. "The Social-Environmental Context of Violent Behavior in Persons Treated for Severe Mental Illness." *American Journal of Public Health* 92 (9): 1523–31.

Swanson, J. W., M. S. Swartz, R. A. Van Dorn, E. B. Elbogen, H. R. Wagner, R. A. Rosenheck, T. S. Stroup, J. P. McEvoy, and J. A. Lieberman. 2006. "A National Study of the Violent Behavior in Persons with Schizophrenia." *Archives of General Psychiatry* 63 (5): 490–9.

Swanson, J. W., M. S. Swartz, R. A. Van Dorn, J. Monahan, T. G. McGuire, H. J. Steadman, and P. C. Robbins. 2009. "Racial Disparities in Involuntary Outpatient Commitment: Are They Real?" *Health Affairs* 28 (3): 816–26.

Swanson, J. W., M. S. Swartz, R. A. Van Dorn, J. Volavka, J. Monahan, T. S. Stroup, J. P. McEvoy, H. R. Wagner, E. B. Elbogen, and J. A. Lieberman. 2008. "Comparison of Antipsychotic Medication Effects on Reducing Violence in People with Schizophrenia." *The British Journal of Psychiatry* 193 (1): 37–43.

Swanson, J. W., R. A. Van Dorn, M. S. Swartz, A. M. Cislo, C. M. Wilder, L. L. Moser, A. R. Gilbert, and T. G. McGuire. 2010. "Robbing Peter to Pay Paul: Did New York State's Outpatient Commitment Program Crowd Out Voluntary Service Recipients?" *Psychiatric Services* 61 (10): 988–95.

Swanson, J. W., R. A. Van Dorn, M. A. Swartz, A. Smith, E. B. Elbogen, and J. Monahan. 2008. "Alternative Pathways to Violence in Persons with Schizophrenia: The Role of Childhood Antisocial Behavior Problems." *Law and Human Behavior* 32 (3): 228–40.

Swartz, M. S., J. W. Swanson, V. A. Hiday, H. R. Wagner, B. J. Burns, and R. Borum. 2001. "A Randomized Controlled Trial of Outpatient Commitment in North Carolina." *Psychiatric Services* 52 (3): 325–29.

Swartz, M. S., J. W. Swanson, H. J. Steadman, P. C. Robbins, and J. Monahan. 2009. *New York State Assisted Outpatient Treatment Program Evaluation.* Durham, NC: Duke University School of Medicine.

Swartz, M. S., H. R. Wagner, J. W. Swanson, V. A. Hiday, and B. J. Burns. 2002. "The Perceived Coerciveness of Involuntary Outpatient Commitment: Findings from an Experimental Study." *Journal of the American Academy of Psychiatry and the Law* 30 (2): 207–17.

Teplin, L. A. 1983. "The Criminalization of the Mentally Ill: Speculation in Search of Data." *Psychological Bulletin* 94 (1): 54–67.

———. 1984. "Criminalizing Mental Disorder: The Comparative Arrest Rate of the Mentally Ill." *American Psychologist* 39 (7): 794–803.

———. 1990. "The Prevalence of Severe Mental Disorder Among Male Urban Jail Detainees: Comparison with the Epidemiologic Catchment Area Program." *American Journal of Public Health* 80 (6): 663–9.

Teplin, L. A., G. M. McClelland, K. M. Abram, and D. A. Weiner. 2005. "Crime Victimization in Adults with Severe Mental Illness." *Archives of General Psychiatry* 62 (8): 911–21.

Treatment Advocacy Center. 2009. "Jails and Prisons." Briefing Paper. Arlington, VA: Treatment Advocacy Center. http://www.treatmentadvocacycenter.org/.

Trupin, E., and H. Richards. 2003. "Seattle's Mental Health Courts: Early Indicators of Effectiveness." *International Journal of Law and Psychiatry* 26 (1): 33–53.

Wallace, C., P. E. Mullen, and P. Burgess. 2004. "Criminal Offending in Schizophrenia Over a 25-Year Period Marked by Deinstitutionalization and Increasing Prevalence of Comorbid Substance Use Disorders." *American Journal of Psychiatry* 161 (4): 716–27.

Washington State Institute for Public Policy. 2004. *Outcome Evaluation of Washington State's Research Based Programs for Juvenile Offenders.* Olympia, WA: Washington State Institute for Public Policy.

Watson, A., P. Hanrahan, D. Luchins, and A. Lurigio. 2001. "Mental Health Courts and the Complex Issue of Mentally Ill Offenders." *Psychiatric Services* 52 (4): 477–81.

Wexler, D. B., and B. J. Winick. 1991. "Therapeutic Jurisprudence as a New Approach to Mental Health Law Policy Analysis and Research." *University of Miami Law Review* 45 (5): 979–87.

Wilper, A. P., S. Woolhandler, J. W. Boyd, K. E. Lasser, D. McCormick, D. H. Bor, and D. U. Himmelstein. 2009. "The Health and Health Care of US Prisoners: Results of a Nationwide Survey." *American Journal of Public Health* 99 (4): 666–72.

Wolff, N. 2002. "Courts as Therapeutic Agents: Thinking Past the Novelty of Mental Health Courts." *Journal of the American Academy of Psychiatry and the Law* 30 (3): 431–7.

Wolff, N., C. L. Blitz, and J. Shi. 2007. "Rates of Sexual Victimization in Prison for Inmates With and Without Mental Disorders." *Psychiatric Services* 58 (8): 1087–94.

Comment   Jeffrey Swanson

The link between mental illness and crime, and whether interventions for one may affect the other, remain challenging topics for research and public policy. Frank and McGuire elucidate key conceptual issues, take stock of relevant literatures, and point the way toward needed future research at the interface of the mental health and criminal justice systems. They also make an important empirical contribution in their own right, offering fresh data analyses to quantify the role of youthful antisocial conduct in later criminal justice contacts, and the net association of mental illness and substance abuse with adults' lifetime probabilities of arrest. Still, their chapter provokes reflection on whether *any* attempt to make broad, general statements about the impact of mental illness and its treatment on crime is bound to come up short.

At the outset, Frank and McGuire distill a complex set of problems into a simple, and seemingly testable, syllogism: If *(a) mental illness causes crime, and (b) mental health treatment reduces mental illness, then (c) mental health treatment reduces crime.* Given evidence for these crisp propositions, the policy implication would clearly follow: *to reduce crime in society, we must increase access to mental health treatment.* In particular, Frank and McGuire entertain the conclusion that people with mental illness who are involved with the criminal justice system should be provided better access, more extensive treatment, and should be subject to sanctions against not adhering to treatment.

Jeffrey Swanson is professor of psychiatry and behavioral sciences at Duke University School of Medicine.

The trouble with the syllogism is not its internal logic but, as Frank and McGuire themselves imply, the elastic meaning of its key external referents—the very subjects and predicates of mental illness, crime, and causation. Serious psychopathology, considered broadly and over the life course, may encompass acute disorders of thought and mood, but also chronic disorders of personality, behavior, and social functioning—even addiction disorders. Crime, for its part, encompasses a vast array of illegal actions that vary widely in their causes and consequences and associated sanctions. And as for the causal arrows between them, over time these tend to run in both directions, take meandering routes, and interact with an untold number of messy variables in the social environment.

That the definitional boundaries of mental illness and crime *overlap* is a semantic problem but hardly a trivial one, insofar as semantics both shape and reflect consequential behavior and interaction—in particular, that of social actors charged with identifying, classifying, controlling, and "treating" deviance. Thus, some illegal behaviors (drug abuse, for example) are also considered pathological, and some psychiatric diagnoses (conduct disorder, for example), may incorporate illegal behaviors as significant indicia. Whether and why particular problems are, in any case, actually *treated* as illnesses, *punished* as crimes, or *controlled* as social threats (or some combination of these) are matters that go beyond the inherent features of behavior; rather, the determination of who gets which interventions may reflect prevailing ideologies and norms; the corresponding organization and financing of social service systems that are designed to uphold such norms and manage those who break them; and, not infrequently, disparities of power and resources and capital in social hierarchies.

More specifically, the intersection of crime and mental illness is a liminal space inhabited by people who could go in either direction—into the mental health service system or into the criminal justice system. In theory, of course, people can receive treatment within the justice system, or justice sanctions within the treatment system. Sometimes involvement in one is used to "leverage" the other; a commitment to enter treatment may be used as a lever to reduce a criminal sentence while, conversely, the threat of a sentence may be used to motivate treatment participation.

The conceptual framework of *therapeutic jurisprudence,* as discussed briefly by Frank and McGuire, represents a set of theoretically driven policies that combine treatment with sanctions. Still, at their core, criminal and mental health interventions remain distinct; they serve different basic purposes, for largely distinct populations, and need to be targeted appropriately. This complicates Frank and McGuire's implicit argument that mental health treatment should substitute wholesale for incarceration of people with serious mental disorders.

Frank and McGuire might have considered several alternative syllogisms, which comprise somewhat more complex but relevant hypotheses about the effects of both criminal justice and mental interventions:

Syllogism 1: If (a) some crimes committed by persons with mental illness are not caused by mental illness, and (b) mental health treatment does not reduce other causes of crime, then (c) mental health treatment does not reduce all crimes committed by persons with mental illness.

Syllogism 2: If (a) incarceration prevents crime directly by incapacitating people who would otherwise commit crimes, and (b) some people with mental illness are inclined to commit crimes and are incarcerated, then (c) incarceration prevents crime in some people with mental illness.

Syllogism 3: If (a) the threat of incarceration deters crime in rational actors, and (b) some persons with serious mental illness who commit crimes are not rational actors, then (c) threat of incarceration does not deter crime in all persons with serious mental illness.

To illustrate, consider a person diagnosed with schizophrenia who commits minor crimes (such as trespassing or disturbing the peace) because she is cognitively impaired, addicted to alcohol, homeless, and wandering the street. Arresting and incarcerating such an individual would serve the immediate interest of public safety by incapacitating a person who might otherwise continue to commit minor crimes. However, there is little reason to expect that, without treatment, any threat of future incarceration would deter such a person from committing the same sorts of crimes upon reentering the community. Alternatively, in such a case, involuntary hospitalization followed by outpatient commitment would serve an equivalent public safety function while also providing treatment, which, in turn, should reduce the likelihood of future crime stemming from the person's acute mental illness and addiction; such is the basic idea underlying many jail diversion programs for justice-involved people with serious mental illness and substance abuse comorbidities. For this clinical population, then, alternative or leveraged mental health treatment—whether inpatient, outpatient or both—may be seen as a sensible crime-prevention policy.

Now consider the very different case of a person with mental illness who is engaged in a lengthy criminal career that is *not* driven by mental illness, but rather follows on a history of antisocial conduct dating back to childhood. In this case, there is little reason to expect that treatment for acute mental illness *per se* would reduce the person's risk of recidivism; indeed, treatment might conceivably *increase* a person's ability to commit crime more effectively. Sorting out these very different kinds of cases is essential for understanding the nature and scope of the problem of crime and mental illness and, ultimately, deciding what to do about them.

There are several ways to think about the scope of the problem of mental illness and crime in society. First, from a broad, longitudinal, social-epidemiological point of view, we would operationally define what counts as mental illness, what counts as crime, and assess their unique and overlapping prevalence in the total population. We would also examine a range of covarying risk factors in relevant domains, assess which comes first in any given case—mental illness or crime—and consider the possible causal role of each in determining the other. Second, from a mental health services and policy point of view, we would start with psychiatric patients—those receiving treatment in various settings—and examine the extent to which antisocial behavior and criminal involvement occur among these patients. And from a criminal justice point of view, we would start with criminal offenders—people who have been arrested, are incarcerated, on probation, or parole—and examine the occurrence of mental illness in these populations.

With respect to the scope of the problem of *mental illness within the justice system,* Frank and McGuire allude to the argument that big city jails have become the new asylums—a tragic testament to the failures of deinstitutionalization and the ill-fated community mental health care system. They cite an estimate by the Treatment Advocacy Center that 1,400 mentally ill individuals inhabit the Los Angeles County Jail on any given day. This appears to be a very large number, but the broader context is that there are between 5,000 and 7,000 inmates in the Los Angeles County Jail population—the largest in the country—and that these are among 2.4 million incarcerated individuals in the United States (Bureau of Justice Statistics 2010).

Even if *all* the people with serious mental illness were released from criminal justice institutions, there would still remain close to two million people in jails and prisons in the United States, which has the highest rate of incarceration among its peer countries. This means that public mental health policy can expect to have only a small impact effect on the overall problem of crime, even if it were to succeed at expanding treatment to people with mental illness, and even assuming that "mental illness causes [some] crime" and "treatment works."

Violent behavior toward others is perhaps the most troubling type of crime and the most closely associated with mental illness in the public mind. And yet the best available data from the United States suggest that only three to five percent of violence acts are attributable to serious mental illness (Swanson 1994).

To ask the question the other way, what is the scope of the problem of *crime and criminal justice involvement in the population with serious mental illness*? Frank and McGuire answer this in their new data analysis mainly by focusing on the overall lifetime arrest rate of people with serious mental illness. This analysis unavoidably combines in a single index vastly different types of illegal behavior, and mixes together those where crime preceded mental illness and vice versa. While a valid gauge of the magnitude of criminal justice involvement, the measure is too blunt to tell us precisely what criminal justice involvement actually means in this population, or what should be done about it. A previous study of patterns of arrest among people with serious mental illness in North Carolina found that 20 percent were arrested over a period of twelve months. However, serious violent crimes accounted for only 10 percent of the arrests, while the vast majority were for so-called "nuisance crimes," such as trespassing or disturbing the peace, and offenses related to substance abuse (Swanson et al. 1999).

Clark, Ricketts, and McHugo (1999) studied patterns and costs of criminal justice involvement among people with co-occurring serious mental illness and substance abuse problems. These researchers found that over a three-year period, 83 percent of the sample had some involvement with law enforcement, but only 44 percent were officially arrested. Two-thirds of the arrests were for minor offenses. The study participants were four times more likely to have a police encounter that did not result in arrest than to be arrested and booked for a crime. Many times police were involved as an ersatz ambulance service, transporting patients in a psychiatric crisis to an emergency treatment facility—with the trappings of criminal arrest. (When we look at crime and mental illness in the United States, are we observing the intersection of illness and illegal behavior *per se,* or are we seeing the peculiarities of our own sometimes dysfunctional public systems of care and crime control, and how they are organized and financed?)

Substance abuse is perhaps the most important single factor that distinguishes justice-involved people with mental illness from their counterparts without criminal involvement. Thus, taking stock of substance abuse comorbidity is central both to understanding the scope of the problem of crime and mental illness, and to designing effective policy solutions. But again, people with comorbid substance abuse are a clinically heterogeneous population. There are several alternative pathways by which substance abuse can, in conjunction with mental illness, influence crime. First, mental illness is associated with increased primary risk for substance abuse; this may be due to common heritable or social-environmental risk factors, or it may reflect self-medication for psychic pain. Substance abuse often involves acquiring and possessing illegal substances, but this may or may not precipitate criminal justice involvement.

Several potential causal pathways may link substance use disorders to violence in persons with a serious mental illness such as schizophrenia. First, acute pharmacological effects of alcohol and certain drugs such as cocaine can increase violence risk; this is true in persons with or without serious mental illness. In patients with underlying mental illness, however, pharmacological effects of alcohol and other substances may increase inherent violence risk by exacerbating psychiatric symptoms. Specifically, violence may become much more likely when substance abuse is added to the mix of impaired impulse control and symptoms such as hostility, threat perception, grandiosity, and dysphoria. Substance use disorders are also associated with treatment nonadherence, which is well-known to elevate the risk for violence in outpatients with serious mental illness.

To sum up, Frank and McGuire have made an important new contribution—both conceptually and empirically—to understanding the ways in which mental health treatment may affect criminal justice outcomes. Going forward, it is important to continue to specify and refine the evidence for effectiveness of policy and interventions to reduce the multilayered problems of crime and mental illness. Outcomes *for whom*? Who are the target populations for *which* interventions? People who commit crimes and people who suffer from mental illnesses represent overlapping and heterogeneous populations. Criminal behavior and mental illness are multidetermined phenomena—to some extent endogenous—but with some common, and some unique exogenous predictors. Our conceptual models and our research inquiries into how these problems emerge and may tumble over each other, as well as our solutions to address them as such—together and separately—need to be equally nuanced and subtle.

References

Bureau of Justice Statistics, accessed April 18, 2010, http://www.ojp.usdoj.gov/bjs.
Clark, R. E., S. K. Ricketts, and G. J. McHugo. 1999. "Legal System Involvement and Costs for Persons in Treatment for Severe Mental Illness and Substance Use Disorders." *Psychiatric Services* 50 (5): 641–47.
Swanson, J. W. 1994. "Mental Disorder, Substance Abuse, and Community Violence: An Epidemiological Approach." In *Violence and Mental Disorder,* edited by J. Monahan and H. Steadman, 101–36. Chicago: University of Chicago Press.
Swanson, J. W., R. Borum, M. S. Swartz, and V. A. Hiday. 1999. "Violent Behavior Preceding Hospitalization among Persons with Severe Mental Illness." *Law & Human Behavior* 23 (2): 185–204.

II

Regulation of Criminal Opportunities and Criminogenic Commodities

5

Rethinking America's Illegal Drug Policy

John J. Donohue III, Benjamin Ewing, and David Peloquin

5.1 Introduction

The United States stands out among developed nations for both its extremely punitive illegal drug policy and the high percentages of its population that have consumed banned substances—particularly marijuana and cocaine. The war against the millions of Americans who use and sell these drugs has cost taxpayers billions of dollars each year and contributed substantially to America's globally unmatched incarceration rate (Walmsley 2009).[1] Yet it has failed to displace America from among the world leaders in use rates for illegal drugs, even if escalating punitiveness may have contributed to declines in US drug consumption from its peaks in the late 1970s and 1980s.

To locate America's illegal drug policy globally and along a spectrum of potential alternatives, it is helpful to consider three broad approaches governments may take toward drugs: (a) legalization—a system in which possession and sale are lawful but subject to regulation and taxation (US policy for alcohol and tobacco);[2] (b) criminalization—a system of proscriptions on

John J. Donohue III is professor of law at Stanford Law School, and a research associate of the National Bureau of Economic Research. Benjamin Ewing is a student at Yale Law School. David Peloquin is a student at Yale Law School.

The authors wish to thank Jonathan Caulkins, Phil Cook, Louis Kaplow, Rob MacCoun, Jeffrey Miron, Peter Reuter, and participants at two NBER conferences and the Harvard Law School Law and Economics workshop for valuable comments. We are also particularly grateful to Jeffrey Miron and Angela Dills for sharing their national time series data on drug enforcement and crime.

1. The United States' incarceration rate of 7.56 per 1,000 people is five to ten times the rate in most western and northern European countries.

2. Under our taxonomy, the libertarian ideal espoused by such scholars as Milton Friedman is a subset of legalization in which taxation and regulation would be kept to a minimum.

possession and sale backed by criminal punishment, potentially including incarceration (US policy for marijuana, cocaine, and other illegal drugs); and (c) depenalization—a hybrid system, in which sale and possession are proscribed, but the prohibition on possession is backed only by such sanctions as fines or mandatory substance abuse treatment, not incarceration[3] (US

3. The terms "depenalization" and "decriminalization" have been used in confusing, misleading, and sometimes contradictory ways. The National Research Council (2001, 192) notes: "The term 'decriminalization' has sometimes been misunderstood to refer to 'legalization' (i.e., making drugs available for nonmedical uses, as in the case of alcohol). However, as used by experts in criminal law and popularized by the National Commission on Marijuana and Drug Abuse [NCMDA] in 1972, 'decriminalization' refers to the repeal of criminal sanctions against possession for personal use, even though the drugs remain contraband and commercial access remains prohibited. The erroneous association between decriminalization and legalization has led some commentators to abandon the term in favor of 'depenalization' to refer to these more lenient marijuana laws." Our taxonomy closely tracks the usage adopted by the European Monitoring Centre for Drugs and Drug Addiction (EMCDDA 2005, 12). The EMCDDA uses decriminalization and depenalization in the following ways: "'[D]ecriminalisation' comprises removal of a conduct or activity from the sphere of criminal law. Prohibition remains the rule, but sanctions for use (and its preparatory acts) no longer fall within the framework of the criminal law (elimination of the notion of a criminal offence). This may be reflected either by the imposition of sanctions of a different kind (administrative sanctions without the establishment of a police record—even if certain administrative measures are included in the police record in some countries, such as France), or the abolition of all sanctions. . . . '[D]epenalisation' means relaxation of the penal sanction provided for by law. In the case of drugs, and cannabis in particular, depenalisation generally signifies the elimination of custodial penalties. Prohibition remains the rule, but imprisonment is no longer provided for, even if other penal sanctions may be retained (fines, establishment of a police record, or other penal sanctions)." We use the term depenalization to describe a regime in which possession is punished with sanctions other than incarceration, reserving decriminalization to refer to regimes in which penalties for possession are not just reduced but are entirely removed or diverted from the realm of criminal law.
   In addition to the erroneous association between decriminalization as used by the NCMDA in the drug context and ordinary understandings of legalization, there are two other important reasons for preferring the term depenalization to decriminalization, when describing the general policy of responding to possession with fines and/or treatment rather than incarceration. First, some Western European countries, for example, make much greater use of fines than the United States for a variety of criminal offenses. While fines may strike Americans as noncriminal sanctions, they are routinely used as criminal sanctions in some other countries. (For example, Green [1988] cites a study from the early 1980s finding that in West Germany the fine was used as the sole penalty for three-quarters of property crime offenders and two-thirds of those convicted of assault.) Hence, even if such a country relies primarily—or even exclusively—on fines and treatment to punish possession, one cannot thereby conclude that possession has necessarily been taken out of the system of criminal law. Second, as Suk (2008) notes with the example of employment discrimination law in France, some of those same countries use criminal law as the primary means of addressing behavior that in the United States is handled primarily through tort law. A more expansive domain for criminal law is structurally related to a heavier use of lesser sanctions, such as fines, in the criminal context, and it may also mean that criminal sanctions do not automatically trigger the degree of stigmatization that they imply in the United States. To the extent that criminal sanctions in general carry less of a stigma in some of the countries with less severe punishments for drug offenses, those countries' variations on depenalization appear closer to decriminalization from the perspective of the American system and its use of incarceration as the basic sanction of criminal law.
   One further clarification is in order: in theory, proscription with sanctions other than incarceration could be applied to sale, in addition to possession. However, because the application of depenalization to both possession and sale would essentially yield a system resembling a highly (though peculiarly) regulated legalization, we do not treat the depenalization of posses-

policy toward alcohol during Prohibition).[4] All three of these approaches have been implemented in the practices of various governments around the world, though to greater and lesser extents. Nearly all countries have criminalized a consistent set of proscribed substances including marijuana, cocaine, heroin, and methamphetamine; most have also legalized other drugs such as alcohol and tobacco; and some have adopted policies of depenalization for substances whose sale, and to some degree possession, remains prohibited.[5]

We begin our analysis in section 5.2 by attempting to define America's illegal drug problem, first sketching consumption patterns, current policy, and the social costs of illegal drugs under America's basic regime of criminalization. Because America's illegal drug policies are an integral part of the context in which those costs arise—and many of those costs, such as those associated with incarceration, would not exist but for America's current policies—we consider current policies and social costs in tandem, distinguishing costs that stem from criminalization and costs that flow from psychopharmacological effects of drugs on their users. Following this overview, we focus in section 5.3 on the particular cases of marijuana and cocaine. For both marijuana and cocaine, we analyze three potential regimes—criminalization, depenalization, and legalization. We also address the two most significant sources of social costs from cocaine: crime and incarceration.

Marijuana is the most widely used illegal drug in America (as elsewhere) and the one with the most vocal advocates for legalization. Cocaine has been an especially acute problem in America, with the prevalence of this drug and its derivative, crack, providing the impetus for the escalation of the War on Drugs in the 1980s and Plan Colombia in the 1990s. We restrict our discussion to these two drugs partly because one of our principal contentions is that analysis of illegal drug policy from a perspective of minimizing social costs requires great focus on the varying burdens of individual drugs given their different toxicological and inherent criminogenic effects, and their distinct patterns of consumption and distribution.

---

sion and sale together as a basic regime. Rather, we implicitly relegate such a regime to a subset of legalization and use the term depenalization to refer to depenalization of possession. (In practice, of course, no depenalization of possession is likely to be complete since states and countries generally set quantity caps defining the limits of noncriminal possession as a way to distinguish ordinary users from sellers.)

4. Contrary to popular perception, Kleiman (2006) notes that depenalization was actually America's policy toward alcohol during prohibition. Alcohol prohibition did not target simple possession but rather manufacture, sale, and transportation, and in that sense it was a policy of extreme depenalization. Cook (2007, 19) notes that even when sanctions were imposed for manufacture, sale, or transportation, in practice these sanctions tended to consist of only a small fine.

5. While there is a growing literature examining the experiences of countries and states that have shifted from criminalization to depenalization—whether that depenalization is effected de jure, as in Portugal's decriminalization, or de facto, as in the case of some other European countries—there is a dearth of evidence on shifts from criminalization to legalization.

Under US criminalization of marijuana, a large number of people are arrested and otherwise punished for possession of a substance that is routinely consumed in today's developed world and is—by various expert accounts and along many measures—less dangerous to users and society than cigarettes or alcohol. This policy not only consumes criminal justice resources and crowds out other valuable social spending, it also creates hard-to-quantify costs in other forms: diminished respect for the law, loss of faith in government warnings about the serious dangers posed by more harmful drugs, and a morally arbitrary arrest lottery undermining the principle that like offenders be treated equally. On the other hand, cocaine is substantially more dangerous than marijuana and under criminalization it is much more socially costly in the aggregate, notwithstanding far lower rates of use. The costs of cocaine under criminalization overwhelmingly stem from crime, violence, and incarceration.

The differing nature of the costs of criminalization for marijuana and cocaine is important because it suggests that the effect of a regime change (e.g., from criminalization to depenalization or legalization) would be different for marijuana than for cocaine. Depenalization and legalization could both potentially reduce perhaps the foremost cost of marijuana criminalization: the extremely high number of arrests for possession, and the concomitant burdens they impose on the criminal justice system's resources and individual arrestees—many of whom are otherwise law-abiding.[6] Legalization, to a much greater extent than depenalization, would reduce the costs of black-market violence and lengthy incarceration for sellers that weigh so heavily in the overall costs of cocaine.

On the other hand, economic theory suggests that reductions in sanctions through depenalization or legalization would lower costs both implicit (such as time spent and risk incurred to obtain the drug) and explicit (the per unit dollar price of the drug), and thereby increase demand and use. By more substantially reducing costs and government disapproval, and by potentially enabling advertising, legalization would be expected to lead to higher levels of consumption than under a regime of depenalization. The possible exception to this claim would be if legalization were accompanied by a sufficiently comprehensive taxation regime that would restrain consumption by maintaining a high enough price to the consumer. The psychopharmacological effects of cocaine are markedly more harmful than those of marijuana, and the costs per additional user would be higher for cocaine than marijuana. Moreover, marijuana consumption is much higher than cocaine consumption so the offsetting effect of tax revenues on the social costs of cocaine would be much less significant than for marijuana.

---

6. Depenalization would reduce these costs less than legalization because criminal justice resources would still be used to impose penalties on sellers and even users. The more extreme the depenalization, the greater would be the expected reduction in these costs.

In sum, legalizing cocaine would pose greater risks and offer greater potential rewards than legalizing marijuana: the decreases in certain categories of costs and increases in others would be much more substantial for cocaine than for marijuana.

Not surprisingly, much of the debate over illegal drug policy and potential reforms hinges on two contentious questions. First, by how much would the prevalence and intensity of a drug's use rise under a different regime?[7] Second, would reductions in other social costs—particularly through lower rates of crime and criminal justice enforcement costs—outweigh the costs of increased consumption?

Our nation's experience with alcohol regulation is instructive. During Prohibition—a regime of decriminalization or extreme depenalization—alcohol consumption was suppressed (from higher rates under legalization) to a degree that noticeably lowered the cost of alcohol abuse. These gains, however, appear to have come at a high cost in terms of crime, which fell sharply after Prohibition ended. While criminal gangs no longer cause mayhem over alcohol distribution, alcohol abuse does lead to belligerence and crime as well as many other social costs ranging from impaired productivity and increased motor vehicle deaths to higher levels of child abuse and neglect. The United States has vastly more alcoholics than drug addicts in part because we have allowed a free market coupled with extensive advertising to promote alcohol consumption, with taxation levels that are well below social costs.

Conjectures from some sources that similarly free markets for cocaine could increase today's relatively small number of cocaine addicts to levels beyond the current number of alcoholics are offered in support of the current war on drugs. Opponents counter by pointing to the enormous criminal violence—here and abroad—that this war has generated, as well as the 500,000 incarcerated Americans whose lost freedom and productivity are among the greatest casualties of the war on drugs. The stakes are high for illicit drug policy, yet unfortunately we must continually choose its contours (for maintaining the status quo is itself a choice) with a less than ideal evidentiary base.

Legalization would almost certainly reduce crime, but such a prospective gain must be weighed against the increase in the costs of substance abuse that would likely follow. The murder and violence of illegal drug dealing, and the hundreds of thousands of ruined lives of prison inmates must be assessed against increased motor vehicle deaths and potentially millions of lives impaired by addiction. These are not pretty or easy choices, and to a significant extent the consequences of various drug policy regimes will depend

7. The answer to this question largely depends upon the specifics of the new regime. For example, depenalization could involve a host of different approaches to enforcement, treatment, and civil penalties, while legalization could entail a wide range of policies regarding taxation, product quality regulation, advertising, and possession by minors.

upon the specifics of design and implementation. Our effort here is directed toward clarifying the tradeoffs by exploring, in the contexts of marijuana and cocaine, the question of which regime—and what set of policies within that overarching framework—would minimize the total cost to society.[8]

5.2   Defining America's Illegal Drug Problem

5.2.1   Consumption Patterns

Consumption Across Users

As figure 5.1 reveals, according to the World Health Organization (WHO) World Mental Health Surveys taken in the 2000s, 42 percent of American adults have tried cannabis, more than twice the take-up rate in any of the seventeen countries studied other than New Zealand, which trailed closely behind the United States (Degenhardt et al. 2008).[9] Figure 5.2 illustrates that the percentage of Americans ever consuming cocaine is even more extreme: 16 percent of American adults have tried cocaine, dwarfing the next highest rates of about 4 percent in Colombia, Mexico, Spain, and New Zealand and the under 2 percent rates in other European countries, the Middle East, Africa, and Asia (Degenhardt et al. 2008). As figure 5.7 and figure 5.8 reveal, annual use figures are naturally lower, but the United States also stands near the top in terms of rates of past-year use. Figure 5.3 and figure 5.4 provide comparable data on lifetime use rates of tobacco and alcohol, the two most socially costly legal drugs. While US consumption levels for these legal substances are not low, they stand out less in the global context than US use rates of marijuana and cocaine.[10] If our severe criminalization has been effective at reducing the prevalence of marijuana

8. A complete normative evaluation of drug policy, even one from a largely consequentalist perspective, must necessarily contend with a host of values not amenable to quantification: welfare, liberty, and justice, to name an important few. Despite such limitations, however, a cost-minimization perspective has a clarity and relative simplicity that makes it a useful guide for any normative discussion of illegal drug reform.

9. There are several reasons for treating these statistics with some caution. First, there are many possible metrics for capturing the extent of drug use, and across countries the percentage of people who have tried a drug once may be only loosely correlated with the percentage who have used the drug often or recently. Second, Room et al. (2008, 60) report: "Since [the] methodology in this study was more uniform than in any previous comparison of cannabis use across countries, it would be [sic] appear to be the most authoritative source for such statements. However, there are large discrepancies between the findings reported in Degenhardt et al. and other well known surveys. . . . Consequently, we have not made use of the WMHS data until these discrepancies, which may represent important methodological differences, are accounted for."

10. For alcohol, Degenhardt et al. (2008) indicate that in terms of cumulative use—that is, the percentage of the population that has ever used a given drug—the United States (at 91.6 percent) is within a few points of several West European nations, including Belgium, France, Germany, the Netherlands, and the Ukraine, rather than the clear outlier it is in terms of marijuana and cocaine. Using this same measure for tobacco, the United States has the highest cumulative incidence of use, 73.6 percent, of any nation studied. However, the United States has had dramatic success in decreasing tobacco consumption since 1985: according to World

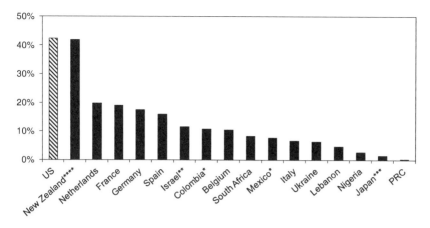

**Fig. 5.1   Percentage reporting use of cannabis in lifetime, population aged 18+,
2001–2005**
Source: Degenhardt et al. (2008, 1057).
*Aged 18–65, **21+, ***20+, ****16+

and cocaine, however, then use rates in the United States are actually markedly lower than they would be were we to follow other countries' examples
and move away from our distinctly punitive approach. One's assessment of
the effectiveness of our illegal drug policy is partly tied to one's assessment
of that counterfactual world.[11]

Health Organization data on regular basis smoking, the United States is far from a leader, with
20 to 29 percent of US men reporting smoking regularly. The analogous percentage is now
higher in most European countries, as well as in China and Russia—where over 60 percent of
men report smoking on a regular basis.

11. If indeed severe sanctions are necessary to keep America's use rates from rising even
higher above those of other countries, it is tempting to conclude that Americans must have a
greater disposition toward recreational drug use. However, in attempting cross-country comparisons of sanctions and use rates, it is important not to lose sight of the broader set of incentives that individuals face. For example, to the extent that potential drug sellers choose among
a set of possible legal and illegal behaviors, the attractiveness of alternative options—including
the quality of social welfare networks, the available legal employment, and the severity of
punishment for other criminal careers—will markedly affect the extent to which each unit of
punishment deters. The United States may need more severe sanctions against drug offenders
than Western European countries to produce comparable degrees of deterrence not only or
simply because Americans have a greater cultural propensity to drug use (although this is possible) but also because alternatives to selling and using are worse in the United States. Lesser
social safety nets and harsher penalties for alternative crimes such as property offenses may
mean that greater punishment is necessary in the United States than in some Western European countries in order to make drug selling less attractive than substitute behaviors. On the
other hand, lower levels of structural unemployment in the United States could militate in the
opposite direction, further complicating the analysis. Thorough analysis of the complex sets
of alternatives that individuals face that impact the deterrent effect of legal sanctions may be
less critical in the drug possession context because drug use and income-producing crimes are
unlikely to be strong substitute behaviors. Still, it is worth remembering that individual users
may choose among broad sets of recreational substances, both legal and illegal, that differ
somewhat across countries.

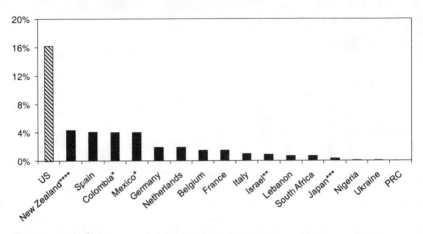

Fig. 5.2   Percentage reporting use of cocaine in lifetime, population aged 18+, 2001–2005
Source: Degenhardt et al. (2008, 1057).
*Aged 18–65, **21+, ***20+, ****16+

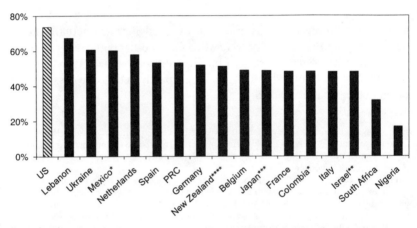

Fig. 5.3   Percentage reporting use of tobacco in lifetime, population aged 18+, 2001–2005
Source: Degenhardt et al. (2008, 1057).
*Aged 18–65, **21+, ***20+, ****16+

A recurring pattern in the distribution of consumption across users holds for a variety of recreational drugs: a small percentage of users account for a large percentage of consumption. This pattern is found for alcohol consumption in the United States (Cook 2007, 57), as well as for cocaine use. For example, one study found that the top 22 percent of users account for 70 percent of cocaine consumption (National Research Council [2001, 60]; see also Rydell and Everingham [1994] finding that heavy cocaine users con-

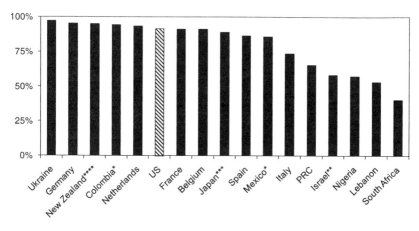

Fig. 5.4   Percentage reporting use of alcohol in lifetime, population aged 18+, 2001–2005
Source: Degenhardt et al. (2008, 1057).
*Aged 18–65, **21+, ***20+, ****16+

sume cocaine at a rate nearly eight times that of light users). The top heaviness of the distribution of cocaine use among consumers is believed to have increased from the early 1980s when consumption was nearly evenly split between light users and heavy users (NRC 2001, 60). Reuter (1999b, 17–8) characterizes cocaine as a "career" rather than an "event," because as they come to appreciate the harmful consequences of the drug, the casual users quit, leaving in place a core of more serious users. Marijuana consumption is concentrated among individuals in their late teens and their twenties. Most consumers use the drug relatively infrequently and for relatively short periods of time (MacCoun and Reuter 2001, 342). Taken as a whole, these drug use distribution patterns suggest that the most severe problems stemming from drug use are concentrated within a relatively small percentage of users.

The National Council on Alcoholism and Drug Dependence (NCADD 2002) relies on a 2001 study by the Schneider Institute for Health Policy at Brandeis University, *Substance Abuse: The Nation's Number One Health Problem,* for the claim that about eighteen million Americans have alcohol problems and five to six million Americans have (illegal) drug problems (SIHP 2001). A similar set of estimates—not of alcoholics and problem users but of abusive or dependent users—comes from the National Survey on Drug Use and Health (NSDUH) from 2007 (Substance Abuse and Mental Health Services Administration 2008). The study found that in 2007, approximately 22.3 million people aged twelve or older had, in the past year, abused or experienced dependence on alcohol, illegal drugs, or both: 15.5 million abused or depended upon alcohol, 3.2 million on alcohol and illegal drugs, and 3.7 million on illegal drugs but not alcohol (SAMHSA 2008, 71).[12]

The NSDUH methodology uses various questions to classify persons as dependent upon or abusing different substances based on the Diagnostic and Statistical Manual of Mental Disorders, 4th edition (DSM-IV). As the report puts it:

> Dependence is considered to be a more severe substance use problem than abuse because it involves the psychological and physiological effects of tolerance and withdrawal. Although individuals may meet the criteria specified here for both dependence and abuse, persons meeting the criteria for both are classified as having dependence, but not abuse. Persons defined with abuse in this report do not meet the criteria for dependence. (SAMHSA 2008, 71)

The plight of drug users who are deemed to be in the thrall of addiction, abuse, or dependence is central to understanding illegal drug policy. Those who advocate maintaining severe criminalization frequently raise the specter of ballooning addiction to make depenalization or legalization seem intolerably reckless.[13] They argue, consistent with the dominant understanding of addiction today as a disease, that once addiction sets in, individuals find themselves caught in a pattern of self-destructive behavior that is nearly impossible to escape. Severe sanctions for use, on this account, offer a strong incentive to avoid initiating the addiction cycle and to get out of it once it begins.

Yet there are fundamental tensions within the viewpoint just described. First, if punitive treatment of users reduces the number of people trying illegal drugs (and perhaps in turn the number who become perpetual users), it may conflict with the aim of providing problem users with the therapeutic treatment they need to wean themselves from drugs. It is not simply that governments with punitive dispositions divert resources that could be used on treatment programs. Punitive criminalization may create

12. The National Survey on Drug Use and Health (NSDUH) is sponsored by the Substance Abuse and Mental Health Services Administration (SAMHSA), which is a part of the Department of Health and Human Services (HHS). The survey itself is carried out by the Research Triangle Institute of North Carolina (RTI). The RTI selects a random sample of households and draws 70,000 individuals ages twelve and over to participate annually. A professional RTI interviewer visits the household to conduct the survey. The actual interview is administered via laptop computer with the respondent entering most answers directly into the computer such that the interviewer does not know the respondent's answers to the questions. Respondents receive $30 in cash following the interview. For further information, see National Survey on Drug Use and Health, https://nsduhweb.rti.org/.

13. For example, Joseph Califano Jr., president of the National Center on Addiction and Substance Abuse at Columbia University (CASA) and former Secretary of Health, Education, and Welfare, uses addiction estimates in just this way, writing: "Today, we have fifty million nicotine addicts, eighteen million alcoholics and alcohol abusers, and six million drug addicts. It is logical to conclude that, if drugs are easier to obtain, less expensive, and socially acceptable, more individuals will use them. With legalization, experts believe the number of cocaine addicts alone could jump beyond the number of alcoholics" (Trebach and Califano 2010).

fears of punishment and demonization that directly discourage users from seeking treatment. *The Economist* recently noted that in Portugal, which decriminalized possession of illegal drugs in 2001, "[t]he number of addicts registered in drug-substitution programmes has risen from 6,000 in 1999 to over 24,000 in 2008, reflecting a big rise in treatment (but not in drug use)" ("Treating, Not Punishing" 2009, 43).[14] The United States has tried a different approach, using criminalization as a vehicle to promote treatment by sometimes offering it as an alternative to, or a means of reducing, criminal penalties.[15]

Second, the generally accepted view—outside of some Chicago school theoretical musings of the late 1960s and early 1970s—has long been that swift and certain sanctions are more salient and effective at deterring use than more distant and uncertain punishments of greater severity. Kleiman (2009) has stressed the intractable tradeoff between swiftness and severity in punishment. As he puts it:

> One problem with the brute-force, high-severity approach is that severity is incompatible with swiftness and certainty. Severity means using a large share of punishment resources on a (relatively) few offenders, and (as the American experience with capital punishment since its reintroduction illustrates) the more severe a sentence is the more reluctantly it will be imposed and the more "due process"—and therefore the more time— it will require. (Kleiman 2009, 3)

The greater deterrence value of more immediate and likely sanctions seems especially important given the apparent risk and time preferences of drug users—individuals whose behavior suggests a present-moment orientation and a heavy discounting of future burdens. An experiment with offenders on probation in Honolulu, for example, which tested the effect of a program oriented around imminent but short incarceration for violators, found that program participants were 55 percent less likely to be arrested for a new crime and 72 percent less likely to test positive for drug use (Hawken and Kleiman 2009, 64).

Third, to the extent that addiction means a lack of voluntariness on the part of the addict, sanctioning addicts with the full brunt of criminal law

14. Speaking on Portugal's experience with decriminalization of illegal drugs, Manuel Cardoso, deputy director of the Institute for Drugs and Drugs Addiction in Portugal, has said: "Before decriminalization, addicts were afraid to seek treatment because they feared they would be denounced to the police and arrested. . . . Now they know they will be treated and not stigmatized as criminals" ("Treating, Not Punishing" 2009).

15. One way for someone caught in possession of marijuana to reduce one's expected sentence is to enter treatment. Many marijuana treatment admissions are criminal justice referrals (Room et al. 2008, 86). In that sense, the rise in arrests for possession of marijuana in the past two decades has been a factor contributing to an increase in the number of marijuana users seeking treatment—although it may be difficult to accurately estimate the number of individuals who did not seek treatment under the current criminalization regime, but who would have sought treatment had marijuana been depenalized or legalized.

is in tension with the core American criminal law requirements of mens rea and actus reus. If drug addiction is characterized by involuntariness, then addicted users appear neither culpable to a degree meriting criminal sanctions nor likely to be deterred by such punishment.[16] On the other hand, if drug addiction is a disorder of choice, as some have recently and compellingly argued on the basis of strong evidence that most addicts recover, then an internalities-based justification of criminalization is weakened: addiction begins to look less like an irreversible step into self-destruction and more like a habit that individuals will struggle over, but quite likely eventually overcome.[17] The greater the degree of choice involved, the less catastrophic is initiation into use and even addiction, and the less justifiable are the costly sanctions designed in large part to keep individuals from ever experimenting with illegal drugs.

The significance of addicts in aggregate marijuana and cocaine consumption is important to bear in mind when considering the effect of changes in price—and policy shifts that would affect a drug's price, such as changes to criminal sanctions, depenalization, or legalization—on the prevalence and intensity of use. Initially, one might assume that nonaddicts and prospective dabblers would be more responsive to changes in price than addicts, whose compulsive behavior is often equated with an inability to quit, rising costs notwithstanding. According to this line of thinking, marginal increases in price—through, say, more severe criminal penalties—would affect casual users much more than heavy users, thus decreasing aggregate harms of use only by changing the behavior of marginal users, without substantially diminishing the core of problem users. A lower price resulting from more lenient policies would induce some new users whose intensity of use would be harder to predict—though a reasonable assumption might be that the new group would contain no greater percentage of addicts than the initial population of users.[18]

However, it is also possible—and consistent with the economic model of rational addiction put forth by Becker and Murphy (1988)—that addicts will

16. In a famous concurrence in Powell v. Texas, Justice White put it this way: "If it cannot be a crime to have an irresistible compulsion to use narcotics . . . I do not see how it can constitutionally be a crime to yield to such a compulsion." Powell v. Texas, 392 U.S. 514, 548 (1968) (White, J., concurring).

17. Reviewing the "four largest, most methodologically rigorous studies of psychiatric disorders and their correlates," Heyman (2009, 69–88) finds that high remission rates are characteristic of addiction. Heyman also finds the widespread belief that addiction is a chronic disorder to be unsupported by the best available data (73–4).

18. This intuitively plausible prediction is backed by evidence demonstrating that addiction is much more or less likely to spread depending upon social context. Heyman (2009, 31–43) reviews the influences of cohort and social context on addiction rates and finds that both are significant, despite the biological basis of addiction. Contrary to received wisdom, Heyman argues convincingly that "[a]ddiction is not an equal-opportunity disorder; indeed there is no psychiatric disorder that is more closely tied to circumstance" (39).

be responsive to price changes over longer time spans.[19] While neither we nor Becker and Murphy believe that all addictive behavior can be explained adequately as the rational pursuit of welfare maximization, their model highlights an important theoretical consideration in attempting to assess the impacts of actual and hypothetical policy changes (and concomitant drug prices) on use: time horizon.[20] One reason among many for caution in extrapolating from the results of short-lived policy experiences is that a policy affecting the use rate of a drug through the price mechanism may have a substantially greater impact if retained over a long period of time. Provocatively, the model put forth by Becker and Murphy suggests that in the long run, consumption of addictive goods may be even more responsive to price changes than consumption of nonaddictive goods.[21] In the long run at least, price changes may indeed expand or contract the core of problem users.

Another factor to take into account when considering consumption across users is the age at which users are most likely to become addicted to illicit substances. In surveys of individuals in the United States, psychiatric researchers have found that drug abuse disorders, excluding alcohol, have a lifetime prevalence of 8.5 percent, and that age nineteen is the median age-of-onset for such disorders (Kessler et al. 2005, 595). More importantly, these same surveys indicate that drug abuse disorders have a narrow age-of-onset range, with an interquartile range of seventeen to twenty-three years (Kessler et al. 2005). This suggests that efforts aimed at curtailing drug use among young people can play a key role in preventing drug addiction. Individuals who do not develop a disorder by their late twenties are much less likely ever to develop such a disorder.[22] Therefore, finding ways to limit

19. Grossman, Chaloupka, and Anderson (1998) find that the Becker-Murphy model—in which demand for addictive goods is sensitive to past, current, and future price—is consistent with some empirical studies of the demand for cigarettes, alcohol, and cocaine, which find negative effects of price on demand, positive effects of past and future consumption on demand, and greater price elasticities of demand over longer time horizons. Other economic models of addiction exist, however, that have treated addicts as myopic or holding inconsistent short- and long-term preferences.

20. Becker and Murphy (1988, 695) put it this way: "We do not claim that all idiosyncratic behavior associated with particular kinds of addictions are consistent with rationality."

21. Becker and Murphy write: "Permanent changes in prices of addictive goods may have a modest short-run effect on the consumption of addictive goods. This could be the source of a general perception that addicts do not respond much to changes in price. However, we show that the long-run demand for addictive goods tends to be more elastic than the demand for nonaddictive goods" (1988, 694–5).

22. The assumption underlying this statement is that the probability of *commencing* abuse drops sharply after adolescence, while those who begin abuse are put on a less favorable subsequent life path. As a result, one would observe that most abusers start early and have worse life outcomes. Of course, this pattern could also appear if there were simply two types of individuals—those prone to abusing drugs (that is, those with high probabilities of commencing abuse and having poor life outcomes) and those not so prone—and individuals in the first

access to drugs among children and teens should be central to any regime—
and any depenalization or legalization proposal.

Consumption Across History

Simply identifying the trends in illegal drug use over time is a difficult task,
given the obvious obstacles to securing accurate information about illegal
behavior over extended periods of time. A number of surveys of illegal drug
use include the percentages of individuals reporting to have used in the past
month, past year, and ever. These are often broken down by drug and user
characteristics—most notably age group. While the percentage of a population using a drug during a given time period is a valuable measure, all such
statistics are limited in that they do not capture other important variables
such as quantities and potencies used by individuals, much less the severity
of harms associated with the instances of use.[23]

Even if one accepts the accuracy of the data, one must also use caution
in analyzing historical data regarding drug use trends. There is a natural—
but potentially misguided—tendency to equate periods of low prevalence
with successful policy and to attribute spikes in the percentage of users with
policy failings. Even if prevalence of use were the sole criterion by which to
measure the success of drug policy, it would remain extremely difficult to
attribute causation to specific policies given the myriad other social factors
that influence use.

With those provisos in mind, it is worth taking a cursory look at historical
trends in the use of marijuana and cocaine in the United States. In figure 5.5

---

group tended to begin abuse in their teen years. Thus, heterogeneity with stable probabilities
could generate the observed pattern in a way that would indicate that delaying initiation of
abuse would not reduce the number of abusers over the life span. Of course, it might still be
desirable to delay addiction to prevent it from stymieing education or growth.

23. In reporting data on drug use over time, it is important to keep in mind the variety
of ways in which use can be measured. Prevalence of use is the most common use measure,
measuring the percentage who have tried a substance, rather than the quantities or potencies
used or distribution of use among users. Prevalence is only a proxy for an ideal measure of
use severity that would somehow incorporate and weight prevalence, intensity, potency, and
other factors contributing to social harms generated by a population's drug problem. Among
prevalence statistics the most commonly reported are lifetime, last year, and last month. Each
of these time horizons carries with it advantages and disadvantages. Lifetime use figures pick
up all those who have ever tried a substance, even if just one time, thus giving a sense of how
common it has been for a member of a given population to try a substance. By looking across
an individual's lifetime, however, such measures necessarily obscure the severity of prevalence
at narrower moments in time (e.g., "now" or "in recent years"). If many people try a drug once
or just several times, but drug use problems stem from perpetual users, the measure can be a
poor proxy for the severity of the current problem of drug use within a population. Looking
at use during the last year or last month illuminates the severity of the drug problem within
a population at a narrower moment in time, and places more emphasis on relatively frequent
users than lifetime use measures. However, these shorter time horizons fail to capture the
likelihood that an individual in a given population will try or come to abuse the drug in the
long-run.

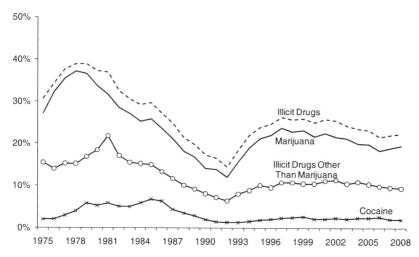

Fig. 5.5   Percentage of 12th graders reporting use of illicit drugs in past 30 days
Source: NIDA (2009, 198–99).

we report data from the Monitoring the Future surveys[24] on the percentage of high school seniors reporting use of marijuana, cocaine, any illegal drug, and any illegal drug other than marijuana, within the past thirty days. While these are relatively narrow measures, we present them not just for the intrinsic significance of use prevalence among late adolescents, but also because they are broadly consistent with overall prevalence and have the important advantage of consistent tracking over a long period of time.

As figure 5.5 suggests, the percentage of high school seniors who recently used marijuana reached a peak during the late 1970s, declined until the early 1990s, rose during the mid-to-late part of that decade and has since leveled and begun to decline in the 2000s. The percentage of high school seniors who recently used cocaine rose through the late 1970s, stayed high in the early 1980s, rose again in the middle of the decade, then declined by its end, falling until the early 1990s, after which time it rose fairly modestly by historical

24. Monitoring the Future (MTF), sponsored by the Institute for Social Research at the University of Michigan, has been a mainstay of data collection regarding drug use in the United States since 1975. Monitoring the Future consists of an annual survey of 16,000 seniors from public and private high schools across the contiguous United States. Random sampling procedures are used to select 133 schools for research, with a maximum of 350 students surveyed within each school. Ten days prior to administration of the survey, students are given a flyer that explains the purpose of the study and provides notice to parents of the study, giving each parent an opportunity to refuse their child's participation. Institute for Social Research staff administer the questionnaire in classrooms during normal class periods following procedures outlined in a project instruction manual. For more information, visit Monitoring the Future: Purpose and Design, http://www.monitoringthefuture.org/purpose.html.

standards, then leveled. The tight correlation between the percentage using marijuana and the percentage using any illegal drug is broadly consistent with drug use trends—not just in the United States, but globally as well. This correlation is quite common across populations because the percentage of individuals around the world using marijuana dwarfs the percentage using all other illegal drugs.

Figure 5.5 might be taken to suggest that the "Just Say No" campaign of the Reagan years led to a major decline in consumption that was reversed during the more permissive Clinton years, although one must consider whether the Reagan campaign influenced reporting behavior as well as drug use. In addition, scholars have offered two reasons to doubt that policy changes in the United States can explain the declines in cocaine and marijuana use from the mid-eighties through the early nineties, the subsequent rise in use during the 1990s or the leveling off in the new century. First, drug use has in a number of instances followed the trajectories of epidemics— wherein use has increased continuously until reaching a plateau, then diminishing, likely due in part to greater awareness of the harmful consequences of use. Second, as Room et al. (2008, 15) note regarding cannabis:

> Interestingly, there seems to be a common pattern over time across countries. For most western nations between 1991 and 1998 there was an increase of about half in the proportion of 18 year olds reporting that they had tried cannabis. Since 1998 in the same countries there has been a substantial decline in that figure, though in 2006 it still remains well above the 1991 level. . . . The common patterns across countries with very different policy approaches reinforce the general impression that penalties for personal use have very little impact on the prevalence of cannabis use in a society.

5.2.2   Current Policy

America's Punitive Approach

> No responsible analysis of the harmful consequences of drug use can ignore the possibility that many of the harms of drug use are either caused or augmented by the legal prohibition against these drugs and its enforcement. Drug prohibition is inevitably a source of government intrusion into citizens' lives. Many (but not all) overdoses occur due to the unknown purity and potency of illegally purchased drugs. The sharing of contaminated syringes is largely a consequence of the artificial scarcity created by their illegality. And much of the criminality and violence associated with drug use (but by no means all) is due to the high price of illegal drugs and the conditions of their sale in illegal markets. (NRC 2001, 63)

Figure 5.6 illustrates that across the array of five broad areas in which the federal government spends resources to control drug use, the dominant growth in spending since the initiation of the war on drugs has come in the

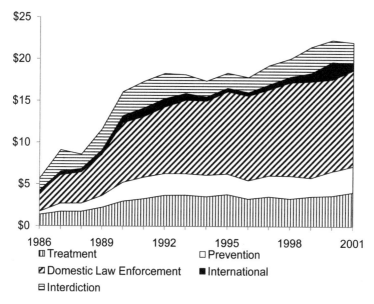

Fig. 5.6   **Federal drug control spending, 1986–2001 (billions of 2008 dollars)**
Source: Nominal figures from ONDCP (2002, 10–11) and ONDCP (1998, 16).
Note: A slight variation on this graph appears in Boyum and Reuter (2005, 38).

area of domestic criminal enforcement. The federal government's categorical classification of drug prohibition spending changed after 2001. However, in the past decade, federal drug policy has continued to shift its emphasis toward the supply side (Office of National Drug Control Policy 2009, 15). As we will later show more directly, disaggregating the costs associated with America's illegal drug problem under the current drug control policy approach underscores that many of the social costs of illegal drugs arise not from drug use per se but rather from drug control.[25] In this section, we examine the punitive side of America's current drug policies, focusing on the costs of incarceration.

Current US drug control policy is largely punitive in nature. In 2007, law enforcement agencies nationwide made over 1.8 million arrests for drug abuse violations, more arrests than for any other category of offense (Bureau of Justice Statistics 2009, 1). Of these arrests, approximately four-fifths were for possession, with 42.1 percent resulting from marijuana possession and 21.5 percent from heroin or cocaine possession (BJS 2009). The Office of National Drug Control Policy (ONDCP) has found that the largest cost

25. This important insight has long been recognized—at least by many advocates of some form of drug legalization. Kleiman and Saiger (1990, 539) note: "A central accomplishment of the consequentialist proponents of legalization has been to stress the vital distinction between the costs of drug abuse and the costs of drug control."

increases in the war on drugs from 1992 to 2002 came as a result of increased incarceration rates for drug offenses and drug-related offenses and from the law enforcement and judicial proceedings needed to put offenders in prison (ONDCP 2004, vi).

Now imprisoning a greater percentage of its population than any other country (Walmsley 2009), the United States has less than 5 percent of the world's population but nearly 25 percent of its prisoners ("A Nation of Jail-birds" 2009). The punitive focus of US drug policy is a major component of our country's record-sized prison populations. The American incarceration rate has increased greatly since President Ronald Reagan's emphasis on the War on Drugs in the early 1980s. The number incarcerated in prison or jail on drug charges is estimated to have risen from about 40,000 in 1980 to about 500,000 today—more than the total number incarcerated for *all* offenses thirty years ago (Mauer 2009, 1). As of 2004, drug offenders constituted an estimated 55 percent of the federal prison population and 21 percent of the state prison population (Mumola and Karberg 2007).[26]

Though most arrests involving drug offenses are for possession, most individuals serving prison sentences for drug offenses are behind bars for trafficking offenses, not just possession. In 1999, the most recent year for which the Bureau of Justice Statistics did a comprehensive report on federal drug offenders, simple possession was the most serious offense for only 2.1 percent of drug offense suspects referred to US Attorneys for prosecution, whereas for 97.5 percent, drug trafficking was the most serious offense (BJS 2001, 2).[27] In terms of drugs involved for defendants actually convicted of federal drug offenses, 30.6 percent involved marijuana, 22.4 percent involved crack cocaine, 21.5 percent involved cocaine powder, 12.5 percent involved methamphetamine, 7.8 percent involved opiates, 0.5 percent involved hallucinogens, and 4.8 percent other substances (BJS 2001, 9).

Unsurprisingly, the percentage of incarcerated drug offenders serving time for possession appears to be significantly greater in state as opposed to federal prisons. Analyzing data from the 2004 Survey of Inmates in State and Federal Correctional Facilities, Mumola and Karberg (2007, 4) report that in 2004, 5.3 percent of drug offenders in federal prisons and 27.9 percent of drug offenders in state prisons were incarcerated for possession. The authors

---

26. The war on drugs increased the number of drug offenders in federal prisons by 26 percent from 2000 to 2006, bringing the number to over 93,000 and accounting for over 53 percent of the increase in the federal prison population during this same time period (Sabol, Couture, and Harrison 2007, 9). Sabol, West, and Cooper (2009, 37–8) report that the numbers of drug offenders in state and federal prison were 265,800 (in 2006) and 95,079 (in 2008), respectively (those in jail are not counted in these numbers).

27. Marijuana possession accounted for 59.8 percent of the cases evaluated for prosecution by US attorneys for simple possession, whereas powder cocaine and crack cocaine accounted for 11 and 10.3 percent, respectively (BJS 2001, 3). For drug trafficking offenses, marijuana was involved in 30.7 percent of evaluated cases, with powder cocaine and crack cocaine being involved in 28.2 and 15.5 percent of cases, respectively.

found that of drug offenders held in state prisons, 61.8 percent reported that cocaine or crack was involved in their offenses, and the analogous figures were 18.6 percent for stimulants, 12.7 percent for marijuana or hashish, 12.2 percent for heroin and other opiates, 2.2 percent for depressants, and 1.7 percent for hallucinogens.[28] One must interpret these data with caution. First, just 20.7 percent of drug offenders in state prisons reported having no prior criminal history (Mumola and Karberg 2007, 4). Second, given the pervasiveness of plea bargaining and the evidentiary ease of prosecuting possession relative to other offenses, the percentage of convicts incarcerated in state prisons whose most severe offense truly is possession remains somewhat illusive.

The price of keeping hundreds of thousands of drug offenders behind bars is high and rising. Locking up approximately a half million drug offenders has a direct budgetary cost in the billions each year—approximately $6.6 billion for state drug prisoners and perhaps that sum over again for federal prisoners and convicts serving time in jail.[29] In addition to the costs of incarceration borne by government and prisoners, a large toll falls on the families of those incarcerated, partly in terms of lost incomes, many of which were lawful ones (Donohue 2009). Fifty-nine percent of male state and federal inmates in prison for drug possession or trafficking have minor children, whereas in the general prison population, only 51 percent have children, indicating an additional cost stemming from high incarceration rates in the form of children with absent fathers (BJS 2008, 4).

There is also a startling racial disparity in imprisonment for drug charges. In state prisons, African Americans account for 38.6 percent of prisoners overall and 45.1 percent of prisoners convicted of drug offenses (Sabol, Couture, and Harrison 2007, 24), though they represent just 13 percent of the US population (US Census Bureau 2008).[30] There is also evidence that

28. Because offenders may have been involved with multiple substances, the figures do not add up to 100 percent.

29. The American Corrections Association estimates that the average cost of incarcerating state prison inmates is $67.55 per day, or around $25,000 per prisoner per year (ACA 2006). Combining this estimate with one from Sabol, West, and Cooper (2009, 21) that 265,800 state prisoners are currently serving sentences for drug offenses yields an annual cost of state drug incarceration of $6.6 billion. If the total population of convicts incarcerated in jail and state and federal prison is approximately a half million, it is reasonable to think that the total costs of incapacitating drug offenders each year may be in the neighborhood of $13 billion.

30. Prevalence of use of illegal drugs is modestly higher among African Americans than Caucasians (SAMHSA 2008, 25). The 2007 NSDUH reported past month illicit drug use rates of 9.5 percent among "blacks or African Americans" and 8.2 percent among whites. While these data are useful at dispelling popular notions that drug use is vastly disproportionate among African Americans, a comparison between the percentage of past-month drug users by race and the percentage of drug-abuse offense prisoners by race does not in and of itself demonstrate disparate enforcement of drug laws against African Americans. Because most people imprisoned for drug-related offenses are imprisoned for drug trafficking and dealing rather than simple possession, and because the indicator of illegal drug use prevalence does not identify either the type of drug or severity of use, the highly aggregated demographic comparison of illicit drug users with individuals incarcerated on drug offenses must be interpreted cautiously.

a substantial portion of racial profiling problems result from the targeting of drug sellers through criminal enforcement efforts, which could be greatly reduced under a less punitive drug policy.

America in a Global Perspective

With the aim of devising rational drug policies based on practical experience rather than predominately ideological concerns, countries throughout Europe are experimenting with drug policy in a variety of ways. In general, European countries have less punitive—and more harm-reduction oriented—approaches to drug policy than the United States. The Action Plan adopted by the German government in 2003 to deal with Germany's drug problem is representative of this approach, claiming: "The 'Action Plan on Drugs and Addiction' advocates a realistic drug policy. It responds more to the concrete reality of life than to any ideological principles. Every addict must have access to appropriate therapy options" (Caspers-Merk 2003, 7). The plan encompasses both legal and illegal substances, recognizing that far more Germans suffer substance abuse problems related to tobacco and alcohol than illegal drugs (11–12).

Portugal has become the poster child of European drug reform following its July 1, 2001, decriminalization of formerly illicit substances.[31] Rather than handle drug possession and use as a criminal matter, the police in Portugal give a civil citation to those caught using or possessing a quantity of drugs less than the average amount sufficient for ten-day use by one person. As Greenwald (2009, 3) notes, these civil citations instruct recipients to appear before a "dissuasion commission" within seventy-two hours. The dissuasion commission, which is designed to avoid all appearances of a criminal tribunal, is made up of a lawyer and two members of the medical profession, and it may order those caught with drugs to pay a fine or undergo a course of treatment. Greenwald reports, however, that fines are a last resort designed to be suspended except for addicts and repeat offenders, who can have their fines suspended as well, if they agree to treatment (3).[32]

Even European countries that have not followed the extreme depenalization approach of Portugal have experimented with less punitive and more treatment-oriented drug policies. In Switzerland, for example, cannabis use remains a criminal offense (Room et al. 2008, 117). However, Switzerland experimented with a regime of open sales of small quantities of illicit drugs,

31. We believe that Portugal's self-described policy of decriminalization is appropriately characterized (whereas some other laws—such as American states' reforms in the 1970s—have been misleadingly called decriminalization) because Portugal has by law explicitly designated short-supply possession as an administrative offence subject only to civil fines (Greenwald 2009; "Treating Not Punishing" 2009).

32. It appears that even treatment imposed as a condition for suspension of a fine may not be enforced rigorously (Greenwald 2009, 3). On the other hand, the Dissuasion Commissions are theoretically empowered to levy other noncriminal sanctions such as the revocation of certain privileges.

such as heroin, in Zurich's Platzspitz (the so-called "Needle Park") (Mac-Coun and Reuter 2005, 264). This experiment lasted only five years, from 1987 to 1992, because the park became unsightly and was viewed as an embarrassment by the city. Instead of resorting to strict punitive measures for drug use, Switzerland then instituted a heroin maintenance program that allowed heroin addicts to receive daily heroin shots supervised by a nurse in a clinical setting. Switzerland has since expanded this program due to evidence that crime rates and unemployment rates among participants drop during participation (266–7). Similar programs have been instituted with encouraging results in Vancouver, Canada, and the Netherlands (Reuter 2009).

But the trend toward decriminalization of drugs is not universal: the United Kingdom has gone in the other direction in recent years, at least with respect to marijuana, by increasing the maximum penalties for marijuana use. Gordon Brown's government decided to reclassify cannabis from a Class C drug to a more serious Class B drug, resulting in a maximum penalty of fourteen years of imprisonment for marijuana supplying, dealing, producing, and trafficking, and five years for possession (Room et al. 2008, 92–3). However, while the potential for such penalties exists, the British Home Office describes the "likely" enforcement steps: for a first possession offense police will issue a warning, for a second they will issue a Penalty Notice for Disorder (a civil citation resulting in an eighty pound fee), and for a third, they will arrest the individual (Home Office 2009). Thus, even in one of Europe's strictest drug regimes, arrests and criminal punishment are reserved for repeat offenders.

While many European countries have more liberal policies toward drug possession, they generally continue to have strict penalties for drug trafficking—though these are appreciably less severe than their counterpart American punishments. As the European Monitoring Centre for Drugs and Drug Addiction puts it, "[o]ver the past ten years, most European countries have moved towards an approach that distinguishes between the drug trafficker, who is viewed as a criminal, and the drug user, who is seen more as a sick person who is in need of treatment" (EMCDDA 2008, 22). For example, in spite of their relatively liberal policies toward drug users, the maximum drug trafficking penalty in the Netherlands is, nominally at least, sixteen years (Drug Enforcement Administration 2005, 255). Even in Portugal, drug trafficking remains a criminal offense because it involves possession in excess of the average dose needed for ten days of personal use (Greenwald 2009, 3). Relative to America, Europe has focused more on helping rather than punishing problem users, while still attempting to disrupt large-scale drug networks.

Europe is not the only region of the world to have largely eliminated or reduced the penalties associated with possessing and using certain drugs. Latin America has also trended toward decriminalization in recent years.

The Argentine Supreme Court decriminalized possession of small amounts of marijuana in August of 2009 (Brice 2009). The court based its ruling on the grounds that it is unconstitutional to punish adults for private use of marijuana if that use does not harm anyone else (Moffett 2009).[33] In declaring unconstitutional a law that provided for sentences of up to two years for drug possession, the court also opened the door for possible decriminalization of other substances, because the specific law overturned was not limited to marijuana. Lower courts might expand the ruling to other drugs. Following the court ruling, the chief of the Argentine cabinet praised the decision for challenging an American-style war on drugs by ending "the repressive policy that the Nixon administration invented" (Brice 2009).

A few days prior to the Argentine court ruling, Mexico enacted decriminalization legislation specifying that individuals in possession of small amounts of marijuana, cocaine, heroin, and methamphetamine will not be criminally prosecuted (Luhnow and de Cordoba 2009; Wilkinson 2009). The new Mexican regime is similar to the Portuguese decriminalization in that those caught by police possessing a small amount of drugs will be encouraged to seek treatment (Luhnow and de Cordoba 2009). After being caught three times with drugs, the user will be required to attend treatment. Unlike the prior presidential administration, which sharply criticized earlier attempts by Mexico to decriminalize drugs, President Obama's drug czar, Gil Kerlikowske, said that the administration would evaluate the new Mexican law using a "wait and see" approach (Luhnow and de Cordoba 2009).

In recent years both Brazil and Ecuador have also signaled that they may follow the path of Argentina and Mexico toward decriminalization (Moffett 2009). Taken together, these developments reflect the dissatisfaction many Latin American governments have with America's punitive war on drugs: a war that was started in large part to combat drug production and trafficking emanating from Latin America. While it is too soon to tell what effects the Argentine and Mexican reforms will have on use rates in those countries, we will show in subsequent sections that the European experience casts doubt on prohibitionist fears that drug use will inevitably jump sharply.

5.2.3 Defining the Costs

Aggregating the Costs

The social costs of recreational drug use in America have been staggering and unabated. According to the ONDCP's most recent estimate, the

33. The Argentine Court's reasoning is similar to that of an earlier Alaska Supreme Court decision. In *Ravin v. State* the Alaska Supreme Court held that Article I, Section 22 of the Alaska Constitution ("The right of the people to privacy is recognized and shall not be infringed") protected people's right to possess marijuana in their own homes for personal use. Ravin v. State, 537 P.2d 494, 511 (Alaska 1975). More recently the Alaska Court of Appeals interpreted *Ravin* as applying only to possession of small amounts of marijuana and upheld an Alaska statute prohibiting possession of eight ounces of marijuana. Walker v. State, 991 P.2d 799, 802–03 (Alaska App. 1999).

economic cost of illegal drug use in the United States in 2002—including lost productivity, health effects, and crime-related costs such as policing expenditures and incarceration—was $180.9 billion, having grown at an average rate of 5.3 percent annually since 1992 (ONDCP 2004, vi).[34] The costs of two legal drugs—alcohol and tobacco—are of a similar order of magnitude. The most recent comprehensive estimate of Harwood (2000) puts the annual economic cost of alcohol use at $184.6 billion in 1998.[35] Rice (1999) estimates the annual economic cost of smoking in 1995 was $138 billion. Placing these figures in constant 2008 dollars provides a set of crude estimates of current annual social costs of alcohol ($244 billion), tobacco smoking ($195 billion), and illegal drugs ($217 billion).[36]

Commentators have rightly pointed out that such cost figures give a misleading impression of precision, ignore the benefits of drug use,[37] and provide scant direction for actual drug policy.[38] We offer these cost estimates for a crude sense of the scale of the problems under the current regime and as a reference point from which to examine the various types of costs associated with drug use—their relative magnitudes, who causes them, and who bears their burdens. It is also worth noting, however, that while such aggregate figures aspire to capture the domestic costs of illegal drugs, the costs imposed on foreign countries by the combination of America's exceptionally large demand for illegal drugs coupled with its severe attempts at prohibition are also high and growing. Organized criminals from the Taliban in Afghanistan to drug cartels in Colombia and Mexico are enriched by America's drug consumption and prohibition policy, with many highly

34. This study uses the cost-of-illness (COI) methodology. The COI methodology evaluates both the direct costs from drug abuse, such as medical expenditures on treatment of drug users, and indirect costs, such as work missed due to drug-induced illness. This method can be contrasted with the willingness-to-pay methodology, which computes the public's willingness to pay for the avoidance of a small amount of additional harm.

35. "As used in this report and throughout most of the literature on economic costs, the term 'alcohol abuse' refers to any cost generating aspect of alcohol consumption. This differs from the clinical definition of the term, which involves specific diagnostic criteria" (Harwood 2000, 1). An early aggregate cost study, Rice, Kelman, and Miller (1991), estimated economic costs for 1988 of $58.3 billion for drug abuse and $85.8 billion for alcohol abuse. A subsequent study, Rice (1999), estimated that in 1995 there were $114.2 billion in costs from drug abuse and $175.9 billion in costs from alcohol abuse.

36. These figures, rounded to the nearest billion, were computed using the CPI-based inflation adjustment calculator of the Bureau of Labor Statistics, available at http://data.bls.gov/cgi-bin/cpicalc.pl.

37. Of course, whether and to what extent drugs benefit their users is not just an empirical question but also a normative one. For a brief and lucid discussion of various perspectives on the role of drug use benefits in policy assessment, see MacCoun and Reuter (2001, 70). The authors note that whereas some economists such as Becker and Murphy argue that the principle of revealed preference evinces benefits for drug users, others such as Kleiman are skeptical of such an argument given that certain drugs "instigate neurological and psychological processes that motivate compulsive use."

38. In noting the limitations of its scope and reliability, the ONDCP's 2004 cost study points to four brief critiques of the value of such estimates: Reuter (1999a), Kleiman (1999), Kopp (1999), and Cohen (1999). For an argument that such economic costs of drug use studies do not help illuminate the relative merits of prohibition or alternative policies, see Miron (2003).

unpleasant consequences. The current American administration has shown some signs of appreciating the magnitude of the role played by American drug demand in fostering crime in foreign countries. Following the recent wave of increasingly deadly gang violence near the Mexican-American border, Secretary of State Hillary Clinton surprised the media by candidly admitting that American drug consumers support crime in Mexico fueled by drug profits (Landler 2009).[39] Consideration of these foreign costs (and their domestic repercussions) might bring total social costs of illegal drugs to equal or exceed those of alcohol.

Disaggregating the Costs

The social costs of drug use come in many different forms. Adapting a list from a 1996 article by MacCoun, Reuter, and Schelling (1996), the National Research Council (NRC 2001, 54) lists sixteen different categories of drug-related harms:

> physical/mental illnesses; diseases transmitted to others; accident victimization; health care costs (drug treatment); health care costs (drug-related illnesses, injuries); reduced performance in school; reduced performance at workplace; poor parenting, child abuse; psychopharmacological crime and violence; economically motivated crime and violence; fear and disorder caused by users and dealers; criminal justice costs; corruption of legal authorities; strain on source country-relations; infringements on liberty and privacy; and violation of the law as an intrinsic harm.

It is striking, though, how large a portion of the social costs of drug use today arise from a single source with a broad reach: drug-related crime. Viewed as an isolated statistic, the ONDCP's estimate of the social costs of drug abuse provides little insight into the nature of America's drug problem. When disaggregated into its component parts, however, it is more revealing.

---

39. Since Secretary Clinton's remarks in March 2009, the news media have reported a flurry of stories concerning the violence in the Mexican drug trade. One particularly gruesome tale published in the *New York Times* in October 2009 reported the arrest of Santiago Meza Lopez who had admitted to disposing of the remains of 300 bodies for a drug cartel by dissolving them in lye. The lye corroded the remains to the point where DNA could not be recovered to identify the bodies. Due to such tactics, many people involved in the Mexican drug trade disappear each year (Lacey 2009). While Mexican drug smugglers are often depicted as cocaine dealers, marijuana remains the largest source of revenue for Mexican drug cartels. Even though Mexican growers are starting to face stiff competition from "mom and pop" US producers of pot, the White House Office of National Drug Control reports that in 2006 over 60 percent of Mexican cartels' revenue ($8.6 billion out of $13.8 billion) came from US marijuana sales (Fainaru and Booth 2009). Mexican traffickers have also established marijuana crops in remote American forests where they have shot at US law enforcement agents, polluted rivers with pesticides and fertilizers, and started large fires. Most recently, the Associated Press has reported on the $25 billion each year in profits from drug trafficking in the United States that Mexican cartels send to Mexico from the United States (AP 2009). In spite of attempts by the US Treasury to stop this flow of funds, the AP reports that $99.75 of every $100 sent by the cartels makes it to Mexico.

Consider the following related estimates from that report, ONDCP (2004), each for the then most recent available year, 2002:

- Of the $180.8 billion in illegal drug costs, $108 billion (nearly 60 percent) were crime-related (IV-7, V-2).
- Over two-thirds of those crime-related costs were in the form of lost productivity for those incarcerated on drug-related charges and costs related to the administration of the criminal justice system (IV-8).
- Incarceration of offenders—475,000 for drug law violations, and 190,000 for drug-related property or violent crimes—resulted in productivity losses of $39 billion and direct outlays of $17 billion at the federal, state, and local levels (III-18, IV-8).
- Health costs constituted a mere 8.7 percent of the total costs of drug abuse (vii).

The ONDCP report goes on to state:

[T]he large majority of these [crime] costs [of illegal drugs] are for drug specific offenses—sales, manufacturing, possession—and the smaller fraction are for drug-related crimes undertaken to finance expensive drug habits. Over 11 percent of arrests in the US are for drug offenses. In addition, appreciable fractions of income generating crimes are attributed to drug abuse: on the order of a quarter of burglaries, personal larcenies and robberies (xii).

While steps toward legalization of currently illegal drugs would likely increase consumption, estimates vary about the extent of this change and how its concomitant costs would compare with gains from decreased law enforcement costs, productivity, and other gains from reducing the levels of incarceration, and potentially substantial decreases in the crime and violence stemming from decreased profitability and scope of black markets.[40] Though our best guess is that moving toward legalization would substantially reduce crime, we qualify this with the word "potentially" because it is possible that a regime shift to depenalization or legalization would increase toxicologically induced crime and thereby offset expected decreases in black market crimes.[41]

---

40. Caulkins and Kleiman (2007, 591) summarize the quandary in the cocaine context: "Unless the taxes and regulations involved in a post-prohibition control regime for cocaine were so high and so tight as to leave the current illicit market largely in place, the result would almost certainly be a very large increase in the number of heavy cocaine users. . . . Against that must be set the enormous reduction in violence and incarceration that would result from abolishing the illicit market in cocaine. (The net impact on property crime is unclear; users, presumably, would steal less, but some dealers, deprived of their customers by legal competition, might switch to theft as a source of illicit income. On the other hand, legalization would free substantial police, prosecution, and prison resources for use against predatory crime.)"

41. Another concern that is difficult to assess is the extent to which current drug dealers would substitute toward other criminal enterprises were a liberalization of illegal drug policy to contract the black market and its profitability.

Citing evidence that a high percentage of arrestees test positive for alcohol and various illegal drugs, advocates of continued criminalization frequently imply, contrary to the implications of the ONDCP cost study, that toxicologically induced crimes are more common or costly than those whose origins are systemic to drug prohibition. Data do show a correlation between crime and illicit drug use that is, upon first consideration, quite distressing: the 2008 Annual Report of the Arrestee Drug Abuse Monitoring Program (ADAM II) found that in 2008, among ten major metropolitan areas across the country, the percentage of arrestees testing positive for the presence of some illicit substance ranged from 49 percent in Washington, DC to 87 percent in Chicago (ONDCP 2009b, 15). However, as we will reiterate in the sections that follow, extrapolating from the ADAM II results a belief that drug criminalization decreases crime or violence (rather than substantially increases both) conflicts with a number of theoretical considerations as well as considerable empirical evidence concerning the relatively greater importance of systemic (compared to toxicologically motivated) offenses.

Three theoretical points should be highlighted. First, as previously noted, the approximately 1.8 million annual arrests for drug abuse violations are more than for any other category of offense (BJS 2009). It is neither surprising nor indicative of a causal relationship between drug use and crime (other than the tautological one produced by criminalization itself) that individuals in this subcategory of arrestees frequently test positive for illegal drugs. Second, any causal extrapolation from the correlation between drug use and crime runs up against the intractable problem of omitted variables bias: it is quite likely that factors that predispose individuals to frequent use of drugs also push them toward both crime and greater likelihood of apprehension by authorities. This is especially true for marijuana: detectable traces may remain in one's system for extended periods of time, so one may test positive upon arrest even if the last instance of use occurred days or even weeks before the arrest, and before or after the commission of the offense (Pacula and Kilmer 2003). Third, the important question is not whether crime systemic to prohibition substantially outweighs toxicologically induced crime—although the best evidence supports this hypothesis. Rather, the appropriate inquiry should be into how the marginal decreases in systemic crime would compare to the marginal increases in toxicologically driven crime given a regime change. Even if lesser penalties, depenalization, or legalization would increase use, the new class of users—individuals formerly deterred by criminalization—would constitute a class much less predisposed to commit other crimes than the group of people already using under criminalization.

Return to the ONDCP's aggregate cost study and three of its key insights: (a) roughly 40 percent of the current costs of illegal drugs in the United States are crime costs borne by offenders via incarceration and the government via administration of the criminal justice system; (b) these costs dominate the victim-borne costs of drug-related crime and health-related costs of abuse; and (c) the greatest driver of these costs is crime systemic to criminalization, rather than crime motivated by toxicology. Together, these propositions suggest that a substantial portion of America's current drug problem is its drug control policy. Since government policies create some of the costliest of all the burdens associated with illegal drugs, a substantial reduction in the social costs of illegal drugs would seem to require a reduction in the costs imposed by the current criminalization regime, not just a restraint of the costs of abuse.

5.3   Reforming America's Illegal Drug Policy[42]

5.3.1   Broad Themes

While many advocates of legalization and continued criminalization of illegal drugs see sufficient similarities across drug classes to paint with broad strokes, we perceive the nature and extent of the harms associated with each drug to call for careful, individualized analysis.[43] That is not to say that recreational drugs do not share certain similarities or that society's experience with legal drugs cannot provide insight into the likely impact of legalizing a currently proscribed drug. The gaping disjunction between the law and policy toward cigarettes and alcohol on the one hand, and toward marijuana, cocaine, and other currently illegal drugs on the other, appears less the result of thoughtful distinction than of inertia and a self-perpetuating myth that drugs accorded legal status are qualitatively similar to each other and different from drugs that are criminalized.[44] But if a unified approach across certain drugs might be desirable for a variety of reasons, only by

42. In this section we consider drug policy primarily from the standpoint of cost-minimization analysis. A final assessment on desirable social policy would consider other important concerns such as individual liberty, distributional justice, and which side of the controversy (those who would maintain the status quo or those who would enact reform) bears the burden of uncertainty. However, due to limited space and our interest in clarifying the social science, we do not give such concerns full treatment, but instead simply note some evidence that might be relevant to the application of these nonefficiency based criteria. For a discussion seeking to reframe the marijuana policy debate in terms of "just deserts" for offenders, see Husak (2007, 189). A comprehensive treatment—and indeed a true cost-benefit analysis—of various schemes would also require serious consideration of the benefits of drugs to their users. To the extent that reforms such as depenalization or legalization would increase the benefits to users through increased consumption, for example, our decision to ignore benefits biases our analysis in favor of the status quo and makes any favorable assessments of such reforms all the more cautiously derived.

43. A persistent critique of arguments for legalization has been that they paint overly rosy pictures of the consequences of legalization by omitting the specifics—such as the forms of regulation, distribution mechanisms, level of taxation, treatment of marketing, and special policies toward young people—that if considered in detail would surely reveal the shortcomings of legalization.

44. At the extreme, this posture often entails language implicitly denying that legal drugs such as alcohol and nicotine are drugs at all. The Drug Enforcement Administration (DEA) exploits

meticulously examining each drug's unique psychopharmacological effects and social attributes can we begin to group together the different drugs that should be treated similarly.[45]

In this section, we consider potential changes to America's policy toward marijuana and cocaine. To oversimplify somewhat, marijuana is the most widely used illegal drug, one of the least dangerous for users across various dimensions, and the frequent subject of debate over policy reform. Likewise, any decrease in social costs stemming from a change to marijuana policy is likely to be far smaller than would result from a comparable policy change concerning a "harder" drug such as cocaine. On the other hand, because the social costs under America's current drug regime are highest for cocaine, changes to policy toward cocaine (as opposed to other narcotics) would change the social cost mitigation calculus in a way that would countenance potential risks and rewards of the greatest magnitude.[46]

5.3.2   Marijuana

Psychopharmacology and Culture

[T]here is a glaring discontinuity between the lived experience of Americans and the drug policies of their governments. Nearly a hundred million of us—forty percent of the adult population, including pillars of the nation's political, financial, academic, and media élites—have smoked (and, therefore, possessed) marijuana at some point, thereby committing an offense that, with a bit of bad luck, could have resulted in humiliation, the loss of benefits such as college loans and scholarships, or worse. More than forty thousand people are in jail for marijuana offenses, and some seven hundred thousand are arrested annually merely for possession. (Hertzberg 2008)

Marijuana is a pivotal substance in the debate over illegal drug policy for many reasons. The World Drug Report 2008 found that cannabis "continues to dominate the world's illicit drug market in terms of pervasiveness of cultivation, volume of production and number of consumers . . . [and its consumer market] dwarfs those for other drugs" (UNODC 2008, 14). In its "Facts and Figures" webpage on marijuana, the ONDCP highlights three

---

this distinction in opposing legalization. "The Legalization Lobby claims drugs are no more dangerous than alcohol," the DEA writes in its summary of the top ten "facts" on legalization (DEA 2003, 3). This statement implicitly perpetuates the myths that (a) alcohol is not a drug; and (b) the substances properly called drugs are illegal.

45. John Kaplan's *The Hardest Drug: Heroin and Public Policy* (1983) provides a classic example of the approach of focusing on the costs and benefits of a single drug, while drawing comparisons with other drugs. Written on the eve of the American crack "epidemic," Kaplan considered the costs of heroin use, formerly considered to be the country's most problematic drug, and explored the costs and benefits of possible systems of legalization and heroin maintenance. Kaplan's careful weighing of costs and benefits for a particular drug provides an example of a strong methodological framework for those conducting research in this area.

46. Caulkins and Kleiman (2007, 564) estimate that "cocaine (including crack) accounts for roughly two-thirds of the social costs associated with illicit drugs in the United States."

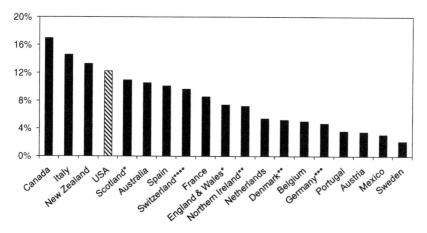

Fig. 5.7   Annual prevalence of cannabis use, population aged 15–64 (2004–2008)
Source: UNODC (2009, 245–9).
*Aged 16–59, **16–64, ***18–64; ****Percentage is the midpoint of a range.

statistics from the 2008 National Survey on Drug Use and Health (NSDUH) (SAMHSA 2009): among Americans aged twelve or older, 102 million (over 40 percent) had tried marijuana in their lifetimes, 25.8 million (over 10 percent) had used in the past year and 15.2 million (over 6 percent) in the past month (ONDCP 2010). As noted in figure 5.1, the United States is a clear outlier with respect to the percentage of its population that has tried marijuana (though this is in part a reflection of the unusually high use rates in the late 1970s and 1980s). Although methodological issues and data availability make cross-country comparison for annual illegal drug use more difficult than for lifetime use, figure 5.7 gives at least a crude sense of the United States in global context by showing the past year cannabis use estimates for the United States and the rest of North America, Australia, New Zealand, and selected countries from western and central Europe.[47] The data suggest that America is also among the world leaders in the percentage of its population using marijuana more regularly.

Far more individuals are arrested for possession of marijuana in the United States than for any other illegal drug. Of the more than 1.8 million

47. "Data from non-western countries are much sparser, but suggest more variation and lower rates" (Room et al. 2008, 61). There are several reasons why lifetime use data are more amenable to cross-country comparison. First, lifetime use figures are likely to fluctuate less over short periods of time because (a) people who have used during their lifetimes will not drop out of the pool of those who have ever used until they die, and (b) those who begin using between sampling periods will make up a smaller percentage of those who have ever used than those who have used during the past year because at any time far more people will have ever used than used in the past year. The most recent use figures for different countries are often for slightly different years. The smaller the expected changes in use from year to year, the lesser the extent to which different sampling years render statistics from two different countries incomparable. Second, lifetime use figures using a uniform methodology are available from at least one recent study, the WHO World Mental Health Surveys, whereas the most comprehensive cross-country

arrests for drug violations in 2007, 42.1 percent—more than 750,000—were for marijuana possession, and when sales and possession arrests are aggregated, 47.4 percent or nearly half of all drug arrests are marijuana-related (FBI Uniform Crime Reporting Program 2007).[48] Marijuana arrests have risen significantly in recent decades; one recent study found that from 1992 to 2002 marijuana arrests increased by 113 percent while overall arrests decreased by 3 percent (King and Mauer 2006).

Room et al. (2008, 22) summarize the basic sensory effects of cannabis on its users:

> Cannabis produces euphoria and relaxation, alters perception, distorts time, and intensifies ordinary sensory experience, such as, eating, watching films, appreciating nature, and listening to music. Users' short-term memory and attention, motor skills, reaction time and skilled activities are impaired while they are intoxicated. . . . Cannabis users are typically seeking one or more of these effects when they use. But use can also result in unsought and adverse effects. The most common unpleasant effects of acute cannabis use are anxiety and panic reactions . . . [these] are a common reason for discontinuing use.

Current evidence suggests that while the harmful health effects of marijuana are not trivial (Browning 2009), they are less troublesome than those of other illegal drugs such as cocaine, heroin, or methamphetamine. Mac-Coun and Reuter (2001, 356, 360) conclude that "[t]he harms of cannabis are clearly no greater that those of alcohol, at the individual level" and "dependence occurs frequently, almost as frequently as for alcohol amongst those who start using the drug . . . [but with seemingly] modest adverse consequences." A recent survey of clinicians and researchers found that the experts perceived cannabis to be less addictive than most other drugs—including caffeine, amphetamine, alcohol, cocaine, methamphetamine, oxycodone, crack, nicotine, and heroin (Gore and Earleywine 2007, 176–85). Similarly, Kershaw and Cathcart (2009) report on a study by the Institute of Medicine that found that of those who tried tobacco, 32 percent went on to become dependent compared to just 9 percent for marijuana (see figure 5.9).[49] Mari-

---

data for past year use of which we are aware come from the World Drug Report 2009, and are pulled together from disparate studies done within individual nations and with somewhat differing methodologies.

48. Far fewer—indeed just a small fraction—are actually imprisoned for marijuana possession. Caulkins and Kleiman (2007, 581) write: "There are more than 1 million arrests per year in the United States for drug possession . . . but few of them result in prison time, or even jail time following a conviction. That is especially true of cannabis possession, even in states where it is not formally 'decriminalized.' Possession of quantities suitable for personal consumption by itself is usually punished, if at all, with probation, fines, community service, or shorter jail terms, not prison sentences."

49. That relatively few marijuana users persist in their habit beyond their youth raises two important questions, however. First, to what extent is this consumption pattern the result of the existing punitive policy? Second, to what extent does uncertainty about the first question undermine our confidence in the long-term consequences of marijuana use?

juana is also far less lethal than nicotine, alcohol, and other prevalent illegal drugs (Gable 2006, 155); fatal overdoses are unheard of, if not virtually impossible. Long-term smoking of marijuana could generate adverse health consequences from breathing smoke, though increased potency reduces the number of inhalations required to achieve the desired effect.

Marijuana use has intruded into mainstream America to a greater degree than any other illegal drug.[50] Moreover, Room et al. (2008) observe that because marijuana's global prevalence so exceeds that of other illegal recreational drugs, the bureaucracies of drug control within individual countries and at the global level depend upon the criminalization of marijuana to broaden the scope of their mission. They note the World Drug Report 2008 estimates that 65 percent of global seizures and 67 percent of "doses" seized were for cannabis and argue, using global use figures, that without cannabis illegal drug use would not be a global population-level issue (89, 92). Finally, the therapeutic potential of marijuana has given rise to a debate over whether doctors should be allowed to prescribe the drug for medicinal purposes.

Perhaps for all these reasons, marijuana has proven an attractive target for advocates of legalization, though many prominent opponents strongly endorse a continued hard-line stand. Growing numbers of commentators in the popular press have advocated the legalization of marijuana (Klein 2009), and assessed the revenue boost legalization might provide states facing cash-strapped budgets (Yamamuru 2009). The debate has been further stimulated in recent months as states have begun reacting to Attorney General Eric Holder's announcement that the DEA will no longer raid state-approved medical marijuana distributors (Woo 2009).

Willingness to consider—if not outright endorse—legalization of marijuana has also grown among academics. Over 500 economists,[51] including three Nobel Laureates,[52] signed an open letter to the President, Congress, governors, and state legislatures expressing skepticism about current marijuana policy and calling for open debate over a shift from prohibition to taxation and regulation. The letter highlights Harvard economist Jeffrey Miron's 2005 report *The Budgetary Implications of Marijuana Prohibition,* which estimates that legalization would save the federal and state governments a combined $7.7 billion in prohibition enforcement expenditures and yield approximately $2.4 billion in tax revenues if taxed like an ordinary good or as much as $6.2 billion if taxed similarly to alcohol or tobacco (Miron 2005, 2–3).[53]

---

50. For example, "in 2004 the three leading Democratic hopefuls—John Kerry, Howard Dean, and John Edwards—all acknowledged without quibbling that they'd smoked pot" (Hertzberg 2008).

51. A list of the names is available at http://www.prohibitioncosts.org/endorsers.html.

52. Milton Friedman, George Akerlof, and Vernon Smith.

53. More recently Miron has expanded upon that report, analyzing the budgetary implications of the prohibition of all other illegal drugs—including cocaine and heroin specifically (Miron 2008).

In the wake of the recent economic downturn, old and new reformers have latched on to the "lost revenues" argument for legalization.

This section first considers the case for reforming marijuana policy, specifically weighing the costs of depenalization and legalization against those of the current system of prohibition.

Criminalization

A defense of marijuana prohibition based on cost-minimization analysis might proceed as follows. First, a completely unregulated market for marijuana would lead to undesirably high levels of consumption—either because of negative externalities (social costs of marijuana use that accrue to those not a party to marijuana use and exchange) or internalities (private costs that accrue to users themselves but that users nevertheless fail to adequately account for in their consumption decisions). Second, regulation and taxation will not adequately correct for these market failures. Third, severe criminal sanctions for users and sellers are cost-justified deterrence mechanisms for reducing use. A more sophisticated version of this third argument would make explicit an important hypothesis frequently left implicit but nevertheless underlying much thought about drug policy: criminalization may not only raise the price for the user (thereby reducing its attractiveness for an individual with given preferences) but also, through the norm-generating or socializing effect of the law, actually alter individuals' preferences such that for any given price, use and distribution hold less appeal.[54]

Though some libertarians argue that the value of individual autonomy dictates allowing marijuana use (irrespective of externalities) and simply sanctioning user behavior when it directly infringes upon the liberty of others, a cost-minimization approach demands consideration of the magnitude of social costs of use before accepting the notion that autonomy can trump all such social costs not generated directly from physical force or fraud. Few dispute that marijuana creates at least some externalities and also internalities—certainly at least in the case of minors not yet capable of adequately processing the risks but also perhaps for the one in eleven who becomes dependent on the drug merely from trying it. The great contention is over which policies can most efficiently mitigate the total costs associated with marijuana use—in other words, which policies will yield the lowest total social costs, combining the costs of use and control.

The crux of the argument in favor of retaining the prohibitions on use, possession, and sale of marijuana is that eliminating any of these sanctions

54. Preferences for drugs are likely to be in significant part endogenous—that is, not independent of, but rather, partly determined by, policy and market structure. However, while most assume that criminalization reduces the aggregate demand for drugs, the policy regime undoubtedly affects individuals in differing ways. For some, the resulting social stigma makes drug use or dealing far less attractive at any given price whereas, for others, a contrary lure of heresy and rebellion makes such activities more desirable at each price.

would increase marijuana use by reducing the cost and decreasing the risk. Full legalization might also stimulate demand by enabling advertisement and brand development. Increased use—either in terms of intensity and frequency or number of users—would in turn increase the costs of use borne by users themselves and society. There are also two related, subsidiary arguments worth addressing. First, it is often contended that marijuana is a "gateway drug" that renders its users more likely to begin using other, more dangerous drugs, and, therefore, an increase in marijuana users as a result of depenalization or legalization would in turn increase the number of users of other illegal drugs.[55] Second, it is sometimes argued that marijuana use induces crime.

Before turning in subsequent sections to the evidence regarding expected increases in marijuana use under depenalization and legalization, it is helpful to consider briefly the insightful analysis of the gateway issues offered by MacCoun and Reuter. Though they believe that "there is little evidence that expanding marijuana use does increase the use of other, more harmful drugs," MacCoun and Reuter present a taxonomy of seven possible meanings of the gateway concept: the first step; the spurious correlation; the early warning; the trap; the tantalizer; the toe in the water; and the foot in the door (MacCoun and Reuter 2001, 245–51).

The basic problems for an econometrician attempting to identify whether—and if so which—gateway hypotheses reflect actual experience are omitted variables bias and endogeneity. At the level of the individual, it is difficult to pinpoint a gateway mechanism because it is quite likely that underlying characteristics that predispose individuals to use marijuana also increase the likelihood of using other drugs. At the population level, it is difficult to assess the effect of marijuana use on the use of other drugs for an additional reason: causality likely runs in both directions.

However, even without precisely estimating the impact of marijuana use on the likelihood of trying other drugs, one may place a rough upper bound on the extent of such an effect by noting how commonly individuals use marijuana without going on to other, more harmful drugs. In their recent cannabis report, Room et al. (2008, 65) write: "Few [marijuana users] go

---

55. A related issue is whether marijuana is an economic substitute for, or complement to, alcohol and cigarettes. Williams et al. (2004), for example, find some evidence that marijuana and alcohol are complements, and therefore increases in the price of alcohol decrease marijuana use. DiNardo and Lemieux (2001), on the other hand, find evidence that increases in the minimum drinking age were associated with slight increases in marijuana use, suggesting a substitution effect. We are skeptical that such studies can resolve the issue of whether marijuana and alcohol or marijuana and cigarettes are substitutes or complements—much less how the overall price decreases in marijuana from depenalization or legalization would affect alcohol or cigarette use—because it is unlikely that marijuana and alcohol or marijuana and cigarettes have stable relationships in individuals' preference relations across social contexts and historical time periods. Even if such a stable relation were uncovered given marijuana criminalization, this would not ensure that the relationship would persist after marijuana reform—especially legalization.

on to use more dangerous illicit drugs; the 1995 US National Household Survey on Drug Abuse found that only 23 percent of twenty-six to thirty-four-year-olds who had used marijuana at some time had also used cocaine during their lives." Similarly, the 2007 NSDUH found that those who used marijuana exclusively constituted 53.3 percent of illegal drug users and 73.2 percent of marijuana users (SAMSHA 2008, 16).

As MacCoun and Reuter remind us, it is also important to understand the mechanism of any gateway effect, assuming one exists at all. If the gateway is a matter of individuals becoming comfortable with illegal behavior and black market consumption, then legalization could undermine this gateway effect, even as it increased consumption directly via lower prices to users.

The most-cited evidence in support of the hypothesis that marijuana users are driven to crime while under the influence is undoubtedly the ADAM II data indicating that in eight of ten major metropolitan areas studied in 2008, over 40 percent of arrestees tested positive for marijuana at the time of arrest (ONDCP 2009b, 17). The weight of auxiliary evidence suggests, however, that this correlation primarily reflects factors other than a causal relationship of crime induction through intoxication.

First, the psychopharmacological effects of marijuana are relatively modest compared to the effects of alcohol, cocaine, and other illegal drugs, and do not suggest, a priori, that intoxicated users are driven to violent, antisocial activity with great frequency.[56] Second, it is clear from the sheer size of marijuana's user base that most users do not resort to nonpossessory crime at all—while intoxicated or otherwise. Third, some empirical evidence suggests that the enforcement of marijuana criminalization may not work even as a "broken windows" policing strategy, much less as a direct measure preventing supposedly toxicologically induced crime.[57] A recent anal-

---

56. Reviewing the literature, two analysts write: "The psychopharmacological model hypothesizes that drug users engage in violent and/or non-violent crime because of the acute psychoactive effects of the substance. . . . There is very little support for this model in the case of marijuana, except for adolescents. Laboratory studies generally show that marijuana, unlike alcohol, temporarily inhibits aggression and violence . . . raising doubt that any association identified in the data is causal in nature. Still, there is some evidence showing a correlation between chronic marijuana use and increased risk of violent behavior" (Pacula and Kilmer 2003, 4). The results of the authors' *own* models, using Arrestee Drug Abuse Monitoring (ADAM) and Uniform Crime Reports (UCR) data, suggest a *possible* causal mechanism between marijuana use and *arrests* for property and income-producing crime, but are too conflicting to affirm or refute the existence of a causal relationship between marijuana use and violent crime arrests. Even if one were to take a leap from their relatively mixed evidence and conclude that a causal relationship between marijuana use and nonviolent crime arrests exists, however, the nature of that relationship remains elusive: perhaps most problematic is the possibility that a positive association between marijuana use and arrest likelihood may be a reflection of marijuana users' greater likelihood of arrest conditional on committing a crime—rather than greater likelihood of committing crimes. At best the authors' analysis offers weak and indirect support for the thesis that marijuana induces nonviolent crime at all, much less toxicologically.

57. So-called "broken windows" policing is a strategy wherein law enforcement cracks down on minor offenses as a means of preventing antisocial behavior from escalating into more serious crimes. The strategy was advanced in James Q. Wilson and George Kelling's article, "Broken Windows: The Police and Neighborhood Safety" (Wilson and Kelling 1982).

ysis of marijuana in public view (MPV) arrests across seventy-five police precincts in New York City from 1989 to 2000 concluded that "there is no good evidence that this 'reefer madness' policing strategy contributed to the decline in the sorts of serious crimes that are of greatest public concern in New York City" (Harcourt and Ludwig 2007, 166).[58] On the contrary: while an initial panel data analysis offered some support for the idea that these misdemeanor marijuana arrests contributed to reductions in violent crime, when the authors restructured their regression model to control for mean reversion, the coefficient on MPV arrests became statistically significant in the opposite direction—suggesting that "an increase in MPV arrests over the period translates into an *increase* in serious crime—not, as the broken windows theory would predict, a decrease in serious crime" (171).

In considering the merits of criminalization, it is also important to remember that even within a system of criminalization, there is much leeway regarding the severity and nature of prohibition enforcement. Moreover, there is significant historical and cross-country evidence to help understand how consumption and costs might change under a less punitive criminal regime. While it is always difficult to isolate the impact of a drug policy, and one must always be wary in generalizing from the experience of other countries to today's America, there is evidence, albeit somewhat conflicting, suggesting that depenalization and even decriminalization of marijuana may not lead to significant increases in use.

Depenalization

It is often said that in the 1970s, eleven states "decriminalized" marijuana (NRC 2001). These states significantly reduced penalties for simple possession of marijuana, in some cases implementing a narrow form of the regime we call depenalization.[59] Evidence on the impact of these marijuana reform laws initially found little or only a weak effect (NRC 2001, 192–3).[60] On the

58. Not only did the authors find evidence against the "broken windows" theory of policing, they also observed that African Americans and Hispanics were much more likely to be arrested for MPV and to fare poorly in the criminal justice system thereafter.

59. Room, et al. (2008, 105), explain: "Predominantly, these state laws downgraded the legal status of marijuana possession offences, defining possession of small amounts as a misdemeanor, i.e. reducing the severity of penalties following violations while retaining them formally as criminally sanctioned offenses under this offense rubric. Thus, while these reforms have widely been labeled as 'decriminalization,' it has been suggested that this may have been a misnomer in strict terms. . . ." In one respect, there is a common denominator among the state reform laws that makes them somewhat like, though not strictly examples of, our particular conception of a depenalization regime: as Pacula et al. (2003, 9) note "[t]he only common denominator across these eleven statutes was the lack of imposition of minimum jail/prison terms." The failure to specify minimum terms of incarceration is not the same as the removal of any incapacitating sanctions, however. If decriminalization strictly refers to a regime of sanctions outside the criminal system, some of the states' reform laws approach this ideal more closely than others: some downgraded possession of a small quantity of marijuana to a misdemeanor while others downgraded the offense to a violation (Pacula et al. 2003).

60. The 2001 NRC report noted that "most cross-state comparisons in the United States . . . have found no significant differences in the prevalence of marijuana use in decriminalized and

other hand, a recent study finds that because other states have also reduced penalties for marijuana possession, "[so called] decriminalized states are not uniquely identifiable based on statutory law as has been presumed by researchers over the past twenty years" (Pacula et al. 2003, 26). The same study also finds, however, that the demand for marijuana among young people is sensitive to variation in penalties. A still more recent study traces the research—which began with studies finding little to no effect but now has become more mixed—and offers two possible explanations for the conflicting findings: (a) the effect of legal variation is different across age groups; and (b) the historical time period may matter (MacCoun et al. 2009, 350). Moreover, the authors find that a reason for minimal effects of depenalization may be that many individuals are unaware of the changes in their state's marijuana law.[61]

Another reason why use rates might not respond to decreased penalties is the extremely low likelihood of being arrested for illegal drug possession: reviewing the data, Boyum and Reuter estimate that in 1999, the "risk of being arrested for marijuana possession, conditional on using marijuana in the previous year, was about 3 percent; for cocaine the figure was 6 percent" (Boyum and Reuter 2005, 56). To the extent that individuals predisposed to illegal drug use also exhibit lower risk aversion and higher discounting of future welfare than the rest of society, they are especially unlikely to find psychologically salient—or change their behavior as a result of—risks characterized by low probabilities and high costs, such as possible arrest for possession.

Probably the most famous example of marijuana reform comes from the Netherlands. There, the 1976 Opium Act ushered in the de facto decriminalization (or extreme depenalization) of possession of small amounts of cannabis for personal consumption (five grams or fewer) and a system of tolerated sale in "coffee shops" that in some sense resembles a form of highly but peculiarly regulated legalization.[62] Under the latter system, registered

---

nondecriminalized states. . . . Even in the few studies that find an effect on prevalence it is a weak one" (NRC 2001, 192–3).

61. MacCoun et al. (2009, 366–7) write: "Our study finds significant associations between the maximum penalty specified in state marijuana laws and a citizen's perceived maximum penalties. But the associations are very small in magnitude. Citizens in decriminalization states are only about 29 percent more likely to believe the maximum penalty for possessing an ounce of marijuana is a fine or probation (relative odds ratio = 1.29). About a third of citizens in each type of state believe the maximum penalty is a jail sentence. People are not oblivious to their marijuana laws, but the average citizen's awareness is pretty tenuous. This fact, combined with prior evidence for only weak effects of perceived sanction severity on offending . . . goes a long way toward clarifying why decriminalization effects are fairly weak and inconsistent."

62. As van der Gouwe, Ehrlich, and van Laar (2009) explain, possession remains illegal and subject to incarceration and fines, but those found in possession of fewer than five grams of cannabis will not be subject to prosecution. Because the Netherlands' policy systematically removes these low-level possession cases from the criminal system, despite retaining nominal prohibition, it may appropriately be termed de facto decriminalization or extreme depenalization.

coffee shop owners that adhere to certain guidelines may, without being targeted for prosecution, possess up to 500 grams of cannabis and sell it in quantities of five grams or fewer (Abraham 1999, 1). The Dutch experience with this controlled form of drug use provides insight into what could happen if the United States were to move down a path toward depenalization, decriminalization, or even legalization of marijuana. MacCoun and Reuter (2005, 264) report that since the 1976 reform, the number of coffee shops has increased steadily so that there now may be between 1,200 and 1,500 such venues in Amsterdam; on the other hand, van der Gouwe, Ehrlich, and van Laar (2009) report a decrease in the number of officially tolerated coffee shops from 1999 to 2007. Marijuana use in the Netherlands increased during the 1980s and early 1990s as the coffee shops became more widespread. However, there is no evidence for the existence of the so-called gateway effect discussed earlier. Notably, there was no increase in use rates of heroin, which is traditionally the most widely used hard drug in the Netherlands, or of cocaine, in spite of the corresponding crack crisis in the United States (MacCoun and Reuter 2005, 264). Indeed, the European School Survey Project on Alcohol and Other Drugs (ESSPAOD 2003), conducted a quarter-century after de facto decriminalization and emergence of the coffee shop system in the Netherlands, found that only 28 percent of Dutch school children surveyed reported smoking cannabis compared with 38 percent in France, whose politicians have been harshly critical of the Dutch approach.[63] Also, as we note in figure 5.1, data from the World Health Organization World Mental Health Surveys indicate that when measured in terms of lifetime cannabis use, the United States has a much higher rate of those over age eighteen who have ever used cannabis (42 percent) compared with the Netherlands (20 percent) (Degenhardt et al. 2008, 1057).

One of the goals of the Dutch scheme involves separating cannabis sales from sales of other illicit drugs in the hopes that cannabis users will not come into contact with sellers of drugs like heroin, thus stopping marijuana users from moving to more serious drugs. Manja Abraham (1999) reported that for users over age eighteen, 48 percent of cannabis purchases took place in coffee shops, whereas relatives and friends supplied 39 percent of cannabis used (3–4). While this demonstrates that a large informal cannabis market exists, only 3.7 percent of users reported obtaining cannabis from a stranger and 5 percent from a home dealer, someone who advertises cannabis sales and delivers them to the home, legally or illegally, depending upon the amount delivered. Among experienced users of cannabis (those who report using the drug more than twenty-five times in their lives), 54 percent reported purchasing cannabis most often in a coffee shop compared with 32 percent for less experienced users (Abraham 1999, 4). This suggests that

---

63. The survey methodology used by the European School Survey Project was modeled after that used by the Monitoring the Future study performed in the United States.

while a large percentage of sales occur outside of the state-sanctioned coffee shops, the heaviest users obtain their cannabis through regulated channels or from people they know, rather than participating in a clandestine market of dealers. The lack of transactions with dealers who are otherwise unrelated to the individual is important because it is such transactions that bring an individual into contact with the black market and its associated crime and violence.

Evidence from Portugal and Australia also suggests that depenalization need not lead to substantial increases in marijuana use or its associated problems. In the period since decriminalization, drug use in Portugal has not spiked, nor has the country been besieged by drug tourists, flocking to the country to use drugs without criminal consequences (Cato Institute 2009). In fact, Portugal continues to have among the lowest rates of cannabis and cocaine use in the European Union, and its rates remain far below their counterparts in the United States (Greenwald 2009, 23–4). Room et al. (2008, 130–3) have pulled together a handful of studies comparing changes in use rates in Australian jurisdictions covered by schemes involving civil penalties for small cannabis offenses with changes in use rates for the rest of Australia still subject to the country's standard criminal penalties for marijuana possession. On the whole, these analyses offer little if any evidence to suggest that use rates increased more in civil penalty jurisdictions than elsewhere.

In the United States, medical marijuana laws have begun to create a subsystem that, under our taxonomy, would be considered a form of decriminalization verging on a highly regulated form of legalization. Medical marijuana laws have introduced a mechanism that allows patients to grow and use marijuana for medical purposes without facing the prospect of state prosecution, while still allowing the states and the federal government to continue prohibiting the large-scale cultivation, distribution, and ordinary possession of marijuana. Fifteen US states have provisions allowing for some type of medical marijuana; however, these subsystems of decriminalization differ from state to state. For example, in Colorado, a constitutional amendment providing for medical marijuana included the requirement that patients using medical marijuana possess a registry identification card issued by the state, and it provided for the establishment of a confidential state registry for this purpose.[64] In California, probably the best-known example of a medical marijuana regime in the United States, the Compassionate Use Act of 1996 simply declares as one of its purposes: "to ensure that patients and their primary caregivers who obtain and use marijuana for medical purposes upon the recommendation of a physician are not subject to crimi-

64. Colo. Const. art. XVIII, § 14, which states that "it shall be an exception from the state's criminal laws for any patient or primary care-giver in lawful possession of a registry identification card to engage or assist in the medical use of marijuana."

nal prosecution or sanction."[65] This act did not create a mandatory registry program for patients using medical marijuana. Rather, in 2004, California introduced a voluntary Medical Marijuana ID card, administered by the county governments.[66]

While California's medical marijuana dispensaries have been the focus of several news stories since the Obama administration announced that agencies in charge of enforcing federal drug laws would no longer raid such dispensaries (Johnson 2009), the legal status of dispensaries remains questionable, and it would be misleading simply to say that California legalized the "sale" of medical marijuana (Wohlsen and Risling 2009; Martin and del Barco 2009). The Compassionate Use Act did not provide for sales through such dispensaries, and the expanded codification of medical marijuana in California occurring in 2003 provided only for multiparty growing of marijuana in collectives and cooperatives.[67] California's attorney general has indicated that for dispensaries to operate legally in California, they must operate as a nonprofit, only sell to members of the collective, verify members' status as qualified patients or primary caregivers, only acquire marijuana from qualified members, and only cultivate and transport amounts required to meet the needs of the collective's members (State of California 2008).

The California courts have also placed limits on the ability of individuals cultivating and selling marijuana to avoid prosecution for possession and sale of the drug by claiming to be the primary caregiver of multiple patients. The California Supreme Court has held that a patient's primary caregiver must establish such status "based on evidence independent of the administration of medical marijuana," and that growth and supply of medical marijuana alone are insufficient to establish oneself as a primary caregiver.[68] The California Supreme Court has also held that employers can fire medical marijuana patients who test positive for marijuana as a result of a urinalysis, because the drug remains illegal at the federal level, and nothing prevents employers from terminating employees who use illegal substances.[69] Thus, while medical marijuana states like California have decriminalized marijuana possession and use for medical marijuana patients, users still face repercussions such as loss of employment and certain limitations on purchases of marijuana that would presumably be reduced or eliminated in a legalization regime.

---

65. Cal. Health & Safety Code § 11362.5 (West 2009).
66. Cal. Health & Safety Code § 11362.71 (West 2009).
67. Cal. Health & Safety Code § 11362.775 (West 2009), which provides that people with valid medical marijuana identification cards who "associate within the state of California collectively or cooperatively to cultivate marijuana for medical purposes, shall not solely on the basis of that fact be subject to state criminal sanctions. . . ."
68. People v. Mentch, 195 P.3d 1061, 1068 (California 2008).
69. Ross v. RagingWire Telecommunications, 174 P.3d 200, 204 (California 2008).

Legalization

From a cost-minimization perspective, the primary expected benefits of legalization over depenalization would be even more substantial reductions in government expenditures on drug control, new tax revenues to offset remaining government spending, the potential for increased government control over product standards and labeling information, and substantial reductions in drug-related crime costs. Government regulation of labeling and product standards could help mitigate the problems of increased potency and user uncertainty regarding whether the drug taken has been laced with, or partly replaced by, other harmful ingredients the consumer did not intend to use—such as PCP. As noted earlier, Miron (2005, 2–3) estimates that the tax revenues from legalized marijuana would indeed be substantial—somewhere between $2.4 and $6.2 billion.[70] By undermining the black market, marijuana legalization could also be expected to reduce systemic or economically motivated marijuana-related crime (as opposed to any toxicologically motivated marijuana crime), and the costs of law enforcement efforts targeted at marijuana. Miron (2005, 2) also estimates that legalization would save the federal and state governments a combined $7.7 billion in prohibition enforcement expenditures. While the assumptions required for such estimates make them imprecise, it is not implausible that for marijuana alone, the combination of tax revenues and diminished enforcement expenditures could boost government coffers by over $10 billion.

However, given the extremely large number of arrests for marijuana possession—far more than for sale—depenalization could achieve many of the same gains in reduced enforcement costs. Moreover, marijuana often has a much shorter distribution chain than cocaine; cultivation by individuals is common and many users receive marijuana from friends for free.[71] These social factors may help explain why violence appears to be significantly less common and severe in black markets for marijuana than in such markets for cocaine.[72] Hence, one of legalization's advantages over depenalization—

---

70. Taxing socially harmful substances will enhance social welfare to the extent that it corrects for externalities (and internalities). The tax revenues themselves are mere transfers from drug users and drug sellers to the government, although to the extent that the drug cartels are outside the United States, there may be some transfer of wealth away from countries such as Mexico to the United States. See generally, Kaplow (2004).

71. "Caulkins and Pacula (2006) analyzed the National Survey on Drug Use and Health and found that most users reported that they acquired their marijuana from a friend (89%) and for free (58%)" (Room et al. 2008, 74).

72. Room et al. (2008, 74–5) put it this way: "Violence is not commonly found in cannabis markets. This is mostly an inference from the absence of reports rather than any positive information that disputes between market participants are resolved amicably and that competition for territory is lacking. . . . The fact that the market is so imbedded in social networks may be an important factor in explaining the lack of violence." Much of the violence over marijuana distribution in the United States is taking place in Mexico, which is plagued by a shocking level of drug cartel-related violence.

its ability to undermine black markets—may be less important for marijuana than for cocaine. Legalization could also be expected to increase use more substantially than depenalization, although social costs of additional marijuana use could be mitigated if marijuana proved a partial substitute—rather than complement—for such drugs as cigarettes and alcohol.

We next consider additional considerations relevant to legalization: advertising, international legal obligations, and informational benefits.

Advertising. Legalization of marijuana in the United States might unleash the power of American advertising to entice consumers to use newly legalized substances while obscuring their dangers. There is some chance that an outright interdiction on advertisements of legalized drugs would be found to violate First Amendment speech protections. Twenty-five years ago, the Supreme Court held in *Posadas de Puerto Rico Associates v. Tourism Company* that if the government can ban a product or an activity like gambling, it can also proscribe advertising of that product or activity.[73] This might suggest that because marijuana and other drugs are currently prohibited, advertising of such products could be banned. More recent decisions, however, have suggested that the government is not necessarily empowered to ban truthful advertising, even of products it could otherwise proscribe.[74]

Steven Duke and Albert Gross (2006, 214–6) have called the *Posadas* decision an aberration and suggested that a complete ban on drug advertising could chill debate about the true dangers of drug use. Instead, these authors argue that a better way to limit advertising would be to withhold trademark protection from companies selling legalized drugs so that they would have no brand names to advertise, unlike today's alcohol and cigarette companies. In addition, Duke and Gross recommend placing warnings on print ads at least as large as the largest type in the ads and prohibiting radio and television advertising, which the Court has held to be immune from First Amendment protections because the airwaves are owned by the public.[75]

Evidence on the value of warning labels comes from Canada where colorful pictures of the damage to the body associated with smoking are placed on cigarette packages and required to cover at least 30 percent of the package material. The Canadian warnings have been found to be far more effective at inhibiting smoking than the bland American "Surgeon General's Warning" (Givel 2007). One of the most touted antidrug advertising campaigns in the United States has been Montana's attempt to counter its methamphetamine problem through television ads and billboards depicting the physical deformities and violent behavior caused by meth use. According to one analysis, two years after the introduction of the "Not Even Once" advertising campaign, meth use in Montana had dropped by one-half (Beale 2008).

73. Posadas de Puerto Rico Associates v. Tourism Company, 478 U.S. 328 (1986).
74. See, for example, 44 Liquormart, Inc. v. Rhode Island, 517 U.S. 484 (1996) (invalidating Rhode Island ban on advertising liquor prices).
75. See Capital Broadcasting Company v. Mitchell, 333 F. Supp. 582 (D.D.C. 1971), *aff'd sub nom.* Capital Broad. Company v. Kleindienst, 405 U.S. 1000 (1972).

Following legalization, rigorous requirements on packaging of newly legalized drugs and explicit counter advertisements could help reduce a sudden surge in demand.

Placing such explicit warnings on newly legalized drug products would raise questions about how to deal with alcohol and tobacco advertising following the legalization of currently illicit substances. If one were to enact strict regulations requiring graphic depictions of the harms of newly legalized drugs like marijuana, it would seem inconsistent to allow cigarette manufacturers to continue packaging cigarettes with the current Surgeon General's Warning, given that in terms of both lethality and addictiveness, marijuana may well be a less dangerous substance than nicotine (Gable 2006, 153). A comprehensive marketing policy on all dangerous substances might be difficult to accomplish, however, for political reasons.

An ongoing case filed in federal district court in Kentucky by several tobacco manufacturers and retailers could determine the extent to which the government may require large or graphic warning labels in print advertisements or product packaging.[76] In this case, the plaintiffs are seeking an injunction against sections of the Family Smoking Prevention and Tobacco Control Act requiring graphic warning labels on cigarette packaging similar to those found in Canada, curtailing the use of color advertising in magazines with over 15 percent readership or two million readers under age eighteen, and prohibiting the advertisement of tobacco products within 1,000 feet of school playgrounds.[77] In January 2010, the US District Court for the Western District of Kentucky granted the plaintiff tobacco companies' motion for summary judgment regarding the Family Smoking Prevention and Tobacco Control Act's provision requiring that all tobacco advertising appear in black text on a white background in magazines with over 15 percent readership or two million readers under the age of eighteen.[78] The court found that the ban violated the First Amendment because it was not narrowly tailored to serve the asserted state interest of protecting minors from tobacco advertising. The court seemed to place heavy emphasis on the fact that barring all color advertising would ban some of the logos and product symbols used by tobacco companies; product symbols whose meanings could not easily be translated into black and white text.[79] However, the court was more tolerant of the new warning requirements that mandate that cigarette packaging contain graphic warnings similar to those used in Canada, finding that these restrictions were narrowly tailored, and thus not in violation of the First Amendment.[80] This case will likely be appealed,

76. Complaint, Commonwealth Brands, Inc. v. United States, No. 00-117 (W.D. Ky. Aug. 31, 2009).

77. Pub. L. No. 111-31, 123 Stat. 1776 (2009).

78. Commonwealth Brands, Inc. v. United States, 678 F. Supp. 2d 512, 525–26 (W.D. Ky. 2010).

79. Ibid.

80. Ibid at 531–2.

and if it reaches the US Supreme Court, which many experts believe it will, its holding could shape the government's ability to restrict the advertisement of legalized drugs for decades to come.

International Law. Another complication for legalization is international law. While many researchers attempt to make international comparisons in studying drugs, one area of drug control policy that receives scant attention is the United Nations Single Convention on Narcotic Drugs of 1961 which binds all UN member nations to maintain prohibition of drugs, including cannabis specifically (Levine and Reinarman 2006, 61). While the Single Convention on Narcotic Drugs requires that countries maintain prohibition of manufacture, sales, and import, it does not require a punitive regime of the type currently found in the United States. Article 36 of the Single Convention, "Penal Provision," specifically allows for treatment programs to either enhance or serve as a substitute for punishment.[81] *The Economist* reports that countries like the Netherlands are able to allow for some innovation in controlling marijuana use through the convention's commentary, which states that its goal is "improvement of the efficacy of national criminal justice systems in the field of drug trafficking" ("A Toker's Guide" 2009). Thus, reforms working within the framework of the existing treaty are possible, though full-scale legalization would require either a country's withdrawal from the treaty or revision thereof.

Perhaps partly due to the Single Convention on Narcotic Drugs, even countries with more liberal narcotics policies than the United States lack full-fledged drug legalization and at most allow for depenalization of marijuana and/or widespread needle exchange programs. As discussed above, in the Netherlands, a country long known for its tolerance of marijuana smoking, the importation and commercial production of cannabis remains illegal (Levine and Reinarman 2006, 64). When considering its own drug reform, Portugal declined to adopt outright legalization likely in part because of its treaty obligations under the 1961 Single Convention (Cato Institute 2009).

Information Under Legalization. America's war on drugs is deeply entrenched, and powerful institutional forces make change difficult. In important ways the case for marijuana reform rests not only on the potential for the institution of an evidence-based, cost-minimizing approach to marijuana policy in its own right, but also on the possibility that marijuana reform might catalyze the use of such an approach in shaping drug policy in general. The National Research Council's *Informing America's Policy on Illegal Drugs: What We Don't Know Keeps Hurting Us* argued that our current form of criminalization severely limits the tools social science needs to study the effects of drugs and drug policies, and it therefore poses a serious obstacle for the possibility of making policy based on sound evidence. Criminalization obscures our knowledge of consumption patterns, prices,

---

81. Single Convention on Narcotic Drugs, art. 36, Mar. 25, 1961.

and potencies, and hence of the responsiveness of prices to policy changes.[82] Perhaps most significantly, because America has no recent experience with the legalization of major currently illegal drugs, there has been too little variation in the data to tease out the causal effects of prohibition or the likely consequences of its repeal.[83] Policy changes resulting in interstate variation in the treatment of marijuana would generate clearer information for analysts and policymakers.

5.3.3   Cocaine

Cocaine has made America's drug problem uniquely severe and has been at the heart of such national policies as President Reagan's push for an increasingly punitive War on Drugs in the 1980s and Plan Colombia in the 1990s. As already noted, the United States is an outlier in cocaine use in terms of the percentage of Americans having ever tried the substance, which is approximately four times that of the next highest use country included in a 2008 World Health Organization survey of international drug use, as seen in figure 5.2. Data from the 2009 World Drug Report, which compiles recent annual use figures from several dozen countries, indicate that in terms of current use rates the United States is no longer such an outlier. Nonetheless, figure 5.8 shows America's past-year prevalence rate is still among the highest in the world.

In order to better recognize the unique attributes of cocaine, we begin by offering a review of the psychopharmacology of the drug and then move into analyses of the problems with mandatory minimum sentencing and differences between the US approach and that of other countries.

Psychopharmacology and Systemic Crime

Much of America's strict prohibition on cocaine is premised on the belief that cocaine is far more damaging psychopharmacologically than other licit or illicit drugs. Regular cocaine use does lead to unquestionable medical and psychological problems. Cocaine is a stimulant, meaning that it causes the body to "speed up" the operation of ordinary functions. At low doses, physical effects of cocaine are similar to those of high doses of caffeine, including "nervousness, jitteriness, sleeplessness and agitation," whereas high doses of cocaine can result in "suspicion, hypervigilance, and paranoia," and extremely high doses can result in "a toxic psychosis, with symptoms similar to the delirium of high fever" (Morgan and Zimmer 1997, 137). As evidenced by the death of "body packers" who swallow balloons filled

82. See, for example, critiques of STRIDE price data (NRC 2001, 108–17).
83. That many authors focus on America's experience with alcohol prohibition and its repeal—notwithstanding the fact that both took place over seventy-five years ago, when social and economic conditions were quite different than today—is evidence of the dearth of American experience with transitions from some form of prohibition to legalization.

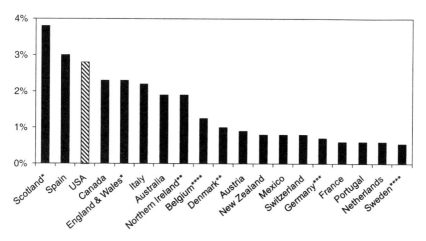

Fig. 5.8   Annual prevalence of cocaine use, population aged 15–64 (2004–2008)
Source: UNODC (2009, 240–4).
*Aged 16–59, **16–64, ***18–64; ****Percentage is the midpoint of a range.

with cocaine in order to transport the substance into the United States, cocaine can be deadly if consumed in large doses (137–8).

Though by nearly all accounts cocaine is more harmful to its users than marijuana, the belief that cocaine is not at all comparable to alcohol or nicotine is undermined by studies on lethality and addictiveness of common drugs. Using a safety ratio measure calculated by taking the lethal dose of a drug (the quantity that causes death in 50 percent of animals) and dividing it by the effective dose (the quantity necessary to produce the desired effect in 50 percent of animal populations), cocaine has a higher ratio (fifteen) than ethanol (ten), indicating that it carries less risk of accidental fatal overdose than alcohol (Gable 2006, 153).

As for the likelihood that one will become addicted to cocaine, sometimes called the "capture ratio," a 1999 study by The Institute of Medicine found that only 17 percent of those who try cocaine go on to become dependent on the substance, whereas the same figure is 32 percent for tobacco users as shown in figure 5.9 (Kershaw and Cathcart 2009). This finding comports with the latest Monitoring the Future study finding that while 7.2 percent of high school seniors report having used cocaine at least once in their lifetime, only 1.9 percent report having used cocaine in the past thirty days (NIDA 2009, 192, 199). This suggests that a large portion of those who try cocaine do not become regular users. A comparison with tobacco proves illustrative, because while 44.7 percent of high school students report having used tobacco at least once during their lifetimes, 20.4 percent report having used the substance in the past thirty days, suggesting that, at least given current law, tobacco has a higher addiction rate than cocaine (192, 199). This evi-

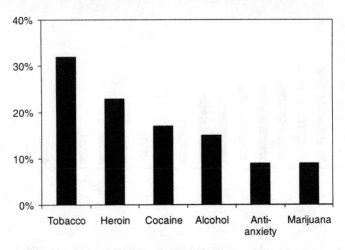

Fig. 5.9   Of those who tried, percentage later dependent, 1999
Source: Kershaw and Cathcart (2009).

dence tends to undermine the view that anyone trying cocaine will all but certainly become an addict.

US drug policy has also reflected exaggeration of differences between the psychopharmacological effects of cocaine and crack. The primary difference between cocaine and crack use stems from the differing routes of administration, with powder cocaine being snorted through the nose, while crack cocaine is generally smoked. Smoking crack leads to a quicker high than snorting powder cocaine because the large surface area of the lungs and the proximity of pulmonary to cerebral circulation allow for rapid absorption of the drug and a direct route to the brain (Belenko 1993, 34–5). This rapid absorption results in a high within five to ten seconds and a subsequent crash once the high wears off (35). Physically, crack smoking, like smoking of other drugs, can lead to a variety of lung problems.[84] Behaviorally, crack smoking is associated with many of the same problems observed in users of powder cocaine, including depression, loss of interest, nervousness, fatigue, sleeplessness, loss of appetite, and thoughts of suicide, though with higher prevalence than for powder cocaine users (38). However, these behavioral problems are gathered from surveys of crack users, and thus come from a self-selected population that may be predisposed to such disorders even without drug use (38).

While differences do exist between cocaine and crack, many of the policy changes, such as the much harsher federal sentencing guidelines for crack as

84. Belenko (1993, 40) reports that studies of crack smokers indicate "injury to the bronchial pathways," "lung irritation and inflammation, resulting in shortness of breath," "decreased ability to exchange air," pulmonary edema, and "pulmonary hemorrhaging possibly caused by the vasoconstricting action of cocaine."

opposed to powder cocaine, now appear to have been enacted partly because of an exaggeration of the differences between the effects of cocaine and crack. Consider, for example, the "crack baby" scare of the 1980s, during which the media highlighted the problem of numerous babies supposedly born addicted to crack. This scare appears to have been sensationalized. Recent research calls into question the supposed link between mothers using crack and children suffering from physical ailments different from those experienced by children whose mothers are not crack users (Morgan and Zimmer 1997, 152–4). Apparently, many of the problems associated with crack babies can be traced to the strong correlation between using crack and the failure of mothers to take other steps associated with prenatal health rather than physiological effects of crack use on the infants.

Psychopharmacological effects have been mischaracterized in other ways as well, beginning with the nature of the relationship between crack use and crime. Many people believe that crack causes crime because of its physical effects on the user. However, while crack was associated with a large increase in violence in American cities during the late 1980s, the psychopharmacological impact of the drug was largely not to blame. In a study of New York City murders committed during a six-month period of 1988—the height of the crack epidemic—researchers attempted to attribute the cause of homicides to three different drug-related factors: (a) psychopharmacological effects of drug use, (b) economic compulsion in which drug addicts kill while committing thefts to fund drug purchases, and (c) systemic effects of participating in the drug market, such as when a dealer kills one of his own agents (Goldstein et al. 1997, 117). These researchers determined that only 7.5 and 1.9 percent of the murders could be attributed solely to either the psychopharmacological effects of drug use or economic compulsion, respectively, (another 4.1 percent fell into multiple categories) whereas 39.1 percent were part of the systemic involvement in the illegal drug markets.[85] This study found that 52.6 percent of homicides in New York City during this peak period of the crack problem were in some way drug related. Nonetheless, the psychopharmacological effects of drugs do not appear to be the primary culprit in the correlation between homicide and crack use. This is underscored by the substantial crime and homicide drops in the 1990s, which, as figure 5.7 reveals, occurred even as the percentage of high school seniors reporting cocaine use in the past month rose through the decade, following a substantial decline in the late 1980s.

In other words, it appears more the clandestine nature of the market in which cocaine is traded rather than the drug itself that leads to violent crime. When two drug dealers or a drug dealer and customer have a dispute

85. 4.1 percent of the murders were categorized as "multidimensional," meaning that they are drug-related but that they fit into more than one of these categories. Of the murders involving drugs, 22 percent involved cocaine and 54 percent involved crack.

regarding a sale or drug turf, they cannot use the legal system to settle the dispute. Rather, they must work problems out on their own, often through violent means.

In a 1999 article, Miron contributed an analysis supportive of the systemic violence view based on national time series data through 1995. The data showed a positive correlation between an index of prohibition expenditures and the homicide rate that was statistically significant across several specifications and persisted even with controls for demographic variables, the unemployment rate, per capita income, the execution rate, and the incarceration rate (Miron 1999). The intuitive causal theory offered by Miron and others is that the more severe the prohibition on illegal drugs, the more attractive is violence relative to other mechanisms of dispute resolution and the greater is the diversion of law enforcement resources from other crimes. Notably, the relationship Miron identified in the data extended beyond the end of Prohibition in 1933—which, as we noted earlier, ushered in a major decrease in homicide (and crime, even in the midst of the Great Depression). Examining figure 5.10, our simple plot of Miron's prohibition enforcement index against the homicide rate, one sees that his national time series correlation appears strong up to the early 1990s (when Miron's original data set ended), after which time the story breaks down.

With more recent data provided to us by Miron and Angela Dills, his coauthor on a more recent paper again using national time series data to analyze the effect of a variety of variables on various measures of crime (Dills, Miron, and Summers 2008), we revisited Miron's original hypothesis and regression specifications.[86] We extended one of Miron's original regressions and several slight variations on that specification to nearly an additional decade of time and two subsets of the available data—1933 to 2004 and 1966 to 2004.[87] The regression from 1933 onward tested the sensitivity of the drug prohibition spending coefficient to the exclusion of early twentieth century data, the accuracy of which is questionable and upon which at least one econometrician has attempted to improve (Eckberg 1995).[88] The regression from 1966 onward tested whether the positive correlation between prohibition enforcement spending and the homicide rate held up for the last third of the twentieth century onward—the time period over which substantial antidrug spending emerged and the war on drugs became entrenched.[89]

---

86. Dills, Miron, and Summers (2008) find that for certain regressions on the homicide rate, an index of drug prohibition spending enters as a statistically significant independent variable. We follow Miron's original paper in using *Vital Statistics* rather than Uniform Crime Rates, for data on the homicide rate (Miron 1999, 90).

87. We used the Hildreth-Lu correction for serial correlation in all our regressions.

88. We also tested the entire available time span using Eckberg's adjusted pre-1933 homicide rate for the same purpose of identifying to what extent Miron's initial finding depended upon the early twentieth century and its questionable data.

89. Given the limitations of national time series data we deliberately chose not to replicate Miron's more heavily controlled specifications—from either his original 1999 paper or his more

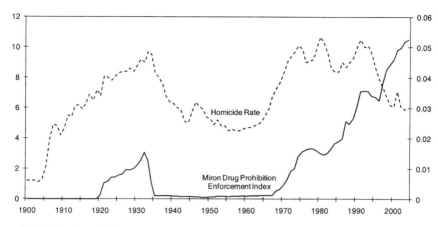

Fig. 5.10   Homicide rate (per 100,000 persons) v. drug prohibition enforcement index (hundreds of 1992 dollars per capita)

Source: Data supplied by Angela Dills and Jeffrey Miron (homicide rate from U.S. Vital Statistics; prohibition enforcement expenditures based on Miron (1999) with data from the Budget of the United States Government (various years)).

Finally, we conducted one additional set of regressions (which we do not report here) as a modest check on how well Miron's prohibition enforcement index proxies for overall spending on drug criminalization. Miron's index tracks the population- and inflation-adjusted expenditures by the one or two federal laws or agencies at any given time devoted exclusively to drug and/or alcohol prohibition, which have at many times been a relatively small component of total antidrug spending.[90] While the current state of available data makes it infeasible to incorporate state-level enforcement spending (which has been estimated to exceed federal spending and the absence of which is a shortcoming of Miron's approach),[91] we were able to test Miron's prohibition enforcement index as a proxy for overall domestic law enforcement spending by running simple, uncontrolled regressions for 1986 through 2001

recent broader study of economic analysis of crime, due to concern about drawing strong conclusions from national time series data and the misleading sense of definitiveness such specifications might suggest. This should in no way diminish the insights into model sensitivity that we reveal here. Indeed to the extent that results differ with certain alternative specifications in Miron's own partial follow-up paper, this only reaffirms the central importance of model specification. Moreover, given our skepticism about the possibility of comprehensively modeling the determinants of homicide using the relatively thin device that is national time series data, the problem of specification cannot simply be solved here by identifying some a priori ideal set of controls and focusing on regressions including them.

90. For a description of Miron's drug prohibition enforcement spending index and a variation thereof using projected rather than actual expenditures, which he also tested, see Miron (1999, 92–3). The drug spending index for which Miron and Dills sent us data was equal to annual spending in hundreds of 1992 dollars per capita.

91. For a brief concise discussion of state versus federal spending on drug control, see Boyum and Reuter (2005, 44). The authors note that state spending data are far sparser than federal spending data but the state data that do exist suggest state spending likely exceeds federal spending and is also probably more enforcement oriented than federal spending.

using total federal domestic law enforcement (population- and inflation-adjusted analogously to Miron's index), after which time the ONDCP's computation methodology radically changed (ONDCP 2002, 10–1; ONDCP 1998, 16). While the short time span is a concern, the general consistency of the results using the two different measures suggests that Miron's index offers a reasonable approximation of changes to at least federal domestic enforcement spending.

The first two columns of table 5.1 show Miron's original specifications through 1995 and the resulting positive coefficient on his drug prohibition spending index, which was significant at the 1 percent level. Our effort at reproducing Miron's original demographics-controlled regression also reveals a positive coefficient, albeit smaller and significant only at the 5 percent level.

When one extends the data beyond 1995, however, the relationship that Miron had established for the previous ninety-five years appears to break down. In our regressions on the homicide rate through 2004, starting in 1900 (with and without Eckberg's adjusted pre-1933 homicide rate), 1933, and 1966, the coefficient on the prohibition spending index is generally smaller and only for 1966 onward does Miron's full specification yield a coefficient on the prohibition spending index that is significant at the 5 percent level. Moreover, the R-squared values for the regressions from 1990 to 2004 are much lower than those for Miron's original regressions from 1900 to 1995.

The regression results do not fatally undermine the hypothesis that drug criminalization increases the homicide rate. They do, however, cast further doubt on the strength of empirical support (which was already only speculative and provisional) for Miron's intuitively plausible theory. Figure 5.10 reveals why the added data from the 1990s onward weakens the estimated relationship between prohibition enforcement expenditures and homicide: federal per capita drug prohibition spending has continued to rise despite a steady fall in the homicide rate.

A number of more general problems potentially plague the basic regression specifications: the enormous difficulty of drawing causal inferences from national time series data; the possibility that causality runs in both directions; and the omission of state enforcement expenditures and other possible explanatory factors. However, bearing in mind these various provisos, Miron's analysis is consistent with, and provides a notable (though tentative and limited) supplement to, more targeted analyses—such as the aforementioned study of New York murders—supporting the theory that criminalization does more harm by the systemic crime and violence it creates than good in any toxicologically induced crime it may prevent.

Costs of Incarceration

The criminalization of cocaine has greatly contributed to our country's vast prison population. Related problems with our current approach to

Table 5.1 Regressions of the homicide rate on prohibition enforcement

	Miron (1999)		Donohue, Ewing & Peloquin								
	1900–1995 (original results)		1900–1995		1900–2004		1900–2004 (Adj. Pre-1933)	1933–2004		1966–2004	
Miron index	***139.2*** (NW t-stat: 3.44) *	***90.1*** (NW t-stat: 3.08) *	**71.40** (32.98)	38.99 (31.26)	**58.99** (27.06)	60.42 (32.13)	42.43 (29.48)	37.64 (38.83)	27.44 (51.96)	**88.88** (35.44)	**94.39** (43.27)
Linear trend	*		***0.43*** (0.08)		−0.01 (0.13)	−0.01 (0.13)	0.08 (0.10)	0.15 (0.20)			−0.13 (0.46)
% Aged 5–14	*	*	49.14 (33.29)		53.28 (40.32)	51.76 (40.72)	**74.25** (35.86)	−6.01 (44.16)		***−345.34*** (109.29)	***−367.77*** (137.83)
% Aged 15–24	*	*	25.15 (18.50)		41.84 (28.90)	41.42 (30.07)	**49.13** (22.81)	8.74 (32.24)		***−201.40*** (60.92)	***−206.03*** (64.89)
% Aged 25–34	*	*	**81.50** (32.73)		70.12 (41.11)	69.10 (41.65)	**90.60** (35.46)	39.64 (37.16)		***−302.64*** (92.35)	***−304.45*** (94.46)
% Aged 35–44	*	*	−5.59 (33.27)		−31.29 (50.13)	−33.15 (50.80)	−4.35 (39.16)	−102.19 (56.43)		***−405.10*** (85.74)	***−394.10*** (92.09)
% Aged 45–54	*	*	−5.11 (36.13)		−8.80 (43.16)	−8.79 (48.94)	−16.26 (42.56)	−53.85 (64.38)		***−280.60*** (70.93)	−247.32 (133.60)
% Aged 55–64	*	*	27.90 (45.94)		−81.38 (68.44)	−85.88 (71.66)	−27.45 (54.65)	***−212.03*** (102.87)		***−558.29*** (115.97)	***−537.64*** (132.90)
% Aged 65+	*	*	**−352.92** (75.82)		53.44 (37.55)	54.03 (116.18)	0.51 (94.03)	−90.55 (199.72)		−138.92 (234.89)	−93.46 (290.42)
Intercept	*	*	−13.84 (21.80)	18.88 (26.45)	−12.50 (27.60)	−10.97 (28.81)	−27.99 (24.07)	37.34 (40.79)	−10.12 (58.46)	***292.01*** (69.18)	***295.51*** (72.00)
ρ	NA	NA	***0.67*** (0.08)	***1.00*** (0.00)	***0.94*** (0.01)	***0.94*** (0.01)	***0.78*** (0.05)	***0.75*** (0.07)	***1.00*** (0.01)	***0.52*** (0.07)	***0.53*** (0.06)
R^2	.53	.94	.72	.02	.20	.20	.45	.60	.01	.81	.80
Adj. R^2	*	*	.70	.01	.13	.12	.40	.54	−.02	.75	.74

Note: In his original paper Miron reported Newey and West *t*-statistics and incorporated a trend term; however, he did not specify in his article a chosen maximum lag order of autocorrelation for the Newey-West approach and did not further elaborate on the construction of his trend term. We regressed the homicide rate on Miron's chosen variables using the Hildreth-Lu correction for serial correlation. We report standard errors in parentheses. Asterisks indicate that the coefficient was not reported. Coefficients in bold are statistically significant at the 5 percent level; coefficients in bold italic are statistically significant at the 1 percent level.

cocaine are mandatory minimum sentences and the differential treatment of crack and powder cocaine. As discussed earlier, there is a large racial disparity between African Americans and Caucasians in terms of the percentage imprisoned for drug-related offenses. Much of this racial disparity is the result of mandatory sentences for possession and trafficking of crack that have been far more severe than those in place for powder cocaine. In the early 1990s, over 90 percent of federal defendants in crack cases were African American compared with only 25 percent of defendants in powder cocaine cases (Caulkins et al. 1997, 20).[92] Mandatory sentencing laws for drugs generally prescribe a sentence based on the quantity of the drug in question. Until just recently, under federal sentencing guidelines a defendant needed to possess an amount of powder cocaine one hundred times greater than the amount of crack cocaine in order to receive an equivalent sentence.[93] Thus a defendant convicted of possessing fifty grams of crack cocaine with intent to distribute faced a mandatory minimum sentence of ten years whereas a defendant would need to possess five kilograms of powder cocaine to expect the same sentence.

Though President Obama recently signed the Fair Sentencing Act, which is set to reduce the sentencing disparity ratio from 100 to 1 to 18 to 1 (CNN Wire Staff 2010), a significant differential will remain, and some states have also adopted more stringent sentences for crack cocaine than powder cocaine (Boyum and Reuter 2005, 52). Differences in state law treatment of the two drugs have the potential to be more important because more prisoners are convicted of crack offenses at the state rather than federal level each year.

In addition to the racial disparities created by mandatory sentencing laws, scholars have also noted additional concerns regarding their implementation. First among these is the fact that drug amounts are determined by mixture weight rather than pure weight. This introduces sentencing distortion because drugs sold in the illicit market vary greatly in their purity. For example, the sale of coca leaf, which contains only 2 percent cocaine, is treated the same as the sale of pure powder cocaine in terms of weight, even though 100 grams of coca leaf has the same amount of cocaine as two grams of pure cocaine (Caulkins et al. 1997, 23). The focus on weight also prevents a distinction between large-scale dealers, the "kingpins" of the

92. The most recent figures from the US Sentencing Commission indicate that in Fiscal Year 2008, 79.8 percent of those sentenced for offenses related to crack cocaine were black, 10.4 percent were white, 8.8 percent were Hispanic, and 1 percent were "other." For powder cocaine, the relevant figures are 30.2 percent black, 16.6 percent white, 52.3 percent Hispanic, and 1.0 percent "other." These data include those sentenced for drug trafficking, drug offenses occurring near a protected location, continuing criminal enterprise, use of a communication facility to facilitate a drug offense, renting or managing a drug establishment, and simple possession (US Sentencing Commission 2008b). As would be expected given the higher mandatory minimum sentences for crack cocaine as compared with powder cocaine, statistics from this same source indicate that defendants convicted on charges involving crack cocaine have median sentences of ninety-seven months, compared with a median of seventy months for those convicted of offenses involving powder cocaine (US Sentencing Commission 2008a).

93. Controlled Substances Act, 21 U.S.C. § 841 (2006).

business, and small time dealers. A kingpin may operate in such a way that he carries very little of a drug substance on him at any given time and thus when caught in possession with an intent to sell, receives a lighter sentence than one of his subordinates, who carries larger quantities of the substance in order to make frequent sales. Without the mandatory minimum sentences, judges would have more discretion to differentiate between the kingpin and the small-time dealer.

Mandatory sentences shift power from judges to prosecutors because prosecutors have discretion concerning whether to charge an individual with a crime carrying a given minimum sentence, whereas once the defendant is convicted, under a mandatory sentencing scheme the judge lacks the discretion to reduce a sentence (Caulkins et al. 1997, 24). Deciding whether it is preferable to grant more power to judges or prosecutors is a judgment call that depends on whether one believes such power should be vested in the executive or judicial branch; however, the shift in power is a clear impact of mandatory minimum sentencing laws.

Given the substantial costs of mandatory minimums, are they necessary or cost-justified deterrence mechanisms? Credible evidence suggests they are not. A 1997 empirical evaluation of the cost-effectiveness of mandatory drug sentences found mandatory minimums are less effective at reducing cocaine use than both conventional enforcement and treatment programs (Caulkins et al. 1997). The authors, part of the RAND Drug Policy Research Center, attempted to measure the effects on cocaine consumption of spending an additional $1 million on conventional enforcement, mandatory minimum sentences, or treatment. Looking at the 184,548 drug dealers convicted in state and federal courts during 1990, the authors estimated that were the federal mandatory minimum drug sentences applied to all of these dealers, the cost to the public for the additional prison time would be $22.5 billion.[94] According to the model tested in this study, longer sentences influence cocaine consumption by raising the price of cocaine as dealers increase prices in order to offset the increased probability of a longer prison sentence. Using an estimate that a drug dealer must be compensated an additional $37,500 per additional year of incarceration and a cost to the public of $25,000 per year of incarceration, they estimated that each dollar spent on longer sentences will translate into a $1.50 increase in total costs to consumers of cocaine. Thus they found that an additional $1 million spent on longer sentences would increase cocaine prices by 0.004 percent.[95] Over

94. The authors focus on federal mandatory minimum sentences because even though most of those imprisoned for possessing and distributing cocaine are in state prisons, they wish to capture the overall impact of mandatory sentencing laws rather than analyzing state-to-state differences in such laws.

95. The exact method by which Caulkins et al. derive the 0.004 percent increase in cocaine prices is as follows. They begin with an estimate from Mark Kleiman that a cocaine dealer needs to be compensated between $25,000 and $50,000 to incur a risk of spending one year in prison, choosing $37,500 because it is in the middle of Kleiman's range. They then divide this $37,500 by $25,000 (the cost of incarcerating a prisoner for one year) to determine that every

a fifteen-year time horizon, given a dealer discount rate of 12 percent and an elasticity of demand for cocaine of one, they determined that each additional $1 million spent on longer sentences reduces cocaine consumption by 12.6 kilograms nationwide (Caulkins et al. 1997, 103). Given estimated total annual consumption of 291,000 kilograms, this represents a change far less than one-hundredth of one percent. If one assumes the relationship to be linear over this range, every increase in incarceration costs of $1 billion per year might be expected to reduce cocaine consumption by about 4.3 percent.

When evaluating treatment programs, the RAND authors relied on Rydell and Everingham's (1994) study of cocaine treatment reporting that 13 percent of cocaine addicts abstain from hardcore cocaine use in the long-run following treatment and that 79 percent abstain during the 0.3 year length of the average treatment program. Given the $1,740 average cost of a treatment program, an extra $1 million could treat 575 heavy cocaine users, resulting in a sixteen kilogram reduction in the first year. Over a fifteen-year time horizon, given that 13 percent of heavy users quit heavy use following treatment, these authors estimated that each $1 million spent on treatment would reduce cocaine consumption by 103.6 kilograms, compared with 12.6 kilograms for longer sentences, making treatment appear much more effective (Caulkins et al. 1997, 105). While the linearity assumption might be more strained over this range, the comparison to the incarceration-increase numbers is revealing: an annual increase of $1 billion in spending on treatment might be expected to reduce cocaine consumption by 35.6 percent.

These findings are in line with Rydell and Everingham's (1994) examination of the effectiveness of treatment (both outpatient and residential programs) compared with three other drug enforcement policies: source country control (eradicating coca leaves in the country where they are grown), interdiction (seizures at the US border to prevent cocaine from entering the country), and domestic enforcement (cocaine seizures, asset seizures, and arrests of drug dealers by federal, state, and local law enforcement agencies). The authors found that the cost of crime and productivity loss from cocaine use decreases by $7.46 for every $1 spent on treatment whereas the same figure for source country control is $0.15 per dollar, $0.32 for interdiction, and $0.52 for domestic enforcement. Rydell and Everingham's initial study was criticized for underestimating the decrease in cocaine use stemming from increases in cocaine prices due to source country control, interdiction, and domestic enforcement. Repeating their study of policy effectiveness in

---

$1 spent by the government on incarceration imposes a cost of $1.50 on dealers, thus meaning that for every $1 million spent on incarceration, cocaine costs increase by $1.5 million. Caulkins et al. then use a cocaine price of $129.20 per gram and a sales quantity of 291,200 kg per year to calculate that $37.6 billion is spent on cocaine in the United States each year. Finally, they divide the $1.5 million increase in the cost of cocaine by $37.6 billion to find a 0.004 percent increase in the price of cocaine for every $1 million spent on incarceration.

2000, assuming a more elastic demand for cocaine, Caulkins, Chiesa, and Everingham (2000) determined that treatment has a four-to-one advantage over domestic enforcement in reducing the costs of crime and productivity losses.

Overall, this evidence on treatment versus severe punishment for those found possessing or dealing cocaine today suggests that mandatory treatment for drug offenders is a more cost-effective solution. As with marijuana policy, there appear to be many potential improvements for cocaine policy, even within the regime of criminalization.

5.4   Conclusion

In the United States—indeed, throughout the world—many individuals are drawn to substances that may harm them greatly. Public policy varies enormously with respect to these substances, partly based on the degree of addiction, the nature of harms, and historical experience. Though sugar, saturated fat, and high fructose corn syrup impose enormous health costs, regulation to discourage consumption of them is virtually nonexistent; in fact, corn subsidies in particular have been criticized for perversely incentivising poor diets. In contrast, tobacco and alcohol are subject to considerable regulation while remaining legal, and a host of drugs ranging from heroin and cocaine to methamphetamine, ecstasy, LSD, and marijuana are banned by state and federal law.

Tobacco imposes high costs on a large proportion of users because the addiction is powerful and the health cost of decades of use will likely be great. Nonetheless, consumption rates tend to be high because the health costs are temporally distant, and governments tend not to prohibit consumption because current productivity and parenting ability are not discernibly impaired. Interestingly, perhaps the greatest domestic success in reducing consumption of harmful substances came for this lawful product, engineered largely through tax hikes via the settlement of tort litigation against the tobacco companies.

Other harmful recreational substances vary in terms of addictiveness and the ability of large numbers of users to enjoy them sporadically and without substantial health cost or productivity impairment for work and parenting. But for sizeable percentages—perhaps 10 percent for marijuana users, 15 percent for alcohol and cocaine users, and almost 25 percent for heroin users (see figure 5.9)—the personal and social costs are dramatic and substantial. It is largely to reduce these costs to this minority of users that governments have banned, and tried to keep as many people as possible away from marijuana, cocaine, methamphetamine, and heroin (and sought to control various legal pharmaceuticals that similarly seem to be used without substantial cost by most while imposing great burdens for some not inconsiderable fraction of users).

Estimates placing the economic costs of illegal drug abuse at levels roughly comparable to those costs for alcohol and tobacco underscore that there are no easy choices when it comes to drug policy. Aggressive efforts to limit consumption through a tough penal approach tend to restrain the costs from drug use while unleashing the high costs of enforcement and incarceration in a context of increased violence centered around the criminal gangs that run the drug trade. Conversely, legalization of alcohol and tobacco drastically reduces enforcement costs with respect to these substances while keeping the costs of consumption high. A cost-minimizing approach to drug policy might move us away from a punitive approach to control of the currently illegal drugs, while entailing aggressive measures to prevent underage consumption and constrain demand.

On the other hand, while thorough consideration of policy toward legal drugs is beyond the scope of the present inquiry, comparisons of their toxicological effects and social costs with those attributable to such illegal drugs as marijuana and cocaine suggest that more vigorous pursuit of demand-restraint policies for alcohol and tobacco may result in a reduction of the social costs of those drugs. At some point, insights from social science and medical testing may be refined enough, and widely enough disseminated, to enable potential users to secure better advance notice regarding their particular susceptibility to the serious consequences of drug and alcohol abuse. At present, many individuals find out the hard way, at great cost to themselves and society. Despite the problem of moral hazard, greater treatment seems to offer a more cost-effective method for dealing with these abusers than criminal penalties.

Our analysis has also underscored that optimal drug policy is likely to differ from one drug to another, since, for example, the impact of government policies—current and hypothetical—may be substantially different for an extremely prevalent drug with relatively mild toxicological effects, such as marijuana, than for a far less common, but more addictive and dangerous drug, such as cocaine. Given the differences in prevalence, user base composition, toxicological effects and distribution networks between marijuana and cocaine, depenalization or legalization would impact the magnitude and distribution of social costs in meaningfully different ways for these two drugs.

Yet if reform's risks and likely impacts upon the distribution of social costs differ from drug to drug, our analysis nevertheless concludes that for both cocaine and marijuana, there is considerable potential for reducing the overall social costs. Our review of theory and empiricism suggests that carefully tailored versions of depenalization or legalization might provide these cost reductions, and additional analytic scrutiny could further clarify their likely impacts.

In light of the admitted uncertainty in empirical predictions of use rates under hypothetical new regimes, and considering the many important values that a cost-minimization approach fails to entertain, we are not surprised that many observers fear or dismiss alternatives to criminalization.[96] Distributional issues, although undertheorized in the illegal drug policy context, arguably underlie much concern about reform. While we follow standard economic analysis and treat a dollar in costs equally across contexts, politicians and voters are attentive to who bears the costs of alternative policies. Particularly troublesome to opponents of legalization—and to a lesser extent depenalization—may be that such reform would redistribute many costs away from current drug users, sellers, and the government and on to a new set of victims: the new drug users and victims of accidents, a group whose ranks could include one's neighbors, relatives, or even one's own children.[97] Upper middle class voters with influence over policy may believe that marijuana prohibition protects their children by placing costs on lower class drug sellers and other countries (such as Mexico). The supporters of prohibition will point to the lower rates of marijuana use by high school seniors today than in the late 1970s as evidence for the success of the prohibitionist approach. But, as figure 5.11 illustrates, substantial historical drops in tobacco and alcohol consumption by high school seniors show that consumption declines by the young can be engineered even for legal substances. Moreover, events from Kabul to Mexico City show that policies of drug prohibition enrich violent forces internationally in ways that can impose large indirect costs on the United States.

While we refrain from analyzing distributional consequences in depth, we are keenly aware of the concern they engender. Our relative optimism about the potential of depenalization or legalization to reduce the costs of certain illegal drugs does not come from a sense that such drugs are not socially harmful. We believe any serious analysis of reform must be especially sensi-

96 We also note that many vocal pundits have vested interests in maintaining the status quo criminalization—a reality that helps explain both much opposition to reform among commentators and the political intractability of illegal drug policy reform. An entire federal bureaucracy, the Drug Enforcement Administration (DEA) has been created to enforce the current prohibition regime, the prison guard unions benefit enormously from the large number of prisoners kept behind bars on drug-related charges, and a multimillion dollar industry has emerged to supply the preemployment drug screening needs of large employers of low-wage workers such as Walmart and Target. The drug testing industry may be the group most opposed to changes involving the reduction of penalties for marijuana use. In the typical urinalysis used in preemployment drug screens, the detection window for marijuana is longer than that for drugs considered more serious, such as cocaine (Boyum and Reuter 2005, 82). Thus, while private employers may continue to require drug screens prior to employment, anything that would make marijuana use more acceptable and thus less of a basis for screening out employment candidates could significantly damage the drug testing industry.

97. While it is easy to appreciate in theory that costs borne by the government are channeled back to society at large through higher taxes and/or forgone spending, such costs are spread diffusely and the individual taxpayer cannot easily measure changes in her burden, if she can perceive them at all.

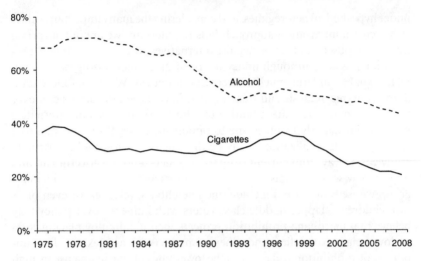

Fig. 5.11   Percentage of 12th graders reporting use of licit drugs in past 30 days
Source: NIDA (2009, 198–9).

tive to policies for tailoring depenalization or legalization to mitigate costs from increases in use.[98] Counteradvertising, treatment, age restrictions, and policies against driving while under the influence—to list just a few such ideas—would together not just alter at the margin but integrally affect a new regime for any currently illegal drug.

In thinking about various options for reforming policy toward marijuana or cocaine, it is helpful to bear in mind that a choice among criminalization, depenalization, and legalization could be made with the aim of minimizing social costs, rather than simply curtailing use—the socially costly goal toward which our current policy of criminalization seems oriented. Maintaining a focus on the social harms of a drug, not just less subtle measures of the prevalence of use, helps to clarify the effects of policies that rely predominantly on tough criminal penalties.

However, even those who would design drug policy principally to minimize use prevalence should not discount the potential of a carefully tailored version of depenalization or legalization to serve that goal. Consider Becker's suggestion that if the goal of reduced consumption (particularly for the young) is largely derived via maintaining high prices, this goal could be achieved at lower social cost by legalizing and taxing up to the level of

98. In at least one important way, increases in use of a legalized drug would be inherently much less harmful than increases in use when a drug is proscribed: they would not contribute to the black market and its associated violence and crime. Would domestic violence and date rape increase? These are concerns, but in periods of declining crime, domestic violence also tends to fall, so the problem might be mitigated.

current price (Becker, Murphy, and Grossman 2006).[99] While the merits of this argument will depend upon the specifics of the legalization policy and the drugs to which it is applied, some general theoretical considerations are worth stressing.

The socializing impact of legalization and possible attendant product advertising could increase individuals' preference for a socially harmful substance, increasing demand for the drug at any given price even if an excise tax were designed to simultaneously keep the price from falling too greatly.[100] Moreover, the greater the excise tax, the less effective legalization would be at shrinking the black market as illegal dealers would find a higher legal price easier to undercut. There is yet another basic tension in Becker's view: while it assumes consumers are responsive predominantly to price rather than the moral command of illegality (and hence its loss under legalization is a minimal cost), it also presumes that consumers will largely turn away from the lower priced illegal drugs that skirt the excise tax.[101]

Yet although legalization with significant taxation would not eliminate the black market for a drug entirely, it would be expected to shrink substantially the size of the illegal market, with the attendant cost reductions from less crime. The remaining black market would also have diminished risk and profit margins, thus providing less economic incentive for participants to engage in costly crime and violence to maintain their stakes. Moreover, the additional tax revenues could be used to fund greater enforcement to protect the underaged (as well as to target the tax evaders), while providing greater vehicles for treatment for those who succumb to the burdens of addiction and abuse. Finally, it is not insignificant that legalization is the only regime that does not contemplate untold numbers of illegal transactions by otherwise law-abiding individuals, and an attendant diminished respect for, and faith in, the rule of law.[102]

Similarly, a well-crafted form of depenalization is not necessarily antithetical to the goal of discouraging drug use. Like legalization, depenalization

99. Becker, Murphy, and Grossman (2006, 38) argue that where demand or supply for a good is inelastic, "a monetary tax could cause a greater reduction in output and increase in price than optimal enforcement against the same good would if it were illegal, even though some producers may go underground to avoid a monetary tax."

100. Depenalization might be less likely to present this particular problem, although it is worth pondering whether a regime of legalization coupled with counteradvertising might be able to avoid the appearance of governmental toleration of drugs and convey an official stance of discouraging use.

101. Greater product information and lesser risk of contamination would provide significant reasons for consumers to prefer the legal markets, but could also, undesirably, stimulate new demand—not just divert existing demand from illegal markets to legal ones.

102. One possible exception to this otherwise straightforward observation is the case of drugs—such as marijuana—that can be produced domestically with relative ease. Full decriminalization of marijuana possession could substantially erode the number of illegal marijuana sales by diverting consumers toward home cultivation for personal use.

could also significantly reduce the enforcement costs and productivity losses from the arrest and legal processing of hundreds of thousands of marijuana possession cases—and some of the costs from analogous proceedings, plus incarceration, in the context of cocaine. Although one might worry that depenalization would expand consumption without contracting the black market, and that full decriminalization of possession would appear hypocritical when combined with the retention of criminal penalties for sale, it is not clear that these concerns would be borne out in practice. Particularly if sanctions were reduced for sale as well as possession, depenalization could, like legalization, reduce the risk and reward for illegal market participants, thus diminishing the likelihood of violence used to protect their market positions. Depenalization of possession alone could not only reduce enforcement costs but also—as the insights of Kleiman (2009) help show—increase the potential swiftness, certainty, and deterrence value per sanction unit, for situations where punishments were applied. It might also help usher in a policy shift toward harm reduction—a new orientation toward helping, rather than punishing, the victims of drug abuse. Rather than being an example of hypocritical or morally ambiguous policy, depenalization could be framed as a new understanding of which activities are sufficiently harm-producing to merit criminalization (i.e., sale) and which are not (i.e., possession). Indeed, the experience of a number of European countries suggests that depenalization could reduce the costs of enforcement, redirect efforts toward helping problem users, and perhaps even reduce the violence of illegal markets, without these gains being outweighed by increased costs from use.[103]

Although our inquiry into illegal drug policy has been a self-conscious search for a cost-minimizing regime, our evaluation of various policy options can also provide a basis for analysis by those who would prefer simply to minimize use cost-effectively or who would conduct a full welfare analysis including the benefits of use for the many casual or moderate users who do not fall victim to costly abuse or dependence.

References

Abraham, Manja D. 1999. "Places of Drug Purchase in the Netherlands." Paper presented at the 10th Annual Conference on Drug Use and Drug Policy, Vienna, Austria. http://proxy.baremetal.com/csdp.org/research/places.pdf.

American Correctional Association (ACA). 2006. *2006 Directory of Adult and Juvenile Correctional Departments, Institutions, Agencies, and Probation and Parole Authorities,* 67th ed. Alexandria, VA: American Correctional Association.

103. Of course, for reasons already mentioned, such comparisons need to be handled with care.

Associated Press (AP). 2009. "U.S. Drug Cartel Crackdown Misses the Money." MSNBC, December 17. http://www.msnbc.msn.com/id/34466436/.

Beale, Jonathan. 2008. "Montana Meth Ads Winning Drug Battle." *BBC News,* August 22. http://fvgroup.com/news/BBC%208.22.08.pdf.

Becker, Gary S., and Kevin M. Murphy. 1988. "A Theory of Rational Addiction." *Journal of Political Economy* 96 (4): 675–700.

Becker, Gary S., Kevin M. Murphy, and Michael Grossman. 2006. "The Market for Illegal Goods: The Case of Drugs." *Journal of Political Economy* 114 (1): 38–60.

Belenko, Steven R. 1993. *Crack and the Evolution of Anti Drug-Policy.* Westport, CT: Greenwood Press.

Boyum, David, and Peter Reuter. 2005. *An Analytic Assessment of U.S. Drug Policy.* Washington, DC: AEI Press.

Brice, Arthur. 2009. "Argentina Ruling Would Allow Personal Use of Pot." CNN, August 25. http://www.cnn.com/2009/WORLD/americas/08/25/argentina.drug.decriminalization/index.html.

Browning, Dominique. 2009. "Reefer Madness." *New York Times,* August 27. http://www.nytimes.com/2009/08/30/books/review/Browning-t.html.

Bureau of Justice Statistics (BJS) 2001. *Federal Drug Offenders, 1999 with Trends 1984–99.* Washington, DC: US Department of Justice, Office of Justice Programs.

———. 2008. *Special Report: Parents in Prison and their Minor Children.* Washington, DC: US Department of Justice, Office of Justice Programs.

———. 2009. *Drugs and Crime Facts.* Washington, DC: US Department of Justice, Office of Justice Programs.

Caspers-Merk, Marion. 2003. *Action Plan on Drugs and Addiction.* Bonn, Germany: German Federal Ministry of Health.

Cato Institute. 2009. "Drug Decriminalization in Portugal." Policy Forum featuring Glenn Greenwald and Peter Reuter, April 3. http://www.cato.org/event.php?eventid=5887.

Caulkins, Jonathan P., James Chiesa, and Susan S. Everingham. 2000. *Response to the National Research Council's Controlling Cocaine Study.* Santa Monica, CA: RAND Corporation.

Caulkins, Jonathan P., and Mark A. R. Kleiman. 2007. "Drug Policy." In *Understanding America: The Anatomy of an Exceptional Nation,* edited by Peter H. Schuck and James Q. Wilson, 563–96. New York: Public Affairs.

Caulkins, Jonathan P., and Rosalie Liccardo Pacula. 2006. "Marijuana Markets: Inferences from Reports by the Household Population." *Journal of Drug Issues* 36 (1): 173–200.

Caulkins, Jonathan P., C. Peter Rydell, William L. Schwabe, and James Chiesa. 1997. *Mandatory Minimum Drug Sentences: Throwing Away the Key or the Taxpayer's Money?* Santa Monica, CA: RAND Corporation.

CNN Wire Staff. 2010. "Obama Signs Bill Reducing Cocaine Sentencing Gap." CNN, August 3. http://articles.cnn.com/2010-08-03/politics/fair.sentencing_1_powder-cocaine-cocaine-sentencing-gap-sentencing-disparity?_s=PM:POLITICS.

Cohen, Mark A. 1999. "Alcohol, Drugs and Crime: Is 'Crime' Really One-Third of the Problem?" *Addiction* 94 (5): 644–47.

Cook, Philip J. 2007. *Paying the Tab: The Economics of Alcohol Policy.* Princeton, NJ: Princeton University Press.

Degenhardt, Louisa, Wai-Tat Chiu, Nancy Sampson, Ronald C. Kessler, James C. Anthony, Matthias Angermeyer, Ronny Bruffaerts, et al. 2008. "Toward a Global View of Alcohol, Tobacco, Cannabis, and Cocaine Use: Findings from the WHO

World Mental Health Surveys." *PLoS Medicine* 5 (7): e141. doi:10.1371/journal.pmed.0050141.

Dills, Angela K., Jeffrey A. Miron, and Garrett Summers. 2008. "What Do Economists Know About Crime?" NBER Working Paper no. 13759. Cambridge, MA: National Bureau of Economic Research, January.

DiNardo, John, and Thomas Lemieux. 2001. "Alcohol, Marijuana, and American Youth: The Unintended Consequences of Government Regulation." *Journal of Health Economics* 20 (6): 991–1010.

Donohue III, John J. 2009. "Assessing the Relative Benefits of Incarceration: The Overall Change over the Previous Decades and the Benefits on the Margin." In *Do Prisons Make Us Safer? The Benefits and Costs of the Prison Boom*, edited by Steven Raphael and Michael Stoll, 269–341. New York: Russell Sage Foundation.

Drug Enforcement Administration (DEA). 2005. "Drug Intelligence Brief: The Changing Face of European Drug Policy." In *Drug War Deadlock: The Policy Battle Continues*, edited by Laura E. Higgins, 247–57. Stanford, CA: Hoover Institution Press.

———. 2003. *Speaking Out Against Drug Legalization*. Washington, DC: US Department of Justice. http://www.justice.gov/dea/demand/speakout/speaking_out-may03.pdf.

Duke, Steven B., and Albert C. Gross. 2006. "Issues in Legalization." In *Drugs and Society: U.S. Public Policy*, edited by Jefferson M. Fish, 201–22. Lanham, MD: Rowman & Littlefield Publishers.

Eckberg, Douglas L. 1995. "Estimates of Early Twentieth Century U.S. Homicide Rates: An Econometric Forecasting Approach." *Demography* 32 (1): 1–16.

European Monitoring Centre for Drugs and Drug Addiction (EMCDDA). 2005. *Illicit Drug Use in the EU: Legislative Approaches*. Lisbon: European Monitoring Centre for Drugs and Drug Addiction.

———. 2008. *Annual Report: The State of the Drug Problem in Europe*. Luxembourg: Office for Official Publications of the European Communities.

European School Survey Project on Alcohol and Other Drugs (ESSPAOD). 2003. *The ESPAD Report 2003: Alcohol and Other Drug Use Among Students in 35 European Countries*. Stockholm: Modintryckoffset. http://www.espad.org/documents/Espad/ESPAD_reports/The_2003_ESPAD_report.pdf.

Fainaru, Steve, and William Booth. 2009. "Cartels Face an Economic Battle." *Washington Post*, October 7. http://www.washingtonpost.com/wp-dyn/content/article/2009/10/06/AR2009100603847.html.

Federal Bureau of Investigation (FBI) Uniform Crime Reporting Program. 2007. *Persons Arrested—Crime in the United States, 2007*. Washington, DC: Federal Bureau of Investigation.

Gable, Robert S. 2006. "Acute Toxicity of Drugs Versus Regulatory Status." In *Drugs and Society: U.S. Public Policy*, edited by Jefferson M. Fish, 149–62. Lanham, MD: Rowman & Littlefield Publishers.

Givel, Michael. 2007. "A Comparison of the Impact of U.S. and Canadian Cigarette Pack Warning Label Requirements on Tobacco Industry Profitability and the Public Health." *Health Policy* 83 (2–3): 343–52.

Goldstein, Paul J., Henry H. Brownstein, Patrick J. Ryan, and Patricia A. Belluci. 1997. "Crack and Homicide in New York City: A Case Study in the Epidemiology of Violence." In *Crack in America: Demon Drugs and Social Justice*, edited by Craig Reinarman and Harry G. Levine, 113–30. Berkeley, CA: University of California Press.

Gore, Robert, and Mitch Earleywine. 2007. "Marijuana's Perceived Addictiveness:

A Survey of Clinicians and Researchers." In *Pot Politics: Marijuana and the Costs of Prohibition,* edited by Mitch Earleywine, 176–88. New York: Oxford University Press.

Greene, Judith A. 1988. "Structuring Criminal Fines: Making an 'Intermediate Penalty' More Useful and Equitable." *Justice System Journal* 13 (1): 37–50.

Greenwald, Glenn. 2009. *Drug Decriminalization in Portugal: Lessons for Creating Fair and Successful Drug Policies.* Washington, DC: Cato Institute.

Grossman, Michael, Frank J. Chaloupka, and Richard Anderson. 1998. "A Survey of Economic Models of Addictive Behavior." *Journal of Drug Issues* 28 (3): 631–43.

Harcourt, Bernard E., and Jens Ludwig. 2007. "Reefer Madness: Broken Windows Policing and Misdemeanor Marijuana Arrests in New York City, 1989–2000." *Criminology and Public Policy* 6 (1): 165–82.

Harwood, Hendrick. 2000. *Updating Estimates of the Economic Costs of Alcohol Abuse in the United States: Estimates, Update Methods, and Data.* Washington, DC: National Institute on Alcohol Abuse and Alcoholism. http://pubs.niaaa.nih .gov/publications/economic-2000/alcoholcost.pdf.

Hawken, Angela, and Mark Kleiman. 2009. *Managing Drug Involved Probationers with Swift and Certain Sanctions: Evaluating Hawaii's HOPE.* Award No. 2007-IJ-CX-0033. Washington, DC: National Institute of Justice, Office of Justice Programs, US Department of Justice.

Hertzberg, Hendrick. 2008. "Higher Standards." *New Yorker,* February 25.

Heyman, Gene M. 2009. *Addiction: A Disorder of Choice.* Cambridge, MA: Harvard University Press.

Home Office. 2009. *Cannabis Reclassification.* Accessed December 20. http://drugs .homeoffice.gov.uk/drugs-laws/cannabis-reclassifications/.

Husak, Douglas. 2007. "Do Marijuana Offenders Deserve Punishment?" In *Pot Politics: Marijuana and the Costs of Prohibition,* edited by Mitch Earleywine, 189–207. New York: Oxford University Press.

Johnson, Carrie. 2009. "U.S. Eases Stance on Medical Marijuana." *Washington Post,* October 20. http://www.washingtonpost.com/wpdyn/content/article/2009/10/19/ AR2009101903638.html.

Kaplan, John. 1983. *The Hardest Drug: Heroin and Public Policy.* Chicago: The University of Chicago Press.

Kaplow, Louis. 2004. "On the (Ir)Relevance of Distribution and Labor Supply Distortion to Government Policy." *Journal of Economic Perspectives* 18 (4): 159–75.

Kershaw, Sarah, and Rebecca Cathcart. 2009. "Marijuana is Gateway Drug for Two Debates." *New York Times,* July 19. Http://www.nytimes.com/2009/07/19/ fashion/19pot.html.

Kessler, Ronald C., Patricia Berglund, Olga Demler, Robert Jin, Kathleen R. Merikangas, and Ellen E. Walters. 2005. "Lifetime Prevalence and Age-of-Onset Distributions of DSM-IV Disorders in the National Comorbidity Survey Replication." *Archives of General Psychiatry* 62 (6): 593–602.

King, Ryan S., and Marc Mauer. 2006. "The War on Marijuana: The Transformation of the War on Drugs in the 1990s." *Harm Reduction* 3:6. doi:10.1186/1477-7517- 3-6.

Kleiman, Mark A. R. 1999. "'Economic Cost' Measurements, Damage Minimization and Drug Abuse Control Policy." *Addiction* 94 (5): 638–41.

———. 2006. "Prohibition: A Rum Do." *Druglink* 22 (4): 14–5.

———. 2009. *When Brute Force Fails: How to Have Less Crime and Less Punishment.* Princeton, NJ: Princeton University Press.

Kleiman, Mark A. R., and Aaron J. Saiger. 1990. "Drug Legalization: The Importance of Asking the Right Question." *Hofstra Law Review* 18 (3): 527–65.

Klein, Joe. 2009. "Why Legalizing Marijuana Makes Sense." *Time,* April 2.

Kopp, Pierre. 1999. "Economic Costs Calculations and Drug Policy Evaluation." *Addiction* 94 (5): 641–44.

Lacey, Marc. 2009. "In Mexican Drug War, Investigators Are Fearful." *New York Times,* October 16. http://www.nytimes.com/2009/10/17/world/americas/17juarez.html.

Landler, Marc. 2009. "Clinton Says U.S. Feeds Mexico Drug Trade." *New York Times,* March 25. http://www.nytimes.com/2009/03/26/world/americas/26mexico.html.

Levine, Harry G., and Craig Reinarman. 2006. "Alcohol Prohibition and Drug Prohibition." In *Drugs and Society: U.S. Public Policy,* edited by Jefferson M. Fish, 43–76. Lanham, MD: Rowman & Littlefield Publishers.

Luhnow, David, and José de Cordoba. 2009. "Mexico Eases Ban on Drug Possession." *The Wall Street Journal,* August 22, A1.

MacCoun, Robert J., Rosalie Liccardo Pacula, Jamie Chriqui, Katherine Harris, and Peter Reuter. 2009. "Do Citizens Know Whether Their State Has Decriminalized Marijuana? Assessing the Perceptual Component of Deterrence Theory." *Review of Law and Economics* 5 (1): 347–71.

MacCoun, Robert J., and Peter Reuter. 2005. "Does Europe Do it Better?" In *Drug War Deadlock: The Policy Battle Continues,* edited by Laura E. Huggins, 262–69. Stanford, CA: Stanford University Press.

———. 2001. *Drug War Heresies: Learning from Other Vices, Times, and Places.* Cambridge, England: Cambridge University Press.

MacCoun, Robert, Peter Reuter, and Thomas Schelling. 1996. "Assessing Alternative Drug Control Regimes." *Journal of Policy Analysis and Management* 15 (3): 330–52.

Martin, Michel, and Mandalit del Barco. 2009. "In California, Medical Marijuana Dispensaries Outnumber Starbucks." National Public Radio, October 15. http://www.npr.org/templates/story/story.php?storyId=113822156.

Mauer, Marc. 2009. *The Changing Racial Dynamics of the War on Drugs.* Washington, DC: The Sentencing Project.

Miron, Jeffrey. 1999. "Violence and the U.S. Prohibition of Drugs and Alcohol." *American Law and Economics Review* 1 (1): 78–114.

———. 2003. *A Critique of Estimates of the Economic Cost of Drug Abuse.* New York: Drug Policy Alliance.

———. 2005. *The Budgetary Implications of Marijuana Prohibition.* Washington, DC: Marijuana Policy Project. http://www.heartland.org/custom/semod_policybot/pdf/17483.pdf.

———. 2008. *The Budgetary Implications of Drug Prohibition.* Silver Spring, MD: Criminal Justice Policy Foundation. http://big.assets.huffingtonpost.com/miron-economic-report.pdf.

Moffett, Matt. 2009. "Argentina Eases Rules on Marijuana." *Wall Street Journal,* August 26, A11.

Morgan, John P., and Lynn Zimmer. 1997. "The Social Pharmacology of Smokeable Cocaine: It's Not All It's Cracked up To Be." In *Crack in America: Demon Drugs and Social Justice,* edited by Craig Reinarman and Harry G. Levine, 131–70. Berkeley, CA: University of California Press.

Mumola, Christopher J., and Jennifer C. Karberg. 2007. *Drug Use and Dependence, State and Federal Prisoners, 2004.* Washington, DC: US Department of Justice, Office of Justice Programs.

National Council on Alcoholism and Drug Dependence (NCADD). 2002. *Alcoholism and Drug Dependence Are America's Number One Health Problem.* Accessed December 20, 2009. http://www.ncadd.org/facts/numberoneprob.html.

National Institute on Drug Abuse (NIDA). 2009. *Monitoring the Future, National Survey Results on Drug Use: 1975–2008, Secondary Students.* Bethesda, MD: National Institute on Drug Abuse. http://www.monitoringthefuture.org/pubs/monographs/vol1_2008.pdf.

National Research Council (NRC). 2001. *Informing America's Policy on Illegal Drugs: What We Don't Know Keeps Hurting Us.* Washington, DC: National Academy Press.

Office of National Drug Control Policy (ONDCP). 1998. *The National Drug Control Strategy 1998: Budget Summary.* Washington, DC: Office of National Drug Control Policy. http://www.ncjrs.gov/ondcppubs/publications/pdf/budget98.pdf.

———. 2002. *National Drug Control Strategy: FY2003 Budget Summary.* Washington, DC: Office of National Drug Control Policy. http://www.whitehousedrugpolicy.gov/publications/pdf/budget2002.pdf.

———. 2004. *The Economic Costs of Drug Abuse in the United States, 1992–2002.* Publication 207303. Washington, DC: Executive Office of the President. www.ncjrs.gov/ondcppubs/publications/pdf/economic_costs.pdf.

———. 2009a. *Office of National Drug Control Policy: FY2010 Budget Strategy.* Washington, DC: Office of National Drug Control Policy. http://www.whitehousedrugpolicy.gov/publications/policy/10budget/index.html.

———. 2009b. *ADAM II: 2008 Annual Report.* Washington, DC: Executive Office of the President. http://www.whitehousedrugpolicy.gov/publications/pdf/adam2008.pdf.

———. 2010. *Marijuana: Facts & Figures.* Washington, DC: Executive Office of the President.

Pacula, Rosalie Liccardo, Jamie F. Chriqui, and Joanna King. 2003. "Marijuana Decriminalization: What Does It Mean in the United States?" NBER Working Paper no. 9690. Cambridge, MA: National Bureau of Economic Research, May.

Pacula, Rosalie Liccardo, and Beau Kilmer. 2003. "Marijuana and Crime: Is there a Connection Beyond Prohibition?" NBER Working Paper no. 10046. Cambridge, MA: National Bureau of Economic Research, October.

Reuter, Peter. 1999a. "Are Calculations of the Economic Costs of Drug Abuse Either Possible or Useful?" *Addiction* 94 (5): 635–38.

———. 1999b. "Drug Use Measures: What Are They Really Telling Us?" *National Institute of Justice Journal* 239:12–19.

———. 2009. Can Heroin Maintenance Help Baltimore? What Baltimore Can Learn From the Experience of Other Countries. Baltimore, MD: The Abell Foundation.

Rice, Dorothy P. 1999. "Economic Costs of Substance Abuse." *Proceedings of the Association of American Physicians* 111 (2): 119–25.

Rice, Dorothy P., Sander Kelman, and Leonard S. Miller. 1991. "Estimates of Economic Costs of Alcohol and Drug Abuse and Mental Illness, 1985 and 1988." *Public Health Reports* 106 (3): 280–92.

Room, Robin, Benedikt Fischer, Wayne Hall, Simon Lenton, and Peter Reuter. 2008. *Cannabis Policy: Moving Beyond Stalemate.* Oxford, England: The Beckley Foundation. http://www.beckleyfoundation.org/pdf/BF_Cannabis_Commission_Report.pdf.

Rydell, C. Peter, and Susan Everingham. 1994. *Controlling Cocaine: Supply Versus Demand Programs.* Santa Monica, CA: RAND Corporation.

Sabol, William J., Heather Couture, and Paige M. Harrison. 2007. *Bureau of Justice Statistics Bulletin: Prisoners in 2006.* Washington, DC: US Department of Justice, Office of Justice Programs.

Sabol, William J., Heather C. West, and Matthew Cooper. 2009. *Bureau of Justice*

Statistics Bulletin: Prisoners in 2008. Washington, DC: US Department of Justice, Office of Justice Programs.

Schneider Institute for Health Policy, Brandeis University (SIHP). 2001. *Substance Abuse: The Nations Number One Health Problem.* Princeton, NJ: The Robert Wood Johnson Foundation.

State of California. 2008. *Department of Justice Guidelines for the Security and Non Diversion of Marijuana Grown for Medical Use.* Sacramento, CA: Department of Justice, State of California. http://ag.ca.gov/cms_attachments/press/pdfs/n1601 _medicalmarijuanaguidelines.pdf.

Substance Abuse and Mental Health Services Administration (SAMHSA). 2009. *Results from the 2008 National Survey on Drug Use and Health: National Findings.* Washington, DC: Department of Health and Human Services. http://www.oas .samhsa.gov/nsduh/2k8nsduh/2k8Results.pdf.

———. 2008. *Results from the 2007 National Survey on Drug Use and Health: National Findings.* Washington, DC: Department of Health and Human Services. http://www.oas.samhsa.gov/nsduh/2k7nsduh/2k7Results.pdf.

Suk, Julie C. 2008. "Procedural Path Dependence: Discrimination and the Civil-Criminal Divide." *Washington University Law Review* 85 (6): 1315–71.

The Economist. 2009. "A Nation of Jailbirds." April 4.

The Economist. 2009. "A Toker's Guide." March 7.

The Economist. 2009. "Treating, not Punishing." August 29.

Trebach, Arnold S., and Joseph A. Califano, Jr. 2010. "Close to Home Online, Viewpoints. Should Illegal Drugs Be Decriminalized?" In *Close to Home: Moyers on Addiction.* Accessed August 30. http://www.pbs.org/wnet/closetohome/viewpoints/ html/decrim.html.

United Nations Office on Drugs and Crime (UNODC). 2008. *World Drug Report 2008.* Vienna, Austria: United Nations Office on Drugs and Crime. http://www .unodc.org/documents/wdr/WDR_2008/WDR_2008_eng_web.pdf.

———. 2009. *World Drug Report 2009.* Vienna, Austria: United Nations Office on Drugs and Crime. http://www.unodc.org/documents/wdr/WDR_2009/WDR 2009_eng_web.pdf.

US Census Bureau. 2008. *2007 Population Estimates.* Washington, D.C.: U.S. Census Bureau. Accessed March 4, 2010. http://www.census.gov/popest/national/asrh/ NC-EST2007-srh.html.

U.S. Sentencing Commission. 2008a. "Average Length of Imprisonment for Each Drug Type." Figure J. Accessed March 4, 2010. http://www.ussc.gov/ANNRPT/ 2008/figj.pdf.

———. 2008b. "Race of Drug Offenders for Each Drug Type." Table 34. Washington, DC: U.S. Sentencing Commission. Accessed March 4, 2010. http://www.ussc. gov/ANNRPT/2008/Table34.pdf.

van der Gouwe, D., E. Ehrlich, and M. W. van Laar. 2009. *Drug Policies in the Netherlands.* Utrecht: Trimbos Institute. http://www.minvws.nl/includes/dl/openbestand .asp?File=/images/fo-drug-policies-_tcm20-180356.pdf.

Walmsley, Roy. 2009. *World Prison Population List, 8th edition.* London: King's College London, International Centre for Prison Studies. http://www.kcl.ac.uk/ depsta/law/research/icps/downloads/wppl-8th_41.pdf.

Wilkinson, Tracy. 2009. "Mexico Moves Quietly to Decriminalize Minor Drug Use." *Los Angeles Times,* June 21. http://articles.latimes.com/2009/jun/21/world/ fg-mexico-decriminalize21.

Williams, J., Rosalie Liccardo Pacula, Frank J. Chaloupka, and Henry Wechsler. 2004. "Alcohol and Marijuana Use Among College Students: Economic Complements or Substitutes?" *Health Economics* 13 (9): 825–43.

Wilson, James Q., and George Kelling. 1982. "Broken Windows: The Police and Neighborhood Safety." *Atlantic Monthly* 249 (3): 29–37.

Wohlsen, Marcus, and Greg Risling. 2009. "Medical Marijuana Shops Abound in California." *Associated Press,* November 5. http://abcnews.go.com/US/wireStory?id=9009353.

Woo, Stu. 2009. "Oakland Council Backs a Tax on Marijuana." *Wall Street Journal,* April 30, A4. http://online.wsj.com/article/SB124105239168771233.html.

Yamamuru, Kevin. 2009. "Governor Asks: What if Pot's Legal and Taxed?" *Sacramento Bee,* May 6, 1A.

Comment   Robert J. MacCoun

Five hundred economists cannot be wrong, can they?

In June 2005, the Marijuana Policy Project (MPP) released Jeffrey Miron's white paper, "The Budgetary Implications of Marijuana Prohibition." Miron provides the most thorough analysis to date on the question of government expenditures on drug prohibition, estimating that legalization could save US taxpayers over $40 billion. Costs are uninformative unless benchmarked to the costs of alternative interventions (cost effectiveness), the benefits they provide (benefit-cost analysis), or our willingess to pay (contingent valuation). Savings on prohibition enforcement might mean little if offset by increased social costs involving public safety, public health, or lost productivity. Such costs are extremely difficult to forecast and involve numerous uncertain parameters—the responsiveness of demand to a change in law, and the responsiveness of these harms to a change in demand.

Nevertheless, Miron's report was released with great fanfare, in tandem with an open letter endorsed by over 500 professional economists, urging the country "to commence an open and honest debate about marijuana prohibition" (Hardy 2005; MPP 2005). That a call for open debate is even necessary says something about the American political climate during the thirty-year war on drugs (1969 to 2009).

But the letter went further, saying: "We believe such a debate will favor a regime in which marijuana is legal but taxed and regulated like other goods." This isn't entirely surprising; an earlier survey of professional economists (Thornton 1991) found that a majority (52 percent vs. 38 percent with 9 percent abstaining) said that they would "favor the decriminalization of illegal drugs." For some economists—most notably the late Milton Friedman—the legalization question seems like a no-brainer. Take a handful of stylized facts about addiction; the conventional wisdom about America's "Great

Robert J. MacCoun is professor of law at the University of California, Berkeley, School of Law, and professor of public policy and affiliated professor in the Department of Psychology at the University of California at Berkeley.

Experiment" with alcohol prohibition; a few back-of-the-envelope calculations; some simple comparative statics diagrams; some optimistic assumptions about taxation, prevention, and treatment; toss in a taste for liberty over paternalism, and you have a seemingly open-and-shut case.

The new analysis by Donohue, Ewing, and Peloquin offers far less certainty, far more candor, and a great deal more complexity and nuance. Donohue and colleagues start with the questions, not the answers. They recognize that there are a great many open empirical questions, and they make some progress toward tackling them—especially their new analyses of the link between drug enforcement and violence. The chapter recognizes and explains a key point that many academic writers fail to grasp: The question of whether and how to legalize drugs is actually a difficult one, and it is difficult in ways that make it more intellectually interesting.

Why is it difficult? There are several reasons (see MacCoun 1998; MacCoun and Reuter 1997, 2001; MacCoun, Reuter, and Schelling 1996). First, one side argues about the risk of increased drug use, while the other side argues about the likely reduction in harm per use. Yet total harm is a function of average harm per dose times the number of doses; if legalization raises use and lowers average harm, the net effect could be either an increase or decrease in total harm. Second, there are many different types of drug-related harm; some are due to prohibition, and some are due to the drugs themselves. Moreover, only some are quantifiable, and legalization might change not just the quantities but their distribution across neighborhoods and age groups. Finally, legalization advocates write as if the burden of proof is on prohibitionists; this may be true in some Rawlsian "original position," but it is dubious as a political position.

But let us not be nihilistic. Presumably experts are good for something in this domain. Put aside the political value (if there is one, see MacCoun and Paletz 2009) of appealing to the collective authority of the economics profession. Normatively, what role should expert consensus play in reasoned deliberation about issues like legalization?

"Appeals to authority" are fallacious as a matter of deductive logic, but they may have inductive value in establishing general professional acceptance, at least under the older Frye standard for admissible expert testimony (*Frye v. United States,* 293 F. 1013, D.C. Cir. 1923). Moreover, there is considerable research showing that when properly elicited, aggregated expert opinions can be far more accurate than those of most individual experts, especially when we do not know which experts are the best ones (Clemen and Winkler 1999; Goossens et al. 2008; Green, Armstrong, and Graefe 2007).

An aggregation of experts is no panacea, and it is possible to oversell "the wisdom of crowds" (Surowiecki 2004). Aggregation cancels out noise, but it can amplify shared group biases (Kerr, MacCoun, and Kramer 1996). And those biases seem particularly likely when the judgments being aggregated occur at a high level of abstraction, where the coloring effects of ideology, emotion, and point-of-view are most likely. But for narrowly focused empirical questions, it can at least give us a rough "current best guess."

5C.1   An Application: Forecasting the Price Effect of Cannabis Legalization

At the time of this writing (April 2010), the State of California faces two roads to the legalization, regulation, and taxation of the commercial retail cannabis: Assembly Bill 2254 in the state legislature,[1] and an initiative to appear on the November 2010 state ballot.[2] Forecasting the effects of these proposals is enormously difficult. How they would be implemented is unclear, and their impact on consumption, tax revenues, public health, and public safety is quite uncertain.

But it would be useful to at least provide a rough order-of-magnitude range for one key outcome—the effect on cannabis consumption—because it helps drive so many of the other outcomes. Laws influence drug use through many different mechanisms (deterrence, price, availability, stigma, and forbidden fruit effects; see MacCoun and Reuter 2001), but the price mechanism is probably the most tractable analytically, and it arguably has the most import for informing policy design.

To produce at least a rough forecast of the price effect of legalization. We consider the current street price of cannabis, plausible estimates of the new posttax retail price, and the price elasticity of demand (the percent change in consumption for a 1 percent change in price).

There are various relevant estimates in the literature, none very solid, and I will not review them here. To reduce the inherent subjectivity of using such estimates, in October of 2009 I informally polled four nationally recognized experts on the economics of drug use, none of whom have endorsed marijuana legalization.[3] I asked them to provide their plausible low and high guesses as to the current street price, their judgment of the likely price under a plausible legalized tax regime, and the price elasticity of demand. I then averaged these low and high estimates with my own (I am "Expert 5" and the least expert in the group, though my independent estimates were close to the median) to come up with the values reported in table 5C.1.

Table 5C.1 provides $5 \times 2 \times 2 \times 2 = 40$ sets of parameter estimates. I narrowed the set by considering only low-low and high-high pairs of past and future prices, leaving $5 \times 2 \times 2 = 20$ sets of estimates.

1. Assembly Bill 2254 ("Marijuana Control, Regulation and Education Act") was introduced in 2009 as AB 390; see http://www.leginfo.ca.gov/pub/09-10/bill/asm/ab_2251-2300/ab_2254_bill_20100218_introduced.pdf.
2. The Regulate, Control and Tax Cannabis Act of 2010; see http://www.taxcannabis.org/index.php/pages/initiative/.
3. I have chosen to keep the experts' identities anonymous to protect the confidentiality of their responses, and because some of them take issue with the implications I derive from their inputs.

Table 5C.1   **Expert poll data**

	Expert						
	1	2	3	4	5	Mean	Median
Street price							
low	$4	$4	$10	$5	$5	$5.60	$5.0
high	$25	$12	$10	$15	$15	$15.40	$15.0
Price elasticity of demand							
low	−0.2	−0.2	−1.0	−0.5	−0.5	−0.48	−0.5
high	−1.4	−0.8	−1.0	−1.5	−1.5	−1.24	−1.4
Price under tax model							
low	$0.50	$4	$6	$5	$3.50	$3.80	$4.0
high	$20	$12	$6	$10	$10.50	$11.70	$10.5

As seen in table 5C.2, I then created twenty forecasts of the price effect of legalization on demand, net of any nonprice mechanisms, under a constant elasticity of demand model, where

$$Q = aP^b$$

and

$$\%\Delta Q = \frac{P_{New}}{P_{Old}} - 1.$$

Note that these are my own inferences from the expert inputs; my experts were not asked to provide such forecasts directly—a point I return to below. But the derived projections suggest an increase in demand of around thirty-five (if the true demand curve is a convex power function).

The highest estimate implies a whopping seventeen-fold increase, though it is an outlier among the twenty estimates I computed; the second highest estimate is 84 percent. The outlier is based on an assumed 88 percent drop in the price, and a subsequent and painstaking analysis I recently published with my colleagues Beau Kilmer, Jonathan Caulkins, Rosalie Pacula, and Peter Reuter (Kilmer et al. 2010) suggests that a pretax drop of 75 to 80 percent is by no means implausible. So the actual effects of a change in policy will be highly sensitive to the posttax price. Kilmer et al. (2010) argue that it is extremely difficult to simply tax the price back up to prelegalization levels because tax evasion is very likely. On the other hand, the equilibrium price could be higher if there is sufficient inelasticity in the supply curve; Kilmer et al. (2010) assume and defend an infinite elasticity of supply, but also note that almost all empirically estimated supply elasticities in the agricultural literature are below five and a great many are below two. And recent steep decreases in alcohol taxes in several Nordic

Table 5C.2   Deriving projections under constant elasticity of demand model

Implied Growth in Demand*	1	2	3	4	5	Mean	Median
low × low	0.52	0.00	0.67	0.00	0.20	0.20	0.12
low × high	17.38	0.00	0.67	0.00	0.71	0.62	0.37
high × low	0.05	0.00	0.67	0.22	0.20	0.14	0.20
high × high	0.37	0.00	0.67	0.84	0.71	0.41	0.65
Average	4.58	0.00	0.67	0.27	0.45	**0.34**	**0.33**

Note: *Ceteris paribus; does not include other effects on demand.

countries have produced less of an impact on consumption than predicted by price elasticity models (Room et al. 2010). So there is not only uncertainty about these estimates, there is uncertainty about what they imply for behavior.

5C.2   Caveats and Two Empirical Benchmarks

These calculations ignore three potential complications that some experts think are important: Short- versus long-term elasticity, the elasticity of participation versus the elasticity of demand, and elasticities per age group. But the whole point of the exercise is to provide a very rough order-of-magnitude forecast to inform the debate. There are plenty of alternative scenarios that could undermine the logic of these calculations, but they are all very speculative, and if we treat them as equally plausible, then we are back to a uniform Bayesian prior, which seems far too pessimistic. Also, as seen in the appendix, these experts considered a very broad range of elasticities relative to what we have observed over a great many years of data in the alcohol and tobacco literatures.

How well do these projections match the available evidence? There are two case studies that in some ways approximate the kind of change that Californians are contemplating.

5C.2.1   The Dutch Experience

MacCoun and Reuter (1997, 2001) examine the de facto legalization of cannabis in the Netherlands in some detail; it is the closest experience we have to full cannabis legalization. Our best available data involve prevalence rather than total demand, so I will focus on past-month users who probably account for the lion's share of the consumption. Although the Dutch depenalized use in the 1970s, there was little impact until the retail coffee shop outlets began proliferating in the 1980s. Past-month prevalence from 8.5 percent to 11.5 percent between 1984 and 1992, and Reuter and I argue that the growth in this period (relative to other nations) was plausibly attributable to aggressive commercialization (later scaled back by Dutch authorities). This implies a potential increase of around 35 percent in past-month use. Importantly, even this increase was short-lived.[4] By 2005, Dutch cannabis prevalence was below that of Spain, England, Italy, and France, and well below that of the United States.[5] But the Dutch system is not a good analog for full-scale legalization because Dutch prices have stayed relatively high, probably due to enforcement against high-level traffickers, as well as retail prices that cover the coffee shop rent and amenities.

5C.2.2   The Drinking Age Experience

Increases in the legal minimum drinking age (usually from eighteen to twenty-one years) are a form of partial prohibition because those who were once able to purchase legally can no longer do so. Although the effects of creating a prohibition and ending a prohibition may not be symmetrical, the drinking age literature provides another real world check on our order-of-magnitude estimates. Estimates of the effect of the raised age requirement on consumption and traffic fatalities are in the 5 percent to 30 percent range (see Wagenaar and Toomey's 2002 meta-analysis of 241 studies from 1960 to 2000; Carpenter and Dobkin 2009). But again, the drinking age did not produce any sizeable price drop.

5.3   What If These Forecasts Are Wrong?

My use of the expert forecasts ignores possible complexities in price effects, and as noted earlier, price is not the only relevant mechanism. Indeed, somewhat surprisingly, prices are not notably lower in the Netherlands, perhaps because they have retained enforcement against high-level traffickers. So if we take the Dutch experience as an estimate of the nonprice effects of legalization, and add it to our price effect to try to get at the total effect on use, then something near a doubling of cannabis consumption seems plausible. Note that I am not predicting a doubling; the evidence does not permit any confident point estimates because there is so much parametric and structural uncertainty. But it is not inconceivable, and advocates for legalization ought to be able to defend the change even under such a scenario.

What would a doubling of past-month prevalence look like? About 3 million Californians aged twelve or older used cannabis at least once in 2006 (11 percent of that population) and about 2 million used in the previous thirty days (7 percent).[6] A doubling would bring past-month use to 3.9 million

4. The later decline is also consistent with our commercialization hypothesis, since government closings reduced the number of cannabis coffee shops (which require a government license) by 40 percent between 1997 and 2007.
5. See http://www.emcdda.europa.eu/; http://www.espad.org/.
6. See http://www.oas.samhsa.gov/2k7State/California.htm.

users—by historic standards, a substantial swing in use. At the same time, that level of use would match the past-month prevalence rate in 1979 (13 percent of the adult population). In other words, a doubling would match our not-too-distant historical experience.

I have not attempted to forecast the social consequences of such an increase in use. Interestingly, between 1975 and 1980, when cannabis use was at its historical peak, fewer than one in twenty American adults cited drugs as "the most important problem" facing the nation in Gallup polls. (In contrast, one in four adults cited drugs as the most important problem in 1989, when cannabis use was near its historical low point for the 1975 to 2010 period.)

Of course, one difference between 1979 and today is that cannabis is now consumed in more potent forms, and it is possible (though not yet established) that this poses greater risks of addiction and hazardous use.[7] This suggests that the public health consequences of cannabis legalization might be mitigated by taxing cannabis by tetrahydrocannabinol (THC) potency rather than by bulk weight, which might discourage high-potency forms, encourage low-potency forms, and encourage users to internalize any costs created by increased intoxication.

And other ways of implementing legalization might have less impact on consumption. As argued in greater detail elsewhere (Kleiman 1992; MacCoun and Reuter 2001), a less risky policy option would be to simply allow the legal cultivation of small numbers of plants for personal use. This is the approach that was adopted by Alaska in the 1970s, readopted there recently, and was also adopted in South Australia. Existing data are sparse, but do not suggest that either jurisdiction experienced significant increases in consumption. A home cultivation policy creates adminstrative and enforcement difficulties, but these are manageable problems—especially relative to our current prohibition or to the complexity of a taxable retail sales model.

Of course, such a model would also bypass one of the major arguments for the current California proposal—its potential for generating revenue.

---

7. Some contest this claim based on very real flaws in government estimates, but an examination of any issue of *High Times* magazine suggests that higher potency is a point of pride in the industry.

Appendix

Table 5CA.1   Parametric range in tobacco and alcohol literatures and in the expert poll

	Price elasticity of demand			
	Lower absolute estimate	Higher absolute estimate	Absolute difference	As % of lower
Tobacco literature (Gallet and List 2002 meta-analysis of 523 estimates)				
Short- vs. long-run	0.40	0.44	0.04	10
Double log vs. linear	0.37	0.45	0.08	22
Myopic vs. rational	0.38	0.44	0.06	16
MLE vs. OLS	0.32	0.40	0.08	25
Alcohol literature (Gallet 2007 meta-analysis of 1172 estimates)				
Short- vs. long-run	0.52	0.82	0.30	58
Beer vs. wine	0.36	0.70	0.34	94
Double log vs. linear	0.60	0.64	0.05	8
Myopic vs. rational	0.67	0.77	0.10	15
MLE vs. OLS	0.43	0.61	0.18	42
Marijuana (my poll of 5 experts)				
Mean low vs. mean high estimate	0.05	1.24	1.19	2483
Lowest vs. highest estimate	0.02	1.50	1.48	7400

References

Carpenter, Christopher, and Carlos Dobkin. 2009. "The Effect of Alcohol Consumption on Mortality: Regression Discontinuity Evidence from the Minimum Drinking Age." *American Economic Journal: Applied Economics* 1 (1): 164–82.

Clemen, Robert T., and Robert L. Winkler. 1999. "Combining Probability Distributions from Experts in Risk Analysis." *Risk Analysis* 19 (2): 187–203.

Goossens, L. H. J., R. M. Cooke, A. R. Hale, and Lj. Rodić-Wiersma. 2008. "Fifteen Years of Expert Judgement at TUDelft." *Safety Science* 46 (2): 234–44.

Green, Kesten C., J. Scott Armstrong, and Andreas Graefe. 2007. "Methods to Elicit Forecasts from Groups: Delphi and Prediction Markets Compared." *Foresight: The International Journal of Applied Forecasting* 8:17–20.

Hardy, Quentin. 2005. "Milton Friedman: Legalize It." *Forbes,* June 2.

Kerr, Nobert L., Robert J. MacCoun, and Geoffrey Kramer. 1996. "Bias in Judgment: Comparing Individuals and Groups." *Psychological Review* 103 (4): 687–719.

Kilmer, Beau, Jonathan P. Caulkins, Rosalie L. Pacula, Robert J. MacCoun, and Peter H. Reuter. 2010. *Altered State? Assessing How Marijuana Legalization in California Could Influence Marijuana Consumption and Public Budgets.* Santa Monica, CA: RAND Corporation.

Kleiman, Mark A. R. 1992. *Against Excess: Drug Policy for Results.* New York: Basic Books.

MacCoun, Robert, J. 1998. "Toward a Psychology of Harm Reduction." *American Psychologist* 53 (11): 1199–208.

MacCoun, Robert J., and Susannah Paletz. 2009. "Citizens' Perceptions of Ideological Bias in Research on Public Policy Controversies." *Political Psychology* 30 (1): 43–65.

MacCoun, Robert J., and Peter Reuter. 1997. "Interpreting Dutch Cannabis Policy: Reasoning by Analogy in the Legalization Debate." *Science* 278 (5335): 47–52.

———. 2001. *Drug War Heresies: Learning From Other Vices, Times, and Places.* Cambridge, England: Cambridge University Press.

MacCoun, Robert J., Peter Reuter, and Thomas Schelling. 1996. "Assessing Alternative Drug Control Regimes." *Journal of Policy Analysis and Management* 15 (3): 330–52.

Marijuana Policy Project. 2005. http://www.prohibitioncosts.org/endorsers.html.

Miron, Jeffrey A. 2005. *The Budgetary Implications of Marijuana Prohibition.* Washington, DC: Marijuana Policy Project. www.prohibitioncosts.org.

Room, Robin, Kim Bloomfield, Gerhard Gmel, Ulrike Grittner, Nina-Katri Gustafsson, Pia Mäkelä, Esa Österberg, Mats Ramstedt, Jürgen Rehm, and Matthias Wicki. 2010. *What Happened to Alcohol Consumption and Problems in the Nordic Countries when Alcohol Taxes Were Decreased and Borders Opened?* Fitzroy, Australia: Turning Point Alcohol and Drug Centre. July 10.

Surowiecki, James. 2004. *The Wisdom of Crowds: Why the Many are Smarter than the Few.* New York: Doubleday Books.

Thornton, Mark. 1991. "Economists on Illegal Drugs: A Survey of the Profession." *Atlantic Economic Journal* 19 (2): 73.

Wagenaar, Alexander C., and Traci L. Toomey. 2002. "Effects of Minimum Drinking Age Laws: Review and Analyses of the Literature from 1960–2000." *Journal of Studies on Alcohol* supp. 14:206–25.

6

Alcohol Regulation and Crime

Christopher Carpenter and Carlos Dobkin

6.1 Introduction

A substantial body of research in economics, criminology, and public health documents an association between alcohol availability, alcohol consumption, and crime.[1] Though much of the literature is focused on violent crime, many studies have also examined the link between alcohol and property crimes, nuisance crimes, and crimes that result directly from alcohol consumption such as driving under the influence (DUI). Most of these have found a large and statistically significant relationship between alcohol consumption and crime.

The very strong correlations between alcohol consumption and crime raise the possibility that alcohol regulations may be effective crime reduction

Christopher Carpenter is associate professor of economics and public policy at the University of California, Irvine, and a research associate of the National Bureau of Economic Research. Carlos Dobkin is associate professor of economics at the University of California, Santa Cruz, and a research associate of the National Bureau of Economic Research.

We thank participants at the preconference on the Economics of Crime Control at the 2009 NBER Summer Institute, participants at the 2010 "Making Crime Control Pay: Cost-Effective Alternatives to Mass Incarceration" conference at UC Berkeley School of Law, Stefano DellaVigna, Jens Ludwig, Steve Raphael, and especially Phil Cook for numerous useful comments. This review has benefited greatly—and draws heavily—from earlier reviews of alcohol and alcohol control policies, including: Cook and Moore (1993, 2000); Chaloupka, Grossman, and Saffer (2002); Room (1983); and others. We gratefully acknowledge grant support from NIH/NIAAA #RO1 AA017302-01. The usual caveats apply.

1. While some crimes such as driving under the influence (DUI) and public intoxication are clearly linked to alcohol use, here we concern ourselves primarily with crimes for which a causal role for alcohol is possible but not obvious or otherwise "mechanical." One reason for this is that the effects of alcohol control policies on DUI and alcohol-related fatalities have been extensively studied and reviewed elsewhere. We focus primarily on the Federal Bureau of Investigation's index crimes, which consist of violent crimes (murder, rape, robbery, and aggravated assault) and property crimes (larceny, burglary, and motor vehicle theft).

tools. Specifically, if alcohol consumption causes people to commit crimes or increases the chance they will be victimized, then laws and regulations designed to reduce the availability of alcohol may reduce crime. However, if the correlation between alcohol use and crime is due in total or in part to unobserved individual factors (such as risk preferences) or to unobserved local factors (such as neighborhood quality), then alcohol regulation may not be an effective crime prevention tool. And even if alcohol consumption by some people does increase the probability that they will commit crimes, it is not obvious that alcohol regulations will significantly reduce consumption in this population; thus it would be possible for certain policies to impose social costs without significantly reducing crime. Despite these concerns, alcohol regulation as a crime reduction strategy is worth examining because alcohol consumption is so strongly associated with crime and because there is wide latitude for changing alcohol regulations in the United States.[2]

In this chapter we offer a critical review of existing research on alcohol and crime from the perspective of economics. Notably, we are not the first to apply economic perspectives to alcohol control policies (see, e.g., Manning et al. 1989; Pogue and Sgontz 1989; Kenkel 1996; Kenkel and Manning 1996; Cook 2007). We review most of the serious policy options that use alcohol control to bring about reductions in crime, but other, less commonly debated policy options exist as well. We are not the first to review the evidence on the effects of alcohol control policies on alcohol consumption and adverse outcomes; indeed, we draw heavily from previous reviews of alcohol control from Cook and Moore (2000), Chaloupka, Saffer, and Grossman (2002), Chaloupka (2004), and others. Those reviews, however, differ from ours in at least two important ways. First, previous reviews have largely (but not exclusively) focused on the monetary price of alcohol and associated tax-based interventions. Second, most earlier reviews have focused on a wider range of alcohol-related outcomes, such as motor vehicle fatalities, accidental injury, risky sexual behavior, and productivity, in addition to crime. This focus on a broader set of outcomes is a natural way to research the effect of price and tax interventions. Here, however, we expand the scope of alcohol regulations under review but focus entirely on their effect on crime. This broader look incorporates a body of evidence from other countries and regions (especially Scandinavia) that have used a variety of natural experiment designs to study the effects of nonprice restrictions on alcohol availability and crime. It also permits examination of several recent high-quality studies that have provided important information about alcohol's causal role in crime using variation in liquor store density, bar closing hours, and age-based alcohol restrictions, among others.

2. Potential changes include alcohol increasing the excise tax, raising the drinking age, adopting tougher drunk-driving laws, restricting liquor license availability, further restricting the hours/days/locations of alcohol sales, and more strictly enforcing existing laws against underage drinking.

We pay particular attention to studies that take the causal inference problem seriously. This focus is appropriate given the chapter's focus on policy-relevant crime control strategies. It is important to accurately assess the strengths and weaknesses of the evidence before deciding to continue using a particular type of regulation, taking into account endogeneity, simultaneity, unobserved heterogeneity, and associated evaluation problems. We also pay close attention to whether alcohol regulations reduce crime rates or just displace crimes to different times or places, and we highlight the need to distinguish between the effects of alcohol restrictions on criminals and the effects on victims.

The chapter proceeds as follows. First, we review evidence from laboratory studies on the pharmacological effects of alcohol consumption on the brain and behavior. We use this and other evidence to lay out several pathways by which alcohol consumption could lead to the commission of crime. We also address the relationship between alcohol and other drugs, with respect to both consumption and regulation. We then review studies on the relationship between alcohol regulations and crime, grouping them by the type of alcohol regulation examined (tax/price restrictions, age-based restrictions, spatial restrictions, temporal restrictions, and regulations not otherwise classified). We summarize what is known about the value of each type of regulation and conclude with a discussion of economic considerations in assessing the importance of alcohol regulations as part of an effective crime control strategy.

6.2   The Pharmacological Effects of Alcohol

Although pharmacological effects are not the only mechanism by which alcohol consumption causes crime, it is a major one. People's blood alcohol concentration (BAC) from drinking affects their level of impairment differently, according to their individual characteristics. The most important is the size of the dose. The number of drinks consumed, the speed with which they are consumed, and the alcohol content of the drinks are the major determinants of the dose. Dose size is moderated by numerous individual characteristics. Heavier and more muscular individuals have more water mass and as a consequence will reach a lower BAC than a smaller, less muscular individual who has consumed the same amount of alcohol. Individuals also differ substantially in the rate at which the liver metabolizes alcohol. For example, there is evidence that older individuals metabolize alcohol more slowly than younger individuals and chronic drinkers metabolize alcohol more rapidly than less frequent drinkers.

Generally speaking, a 160-pound man will reach a BAC of .02 percent (or 2 grams per 100 milliliters of blood) after one standard-sized drink (roughly one shot [1–1.5 ounces] of liquor, one 12-ounce beer, or one 5-ounce glass of wine). That same man will reach a BAC of .05 percent, .07 percent, .09 percent, and .12 percent after two, three, four, and five drinks, respectively, and will accordingly reach increasingly higher blood alcohol concentrations with successive drinks (assuming no time between drinks). A similarly sized woman will, on average, reach a higher BAC after the same number of drinks due to sex-specific differences in body composition.

Though the exact level of impairment at a given BAC varies from person to person, intoxication due to alcohol usually follows several stages associated with different BAC levels. At low BACs (below .05 percent), alcohol can induce enjoyment, happiness, and euphoria characterized by increased sociability and talkativeness. Loss of inhibitions and reduced attention are also characteristic of this level of intoxication. At higher BACs (.06 percent–.10 percent), disinhibition is more apparent, as are impairments in judgment, coordination, concentration, reflexes, depth perception, distance acuity, and peripheral vision. Because these impairments can be dangerous in certain environments, many countries set the BAC at which a driver is considered legally impaired at either .05 percent or .08 percent (often lower for younger or less experienced drivers). In the range .11 percent–.30 percent, individuals experience exaggerated emotional states, including anger and sadness; they may also have a higher pain threshold, reduced reaction time, loss of balance, slurred speech, and moderate to severe motor impairment. At extremely high BACs (above .35 percent), individuals are likely to suffer from incontinence or impaired respiration, or they may lose consciousness and even die from respiratory arrest. For lower levels of BAC, many of the effects have been documented in controlled laboratory settings, particularly impairments of driving-related skills and tasks.

Laboratory experiments have been used extensively to estimate whether and to what extent acute alcohol consumption increases aggressive behaviors in humans.[3] In the most common experimental design, individuals are told they will be competing against a competitor in a different location, with the winner of each task choosing the severity of the electric shock that the loser receives. In reality, there is no competitor in these experiments, and the outcomes (i.e., whether the subject wins or loses the timed task) are predetermined. The magnitude and severity of the shocks chosen by the subjects provide a measure of aggression. The subjects are told either that they will be served an alcoholic beverage or that they will be served a nonalcoholic beverage. Individuals in each group are randomly served an alcoholic beverage or a nonalcoholic beverage. Comparing the level of the electric shocks chosen by the people in the four groups allows researchers to separate the effects of alcohol from the effects due to alcohol-based expectations. These experiments typically find that people who consume the bever-

---

3. Notably, the increases in aggression attributable to alcohol have also been documented in controlled experiments with mice and primates, suggesting a fundamental biological link between alcohol and aggression.

age with alcohol, whether they were expecting it or not, choose to give larger shocks than those that did not get alcohol.[4]

6.3   Possible Causal Pathways and Mechanisms from Alcohol to Crime

In this section we examine several of the causal pathways through which alcohol consumption leads to crime (Fagan 1990; Pernanen 1981).[5] Most public policies targeting alcohol consumption have the potential to influence more than one causal pathway, making it challenging to determine exactly how important each pathway is. As a result, it is not possible to rank them perfectly; however, we discuss the pathways in what we believe is roughly their order of importance: (a) direct pharmacological effects on aggression and cognitive functioning; (b) the "excuse" mechanism; and (c) the role of social interactions and venues.

Arguably the most direct pathway from alcohol consumption to crime is through its direct pharmacological effects. By increasing aggression and heightening emotional responses, acute alcohol use may cause increases in interpersonal violence, including murder, rape, robbery, and assault. And by reducing cognitive functioning and altering normal judgment and decision-making abilities, drinking may lead to alcohol-induced myopia or shortsightedness. Individuals so afflicted may engage in criminal activity because they fail to recognize the social and legal consequences of their actions. The pharmacological effects of alcohol may also have a causal effect on crime by increasing the risk of victimization. Excessively large doses of alcohol, for example, lead to sedation rather than aggression, which may make intoxicated individuals easy targets of various types of crime. And impaired cognitive functioning and decision making may place individuals in situations where they are at increased risk of victimization. Unfortunately, for reasons outlined later, it is difficult to disentangle alcohol's effect on crime commission from its effect on criminal victimization, and as a result very little research has been conducted on this important question.

4. It is worth noting that the majority of the experiments examining how alcohol affects aggression have studied either college undergraduates or alcoholics, somewhat limiting the generalizability of the findings. Also, the dose-response relationship observed between alcohol consumption and aggression is highly nonlinear: although through much of the range of BAC alcohol increases aggression, at very high levels it results in sedation. Finally, the pharmacological effects of alcohol can differ markedly from the effects of other drugs; we discuss this later in section 6.4.

5. It is important to acknowledge that some sociologists and criminologists suggest that the links among alcohol, crime, and violence do not result from a causal mechanism of the type we describe here. Some common alternative hypotheses include the possibility that unobserved factors such as risk preference or taste for deviance cause both variation in alcohol consumption and variation in crime or that some income-producing crime is itself a cause (not a consequence) of alcohol and other drugs (Fagan 1993 and others). That these types of explanations would produce the same observed associations between alcohol use and crime as a true causal effect (defined later) is why we focus on studies that seriously address the possibility of omitted variables bias.

Alcohol may also increase crime by providing an "excuse motive" for crime commission. It is conceivable that someone considering a criminal act could believe that being inebriated would lessen the punishment for a crime if the case came to trial. Alcohol consumption may also lead a person to justify antisocial activities to himself or the people around him. Policies that succeeded in reducing alcohol availability could remove the excuse motive in some instances.

Alcohol consumption may also increase the incidence of interpersonal violence by increasing social contact, which again may be relevant both for crime commission and for criminal victimization. A closely related mechanism is venue: alcohol regulations can dictate the location and setting of alcohol use either directly (e.g., through bar closing hours or licensing of on-premises outlets where alcohol is consumed at the same location after purchase) or indirectly (e.g., by lowering the drinking age and thereby increasing the number of public venues where youths can legally consume alcohol). When people consume alcohol in public places such as bars they will have more interactions than they would if they had stayed home. Even in private venues alcohol is often enjoyed in social group settings. Indeed, one of alcohol's pharmacological effects is to make individuals more talkative and outwardly social in the short term. Alcohol use may therefore increase the number of interpersonal interactions at risk for a criminal incident, and in public venues those interactions are more likely to be with strangers and involve negotiations over personal space, further increasing the risk of a violent conclusion to the interaction.

Most of the studies of the impact of alcohol regulations are ecological studies, which find that regulations can plausibly impact more than one of the mechanisms described earlier. Because the individual effect of each mechanism is difficult to determine, it is also difficult to predict how a new regulation that targets only one mechanism is likely to affect crime rates. However, the reduced-form findings are still of substantial value since most new policies are likely to have characteristics similar to those of existing policies.

6.4   Alcohol and Crime versus Other Drugs and Crime

Our focus here is on the relationship between alcohol regulations and crime as distinct from the relationship between the regulation of illicit drugs (such as marijuana, methamphetamines, heroin, and cocaine) and crime, which is the focus of other work in this volume (see chapter 3 by Pollack, Reuter, and Sevigny). One reason for this distinction is that the production, purchase, sale, and distribution of alcohol are not criminogenic in the same way as the production, purchase, sale, and distribution of illicit drugs such as opiates and cocaine. Because marijuana and hard drugs are illegal, a substantial portion of the crime associated with these drugs is caused by the dangerous nature of the illicit markets. Evaluating policies that target illegal drugs is therefore even more complex than evaluating policies aimed at alcohol abuse.

Another reason to distinguish alcohol from other drugs when considering the effects of their consumption on crime is that the pharmacological and behavioral effects of alcohol differ significantly from those of the most commonly consumed illicit drugs. While several laboratory studies and reviews of the literature (described previously) have documented a causal effect of alcohol consumption on aggression and disinhibition, controlled experiments in animals and humans that examine other substances indicate a range of behavioral effects. Probably the closest to alcohol in its pharmacological effects is cocaine, which has similarly been shown to increase aggression, reduce self-control, and increase irritability (Washton 1987). Amphetamines can also produce an increase in aggression; however, unlike the aggression induced by alcohol it is sometimes accompanied by a paranoid psychotic state that independently may contribute to violent acts. In contrast, marijuana has generally been found to inhibit (rather than promote) aggressive behavior in humans, mice, fish, and primates (Miczek et al. 1994). Similarly, opiates have been shown to decrease aggressive behavior and hostility in animals and humans, though the period of opiate withdrawal is usually characterized as increasing risk for aggressive behaviors. Thus alcohol has a pharmacological profile that is significantly different from that of the most commonly consumed illicit drugs.

The differential pharmacological effects of alcohol and other drugs on human behavior raise a potentially important issue regarding the role of alcohol regulation and crime control. Specifically, it is possible that alcohol use is related to the use of other drugs in an underlying structural way. If alcohol and other drugs are complements in consumption, then an increase in the price of alcohol (through, for example, stricter regulations) will reduce not only drinking (through the own-price effect) but also use of other drugs (through a cross-price effect). In contrast, if alcohol and other drugs are substitutes in consumption, then an increase in the price of alcohol will reduce drinking but will lead to an increase in the use of other drugs. Existing research is mixed on this question and has focused primarily on the study of marijuana. While some studies find evidence that alcohol and marijuana are substitutes in consumption (DiNardo and Lemieux 2001; Conlin, Dickert-Conlin, and Pepper 2005), others find that the two are complements (Pacula 1998).[6] The relationship is potentially important because some research has

6. DiNardo and Lemieux (2001) use variation induced by state drinking age changes (described in more detail following in the review of age-based alcohol restrictions) and find that exposure to a more restrictive drinking age significantly reduced alcohol consumption by high school seniors but significantly increased marijuana consumption, suggesting that alcohol and marijuana are substitutes in consumption among youths. Conlin, Dickert-Conlin, and Pepper (2005) use changes between wet and dry status from local prohibition referenda in

suggested a direct causal effect of marijuana on the commission of income-producing and property crimes (Pacula and Kilmer 2003).[7]

Why might this matter? The vast majority of the empirical research reviewed that follows relies on estimating reduced-form relationships between alcohol control policies and crime. If alcohol control policies influence both the consumption of alcohol and illicit drugs, we will observe the total or net effect of these two mechanisms.

6.5 A Critical Evaluation and Summary of Research on the Effects of Alcohol Regulations on Alcohol Consumption and Crime

A key reason that alcohol control merits attention as a possible crime control strategy is that access to alcohol is highly manipulable by public policy through various types of regulations. Indeed, much of the research we review compares the effects of regulations across areas and changes within areas over time as a way of identifying alcohol's causal role in the commission of crime. We group our review by types of alcohol regulation, which broadly correspond to different types of research designs that have been used to identify the effects of alcohol on crime. These include: excise taxes on alcohol; age-based restrictions such as minimum legal drinking ages; spatial restrictions on alcohol outlet density and availability; temporal restrictions on alcohol sale; and other "circumstance" regulations that combine elements of spatial and temporal alcohol availability restrictions. We discuss each of these—and the relevant literature employing each design—in turn.[8]

Texas in a quasi-experimental framework and find a significant inverse relationship between alcohol availability and illicit drug-related crimes, suggesting that alcohol and illicit drugs are substitutes. Pacula (1998) uses data from the National Longitudinal Survey of Youths and finds that increases in the beer tax reduce both drinking and marijuana use among young adults, suggesting the two goods are complements in consumption.

7. Pacula and Kilmer (2003) use Arrestee Drug Abuse Monitoring (ADAM) and Uniform Crime Reports (UCR) data to estimate fixed-effects models of crime with controls for alcohol, cocaine, and marijuana prices. They find that higher marijuana prices (which should be associated with lower marijuana use) were associated with lower rates of income-producing and property crime but not violent crime, which is consistent with pharmacological evidence suggesting that marijuana decreases aggression in the short term. As noted earlier, there is less research addressing whether alcohol and illicit drugs other than marijuana are substitutes or complements. Again, this may be important because some previous research suggests a causal effect of cocaine consumption on crime. Desimone (2001), for example, uses data from twenty-nine large cities in the period 1981 to 1995 and instruments for the endogeneity of cocaine prices with wholesale supply factors and retail enforcement intensity and finds a significant negative association between the price of cocaine and every index crime except assault. His results suggest that there are independent causal effects of cocaine use (i.e., consumption) on crime apart from effects on criminality associated with the production, sale, and distribution of the drug.

8. In addition to these categories, there are others that may prove fruitful in future research, including: restrictions on alcohol advertising, alcohol education regulations in schools, requirements that parolees and other alcohol offenders abstain from alcohol (e.g., through 24/7 sobriety programs), restrictions on price promotions and other point-of-sale regulations such as

6.5.1   Regulations on the Tax/Price of Alcohol

Economists studying the relationship between alcohol and crime have largely focused on alcohol control policies that change the full price of alcohol either directly (through alcohol excise taxes) or indirectly (through other nonprice availability restrictions). In this section we review and evaluate studies that have leveraged variation in excise taxes to identify alcohol's role in crime. Studies of this variety have natural appeal to economists because they are firmly grounded in economic theory: a tax-induced increase in the price of alcohol should reduce alcohol consumption by the law of demand. Moreover, there is a great deal of variation across states and countries in alcohol excise taxes, and there is also some variation within areas over time, which allows estimation of more credible fixed-effects models of the effects of taxes on alcohol prices, drinking, and crime. Indeed, previous research confirms that alcohol taxes are passed through to prices (a necessary condition for taxes to affect alcohol consumption and crime). Young and Bielinska-Kwapisz (2002) and Stehr (2007) both use quasi-experimental approaches to document that taxes are fully shifted to prices by matching tax information to commonly used local price data from the ACCRA (the American Chamber of Commerce Researchers Association, now known as the Council on Community Economic Research, or C2ER). Kenkel (2005) also finds that taxes are more than fully shifted to prices using original survey data from before and after a large alcohol tax hike in Alaska. Finally, a focus on alcohol taxes has substantial policy relevance as several states have debated and implemented significant increases in alcohol taxes in the past few years.

There is a now enormous body of evidence showing an inverse relationship between alcohol taxes and various measures of alcohol consumption; it has been reviewed extensively elsewhere (Chaloupka, Saffer, and Grossman 2002; Cook and Moore 2001; and others). Some of this evidence comes from cross sectional studies that use tax-induced price variation (Grossman, Coate, and Arluck 1987; Grossman et al. 1994; Coate and Grossman 1988; and others), but some of the earliest work on this topic used more credible panel data evaluation methods. Cook and Tauchen (1982), for example, showed that increases in state liquor taxes significantly reduced mortality from cirrhosis of the liver, a common proxy for chronic heavy drinking. This study effectively introduced the two-way fixed effects design to studies of alcohol control policies, and it has become the standard for these types of evaluations. Although some research has called the relationship between

"Happy Hours," laws that assign liability to bar owners for serving intoxicated persons, alcohol-involved driving regulations (e.g., ignition interlock programs), fines and penalties for alcohol violations, and others. To our knowledge these regulations have not been studied extensively by economists in the context of crime or violence outcomes (other than crime and violence related to driving under the influence), so we do not discuss them here.

state beer taxes and alcohol consumption into question, particularly for young adults (see Dee 1999; Mast, Benson, and Rasmussen 1999; and others), other recent research has confirmed that tax-induced price increases for ethanol are associated with decreases in drinking (Cook and Moore 2001; Carpenter et al. 2007; and others).

Several studies in economics by Markowitz and colleagues have used the inverse relationship between alcohol taxes and consumption to estimate models of the effect of alcohol consumption on violence by using alcohol taxes as instruments or by directly estimating the reduced-form association between alcohol taxes and individual measures of violence. Markowitz and Grossman (1998), for example, using one cross-section of data from the 1976 National Family Violence Survey, found that state excise taxes on beer were significantly negatively related to the probability of child abuse. In a related study Markowitz and Grossman (2000) added data from the 1985 wave of the same survey, which allowed them to estimate the sensitivity of the beer tax estimates to the inclusion of state fixed effects (thus identifying the effects of beer taxes from changes in state tax rates). They found that beer taxes were negatively related to child abuse committed by women, but these results were only statistically significant when state fixed effects were excluded. These studies do not include direct information on alcohol consumption, so the first stage relationship cannot be directly tested. Markowitz (2000) also examined spousal violence using the 1985, 1986, and 1987 waves of the National Family Violence Survey. In models with individual fixed effects, she estimated that a 1 percent increase in price would reduce abuse aimed at wives by 5.34 percent. Markowitz (2005) analyzes panel data on individuals from the 1992, 1993, and 1994 National Crime Victimization Surveys. She finds that higher beer taxes have a (marginally) significant inverse relationship with physical assault but no substantive relationship with rape/sexual assault or robbery. Markowitz (2001a) uses data from the 1989 and 1992 cross-sections of the International Victimization Survey. Controlling for the country-specific price of alcohol, she finds that these prices exhibit significant negative associations with the rates of assault, robbery, and sexual assault against women in the cross-section but that the associations are no longer statistically significant when country fixed effects are included in the regressions.

Markowitz and colleagues have also used similar strategies to relate beer taxes to violence among youths and young adults. Markowitz (2001b), for example, uses data from the 1991, 1993, and 1995 Centers for Disease Control and Prevention's Youth Risk Behavior Surveys (YRBS) to examine the relationship between alcohol use and the probability of being in a physical fight or carrying a weapon. An advantage of the YRBS data is that they include information on youth drinking participation and heavy episodic drinking. Using beer prices as instruments for youth drinking, Markowitz estimates that alcohol consumption significantly increases the probability of being in a physical fight but does not affect weapon-carrying behavior. However, the first-stage and reduced-form relationships are estimated entirely from cross-sectional variation across states (net of state economic and religious characteristics). Finally, Grossman and Markowitz (2001), using data from the 1989, 1990, and 1991 Core Alcohol and Drug Surveys of College students, find that state beer taxes are inversely related to the probability that college students reported getting into trouble with the police, being involved in property damage, getting into a verbal or physical fight, and being involved in violence. They control directly for observed measures of antidrinking sentiment in a state (such as religiosity) but do not include state (or other area) fixed effects in their models.

In a related analysis, using data on individuals aged twelve and older from the 1991 National Household Survey on Drug Abuse, Saffer (2001) found that state beer taxes were significantly and inversely related to the probability of being arrested, the probability of engaging in property crime, the probability of engaging in property damage, and the probability of an individual using force to obtain something from someone. These effects were generally larger for youths under age twenty-one. Apart from individual demographic characteristics, however, no other state policies or economic/demographic characteristics were included in the model except for state drug control spending.

Arguably the most compelling direct evidence that higher alcohol taxes would reduce crime rates comes from a series of panel evaluations. The first of these was conducted by Cook and Moore (1993), who regressed state violent crime rates for the period 1979 to 1987 on state excise taxes on beer, state fixed effects, and year fixed effects. In this parsimonious specification, they found a significant inverse relationship between a state's beer tax and rates of rape and robbery (but not homicide or assault) within the state. They did not consider property or nuisance crimes, however, and they did not control for other state demographic characteristics or other relevant prices or policies. To the extent that these omitted characteristics were invariant within states over this period, however, the inclusion of state fixed effects largely shields Cook and Moore's 1993 study from these criticisms.

More recently, Desimone (2001) effectively replicates and extends the findings of Cook and Moore (1993), despite the fact that Desimone's focus is on the money price of cocaine, not alcohol. Using panel data on crimes in twenty-nine large cities for the period 1981 to 1995, Desimone estimates fixed-effects models that include controls for the excise tax on beer in addition to a host of city-level demographic characteristics such as the local age structure, unemployment rates, per capita income, the fraction that is female, and the fraction that is racial and ethnic minorities. Like Cook and Moore (1993), he too finds that beer taxes are significantly negatively related to rape, and he also finds a significant negative association between beer taxes and rates of assault, larceny, and motor vehicle theft.

Finally, Matthews, Shepherd, and Sivarajasingam (2006) and Sivarajas-ingam, Matthews, and Shepherd (2006) study the relationship between beer prices and rates of injury-related violence using a panel of emergency department (ED) admissions over the period 1995 to 2000 in England and Wales. They estimated fixed-effects models of outcomes and found that higher beer prices were significantly associated with lower rates of violence-related injury as proxied by ED admissions, consistent with a causal relationship between alcohol prices and violence. These studies did not, however, address the mechanisms that drive regional or temporal price variations in beer.

Critiques of the Literature on Tax/Price Restrictions

Although the literature on alcohol taxes and criminal outcomes is extensive, most studies focus exclusively on violent crimes, so much less is known about the impact of alcohol taxes on nuisance or property crimes. In addition, these studies cannot disentangle crime commission from criminal victimization since taxes should theoretically affect consumption among both populations.

A more serious problem is that over the 1980s and 1990s (the period studied in most existing research) there were very few changes in state alcohol tax rates, making it difficult to precisely measure the effect of taxes on drinking and crime using models with fixed effects. Therefore much of the research using taxes to identify the effects of alcohol on crime—particularly the studies using individual level data to examine violence—has been cross-sectional, which raises standard concerns that unobserved factors associated with both the level of the state's beer tax and the state's crime rate cannot be ruled out as an alternative explanation. This critique has been previously articulated by Dee (1999) and others in the context of youths. A related issue is that since alcohol taxes affect everyone within the taxed jurisdiction there is no clean way to define within-area treatment and control groups that would make it possible to difference out these possible biases.

Indeed, a central question for evaluating the usefulness of tax/price strategies is: what causes the observed variation in the level of alcohol taxes across space and time? Studies of taxes and prices may be biased if population preferences about alcohol control (or changes in these preferences) are correlated with tax rates (or changes in these rates). Arguably, these preferences are more likely problematic for evaluations of direct restrictions on spatial and temporal alcohol availability (reviewed later), in part because concern about alcohol-related problems directly underlies many of those policies. Taxes are somewhat shielded from this concern because they are often imposed as revenue-raising devices. Researchers must still be careful, however, because other determinants of crime rates such as resources available to police are also likely to be affected by budget shortfalls.

Overall Evaluation: Tax/Price Restrictions

Alcohol taxes in real terms have been falling steadily for decades, and economists commonly argue that alcohol taxes are "too low" (Manning et al. 1989; Cook 2007; and others). Economic theory predicts that higher alcohol taxes should reduce both alcohol consumption and crime, to the extent that crime is caused by drinking. Yet the evidence on the effects of alcohol taxes has been limited by the fact that there have not been many significant changes in the rate at which alcohol is taxed. As a result, most of the papers in the literature on the effect of alcohol taxes on violence are identified off cross-sectional variation, so omitted variables bias is a serious concern. However, the two studies that leverage within-state variation find that alcohol taxes are negatively related to rates of various violent crimes. Several recent alcohol tax increases may be fruitful subjects for future panel evaluations of the effects of taxes on alcohol consumption crime and may help to shed light on previous debates in this literature about the importance of price.

6.5.2 Age-Based Alcohol Restrictions

One of the most direct forms of alcohol regulation in the United States and elsewhere is the minimum legal drinking age (MLDA). Most economists view drinking-age policies as affecting the full price of obtaining alcohol. Studies of age-based restrictions benefit from several advantages. First, like alcohol taxes, they are highly policy relevant. The country has been actively engaged in a debate about the appropriateness of an age-twenty-one drinking age, led by the Amethyst Initiative, a group of college and university leaders who have called for a reexamination of US minimum drinking age policies. Second, studies of drinking ages benefit from naturally sharp predictions about which groups of people should be affected by the policy in question: youths under the drinking age should have their consumption (and by implication, criminal activity) constrained by the MLDA, while youths at or above the drinking age should be largely unaffected. Third, drinking age studies benefit from numerous changes in the drinking age, which can be used to estimate the effects of age-based alcohol regulations. In the early 1970s, for example, all states had an MLDA of twenty-one, but later that decade several states experimented with reducing the MLDA to eighteen, nineteen, or twenty. In response to research showing that youth alcohol-related fatalities increased following these age-based liberalizations, the federal government passed the 1984 Uniform Minimum Drinking Age Act, which required states to adopt an age-twenty-one MLDA or risk losing 10 percent of their federally provided highway funds. By 1988, all states had returned to an MLDA of 21. Because states adopted lower and then higher drinking ages in a staggered fashion (i.e., different states changed their laws in different years), it is possible to leverage within-state variation in the drinking age for identification. Moreover, the age-based criteria for the laws allows researchers to use people too young or too old to be affected by the laws as a control group.

Given the strengths of age-based research designs, it is not surprising that the effect of these laws on alcohol consumption has been clearly documented. Multiple studies have shown that exposure to a lower drinking age increased both drinking participation and heavy episodic drinking. Using pooled cross-sections of reports of alcohol consumption by high school seniors from the school-based Monitoring the Future (MTF) study of 1976 to 1992, Dee (1999) found that exposure to a permissive drinking age significantly increased drinking participation and heavy episodic drinking; this result was confirmed in analyses of other policies that also used MTF data (see, e.g., DiNardo and Lemieux 2001; Carpenter et al. 2007). Cook and Moore (2001) found a similar result using data on young adults from the National Longitudinal Survey of Youths. Multiple studies have also shown that states' drinking age experiments were predictably associated with significant changes in alcohol-related traffic fatalities, which is partly what prompted the 1984 federal action (see Wagenaar and Toomey 2001 for a comprehensive review).

Two studies have documented that the state drinking age changes—in addition to affecting alcohol use—also affected crime. Using age-specific arrest data from the Uniform Crime Reports, Joksch and Jones (1993) found that increasing the drinking age reduced nuisance crimes and simple assaults among young adults in the affected age groups. Carpenter (2005) also found that drinking age increases were associated with significant reductions in arrests for nuisance crimes among youths in the targeted group. Taken together, these two studies suggest a causal relationship between alcohol availability, alcohol consumption, and the commission of some types of crime.

More recently, Carpenter and Dobkin (2010) used a different approach to evaluate drinking ages and their effect on alcohol consumption and crime. Specifically, their regression discontinuity (RD) design uses the fact that the costs of obtaining alcohol fall discretely at the MLDA. Since all other observed and unobserved determinants of crime are likely to trend smoothly across the MLDA threshold, the observed changes in drinking and crime precisely at age twenty-one (net of birthday effects) can be used to identify the effect of easier alcohol availability on crime. Using alcohol consumption data from the 2001 to 2007 California Health Interview Surveys (which gives subjects' exact age in months at the time they were interviewed), they find that drinking participation increases sharply at age twenty-one by about 30 percent.[9] They then use data on the universe of arrests in California for

---

9. In related work, Carpenter and Dobkin (2009) also document a similar discontinuity nationally using data from the 1997 to 2003 National Health Interview Surveys.

the period 2000 to 2008 (including subjects' exact age in days at time they were arrested) from the Monthly Arrest and Citation Register and find significant increases in arrest rates for nuisance and violent crimes precisely at age twenty-one. Assaults accounted for most of the sharp increase in arrests for violent crimes exactly at age twenty-one. The RD approach in Carpenter and Dobkin (2009) leverages an abrupt change in alcohol availability; as a result the estimates from this research design are less likely to be contaminated by population policy preferences than estimates from research designs that leverage statewide changes in policies regulating alcohol.

Critiques of the Literature on Age-Based Restrictions

Although studies of age-based restrictions on alcohol have several strengths, they also have limitations. First, there is limited evidence on enforcement of drinking age laws, either historically or present day. However, numerous researchers have documented the first-stage effect of age-based restrictions on alcohol consumption, somewhat easing this concern. Second, most of the studies using age-based alcohol regulations use arrest data instead of reported crimes data (since the age of the offender is typically not known). This raises the usual concern that alcohol use independently increases the probability of being arrested if one has committed a crime, thus resulting in an overstatement of the effect of age-based restrictions. The fact that these studies generally find effects for some crime types but not others mitigates this concern somewhat.

Third, the alcohol/crime relationship using variation in drinking age laws is complicated by the fact that individuals legally old enough to drink not only can obtain alcohol more cheaply, but also can obtain it in more places and venues (an additional dimension of the "full price" of alcohol). This means that it is difficult to distinguish whether it is the alcohol consumption, the increased social interaction with other potentially intoxicated individuals, or the interaction of the two that is the key causal determinant in increased crime.[10] Since very few large-scale surveys in the United States ask detailed questions about the location and circumstances of alcohol use, these age-based studies usually cannot rule out the possibility that changes in both the quantity of alcohol consumed and the circumstances of consumption independently contribute to changes in the incidence of crime.

Finally, there are two related critical issues dealing with external validity and whether drinking age laws induce temporary displacements of drinking and crime outcomes or permanent reductions. Carpenter and Dobkin's RD design suggests that the increases in crime attributable to easier alcohol access at age twenty-one persist through at least age twenty-three, though extrapolation away from the discontinuity for the purposes of informing

---

10. This limitation is less salient for the evidence on property and nuisance crimes, since they are less likely to involve interpersonal interactions.

policy is particularly difficult in this setting. Indeed, one of the most salient challenges to age-based designs is that their key advantage—tight information about which individuals should and should not have been affected by the restrictions according to single year of age (in the panel evaluation design) or exact age (in the RD design)—comes at a cost: questionable generalizability beyond young adults. That is, it is not obvious that a proportional reduction in alcohol consumption at age fifteen, thirty-five, or fifty would have the same effects on crime as indicated in the drinking age studies (whose focus is ages eighteen to twenty-one). The weight of this limitation, however, is somewhat mitigated by the fact that the age profiles for both drinking and crime peak in late adolescence and early adulthood. This suggests that though estimates are specific to young adults, they are still of substantial general interest.[11]

Overall Evaluation: Age-Based Alcohol Restrictions

In the 1970s and 1980s many states lowered their drinking age to eighteen or nineteen before raising it back to twenty-one; the minimum legal drinking age in every state has been set at twenty-one since then. The literature has produced a great deal of evidence that lowering the drinking age would increase youth drinking, and results from both panel evaluations and a regression discontinuity design indicate that lowering the drinking age would also increase several types of crime, including violent crime, committed by young adults.

6.5.3   Space-Based Restrictions on the Availability and Density of Alcohol Outlets

There are numerous studies in the addiction, criminology, and public health literature that have found a strong spatial relationship between alcohol and crime. If these correlations are due to an underlying causal relationship between alcohol availability and crime, then local restrictions on the availability of alcohol—such as prohibiting the sale of alcohol in residential zones or within a certain radius of schools—may be effective crime control tools.

Studies of this type typically use sophisticated geographic information system (GIS) methods and very detailed data on locations of alcohol outlets and the places where crimes are committed to estimate spatial correlations. Since these studies typically focus on crime committed in very small areas around where alcohol is available, concerns about ecological inference problems are mitigated. Also, some of the studies allow disaggregation by type of alcohol outlet (e.g., liquor store versus bar) to provide more detailed evi-

---

11. Note that if age-based alcohol control policies have longer-term effects on drinking outcomes (as suggested by Norberg, Bierut, and Grueza 2009 and Kaestner and Yarnoff 2009), then there may also be an additional rationale for age-based restrictions.

dence on which types of outlets are more strongly associated with crime. The pharmacological evidence reviewed earlier suggests that on-premises outlets should be more strongly related to aggression-related crimes than off-premises outlets in the presence of a true causal effect.

Most of the early research using spatial variation relied on cross-sectional variation in alcohol outlets in particular cities. One of the earliest and most often cited studies of this kind was conducted by Scribner, MacKinnon, and Dwyer (1995) using detailed information on the location of assaults in seventy-five communities in Los Angeles. They found that one additional alcohol outlet was associated with 3.4 additional violent assaults (from a base of 570). In a related study, Scribner et al. (1999) examined 155 neighborhoods in New Orleans and found that a 10 percent increase in off-premises alcohol outlets was significantly associated with a 2.4 percent higher homicide rate.[12] Livingston (2008) performed a similar study for 223 neighborhoods in Melbourne, Australia, and found statistically significant relationships between general alcohol outlet density and assault and on-premises alcohol outlet density and assault, but other research that has disaggregated alcohol outlets by type has reached different conclusions.[13] A 2006 study by Gruenewald and colleagues, for example, examined California hospital admission for assaults and found that assaults were more common in areas with many alcohol outlets that required off-premises consumption such as liquor stores than in areas with many outlets where alcohol is consumed on the premises, such as bars. In fact, Gruenewald et al. (2006) found that bar density increased the assault rate only in low-income, poor communities and rural communities, but not in stable, wealthy communities.

The relationships between space-based restrictions, alcohol consumption, and crime-related outcomes have also been studied extensively in the context of college students. Multiple studies have used the Harvard College Alcohol Study (CAS)—a large, nationally representative survey of college youths' risk behaviors related to alcohol use—to show that proximity of the campus to alcohol outlets is significantly related to drinking participation and heavy episodic drinking (see, e.g., Chaloupka and Wechsler 1996; Weitzman et al. 2002). Wechsler et al. (2002) fielded a telephone survey of households around college campuses with varying rates of binge drinking. They found that people living near college campuses with high binge-drinking rates reported significantly more nuisance crimes such as drunkenness, vandalism, public urination, and other disorderly conduct than people living farther away.

---

12. Not all such studies have found similar effects, however. Gorman et al. (1998) perform a similar analysis for New Jersey and find no spatial relationship between alcohol outlets and violence.

13. We review only a handful of representative articles from the public health and criminology literature here. For others see, for example, Lipton and Gruenewald (2002); Roncek and Maier (1991); Zhu, Gorman, and Horel (2004); Gorman et al. (1998).

Of course, a significant issue with these cross-sectional analyses of spatial variation in liquor outlets is that unobserved local factors that contribute to both crime and alcohol outlet density may bias the estimates presented in these studies. Researchers have tried to address this challenge in a variety of ways. The most common approach is to include tract-level controls for multiple observable dimensions of local neighborhood quality. Adjusting for observable differences between neighborhoods in this fashion may reduce the problem of omitted variables bias.

An alternative way to address the problem that neighborhood characteristics are probably correlated with both liquor outlet availability and crime is to identify an instrumental variable that affects liquor availability but does not directly affect crime (i.e., a variable that only affects crime through its effect on liquor outlets). Gyimah-Brempong (2001) uses the number of gas stations in a census tract as an instrument for alcohol outlet density in Detroit, with the idea that the fixed costs of operating an alcohol outlet are lower in commercial zones. He uses median rent as an additional instrument with the reasoning that higher rents will make it more expensive to operate an alcohol outlet. He finds that both uncorrected and corrected specifications suggest a strong positive relationship between alcohol outlets and property and violent crimes. A difficulty with this approach is that it is not clear that the instruments satisfy the necessary exclusion restrictions for valid identification.

A third approach for addressing concerns about omitted variables bias is to examine how the opening and closing of alcohol outlets affects crime rates. Teh (2008) employs this type of strategy in an event-study framework using data on liquor outlets in Los Angeles. Her empirical specifications include area fixed effects, which ease concerns about the time-invariant characteristics of neighborhoods that might affect both crime rates and the probability that a liquor store is located in the neighborhood. In her main specifications the effects of liquor availability are identified from liquor store openings and closings. She finds that both property and violent crimes increase immediately after an alcohol outlet opens, and these effects are larger in the immediate vicinity of the outlet and in low-income neighborhoods.

Critiques of the Space-Based Literature on Alcohol Outlets

Despite these innovations for addressing the evaluation problem in the context of spatial alcohol availability and crime, several challenges remain. First, it is not obvious that the designs used in this literature adequately address concerns about omitted variables bias. As noted previously, the cross-sectional comparisons are vulnerable to omitted variables bias. Even the panel and interrupted time-series designs in this literature may still produce biased estimates if changing population preferences toward alcohol contribute to political processes that generate spatial restrictions.

Second, the mechanisms underlying any crime reduction in these studies are not well understood. For example, spatial studies face the challenge that alcohol outlets may *attract* crime (in addition to or instead of causing it), so estimates from this design may overstate the benefits of reducing liquor store or bar density. Similarly, it is difficult to disentangle whether it is variation in alcohol consumption, variation in social interaction around liquor outlets, or the interaction of the two that causes crime. Also, little is known about how liquor store placement and alcohol outlet density affect alcohol consumption. Most survey data on alcohol use are not well suited for these types of detailed spatial analyses since surveys generally do not ask about the precise location of consumption. Studies have used data on the location of alcohol sales (Stevenson, Lind, and Weatherburn 1999), though this may be a poor measure of the location of consumption, particularly for consumption away from the location where the alcohol was purchased.

Third, most studies in the spatial availability literature have focused on violent crime; a more comprehensive analysis of all crime types would be useful, particularly an examination of alcohol-related crimes (e.g., public intoxication) to strengthen the evidence that alcohol outlets actually increase consumption. Fourth, most studies lack information on spatial dimensions of police enforcement. Such studies may produce biased estimates of the effects of, say, liquor outlets on crime if enforcement is systematically higher around liquor outlets (either at a point in time or over time in a way that is correlated with alcohol outlet openings and closings). Fifth, studies in this literature cannot disentangle whether alcohol use causes crime commission, criminal victimization, or both. Having an alcohol outlet in a neighborhood could plausibly increase the alcohol consumption of both perpetrators and victims, and there is no way to separately identify these two effects.

Finally, and perhaps most important, few of the studies in the spatial availability literature provide evidence on the critical question of whether the policies simply shift the location of alcohol consumption and crime or whether they actually affect the overall crime rate. While social welfare may be enhanced in the presence of consumption or crime displacement across space (if, for example, alcohol consumed and crime committed away from schools were less socially harmful than the same level of consumption and crime near schools), a full accounting of the costs and benefits of these policies requires a complete understanding of the total effects of the regulations on outcomes.

Overall Evaluation: Space-Based Regulations on Alcohol Outlets

The existing evidence suggests a link between alcohol outlets and some types of crime, but strong conclusions are not yet warranted because studies of spatial availability restrictions have yet to convincingly overcome key identification problems. Even the best studies in this literature do not establish that the opening of an alcohol outlet will increase crime rather than just attract it. We conclude that the evidence is not sufficient to establish that spatial availability restrictions are effective at reducing crime.

6.5.4   Temporal Restrictions on the Hours and/or Days of Alcohol Sales

In addition to explicitly space-based regulations, there are also several types of alcohol regulations that specify when alcohol can be purchased or consumed. These include laws that prevent Sunday sales of alcohol in the United States and Australia and Saturday sales in Scandinavia, and laws that regulate the hours of operation of venues where alcohol is consumed, such as bars and restaurants.

Studies of temporal availability restrictions have the advantage that there have been many changes in laws governing when alcohol can be sold. This allows researchers to implement fairly compelling pre-/post- and interrupted time-series designs, thus reducing some concerns about omitted variables bias to the extent that time-invariant unobservables are controlled for through the inclusion of location fixed effects. Since these types of policies are routinely debated in many jurisdictions, studies that can evaluate their efficacy are of particular interest.

Much of the research exploiting temporal variation in alcohol availability has focused on repealing prohibitions of alcohol sales, particularly restrictions on Sunday alcohol sales. Commonly termed "blue laws," these policies are still prevalent in many areas in the southern United States. In the past decade, however, several places have lifted their Sunday sales restrictions, in part to increase state revenue from sales taxes. Evidence suggests that such policy liberalizations do increase alcohol sales. Stehr (2007) uses aggregate data on beer, wine, and spirits sales to study the effect of various US states' repeal of Sunday sales restrictions. His fixed-effects estimates indicate that Sunday sales policies significantly increased spirits sales. Evidence that such policies affect actual alcohol consumption (as distinct from alcohol sales) is more limited, though Carpenter and Eisenberg (2009) show that Sunday sales liberalization in Ontario, Canada, increased Sunday-specific drinking by seven to 15 percent, with some evidence of substitution away from consumption on Fridays and Saturdays.[14]

Evidence that these types of temporal restrictions on alcohol sales and availability reduce crime rates is fairly limited. Ligon and Thyer (1993) showed that a ban on Sunday alcohol sales reduced arrests for driving under the influence (DUI). McMillan and Lapham (2006), using data on day-specific traffic fatalities in New Mexico before and after its 1995 Sunday sales liberalization, found very large increases in Sunday fatalities, though more

---

14. Gruber and Hungerman (2008) examine earlier repeals of blue laws in the United States that increased a variety of economic activities on Sundays (not just alcohol sales). While alcohol consumption was not the primary focus of their paper, they did find that blue law repeals increased drinking by 16 percent among individuals who had previously attended church services (and whose behavior would be most likely affected by the blue law repeal).

recent analyses have suggested far more modest effects (Maloney and Rudbeck 2009; Lovenheim and Steefel 2009). A related series of papers by Smith (1988a, 1988b, 1990, and others) showed that increases in the hours/days of availability in Australia were associated with increases in alcohol-related fatalities.

Some of the best evidence of the impact of temporal availability restrictions on crime rates comes from Scandinavia, where multiple policy changes make it possible to implement relatively compelling interrupted time-series designs.[15] Olsson and Wikstrom (1982) studied Sweden's short-term closing of its state monopoly liquor stores on Saturdays in the summer of 1981. They found that offenses related to drunkenness, domestic disturbances, public disturbances, and assaults fell on both Saturdays and Sundays relative to other days of the week during the period of the experiment. Interestingly, they found no effects on outcomes related to vandalism, acute medical care, and road accidents, and there is also no evidence from this policy experiment that the reduction in Saturday availability reduced total alcohol consumption. These results raise the possibility of across-day substitution (e.g., a displacement of consumption and/or crime from weekends to weekdays) and suggest the need for more detailed data on the circumstances of alcohol consumption.[16]

In a series of studies examining the effects of Sweden's staggered adoption of longer Saturday retail hours in its monopoly-run liquor stores (first in a limited geographic area in February 2000 and then countrywide in 2001), Norstrom and Skog (2003, 2005) found that increased alcohol availability was associated with modest increases in sales of beer and spirits (but not wine) of about 3.6 percent during both phases of the experiment. The increased alcohol sales from the first liberalization (but not the second) were associated with significant increases in alcohol-involved driving, while assaults exhibited no significant change in either period. Norstrom and Skog argue that the increase in drunk-driving arrests that resulted from the 2000 policy change is at least partly attributable to changes in police enforcement. They also note that such modest changes in overall alcohol sales make it difficult to precisely estimate the relationship between alcohol sales and assaults. Norstrom and Skog did not examine whether their outcomes exhibited cross-day substitution in response to the Saturday-specific increase in availability.

15. In addition to the peer-reviewed studies on Scandinavian policy changes described here and in the next section, see the comprehensive treatment by Room (2002).

16. The lack of effects on overall alcohol consumption from modest changes in the days or hours of sale is a common finding in this literature. Duffy and Plant (1986), for example, studied Scotland's 1976 alcohol liberalization, which extended bar closing hours from 10:00 p.m. until 11:00 p.m. and allowed "public houses" (not just bars in hotels) to be open on Sundays. Using changes in alcohol-related outcomes in England and Wales as a control condition, they found no evidence that these temporal restrictions affected overall alcohol consumption or alcohol-related harm except for a reduction in public order offenses such as drunkenness.

Finally, we review studies of laws that regulate the hours of alcohol availability. Chikritzhs and Stockwell (2002) studied later closing times for bars in licensed hotels in Perth, Australia, using data on assaults reported to the police. Over their 1991 to 1997 sample period, about a quarter of hotels applied for and were granted a permit to extend alcohol sales from midnight until 1:00 a.m. They found that, relative to hotels that were not granted such permits, hotels with extended trading hours exhibited significantly greater wholesale alcohol purchases (their proxy for increased alcohol consumption) and had significantly higher rates of assault in the immediate vicinity of the hotel. Vingilis et al. (2005) studied the effects of Ontario, Canada's 1996 extension of its bar closing hours from 1:00 a.m. to 2:00 a.m. They examined administrative data on hospital admissions for each hour of availability from 11:00 p.m. to 3:00 a.m. for the four years before and three years after the policy change. They found reductions in motor vehicle collision admissions between 11:00 p.m. and midnight and between 1:00 and 2:00 a.m. but no significant change for the 2:00 to 3:00 a.m. period, which they attribute to concurrent increased enforcement and road safety initiatives. For other types of injuries not related to motor vehicle collisions, they found significant increases for the 2:00 to 3:00 a.m. period.[17]

One of the strongest examples of this type of research used the adoption of mandatory bar and restaurant closing hours in Sao Paolo, Brazil. Biderman, DeMello, and Schneider (2010) use a difference-in-differences design to examine the effects of these "dry" laws on violent crime. Between March 2001 and August 2004, sixteen of thirty-nine municipalities in the Sao Paolo metropolitan area prohibited alcohol sales during the late-night and early-morning hours; prior to this most bars were allowed to remain open twenty-four hours a day. In models with city and period fixed effects as well as controls for varying city/period demographic characteristics, police enforcement, and lags in the homicide rate, Biderman and colleagues found that adoption of the dry law was associated with a statistically significant reduction in both homicides and battery of about 10 percent.[18]

Changes in temporal restrictions are not uniformly effective, however, as evidenced by recent evaluations of another high-profile policy experiment regarding bar closing hours that was intended to reduce crime—England and Wales's Licensing Act of 2003—but that have not returned uniformly strong evidence of crime reductions (Hough and Hunter 2008; Humphreys and Eisner 2010; and others). That policy liberalized restrictions on bar

17. A study related to research on bar closing hours is by Jackson and Owens (2010), who use the extension of late-night hours of Metro rail service in Washington, DC, which allowed individuals to stay at bars and restaurants until those establishments closed. They show that a series of these policy changes predictably affected DUIs and alcohol-related crimes.

18. Biderman et al.'s (2010) results confirm the findings of an earlier single-city analysis of the Brazilian city of Diadema, which found that homicides fell significantly after the imposition of a mandatory 11:00 p.m. closing hour (Duailibi et al. 2007).

closing hours and encouraged licensed premises to apply for rights to serve alcohol later than previously allowed. The rationale for the policy was to reduce the problems associated with a fixed, common bar closing time, which generally resulted in large numbers of inebriated individuals coming into close contact with each other in small spaces. Staggering bar closing hours, it was thought, would dramatically reduce crimes such as assaults that occur at very high rates when all bars close at once in the early hours of the morning. Results have generally shown no meaningful effects on either alcohol consumption or measures of violent crime (Hough and Hunter 2008). Some scholars have noted that because the law did not require staggered closing hours but rather made them voluntary, in reality there was rather limited variation in the treatment of interest (Treno 2010; Frattaroli 2010).

Critiques of the Literature on Temporal Availability Restrictions

Studies of temporal availability restrictions have several of the same limitations as the spatial availability research described earlier. While these studies arguably do a better job of dealing with the possibility of omitted variables correlated with both the temporal availability restriction and outcomes, one might still worry that changing attitudes toward alcohol will drive the adoption of these policies and also directly affect outcomes. Though Sunday sales liberalizations seem to be driven by a desire to increase state tax revenues, endogenous policy adoption may be an issue for the other studies examined in this subsection, such as the imposition of mandatory bar closing times in Brazil or liberalized/staggered bar closing times in England and Wales.[19] A related question about generalizability arises in examining changes in temporal availability restrictions: while a handful of studies have examined the effects of changes in the days and hours of alcohol availability on alcohol consumption and DUI outcomes in the United States, none of these has examined crime or violence more generally. The studies that do examine crime leverage policy changes in countries and time periods where the basic patterns of alcohol control and crime differ markedly from those in the United States.

There are other limitations as well. As with the spatial availability studies, the research on temporal restrictions provides almost no insight into how these policies affect the extent or conditions of alcohol consumption, as most evidence comes from imperfect proxies such as aggregate sales. And, like the spatial literature, most studies of restrictions on the days or hours of alcohol sales lack information on temporal dimensions of police enforcement. If enforcement is systematically lower during the periods when alcohol sales are restricted, the observed effect of a change in temporal

19. Duailibi et al. (2007) note, for example, that the mandatory bar closing hour policy in Diadema was instituted because the mayor was concerned about the high murder rate, and police records showed that most murders occurred in or near bars.

availability restrictions on crime will be dampened. Studies in the temporal literature also cannot separately identify whether alcohol use causes crime commission, criminal victimization, or both. Finally, and again perhaps most important, few of the temporal availability studies provide compelling evidence on whether the policies simply shift the timing of alcohol consumption and crime or permanently reduce them.

Overall Evaluation: Temporal Availability Restrictions

Research examining temporal restrictions on the hours and days on which alcohol may be sold share many of the strengths and weaknesses of studies that exploit detailed spatial variation in the availability of alcohol outlets. These studies tend to examine a limited number of types of crime and do not address the broader question of whether temporal availability restrictions simply redistribute crime across different time periods or reduce it. We conclude that there is compelling evidence that temporal availability restrictions change the times at which crimes are committed, but that the evidence that they actually reduce overall alcohol consumption and crime rates is weaker.

6.5.5   Other "Circumstance" Regulations not Elsewhere Classified and Indirect Evidence on Alcohol and Crime

The preceding sections reviewed evidence from studies of alcohol regulations that were either spatial or temporal in nature. There are, in addition, other types of alcohol restrictions that combine elements of both. These "circumstance" regulations control the conditions under which alcohol is made available and include alcohol rationing and privatizations of government liquor sales monopolies (which generally lead to increases in alcohol availability through increases in outlet density and reductions in prices). In this section we also review a handful of studies that do not explicitly evaluate alcohol control policies but do provide important and useful evidence on the nature and extent of the causal links between alcohol availability, alcohol consumption, and the commission of crime.

One type of circumstance regulation that has been studied in the context of crime is drunk-driving policy. Specifically, Carpenter (2007) examined the reduced-form relationship between age-targeted "zero tolerance" (ZT) drunk-driving laws and age-specific crime (as proxied by age-specific arrests).[20] The ZT laws were adopted by every US state during the 1990s; they make it illegal for youths under age twenty-one to drive with *any* alcohol in their blood (the relevant standard for adults in most states at the time was a BAC of 0.08 or 0.10); thus, these laws dramatically lowered the relevant

---

20. Alcohol-involved driving regulations may be useful for future studies of alcohol and crime, but we are not aware of any research that has used them in this way other than that by Carpenter (2007).

BAC threshold for youths under age twenty-one but had no independent effect on the legal environment for young adults over age twenty-one. Carpenter (2007) showed that adoption of ZT laws, which reduced youth drinking among eighteen to twenty-year-olds by 13 percent (Carpenter 2004), also reduced property and nuisance crime arrests among young adults aged eighteen to twenty by 5 percent but had no effect on arrests among slightly older adults aged twenty-two to twenty-four who were unaffected by ZT laws. He did not find significant effects on violent crime.

Another type of circumstance regulation is a local prohibition on alcohol (i.e., whether a city or county is "wet" or "dry"). Such restrictions remain especially common in the southern United States. Conlin, Dickert-Conlin, and Pepper (2005) studied the effects of changes in local prohibitions at the county level in Texas using data from 1978 to 1996. In fixed-effects models with county and year fixed effects, they found that a county's movement to wet status *decreased* illicit drug crimes (and mortality associated with illicit drug use). They interpret this as evidence that alcohol and illicit drugs are substitutes.

Several studies have examined large-scale reductions in alcohol consumption associated with major world or country-specific events. During Russia's antialcohol campaign of 1985 to 1988, alcohol was banned in public places, prices quadrupled, and state production and sale of alcohol was dramatically limited. Over this period, population alcohol consumption fell by 25 percent, and the homicide rate fell by about 40 percent (Shkolnikov and Nemtsov 1997). Lenke (1982) reports on a series of studies in Scandinavia that have suggested a strong link between availability and crime using historical records. First, he shows that alcohol rationing as part of a broader food shortage during World War I resulted in a two-thirds decline in alcohol consumption. This was soon followed by significant reductions in assault but overall increases in other types of crime. Lenke also reports on the end of Sweden's rationing system in 1955, which led to a sharp increase in alcohol consumption of about 25 percent and a more modest increase in assaults (8 percent). In another study, Lenke (1982) reports on a policy experiment that introduced "middle-strong" beer into general food stores in 1965. Prior to 1965, beer above a certain alcohol content could only be sold in government-run monopoly stores. From 1960 to 1970, alcohol consumption increased in Sweden by 40 percent and assaults increased by 50 to 100 percent, with particularly large increases among youths and in rural areas. Lenke reports similar patterns from a closely related policy experiment in Finland in 1969. Notably, however, when Sweden ended the sale of middle-strong beer in general food stores in 1977, alcohol consumption fell only modestly—on the order of 10 percent—and assaults did not fall. These studies do not include explicit control groups, raising some concerns that the estimates may be biased.

Temporary suspensions of alcohol availability associated with labor strikes affecting monopoly-run alcohol outlets have also provided strong evidence of a link between alcohol availability and crime. Lenke (1982) reports on a three-month strike at the state monopoly liquor stores in Sweden in 1963. During the strike (when alcohol was much more difficult to obtain), aggravated assault fell. There were similar reductions in Finland during strikes by workers at state liquor stores in 1972, which caused an abrupt and large reduction in alcohol availability. Over this period, it is estimated that alcohol consumption fell by 30 percent, with concomitant reductions in public drunkenness, resisting arrest, disturbing the peace, and aggravated assault. Inflicted injuries as measured by admissions to emergency clinics for murder, manslaughter, assault, and battery also fell sharply coincident with the reduced availability (Makela 1980; Karaharju and Stjernvall 1974; Takala 1973). Similar strikes in Norway's monopoly liquor stores in 1978 also reduced alcohol consumption by 5 to 10 percent and reduced domestic violence (Horverak 1981, as reported in Room 1983). Although these circumstances were not brought about by intentional policy manipulations, the studies do provide strong evidence that liberalizing alcohol availability through increased retail availability would increase alcohol consumption and crime.

Finally, we note that several studies have shed light on a possible link between alcohol and crime while not directly studying alcohol control or alcohol consumption. Dahl and DellaVigna (2009), for example, find that the release of violent movies is associated with reductions in violent crime during evening hours; they hypothesize that moviegoing may displace alcohol consumption, which would result in fewer acts of violence if alcohol use causes violent behavior. Rees and Schnepel (2009) examine the relationship between college football games and crime, finding that cities hosting Division I-A football games experience sharp increases in arrests for assault, vandalism, and disorderly conduct on game days. Importantly, they find some of the largest effects on liquor law violations which, combined with anecdotal evidence, suggests that alcohol may play a causal role in game-day crime. Card and Dahl (2009) study the effects of emotional cues on domestic violence; they examine the days on which professional football games are played and show that unexpected home team losses significantly increase acts of domestic violence. Again, alcohol use may be one mechanism contributing to this effect. These and other studies suggest alcohol is a substantial cause of violence and that situation-specific regulations may be effective at reducing alcohol consumption and some of the crime it generates.

6.6   Common Limitations and Proposed Future Directions

While each of the literatures we have reviewed previously has specific strengths and weaknesses, there are also some broad gaps in the literature on alcohol control policy and crime that are worth mentioning in the hope of spurring researchers to address them.

One of the most serious gaps in the literature is that little is known about how much and in what ways alcohol regulations affect alcohol consumption. Understanding how regulations affect the levels, patterns, and circumstances of alcohol use would be of substantial value. For example, information on how each regulation affects total drinking, binge drinking, and drinking by high-risk groups would provide more insight into the mechanisms through which the policies reduce crime (if indeed they do) and would subsequently allow policymakers to craft more effective regulations. An additional benefit of having estimates of how different policies affect the level of alcohol consumption by different groups (e.g., heavy versus light drinkers) is that we would be able to better characterize specific policies' social costs. Existing evidence suggests that even heavy and "problem" drinkers respond to price (Cook and Tauchen 1982), though which groups are particularly sensitive to tax-induced price changes is not well documented.

Another limitation of the literature reviewed here is that it is focused largely on homicides and other violent crimes such as rape and assault, presumably because of the strong pharmacological links between alcohol and aggression. Property crimes (e.g., larceny, motor vehicle theft), drug crimes (e.g., possession, sale, use), and social nuisance crimes (e.g., vandalism, disorderly conduct, prostitution) have received much less attention, perhaps because they are considered less serious. However, these crimes are far more common than violent crimes, so failing to examine them closely may lead us to miss a substantial part of the social costs of alcohol consumption.

A final shortcoming of the entire literature on alcohol and crime is the disproportionate focus on alcohol's role in the commission of crime as opposed to criminal victimization (with the exception of homicide victimization, for which there is a substantial public health and criminology literature). The lack of research attention to how alcohol affects the probability of criminal victimization is probably due in part to the lack of high quality victimization data. The National Crime Victimization Surveys, for example, provide some of the best data for studying criminal victimization, but they do not include geographic identifiers. It is not possible, therefore, to conduct state/year panel evaluations of the effects of alcohol control policies on criminal victimization. Yet even with credible victimization data there is another methodological and conceptual challenge for understanding how alcohol regulations affect criminal victimization: specifically, most alcohol control policies probably affect the alcohol consumption of both criminals and their victims, but it is impossible to distinguish between these two causal mechanisms without very rich individual-level data. Beer taxes, for example, likely affect drinking among both individuals committing crime and their victims, as do spatial and temporal restrictions on alcohol availability.

There are at least two recent encouraging developments for researchers interested in the important question of how alcohol affects crime. The first is that excellent data sources such as the National Epidemiologic Survey on Alcohol Related Conditions (NESARC) are becoming more broadly available. The NESARC is a two-wave panel (completed in 2001 and 2004–2005) of the alcohol consumption behaviors of over 40,000 adult residents of the United States performed by the National Institute on Alcohol Abuse and Alcoholism (NIAAA). Limited-access data files with geographic identifiers will be made available to researchers. These data are likely to be particularly useful for understanding the settings in which alcohol is consumed because the survey includes detailed questions about the location, timing, and frequency of recent alcohol consumption. Most US surveys such as the National Health Interview Survey contain far less detailed information on alcohol consumption and/or lack a longitudinal component. Another useful data set increasingly being used by economists is the National Incident Based Reporting System (NIBRS). It contains detailed information on crimes known to the police (not just crimes resulting in an arrest) and includes among other variables one that records if the crime involved alcohol. With this information, NIBRS can support state/year panel evaluations of alcohol control regulations on various measures of crime and violence, including incidents of criminal victimization. Finally, we are encouraged by the increased availability of large administrative data sets at the state and federal levels on mortality, arrests, and hospital and emergency room admissions; they broaden the set of outcomes that researchers can examine in the contexts of crime and violence.

A second encouraging development is the substantial number of recent state- and province-level policy changes. Some of the policy changes are the consequence of the recent economic downturn, which seriously diminished state budget coffers and led many states to increase excise taxes on beer, wine, and spirits as revenue-raising devices. For example, the Tax Foundation lists nineteen legislated increases in state beer taxes in the period 2002 to 2008, including several very large tax hikes (e.g., in Alaska from thirty-five cents to $1.07 per gallon in 2002); in the entire prior decade there were just fifteen increases (and most of these were small). These changes are particularly welcome for analyses of the effects of beer taxes, since one limitation of research in this area is that there historically have been too few large scale state-specific tax increases to get precise estimates from panel regression models (Dee 1999). Budget shortfalls have also led twelve states since 2000 to repeal longstanding restrictions on Sunday alcohol sales (Stehr 2007). The staggered timing of adoption of these policies at the state level should prove useful for understanding not only how these regulations affect alcohol consumption but also how they affect crime. Finally, a handful of US states and Canadian provinces have begun to privatize their systems of liquor control. Iowa, West Virginia, and Alberta did so in the late 1980s and early 1990s with dramatic effect on alcohol sales (Holder and Wagenaar 1995; Cook 2007). More recently, British Columbia undertook a partial privatization that has resulted in very large increases in alcohol availability; when combined with detailed information on consumption, violence, and crime, this should provide useful new insight into both the structural relationships underlying alcohol and crime as well as direct policy guidance for other states, such as Virginia, that are actively debating privatization (Stockwell et al. 2009).

In summary, the increased availability of high-quality survey and administrative data and the numerous recent policy changes suggest that future work on alcohol regulations, alcohol consumption, and crime can address some of the limitations that are common to the now substantial literature on this important and complex topic.

6.7   Policy Options and Economic Considerations

We conclude our review with a discussion of the economic considerations that are relevant when considering whether alcohol regulations should be implemented in an attempt to reduce crime. Doing so requires us to identify the main feature distinguishing the public health perspective from the economic perspective: the latter takes into account the valuation of the utility loss borne by moderate drinkers whose responsible alcohol consumption is not criminogenic. In a typical policy analysis from a public health perspective, these utility losses are not included in the cost/benefit calculations of alcohol control policies. Instead, the value of the crime reduction (as measured by the direct dollar values of reduced property and nuisance crimes and the present value of the stream of increased quality-adjusted life years gained from reducing crime) is compared with the direct costs of the stricter regulation (e.g., the personnel and administrative costs associated with increased enforcement of alcohol control regulations). The economic approach, however, recognizes that adoption of stricter alcohol control policies for the purposes of crime reduction imposes deadweight loss on moderate, responsible consumers. Higher taxes, for example, may reduce alcohol consumption by people whose drinking leads them to commit crimes, but may also reduce the consumption by law-abiding drinkers. Since the majority of the population consumes alcohol and does so in a responsible way, the foregone value of alcohol consumption by this group should not be easily dismissed.[21]

The situation is further complicated by the fact that alcohol may confer

---

21. Cook (2008), however, argues that this concern about alcohol taxes—that they penalize moderate drinkers—is weakened to the extent that revenue raised from alcohol taxes can be used to reduce other tax rates or create public programs that benefit those same moderate drinkers. Moreover, the costs associated with implementing more targeted interventions (e.g., setting up counseling programs for drinkers, enforcing stronger sanctions against alcohol-related crimes) also impose costs on moderate drinkers.

nontrivial benefits to drinkers and to society. There is a large body of medical research suggesting that moderate drinking reduces heart disease risk among men, although Cook, Ostermann, and Sloan (2005) find no long-term net effect on mortality for moderate drinkers. There is also evidence that moderate and social drinkers have higher earnings than abstainers, raising the possibility that responsible consumption of alcohol might make people more productive. If these literatures document a causal relationship, regulations that lead to lower alcohol consumption would impose costs on society.

Notably, stricter regulations of alcohol such as higher excise taxes are likely to have effects on a range of important social outcomes. Although our review here has focused on studies that convincingly tackle alcohol's causal role in crime, there are large bodies of research on other adverse outcomes of alcohol consumption, including: drunk-driving mortality, mortality due to accidents and other causes, accidental injury, and risky sexual behavior (for reviews, see Cook and Moore 2000; Chaloupka 2004; and others). Measured in economic terms, the value of the changes in these other alcohol-related outcomes may be substantially greater than the direct and indirect costs of stricter alcohol control.

What, then, are we to conclude about the relative value of alcohol control policies available to local, state, and federal lawmakers? First, changing the availability of alcohol with marginal spatial or temporal restrictions (or some combination of these) is unlikely to yield major reductions in crime because individuals can—and do—respond to such restrictions by shifting the venue or circumstances of their consumption, thus undoing the effects of the regulation. The most credible existing evidence on the repeal of Sunday sales, for example, suggests that it has no effect on overall alcohol consumption and very modest effects on the outcome that is arguably the most direct consequence of problem alcohol consumption: alcohol-related fatalities (Carpenter and Eisenberg 2009; Lovenheim and Steefel 2009). And while there is credible evidence that Sao Paolo's introduction of mandatory bar closing times significantly reduced violent crime, the change was of a very different type and magnitude than is relevant for the vast majority of the United States (where very few bars are open twenty-four hours a day). We do see potential value in mandating staggered bar closing hours (a voluntary variant of which was tried with seemingly little success in the UK Licensing Act of 2003), but the political viability of this option is unclear. Moreover, while most alcohol outlet policies with respect to licensing disrupt the location or timing of on-premises drinking, in theory a larger scale supply-side restriction on alcohol licenses (such as increasing licensing fees or directly restricting the supply of available licenses) would reduce alcohol-related adverse outcomes such as crime and violence by driving up alcohol prices, though this is an understudied research area.

Second, we conclude that lowering the minimum drinking age in the United States—a policy option being considered by several states (Florida,

Wisconsin, Vermont, and others) at this writing in 2010—would lead to significant increases in crime and violence among young adults and overall. Both the state/year panel evaluation based on historical state policy changes (Joksch and Jones 1993) and evidence from a regression discontinuity design examining a more recent time period (Carpenter and Dobkin 2010) confirm that drinking ages have large and economically meaningful effects on alcohol consumption and crime among young adults (who are at the peak of the age-crime profile). Were individual US states to return to the 1970s-era regime of allowing youth aged eighteen to twenty-one to legally drink alcohol, the results from these studies indicate that nuisance and violent crime would significantly increase among this age group.[22] And while a drinking age of twenty-one may shift some alcohol consumption to later in the life cycle, this shift is still likely to result in less crime overall because: (a) by this age youths are on the downward slope of the age-crime profile; and (b) brain development and maturation in young adults continues through the mid-20s, such that the degree of crime-inducing cognitive deficits from alcohol use later in life is likely to be lower than in the late teens and early twenties (Brown et al. 2000; Pyapali et al. 1999; and others).

In contrast to the active discussion about lowering drinking ages in some states, there currently is no political interest in raising the minimum drinking age above twenty-one in the United States, despite the fact that such an increase would likely reduce crime and other adverse outcomes in the affected age range. How, then, could current drinking age policy be improved for the purpose of further reducing crime? One possibility is to increase enforcement of the law. Little research, however, has credibly evaluated the effects of better drinking age enforcement, in part because enforcement is likely strongly endogenous to youth drinking and crime outcomes (e.g., communities may be expected to get tough on drinking age violations after spikes in underage drinking problems). Some recent work, however, has used more credible multicommunity controlled time-series methods to evaluate the effects of drinking age enforcement training for employees at alcohol outlets and police enforcement checks of these outlets. That research shows no evidence that training programs are effective and some evidence that increased enforcement checks reduce sales to minors (and, by implication, underage drinking) (Wagenaar, Toomey, and Erickson 2005). This research suggests that increasing enforcement of current drinking ages through police checks would further reduce youth drinking and associated crime.

Third, our research suggests that increases in excise taxes on alcohol are likely to reduce crime. As others have shown, the real price of ethanol has

22. Different drinking ages across states also raise serious issues about adverse consequences (including crime, alcohol-related traffic fatalities, and other events) for youths traveling across state lines to purchase and consume alcohol. For evidence on this, see Lovenheim and Slemrod (2010). These issues are also relevant for analyses of differential excise taxes across states; for recent evidence on this, see Stehr (2007).

fallen steadily over the past two decades (see, e.g., Cook 2007, 2008). While our review of the literature examining the impact of alcohol taxes on crime illustrates some important limitations to those studies, we think there is sufficient evidence on the underlying structural relationship between taxes and prices, prices and alcohol consumption, and alcohol consumption and crime to conclude that a tax-induced price increase would reduce drinking and crime.[23] Such an increase is likely to be most effective when it is sizable and does not exacerbate cross-state tax differentials.[24]

As noted earlier, alcohol tax increases are increasingly common revenue-raising devices in states facing serious budget shortfalls. A natural question is: how much crime reduction would a representative tax increase buy? One recent estimate is that a 10 percent increase in the price of alcohol would reduce youth drinking by a similar amount (Carpenter et al. 2007); price elasticity estimates for older adults are generally smaller in magnitude. Carpenter and Dobkin (2010) estimate that a 10 percent increase in drinking probability increases the likelihood of being arrested for any crime by about 2 percent for young adults, with most of these effects attributable to reductions in violent crime, such as aggravated assault. These estimates imply modest but meaningful effects on overall crime given common estimates that about 40 percent of violent crimes involve alcohol (Greenfield and Hennenberg 2001). Another, more direct way to predict the likely effects of alcohol tax increases on crime is to use estimates from state panel evaluations described previously. For example, Cook and Moore (1993) estimate that a 10 percent increase in the beer tax (roughly twenty-five cents per six pack of twelve-ounce beer measured in 2009 dollars) would reduce murder, rape, assault, and robbery by 0.3, 1.3, 0.3, and 0.9 percent, respectively.

Finally, although we have reviewed most of the serious policy options that use alcohol control to bring about reductions in crime, less commonly debated policy options also exist. Most of the alcohol restrictions we have discussed here work by altering the costs of alcohol consumption (e.g., directly, by raising prices, or more commonly, through sanctions and availability restrictions). Other potential interventions might target changes in actual or perceived benefits of alcohol consumption, such as responsible drinking campaigns, alcohol advertising regulations, and/or product placements in mainstream media. If these approaches were effective at reducing irresponsible drinking they might reduce crime with less deadweight loss than other policies.

---

23. We do not think the literature is definitive with respect to taxation of, say, beer versus wine or spirits. In part this is because the most common empirical approach is to control for beer taxes, since this is the most commonly consumed alcoholic beverage in the United States. This is an important issue for future work.

24. Cook (2008) provides perspective to and arguments against the idea that alcohol tax increases are inferior because they are poorly focused and penalize moderate drinkers. Of course, to the extent that higher alcohol taxes also reduce other harms besides crime (e.g., motor vehicle fatalities), the case for tax increases is strengthened.

6.8   Conclusion

We began this review with the goal of identifying whether the strong observed associations between alcohol and crime reflect true causal effects of alcohol consumption (pharmacologically driven or otherwise) or whether they reflect unobserved heterogeneity, with the goal of informing alcohol regulation-based efforts to reduce crime. Our final assessment is that there is ample evidence to conclude that at least some of the extensively documented correlations between alcohol availability, alcohol consumption, crime, and violence do, in fact, represent true causal effects of alcohol use on crime commission. This seems especially true for interventions that induce very large and stark changes in alcohol consumption (e.g., large price or availability changes), as well as for alcohol control policies that effectively manipulate not only alcohol consumption but also potential and realized social interactions (e.g., mandatory closing hours and drinking ages). Taken together, our review suggests that, to the extent that inebriation plays a causal role in crime, the control of alcohol consumption should be taken seriously and deserves a place on the policy agenda.

References

Biderman, Ciro, João M. P. De Mello, and Alexandre Schneider. 2010. "Dry Laws and Homicides: Evidence from the São Paulo Metropolitan Area." *The Economic Journal* 120 (543): 157–82.

Brown, Sandra, Susan Tapert, Eric Granholm, and Dean Delis. 2000. "Neurocognitive Functioning of Adolescents: Effects of Protracted Alcohol Use." *Alcoholism: Clinical and Experimental Research* 24 (2): 164–71.

Card, David, and Gordon Dahl. 2009. "Family Violence and Football: The Effect of Unexpected Emotional Cues on Violent Behavior." NBER Working Paper no. 15497. Cambridge, MA: National Bureau of Economic Research, November.

Carpenter, Christopher. 2004. "How Do Zero Tolerance Drunk Driving Laws Work?" *Journal of Health Economics* 23 (1): 61–83.

———. 2005. "Heavy Alcohol Use and the Commission of Nuisance Crime: Evidence from Underage Drunk Driving Laws." *American Economic Review Papers and Proceedings* 95 (2): 267–72.

———. 2007. "Heavy Alcohol Use and Crime: Evidence from Underage Drunk Driving Laws." *Journal of Law and Economics* 50 (3): 539–57.

Carpenter, Christopher, and Carlos Dobkin. 2009. "The Effect of Alcohol Access on Consumption and Mortality: Regression Discontinuity Evidence from the Minimum Drinking Age." *American Economic Journal: Applied Economics* 1 (1): 164–82.

———. 2010. "The Drinking Age, Alcohol Consumption, and Crime." University of California. Working Paper.

Carpenter, Christopher, and Daniel Eisenberg. 2009. "The Effects of Sunday Sales Restrictions on Overall and Day-Specific Alcohol Consumption: Evidence from Canada." *Journal of Studies on Alcohol and Drugs* 70 (1): 126–33.

Carpenter, Christopher, Deborah D. Kloska, Patrick O'Malley, and Lloyd Johnston. 2007. "Alcohol Control Policies and Youth Alcohol Consumption: Evidence from

28 Years of Monitoring the Future." *The B. E. Journal of Economic Analysis and Policy* 7 (1, Topics): Article 25. doi: 10.2202/1935-1682.1637.

Chaloupka, Frank. 2004. "The Effects of Price on Alcohol Use, Abuse, and their Consequences." In *Reducing Underage Drinking: A Collective Responsibility,* edited by Richard Bonnie and Mary Ellen O'Connell, 541–64. Washington, DC: The National Academies Press.

Chaloupka, Frank, Michael Grossman, and Henry Saffer. 2002. "The Effects of Price on Alcohol Consumption and Alcohol-Related Problems." *Alcohol Research and Health* 26:22–34.

Chaloupka, Frank, and Henry Wechsler. 1996. "Binge Drinking in College: The Impact of Price, Availability, and Alcohol Control Policies." *Contemporary Economic Policy* 14 (4): 112–24.

Chikritzhs, Tanya, and Tim Stockwell. 2002. "The Impact of Later Trading Hours for Australian Public Houses (Hotels) on Levels of Violence." *Journal of Studies on Alcohol* 63:591–9.

Coate, Douglas, and Michael Grossman. 1988. "Effects of Alcoholic Beverage Prices and Legal Drinking Ages on Youth Alcohol Use." *Journal of Law and Economics* 31:145–71.

Conlin, Michael, Stacy Dickert-Conlin, and John Pepper. 2005. "The Effect of Alcohol Prohibition on Illicit Drug-Related Crimes." *Journal of Law and Economics* 48:215–34.

Cook, Philip. 2007. *Paying the Tab: The Costs and Benefits of Alcohol Control.* Princeton, NJ: Princeton University Press.

———. 2008. "A Free Lunch." Journal of Drug Policy Analysis 1 (1): Article 2. doi: 10.2202/1941-2851.1001.

Cook, Philip, and Michael Moore. 1993a. "Economic Perspectives on Reducing Alcohol-Related Violence." In *Alcohol and Interpersonal Violence: Fostering Multidisciplinary Perspectives,* edited by Susan E. Martin, Research Monograph 24. Washington, DC: National Institute on Alcohol Abuse and Alcoholism.

———. 1993b. "Violence Reduction through Restrictions on Alcohol Availability." *Alcohol Health & Research World* 17:151–7.

———. 2000. "Alcohol." In *Handbook of Health Economics Vol. 1A,* edited by Anthony Cuyler and Joseph Newhouse, 1629–73. Amsterdam: North Holland Press.

———. 2001. "Environment and Persistence in Youthful Drinking Patterns." In *Risky Behavior Among Youths: An Economic Analysis,* edited by Jonathan Gruber, 375–437. Chicago: University of Chicago Press.

Cook, Philip, Jan Ostermann, and Frank Sloan. 2005. "The Net Effect of an Alcohol Tax Increase on Death Rates in Middle Age." *The American Economic Review* 95:278–81.

Cook, Philip, and George Tauchen. 1982. "The Effect of Liquor Taxes on Heavy Drinking." *Bell Journal of Economics* 13:379–90.

Dahl, Gordon, and Stefano DellaVigna. 2009. "Does Movie Violence Increase Violent Crime?" *Quarterly Journal of Economics* 124:677–734.

Dee, Thomas. 1999. "State Alcohol Policies, Teen Drinking and Traffic Fatalities." *Journal of Public Economics* 72:289–315.

Desimone, Jeffrey. 2001. "The Effect of Cocaine Prices on Crime." *Economic Inquiry* 39:627–43.

DiNardo, John, and Thomas Lemieux. 2001. "Alcohol, Marijuana, and the American Youth: The Unintended Consequences of Government Regulation." *Journal of Health Economics* 20:991–1010.

Duailibi, Sergio, William Ponicki, Joel Grube, Ilana Pinsky, Ronaldo Laranjeira, and Martin Raw. 2007. "The Effect of Restricting Opening Hours on Alcohol-Related Violence." *American Journal of Public Health* 97:2276–80.

Duffy, John, and Martin Plant. 1986. "Scotland's Liquor Licensing Changes: An Assessment." *British Medical Journal* 292:36–9.

Fagan, Jeffrey. 1990. "Intoxication and Aggression." In *Drugs and Crime: Crime and Justice, A Review of Research, Vol. 13*, edited by Michael Tonry and James Q. Wilson 241–320. Chicago: The University of Chicago Press.

———. 1993. "Interactions Among Drugs, Alcohol and Violence." *Health Affairs* 4:65–79.

Frattaroli, Shannon. 2010. "Why Implementation Matters: Recent Experience with the UK Licensing Act (2003)." *Criminology & Public Policy* 9:77–83.

Gorman, D. M., P. W. Speer, E. W. Labouvie, and A. P. Subaiya. 1998. "Risk of Assaultive Violence and Alcohol Availability in New Jersey." *American Journal of Public Health* 88 (1): 97–100.

Greenfield, Lawrence A., and Maureen Henneberg. 2001. "Victim and Offender Self-Reports of Alcohol Involvement in Crime." *Alcohol Research and Health* 25:20–31.

Grossman, Michael, Frank Chaloupka, Henry Saffer, and Adit Laixuthai. 1994. "Effects of Alcohol Price Policy on Youth: A Summary of Economic Research." *Journal of Research on Adolescence* 4:347–64.

Grossman, Michael, Douglas Coate, and Gregory Arluck. 1987. "Price Sensitivity of Alcohol Beverages in the United States." In *Control Issues in Alcohol Abuse Prevention: Strategies for States and Communities,* edited by Harold Holder, 169–98. Greenwich: JAI Press.

Grossman, Michael, and Sara Markowitz. 2001. "Alcohol Regulation and Violence on College Campuses." In *Economics of Substance Abuse,* edited by Michael Grossman and Chee-Ruey Hsieh, 257–89. United Kingdom: Edward Elgar Limited.

Gruber, Jonathan, and Daniel M. Hungerman. 2008. "The Church Versus the Mall: What Happens When Religion Faces Increased Secular Competition?" *Quarterly Journal of Economics* 123 (2): 831–62.

Gruenewald, Paul, Bridget Freisthler, Lillian Remer, Elizabeth LaScala, and Andrew Treno. 2006. "Ecological Models of Alcohol Outlets and Violent Assaults: Crime Potentials and Geospatial Analysis." *Addiction* 101:666–77.

Gyimah-Brempong, Kwabena. 2001. "Alcohol Availability and Crime: Evidence from Census Tract Data." *Southern Economic Journal* 68:2–21.

Holder, Harold, and Alexander Wagenaar. 1995. "Changes in Alcohol Consumption Resulting from the Elimination of Retail Wine Monopolies: Results from Five U.S. States." *Journal of Studies on Alcohol* 56:566–72.

Horverak, O. 1981. "The 1978 Strike at the Norwegian Wine and Spirits Monopoly: Effects on the Supply and Consumption of Alcohol and on some Alcohol-Related Problems." Paper presented at the 27th International Meeting of Epidemiology Section, Institute on the Prevention and Treatment of Alcoholism. June, Vienna, Austria.

Hough, Mike, and Gillian Hunter. 2008. "The 2003 Licensing Act's Impact on Crime and Disorder: An Evaluation." *Criminology and Criminal Justice* 8:239–60.

Humphreys, David, and Manuel Eisner. 2010. "Evaluating a Natural Experiment in Alcohol Policy: The Licensing Act (2003) and the Requirement for Attention to Implementation." *Criminology & Public Policy* 9:41–67.

Jackson, Kirabo, and Emily Owens. 2010. "One for the Road: Public Transportation, Alcohol Consumption, and Intoxicated Driving." NBER Working Paper no. 15872. Cambridge, MA: National Bureau of Economic Research, April.

Joksch, Hans, and Ralph Jones. 1993. "Changes in the Drinking Age and Crime." *Journal of Criminal Justice* 21:209–21.

Kaestner, Robert, and Benjamin Yarnoff. 2009. "Long Term Effects of Minimum Legal Drinking Age Laws on Adult Alcohol Use and Driving Fatalities." NBER Working Paper no. 15439. Cambridge, MA: National Bureau of Economic Research, October.

Karaharju, E., and L. Stjernvall. 1974. "The Alcohol Factor in Accidents." *Injury* 6:67–9.

Kenkel, Donald. 1996. "New Estimates of the Optimal Tax on Alcohol." *Economic Inquiry* 34:296–319.

———. 2005. "Are Alcohol Tax Hikes Fully Passed Through to Prices: Evidence From Alaska." *American Economic Review* 5 (2): 273–7.

Kenkel, Donald, and Willard Manning. 1996. "Perspectives on Alcohol Taxation." *Alcohol Health & Research World* 20:230–8.

Lenke, Leif. 1982. "Alcohol and Crimes of Violence: A Causal Analysis." *Contemporary Drug Problems* 11:355–65.

Ligon, Jan, and Bruce Thyer. 1993. "The Effects of a Sunday Liquor Sales Ban on DUI Arrests." *Journal of Alcohol and Drug Education* 38:33–40.

Lipton, Robert, and Paul Gruenewald. 2002. "The Spatial Dynamics of Violence and Alcohol Outlets." *Journal of Studies on Alcohol* 63 (2): 187–95.

Livingston, Michael. 2008. "Alcohol Outlet Density Assault: A Spatial Analysis." *Addiction* 103 (4): 619–28.

Lovenheim, Michael, and Joel Slemrod. 2010. "The Fatal Toll of Driving to Drink: The Effects of Minimum Drinking Age Evasion of Traffic Fatalities." *Journal of Health Economics* 29:62–77.

Lovenheim, Michael, and Daniel Steefel. 2009. "Do Blue Laws Save Lives? The Effects of Sunday Sales Bans on Fatal Vehicle Accidents." Cornell University. Working Paper.

Makela, Klaus. 1980. "Differential Effects of Restricting the Supply of Alcohol: Studies of a Strike in Finnish Liquor Stores." *Journal of Drug Issues* 10: 131–44.

Maloney, Michael T., and Jason C. Rudbeck. 2009. "The Outcome from Legalizing Sunday Packaged Alcohol Sales on Traffic Accidents in New Mexico." *Accident Analysis and Prevention* 41 (5): 1094–8.

Manning, W., E. Keller, J. Newhouse, E. Sloss, and J. Wasserman. 1989. "The Taxes of Sin: Do Smokers and Drinkers Pay Their Way." *Journal of the American Medical Association* 261 (11): 1604–9.

Markowitz, Sara. 2000. "The Price of Alcohol, Wife Abuse, and Husband Abuse." *Southern Economic Journal* 67:279–303.

———. 2001a. "Criminal Violence and Alcohol Beverage Control: Evidence from an International Study." In *The Economic Analysis of Substance Use and Abuse: The Experience of Developed Countries and Lessons for Developing Countries,* edited by Michael Grossman and Chee-Ruey Hsieh, 309–36. United Kingdom: Edward Elgar Limited.

———. 2001b. "The Role of Alcohol and Drug Consumption in Determining Physical Violence and Weapon Carrying by Teenagers." *Eastern Economic Journal* 27:409–32.

———. 2005. "Alcohol, Drugs and Violent Crime." *International Review of Law and Economics* 25:20–44.

Markowitz, Sara, and Michael Grossman. 1998. "Alcohol Regulation and Domestic Violence Towards Children." *Contemporary Economic Policy* 16:309–20.

———. 2000. "The Effects of Beer Taxes on Physical Child Abuse." *Journal of Health Economics* 19:271–82.

Mast, Brent D., Bruce L. Benson, and David W. Rasmussen. 1999. "Beer Taxation and Alcohol-Related Traffic Fatalities." *Southern Economic Journal* 66 (2): 214–49.

Matthews, Kent, Jonathan Shepherd, and Vaseekaran Sivarajasingam. 2006. "Violence-Related Injury and the Price of Beer in England and Wales." *Applied Economics* 38:661–70.

McMillan, Garnett, and Sandra Lapham. 2006. "Effectiveness of Bans and Laws in Reducing Traffic Deaths: Legalized Sunday Packaged Alcohol Sales and Alcohol-Related Traffic Crashes and Crash Fatalities in New Mexico." *American Journal of Public Health* 96:1944–8.

Miczek, Klaus A., Joseph F. DeBold, Margaret Haney, Jennifer Tidey, Jeffrey Vivian, and Elise M. Weerts. 1994. "Alcohol, Drugs of Abuse, Aggression, and Violence." In *Understanding and Preventing Violence: Vol. 3, Social Influences,* edited by Albert J. Reiss, Jeffrey A. Roth, and Klaus A. Miczek, 377–468. Washington, DC: National Academy Press.

Norberg, Karen, Laura Bierut, and Richard Grucza. 2009. "Long-Term Effects of Minimum Drinking Age Laws on Past-Year Alcohol and Drug Use Disorders." *Alcoholism: Clinical and Experimental Research* 33:2180–90.

Norstrom, Thor, and Ole-Jorgen Skog. 2003. "Saturday Opening of Alcohol Retail Shops in Sweden: An Impact Analysis." Journal of Studies on Alcohol 64 (3): 393–401.

———. 2005. "Saturday Opening of Alcohol Retail Shops in Sweden: An Experiment in Two Phases." *Addiction* 100:767–76.

Olsson, Orvar, and Perl-Olaf Wikstrom. 1982. "Effects of the Experimental Saturday Closing of Liquor Retail Stores in Sweden." *Contemporary Drug Problems* 11: 325–53.

Pacula, Rosalie. 1998. "Does the Beer Tax Reduce Marijuana Consumption?" *Journal of Health Economics* 17:557–85.

Pacula, Rosalie, and Beau Kilmer. 2003. "Marijuana and Crime: Is There a Connection Beyond Prohibition?" NBER Working Paper no. 10046. Cambridge, MA: National Bureau of Economic Research, October.

Pernanen, Kai. 1981. "Theoretical Aspects of the Relationship between Alcohol Abuse and Crime." In *Drinking and Crime: Perspectives on the Relationship Between Alcohol Consumption and Criminal Behavior,* edited by James J. Collins, 1–69. New York: Guilford.

Pogue, Thomas, and Larry Sgontz. 1989. "Taxing to Control Social Costs: The Case of Alcohol." *American Economic Review* 791:235–43.

Pyapali, G., D. Turner, W. Wilson, and S. Swartzwelder. 1999. "Age and Dose-Dependent Effects of Ethanol on the Induction of Hippocampal Long-term Potentiation." *Alcohol* 19:107–11.

Rees, Daniel, and Kevin Schnepel. 2009. "College Football Games and Crime." *Journal of Sports Economics* 10:68–87.

Roncek, Dennis W., and Pamela A. Maier. 1991. "Bars, Blocks, and Crime Revisited: Linking the Theory of Routine Activities to the Empiricism of 'Hot Spots.'" *Criminology* 29 (4): 725–53.

Room, Robin. 1983. "Behavioral Aspects." In *Encyclopedia of Crime and Justice, Vol. 1,* edited by Sanford Kadish, 35–44. New York: The Free Press.

———. 2002. "The Effects of Nordic Alcohol Policies: What Happens to Drinking and Harm When Alcohol Controls Change?" Publication no. 42. Helsinki: Nordic Council for Alcohol and Drug Research.

Saffer, Henry. 2001. "Substance Abuse Control and Crime: Evidence from the National Household Survey of Drug Abuse." In *The Economic Analysis of Substance Use and Abuse,* edited by Michael Grossman and Chee-Ruey Hsieh, 291–308. United Kingdom: Edward Elgar Limited.

Scribner, Richard, Deborah Cohen, Stephen Kaplan, and Susan H. Allen. 1999. "Alcohol Availability and Homicide in New Orleans: Conceptual Considerations for Small Area Analysis of the Effect of Alcohol Outlet Density." *Journal of Studies on Alcohol* 60 (3): 310–16.

Scribner, Richard, David MacKinnon, and James Dwyer. 1995. "The Risk of Assaultive Violence and Alcohol Availability in Los Angeles County." *American Journal of Public Health* 85:335–40.

Shkolnikov, Vladimir, and Aalexander Nemtsov. 1997. "The Anti-Alcohol Campaign and Variations in Russian Mortality." In *Premature Death in the New Independent States,* edited by Jose Bobadilla, Christine Costello, and Faith Mitchell, 239–61. Washington, DC: National Academies Press.

Sivarajasingam, Vaseekaran, Kent Matthews, and Jonathan Shepherd. 2006. "Price of Beer and Violence-Related Injury in England and Wales." *Injury, International Journal of the Care of the Injured* 37:388–94.

Smith, D. Ian. 1978. "Impact on Traffic Safety of the Introduction of Sunday Alcohol Sales in Perth, Western Australia." *Journal of Studies on Alcohol* 39:1302–4.

———. 1988a. "Effect on Casualty Traffic Accidents of the Introduction of 10pm Monday to Saturday Hotel Closing in Victoria." *Australian Drug and Alcohol Review* 7:163–6.

———. 1988b. "Effect on Traffic Accidents of Introducing Sunday Alcohol Sales in Brisbane, Australia." *The International Journal of the Addictions* 23:1091–9.

———. 1990. "Effect on Casualty Traffic Accidents of Changing Sunday Alcohol Sales Legislation in Victoria, Australia." *Journal of Drug Issues* 20:417–26.

———. 1987. "Effect on Traffic Accidents of Introducing Sunday Hotel Sales in New South Wales, Australia." *Contemporary Drug Problems* 14:279–94.

Stehr, Mark. 2007. "The Effect of Sunday Sales Bans and Excise Taxes on Drinking and Cross-Border Shopping for Alcoholic Beverages." *National Tax Journal* 60:85–105.

Stevenson, Richard, Bronwyn Lind, and Don Weatherburn. 1999. "The Relationship between Alcohol Sales and Assault in New South Wales, Australia." *Addiction* 94:397–410.

Stockwell, Tim, Jinhui Zhao, Scott Macdonald, Basia Pakula, Paul Gruenewald, and Harold Holder. 2009. "Changes in Per Capita Alcohol Sales during the Partial Privatization of British Columbia's Retail Alcohol Monopoly 2003–2008: A Multi-level Local Area Analysis." *Addiction* 104:1827–36.

Takala, H. 1973. "Alkoholstrejkens inverkan pa uppdagad brottslighet [The Effect of the Alcohol Strike on Reported Crime]." *Alkoholpolitik* 1:14–6.

Teh, Bing-Ru. 2008. "Do Liquor Stores Increase Crime and Urban Decay? Evidence from Los Angeles." University of California, Berkeley. Working Paper.

Treno, Andrew. 2010. "Evaluation of the Licensing Act of 2003: A Look inside the Black Box." *Criminology & Public Policy* 9:35–9.

Vingilis, Evelyn, A. Ian McLeod, Jane Seeley, Robert Mann, Doug Beirness, and Charles Compton. 2005. "Road Safety Impact of Extending Drinking Hours in Ontario." *Accident Analysis and Prevention* 37:549–56.

Wagenaar, Alexander, and Traci Toomey. 2001. "Effects of Minimum Drinking Age Laws: Review and Analyses of the Literature from 1960 to 2000." *Journal of Studies on Alcohol* Suppl(14):206–25.

Wagenaar, Alexander, Traci Toomey, and Darin Erickson. 2005. "Complying with the Minimum Drinking Age: Enforcement and Training Interventions." *Alcoholism: Clinical and Experimental Research* 29:255–62.

Washton, Arnold. 1987. "Cocaine: Drug Epidemic of the '80's." In *The Cocaine Crisis,* edited by David Allen, 45–63. New York: Plenum Press.

Wechsler, Henry, Jae Eun Lee, John Hall, Alexander Wagenaar, and Hang Lee. 2002. "Secondhand Effects of Student Alcohol Use Reported by Neighbors of Colleges: The Role of Alcohol Outlets." *Social Science and Medicine* 55:425–35.

Weitzman, Elissa, Alison Folkman, Kerry Folkman, and Henry Wechsler. 2002. "The Relationship of Alcohol Outlet Density to Heavy and Frequent Drinking and Drinking-Related Problems among College students at Eight Universities." *Health and Place* 9:1–6.

Young, Douglas, and Agnieszka Bielinska-Kwapisz. 2002. "Alcohol Taxes and Beverage Prices." *National Tax Journal* 55:57–74.

Zhu, L., D. M. Gorman, and S. Horel. 2004. "Alcohol Outlet Density and Violence: A Geospacial Analysis." *Alcohol & Alcoholism* 39:369–75.

7

The Role of Private Action
in Controlling Crime

Philip J. Cook and John MacDonald

Private actors have a pervasive role in crime prevention and control. Here are some examples: pedestrians avoiding dark alleys at night; domestic partners moving out to end an abusive relationship; households installing burglar alarms, acquiring guns and watchdogs, and relocating to a safer community; banks, retailers, residential communities, and business improvement districts hiring security guards; credit card companies monitoring activity and suspending cards that appear to be fraudulent; individuals, households, and businesses utilizing locks, barriers, closed-circuit cameras, and electronic sensors to reduce merchandise theft.

Of course, the criminal justice system does have a considerable influence on crime, but there again private-sector actions are of vital importance. Few crimes would be solved without citizens voluntarily reporting to the police and cooperating with investigations. Given that such cooperation is costly to the private citizens and usually has no extrinsic reward, theory predicts (and the evidence supports) that this cooperation is undersupplied. The propensity of potential victims to cooperate with the criminal justice system is an attribute of criminal opportunities. Tourists and drug dealers are attractive targets for robbers, not only because of the valuables they carry, but also

Philip J. Cook is the ITT/Terry Sanford Professor of Public Policy and professor of economics and sociology at Duke University, where he is also senior associate dean for faculty and research. He is a research associate of the NBER and a codirector of the NBER Working Group on the Economics of Crime. John MacDonald is associate professor of criminology and undergraduate chair at the University of Pennsylvania.

Acknowledgments: Seunghoon Han and Maeve Gearing provided excellent research assistance. Partial support for this research was provided through a cooperative agreement from the Centers for Disease Control and Prevention (CDC) (1U49CE000773). Thanks to Jens Ludwig, Tracey Meares, and conference attendees for their suggestions on an earlier draft. The opinions expressed in this document are those of the authors only.

because perpetrators know they are not likely to report their victimization to the police if robbed.

Given the central role of private individuals and firms in determining the effectiveness of the criminal justice system, and the quality and availability of criminal opportunities, private actions arguably deserve a more central role in the analysis of crime and crime prevention policy.[1] But the leading scholarly commentaries on the crime drop during the 1990s have largely ignored the role of the private sector (Levitt 2004; Blumstein and Wallman 2000; Zimring 2007). Among the potentially relevant trends: growing reporting rates, the growing sophistication and use of alarms, monitoring equipment and locks; the considerable increase in the employment of private security guards; and the decline in the use of cash.

Criminal opportunity theory (Cook 1986) helps explain observed crime patterns and trends, and may also provide some guidance in designing cost-effective crime-control policy. Private actions to protect property and avoid victimization can be encouraged or discouraged through regulation of the insurance industry and other means. Private actions to avoid, mitigate, and respond to crime tend to have substantial externalities. The resulting misallocation of resources, properly understood, may justify changes in government policy. In particular, private cooperation with the criminal justice system may be enhanced through reducing the risks and costs of cooperation, and increasing the rewards.

One creative method to harness private action to cost-effective crime control is the creation of business improvement districts (BIDs). A BID is a nonprofit organization created by neighborhood property owners to provide local public goods, including public safety. The organization has the power to tax all the owners in the district, including those who did not sign the original petition. Previous evaluations of BIDs in Los Angeles indicate that they are successful in reducing crime rates (Brooks 2008; MacDonald et al. 2009). We analyze the costs and benefits of these BIDs in what follows, including the effect on arrests and spillovers, and report a dose-response relationship for private expenditures. The rules for creating BIDs differ widely among jurisdictions, and Los Angeles appears to be a model for how to facilitate this sort of private collective action.

We conclude that the social benefits of Los Angeles BID expenditures on security are a large multiple (about twenty) of the private expenditures. We also provide an extended discussion of motor vehicle theft, where new technology appears to get much of the credit for the dramatic reductions in theft rates. These two examples, among others, illustrate our fundamental

---

1. The theory of how private action to prevent and avoid crime interacts with observed crime rates has been developed by Clotfelter (1978), Ehrlich (1981), Cook (1986), Shavell (1991), Philipson and Posner (1996), and others. Gary Becker's (1968) seminal article on crime and punishment includes a brief discussion of optimal private expenditures on actions to influence the probability of victimization (200 ff.).

conclusion; namely, that that there are substantial crime-reduction benefits associated with government policies that encourage certain types of private action to prevent and control crime.

We begin by discussing the downward trend in crime during the last three decades, and the possible explanations for that trend, including increases in private security. Section 7.2, on the incentives and consequences of private prevention activities, sketches the conceptual issues and notes that private action can be either socially beneficial or harmful. Section 7.3 then considers motor vehicle theft as a case where increasingly effective private action, resulting from technical innovation and government regulation, appears particularly beneficial. Section 7.4 considers another important issue, the extent to which citizens voluntarily report crimes to the police and cooperate with the investigation. The likelihood that crimes will be reported to the police has increased over the last two decades, but there is a strong case to be made that the voluntary cooperation is undersupplied. Section 7.5 then considers the costs and benefits of business improvement districts, reporting results on the effects of BIDs in Los Angeles. Section 7.6 concludes.

7.1   Trends in Crime and Its Prevention

The great crime decline during the last three decades represents something of a happy mystery. We know the trend is real, rather than an artifact of the available data, since it is found in three independent sources—the FBI's Uniform Crime Reports, the National Crime Victimization Survey, and the homicide series in the Vital Statistics (Cook and Laub 2002). The causes of this decline have been the subject of much speculation. A surprising feature of this speculation is the absence of attention to the role of private actions to prevent and avoid crime.

Figure 7.1 depicts robbery and homicide rates since 1973, when the National Crime Victimization Survey (NCVS) was initiated.[2] Victimization rates for robbery (and other violent crimes) varied in a narrow range until 1994, and then dropped to one-third of its 1994 level by 2004. Criminal homicide followed a remarkably similar pattern until 1999.

Property crime rates began their slide two decades earlier, and have declined rapidly since 1980. Recent rates, as estimated by the NCVS, are just one-fifth the peak level (figure 7.2). Residential burglaries (break-ins

2. The US Department of Justice implemented a survey for measuring rates of violence and other common crime in 1973. Since then the National Crime Victimization Survey (NCVS) has contacted large samples of households (currently about 45,000) to inquire whether any members age twelve and over have become crime victims during the preceding six months, and if so to provide details. The resulting estimates tend to be substantially larger than the counts recorded by the police, and are also useful in providing the statistical basis for analyzing demographic patterns of violence—both of the victims and of the perpetrators (based on respondents' reports of their impression of the age, race, sex, and number of assailants).

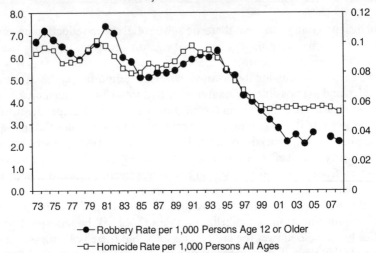

Fig. 7.1 Trend in robbery and homicide

Source: Robbery rates are from the National Crime Victimization Survey (NCVS). Criminal homicide rates are from the FBI's Uniform Crime Reports.

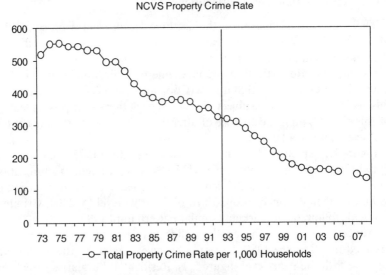

Fig. 7.2 NCVS property crime rates since 1973

Source: The National Crime Victimization Survey (NCVS) (http://bjs.ojp.usdoj.gov/content/glance/house2.cfm).

Notes: Property crimes include burglary, theft, and motor vehicle theft. The National Crime Victimization Survey redesign was implemented in 1993. The data before 1993 are adjusted to make them comparable with data collected since the redesign. The adjustment methods are described in Criminal Victimization 1973–1995. Estimates for 1993 and beyond are based on collection year while earlier estimates are based on data year. Changes to the NCVS and their impact upon the survey's estimates in 2006 are discussed in the Criminal Victimization, 2006 Technical Notes.

and attempts) in particular have declined 70 percent since 1976 (from 107 to 30 per 1,000 households).

The extraordinary reduction in violent crime during the 1990s has been the subject of extensive exegesis by scholars (Blumstein and Wallman 2000, 2006; Cook and Laub 2002; Zimring 2007). No expert predicted this decline, and any explanation is necessarily speculative. Levitt (2004) provides a survey of potential causes. He first notes that the decline was quite universal, affecting all demographic groups and geographic areas. With respect to urbanicity, Levitt observes that the greatest percentage improvements occurred within metropolitan statistical areas (MSAs) and especially among large cities with populations over 250,000. In fact, all of the twenty-five largest cities experienced noteworthy declines in homicide rates from their peak year (mostly in the early 1990s) to 2001, declines that ranged as high as 73 percent for New York and San Diego. Based on his analysis, Levitt ends up awarding partial credit for the crime drop to increases in the number of police, the rising prison population, the receding crack epidemic, and the legalization of abortion through *Roe v. Wade*. His claim for the importance of abortion liberalization is controversial to say the least (Joyce 2004), but the rest of the list is widely (though not universally) endorsed by experts. His judgment about what is *not* important to the crime drop includes the sustained economic growth in the 1990s, and the much-ballyhooed innovations in policing in New York and elsewhere.

A surprising feature of Levitt's analysis is the lack of discussion of private measures to prevent crime. Private crime-prevention efforts include everything from homeowners locking their doors and leaving a light on, to the employment of armed guards and armored vehicles to move large amounts of cash or valuables. The sum total of these efforts is difficult to estimate (Anderson 1999), but the private actions that can be readily measured are of the same order of magnitude as public expenditures for the criminal justice system—and they are expanding more quickly.

The Economic Census (conducted once every five years by the US Census Bureau) provides an estimate of receipts of the private security industry in 2007 as $40 billion, as compared to $99 billion in public expenditures on police protection in 2006.[3] Estimates of the number of employees suggest something close to parity. According to Bureau of Labor Statistics' estimates of occupational employment, there were just over 800,000 police officers in 2008, but more than one million security guards, with very similar upward trends since the mid-1980s (figure 7.3). Some of the security guards are

---

3. The receipts and employment for the private security industry are taken from the Economic Census for 2007, industry NAICS 5616 (excluding locksmiths). See the 2007 Census Factfinder for more information (http://factfinder.census.gov/servlet/IBQTable?_bm=y&-geo_id=&-ds _name=EC0756I1&-_lang=en). Public expenditures on police protection in 2007 are not available yet.

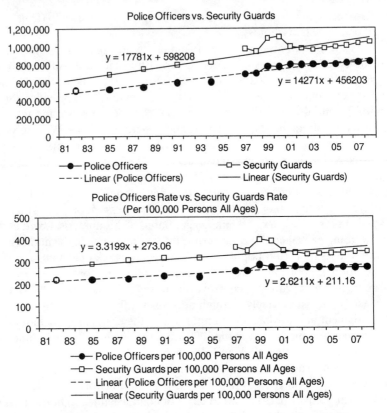

Fig. 7.3   **Trends in employment of police officers and security guards, counts and rates**

Sources: 1) Occupation data of Police Officers and Security Guards: Bureau of Labor Statistics, Occupational Employment and Wage Estimates, each year (1981–1995: paper version, 1997–2008: http://www.bls.gov/oes/oes_data.htm). 2) Population: Population Distribution and Population Estimates Branches, US Bureau of the Census (http://www.census.gov/popest/national/national.html).

employed directly by the public sector; the Economic Census estimated the number of private security employees in 2007 as 820,000.[4]

The scope of private security and protection is suggestive of its importance in influencing crime rates, but stops short of demonstrating that importance. In what follows we discuss the conceptual issues and provide detailed discussions of theft prevention for motor vehicles, of crime reporting, and of the security expenditures by Business Improvement Districts.

4. Two other national surveys also provide estimates of the number of private security industry employees, the Current Population Survey, and the US Census Bureau's County Business Patterns. Estimates for 2007 from the three sources are in rough agreement: 820,000 (Economic Census), 780,000 (Current Population Survey), and 760,000 (County Business Patterns).

7.2   Incentives and Consequences of Private Prevention Activities

Private security, and private crime-control efforts more generally, constitute an unwritten chapter in the recent literature on "what works" in crime-control policy. Observed crime rates and patterns reflect private choices regarding cooperation and self-protection (Clotfelter 1977; Cook 1986; Ehrlich 1996; Cornish and Clarke 2003). A systematic approach to public crime control requires understanding of the potential interactions between private and public efforts.

A place to begin the discussion of this complex topic is with the private security industry, which is ubiquitous. On any given outing, we are more likely to encounter a private security guard than a uniformed officer (Sklansky 2008, 124–25). The industry encompasses proprietary (in-house) security, guard and patrol services, alarm services, private investigations, armored car services, and security consultants, as well as security equipment (Cunningham, Strauchs, and Van Meter 1990). Private security supplements and in some cases substitutes for public action: for example, businesses in many cases investigate and resolve employee theft and fraud without ever going public. More generally, as noted by Brian Forst, "the central functions of policing—preserving domestic peace and order, preventing and responding to crimes—have always been conducted first, foremost, and predominantly by private means . . . Most crimes still are not reported to the police" (1999, 19).

Private security guards (and police officers who moonlight as private security guards) serve a narrow purpose; namely, to protect the property and people they are hired to protect. The term of art is "situational crime prevention" (Clarke 1983). The guard's job is accomplished if the robbers avoid his bank, or his corporate executive is not kidnapped, or rowdy teenagers are successfully kicked out of his shopping mall, or the would-be burglar does not enter his gated community. One partial exception is the security hired by BIDs, whose assignment is to protect an entire neighborhood.

Unfortunately there is little systematic evidence on the crime-prevention effects of private security guards (Eck 2006; Welsh and Farrington 2009). An obvious possibility is that the crime will be displaced to other, unguarded victims and places. If private security simply redistributes crime, then its public value (as opposed to private) is nil, and it creates serious equity concerns.[5]

While displacement is a legitimate concern, whether it occurs in practice, and to what degree, is an empirical matter. Guerette and Bowers (2009) reviewed 102 evaluations of situational crime prevention interventions, which included 574 observations. They report that displacement was about as likely as the opposite, *diffusion* of benefits, and that if displacement did occur, it

---

5. Further, there is a danger that affluent people will become less willing to support public policing if they are purchasing effective private protection (Bayley and Shearing 2001, 30).

tended to be less than the direct effect. Draca, Machin, and Witt (2010) report that a surge in police presence in London following terrorist attacks reduced crime in the targeted boroughs without any evidence of displacement, a null finding that is typical of evaluations of hot spots policing and related interventions.

There is also a conceptual point to be made. Lucrative opportunities, if unguarded, are likely to generate crime that would not otherwise occur. In Isaac Ehrlich's (1974) classic formulation, the supply of offenses is a function of the relative wage rates for licit and illicit activities. An increase in the net return (payoff per unit of effort) to crime will stimulate participation in criminal activity. He postulates that the payoffs to property crimes "depend, primarily, on the level of transferable assets in the community, that is, on opportunities provided by potential victims of crime" (87). But if the most lucrative "transferable assets" are well protected, then the payoff to crime is reduced. Of course, it is the most lucrative targets that tend to be most closely guarded. Banks invest more in security against robbery than, say, travel agencies. Jewelry stores display costume jewelry on open racks but keep the real thing in glass cases wired with alarms. People with meager assets do not need bodyguards to protect against being kidnapped for ransom. Credit card companies have instituted elaborate systems for preventing fraudulent use.

The social welfare implications of private action to avoid victimization depend on how well private incentives coincide with social costs. To the extent that private protection *does* have the effect of displacing rather than (or as well as) preventing crime, then such measures will tend to be oversupplied, since the private benefit will exceed the social benefit. That tendency may be exacerbated if the private action is subsidized by the public, as in the case of residential alarms that mobilize the police at no cost to the owner.

7.2.1   Socially Harmful Private Precautions

Some forms of private precautionary action may be harmful in the aggregate, even though they seem individually rational. Car alarms may be in this category, since they contribute to noise pollution in cities and have so many false positives that they have lost much of their ability to garner attention by passersby.[6] Burglary alarms are also problematic: over 94 percent (and possibly as much as 99 percent) of all alarms are false, and in 2000, the police responded to 36 million false alarms at a public cost of $1.8 billion (Blackstone, Buck, and Hakim 2005). Determining whether that cost is warranted requires comparison with the (unknown) effect on burglary rates.

Also important is the tendency of those with the financial means to avoid higher-crime communities, thus depriving those communities of resources

---

6. A plausible case for a ban has been argued by Friedman, Naparstek, and Taussig-Rubbo (2003).

and social capital and contributing to a self-reinforcing process of decline. Similarly, social relations are strained in public places by private actions to avoid contact with those deemed threatening based on their appearance—youthful minority males, for example. The private actions that have been most extensively studied are keeping and carrying a handgun for self-protection; here too there is evidence of profound harm to the community.

For some people, the ready availability of a firearm provides a sense of security against intruders, including the nightmare scenario of home invasion by violent criminals. That sense of security may be worth a great deal, whether or not it is based on a rational assessment of the chances that a handgun will be needed for this purpose, or if needed will actually be successfully deployed. Unfortunately, it is also true that handguns kept in the home are sometimes used to threaten other family members or to act on a suicidal impulse. Further, other family members, including adolescents and children, may misappropriate them and do great harm. Someone deciding whether to keep a handgun in the home thus faces a situation of competing risks—without a gun, there is a possibly greater risk of being unable to defend against a criminal intrusion, while with a gun, there are multiple risks of accident and misuse. The magnitudes of these competing risks will differ widely depending on how the handgun is stored, as well as other factors—such as whether there are children at home, and whether household members abuse alcohol and drugs, are inclined to violence, or suffer from depression or other mental illness.

Keeping guns in the home also generates externalities for the community. Whether such externalities are positive or negative on balance is not clear a priori, but is well established by evidence. There are several logical mechanisms. A burglar may be deterred by the threat of encountering an armed householder during a break-in. On the other hand, guns have high value to burglars, and a gun-rich neighborhood, other things equal, will be a more profitable site for burglars. Guns kept in the home also become a major source to youths and criminals, with the result that the proportion of robberies and assaults involving guns increases with the density of gun ownership in urban communities. Extensive econometric and other evidence support a conclusion that private gun ownership has a net positive effect on burglary and criminal homicide rates (Cook and Ludwig 2003, 2006). The elasticity of homicide with respect to gun density is at least $+0.1$. From that effect alone, the negative externality associated with keeping an additional handgun amounts to several hundred dollars per year.

Keeping a handgun for self-defense generates negative externalities, and hence is an example of an activity that is more attractive individually than collectively. There is also a reasonable concern that some private precautionary activities are *under*supplied as a result of the moral hazard created by insurance and even by the criminal justice system. Motor vehicle theft provides an illuminating case study of these possibilities.

7.3   Motor Vehicle Theft and Criminal Opportunity

The stakes in the prevention of auto theft are high. About one in eight property crimes reported to the police in the United States are thefts of motor vehicles. (This figure does not include thefts *from* vehicles, which is a still higher number.) Of the $17 billion lost by victims of property crime in 2003, over half was the result of auto theft (FBI 2004).[7] The prevention of auto theft has been an active concern of government since the introduction of state registration systems in the 1920s and 1930s.

In recent decades, technological development in electronics and information processing have created increasingly sophisticated locks, alarms, video surveillance systems, and tracking devices, which arguably have taken much of the profit out of motor vehicle theft. (They are also important in the prevention of such diverse crimes as shoplifting, robbery, and credit card fraud.) Figure 7.4 depicts the sharp downward trend in motor vehicle theft rates in recent years, as evident in both NCVS and Uniform Crime Reports (UCR) data. The absolute number of thefts reported to the police in 2008 is lower than the count in 1989, when there were half as many vehicles on the road. It is entirely plausible that the sharp declines are due in part to tracking systems and "target hardening" locks—that is, to investments in private prevention. A spokesman for Highway Loss Data Institute opined that "It's a much tougher job to be a car thief today" (Leinwand, 2009).

From the potential motor-vehicle thief's perspective, the opportunities created by unoccupied vehicles differ widely in terms of their "quality," which can be defined by the dimensions that guide purposeful choice: the effort and skill required to succeed in the theft, the payoff if successful, the likelihood of arrest, and the legal and private consequences if arrested. Each of these dimensions is arguably affected by private crime-prevention efforts.

7.3.1   Types of Prevention

Prevention efforts by the owner/driver can be sorted into three clusters: (a) care exercised when deciding where to park and whether to lock up; (b) investment in locking devices that make it more difficult to enter the car (when locked) and to drive off; and (c) investment in devices that make it easier to track a stolen vehicle and identify it as such, including LoJack and OnStar.[8] There is a public stake in the decisions made by private actors in each of these cases; theft imposes costs on the public as well as the owner

7. Keep in mind, however, that auto theft is more likely to be reported than other types of property crime, and hence is disproportionately represented in the Uniform Crime Reports.
8. Using the Ehrlich-Becker (1972) dichotomy, the first two clusters are primarily self-protection, since they reduce the chance of victimization (both theft of vehicle and theft from the vehicle), while the third is primarily self-insurance, since it reduces the expected loss by increasing the chances of recovery if the vehicle is stolen. In their analysis, the third is unambiguously a substitute for insurance.

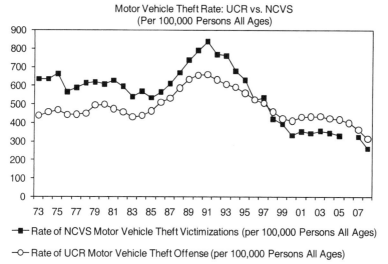

Fig. 7.4   UCR and NCVS trends on motor vehicle theft

Sources: 1) UCR MVT: 1973–2007 data from Crime trends, BJS homepage (http://bjs.ojp
.usdoj.gov/dataonline/Search/Crime/State/RunCrimeTrendsInOneVar.cfm); 2008 data from
Crime in the United States (http://www.fbi.gov/ucr/ucr.htm). 2) NCVS MVT: *Criminal Victimization in the US,* various years. 3) Population: Population Distribution and Population Estimates Branches, US Bureau of the Census (http://www.census.gov/popest/national/national
.html).

and his insurance company. Furthermore, since the private incentives do not
match up well with social costs, there is the usual justification for government intervention.

To develop these points, consider an individual who is deciding whether
to park her vehicle overnight in a secure parking structure or in a dark
alley. Parking in the alley raises the probability that the car will be stolen.
If she carries comprehensive insurance she will only bear a fraction of the
immediate loss. If the car ends up being stolen and the police are notified,
which they almost always are, then the subsequent investigation and possible recovery, arrest, court processing, and sanction will all be conducted
primarily at public expense. (While the police could choose not to respond
to the theft report, that inaction would ensure a failure to arrest, which
would dilute the general deterrent and possibly increase the auto-theft rate.)
Thus the cost of theft to the owner is less than to the public, creating a moral
hazard to be negligent about parking the car—both because of insurance,
and also because of the chance that the police will probably recover the car.
For that reason we expect that there will be more vehicles parked in alleys
than is socially optimal.

But that conclusion presumes that the overall auto-theft rate is influenced
by her decision of where to park. If the auto theft rate is not influenced by
the density of accessible vehicles, but only by the supply of thieves, then her

decision would be of little or no public concern. Indeed, under the assumption that the theft rate is independent of the density of attractive opportunities, her parking in the alley would reduce the likelihood that another car was stolen, conveying a positive externality on other owners without imposing any net cost on the police or public. If private prevention actions displace crime without reducing it, then the result will be excessive prevention (Clotfelter 1978; Shavell 1991). There will be too few vehicles parked in the alley.

In reality, there is good reason to expect that displacement will not be complete. If motor-vehicle thieves are heterogeneous with respect to skill and motivation, then private precautions would likely affect the overall rate of auto theft. For example, since some potential thieves are unskilled opportunists (i.e., "joyriders"), then a general increase in driver precaution in this regard will reduce theft rates by making an encounter with a suitable target less likely. Indeed, there is evidence that improved locking devices on motor vehicles have had a disproportionate effect on joyriders, relegating them to stealing cars that are parked with the key left in the ignition (Tremblay, Clermont, and Cusson 1994; Copes and Cherbonneau 2006). One indicator is that the percentage of arrests for auto theft involving juveniles has declined from 44 percent in 1994 to 25 percent in 2006.[9]

For professional thieves, who steal to order for a chop shop or illegal exporter, the value of the vehicle matters. If owners of the most valuable vehicles tend to take the most effective precautions against theft, then while theft displacement to older and cheaper models will occur, the precautions are not without consequence for the theft rate, since they tend to reduce the overall profitability of professional auto theft.

Unfortunately there is not much empirical evidence on this matter. One analysis by the UK Home Office assessed the effect of steering column locks, providing some evidence that they reduced theft rates (Webb 1994). Germany was the first nation to mandate such locks; in 1961 all motor vehicles were required to have them, even if it required retrofitting. The sharp drop in theft rates that followed is likely due in part to the large effect on joyriding (Clarke and Harris 1992). US auto makers began incorporating steering column locks in 1969 as a result of a federal mandate, but only on new vehicles. The effect on overall theft rates, if any, would logically have been gradual, and is not readily isolated from other trends (Webb 1994).

Most vehicles are now equipped with an ignition immobilizer, an electronic device that blocks the engine from starting unless the key with the correct microchip is present. Immobilizers have been mandatory in all new cars sold in the United Kingdom (since 1998), Australia, and Canada. In

9. The percentage of arrests (of those under eighteen) for other property crimes also declined during this period, but not by as much: for example, the arrest percentage for larceny declined from 33 percent to 25 percent. http://www.ojjdp.ncjrs.gov/ojstatbb/ezaucr/asp/ucr _display.asp.

the United States 86 percent of new cars are built with the device, compared with fewer than 5 percent in 1989 (Leinwand 2009). We know of no scholarly evaluation of these devices, but the Insurance Bureau of Canada states on their website: "After extensive research, IBC determined that electronic engine immobilizers are the most effective means of automobile theft deterrence."[10] What is left for the thieves is to somehow obtain a key with the right microchip, or carjack the vehicle, or haul it away—or steal an older vehicle from a dwindling and aging stock.

7.3.2   Private Actions to Aid Police Investigation

The third cluster of private actions to prevent motor vehicle theft are those intended to track the vehicle and facilitate recovery, arrest, and successful prosecution. The original device was simply the Vehicle Identification Number (VIN) that, when affixed to the vehicle and registered with a public agency could be used to identify stolen vehicles. Manufacturers began using public VINs in the mid-1960s in response to the Highway Safety Act of 1966. In 1984 Congress adopted legislation that resulted in a requirement that manufacturers of designated high theft passenger car lines inscribe the VIN onto the engine, the transmission, and twelve major body parts. The goal was to deter professional thieves who steal cars for their parts. An analysis by the National Highway Traffic Safety Administration (NHTSA 1998) found that parts marking cost just $4.92 per vehicle, and that a 2 percent reduction in the theft rate would create consumer benefits exceeding that cost. The analysis found that the implementation of the standard was accompanied by a marked shift in theft rates from new (marked) vehicles to older (unmarked) vehicles; this effect was as large as 20 percent when cars were new, but it weakened as they became older (NHTSA 1998).

The only device that has been subjected to a thorough cost-benefit analysis is LoJack (Ayres and Levitt 1998). LoJack is installed at the dealership for a onetime cost to the owner of $695. It consists of a small FM radio transponder that can be hidden in one of twenty different places, and is switched on after the police have been notified of a theft. It then sends a silent signal to local police vehicles equipped with LoJack vehicle tracking units. It claims a 90 percent recovery rate, compared with a 63 percent chance of recovery of a typical car without Lojack.[11] More important from a social benefit perspective is that it serves as a powerful deterrent to car theft; Ayres and Levitt (1998) found that each dollar spent on LoJack resulted in a reduction in the costs of auto theft of about $10. The substantial reduction in the rate of auto theft associated with the introduction of LoJack into a city, even with market penetration amounting to a few percentage points, appears to result

---

10. http://www.ibc.ca/en/Insurance_Crime/Prevention_Investigation/Immobilizers/Immobilizer-FAQs.asp

11. Joanne Helperin (2009). See also Ayres and Nalebuff (2005).

from its ability to assist law enforcement in making arrests of professional thieves and chop-shop owners—individuals who may be very active in this market and not otherwise likely to be arrested. A thief who steals 100 cars per year is almost sure to steal at least one LoJack-equipped vehicle even if only 2 or 3 percent of all vehicles are so equipped—because the thief has no indication of whether any particular vehicle is equipped. Interestingly, LoJack enhances the deterrent effect by prohibiting any visible indication that LoJack has been installed.[12]

While LoJack provides owners with some reduction in expected theft loss, the main beneficiaries of an individual's decision to acquire LoJack are the public at large—and the insurance companies, if rates for comprehensive insurance do not adjust to reduced payouts. Ayres and Levitt estimate that the positive externality of one LoJack device is over $1,300 *annually.* Though this value is somewhat less in cities with relatively low rates of auto theft, it appears that it would be in the public interest for additional regions to license LoJack and for individuals to be subsidized or otherwise encouraged to install it. In a few states, most notably Massachusetts, insurance companies are required to provide a discount on premiums for comprehensive insurance, and some companies provide such a discount voluntarily. But the company that insures an individual who installs LoJack only enjoys a fraction of the benefit (in proportion to their market share) and is unlikely to pass on anything like the full social value to the premium holder.

LoJack is not the only vehicle recovery system. Some manufacturers offer factory-installed systems. Most prominent is GM's OnStar, which combines a GPS transmitter and cellular technology and has a number of features that provide private benefits lacking for LoJack—for example, automatic emergency notification of a crash, and the ability to locate the vehicle when someone else (a thief, or a teenage son) is driving it. The GPS technology requires an unobstructed line of site to satellites, and so will not help locate the vehicle when it is parked in a building. But it does provide an increased chance of tracking and recovery, with a greater private payoff.

7.3.3   Conclusions

The case of auto theft is of interest both because it dominates statistics on property loss due to theft, and because it has been an active area of private innovation. But there are similar issues with the prevention of burglary, shoplifting, credit card fraud, and other property crimes.

In reviewing the three clusters, we are left with several conclusions. First,

---

12. Gonzalez-Navarro (2008) analyzes the results of a program in Mexico where some Ford models in some states were equipped with LoJack at company expense. The result was to cut theft rates for those models by over half, without displacement to other models. But there was geographic displacement—states not included in the LoJack experiment experienced an increase in theft for the included models.

new technology has been incorporated in locking devices to the point where the amateur thieves of old (the joyriders) are limited to opportunities created by exceptional carelessness or a dwindling number of older cars. Even the professionals find it difficult to start and drive away the new models. This target-hardening trend is broad enough to suggest that it deserves partial credit for the dramatic reduction in auto theft rates since the early 1990s. Second, private prevention actions may displace theft to other vehicles, but the extent of displacement depends on the circumstances. If adoption of effective locking technology is broad enough, the scope for displacement, at least within the realm of auto theft, is limited. Third, the most effective device for preventing theft appears to be LoJack, which works as a general deterrent by increasing the likelihood that professional thieves and chop shop owners will be arrested and punished. This is a classic case of public-private coproduction of prevention, where motor vehicle owners invest in a device that provides exceptionally useful information to police investigations.

The public has a stake in reducing auto theft; a general reduction in the risk of victimization is a local public good. For LoJack, and perhaps some other devices, the owner's payoff to adopting is far less than the social value. This misalignment of private and public payoffs can be dealt with by government regulation of manufacturers, public subsidies, or insurance. Only nine states have regulations requiring insurers to provide car owners with discounts for comprehensive insurance for antitheft devices. The amount of the discount differs but is typically 15 to 20 percent for passive devices that are automatically activated when the vehicle is locked. Massachusetts leads the way with a minimum 25 percent discount if they have both an antitheft device and an auto recovery system like LoJack.[13] The fact that most states do not have such insurance regulations is more likely the result of political failure than of objective differences in costs and benefits.

Most difficult, perhaps, is to regulate carelessness. It is entirely possible that there is excess carelessness given the moral hazards created by insurance and the fact that the police do not charge for recovering a vehicle. If it is less costly at the margin to reduce theft by reducing private carelessness than to increase public enforcement, we could institute penalties for, say, leaving a car unlocked in a public place with the key in the ignition, or allowing insurance companies to refuse to pay off if such a vehicle is stolen, or charging the owner for the police resources devoted to tracking down the vehicle. Such measures may pass a cost-benefit test, but are not likely to be popular with the public.

13. Insurance Information Institute, "Auto Theft" (December 2009), http://www.iii.org/ IU/Auto-Theft/. Blackbox GPS lists insurance companies that offer discounts: http://www .tessco.com/yts/partner/manufacturer_list/vendors/deluo_gps/pdf/Insurance-Discounts.pdf.

7.4   Private Cooperation with the Criminal Justice System

While improved locking devices no doubt deserve some credit for the decline in auto theft, the evidence in support of effectiveness is much stronger for LoJack. As we discussed, the mechanism by which LoJack achieves its remarkable results is by providing law enforcement with timely information on the location of the stolen vehicle, and thus greatly enhancing the likelihood of successfully arresting and putting out of business the professional thieves and chop shop operators. LoJack is an example of effective coproduction of crime prevention from a combination of private inputs (the LoJack transmitter) and public inputs (the police investigation). There is nothing unusual about public-private coproduction in law enforcement (Clotfelter 1993). In fact, for the criminal justice system to prevent property and violent crimes requires private cooperation throughout the enforcement process (Gottfredson and Gottfredson 1988; Kruttschnitt and Carbone-Lopez 2009).

The first step in this coproduction process is that a private citizen—usually the victim—notifies the police of a crime. (The typical process for detecting consensual transactions of illicit drugs, vice, or corruption is quite different, since such crimes usually become known to the law enforcement only through police investigation.) Since reporting a crime is in most circumstances a public service provided at some private cost and little benefit, it is not surprising that a majority of crimes of theft and violence are never made known to the police. Among the exceptions are criminal homicide and auto theft, the latter because the police are usually able to recover a vehicle if they know it has been stolen, and because insurance companies will not pay off if the police have not been notified.

7.4.1   Recent Trends

During the last two decades reporting rates for property and violent crimes have trended upward. Figure 7.5 documents this trend since 1973 for four crimes: noncommercial robbery, aggravated assault, residential burglary, and auto theft. For each type of crime we offer two indicators. The first is from the NCVS, and is based on the respondent's statement of whether a criminal victimization was made known to the police. Since that measure may be biased (the respondent may be reluctant to admit that she did not report a crime), we also offer a second indicator, the ratio of "crimes known to the police" from the UCR, to the NCVS estimate of the number of such crimes.[14] For all four crimes we observe that both indicators have an upward trend. The trend lines in the figure are broken between 1992 and 1993 to

14. The "crimes known" variable is reported by the FBI's Uniform Crime Reports based on administrative data submitted by local police departments. For robbery and burglary, the UCR count is adjusted to exclude crimes against businesses and organizations, since such crimes are excluded from the NCVS sampling frame.

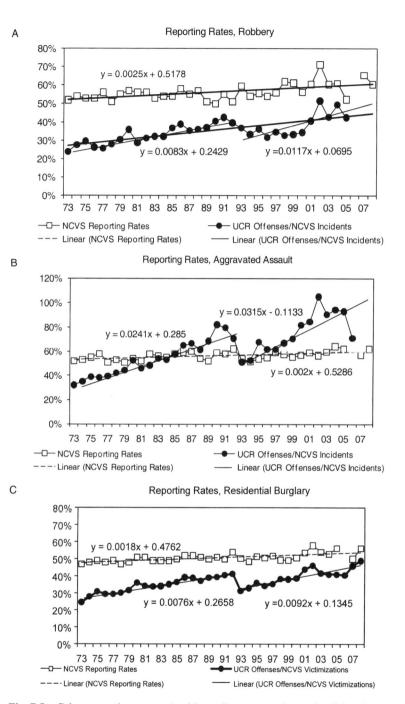

Fig. 7.5   Crime reporting rates: *A*, robbery; *B*, aggravated assault; *C*, burglary; and *D*, motor vehicle theft

D

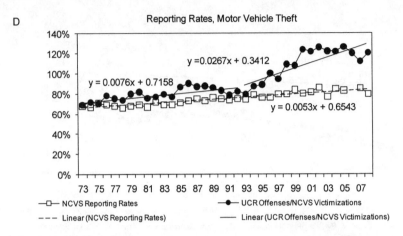

Fig. 7.5   (continued)

reflect the redesign of the NCVS, which had the effect of increasing the estimates for some types of crime (Kindermann, Lynch, and Cantor 1997).

As expected, the NCVS self-report measure (with its potential bias) exceeds the UCR/NCVS measure for robbery and burglary. Strangely, however, that is not the case for aggravated assault or auto theft. Indeed, for auto theft the UCR/NCVS measure goes as high as 120 percent. If the NCVS estimate of the volume of auto theft is accurate, then a ratio above 100 suggests that a substantial fraction of reports to the police are false. A benign possibility is that sometimes owners report a vehicle stolen when really it has been misplaced. The malign possibility is a fraudulent attempt to collect insurance money on a vehicle that may only exist on paper, or for which the actual value is less than the insured value. In any event, the fact that the NCVS item on reporting also indicates an upward trend suggests that the upward trend does not result just (or only) from an increase in false reports.

Since making a crime known to law enforcement is the first step in the process by which the criminal justice system sanctions crime, it is plausible that the upward trends account for a portion of the crime drop during this period. But neither the reasons for these trends nor their consequences have been systematically analyzed. What we do know, thanks to a careful study by Eric Baumer and Janet Lauritsen (2010), is that the upward trend in the NCVS reporting rates is not the result of trends in the mix of crime; they find that a strong upward trend in the NCVS measure persists after controlling for victim-offender relationship, socioeconomic characteristics of the victim, injury, weapon type, and demographic characteristics of the victims and offenders.[15]

---

15. Baumer and Lauritsen (2010) conclude that reporting rates (based on NCVS items) followed an upward trend since 1978 for aggravated assault, sexual offenses, burglary, motor vehicle theft, and larceny. They find a primarily downward trend for robbery, which contradicts our finding. They did not consider our alternative measure, the UCR/NCVS ratio.

In what follows we consider the incentives for cooperating with the system as a way to identify potential policy levers for sustaining this trend, whatever its cause in the past.

7.4.2   Incentives for Cooperation

Under some circumstances it is in the self-interest of the victim to report a crime. Reporting may be required by insurance companies, or may be warranted just from the prospect of recovering stolen property. There may also be a financial incentive for a victim to report a violent crime if he is eligible for payments under a state victim compensation program (which mandates that the victim cooperate), or has hope that the offender, if caught and convicted, may be required to pay restitution as part of a settlement or sentence. In unusual cases there is a possibility of a remunerative tort case against the offender, which would be facilitated by a criminal prosecution. Retail businesses may routinely report shoplifting and other crimes in the hope of acquiring a reputation that will have deterrent value.

The decision to report is not always or even predominantly based on a financial calculation. A sense of public duty, or desire for revenge, may play a role. Related findings are that victims are more likely to report if they believe that the police will be able to do something about the crime, and if the crime is serious (Reiss 1971; Levitt 1998; Baumer and Lauritsen 2010). (A downward trend in crime could therefore increase reporting because residents perceive that police are more effective, and because they actually are, given their lighter workload.) Officials are *required* to report certain crimes that become known to them—some states require serious offenses occurring in schools to be reported, and medical providers are required to report gunshot wounds and suspected child abuse. Victims may report domestic violence in the hope that the violent partner will learn a lesson and desist.

On the other side of the ledger are the private costs of reporting and cooperating with an investigation. In most cases it is just a matter of taking the time to give a report, but sometimes there is reason to fear more serious consequences. Many victims may wish to avoid contact with authorities because of their immigration status or their own illicit activities—which is what makes undocumented aliens and prostitutes so vulnerable to predators. Of course there is a reasonable fear of retaliation, especially when dealing with criminal gangs or acquaintances. There may also be a general distrust or disaffection of the police, coupled with a "no snitching" norm in the neighborhood.

Given this list of considerations on both sides of the ledger, there are a variety of possible explanations for the upward trend in reporting. There are potentially positive effects of technology—the introduction of mobile phones (which reduce the cost of reporting) and of improvements in 911 systems—and of concerted efforts to improve the relationship between police and public through community policing with its neighborhood watch and related community-participation programs, and efforts to improve the perception of the fairness and legitimacy of policing (Tyler and Fagan 2008; Skogan and Frydl 2004). "Consistent with this claim, survey data reveal that the percentage of citizens who rate the police highly in terms of honesty and ethical behavior has risen from about 37% in the mid-to-late 1970s to about 61% by the middle of the present decade" (Baumer and Lauritsen 2010, 137). Whether the private incentive to cooperate with the criminal justice system has grown over this period is an intriguing possibility.

7.4.3   Policies to Improve Cooperation

In recent years conditional cash transfers have been touted as a potentially effective ingredient for a variety of social programs that are intended to change private behavior (Corby et al. 2000). The possibility of paying for information that would be helpful to law enforcement is not a new one—for example, the national nonprofit organization CrimeStoppers got its start in 1976. Community chapters of CrimeStoppers collect private contributions and use the funds to pay rewards (up to $1,000) for anonymous information leading to arrest. Other "tip" programs have been set up by police departments, focusing on particular problems such as illegal gun possession. In a sense it is difficult to see how such programs could *not* be cost-effective (assuming they are well managed), since a tip that is key to arresting a perpetrator of serious crime is presumably worth far more than $1,000—but we are not aware of any systematic evaluations.

More generally, victims who cooperate with law enforcement have been treated better over the years, starting with the victims' rights movement during the 1970s. President Reagan appointed a task force that offered over sixty action recommendations that "encouraged the expansion of victim services and suggested practices to make the criminal justice process and related victim service delivery system more 'victim friendly'" (Tobolowsky 2001, 9). The report helped inspire state and federal legislation. "Currently, the federal government and all of the states have statutory victim compensation programs and restitution provisions which authorize restitution as a probation condition or as an independent sentence, or both. A victim right to restitution is also included in several of the state constitutions" (11). Since 1984, the federal government has provided states with grants to support victim compensation and victim services.

It seems reasonable to suppose that the promise of victim compensation and restitution would motivate victims to report to the police and cooperate with the investigation and trial. But in practice restitution is usually not required as part of a felony sentence in state courts: in 2006, 18 percent of violent-crime defendants and 27 percent of property-crime defendants were required to pay restitution.[16] Even when it is part of the sentence, there is no guarantee that it will be collected and transferred to the victim.

16. See Rosenmerkel and Durose (2009).

Victim compensation programs also tend to offer less than meets the eye, although they do play a role. The first such program was created in California in 1965, and spread rapidly (with a federal assist in the 1980s). They have been operating in every state since at least the 1990s. In these programs the government is typically payer of last resort, and only for certain expenses incurred in violent crimes: medical expenses not otherwise covered, some lost wages, funeral expenses. They have garnered little public notice. In FY 2009, California reported about 200,000 serious violent crimes and received 54,572 applications for compensation, paying out $94 million, or about $1,700 per claim (http://www.boc.ca.gov/docs/stats/CountyCompApps.pdf). We know of no evaluations of victim programs from the point of view of whether and how much they induce reporting and cooperation.

7.5   An Evaluation of Business Improvement Districts in Los Angeles

Business improvement districts offer an interesting example of private action that combines situational crime prevention with a close working relationship with the police, and which, while nongovernmental, are the result of collective action. These self-taxing entities raise money to pay for private security guards, combat disorder, and generally to repair "broken windows" directly, while also advocating for improved policing and other city services (MacDonald and Stokes 2006). Services provided by BID organizations within a defined district are typically supplemental to those provided by public agencies. The BID services often include trash collection, private security officers, and closed-circuit television (CCTV) cameras, as well as marketing and place promotion, and development planning. The BIDs exist in urban areas "to make places attractive—safer, cleaner, and more marketable" (Mitchell 2008, 3).

Business improvement districts emerged out of legal institutions that have been used by urban municipalities in America since the early 1800s to finance improvements in local infrastructure like sidewalks, street lighting, and sewers that directly benefit adjacent property owners. Briffault (1999, 415) notes that the public benefit "justifies public action to provide the improvement; the private benefit justifies requiring landowners to defray a portion of the municipality's expenses." The BID model is a form of special-purpose district that has the power to assess local landowners and is consistent with common-use service arrangements (Houstoun 1997).

The BIDs are private entities but they are typically chartered by state legislation and regulated by local governments (Mitchell 2001). The method for collecting assessments for BIDs differs across jurisdictions. In some states the assessments are collected by municipal agencies and then transferred to a private sector nonprofit organization that manages the operations of the BID. In other locales assessments are collected by the nonprofit organizations managing the BIDs. Relying on nonprofit agencies to collect assessments can create difficulties when property owners are delinquent in paying. Frankford Special Services District in Philadelphia, for example, reported collecting only $39,000 of its mandated $85,000 assessment in 1997, and the city had to make up for the budget shortfall through federal community development block grants (Stokes 2006). Not surprisingly, some businesses and property owners resent being asked "to make an additional payment to finance services they think should be paid for out of their existing tax dollars" (Briffault 1999, 385). Despite differences in state-enabling legislation and methods of administration, the popularity of BIDs is evident from their growth in US cities. In 1999 there was an estimated 404 BIDs in the United States (Mitchell 2001). The International Downtown Association estimates there are over 800 BIDs in the United States in 2009.

In Los Angeles (LA), California, BIDs are managed and operated by private nonprofit organizations, but they are chartered and regulated by the city government. The LA city clerk's Administrative Services Division manages the city's BID program. The city levies an assessment on the BID's behalf through property or business tax collection, charges each BID a fee for the transaction, and then transfers the funds to the nonprofit organization managing the daily operations of each BID (MacDonald et al. 2009).

The adoption of a BID in LA requires extensive planning and support from business and property owners. A formal planning phase for the BID must be outlined and presented to the LA city clerk's office. In the planning phase LA requires the use of outside consultants to develop a formal BID plan including a membership database, the design and geography to incorporate the BID, an assessment formula for financing services, and a plan to incorporate a nonprofit organization to manage daily operations of the BID. At least 15 percent of the business owners or more than 50 percent of the property owners must sign supporting petitions for a formal BID proposal to be accepted by the city. Subsequent to a formal proposal being approved by the LA city clerk's and city attorney's office a laborious process of legal and legislative oversight ensues, including: a formal vote of the majority of property owners and merchants weighted by level of property assessment; a five-year service and budget plan for operating the BID; and a review of documents by the LA city clerk's and city attorney's office. After all planning stages have been successfully met, a series of public meetings are held prior to an enabling vote by the LA city council that officially charters BIDs (City of Los Angeles Office of the City Clerk; MacDonald et al. 2009). After five years, the BID has to be reauthorized by another formal plan and vote of property owners to continue its operations. Los Angeles offers some financial assistance for BID formation planning (City of Los Angeles Office of the City Clerk).

Los Angeles has also embedded several accountability measures to regulating BIDs. For example, the nonprofit organizations managing BIDs are required to provide the city with financial reports, and the city can audit and shut down any BID organization whose operations are deemed to be out of compliance with the proposed service plan, or for financial irregularities (City of Los Angeles Office of the City Clerk; MacDonald et al. 2009).

Many of the BIDs in LA focus their services on sanitation and private security of common public-space area enhancements to the existing publicly-funded sanitation and police services. "Clean" and "safe" are common terms used by BIDs in LA. Eleven of the thirty BIDs operating in LA in 2005 spent more than $200,000 a year on private security operations, with nearly equal amounts being spent on sanitation services. The Figueroa Corridor BID and Hollywood Entertainment BID provide good examples of BIDs with a focus on sanitation and safety. The Figueroa Corridor BID was formed in 1998 by business property owners in direct response to economic decline and a concern with area crime. From the outset, its efforts were focused on improving community safety by employing uniformed private security workers (Safety Ambassadors) who patrol the district on foot, bike, and evening vehicle patrols and assist in keeping order. It spends close to $500,000 a year, or almost half of its operational budget, on these officers. This BID also employs cleaning crews that remove trash, debris, and graffiti (Holter 2002). On a monthly basis the BID collects and removes more than 3,000 to 4,000 bags of trash and 1,000 to 5,000 square feet of graffiti.[17]

The Hollywood Entertainment BID employs armed private security officers who are retired law-enforcement officers. These officers patrol the Hollywood district seven days a week during evening hours, initiate citizen arrests when they observe violations of the law, and work closely with the LAPD. It spends just over $1 million a year on private security, or approximately 47 percent of its operating budget. It has also installed eight CCTV cameras at intersections in the district for use by the LAPD (http://www.hollywoodbid.org/).

Brooks (2008) conducted an evaluation of the effects of BIDs on changes in crime in LA neighborhoods and found that their adoption was associated with a significant drop in the number of serious crimes reported to the police between 1990 and 2002. Her analysis of BID effects on crime controlled for time-stable differences between neighborhoods, and used as a control group BID neighborhoods that proposed BIDs but did not end up adopting them. A more recent analysis by MacDonald and colleagues (2009) using data from 1994 to 2005 in LA found significant pre-post declines in robbery and violent crimes in areas that adopted BIDs.

These evaluations did not fully consider the cost of BIDs to the public, and in particular the use of police services. The BID provides greater capacity to mobilize the police, and BIDs have been criticized for encouraging the increased use of police arrest powers in their districts and displacing

17. http://www.figueroacorridor.org/uploads/Spring2008Newsletter.pdf — sum2007.pdf.

disorder and crime to adjacent areas (Harcourt 2005). If BIDs reduce crime by increasing arrests in their districts, the additional cost to the public of arrests, related prosecutions, and incarcerations should be incorporated in the cost-benefit analysis.

We examined the effect of BIDs on crime and arrests in LA, applying quasi-experimental statistical methods to fine-grained annual crime data for the years 1994 to 2005. We used the year of BID implementation to reflect the exposure to the BID intervention and examine the pre-post changes in the incidence of crime and arrests in affected neighborhoods, controlling for overall time trends. Our innovations, with respect to the existing literature, included an analysis of the impact on arrests, an analysis of spillover effects, and an estimate of the dose-response relationship with an associated cost-benefit analysis. A detailed report of methods and results is presented in our recent paper (Cook and MacDonald, forthcoming).

The results from our analyses indicate a substantial effect of BIDs on crimes and arrests. The introduction of BIDs is associated with roughly twenty-eight fewer total serious crimes per neighborhood. Interpreting this estimate from the sample mean of 249 crime incidents per BID neighborhood suggests an 11 percent relative decline in crime associated with BID implementation. In terms of crime motivated by environmental opportunities the results appear to be particularly strong. The largest marginal shift in crime occurs for robberies, followed by burglary and auto theft. For example, interpreting the estimate of robberies from the sample mean of twenty-seven incidents per BID neighborhood suggests an 18 percent reduction associated with BIDs.

Additionally, BID introduction is not associated with increased use of arrest powers by the police. On the contrary, across all models BIDs are associated with significantly fewer police arrests over time. The introduction of BIDs is associated with an average BID neighborhood reduction in 9.62 arrest incidents, reflecting a 32 percent decline. Importantly, these models we estimated controlled for crime and arrest trends in adjacent reporting districts through the inclusion of police division*year interaction terms. The substantive results for BID effects are also the same across all crime and arrest outcomes when we control for the two years leading up to and after BID adoption.

These results we just discussed treat BIDs as binary, either present or not. In fact, they are highly heterogeneous with respect to resources devoted to crime prevention. We used as a measure of private security dosage the expenditure per reporting district. The results, shown in table 7.1, are consistent with those for BID presence, but specifically indicate that BIDs with greater private security expenditures per neighborhood (denoted *Security$*) have greater reductions in crime and arrests. (Note that these regressions include an indicator for BIDs that did not spend on security.) We conclude that an additional $10,000 per neighborhood spent by BIDs on private security

Table 7.1   Effect of BID private security spending on crimes and arrests

	Regression estimates				
	Total	Robbery	Assault	Burglary	Auto theft
Crime					
Security$	−3.371[a]	−0.590[a]	−0.431[b]	−0.533[a]	0.166
($10,000)	(2.89)	(3.98)	(2.01)	(2.87)	(0.64)
ZeroSecurity$	−5.66	−3.80[a]	−0.354	−1.320	0.223
(0–1 variable)	(0.50)	(2.78)	(0.16)	(0.63)	(0.07)
Arrest					
Security$	−1.658[a]	−0.505[a]	−0.558[a]	−0.199[a]	−0.205[a]
($10,000)	(3.28)	(5.06)	(3.02)	(3.48)	(2.65)
ZeroSecurity$	−0.907	−1.515	−4.049	−0.746	−0.151
(0–1 variable)	(0.11)	(1.92)	(0.90)	(0.90)	(0.29)

Notes: Each column reports estimates from two regressions, first with a crime count as the dependent variable (top half) and then for an arrest count (bottom half). *t*-values reported in parentheses. Coefficients are multiplied by 10,000 for Security$. All regressions include neighborhood and division*year fixed effects. Standard errors were adjusted for larger variances within higher crime neighborhoods. N = 12,864 (1,072 reporting districts*12 years).
[a]$p < .01$
[b]$p \leq .05$

reduces the average number of crimes per neighborhood by 3.37. Separate regressions by crime type indicate that an additional $10,000 per neighborhood reduces robbery, assault, and burglary counts by about 0.5 incidents. The only exception to this pattern is auto theft, which has no discernible association with BID spending on private security. The BID expenditures on private security also appear to be associated with a decreased use of arrest powers by the police. Across all models a greater amount of BID spending on private security per neighborhood is associated with significantly fewer police arrests. An additional $10,000 of spending per neighborhood by BIDs is associated with 1.65 fewer arrests. Crime-specific results indicate that most of the reduction in crime is for robbery and assault.

An additional expenditure of $10,000 per neighborhood (reporting district) would represent a 19.3 percent increase above the average amount spent ($51,906) for the twenty-one BIDs that provide private security to their neighborhoods. The Hollywood Entertainment and Downtown Industrial BIDs have the highest dosage of private security expenditures per neighborhood at $190,120 and $194,712, respectively.

What effect do BIDs have on neighboring, non-BID areas? It is possible that BID effects may be confined to their neighborhoods and have no impact on their closest neighbors. Alternatively, BIDs may displace crime to their neighboring areas as their districts become less attractive for criminal opportunities. The BIDs could also generate spillover effects and reduce crime for their adjacent neighbors by enhancing the overall level of crime prevention in their districts and making even their next-door neighborhoods less attractive to criminals. In any event, when we tested for spillovers directly, we found no evidence of either positive or negative effects.

7.5.1   Effects of BIDs on Crime-Related Social Costs

Next, we consider direct crime and criminal justice cost savings resulting from BID investments in area-specific services. As we have seen, adoption of BIDs reduced the average number of crimes and arrests in affected neighborhoods. How much are these reduction worth? The social costs of crime victimization include direct costs related to medical and mental health services, productivity losses (wages, housework, etc.), and pain and suffering. Two methods have been used to monetize the consequences of crime. Most common has been to infer crime costs from jury awards for torts that have the elements of crimes like robbery or assault. This ex-post compensatory approach has most recently been pursued by Roman (2009). In principle the more valid approach is to estimate the willingness-to-pay (WTP) for a reduced probability of victimization, which provides an ex-ante assessment that should include the costs of crime avoidance and concerns about family and friends as well as self. Ludwig and Cook (2001) utilized a contingent-valuation survey to estimate willingness to pay for a reduction in gun violence, and Cohen et al. (2004) applied this method to estimating the value of reducing several other types of crime. Estimates utilizing both approaches are reported in table 7.2.[18] Note that the unit social cost of a robbery is quite similar in the two methods, but that the jury-award method produces a higher estimate for assault. Jury awards and WTP show that an additional spending of $10,000 per neighborhood by BIDs yields a social-cost savings of $149,362 to $155,242 for robberies and $34,217 to $52,812 for assaults.[19] The conclusion is clear in either case—even if we just limit the assessment to robbery and assault, the social benefit of crime reduction is a large multiple (about twenty) of private expenditure.

This conclusion is strengthened when the savings from reduced arrest rates are included. The average cost of an arrest and related prosecution in LA (in 2005 dollars) has been previously documented by investigators at the RAND Corporation (see Turner, et al. 2007). An average arrest by the LAPD was estimated to cost $473, which includes the cost of officers at the crime scene and police station booking an offender (four hours total at $34.90 per hour), the cost of case review by a detective (one-and-a-half hours at $42.82 per hour), a citation package delivered to the LA district attorney (one hour at

18. The average direct victim injury cost is much lower and estimated to be $30,690 per robbery and $23,212 per assault (Miller, Cohen, and Rossman 1993). These cost estimates are conservative because they exclude a number of external social costs including how crime influences decisions about travel, housing, business locations, prices of insurance, the value that individuals place on avoiding victimization, and other factors.
19. A separate estimate using direct injury costs per crime from Miller, Cohen, and Rossman (1993) indicates that an additional $10,000 in BID spending on private security is associated with $18,199 social injury-costs savings for robberies and $10,027 for assaults averted.

Table 7.2   Cost savings from BIDs for crimes and arrests per neighborhood

Incident costs	Per $10,000 private security	95% conf. interval
Robbery ($263,122)[a]	$155,242	$78,011–$232,473
Assault ($79,390)[a]	$34,217	$511–$67,923
Robbery ($253,156)[b]	$149,362	$75,056–$223,668
Assault ($122,249)[b]	$52,689	$786–$104,592
Arrest ($2,947)[c]	$4,863	$1,963–$7,798

Note: Estimates of costs/crime taken from the publications and converted into 2005 dollars.
[a]Estimate taken from Cohen et al. (2004).
[b]Estimate taken from Roman (2009).
[c]Estimate taken from Turner et al. (2007).

$34.90 per hour), and a booking fee of $25. The total cost of each court appearance related to an arrest was estimated to be approximately $2,474. Court costs included the costs associated with the district attorney's prosecution, the public defender representation, and the costs of a case appearing in court. The average costs of an arrest and court prosecution is estimated at $2,947. These criminal justice cost estimates are conservative because they exclude the average cost of jail, future prison, and potential lost wages due to incarceration.

Taking the estimated average reduction 1.65 arrests per additional $10,000 BID expenditures on private security per neighborhood and multiplying that by the average costs of an arrest and court prosecution ($2,947) translates into an approximate savings of $4,863. This suggests that there is a substantial benefit to the public in reduced criminal justice expenditures for money spent by BIDs on private security, with no indication that these benefits are offset by arrests going up in neighboring locations.

The bottom line is that the local security provided by BIDs in Los Angeles reduces crime and the number of people who are arrested and processed in the criminal justice system. These effects provide a social benefit that is a multiple of the private expenditure. While we do not have estimates of the effects of BID security on the profitability of the constituent businesses, the popularity of BIDs suggests that the participants are satisfied. In effect, BIDs may well increase the profitability of doing business in the central city.

7.6   Conclusion

Criminal justice policy is mostly concerned with how best to use public resources to reduce crime by reducing the population of active criminals through deterrence, incapacitation, and rehabilitation of criminals. That formulation of the policy problem tends to downplay the role of private action. In fact, the volume and distribution of crime is not solely determined by the population of active criminals. Individuals choose whether to commit crime, and what crimes to commit, based in part on the characteristics of available opportunities. Those criminal opportunities are created primarily by private action. Expressed differently, private individuals and firms produce private security, providing the first line of defense in reducing the supply of tangible opportunities for crime, and to some extent making crime less attractive and profitable. If policymakers ignore the fundamental role of private action, they are in danger of misunderstanding observed trends and patterns in crime—and of failing to recognize effective tactics for reducing the costs of crime.

It is also true that the productivity of the criminal justice system depends crucially on private inputs. A successful investigation leading to arrest and conviction of a criminal usually requires private citizens to voluntarily provide the necessary information, beginning with the crime report. Since private cooperation tends to be costly to the provider and have little tangible payoff, it is likely to be undersupplied—the public benefit of cooperation is greater than the private benefit. In the coproduction process by which the private and public sectors serve to influence the crime rate, greater public effort to enhance private inputs is a promising avenue to efficient crime control.

While there is a good *prima facie* case for positive marginal social benefit of private inputs into the criminal-justice process, the case is less clear for the provision of private security. We have argued that some private-security actions have negative externalities, such as keeping a handgun for self-defense and thereby providing a lure to burglars and an enhanced supply of guns to criminals. Likewise, normal precautions in protecting property may cause displacement to other targets. So there can be no general claim that there is too little private security. The effects must be assessed on a case-by-case basis. For example, it is entirely plausible that the near-universal adoption of sophisticated locking devices for motor vehicles gets part of the credit for greatly reduced rates of auto theft (whereas car alarms have little effect and substantial social cost). The dissemination of steering-column locks and immobilizers has been encouraged by government regulation of auto manufacture and of rate setting in comprehensive insurance, and more could be done along these lines. A similar analysis could be applied to other types of property crime.

More important is the challenge of finding cost-beneficial policies to increase private inputs to the criminal justice process. There are a number of policy instruments available. Tangible costs and benefits can be enhanced through monetary rewards, expansions in victim compensation and restitution, and respectful treatment of citizens who do come forward. Overcoming distrust of the police and "no snitching" norms (with the implied threat of retaliation) may be more difficult, but is surely important. For whatever reasons, we have seen steady increases in crime reporting over the last three decades. (The growing trust in police may get part of the credit.) The *quality* of private inputs may also be improving, due to technological change. The most carefully studied example is LoJack, which provides police investigators with the exact location of the stolen car. The advent of cell phones may also have increased the provision of timely reports to the police.

Security guards, most of whom are privately employed, surely play a role in improving cooperation with the police. The number of security guards exceeds the number of police, and the two sorts of employment have grown apace. Of particular interest is the formation of business improvement districts that focus much of their efforts on controlling crime in public spaces around commercial districts. By hiring private security and working closely with the police, BIDs coproduce crime control—a local public good. We have demonstrated that BIDs reduce crime, and that the reduction in crime is coupled with reductions in arrest rates. The BIDs in Los Angeles clearly pass a cost-benefit test. Indeed, the social cost savings from BID security expenditures is an order of magnitude greater than expenditures, just as is true for Lojack. If BIDs as successful as LA's are to emerge elsewhere, one key is to provide the legal framework that facilitates the formation and funding of BIDs.

References

Anderson, David A. 1999. "The Aggregate Burden of Crime." *Journal of Law and Economics* 42 (2): 611–42.

Ayres, Ian, and Steven D. Levitt. 1998. "Measuring Positive Externalities from Unobservable Victim Precautions: An Empirical Analysis of Lojack." *Quarterly Journal of Economics* 113 (1): 43–77.

Ayres, Ian, and Barry Nalebuff. 2005. "Stop thief!" *Forbes,* January 10.

Baumer, Eric P., and Janet L. Lauritsen. 2010. "Reporting Crime to the Police, 1973–2005: A Multivariate Analysis of Long-term Trends in the National Crime Survey (NCS) and National Crime Victimization Survey (NCVS)." *Criminology* 48 (1): 131–85.

Bayley, David, and Clifford Shearing. 2001. "The New Structure of Policing: Description, Conceptualization, and Research Agenda." Research Report. Washington, DC: National Institute of Justice.

Becker, Gary S. 1968. "Crime and Punishment: An Economic Approach." *Journal of Political Economy* 76 (2): 169–217.

Blackstone, Erwin A., Andrew J. Buck, and Simon Hakim. 2005. "Evaluation of Alternative Policies to Combat False Emergency Calls." *Evaluation and Program Planning* 28 (2): 233–42.

Blumstein, Alfred, and Joel Wallman. 2000. *The Crime Drop in America.* New York: Cambridge University Press.

———. 2006. "The Crime Drop and Beyond." *Annual Review of Law and Social Science* 2:125–46.

Briffault, Richard. 1999. "A Government for Our Time? Business Improvement Districts and Urban Governance." *Columbia Law Review* 99 (2): 365–477.

Brooks, Leah. 2008. "Volunteering to Be Taxed: Business Improvement Districts and the Extra-Governmental Provision of Public Safety" *Journal of Public Economics* 92 (1–2): 388–406.

City of Los Angeles Office of the City Clerk. Undated. Business Improvement Districts. Accessed January 7, 2010. http://cityclerk.lacity.org/bids/.

Clarke, Ronald V. 1983. "Situational Crime Prevention: Its Theoretical Basis and Practical Scope." In *Crime and Justice: An Annual Review of Research, volume 4,* edited by Michael Tonry and Norval Morris, 225–56. Chicago: University of Chicago Press.

Clarke, Ronald V., and Patricia M. Harris. 1992. "Auto Theft and its Prevention." *Crime and Justice* 16 (1): 1–54.

Clotfelter, Charles T. 1977. "Public Services, Private Substitutes, and the Demand for Protection against Crime." *American Economic Review* 67 (5): 867–77.

———. 1978. "Private Security and the Public Safety." *Journal of Urban Economics* 5 (3): 388–402.

———. 1993. "The Private Life of Public Economics." *Southern Economic Journal* 59 (4): 579–96.

Cohen, Mark A., Roland Rust, Sara Steen, and Simon Tidd. 2004. "Willingness-to-Pay for Crime Control Programs." *Criminology* 42 (1): 86–106.

Cook, Philip J. 1986. "The Demand and Supply of Criminal Opportunities." *Crime and Justice* 7 (1): 1–27.

———. 2009. "Crime Control in the City: A Research-based Briefing on Public and Private Measures." *Cityscape: A Journal of Policy Development and Research* 11 (1): 53–79.

Cook, Philip J., and John H. Laub. 2002. "After the Epidemic: Recent Trends in Youth Violence in the United States." In *Crime and Justice: A Review of Research,* edited by Michael Tonry, 117–53. Chicago: University of Chicago Press.

Cook, Philip J., and Jens Ludwig. 2003. "The Effects of Gun Prevalence on Burglary: Deterrence vs. Inducement." In *Evaluating Gun Policy,* edited by Jens Ludwig and Philip J. Cook, 74–118. Washington, DC: Brookings Institution Press.

———. 2006. "The Social Costs of Gun Ownership." *Journal of Public Economics* 90 (1–2): 379–91.

Cook, Philip J., and John MacDonald. Forthcoming. "Public Safety through Private Action: An Economic Assessment of BIDs." *The Economic Journal.*

Copes, Heith, and Michael Cherbonneau. 2006. "The Key to Auto Theft: Emerging Methods of Auto Theft from the Offenders' Perspective." *British Journal of Criminology* 46 (5): 917–34.

Corby, Elizabeth A., John M. Roll, David M. Ledgerwood, and Charles R. Schuster. 2000. "Contingency Management Interventions for Treating the Substance Abuse of Adolescents: A Feasibility Study." *Experimental and Clinical Psycholpharmacology* 8 (3): 371–76.

Cornish, Derek, and Ronald V. Clarke. 2003. "Opportunities, Precipitators, and Criminal Decisions: A Reply to Wortley's Critique of Situational Crime Prevention" In *Theory for Practice in Situational Crime Prevention,* edited by Martha J. Smith and Derek B. Cornish, 41–96. Monsey, NY: Criminal Justice Press.

Cunningham, William C., John J. Strauchs, and Clifford W. Van Meter. 1990. *Private Security Trends 1970 to 2000: The Hallcrest Report II.* Boston: Butterworth-Heinemann.

Draca, Mirko, Stephen Machin, and Robert Witt. 2010. "Crime Displacement and Police Interventions: Evidence from London's 'Operation Theseus.'" In *The Eco-*

nomics of Crime: Lessons for and from Latin America, edited by Rafael Di Tella, Sebastian Edwards, and Ernesto Schargrodsky, 359–74. Chicago: University of Chicago Press.

Eck, John E. 2006. "Preventing Crime at Places." In *Evidence-Based Crime Prevention,* revised edition, edited by Lawrence W. Sherman, David P. Farrington, Brandon C. Welsh, and Doris Layton MacKenzie, 241–94. New York: Routledge.

Ehrlich, Isaac. 1974. "Participation in Illegitimate Activities: An Economic Analysis." In *Essays in the Economics of Crime and Punishment,* edited by Gary S. Becker and William M. Landes, 68–134. New York: National Bureau of Economic Research.

———. 1981. "On the Usefulness of Controlling Individuals: An Economic Analysis of Rehabilitation, Incapacitation and Deterrence. *American Economic Review* 71 (3): 307–22.

———. 1996. "Crime, Punishment, and the Market for Offenses." *Journal of Economic Perspectives* 10 (1): 43–67.

Ehrlich, Isaac, and Gary S. Becker. 1972. "Market Insurance, Self-Insurance, and Self-Protection." *Journal of Political Economy* 80 (4): 623–48.

Forst, Brian. 1999. "Policing with Legitimacy, Efficiency, and Equity." In *The Privatization of Policing: Two Views,* edited by Brian Forst and Peter Manning, 1–48. Washington, DC: Georgetown University Press.

Friedman, Aaron, Aaron Naparstek, and Mateo Taussig-Rubbo. 2003. "Alarmingly Useless: The Case for Banning Car Alarms in New York City." Transportation Alternatives. http://www.transalt.org.

Gonzalez-Navarro, Marco. 2008. "Deterrence and Displacement in Auto Theft." Working Paper. Princeton University, October 15.

Gottfredson, Michael R., and Don M. Gottfredson. 1988. *Decision Making in Criminal Justice: Toward the Rational Exercise of Discretion,* 2nd edition. New York: Plenum.

Guerette, Rob T., and Kate J. Bowers. 2009. "Assessing the Extent of Crime Displacement and Diffusion of Benefits: A Review of Situational Crime Prevention Evaluations." *Criminology* 47 (4): 1331–68.

Harcourt, Bernard E. 2005. "Policing L.A.'s Skid Row: Crime and Real Estate Development in Downtown Los Angeles (An Experiment in Real Time)." *University of Chicago Legal Forum* May: 325–404.

Helperin, Joanne. 2009. "Evaluating Stolen Vehicle Recovery Systems: The Pros, Cons and Pricing." Edmunds, Inc. Posted November 20, 2009. www.edmunds.com/ownership/articles/128786/article.html.

Holter, Darryl. 2002. *Four: The "Business Improvement Districts" Revolution.* California Policy Options Paper 943, January 1. Los Angeles, CA: UCLA School of Public Affairs. Accessed January 2, 2009. http://repositories.cdlib.org/uclaspa/cpo/943.

Houstoun, Lawrence O. 1997. *BIDs: Business Improvement Districts.* Washington, DC: Urban Land Institute in cooperation with the International Downtown Association.

Joyce, Theodore. 2004. "Did Legalized Abortion Lower Crime?" *Journal of Human Resources* 39 (1): 1–28.

Kindermann, Charles, James P. Lynch, and David Cantor. 1997. *The Effects of the Re-design on Victimization Estimates.* Washington, DC: Bureau of Justice Statistics.

Kruttschnitt, Candace, and Kristin Carbone-Lopez. 2009. "Customer Satisfaction: Crime Victims' Willingness to Call the Police." Research Paper. Washington, DC: The Police Foundation.

Leinwand, Donna. 2009. "Car Theft Slows to Lowest in 20 Years." *USA Today.* Accessed February 18, 2011. http://www.usatoday.com/NEWS/USAedition/2009 -10-19-1Aautotheft19_ST_U.htm.

Levitt, Steven D. 1998. "The Relationship between Crime Reporting and Police: Implications for the Use of Uniform Crime Reports." *Journal of Quantitative Criminology* 14 (1): 61–81.

———. 2004. "Understanding Why Crime Fell in the 1990s: Four Factors That Explain the Decline and Six That Do Not." *Journal of Economic Perspectives* 18 (1): 163–90.

Ludwig, Jens, and Philip J. Cook. 2001. "The Benefits of Reducing Gun Violence: Evidence from Contingent-Valuation Survey Data." *Journal of Risk and Uncertainty* 22 (3): 207–26.

MacDonald, John, Ricky Bluthenthal, Aaron Kofner, Robert Stokes, Amber Sehgal, Terry Fain, and Leo Beletsky. 2009. *Neighborhood Effects on Crime and Youth Violence: The Role of Business Improvement Districts in Los Angeles.* Santa Monica, CA: RAND Corporation.

MacDonald, John, and Robert J. Stokes. 2006. "Cities Should Enlist Business in Their Battle Against Crime." Commentary. Santa Monica, CA: RAND Corporation. http://www.rand.org/commentary/2006/07/03/LABJ.html.

Miller, Ted R., Mark A. Cohen, and Shelli B. Rossman. 1993. "Victim Costs of Violent Crime and Resulting Injuries." *Health Affairs* 12 (4): 186–97.

Mitchell, Jerry. 2001. "Business Improvement Districts and the 'New' Revitalization of Downtown." *Economic Development Quarterly* 15 (2): 115–23.

———. 2008. *Business Improvement Districts and the Shape of American Cities.* Albany: SUNY Press.

National Highway Transportation Safety Administration. 1998. "Auto Theft and Recovery: Effects of the Anti Car Theft Act of 1992 and the Motor Vehicle Theft Law Enforcement Act of 1984: Report to the Congress." NHTSA Report Number DOT HS 808 761. Accessed November 22, 2009. http://www.nhtsa.dot.gov/cars/ rules/regrev/evaluate/808761.html.

Philipson, Tomas J., and Richard A. Posner. 1996. "The Economic Epidemiology of Crime." *Journal of Law and Economics* 39 (2): 405–33.

Reiss, Albert J. 1971. *The Police and the Public.* New Haven, CT: Yale University Press.

Roman, Jonathan K. 2009. "What is the Price of Crime? New Estimates of the Cost of Criminal Victimization." PhD diss., University of Maryland. http://www.lib .umd.edu/drum/handle/1903/9868.

Rosenmerkel, Sean, and Matthew Durose. 2009. "National Judicial Reporting Program Felony Sentences in State Courts, 2006." NCJ 226846, December. Table 1.5.

Shavell, Steven. 1991. "Individual Precautions to Prevent Theft: Private versus Socially Optimal Behavior." *International Review of Law and Economics* 11 (2): 123–32.

Sklansky, David A. 2008. *Democracy and Police.* Stanford, CA: Stanford University Press.

Skogan, Wesley, and Kathleen Frydl, editors. 2004. *Fairness and Effectiveness in Policing.* Washington, DC: National Academy Press.

Stokes, Robert J. 2006. "Business Improvement Districts and Inner City Revitalization: The Case of Philadelphia's Frankford Special Services District." *International Journal of Public Administration* 29 (1–3): 173–86.

Tobolowsky, Peggy M. 2001. *Crime Victim Rights and Remedies.* Durham, NC: Carolina Academic Press.

Tremblay, Pierre, Yvan Clermont, and Maurice Cusson. 1994. "Jockeys and Joyriders: Changing Patterns in Car Theft Opportunity Structures." *British Journal of Criminology* 34 (3): 307–21.

Turner, Susan, Terry Fain, John MacDonald, Amber Sehgal, with Jitahadi Imara, Felicia Cotton, Davida Davies, and Apryl Harris. 2007. *Los Angeles County Juvenile Justice Crime Prevention Act: Fiscal Year 2004–2005 Report.* Santa Monica, CA: RAND Corporation.

Tyler, Tom R., and Jeffrey Fagan. 2008. "Legitimacy and Cooperation: Why Do People Help the Police Fight Crime in their Communities?" *Ohio State Journal of Criminal Law* 6 (1): 231–75.

Webb, Barry. 1994. "Steering Column Locks and Motor Vehicle Theft: Evaluations from Three Countries." London: Home Office Police Research Group.

Welsh, Brandon C., and David P. Farrington. 2009. *Making Public Places Safer: Surveillance and Crime Prevention.* New York: Oxford University Press.

Zimring, Franklin E. 2007. *The Great American Crime Decline.* New York: Oxford University Press.

Social Policy

8

Decreasing Delinquency, Criminal Behavior, and Recidivism by Intervening on Psychological Factors Other Than Cognitive Ability
A Review of the Intervention Literature

Patrick L. Hill, Brent W. Roberts, Jeffrey T. Grogger, Jonathan Guryan, and Karen Sixkiller

8.1 Introduction

Research on the causes of crime and delinquency has a long history, with philosophical and theoretical commentary on the topic dating back centuries (see for a review, Binder 1987; Emler and Reicher 1995). This work often has been directly or indirectly catalyzed by efforts to define laws and penalties appropriate to juvenile offenders. If one deems a youth to be a cognitively mature decision maker, then the youth might be more "deserving" of penalties similar to adult offenders. If one instead is sympathetic to the turmoil and tumult inherent in the adolescent experience (see, e.g., Blos 1962; Erikson 1950, 1968), more lenient penalties may be in order. Given the legal implications, it is unsurprising that most efforts to decrease delinquency focus on addressing its cognitive ability catalysts. Another benefit to a cognitive ability approach is that it seems to explain the decrease in illegal activity with age. Adults are assumed to have better cognitive capabilities than adolescents, and thus are able to make better decisions.

Three issues confront researchers who focus solely on cognitive ability antecedents to delinquency and criminality. First, focusing on cognitive ability assumes that adults make more conservative judgments about the

Patrick L. Hill is a postdoctoral fellow in the Department of Psychology at the University of Illinois, Urbana-Champaign. Brent W. Roberts is professor of psychology at the University of Illinois, Urbana-Champaign. Jeffrey T. Grogger is the Irving Harris Professor in Urban Policy in the Harris School of Public Policy, University of Chicago, and a research associate of the National Bureau of Economic Research. Jonathan Guryan is a faculty fellow at the Institute for Policy Research and associate professor of human development and social policy and of economics at Northwestern University, and a research associate of the National Bureau of Economic Research. Karen Sixkiller is a graduate student in the department of psychology at the University of Illinois, Urbana-Champaign.

consequences of their risky decisions. However, some research suggests that adults may actually feel *more* "invulnerable" to risks than adolescents (e.g., Millstein and Halpern-Felsher 2002a, 2002b; Quadrel, Fischhoff, and Davis 1993). Indeed, adolescents have reported greater personal risks for negative events (e.g., injury, having an accident while driving drunk) than young adults (Millstein and Halpern-Felsher 2002a, 2002b). This work suggests that adolescents are not relatively more optimistic in their risk assessments. Such evidence sheds doubt on the idea that faulty decision-making skills are solely to blame for adolescents' increased risk-taking tendencies.

Second, recent work has demonstrated that skills other than cognitive ability predict a number of developmental outcomes in both the economic (e.g., Borghans et al. 2008; Cunha and Heckman 2009; Heckman 2008; Heckman, Stixrud, and Urzua 2006) and psychological literatures (e.g., Ozer and Benet-Martínez 2006; Lodi-Smith and Roberts 2007; Roberts et al. 2007). For example, personality traits appear to predict significant life outcomes (e.g., divorce, occupational attainment, and mortality) as well as socioeconomic status or cognitive ability (Roberts et al. 2007). Moreover, there is evidence that emotional and behavioral skills motivate cognitive skill development, but the reverse does not appear to hold (Cunha and Heckman 2008). Therefore, not only do psychological factors other than cognitive ability predict developmental outcomes, but they also may indirectly influence outcomes through promoting cognitive development.

Economists refer to these as "noncognitive" factors, which, taken literally, is nonsensical from several perspectives. What is really meant by the term "noncognitive" is "all things that are not cognitive ability," which is quite a bit different from the literal meaning of noncognitive. Many of the factors other than cognitive abilities are clearly cognitive in nature. When people set goals they clearly think about what they want or desire. Thus, the term needlessly characterizes everything that is not cognitive ability as an omission (i.e., "non").

Rather than lump all sources of individual heterogeneity that are not measured by IQ tests into a single category, it is useful to separate these characteristics and skills more finely. There are fields, terms, and systems already in place that are used to be more descriptively accurate. Several of the authors of this chapter refer to themselves as personality psychologists, which is a field that subsumes all individual differences, including cognitive abilities. Although there are several alternatives, we have proposed that there are at least four categories of individual differences contained within the study of personality: cognitive abilities, personality traits, motivations, and narratives (Roberts and Wood 2006). We have distinguished among these four domains because constructs found within each grouping tend to be conceptually and empirically distinct. Or, to put it in terms similar to the ideas outlined by economists, important life achievements, such as status in work or marital stability, can be predicted independently from IQ, personality traits, motives, and individual experience (narratives; Roberts et al. 2007).

A third reason the sole focus on cognitive ability is problematic is that research has consistently demonstrated that psychological factors other than cognitive ability predict one's likelihood for delinquent action (for a review, see Dodge, Coie, and Lynam 2006; Hirschi 1969). For example, in a sample of sixth- to tenth-graders, personality traits significantly predict a number of antisocial behaviors, including conduct problems, aggression, and symptoms of antisocial personality disorder (Miller, Lynam, and Leukefeld 2003). In that study, facets of conscientiousness, neuroticism, and particularly agreeableness were strongly related to these antisocial outcomes. Similarly, evidence suggests that delinquents' personality traits predicted their likelihood to recidivate (Steiner, Cauffman, and Duxbury 1999).

When one examines the effect sizes associated with various risk factors for crime it is hard to understand why research has focused so strongly on cognitive ability. Table 8.1 provides representative effect sizes from several reviews and meta-analyses examining the relative importance of different risk factors (Cottle, Lee, and Heilbrun 2001; Gerard and Buehler 2004; Loeber et al. 2007). Although statistically significant predictors, cognitive and environmental factors typically have effect sizes that are relatively modest in nature. In contrast, factors such as "nonsevere pathology" (e.g., stress and anxiety; Cottle, Lee, and Heilbrun 2001), hostility (Loeber et al. 2005), and impulsiveness (Farrington, Ttofi, and Coid 2009) are as important if not more important than cognitive ability. For example, compare the results in table 8.1 to the magnitude of the correlations found by Miller, Lynam, and Leukefeld (2003) between personality facets and the stability of conduct problems: neuroticism (–.02 to .30), agreeableness (–.06 to –.47), and conscientiousness (–.15 to –.35). Indeed, these correlations are often stronger in magnitude than several of the risk factors assumed to be most important for predicting delinquency. Overall, it is clear that intervention research must move past the sole focus on cognitive factors.

The existence of factors other than cognitive ability that predict criminality and delinquency invites questions about the ability to intervene and change these characteristics. The potential for intervening to change the personalities of children and adolescents rather than intervening to change abilities was made clear recently by work with the Perry Preschool Project (Heckman, Malofeera et al. 2009; Heckman, Moon et al. 2009; Heckman, Moon, Pinto et al. 2009). The Perry Preschool Project is a well-known intervention program that was intended to promote academic skill development among at-risk youth. The effects of the intervention in the Perry Preschool Project on cognitive skills were relatively disappointing, with no evidence for long-term differential gains in academic or cognitive skills. However, recent analyses have demonstrated that intervention participants outperformed nonparticipants on a number of important life outcomes, such as employment and criminal behavior. Heckman and colleagues found that cognitive ability factors contribute relatively little to these outcomes, and concluded instead that the Perry Preschool Program seemed to benefit its participants

Table 8.1   **A comparison of cognitive, environmental, and noncognitive predictors of different criminality outcomes in selected studies**

Predicting moderate/serious delinquency in males (Loeber et al. 2007)

Cognitive factors (top four)	
High verbal IQ	−.16
Good performance on Continuous Performance task	−.13
Low delayed visual memory	.12
Low immediate visual memory	.11
High delayed verbal memory	−.10
Child factors (top five)	
High marijuana use	.43
High drug selling	.42
High truancy	.39
High alcohol use	.37
High tobacco use	.34
Family factors (top three)	
High parental supervision	−.22
High parental stress	.13
Low positive parenting	.12
Peer factors	
High peer delinquency	.36
Community factors (top four)	
Low community crime (youth report)	−.26
Good housing quality	−.19
Low community crime (parent report)	−.18
Poor housing quality	.07

Predicting desistance from delinquency in males (Loeber et al. 2007)

Cognitive factors (top three)	
Low immediate visual memory	.12
High spatial IQ	−.06
Poor performance on Continuous Performance task	.06
Child factors (top five)	
High interpersonal callousness	.18
High tobacco use	.16
High drug selling	.14
High alcohol use	.13
High perceived likelihood of being caught	.12
Family factors (top four)	
High parental supervision	−.07
High parental stress	.05
High physical punishment	.04
High positive parenting	−.03
Peer factors	
High peer delinquency	.18
Community factors	
Low community crime (parent report)	−.10
Poor housing quality	.07
High community crime (youth report)	.04
High community crime risk (parent report)	.02

Predicting recidivism (meta-analysis by Cottle, Lee, and Heilbrun 2001)

Cognitive factors (top five)	
Standardized achievement score	−.15
Full scale IQ score	−.14
History of special education	.13
Verbal IQ score	−.11
Performance IQ score	−.03

Table 8.1   (continued)

Child factors (top five)	
Nonsevere pathology (e.g., stress, anxiety)	.31
Conduct problems	.26
Effective use of leisure time	.23
Substance abuse	.15
Severe pathology	.07
Family factors	
Family problems	.28
History of abuse	.11
Single parent	.07
Parent pathology	.05
Peer factors	
Delinquent peers	.20

Predicting conduct problems (Gerard and Buehler 2004)

Cognitive factors	
Scholastic achievement	−.24
Child factors	
School detachment	.33
Self-esteem	−.20
Perceived prejudice by students	.08
Family factors (top five)	
Family detachment	.31
Parent's relationship quality	−.17
Parent's marital status	−.13
Parental involvement	−.13
Household size	.10
Peer factors	
Trouble with peers	.20
Peer support	−.17
Community factors	
Neighborhood satisfaction	−.13
Neighborhood safety	−.09
Neighborhood quality	−.07
Neighborhood problems	.07

Predicting stability of conduct problems from personality (Miller, Lynam, and Leukefeld 2003)

Neuroticism (top five)	
Angry hostility	.30
Impulsiveness	.22
Depression	.15
Self-consciousness	.02
Vulnerability	.03
Agreeableness (top five)	
Straightforwardness	−.47
Compliance	−.37
Altruism	−.30
Trust	−.24
Tendermindedness	−.12
Conscientiousness (top five)	
Deliberation	−.35
Dutifulness	−.23
Competence	−.22
Achievement striving	−.15
Self-discipline	−.15

primarily through its effect on personality factors. This work provides a clear example of the importance of personality variables, given that the program would largely be viewed as unsuccessful if one looked only at cognitive ability outcomes. It also highlights the fact that psychological factors other than cognitive ability, such as personality, are a potential fruitful focus for intervention research. These attributes appear to be changeable, especially in childhood and adolescence, and the changes gained through intervention lead to concrete gains in human capital above and beyond cognitive ability and socioeconomic status. We therefore suggest that interventions that focus solely on cognitive skills, though sometimes beneficial, may fail to address the totality of the effective ways to intervene to diminish the likelihood of criminal behavior. In the following review, we provide an overview of interventions that focus on changing psychological factors other than cognitive ability.

8.2   Outline for the Review

Two issues often bias reports of intervention results. First, most evaluations of intervention efficacy are performed by the developers of the intervention program. Accordingly, such results can be colored by the researchers' desire to find positive results of their hard work. Second, given the costs involved in testing interventions, researchers often employ smaller samples for evaluation tests, leading to questions regarding their generalizability or lack of statistical power. For these reasons, we focus on reviewing only those studies that have garnered "strong" empirical support. We followed two criteria for defining strong support: (a) that any positive results for a program (or program category) have been replicated at least once; (b) that support for a program has come from multiple research groups.

To help address these issues, we let past meta-analyses of the literature guide our review. It is worth noting that these guidelines often paint a different picture than that portrayed in the literature. One prominent example is the frequent assumption in the literature that longer interventions should have more significant effects (Dodge 2008; Kazdin 1987). However, meta-analyses of intervention efficacy have been more equivocal on this topic; some fail to demonstrate a significant effect for study duration (e.g., Garrard and Lipsey 2007; Wilson and Lipsey 2007), while others do find a "dosage" effect (Lipsey and Wilson 1998). Given this discrepancy, and the emphasis that has been placed on study duration in the literature, we first classified interventions according to whether they were short-term or long-term in nature. In one meta-analysis of interventions across multiple domains, the median study duration was twenty-one to thirty weeks (Lipsey and Wilson 1998). Accordingly, we considered interventions with an average duration of up to six months (about twenty-six weeks) to be short term, and any intervention that exceeds this threshold to be long term.

Such an approach also has inherent value for economic analyses of these interventions. Given that only a few of the interventions discussed have yet to receive formal cost-benefit analysis, duration period provides at least some indication of the inherent costs. Long-term interventions have greater costs than short-term ones, and therefore, need to demonstrate larger effects in order to be cost-effective. To this end, we characterize the reviewed literature according to its duration, and whether it has demonstrated consistent support. In table 8.2, we provide an organizing framework for our review, showing how we classified the different intervention programs according to these two factors. It is worth noting that most interventions were short term in nature, as one would expect given the costs of long-term approaches. More often than not, it appears that efficacy is not contingent upon duration. Indeed, several short-term interventions have demonstrated consistently positive effects.

Moreover, in table 8.2, we have included the estimates of benefits associated with some of the interventions we review from a recent comparison of the costs and benefits of different intervention programs (Drake, Aos, and Miller 2009). As noted, only a subset of the reviewed interventions has received cost-benefit review. Indeed, even some of the studies reviewed did not have appropriate benefit *and* cost information, as noted by the asterisks in the table. In addition, programs such as boot camps look somewhat beneficial; however, this program demonstrated no benefits and only reduced costs compared to institutionalization. To preface our remarks following, this work does coincide with the results of the studies and meta-analyses, as many of the programs that we label as "positive" also are cost-effective.

Table 8.2   A framework for reviewing noncognitive interventions

Positive	Negative/inconclusive
Short-term	
School-based	Juvenile awareness programs
After-school programs	"Scared Straight" (–$17,470)
Social skills training	Prison visits
Family interventions	Boot camps ($8,325)
Parent management training	Incarceration
Functional family therapy ($49,776)	Job and vocational training
Multisystemic therapy ($17,694)	
Multidimensional treatment foster care ($88,953)	
Health-based intervention	
Long-term	
Olweus Bullying Program	Positive youth development
Life skills training[a]	Prison-based interventions
Seattle Social Development Program[a]	Social cognitive skills training

[a]Indicates no viable information for either costs or benefits in the Drake, Aos, and Miller (2009) review.

Those programs labeled as "negative" exhibit little to no benefits, and thus have poorer cost-benefit ratios. In sum, the little extant cost-benefit work does correspond to our determination of intervention efficacy, and when available, we report program-specific cost-benefit studies in the following.

Within these four cells, we also limited our review to interventions that attempted to intervene on psychological risk factors other than cognitive ability or environmental factors, such as poverty. In this effort, we tried to be as inclusive as possible, and it became clear that many of the interventions focus on proximal mechanisms that researchers presume they can change. So, for example, researchers may focus on improving "aggressive cognitions," not on "aggression" per se, because the trait of aggression incorporates its cognitive nature as well as the biological, behavioral, and emotional factors involved (see Roberts and Jackson 2008). While this seems a reasonable approach, it creates an interesting mismatch between the risk factors to crime and delinquency and the focus of psychologically-oriented interventions. Most of the risk factors appear to be relatively stable personality factors that are akin to cognitive ability. That is, they are difficult to change. Yet the interventions focus on components of those personality domains that are presumed to be more changeable. It is unclear whether the target of many of the interventions results in change on the psychological risk factors most consistently linked to criminal outcomes. We will return to these ideas in our summary.

8.3   Short-Term Positive Interventions

Short-term promising interventions can be generally classified into four sections. First, a number of programs have addressed antisocial behavior from the classroom, likely because schools provide researchers with easy opportunities to sample several youth in one setting. Second, programs have addressed the social skills of youth, given the strong influence that peers have on youth delinquency. Third, intervening in the family system often demonstrates positive outcomes. Fourth, recently, some more provocative studies have demonstrated that changes in nutrition might have an impact on aggression and delinquency.

8.3.1   School-Based Programs

Given that school-based programs are among the more frequently employed, this area has received more attention in literature reviews and meta-analyses (e.g., Garrard and Lipsey 2007; Gottfredson et al. 2004; Wilson and Lipsey 2007). We therefore focus on the overarching themes presented by these reviews. Before discussing specific study characteristics, a clear emphasis espoused by this literature is the need for rigorous implementation. For example, in one meta-analysis, the average effect size for well-implemented school-based conflict resolution programs was .42, compared to .04 to .08 for programs that experienced some implementation problems (Garrard and Lipsey 2007). Indeed, more than any other variable, it has been suggested that the best predictor of efficacy in school interventions is the school's ability to carry out the intervention (Wilson and Lipsey 2007).

When evaluating more specific characteristics, one of particular interest is the student's age. For interventions within the family system, it has been frequently suggested that early interventions are preferable (e.g., Cummings, Davies, and Campbell 2000; Greenberg, Domitrovich, and Bumbarger 2001), because it is best to address parenting or family issues before they have become too ingrained. Evaluations of school-based interventions, however, have provided more equivocal results. When examining the effects of conflict resolution education on antisocial behavior, older children have been shown to benefit *more* than younger children (Garrard and Lipsey 2007). However, the results are more nuanced when considering interventions for aggressive behavior (Wilson and Lipsey 2007). If these programs are implemented universally (to classrooms as a whole), they tend to work better with younger students. Programs that target at-risk or problem youth, however, show no systematic age differences. While such results are clearly mixed, we point them out to counter the frequently held belief that interventions *must* start in childhood to prove effective. On the contrary, some interventions appear to work better for adolescents.

This claim also receives support from the literature on after-school programs. One review of the literature suggests that participation in these programs was effective in reducing delinquency among older (grades 6 through 8) students but not for younger (grades 4 through 5) students (Gottfredson et al. 2004). The reviewed programs all included academic and social skills development, as well as recreational services. When looking at the mediators of these effects among older students, the results presented two possibilities. First, after-school program participation was positively related to intentions to *not* use drugs. Second, there is some evidence that these programs also promote positive peer associations. Moreover, the intervention effect sizes were greatest for those programs that emphasized social skills and character development. These results suggest that after-school programs might be effective not because they emphasize academic skills or participation in constructive activities, but rather because they decrease youths' intentions to use drugs and promote their social competence.

Promoting positive peer relations is an important theme for conflict resolution programs in the school as well. Interventions that include peer mediation appear to demonstrate stronger effect sizes, although such programs are few in number (Garrard and Lipsey 2007). Broadly speaking, conflict resolution programs are generally quite effective in reducing antisocial behavior among youth. The efficacy of conflict resolution programs is most likely the result of their focus on interpersonal and behavioral skills, which have demonstrated some promise in reducing problem behavior, both in and outside of the school environment.

8.3.2   Social Skills Training

A wealth of research has demonstrated the effects of peer influence on delinquency and risky decision making (e.g., Dishion 2000; Elliott and Menard 1996; Gifford-Smith et al. 2005; Thornberry and Krohn 1997). Indeed, Thornberry and Krohn (1997) suggest that the negative effects of associating with deviant peers are among the most replicated findings in the field. As noted before, documented increases in delinquency following ineffective interventions might result from the fact that these programs congregate deviant adolescents together. It thus is not surprising that Lipsey and Wilson (1998) suggest that treatments that emphasized interpersonal skills are among the most effective both for institutionalized and noninstitutionalized juvenile offenders.

Social skills training (SST) was initially employed for use with psychiatric patients (e.g., Argyle 1969), but was adapted for work with delinquents soon thereafter. Social skills training is intended to help those individuals lacking in even the most basic interaction abilities, such as making "small talk" and maintaining eye contact. Some of the initial work on SST found that it had positive effects on basic social interaction skills (Spence and Marzillier 1979), but that its long-term effects on social problems were more mixed (Spence and Marzillier 1981). One SST program that has demonstrated efficacy is Aggression Replacement Training (ART) (Glick and Goldstein 1987). Over a ten-week period, intervention participants were taught moral education, anger control skills, and other social skills, such as basic social interaction abilities, stress-coping skills, planning skills, and dealing with feelings. These skills were taught through a combination of observation, discussion, and role-playing in which individuals learned more effective behavioral responses to anger. Compared to controls at post-test, intervention participants had fewer behavioral incidents and scored lower on impulsiveness. They also scored better on a number of social skills, including expressing complaints, keeping out of fights, and responding to anger; moreover, there was evidence that intervention participants were also able to transfer these skills to different contexts. A second study with youth who committed serious crimes replicated some but not all of these results. Another social skills program, ASSET, has similarly reported decreases in recidivism among the intervention group, and retention of social skills at eight-month follow-up (Hazel et al. 1981, 1982).

However, there are some conflicting results on social skills interventions. For example, Bailey and Ballard (2006) found few differences between intervention and control groups across a variety of outcomes. In their discussion, they note that the ten-week program might not be long enough to allow for real, consequential skill development. Another possibility is that social skills programs might work best if included as part of a broad approach. For example, Serna, Schumacher, Hazel, and Sheldon (1986) found promising results for a program that taught social skills to both adjudicated youth and their parents.

These results point to two important conclusions. First, while the broad category of "social skills training" has received empirical support from multiple labs, as well as support from meta-analyses, the results of individual social skills programs have been more mixed. Second, it seems that social skills programs might work best when implemented in tandem with other types of interventions. As noted before, school programs with social skills training were among the more efficacious. Moreover, social skills might be taught best within the family. As with most things, social interactions are first taught in the home.

8.3.3   Family Interventions

One common thread in the developmental research on delinquency is the importance placed on the family environment. Several family indicators have been invoked as possible risk factors for delinquency and conduct disorder, such as being raised by a single parent, marital troubles between parents, and parental drug use and depression (e.g., Brandt 2006; Hirschi 1969; Loeber 1990; Loeber and Farrington 2000). The family system often serves as a primary predictor of many developmental and behavioral problems and is integrally tied to the other subsystems discussed here (for a review, see Cummings, Davies, and Campbell 2000). Accordingly, it appears as though family therapy works best when part of a multifaceted approach (Lipsey 1999), which we discuss with respect to broad interventions. However, a few more narrow family counseling programs have demonstrated promise.

One example is parent management training (PMT), which focuses on teaching parents better disciplinary techniques (Kazdin 2005). Typically, such programs ask parents to meet with therapists, and they work together to decide on appropriate punishment programs for their children, and on how to be more responsive to the child's needs. These techniques have received widespread empirical support (e.g., Eyberg, Nelson, and Boggs 2008; Kazdin 2005; Nixon 2002), and work well with children who have conduct or externalizing problems (Brestan and Eyberg 1998; Hautmann et al. 2009). Unlike the research on school-based interventions, parental training programs tend to be most efficacious when implemented with parents who have younger children, as it is best to address parenting issues earlier rather than later.

One program though that has shown consistent efficacy with adolescents is functional family therapy (FFT) (Alexander and Parsons 1982; Sexton and Alexander 2000). Functional family therapy works with the family unit as a whole to promote more positive family interactions and problem-solving. Desired outcomes include more empathetic responding to family members, better discussions of family issues, and general family cohesion. On average, families take part in twelve sessions over the course of three months, mostly occurring within the home. Results have consistently supported FFT as a means for decreasing problem behavior and recidivism (e.g., Alexander and Parsons 1973; Gordon et al. 1988). For example, when looking at misdemeanors and felonies, Gordon, Graves, and Arbuthnot (1995) reported an 8.7 percent recidivism rate for FFT delinquents compared to 40.9 percent for the comparison youth at thirty-two-month follow-up. These studies provide support that FFT is among the best performing short-term programs with respect to its long-term effects on recidivism.

Two additional programs are worth noting that tend to be more comprehensive in nature. Given the intensive nature of these two interventions, researchers have been more interested in their cost-benefit analysis compared to the aforementioned interventions. We note these analyses following, but generally speaking, they do appear to be relatively cost-effective. Accordingly, we count them among the interventions that have "worked."

Multisystemic Therapy

Multisystemic therapy (MST) was initially developed by Henggeler and colleagues (Henggeler and Borduin 1990; Henggeler et al. 1998) in an effort to treat severely antisocial children and adolescents (typically around fourteen to sixteen years old). It is assumed that those youth who enter into MST have multiple issues across multiple domains, which necessitates intensive therapy. Each program is individually tailored to the adolescent, and typically starts with daily sessions that become less frequent over the three- to five-month course of treatment (Burns et al. 2000). Due to this flexibility, this program avoids the issues mentioned earlier with respect to job and vocational training; namely, that programs drafted for the population writ large may fail to address the individual needs of the specific juvenile delinquent.

The MST was conceptualized according to the ideals of Bronfenbrenner's (1979) ecological systems theory. Bronfenbrenner strongly emphasized that a child's development cannot be accurately viewed by examining it within a single domain. Instead, development occurs within several subsystems and the more proximal systems (e.g., family, school, friends) are all interconnected, which also follows from systems theory (Plas 1992). Moreover, these proximal systems are subsumed within the broader context of the child's environment (culture, government, economy). Accordingly, MST treats the delinquent by considering his or her problem within the broader context of these interrelated and hierarchical systems, rather than focusing more narrowly on a single domain. Indeed, Bronfenbrenner's theory can be viewed as the general rationale behind why broad interventions are generally preferable to narrow ones.

The MST programs have received widespread empirical support for their efficacy in reducing behavioral problems. Studies suggest that MST generally leads to fewer rearrests, less drug use, and decreased incarceration and drug use in comparison to usual juvenile justice services (Henggeler et al. 1991; Henggeler, Melton, and Smith 1992). Among first-time offenders, it leads to decreased delinquency and reoffending, and to increased school and family functioning (Sutphen, Thyer, and Kurtz 1995). Moreover, MST effects have been demonstrated more than two years after intervention (Henggeler et al. 1993), and one study reports that MST decreased recidivism by 50 percent in comparison to individual therapy at follow-up over a decade postintervention (Schaeffer and Borduin 2005).

Given the consistent evidence for its efficacy, research has investigated the possible costs involved in widespread implementation of MST. The typical cost per child ranges from $4,000 to $12,000 per child (Brown et al. 1997; Schaeffer and Borduin 2005; Sheidow et al. 2004). While these costs are prohibitive enough to discourage large-sample evaluations of MST, this is relatively cheap in comparison to traditional juvenile justice services (i.e., incarceration). Indeed, MST was the most cost-effective intervention for juvenile offenders among the eleven programs reviewed by the state of Washington (Washington State Institute for Public Policy 1998).

Multidimensional Treatment Foster Care

The MST programs sometimes are implemented as a last resort before having to displace the juvenile offender. However, when the adolescent needs to be removed from his or her home, one of the most effective options is to place them in multidimensional treatment foster care (MTFC) (Chamberlain and Reed 1998; Fisher and Chamberlain 2000). As part of this program, children are taken from their homes and placed in foster care until they reach a set of behavioral benchmarks. After return to their natural family, counseling is provided on a need basis in the following months. Given the intensive nature of this program, some youth can stay in the program for nearly two years. However, Leve and Chamberlain (2005) reported that the average intervention dosage was around six to seven months in their study.

When in foster care, intervention participants are cared for by several personnel both in and out of the foster home. The first line of treatment comes from the foster parents, who provide consistent positive reinforcement when encouraging social, prosocial, and personal skill development. In addition, youth are provided with opportunities for counseling, and a behavior support specialist to help modify their social interaction skills. While the youth is presented with these opportunities in foster care, the child's natural family also receives therapy sessions to indoctrinate a more positive family environment. A case manager or team supervisor oversees all of these activities, which is particularly important given the number of people involved in this type of intervention.

The MTFC interventions have consistently demonstrated promise for reducing delinquency and recidivism. Boys in the intervention committed fewer delinquent actions after one year, and fewer serious offenses at the two-year follow-up than nontreated youth (Chamberlain and Reed 1998; Eddy, Whaley, and Chamberlain 2004), and similar trends have been reported with girls as well (Chamberlain, Leve, and DeGarmo 2007; Leve and Chamberlain 2004; Leve, Chamberlain, and Reid 2005). Mediators of these effects include supervision efficacy, disciplinary practices, and decreased exposure to deviant peers (Eddy and Chamberlain 2000; Leve and Chamberlain 2005). Such results again speak to the importance of consistent intervention implementation, and the negative effects of deviant peer association.

While MTFC interventions are quite intensive in nature, studies do suggest that they are generally cost-effective. When considering the costs of prevented crimes and incarcerations, Aos et al. (1999, 2001) report that MTFC saves taxpayers from $21,836 to $87,622 per youth (reported in Chamberlain, Leve, and DeGarmo 2007). As another mark of its effectiveness, researchers have begun to modify MTFC programs to instruct regular foster care parents as well (Price et al. 2009). Preliminary results suggest that MTFC might be effective not only for reducing problem behavior among youth needing intervention, but also for use with "normal" foster-care children.

8.3.4   Health-Based Interventions

Among the more provocative efforts toward reducing crime have been those that target the participants' nutrition. For centuries, it was assumed that psychological issues resulted from physical or nutritional problems. With the advent of more modern psychological theories, researchers have moved toward new methods for treating mental and behavioral problems. However, in doing so, researchers may have overly discounted the role of physical health on mental health. Indeed, evidence continues to accumulate in favor of the idea that diet can have a profound influence on mood (Kaplan et al. 2007), as well as on antisocial and criminal behavior (Benton 2007).

For example, one line of work has demonstrated that providing participants with essential fatty acids (EFA), often found in fish oil, can decrease levels of aggression (e.g., Gesch et al. 2002; Hamazaki and Hamazaki 2008; Itomura et al. 2005; Buydens-Branchey, Branchey, and Hibbeln 2008). In an initial study, young adult prisoners who were given vitamin supplements (which included, among other things, essential fatty acids) demonstrated significant decreases in violent prison offenses compared to a placebo group (Gesch et al. 2002). Fatty acid supplements have also been shown to decrease both aggression in young girls (Itomura et al., 2005), as well as anger and anxiety in substance users (Buydens-Branchey, Branchey, and Hibbeln 2008). One reason why these effects may occur is because these supplements help participants' serotonergic functioning (Hamazaki and Hamazaki 2008). Serotonin deficiency is related to increased impulsive behavior (Mann 1999), and such deficiencies have been linked to decreased intake of fatty acids. Therefore, providing individuals with needed fatty acids might help those with underdeveloped serotonergic systems, who otherwise would be predisposed to aggressive behavior.

Similarly, work has suggested that correcting chemical imbalances and vitamin deficiencies can reduce antisocial behavior. In a study of patients diagnosed with a behavioral disorder, researchers found that a majority had clear chemical imbalances (Walsh, Glab, and Haakenson 2004). The researchers then provided participants with supplements designed specifically for each individual. Participants showed significant decreases in assaultive and destructive behaviors after four to eight months of treatment. It is worth noting that, given the idiographic nature of the intervention, the authors did not employ a placebo group. However, these results are promising for future efforts to decrease behavioral disorders through biochemical interventions.

Before concluding this section, it is interesting to note how these studies might relate to cognitive interventions. One longitudinal study found that malnutrition at age three predicted behavioral problems at ages eight, eleven, and seventeen (Liu et al. 2004). This link was mediated at ages eight and eleven by participants' cognitive ability, but this was not true for the results at age seventeen. Clearly these results point to the long-term importance of nutrition on externalizing behavior. Moreover, they suggest that it might prove as efficacious to provide early interventions for nutrition, as it is to provide early cognitive interventions. If nutrition influences cognitive ability, which in turn decreases problem behaviors, it seems that one can better address the problem by intervening at the "root." This speculation is supported further by the fact that the mediational tests were not significant at age seventeen, suggesting that the long-term effects of malnutrition on externalizing cannot be fully explained by cognitive ability.

8.3.5   Summary

In summary, four areas provide promise for addressing issues of antisocial behavior using relatively short-term interventions: school, social skills, family, and nutrition. Of the four, the area most in need of future work appears to be social skills interventions; the category as a whole appears effective, but there is greater uncertainty at the individual program level. While all benefit economically from being short in duration, it does appear that some clearly cost more than others. For example, providing necessary nutrients involves little to no labor (other than possibly the initial diagnosis stage) and few institutional resources. On the contrary, intensive therapy programs such as MTFC will cost much more per participant. However, one might also expect such programs to demonstrate larger effects. Future research is certainly needed to provide cost-benefit comparisons between these short-term interventions, especially given their disparate nature.

8.4   Short-Term Interventions with Negative and Inconclusive Effects

As noted before, most intervention programs tend to be short-term in nature, given the lesser costs involved in their implementation. Not surprisingly then, there are nearly as many ineffective short-term programs as there are effective ones. Unfortunately, in some cases, these ineffective programs have received as much or more media acclaim as the effective ones. This likely has been one reason behind their perseverance in the face of their disappointing results. Most of these programs can be characterized as being "tough" on delinquency, which can often lead to results opposite of those intended.

8.4.1   Juvenile Awareness Programs, Boot Camps, and Incarceration

Possibly the most publicized interventions are those that either incarcerate youth or attempt to rehabilitate them by scaring them with that possibility. The documentary "Scared Straight!" (Shapiro 1978) and its subsequent sequels brought widespread attention to efforts toward this latter goal. Accordingly, most people would be surprised to learn that these programs have received almost no empirical support, and that some of these programs may even promote increased delinquency (e.g., Finckenauer 1982; Finckenauer and Gavin 1999; Petrosino, Turpin-Petrosino, and Buehler 2003).

Petrosino, Turpin-Petrosino, and Buehler (2003) reviewed the literature on juvenile awareness programs, a category that broadly includes all programs for which juvenile delinquents are confronted with the prison environment (either through prison visits or interactions with prisoners). They chose only those studies that randomly assigned delinquents into no-treatment control or intervention (awareness) groups. In a meta-analysis of recidivism rates, the authors found that delinquents placed in the intervention programs were actually *more* likely to recidivate than those in the control groups. Indeed, none of the reviewed programs demonstrated a decrease for the intervention group. Lipsey (1992) reported similar results in his meta-analysis of these programs, suggesting that intervention participants were on average 7 percent more likely to recidivate than controls. Moreover, it appears to be even less effective to actually imprison delinquents than to simply scare them with the possibility. Multiple studies have reported recidivism rates for adjudicated youth at or above 50 percent (e.g., Beck and Shipley 1987; Snyder and Sickmund 2006).

A fellow traveler to these programs is the "boot camp" intervention. The boot camp approach places delinquents in a militaristic lifestyle, assuming that increased discipline and structure should promote self-control and decrease future recidivism (e.g., Empey, Stafford, and Hay 1999; Gottfredson and Hirschi 1990). Similar to juvenile awareness programs, the primary assumption underlying the boot camp approach is that it will scare first-time delinquents out of pursuing lifelong criminal activity (MacKenzie and Parent 1991). However, these programs also have proven largely ineffective in reducing recidivism (e.g., Burns and Vito 1995; Jones 1996; MacKenzie 1991; MacKenzie and Shaw 1993). Some studies even suggest that these programs may even have detrimental effects (Jones and Ross 1997; Morash and Rucker 1990).

Another widely publicized program that has received little to no support is DARE (Drug Abuse Resistance Education). The DARE programs attempt to decrease drug use largely through informing students of its prevalence and inherent risks. However, ever since DARE programs were introduced in 1983, most evaluations of their efficacy suggest that they either have no effect or in fact increase drug use (Lynam et al. 1999; MacKillop et al. 2003; Werch and Owen 2002). Indeed, Lilienfeld (2007) recently provided DARE as an example of a program that "does harm" to its participants.

Why do these programs perform so poorly? And furthermore, why do programs with so little empirical support continue to receive government funding? With respect to the first question, one issue is that delinquents are subject to a variety of iatrogenic effects (Rhule 2005). Once one has been labeled as an adjudicated youth, this can lead to differential treatment by those in the youth's social environment (Caprara 1993; Dweck and Leggett 1988). People in the community are likely to treat the adjudicated youth as less competent and trustworthy, which significantly complicates the readjustment process postintervention. Indeed, others in the community are more likely to make negative attributions of the delinquent's actions (Dodge 1980), and in turn may be more prone to aggression toward the child (Dodge and Frame 1982). Finally, by congregating antisocial youth together in intervention groups, they might adopt more negative social norms because they now view antisocial activities as more ubiquitous and socially acceptable (e.g., Morash and Rucker 1990; Stormshak et al. 1999). Youth in this situation also might increase antisocial behavior in an effort to "prove" to peers that the youth was not deterred or scared by the program.

With respect to the second question, a few reasons have been suggested regarding why these programs persist despite a lack of empirical support (Finckenauer 2005). One follows from the field's general focus on cognitive ability factors. If one believes that delinquent activities result from deliberative decision making, it seems logical that adolescents would engage in fewer risky actions if the negative consequences of these actions were made more salient. Another issue involves what is meant by program "efficacy." As demonstrated by the public interest in the "Scared Straight" documentaries, it is easy to get people to believe in a program by reporting on individual success stories. Compelling anecdotes lead people to believe that programs are making a difference if they can help "just one person." Finally, these programs, especially boot camps, have inherent appeal for those who believe that we need to "get tough" on delinquents. People who believe in a strict morality are likely to approve of these seemingly harsher penalties (Lakoff 2002), regardless of their lack of empirical support. This claim also provides rationale for why school suspensions and expulsions continue despite the fact that they often fail to reduce school violence (Skiba 2002).

8.4.2   Job and Vocational Training

Counter to these approaches that take a hard line on delinquency, some programs seek to reduce delinquency by motivating youth toward more adaptive life commitments. Research frequently suggests that having adolescents commit to age-appropriate roles can decrease their likelihood for delinquency (Hirschi 1969; Laub and Sampson 2003; Sampson and Laub 1993). However, adolescents who prematurely adopt adult roles might actually be more likely to commit delinquent acts (Hirschi 1969). One example of an adolescent-appropriate role commitment is their entry into the workplace. Accordingly, research frequently has examined whether job training and vocational programs might help reduce delinquency.

Generally, the results of such programs are equivocal at best. In a meta-analysis of studies with juvenile offenders, job skills programs were found to have limited effects on recidivism (Lipsey 2009). Another meta-analysis suggests that vocational education programs may even increase recidivism rates (Lipsey and Wilson 1998; see also Bloom et al. 1994). Two points temper any strong negative conclusions. First, employment-related programs appear more efficacious for noninstitutionalized than for institutionalized offenders (Lipsey and Wilson 1998). Second, there is great variability in this area with respect to program goals and methodological rigor, which can influence their reported effectiveness (Bouffard, MacKenzie, and Hickman 2000). Given these points, it is difficult to make any broad conclusions regarding job-training programs other than that they work for some delinquents some of the time.

8.4.3   Summation

The current section makes two important points. First, some short-term interventions work. It is clearly not the case that small investments must necessarily result in small rewards. Changing nutrition or working with families are interventions that can be done in an expedient manner, and they appear to have lasting effects on criminal behavior. Second, not all short-term interventions work; while duration is important in determining cost, it is less important for efficacy than the content of the intervention and how well it is implemented. Before drawing firm conclusions we examine the longer interventions. Afterwards, we will discuss common features of effective interventions regardless of duration.

8.5   Long-Term Positive Interventions

We now discuss interventions that take longer than six months on average. It clearly requires more resources in general to implement these interventions, but more time is also required before strong conclusions can be drawn regarding their long-term benefits. Accordingly, less empirical support is available for these programs, and it is rare to find any that have been replicated by researchers outside of the lab that first created them.

Moreover, given the relative lack of evaluations of long-term interventions, long-term interventions also are underrepresented in meta-analyses. We therefore sought other sources for direction in selecting studies to review, and decided to follow the suggestions of the "Blueprints for Violence Prevention" program at the University of Colorado (Center for the Study and Prevention of Violence 2009). The Blueprints program has evaluated hundreds of interventions and has nominated a few programs as being either "models" or "promising" for decreasing violent and antisocial behavior. In the following, we review three of these programs as our examples of long-term positive interventions. It is worth noting that some of the short-term interventions mentioned earlier were also nominated, including multisystemic therapy, multidimensional treatment foster care, and the Perry Preschool Project.

8.5.1   Olweus Bullying Program

We begin this section with one of the most consistent and well-received intervention programs to reduce aggressive behavior. The Olweus Bullying Program (Olweus 1993, 1994, 1995) seeks to reduce bullying in schools using a multifaceted approach with training for students, teachers, and parents. The Olweus Program seeks to address the problem of bullying by first dissuading some myths on the topic. For example, bullying does not occur because of larger class sizes, failure in school, or differences in students' appearances. Instead, bullies are marked by their generally aggressive and antisocial dispositions, an important point given its implications for interventions.

At the school level, teachers receive training to better diagnose and monitor bullying behavior. They also are taught how to engender better social skills among their students. In class, students engage in role-playing scenarios and cooperative groups to practice better social interactions. When bullying does occur, either in the classroom or on the playground, teachers have serious discussions with both the bully and victim. It is of the utmost importance that teachers do not allow even minor cases of bullying behavior to persist in the classroom. Moreover, teachers report these problems to the parents of the students, who also play an important role in discouraging bullying behavior.

At the family level, parents also receive training on how to discern the signs of aggression and bullying at home. They are expected to maintain consistent rules and disciplinary practices to deter their children from aggressive behavior. Parents are taught to identify even seemingly minor signs of bullying and aggression, such as damaged schoolbooks and cuts or bruises. These small signs can be indicative of victimization, and should be reported to teachers and staff during parent-school meetings. In addition, parents should keep a close eye on their child's friends and social activities, which will help teachers get a better idea of which students are involved.

Olweus (1991, 1995) reviewed the evidence on program effectiveness in a large sample of students from grades four to seven, following these students over a span of 2.5 years. Bullying decreased by at least 50 percent, and general antisocial behavior was markedly reduced. More broadly, the program had positive effects on the general school environment. Teachers reported more positive peer interactions, and better attitudes toward schoolwork. Although other reviews have demonstrated somewhat smaller effect sizes, the program has consistently demonstrated reductions in bullying behavior over the past two decades (Limber 2006; Olweus 2005). Moreover, these effects tend to get stronger with time (Olweus 2005), demonstrating significant dosage effects. While future work is needed to better investigate possible moderators and mediators of these effects (Limber 2006), this program remains one of the most effective for reducing aggressive and antisocial behavior in the literature.

8.5.2   Life Skills Training

Life skills training programs (LST) (Botvin, Eng, and Williams 1980; Botvin and Griffin 2004) seek to discourage drug use among early adolescents. Intervention sessions involve teaching adolescents self-management skills (goal-setting, problem-solving), social skills (ability to interact with others), and drug-related information (consequences and skills to reduce peer drug influences). Often these sessions occur in the school with teacher assistance, because schools provide a ready opportunity to sample several adolescents at the same time. With respect to its goals and methods, LST clearly mirrors some of the social skills programs mentioned earlier. However, LST includes "booster" sessions on these topics for an additional two years' time.

The LST programs have consistently demonstrated efficacy in reducing drug use in both small-scale and large-scale study implementations (for a review, see Botvin and Griffin 2004). For example, Botvin et al. (2001) report that intervention participants were less than half as likely to report binge drinking than control adolescents at both one- and two-year follow-ups, demonstrating the long-term effects of LST programs. Using the wealth of data on these programs, researchers have been able to identify a number of mediating variables that might partially account for the evidenced decreases in drug use (Botvin and Griffin 2004). Some possible mediators include participants' attitudes toward drugs, their perceived norms of drug use, assertiveness, decision making, and refusal skills. It is worth noting that several of these are similar to those mentioned before, with respect to the short-term interventions.

8.5.3   Seattle Social Development Project

The Seattle Social Development Project (SSDP) is a school-based approach that extends into the family environment (Hawkins et al. 1992; Hawkins et al. 2007). The program posits that children can follow either a prosocial path, which serves as a protective buffer, or an antisocial path, which serves to promote delinquent and problem behaviors. The overarching goal of the program is to motivate youth toward the prosocial path, and away from the influence of deviant and delinquent peers.

The first stage of implementation occurs at the teacher level. Teachers are trained to implement more prosocial and cooperative activities in their classrooms. Emphasis is placed on providing students with opportunities to learn in small groups, and implementing consistent disciplinary and reward practices. Methods are specifically tailored to provide age-appropriate instruction for students from first to sixth grade. After appropriate training, teachers are told to integrate these practices into their daily curriculum, providing students with consistent doses of the intervention. Students then progress through the school years, receiving the preventive intervention for as many years as their school system allows. This allows for the long-term development of communication, social, and decision-making skills.

The second stage of intervention involves parent-training sessions. Again, these sessions are tailored to provide parents with information specific to their child's current stage of development. Early on, parents are taught appropriate disciplinary techniques, including child-monitoring skills. Later they learn methods for discouraging their child's drug use. Each year, parents are provided with the opportunity to take part in these training sessions, which are not particularly time consuming (only four to seven sessions per year).

The SSDP has demonstrated efficacy in addressing its primary program goals. Receiving two years of the intervention reduced aggressive and antisocial behavior among Caucasian boys compared to the control group (Hawkins, Von Cleve, and Catalano 1991). After receiving four years of treatment, intervention participants scored better on a number of family and school outcomes, including family management and communication, and school commitment and attachment (Hawkins et al. 1992). In addition, intervention students reported less initiation of delinquent and alcohol-related behaviors. Finally, studies have assessed whether these effects are lasting by sampling intervention participants at age 21 (Hawkins et al. 2005; Lonczak et al. 2002). Overall, full intervention participants performed better on several measures of general life outcomes (high school graduation, current employment), mental health, crime, and sexual behavior (see Hawkins et al. [2007] for a review). Therefore, it appears that the intervention continued to lead to positive outcomes even into emerging adulthood. However, since the long-term effects of this intervention are sometimes small and nonsignificant (see e.g., Hawkins et al. 1999), further research is needed to investigate possible mediators and moderators of intervention efficacy.

8.6   Long-Term Negative and Inconclusive Interventions

Obviously a number of projects could be reviewed in our final category, since most long-term interventions can be considered as having "inconclusive" support. We therefore chose to mention a couple in hopes of sparking interest for future work. It is worth emphasizing that we are not saying these are *negative* programs, but rather that "the jury is still out" regarding their effectiveness.

8.6.1   Positive Youth Development

Positive youth development (PYD) programs counter the traditional approach of identifying "negatives" and addressing them. Instead, PYD programs posit that youth possess the potential for "good," which should be nurtured by the community (Benson 2003; Lerner 2004; Lerner et al. 2005). The PYD programs focus on promoting social competence and connectedness, resilience, and the adoption of prosocial standards. To achieve these ends, PYD programs often work with youth throughout their development in multiple areas (family, school, and community). This movement is relatively recent, and thus these programs have had relatively fewer empirical tests. However, recent work does support the claim that PYD programs can decrease youth's propensity to take part in delinquent activities.

Lerner and colleagues (Jelicic et al. 2007; Lerner et al. 2005) have investigated PYD using a longitudinal investigation of 4-H programs, which provide youth with opportunities to learn about science and farming using cooperative group activities (4-H 2009). Youth are able to participate in these programs from early childhood into adolescence. Jelicic et al. (2007) assessed 4-H participants as fifth and sixth graders on indicators of the five primary PYD goals (caring, character, connection, competence, and confidence), as well as adaptive and maladaptive outcomes. They demonstrate that youth higher on the PYD goals at fifth grade were less likely to take part in risk behaviors at sixth grade (delinquency and substance use). It thus appears that promoting PYD can decrease crime behaviors among youth.

While researchers are increasingly looking into PYD approaches (see Catalano et al. [2002] for a review), the 4-H study and the SSDP are two of the few PYD programs that have systematically assessed their efficacy in reducing problem behaviors. Given that the PYD movement has emphasized its distinction from past risk-prevention approaches, it is unsurprising that most programs tend to focus on the positive (Schwartz et al. 2007). However, most of the PYD goals clearly resemble those mentioned before as detractors to crime and delinquency, such as social competence and cooperation. One, therefore, would predict that PYD approaches should similarly prove efficacious in reducing problem behaviors. To this end, Schwartz et al. (2007) suggest that future research on interventions need to integrate ideas from risk-protection and PYD approaches to provide the most thorough solutions to the problems of youth.

8.6.2   Prison-Based Interventions

A second set of interventions with inconclusive results focuses on rehabilitation programs within prison populations. While these intervention programs sometimes last less than six months, we classified these as long-term given that the length of imprisonment itself probably should be included when considering whether they decrease recidivism postrelease. A recent meta-analysis suggests that prison interventions can be effective in reducing prison misconduct (French and Gendreau 2006). Moreover, the interventions that proved effective in reducing misconduct also were shown to decrease levels of recidivism after release. Therefore, although imprisonment itself might be a poor deterrent, as noted earlier, there are ways to help decrease recidivism even within the prison environment.

In the meta-analysis, behavioral programs appeared to be most effective for reducing problem behavior (French and Gendreau 2006). It is worth noting that this category was rather inclusive in nature, containing approaches using behavioral, cognitive-behavioral, and social learning techniques. This was contrasted against "nonbehavioral" programs that included everything from group interventions to nutrition programs. Clearly, there is great heterogeneity in the types of interventions employed in prisons. Moreover, the meta-analysis indicated large levels of heterogeneity in the results of these programs, with some fairly strong outliers. This is one reason why we chose to consider the evidence on prison interventions as inconclusive, despite the positive effects on average for both behavioral and nonbehavioral programs. Another reason to classify this initial evidence as inconclusive is that several elements of the prison system impede the ability for rigorous evaluation of these programs. For one, levels of overcrowding differ dramatically across prisons, which can have profound effects on implementation efficacy. Therefore, interventions might work for some prisons and for some prisoners that fail to show effects in other contexts. Future research thus needs to conduct more thorough on-site evaluations, and focus on rigorous program implementation (French and Gendreau 2006).

8.6.3   Social Cognitive Skills Training

We end our review of long-term negative and inconclusive interventions by examining recent work on programs to develop interpersonal skills from a social cognitive framework. Deviant youth have been shown to interpret social situations differently from "normal" youth. Aggressive youth are more likely to attribute others' actions as signs of hostility (e.g., Dodge et al. 1990; MacBrayer, Milich, and Hundley 2003; Slaby and Guerra 1988). Moreover, hostile and aggressive individuals appear to attend more to aggressive cues and actions than nonaggressive individuals (Dodge et al. 1997; Zelli, Huesmann, and Cervone 1995). To address these issues, social cognitive interventions target the youth's social information processing skills on several levels. These interventions intend to lead youth toward (a) better attention to and interpretation of social cues, (b) more adaptive action goals and scripts, and (c) better activation and retrieval of these scripts, which in turn promotes more adaptive responses to social situations (see e.g., Crick and Dodge 1994; Huesmann 1998). These efforts often take place over multiple years, and incorporate teachers, counselors, and parents in the intervention process.

Evidence for these programs, however, can be viewed as, at best, equivocal. They can be successful in targeting their proximal outcomes, such as social cognitive skills (for a meta-analysis, see Beelmann, Pfingsten, and Lösel [1994]). There is much less support for the long-term nature of these effects, or that these interventions in fact decrease problem behaviors. One study reported moderate, but significant, decreases in conduct problems between the intervention and control groups (Conduct Problems Prevention Research Group 2002). However, not all indicators of conduct behaviors showed significant differences, and even some indicators of social cognitive skills failed to reach significance. More recent work paints an even less promising picture. A multisite study evaluation was recently conducted for the GREAT program (Guiding Responsibility and Expectations in Adolescents Today and Tomorrow) (Meyer et al. 2004; Orpinas, Horne, and Multisite Violence Prevention Program 2004; Smith et al. 2004), which demonstrated that social cognitive interventions might instead have detrimental effects (Multisite Violence Prevention Project 2009). Indeed, youth who received the universal intervention (participants were not selected based on risk) demonstrated significant *increases* in aggression and the endorsement of norms supporting aggression.

Generally, two points are worth noting with respect to social cognitive skills interventions. First, these interventions appear more effective for high-risk children, and thus should not be universally applied. While the program had negative effects when applied universally, the effectiveness of the GREAT program was moderated by the child's level of risk (Multisite Violence Prevention Project 2008, 2009). Children appeared to benefit more (or in some cases, be less negatively affected) when they were classified as having multiple risk factors. However, even in these studies, often only those participants reporting with at least half of the examined risk factors actually demonstrated positive effects. Second, such programs appear to be cost-effective only for the highest-risk group (Foster and Jones 2007), given that the cost per child can exceed $50,000 and, more importantly, that they only seem to decrease criminal activity for the highest-risk youth. Perhaps the most optimistic appraisal of these interventions is that they are burdened by the idiosyncrasy and nuance of their effects. These programs only appear to help a select group of youth, and at a particularly prohibitive cost. Indeed, this idiosyncrasy is underscored by research in Scotland that found much more variation between different schools within a treatment category than between schools from different treatment categories (Sharp and Davids 2003).

8.7   Summary and Conclusion

In this review, we examined the initial work on interventions for antisocial behavior that addressed the problem by focusing on factors other than cognitive ability. As is evident throughout, a number of these programs show promise in their ability to reduce delinquent actions. A few common themes across this review are worth noting. First, with respect to intervention duration, the conclusions are more ambiguous than portrayed in the literature. It does appear that single-dose interventions are unlikely to demonstrate strong results. However, short-term interventions can demonstrate significant effects, and often there is more evidence in favor of their efficacy than currently available for long-term programs. Therefore, conclusions about duration are tempered by what one means by "short" and "long." Our review does contradict a strict interpretation of duration benefits, insofar that longer is not always better. We would hasten to add that extremely short-term approaches seem ineffective. Possibly the best message to take home regarding duration is that it is not as clear a predictor of efficacy as it has been portrayed at times in the literature.

Second, in order to reduce delinquency, interventions in any domain could emphasize rigorous and consistent implementation. For example, with respect to school-based programs, reducing delinquency requires teachers and parents to set forth clear directions and rules for youth, and those who break these rules must be disciplined in a consistent fashion. Several programs reviewed sought to train teachers and parents to better identify and respond to youth problems. Therefore, it appears that one mark of an effective intervention is whether it is rigorously implemented. Indeed, meta-analyses show that implementation integrity is a significant predictor of program efficacy (Lipsey and Wilson 1998), and even suggest that the best advice for schools is to choose the program that they have the most faith that they can implement (Wilson and Lipsey 2007).

Third, to maximize the chance of promoting cognitive development, interventions could incorporate the family environment in some capacity. This is evident both with respect to the short-term effective programs (e.g., functional family therapy and parent management training), and the long-term ones (e.g., the Olweus program and the SSDP). The family system is the most proximal to the youth (Bronfenbrenner 1979), and thus it is unsurprising that programs are most effective when they target the family. Family-based programs also tend to be among those deemed most effective in meta-analyses (Lipsey 2009; Lipsey and Wilson 1998).

Fourth, as made evident by programs emphasizing social skills, interventions that are most likely to result in reduced criminal activity would motivate youth to develop more effective strategies for dealing with social situations. Youth offenders often are less adept at interpreting social situations (Dodge et al. 2003; Gouze 1987), which can serve as a catalyst for deviant activities. Social skills training thus can help youth not only by teaching them appropriate social schemata for future use, but also by providing youth the opportunity to practice these skills. Through practice, such skills can become routinized and readily accessible to the youth for use in future interactions. Given the lack of efficacy for social cognitive interventions, this points to a potential significant insight. Learning interpersonal rituals that are routinized and thus no longer "cognitive" is a very effective means of reducing delinquent behavior. Thus, cultural rituals for "proper" or polite interpersonal behavior, which is often the focus of life skills or interpersonal training, may provide simple, but effective ways of decreasing delinquency.

We again note the correspondence between the cost-benefit comparisons provided by Drake, Aos, and Miller (2009) and our review. It is worth further to note that they found little relation between the percent change in crime outcomes and the cost of the program. For example, in their review, functional family therapy (FFT) demonstrated the greatest reduction in crime outcomes, yet was only around the median of reviewed interventions with respect to costs. To compare its effects to a therapy program the reader may better know, cognitive-behavioral treatment (CBT), this reduction was over six times greater than that evidenced by CBT, which focuses instead on correcting aberrant emotions and behaviors by attempting to retrain the way individuals think and their behavior in specific situations. On the other hand, programs like boot camps and "Scared Straight" can be implemented with little to no cost, yet fail to have any beneficial effect on crime. Moreover, this cost-benefit comparison accounted for the methodological rigor of the studies, by both attenuating effect sizes for studies with less than ideal designs (i.e., not having a true control group and randomized design) and eliminating all studies that failed to meet a set methodological rigor. Therefore, even though we sought to provide a broader review of the intervention literature, one comes to the same conclusions even when assessing interventions using cost-benefit analyses based on only rigorous program evaluations.

The gestalt one takes from the effective interventions is that they either affect physiological systems or entail a high degree of immersion, which we would differentiate from dose or length of intervention. By immersion, we mean that a significant portion of the juvenile's social structures are all dedicated to changing or limiting the behavior of the juvenile. So, for example, family appears to be an effective vector for intervention, presumably because family constitutes one of the most important, multifaceted structures in the lives of children and juveniles. Similarly, interventions like the Olweus Bullying program act on all of the major social structures that children face, such as school, peers, and family, and are highly effective. In turn, physiological interventions, though apparently nonimmersive, may mimic some of the effects of pervasive social control on psychological outcomes. One possibility is that the serotonergic system is at the root of the psychological systems responsible for the variety of behaviors associated with delinquency and criminality.

Moreover, this gestalt coincides with theories of developmental psychopathology, which attempt to describe the developmental trajectories of psychological and skill deficits starting early in youth (Cummings, Davies, and Campbell 2000). In line with our review, these developmental pathways are complex and incorporate factors across different domains (family, social, environmental, biological). Moreover, an individual is never destined for adaptive or maladaptive development (Sroufe 1997), suggesting that interventions can be successful even for children at the highest risk. Indeed, "resilience" can be conceptualized similarly to recent views on personality traits (e.g., Roberts 2009), insofar that while resilience demonstrates continuity over time, it is not static and unchanging (Luthar 1991, 1995; Luthar, Doernberger, and Zigler 1993). This view of development thus argues against focusing on any single predictor (e.g., cognitive ability), and provides rationale why immersive programs may best benefit youth as they address a wider range of social and environmental factors that put youth at risk for criminal activity.

Interestingly, pervasive and consistent social environments have been hypothesized to be the most likely types of environments to affect change in personality traits (Roberts and Jackson 2008). Ironically, despite the fact that personality traits are clear risk factors for criminal activities, the interventions we reviewed seldom assessed changes in personality, presumably because researchers often make the mistake that they are unchangeable (Roberts and Caspi 2001). That being said, many of the interventions detailed earlier may be working exactly because they are facilitating fundamental changes in the personalities of the children and adolescents who are participating in the interventions. Changing personality traits, as opposed to more "changeable" constructs, such as very specific thoughts and behaviors, may be a more effective intervention because of the simple fact that people take their personalities with them across situations.

For example, several of the desired intervention outcomes can be readily designated as facets of conscientiousness (Roberts et al. 2004). Conscientiousness is a family of traits marked by subfacets such as industriousness, impulse control, deciveness, orderliness, responsibility, and conventionality;

the latter focusing on following rules and norms. Any decrease in crime and delinquency implicitly suggests that the delinquent is demonstrating better adherence to the rules of conventions of society, as well as improved impulse control. Even having to adhere to intervention guidelines should motivate one to be more reliable and punctual, and to follow the order and conventions of the specific intervention. Second, several programs emphasized problem-solving and decision-making skills, often in social or family contexts, which are direct initiatives to promote decisiveness. Third, to the extent that job training or educational initiatives work, these types of programs appear to be directly designed to promote industriousness. Accordingly, developing interventions for conscientiousness should serve as a primary goal for future research.

It is also worth noting that some programs might also serve to promote greater agreeableness. Agreeable individuals are marked by their cooperation and trustfulness (e.g., McCrae and Costa 1992). It thus is unsurprising that several of the most effective programs were those that taught youth better social and life skills. In addition, the more effective school-based programs were those able to motivate agreeableness at the school level (e.g., general school ethos and affection). Moreover, it is clear that the family context would be a primary target for interventions to increase agreeableness, because temperament quality and emotional stability early in childhood might serve as antecedents for the display of agreeableness later in life (e.g., Graziano and Eisenberg 1997). It even appears that the recent PYD movement posits the promotion of agreeable behavior as a primary objective. Indeed, three of the five indicators of PYD (Lerner et al. 2005)—character, connection, and caring/compassion—would be similarly indicative of an agreeable individual. Since agreeableness counterindicates delinquency (Miller et al. 2003), we believe that PYD programs have promise for decreasing rates of crime and delinquency among youth, even though they currently have relatively less empirical support.

Of course, there are very little direct data to support the idea that these interventions are affecting change in personality. In fact, despite focusing so strongly on bullies, even the Olweus Bullying program has failed to track whether the personality of bullies changes over time as a result of intervention. However, there are some indirect data to support this inference. First, personality traits do change and often change at ages typically not entertained, such as middle age (Roberts, Walton and Viechtbauer 2006). Moreover, the changes in personality traits found in young adulthood and middle age are often correlated with social environmental factors associated with overcoming criminal activities, such as stable marriages (Robins, Caspi, and Moffitt 2002; Roberts and Bogg 2004), and successful occupational experiences (Roberts, Caspi, and Moffitt 2003). These associations are surprisingly similar to the theories of social control that propose that experiences in work and marriage can lead to a desistance from a life of crime (Sampson and Laub 1990). Finally, there is a nascent literature on the changeability of personality through direct therapeutic intervention. Several studies have shown that personality traits change when individuals successfully complete some form of therapy for disorders such as depression (Piedmont and Ciarrocchi 1999; De Fruyt et al. 2006). More recently it was shown that a mindfulness intervention for doctors also resulted in personality trait change, especially in the domains of conscientiousness and neuroticism (Krasner et al. 2009). Finally, coming full circle with the nutrition interventions that appear to be affecting serotonergic functioning, a recent study showed that taking serotonin reuptake inhibitors resulted in personality trait change and that the reductions seen in depression were largely a result of this change (Tang et al. 2009).

We therefore suggest that several of the programs reviewed here might demonstrate positive effects by virtue of their ability to change personality traits. To this end, one clear direction for research is to design and implement interventions for promoting more adaptive personality traits, such as conscientiousness, agreeableness, social self-confidence, and emotional stability. We nominate these personality dimensions because they have been previously designated as indicators of greater maturity (Hogan and Roberts 2004), a construct seemingly antagonistic to delinquent and unlawful action.

8.7.1   Conclusion

We wish to end on the positives rather than the negatives. Throughout this review, it is clear that youth are not condemned to a life of crime. Instead this work demonstrates the multifinality inherent in this population. Accordingly, one must not characterize these youth as "hopeless," which in turn leads one to avoid intervening. Moreover, in our review, we hope to have debunked two myths regarding how to intervene. First, researchers need not be overwhelmed by the perceived demands of implementing intervention programs. Our review demonstrates that relatively short-term and easy-to-implement programs can demonstrate significant effects (e.g., health-based interventions). Second, noncognitive interventions can have as strong, if not stronger, effects than programs targeting IQ or the environment. Several factors influence the development of delinquency, and accordingly, a single-minded focus on intelligence seems misguided. While Descartes famously decreed, "I think, therefore I am," intervention researchers should take note that we are more than what we think.

References

Alexander, James F., and Bruce V. Parsons. 1973. "Short-term Behavioral Intervention with Delinquent Families: Impact on Family Process and Recidivism." *Journal of Abnormal Psychology* 81 (3): 219–25.

———. 1982. *Functional Family Therapy: Principles and Procedures.* Pacific Grove, CA: Brooks/Cole.

Aos, S., P. Phipps, R. Barnoski, and R. Leib. 1999. *The Comparative Costs and Benefits of Programs to Reduce Crime: A Review of National Research Findings with Implications for Washington State.* Olympia, WA: Washington State Institute for Public Policy.

———. 2001. *The Comparative Costs and Benefits of Programs to Reduce Crime.* Document no. 01-05-1201. Olympia, WA: Washington State Institute for Public Policy.

Argyle, Michael. 1969. *Social Interaction.* London: Methuen.

Bailey, K. A., and J. D. Ballard. 2006. "Social Skills Training: Effects on Behavior and Recidivism with First-Time Adjudicated Youth." *Applied Psychology in Criminal Justice* 2 (1): 26–42.

Beck, A. J., and B. E. Shipley. 1987. "Recidivism of Young Parolees." Special Report. Washington, DC: United States Bureau of Justice Statistics. May.

Beelmann, Andreas, Ulrich Pfingsten, and Friedrich Lösel. 1994. "Effects of Training Social Competence in Children: A Meta-Analysis of Recent Evaluation Studies." *Journal of Clinical Child Psychology* 23 (3): 260–71.

Benson, Peter L. 2003. "Developmental Assets and Asset-Building Community: Conceptual and Empirical Foundations." In *Developmental Assets and Asset-building Communities: Implications for Research, Policy, and Practice,* edited by Richard M. Lerner and Peter L. Benson, 19–43. New York: Kluwer Academic/Plenum Publishers.

Benton, David. 2007. "The Impact of Diet on Anti-Social, Violent, and Criminal Behaviour." *Neuroscience and Biobehavioral Review* 31 (5): 752–74.

Binder, A. 1987. "An Historical and Theoretical Introduction." In *Handbook of Juvenile Delinquency,* edited by Herbert C. Quay, 1–32. New York: John Wiley & Sons.

Bloom, H., L. L. Orr, G. Cave, S. H. Bell, F. Doolittle, and W. Lin. 1994. *The National JTPA Study: Overview of Impacts, Benefits, and Costs of title IIA.* Cambridge, MA: Abt Associates.

Blos, Peter. 1962. *On Adolescence: A Psychoanalytic Interpretation.* New York: Free Press.

Borghans, Lex, Angela Lee Duckworth, James J. Heckman, and Bas ter Weel. 2008. "The Economics and Psychology of Personality Traits." *Journal of Human Resources* 43 (4): 972–1059.

Botvin, Gilbert J., Anna Eng, and Christine L. Williams. 1980. "Preventing the Onset of Cigarette Smoking through Life Skills Training." *Preventive Medicine* 9 (1): 135–43.

Botvin, Gilbert J., and Kenneth W. Griffin. 2004. "Life Skills Training: Empirical Findings and Future Directions." *The Journal of Primary Prevention* 25 (2): 211–32.

Botvin, Gilbert J., Kenneth W. Griffin, Tracy Diaz, and Michelle Ifill-Williams. 2001. "Preventing Binge Drinking during Early Adolescence: One- and Two-Year Follow-up of a School-Based Preventive Intervention." *Psychology of Addictive Behaviors* 15 (4): 360–65.

Bouffard, Jeffrey A., Doris Layton MacKenzie, and Laura J. Hickman. 2000. "Effectiveness of Vocational Education and Employment Programs for Adult Offenders: A Methodology-Based Analysis of the Literature." *Journal of Offender Rehabilitation* 31 (1 and 2): 1–41.

Brandt, David E. 2006. *Delinquency, Development, and Social Policy.* New Haven, CT: Yale University Press.

Brestan, Elizabeth V., and Sheila M. Eyberg. 1998. "Effective Psychosocial Treatments of Conduct-Disordered Children and Adolescents: 29 Years, 82 Studies, and 5,272 Kids." *Journal of Clinical Child and Adolescent Psychology* 27 (2): 180–9.

Bronfenbrenner, Urie. 1979. *The Ecology of Human Development: Experiments by Nature and Design.* Cambridge, MA: Harvard University Press.

Brown, Tamara L., Cynthia Cupit Swenson, Phillippe B. Cunningham, Scott W. Henggeler, Sonja K. Schoenwald, and Melissa D. Rowland. 1997. "Multisystemic Treatment of Violent and Chronic Offenders: Bridging the Gap between Research and Practice." *Administration and Policy in Mental Health* 25 (2): 221–38.

Burns, Barbara J., Sonja K. Schoenwald, John D. Burchard, Leyla Faw, and Albert B. Santos. 2000. "Comprehensive Community-Based Interventions for Youth with Severe Emotional Disorders: Multisystemic Therapy and the Wraparound Process." *Journal of Child and Family Studies* 9 (3): 283–314.

Burns, J. C., and G. F. Vito. 1995. "An Impact Analysis of the Alabama Boot Camp Program." *Federal Probation* 59:63–67.

Buydens-Branchey, Laure, Marc Branchey, and Joseph R. Hibbeln. 2008. "Associations between Increases in Plasma n-3 Polyunsaturated Fatty Acids following Supplementation and Decreases in Anger and Anxiety in Substance Abusers." *Progress in Neuro-Psychopharmacology and Biological Psychiatry* 32 (2): 568–75.

Caprara, Gian Vittorio. 1993. "Marginal Deviations, Aggregate Effects, Disruption of Continuity and Deviation Amplifying Mechanisms." In *Foundations of Personality,* NATO ASI Series: D, Behavioural and Social Sciences, volume 72, edited by Joop Hettema and Ian J. Deary, 227–44. Dordrecht, the Netherlands: Kluwer Academic Publishers.

Catalano, Richard F., M. Lisa Berglund, Jean A. M. Ryan, Heather S. Lonczak, and J. David Hawkins. 2002. "Positive Youth Development in the United States: Research Findings on Evaluations of Positive Youth Development Programs." *Prevention & Treatment* 5 (1). doi: 10.1037/1522-3736.5.1.515a.

Chamberlain, Patricia, Leslie D. Leve, and David S. DeGarmo. 2007. "Multidimensional Treatment Foster Care for Girls in the Juvenile Justice System: 2-Year Follow-up of a Randomized Clinical Trial." *Journal of Counseling and Clinical Psychology* 75 (1): 187–93.

Chamberlain, Patricia, and John B. Reid. 1998. "Comparison of Two Community Alternatives to Incarceration for Chronic Juvenile Offenders." *Journal of Consulting and Clinical Psychology* 66 (4): 624–33.

Conduct Problems Prevention Research Group. 2002. "Evaluation of the First 3 Years of the Fast Track Prevention Trial with Children at High Risk for Adolescent Conduct Problems." *Journal of Abnormal Child Psychology* 30 (1): 19–35. http://www.springerlink.com/content/0091-0627/30/1/.

Cottle, Cindy C., Ria J. Lee, and Kirk Heilbrun. 2001. "The Prediction of Criminal Recidivism in Juveniles: A Meta-Analysis." *Criminal Justice and Behavior* 28 (3): 367–94.

Crick, Nicki R., and Kenneth A. Dodge. 1994. "A Review and Reformulation of Social Information-Processing Mechanisms in Children's Social Adjustment." *Psychological Bulletin* 115 (1): 74–101.

Cummings, E. Mark, Patrick T. Davies, and Susan B. Campbell. 2000. *Developmental Psychopathology and Family Process: Theory, Research, and Clinical Implications.* New York: Guilford.

Cunha, Flavio, and James J. Heckman. 2008. "Formulating, Identifying, and Estimating the Technology of Cognitive and Noncognitive Skill Formation." *Journal of Human Resources* 43 (4): 738–82.

————. 2009. "The Economics and Psychology of Inequality and Human Development." *Journal of European Economic Association* 7 (2–3): 320–64.

De Fruyt, Filip, Karla Van Leeuwen, R. Michael Bagby, Frederic Rouillon, and Jean-Pierre Rolland. 2006. "Assessing and Interpreting Personality Change and Continuity in Patients Treated for Major Depression." *Psychological Assessment* 18 (1): 71–80.

Dishion, Thomas J. 2000. "Cross-Setting Consistency in Early Adolescent Psychopathology: Deviant Friendships and Problem Behavior Sequelae." *Journal of Personality* 68 (6): 1109–26.

Dodge, Kenneth A. 1980. "Social Cognition and Children's Aggressive Behavior." *Child Development* 51 (1): 162–70.

————. 2008. "Framing Public Policy and Prevention of Chronic Violence in American Youths." *American Psychologist* 63 (7): 573–90.

Dodge, Kenneth A., John D. Coie, and Donald R. Lynam. 2006. "Aggression and Antisocial Behavior in Youth." In *Handbook of Child Psychology, Sixth Edition, Volume 3: Social, Emotional, and Personality Development,* edited by Nancy Eisenberg, 719–88. New York: John Wiley & Sons.

Dodge, Kenneth A., and Cynthia L. Frame. 1982. "Social Cognitive Biases and Deficits in Aggressive Boys." *Child Development* 53 (3): 620–35.

Dodge, Kenneth A., Jennifer E. Lansford, Virginia Salzer Burks, John E. Bates, Gregory S. Pettit, Reid Fontaine, and Joseph M. Price. 2003. "Peer Rejection and Social Information-Processing Factors in the Development of Aggressive Behavior Problems in Children." *Child Development* 74 (2): 374–93.

Dodge, Kenneth A., John E. Lochman, Jennifer D. Harnish, John E. Bates, and Gregory S. Pettit. 1997. "Reactive and Proactive Aggression in School Children and Psychiatrically Impaired Chronically Assaultive Youth." *Journal of Abnormal Psychology* 106 (1): 37–51.

Dodge, Kenneth A., Joseph M. Price, Jo-Anne Bachorowski, and Joseph P. Newman. 1990. "Hostile Attributional Biases in Severely Aggressive Adolescents." *Journal of Abnormal Psychology* 99 (4): 385–92.

Drake, Elizabeth K., Steve Aos, and Marna G. Miller. 2009. "Evidence-based Public Policy Options to Reduce Crime and Criminal Justice Costs: Implications in Washington State." *Victims and Offenders* 4 (2): 170–96.

Dweck, Carol S., and Ellen L. Leggett. 1988. "A Social-Cognitive Approach to Motivation and Personality." *Psychological Review* 95 (2): 256–73.

Eddy, J. Mark, Rachel Bridge Whaley, and Patricia Chamberlain. 2004. "The Prevention of Violent Behavior by Chronic and Serious Male Juvenile Offenders: A 2-Year Follow-up of a Randomized Clinical Trial." *Journal of Emotional and Behavioral Disorders* 12 (1): 2–8.

Eddy, J. Mark, and Patricia Chamberlain. 2000. "Family Management and Deviant Peer Association as Mediators of the Impact of Treatment Condition on Youth Antisocial Behavior." *Journal of Counseling and Clinical Psychology* 68 (5): 857–63.

Elliott, Delbert S., and Scott Menard. 1996. "Delinquent Friends and Delinquent Behavior: Temporal and Developmental Patterns." In *Delinquency and Crime: Current Theories,* edited by J. David Hawkins, 28–67. New York: Cambridge University Press.

Emler, Nicholas, and Stephen Reicher. 1995. *Adolescence and Delinquency: The Collective Management of Reputation.* Cambridge, MA: Blackwell.

Empey, Lamar T., Mark C. Stafford, and Carter H. Hay. 1999. *American Delinquency: Its Meaning and Construction,* 4th edition. Belmont, CA: Wadsworth.

Erikson, Erik H. 1950. *Childhood and Society.* New York: Norton.

————. 1968. *Identity: Youth and Crisis.* New York: Norton.

Eyberg, Sheila M., Melanie M. Nelson, and Stephen R. Boggs. 2008. "Evidence-Based Psychosocial Treatments for Children and Adolescents with Disruptive Behavior." *Journal of Clinical Child and Adolescent Psychology* 37 (1): 215–37.

Farrington, David P., Maria M. Ttofi, and Jeremy W. Coid. 2009. "Development of Adolescence-Limited, Late-Onset, and Persistent Offenders from Age 8 to Age 48." *Aggressive Behavior* 35 (2): 150–63.

Finckenauer, James O. 1982. *Scared Straight! and the Panacea Phenomenon.* Englewood Cliffs, NJ: Prentice-Hall.

————. 2005. "Ruminating about Boot Camps: Panaceas, Paradoxes, and Ideology." *Journal of Offender Rehabilitation* 40 (3–4): 199–207.

Finckenauer, James O., and Patricia W. Gavin. 1999. *Scared Straight: The Panacea Phenomenon Revisited.* Prospect Heights, IL: Waveland Press.

Fisher, Philip A., and Patricia Chamberlain. 2000. "Multidimensional Treatment Foster Care: A Program for Intensive Parenting, Family Support, and Skill Building." *Journal of Emotional and Behavioral Disorders* 8 (3): 155–64.

Foster, E. Michael, and Damon E. Jones. 2007. "The Economic Analysis of Prevention: An Illustration Involving Children's Behavior Problems." *The Journal of Mental Health Policy and Economics* 10 (4): 165–75.

4-H. 2009. "The 4-H Story." http://4-h.org/4hstory.html.

French, Sheila A., and Paul Gendreau. 2006. "Reducing Prison Misconducts: What Works!" *Criminal Justice and Behavior* 33 (2): 185–218.

Garrard, Wendy M., and Mark W. Lipsey. 2007. "Conflict Resolution Education and Antisocial Behavior in US Schools: A Meta-Analysis." *Conflict Resolution Quarterly* 25 (1): 9–38.

Gerard, J. M., and C. Buehler. 2004. "Cumulative Environmental Risk and Youth Maladjustment: The Role of Youth Attributes." *Child Development* 75 (6): 1832–49.

Gesch, C. Bernard, Sean M. Hammond, Sarah E. Hampson, Anita Eves, and Martin J. Crowder. 2002. "Influence of Supplementary Vitamins, Minerals, and Essential Fatty Acids on the Antisocial Behaviour of Young Adult Prisoners: Randomised, Placebo-controlled Trial." *British Journal of Psychiatry* 181 (1): 22–28.

Gifford-Smith, Mary, Kenneth A. Dodge, Thomas J. Dishion, and Joan McCord. 2005. "Peer Influence in Children and Adolescents: Crossing the Bridge from Developmental to Intervention Science." *Journal of Abnormal Child Psychology* 33 (3): 255–65.

Glick, Barry, and Arnold P. Goldstein. 1987. "Aggression Replacement Training." *Journal of Counseling and Development* 65 (7): 356–62.

Gordon, Donald A., Jack Arbuthnot, Kathryn E. Gustafson, and Peter McGreen. 1988. "Home-Based Behavioral-Systems Family Therapy with Disadvantaged Juvenile Delinquents." *American Journal of Family Therapy* 16 (3): 243–55.

Gordon, Donald A., Karen Graves, and Jack Arbuthnot. 1995. "The Effect of Functional Family Therapy for Delinquents on Adult Criminal Behavior." *Criminal Justice and Behavior* 22 (1): 60–73.

Gottfredson, Denise C., Stephanie A. Gerstenblith, David A. Soulé, Shannon C. Womer, and Shaoli Lu. 2004. "Do After School Programs Reduce Delinquency?" *Prevention Science* 5 (4): 253–66.

Gottfredson, Michael R., and Travis Hirschi. 1990. *A General Theory of Crime.* Palo Alto, CA: Stanford University Press.

Gouze, Karen R. 1987. "Attention and Social Problem Solving as Correlates of Aggression in Preschool Males." *Journal of Abnormal Child Psychology* 15 (2): 181–97.

Graziano, William G., and Nancy H. Eisenberg. 1997. "Agreeableness: A Dimension of Personality." In *Handbook of Personality Psychology*, edited by Robert Hogan, John Johnson, and Stephen Briggs, 795–824. San Diego: Academic Press.

Greenberg, Mark T., Celene Domitrovich, and Brian Bumbarger. 2001. "The Prevention of Mental Disorders in School-Aged Children: Current State of the Field." *Prevention & Treatment* 4 (1). doi: 10.1037/1522-3736.4.1.41a.

Hamazaki, Tomohito, and Kei Hamazaki. 2008. "Fish Oils and Aggression or Hostility." *Progress in Lipid Research* 47 (4): 221–32.

Hautmann, Christopher, Petra Stein, Charlotte Hanisch, Ilka Eichelberger, Julia Plück, Daniel Walter, and Manfred Döpfner. 2009. "Does Parent Management Training for Children with Externalizing Problem Behavior in Routine Care Result in Clinically Significant Changes?" *Psychotherapy Research* 19 (2): 224–33.

Hawkins, J. David, Richard F. Catalano, Rick Kosterman, Robert Abbott, and Karl G. Hill. 1999. "Preventing Adolescent Health-Risk Behaviors by Strengthening Protection during Childhood." *Archives of Pediatrics and Adolescent Medicine* 153 (3): 226–34.

Hawkins, J. David, Richard F. Catalano, Diane M. Morrison, Julie O'Donnell, Robert D. Abbott, and L. Edward Day. 1992. "The Seattle Social Development Project: Effects of the First Four Years on Protective Factors and Problem Behaviors." In *Preventing Antisocial Behavior: Interventions from Birth through Adolescence*, edited by Joan McCord and Richard E. Tremblay, 139–61. New York: Guilford Press.

Hawkins, J. David, Rick Kosterman, Richard F. Catalano, Karl G. Hill, and Robert D. Abbott. 2005. "Promoting Positive Adult Functioning through Social Development Intervention in Childhood: Long-Term Effects from the Seattle Social Development Project." *Archives of Pediatrics and Adolescent Medicine* 159 (1): 25–31.

Hawkins, J. David, Brian H. Smith, Karl G. Hill, Rick Kosterman, Richard F. Catalano, and Robert D. Abbott. 2007. "Promoting Social Development and Preventing Health and Behavior Problems during the Elementary Grades: Results from the Seattle Social Development Project." *Victims and Offenders* 2 (2): 161–81.

Hawkins, J. David, Elizabeth Von Cleve, and Richard F. Catalano. 1991. "Reducing Early Childhood Aggression: Results of a Primary Prevention Program." *Journal of the American Academy of Child and Adolescent Psychiatry* 30 (2): 208–17.

Hazel, J. S., J. B. Schumaker, J. A. Sherman, and J. B. Sheldon-Wildgren. 1981. "The Development and Evaluation of a Group Skills Training Program for Court Adjudicated Youths." In *Behavioral Group Therapy, 1981: An Annual Review*, edited by Dennis Upper and Steven M. Ross, 113–52. Champaign, IL: Research Press.

———. 1982. "Group Training for Social Skills: A Program for Court-Adjudicated, Probationary Youths." *Criminal Justice and Behavior* 9 (1): 35–53.

Heckman, James J. 2008. "Schools, Skills, and Synapses." *Economic Inquiry* 46 (3): 289–324.

Heckman, J. J., L. Malofeeva, R. Pinto, and P. A. Savelyev. 2009. "The Effect of the Perry Preschool Program on the Cognitive and Non-cognitive Skills of its Participants." Working Paper. University of Chicago, Department of Economics.

Heckman, J. J., S. H. Moon, R. Pinto, P. A. Savelyev, and A. Q. Yavitz. 2009. "A Reanalysis of the High/Scope Perry Preschool Program." Working Paper. University of Chicago, Department of Economics.

Heckman, J. J., S. H. Moon, R. Pinto, and A. Q. Yavitz. 2009. "The Rate of Return to the Perry Preschool Program." Working Paper. University of Chicago, Department of Economics.

Heckman, James J., Jora Stixrud, and Sergio Urzua. 2006. "The Effects of Cognitive and Noncognitive Abilities on Labor Market Outcomes and Social Behavior." *Journal of Labor Economics* 24 (3): 411–82.

Henggeler, Scott W., and Charles M. Borduin. 1990. *Family Therapy and Beyond: A Multisystemic Approach to Treating the Behavior Problems of Children and Adolescents.* Pacific Grove, CA: Brooks/Cole.

Henggeler, S. W., C. M. Borduin, G. B. Melton, B. J. Mann, L. Smith, J. A. Hall, L. Cone, and B. R. Fucci. 1991. "Effects of Multisystemic Therapy on Drug Use and Abuse in Serious Juvenile Offenders: A Progress Report from Two Outcome Studies." *Family Dynamics of Addiction Quarterly* 1:40–51.

Henggeler, Scott W., Gary B. Melton, and Linda A. Smith. 1992. "Family Preservation using Multisystemic Therapy: An Effective Alternative to Incarcerating Serious Juvenile Offenders." *Journal of Consulting and Clinical Psychology* 60 (6): 953–61.

Henggeler, Scott W., Gary B. Melton, Linda A. Smith, Sonja K. Schoenwald, and Jerome H. Hanley. 1993. "Family Preservation Using Multisystemic Treatment: Long-Term Follow-up to a Clinical Trial with Serious Juvenile Offenders." *Journal of Child and Family Studies* 2 (4): 283–93.

Henggeler, Scott W., Sonja K. Schoenwald, Charles M. Borduin, Melisa D. Rowland, and Phillippe B. Cunningham. 1998. *Multisystemic Treatment of Antisocial Behavior in Children and Adolescents.* New York: Guilford.

Hirschi, Travis. 1969. *Causes of Delinquency.* Berkeley, CA: University of California Press.

Hogan, Robert, and Brent W. Roberts. 2004. "A Socioanalytic Model of Maturity." *Journal of Career Assessment* 12 (2): 207–17.

Huesmann, L. Rowell. 1998. "The Role of Social Information Processing and Cognitive Schema in the Acquisition and Maintenance of Habitual Aggressive Behavior." In *Human Aggression: Theories, Research, and Implications for Social Policy,* edited by Russell G. Green and Edward Donnerstein, 73–109. New York: Academic Press.

Jelicic, Helena, Deborah L. Bobek, Erin Phelps, Richard M. Lerner, and Jacqueline V. Lerner. 2007. "Using Positive Youth Development to Predict Contribution and Risk Behaviors in Early Adolescence: Findings from the First Two Waves of the 4-H Study of Positive Youth Development." *International Journal of Behavioral Development* 31 (3): 263–73.

Jones, M. 1996. "Do Boot Camp Graduates Make Better Probationers?" *Journal of Crime and Justice* 19 (1): 1–14.

Jones, Mark, and Darrell L. Ross. 1997. "Is Less Better? Boot Camp, Regular Probation and Rearrest in North Carolina." *American Journal of Criminal Justice* 21 (2): 147–61.

Kaplan, Bonnie J., Susan G. Crawford, Catherine J. Field, and J. Steven Simpson. 2007. "Vitamins, Minerals, and Mood." *Psychological Bulletin* 133 (5): 747–60.

Kazdin, Alan E. 1987. "Treatment of Antisocial Behavior in Children: Current Status and Future Directions." *Psychological Bulletin* 102 (2): 187–203.

———. 2005. *Parent Management Training: Treatment for Oppositional, Aggressive, and Antisocial Behavior in Children and Adolescents.* New York: Oxford University Press.

Krasner, Michael S., Ronald M. Epstein, Howard Beckman, Anthony L. Suchman, Benjamin Chapman, Christopher J. Mooney, and Timothy E. Quill. 2009. "Association of an Educational Program in Mindful Communication with Burnout, Empathy, and Attitudes among Primary Care Physicians." *Journal of the American Medical Association* 302 (12): 1284–93.

Lakoff, George. 2002. *Moral Politics: How Liberals and Conservatives Think.* Chicago: University of Chicago Press.

Laub, John H., and Robert J. Sampson. 2003. *Shared Beginnings, Divergent Lives: Delinquent Boys to Age 70.* Cambridge, MA: Harvard University Press.

Lerner, Richard M. 2004. *Liberty: Thriving and Civic Engagement among America's Youth.* Thousand Oaks, CA: Sage Publications.

Lerner, Richard M., Jacqueline V. Lerner, Jason B. Almerigi, Christina Theokas, Erin Phelps, Steinunn Gestsdottir, Sophie Naudeau, et al. 2005. "Positive Youth Development, Participation in Community Youth Development Programs, and Community Contributions of Fifth-Grade Adolescents: Findings from the First Wave of the 4-H Study of Positive Youth Development." *Journal of Early Adolescence* 25 (1): 17–71.

Leve, Leslie D., and Patricia Chamberlain. 2004. "Female Juvenile Offenders: Defining an Early-Onset Pathway for Delinquency." *Journal of Child and Family Studies* 13 (4): 439–52.

———. 2005. "Association with Delinquent Peers: Intervention Effects for Youth in the Juvenile Justice System." *Journal of Abnormal Child Psychology* 33 (3): 339–47.

Leve, Leslie D., Patricia Chamberlain, and John B. Reid. 2005. "Intervention Outcomes for Girls Referred from Juvenile Justice: Effects on Delinquency." *Journal of Consulting and Clinical Psychology* 73 (6): 1181–85.

Lilienfeld, Scott O. 2007. "Psychological Treatments that Cause Harm." *Perspectives on Psychological Science* 2 (1): 53–70.

Limber, S. P. 2006. "The Olweus Bullying Prevention Program: An Overview of Its Implementation and Research Basis." In *Handbook of School Violence and School Safety: From Research to Practice,* edited by Shane R. Jimerson and Michael J. Furlong, 293–307. Mahwah, NJ: Lawrence Erlbaum Associates.

Lipsey, Mark W. 1992. "Juvenile Delinquency Treatment: A Meta-Analytic Inquiry into the Variability of Effects." In *Meta-Analysis for Explanation: A Casebook,* edited by Thomas D. Cook, Harris Cooper, David S. Cordray, Heidi Hartmann, Larry V. Hedges, Richard J. Light, Thomas A. Louis, and Frederick Mosteller, 83–127. New York: Russell Sage Foundation.

———. 1999. "Can Intervention Rehabilitate Serious Delinquents?" *Annals of the American Academy of Political and Social Science* 564 (1): 142–66.

———. 2009. "The Primary Factors that Characterize Effective Interventions with Juvenile Offenders: A Meta-Analytic Overview." *Victims and Offenders* 4 (2): 124–47.

Lipsey, Mark W., and David B. Wilson. 1998. "Effective Intervention for Serious Juvenile Offenders: A Synthesis of Research." In *Serious and Violent Juvenile Offenders: Risk Factors and Successful Interventions,* edited by Rolf Loeber and David P. Farrington, 313–45. Thousand Oaks, CA: Sage Publications.

Liu, Jianghong, Adrian Raine, Peter H. Venables, and Sarnoff A. Mednick. 2004. "Malnutrition at Age 3 years and Externalizing Behavior Problems at Ages 8, 11, and 17 Years." *American Journal of Psychiatry* 161 (11): 2005–13.

Lodi-Smith, Jennifer, and Brent W. Roberts. 2007. "Social Investment and Personality: A Meta-Analytic Analysis of the Relationship of Personality Traits to Investment in Work, Family, Religion, and Volunteerism." *Personality and Social Psychology Review* 11 (1): 68–86.

Loeber, Rolf. 1990. "Development and Risk Factors of Juvenile Antisocial Behavior and Delinquency." *Clinical Psychology Review* 10 (1): 1–41.

Loeber, Rolf, and David P. Farrington. 2000. "Young Children who Commit Crime: Epidemiology, Developmental Origins, Risk Factors, Early Interventions, and Policy Implications." *Development and Psychopathology* 12 (4): 737–62.

Loeber, Rolf, Dustin Pardini, D. Lynn Homish, Evelyn H. Wei, Anne M. Crawford, David P. Farrington, Magda Stouthamer-Loeber, Judith Creemers, Steven A. Koehler, and Richard Rosenfeld. 2005. "The Prediction of Violence and Homicide in Young Men." *Journal of Consulting and Clinical Psychology* 73 (6): 1074–88.

Loeber, Rolf, Dustin A. Pardini, Magda Stouthamer-Loeber, and Adrian Raine. 2007. "Do Cognitive, Physiological, and Psychosocial Risk and Promotive Factors Predict Desistance from Delinquency in Males?" *Developmental and Psychopathology* 19:867–87.

Lonczak, Heather S., Robert D. Abbott, J. David Hawkins, Rick Kosterman, and Richard F. Catalano. 2002. "Effects of the Seattle Social Development Project on Sexual Behavior, Pregnancy, Birth, and Sexually Transmitted Disease Outcomes by Age 21 Years." *Archives of Pediatrics and Adolescent Medicine* 156 (5): 438–47.

Luthar, Suniya S. 1991. "Vulnerability and Resilience: A Study of High-Risk Adolescents." *Child Development* 62 (3): 600–16.

———. 1995. "Social Competence in the School Setting: Prospective Cross-Domain Associations among Inner-City Teens." *Child Development* 66 (2): 416–29.

Luthar, Suniya S., Carol H. Doernberger, and Edward Zigler. 1993. "Resilience is Not a Unidimensional Construct: Insights from a Prospective Study of Inner-City Adolescents." *Development and Psychopathology* 5 (4): 703–17.

Lynam, Donald R., Richard Milich, Rick Zimmerman, Scott P. Novak, T. K. Logan, Catherine Martin, Carl Leukefeld, and Richard Clayton. 1999. "Project DARE: No Effects at Ten-Year Follow-up." *Journal of Consulting and Clinical Psychology* 67 (4): 590–93.

MacBrayer, Elizabeth Kirby, Richard Milich, and Mary Hundley. 2003. "Attributional Biases in Aggressive Children and Their Mothers." *Journal of Abnormal Psychology* 112 (4): 698–708.

MacKenzie, Doris Layton, and Dale G. Parent. 1991. "Shock Incarceration and Prison Crowding in Louisiana." *Journal of Criminal Justice* 19 (3): 225–37.

MacKenzie, Doris Layton, and James W. Shaw. 1993. "The Impact of Shock Incarceration on Technical Violations and New Criminal Activities." *Justice Quarterly* 10 (3): 463–88.

MacKillop, James, Stephen A. Lisman, Allison Weinstein, and Deborah Rosenbaum. 2003. "Controversial Treatments for Alcoholism." In *Science and Pseudoscience in Clinical Psychology,* edited by Scott O. Lilienfeld, Steven Jay Lynn, and Jeffrey M. Lohr, 273–305. New York: Guilford Press.

Mann, J. John. 1999. "Role of the Serotonergic System in the Pathogenesis of Major Depression and Suicidal Behavior." *Neuropsychopharmacology* 21 (supp. 1): S99–S105. http://www.nature.com/npp/journal/v21/n1s/index.html.

McCrae, Robert R., and Paul T. Costa, Jr. 1992. "Discriminant Validity of the NEO-PIR Facet Scales." *Educational and Psychological Measurement* 52 (1): 229–37.

Meyer, Aleta L., Kevin W. Allison, LeRoy E. Reese, Franklin N. Gay, and Multisite Violence Prevention Project. 2004. "Choosing to Be Violence Free in Middle School: The Student Component of the GREAT Schools and Families Universal Program." *American Journal of Preventive Medicine* 26 (1, supp. 1): 20–28.

Miller, Joshua D., Donald Lynam, and Carl Leukefeld. 2003. "Examining Antisocial Behavior through the Lens of the Five Factor Model of Personality." *Aggressive Behavior* 29 (6): 497–514.

Millstein, Susan G., and Bonnie L. Halpern-Felsher. 2002a. "Judgments about Risk and Perceived Invulnerability in Adolescents and Young Adults." *Journal of Research on Adolescence* 12 (4): 399–422.

———. 2002b. "Perceptions of Risk and Vulnerability." *The Journal of Adolescent Health* 31 (1, supp. 1): 10–27.

Morash, Merry, and Lila Rucker. 1990. "A Critical Look at the Idea of Boot Camp as a Correctional Reform." *Crime & Delinquency* 36 (2): 204–22.

Multisite Violence Prevention Project. 2008. "The Multisite Violence Prevention Project: Impact of a Universal School-Based Violence Prevention Program on Social-Cognitive Outcomes." *Prevention Science* 9 (4): 231–44.

———. 2009. "The Ecological Effects of Universal and Selective Violence Prevention Programs for Middle School Students: A Randomized Trial." *Journal of Consulting and Clinical Psychology* 77 (3): 526–42.

Nixon, Reginald D. V. 2002. "Treatment of Behavior Problems in Preschoolers: A Review of Parent Training Programs." *Clinical Psychology Review* 22 (4): 525–46.

Olweus, Dan. 1991. "Bully/victim Problems among Schoolchildren: Basic Facts and Effects of a School-Based Intervention Program." In *The Development and Treatment of Childhood Aggression,* edited by Debra J. Pepler and Kenneth H. Rubin, 411–48. Hillsdale, NJ: Lawrence Erlbaum Associates, Inc.

———. 1993. *Bullying at School: What We Know and What We Can Do.* Cambridge, MA: Blackwell.

———. 1994. "Bullying at School: Basic Facts and Effects of a School Based Intervention Program." *Journal of Child Psychology and Psychiatry* 35 (7): 1171–90.

———. 1995. "Bullying or Peer Abuse at School: Facts and Intervention." *Current Directions in Psychological Science* 4 (6): 196–200.

———. 2005. "A Useful Evaluation Design, and Effects of the Olweus Bullying Prevention Program." *Psychology, Crime, & Law* 11 (4): 389–402.

Orpinas, Pamela, Arthur M. Horne, and Multisite Violence Prevention Program. 2004. "A Teacher-Focused Approach to Prevent and Reduce Students' Aggressive Behavior: The GREAT Teacher Program." *American Journal of Preventive Medicine* 26 (1, supp. 1): 29–38.

Ozer, Daniel J., and Verónica Benet-Martínez. 2006. "Personality and the Prediction of Consequential Outcomes." *Annual Review of Psychology* 57:401–21.

Petrosino, Anthony, Carolyn Turpin-Petrosino, and John Buehler. 2003. "Scared Straight and Other Juvenile Awareness Programs for Preventing Juvenile Delinquency: A Systematic Review of the Randomized Experimental Evidence." *Annals of the American Academy of Political and Social Science* 589 (1): 41–62.

Piedmont, Ralph L., and Joseph W. Ciarrocchi. 1999. "The Utility of the Revised NEO Personality Inventory in an Outpatient, Drug Rehabilitation Context." *Psychology of Addictive Behaviors* 13 (3): 213–26.

Plas, J. M. 1992. "The Development of Systems Thinking: A Historical Perspective." In *The Handbook of Family-School Intervention: A Systems Perspective,* edited by Marvin J. Fine and Cindy Carlson, 45–56. Needham Heights, MA: Allyn & Bacon.

Price, Joseph M., Patricia Chamberlain, John Landsverk, and John Reid. 2009. "KEEP Foster-parent Training Intervention: Model Description and Effectiveness." *Child & Family Social Work* 14 (2): 233–42.

Quadrel, Marilyn Jacobs, Baruch Fischhoff, and Wendy Davis. 1993. "Adolescent (In)vulnerability." *American Psychologist* 48 (2): 102–16.

Rhule, Dana M. 2005. "Take Care To Do No Harm: Harmful Interventions for Youth Problem Behavior." *Professional Psychology: Research and Practice* 36 (6): 618–25.

Roberts, Brent W. 2009. "Back to the Future: Personality and Assessment and Personality Development." *Journal of Research in Personality* 43 (2): 137–45.

Roberts, Brent W., and Timothy Bogg. 2004. "A Longitudinal Study of Relationships between Conscientiousness and the Social-Environmental Factors and Substance-Use Behaviors That Influence Health." *Journal of Personality* 72 (2): 325–54.

Roberts, Brent W., and Avshalom Caspi. 2001. Personality Development and the Person-Situation Debate: It's Déjà Vu All Over Again. *Psychological Inquiry* 12: 104–09.

Roberts, Brent W., Avshalom Caspi, and Terrie E. Moffitt. 2002. "It's Not Just Who You're with, It's Who You Are: Personality and Relationship Experiences across Multiple Relationships." *Journal of Personality* 70:925–64.

———. 2003. "Work Experiences and Personality Development in Young Adulthood." *Journal of Personality and Social Psychology* 84 (3): 582–93.

Roberts, Brent W., and Joshua J. Jackson. 2008. "Sociogenomic Personality Psychology." *Journal of Personality* 76 (6): 1523–44.

Roberts, Brent W., Nathan R. Kuncel, Rebecca Shiner, Avshalom Caspi, and Lewis R. Goldberg. 2007. "The Power of Personality: The Comparative Validity of Personality Traits, Socioeconomic Status, and Cognitive Ability for Predicting Important Life Outcomes." *Perspectives in Psychological Science* 2 (4): 313–45.

Roberts, Brent W., Kate E. Walton, and Wolfgang Viechtbauer. 2006. "Patterns of Mean-Level Change in Personality Traits across the Life Course: A Meta-Analysis of Longitudinal Studies." *Psychological Bulletin* 132 (1): 1–25.

Roberts, Brent W., and Dustin Wood. 2006. "Personality Devleopment in the Context of the Neo-Socioanalytic Model of Personality." In *Handbook of Personality Development*, edited by D. Mroczek and T. Little, 11–39. Mahwah, NJ: Lawrence Erlbaum Associates.

Sampson, Robert J., and John H. Laub. 1990. "Crime and Deviance over the Life Course: The Salience of Adult Social Bonds." *American Sociological Review* 55 (5): 609–27.

———. 1993. *Crime in the Making: Pathways and Turning Points through Life.* Cambridge, MA: Harvard University Press.

Schaeffer, Cindy M., and Charles M. Borduin. 2005. "Long-Term Follow-up to a Randomized Clinical Trial of Multisystemic Therapy with Serious and Violent Juvenile Offenders." *Journal of Consulting and Clinical Psychology* 73 (3): 445–53.

Schwartz, Seth J., Hilda Pantin, J. Douglas Coatsworth, and José Szapocznik. 2007. "Addressing the Challenges and Opportunities for Today's Youth: Toward an Integrative Model and its Implications for Research and Intervention." *The Journal of Primary Prevention* 28 (2): 117–44.

Serna, Loretta A., Jean B. Schumaker, J. Stephen Hazel, and Jan B. Sheldon. 1986. "Teaching Reciprocal Social Skills to Parents and their Delinquent Adolescents." *Journal of Clinical Child Psychology* 15 (1): 64–77.

Shapiro, Arnold. 1978. *Scared Straight!* Santa Monica, CA: Pyramid Films.

Sharp, Stephen, and Engelina Davids. 2003. "Early Intervention in Behaviour: A Study of the FAST-Track Programme." *Emotional and Behavioral Difficulties* 8 (3): 173–88.

Sheidow, Ashli J., W. David Bradford, Scott W. Henggeler, Melisa D. Rowland, Colleen Halliday-Boykins, Sonja K. Schoenwald, and David M. Ward. 2004. "Treatment Costs for Youths Receiving Multisystemic Therapy or Hospitalization After a Psychiatric Crisis." *Psychiatric Services* 55 (5): 548–54.

Skiba, Russell J. 2002. "Special Education and School Discipline: A Precarious Balance." *Behavioral Disorders* 27 (2): 81–97.

Slaby, Ronald G., and Nancy G. Guerra. 1988. "Cognitive Mediators of Aggression in Adolescent Offenders: Part 1, Assessment." *Developmental Psychology* 24 (4): 580–88.

Smith, Emilie Phillips, Deborah Gorman-Smith, William Quinn, David Rabiner, Patrick Tolan, Donna-Marie Winn, and Multisite Violence Prevention Project. 2004. "Community-Based Multiple Family Groups to Prevent and Reduce Violent and Aggressive Behavior: The GREAT Families Program." *American Journal of Preventive Medicine* 26 (1, supp. 1): 39–47.

Snyder, Howard N., and Melissa Sickmund. 2006. *Juvenile Offenders and Victims: 2006 National Report.* Washington, DC: US Department of Justice, Office of Justice Programs, Office of Juvenile Justice and Delinquency Prevention.

Spence, Susan H., and John S. Marzillier. 1979. "Social Skills Training with Adolescent Male Offenders: I. Short-Term Effects." *Behavioral Research & Therapy* 17 (1): 7–16.

———. 1981. "Social Skills Training with Adolescent Male Offenders: II. Short-Term, Long-Term and Generalized Effects." *Behavioral Research & Therapy* 19 (4): 349–68.

Sroufe, L. Alan. 1997. "Psychopathology as an Outcome of Development." *Development and Psychopathology* 9 (2): 251–68.

Steiner, Hans, Elizabeth Cauffman, and Elaine Duxbury. 1999. "Personality Traits in Juvenile Delinquents: Relation to Criminal Behavior and Recidivism." *Journal of the American Academy of Child & Adolescent Psychiatry* 38 (3): 256–62.

Stormshak, Elizabeth A., Karen L. Bierman, Carole Bruschi, Kenneth A. Dodge, John D. Coie, and the Conduct Problems Prevention Research Group. 1999. "The Relation between Behavior Problems and Peer Preference in Different Classroom Contexts." *Child Development* 70 (1): 169–82.

Sutphen, Richard D., Bruce A. Thyer, and P. David Kurtz. 1995. "Multisystemic Treatment of High-Risk Juvenile Offenders." *International Journal of Offender Therapy and Comparative Criminology* 39 (4): 327–34.

Tang, Tony Z., Robert J. DeRubeis, Steven D. Hollon, Jay Amsterdam, Richard Shelton, and Benjamin Schalet. 2009. "Personality Change during Depression Treatment: A Placebo-Controlled Trial." *Archives of General Psychiatry* 66 (12): 1322–30.

Thornberry, Terence P., and Marvin D. Krohn. 1997. "Peers, Drug Use, and Delinquency." In *Handbook of Antisocial Behavior,* edited by David M. Stoff, James Breiling, and Jack D. Maser, 218–33. Hoboken, NJ: John Wiley & Sons.

Walsh, William J., Laura B. Glab, and Mary L. Haakenson. 2004. "Reduced Violent Behavior Following Biochemical Therapy." *Physiology & Behavior* 82 (5): 835–9.

Washington State Institute for Public Policy. 1998. "Watching the Bottom Line: Cost-Effective Interventions for Reducing Crime in Washington." Preliminary Technical Report, January. Olympia, WA: Washington State Institute for Public Policy.

Werch, Chudley E., and Deborah M. Owen. 2002. "Iatrogenic Effects of Alcohol and Drug Prevention Programs." *Journal of Studies on Alcohol* 63 (5): 581–90.

Wilson, Sandra Jo, and Mark W. Lipsey. 2007. "School-Based Interventions for Aggressive and Disruptive Behavior: Update of a Meta-Analysis." *American Journal of Preventive Medicine* 33 (2, supp. 1): S130–43.

Zelli, Arnaldo, L. Rowell Huesmann, and Daniel Cervone. 1995. "Social Inference and Individual Differences in Aggression: Evidence for Spontaneous Judgments of Hostility." *Aggressive Behavior* 21 (6): 405–17.

Comment   Kenneth A. Dodge

Processes in the Prevention of Crime and Delinquency

Hill, Roberts, Grogger, Guryan, and Sixkiller (chapter 8, this volume) are to be congratulated for their review of interventions to decrease delinquency, criminal behavior, and recidivism, particularly for their insight in bringing a focus to this review on psychological processes that might mediate the impact of intervention on long-term outcomes. This commentary will highlight the contribution made by Hill and colleagues, provide a different conceptualization of psychological processes in delinquency, and then propose a broader model of possible intervention targets in delinquency prevention.

Why Focus on Psychological Processes?

Traditional perspectives on the prevention of criminal behavior within economics have treated the individual as a "black box" without concern for how a program might achieve success, beyond presumed-but-untested influence on an individual's appraisal of the costs and benefits of a decision to engage in crime. However, an understanding of the psychological mechanisms through which a program operates successfully is crucial to future program planning, implementation, and public policy, for two reasons. First, it is unlikely that programs that have been evaluated through small-scale randomized controlled trials will ever be disseminated at scale in precisely the same manner in which they had been implemented originally. The original program might have been implemented decades ago in a different policy era, with children of a limited range in ethnicity, with interventionists who are graduate students or university employees who are supervised by program developers, or with participants who are volunteers who have consented to be studied.

Planned adaptations as well as unanticipated problems in scaling up will bring a different "look" to disseminated programs. Adaptations are often planned when a program is implemented with a different age, gender, or cultural group than the one for which it had been created. These changes are viewed as "improvements," albeit without careful evaluation. Problems in scaling up a program may lead to degradation in training of interventionists, supervision, caseload, adherence to fidelity, and infrastructure support. Welsh et al. (2010) have reviewed studies of scaling up early intervention programs for families with young children at risk for delinquency and have concluded that scaling-up degrades impact by 15 to 40 percent, called the

Kenneth A. Dodge is the William McDougall Professor of Public Policy, professor of psychology and neuroscience, and director of the Center for Child and Family Policy at Duke University.

"scale-up penalty." The net result of these planned and unplanned changes is that scaled-up and disseminated programs rarely mimic the original program precisely.

Whether the sum of planned and unplanned changes improves or degrades the long-term impact of a disseminated program on preventing delinquency and crime will not be evident to program officials immediately, but they cannot wait for these long-term outcomes to determine a program's merit. They need an early signal of program effectiveness. Thus, the second reason for focusing on proximal psychological processes is to evaluate whether a program is changing a targeted child in the desired direction. A contribution of the Hill et al. review is to begin to identify these optimal proximal targets by reviewing the impact of programs on cognitive abilities and personality.

The importance of identifying optimal proximal targets can be understood through an analogy to interventions in a very different domain, cardiovascular disease prevention. Some of these interventions aim to have a long-term impact on myocardial infarctions by addressing exercise, diet, stress, and lifestyle. But which exercise programs, which diets, and which lifestyle changes are effective, and which components of these programs must be preserved in dissemination? Few of these interventions have been evaluated for long-enough time periods to know whether they lower the risk of heart attacks. However, basic epidemiological research has identified an important process and early predictor of cardiovascular disease in the measure of blood pressure. New behavioral health programs and pharmacologic interventions that aim to prevent heart attacks are evaluated based on their proficiency in lowering blood pressure in individuals, at least until long-term follow-up can be completed to determine efficacy in preventing heart attacks. Furthermore, blood pressure has become the proximal target of pharmacologic interventions to prevent heart disease. These interventions are rarely disseminated with a static dose for all patients; instead, the physician titrates the dose until an optimal blood pressure level is achieved. If an intervention lowers blood pressure, it is assumed also to lower the risk of cardiovascular disease.

Similarly, evaluation of new delinquency prevention programs and policies cannot wait until their participants age out to determine their worthiness. They will be evaluated with regard to their efficacy in having an impact on important proximal processes in development. Likewise, programs that have been found to be effective in long-term delinquency prevention through small-scale trials are unlikely to be scaled up precisely as planned. In scaling up programs, instead of trying to mimic program features that might or might not be crucial to long-term delinquency prevention, it is important to maintain focus on optimal proximal targets. Hence, Hill et al. push the field forward by focusing discourse on identifying processes in the development of serious delinquency and optimal proximal targets for interventions.

They fall short, however, in their conceptualization and labeling of crucial proximal processes.

Cognitive and Noncognitive Targets of Intervention

Hill et al. organize the world of preventive intervention in delinquency into cognitive and noncognitive factors and short-term (less than six months) and long-term programs. The latter distinction seems arbitrary and not likely to catch on as an organizing framework because many short-term programs sometimes last more than six months in reality and some have "booster" interventions in subsequent years.

It is understandable how Hill and colleagues come to the cognitive-noncognitive distinction: the original Head Start program sought to yield long-term impact by changing young children's intelligence. They also argue that the legal basis for differentiating juvenile and adult adjudication is predicated on an assumption that the primary difference between children and adults is intelligence. Further, they note that Heckman (Cunha and Heckman 2008; Heckman 2008) has divided the world this way. He has examined the superiority of noncognitive abilities over cognitive abilities in predicting labor market outcomes (Heckman, Stixrud, and Urzua 2006) and has been taking aim at cognitive factors in his reanalyses of the data from the Perry Preschool Project (Heckman et al. 2010). Finally, Hill et al. claim, without citation of a single study, that "most efforts to decrease delinquency focus on addressing its cognitive ability catalysts." They define cognitive ability here as the intelligence quotient (IQ), and they suggest that interventions that address intelligence dominate the field but have not been successful. They argue that the focus should be on "psychological factors other than cognitive ability."

It seems that they have set up a straw man here in claiming that intelligence has been the target of most interventions and that this target should shift. Psychologists have long ago stopped trying to change intelligence in a traditional way, which has come to be viewed either as irrelevant or more commonly as a genetically endowed characteristic that is shaped by the environment to affect skills, abilities, performances, and achievements. There is a sharp distinction between the intelligence quotient and the large array of mental abilities and skills that are involved in behavioral decision making, and the focus of psychological research has been on identifying the key processes and skills in behavior.

Contemporary interventions and policies are directed toward this array without targeting intelligence per se. The US Supreme Court (*Roper v. Simmons,* 543 US 551, 2005, and *Graham v. Florida,* 560, US, 2010) has ruled twice that legal sanctions (first, death penalty, and, second, life in prison without parole) must differ for juveniles and adults, not because the two groups differ in the intelligence quotient but because of scientific findings that adolescent brain development is not yet complete. In early adolescence, the brain undergoes rapid changes in myelination, growth, and pruning that alter the individual's ability to understand social events and make decisions about one's behavior. Full self-control, termed executive function, is not achieved until well into adulthood. It seems contradictory to term these processes "noncognitive" when they obviously involve brain activity and mental processes. The scientific field is just now sorting out the array of psychological processes that constitute executive function. Preventive interventions for children are targeted toward these psychological processes, but the field seeks a coherent taxonomy.

Targeting Personality

Hill et al. suggest that the target of interventions should be personality change; specifically, cognitive abilities (not intelligence), personality traits, motivations, and narratives. They note that "Most of the risk factors (for delinquency) appear to be relatively stable personality factors that are akin to cognitive ability," and they cite the work of Miller, Lynam, and Leukefield (2003), which showed that self-report measures of the Five Factor Model of personality (known as the Big Five), particularly Conscientiousness and Agreeableness, are strong predictors of later self-reported antisocial behavior.

Although Hill et al. are to be commended for seeking psychological constructs that might mediate behavior change, the Big Five model that they target is not an optimal choice for a guiding framework. This model is not consistent with the premise of intervention; namely, that personality constructs are amenable to change by exogenous intervention. In personality theory, the Big Five factors are typically theorized as genetically endowed, static characteristics that cause behavior (McCrae and Costa 1997). It is hypothesized that lack of agreeableness "causes" one to behave with crime and delinquency. No explanation is offered about the origins of agreeableness, other than genetic endowments. Agreeableness does not change or develop, just as intelligence does not change. The notion that agreeableness might be altered by environmental experiences or intervention is foreign to the theory itself. In actuality, because of the way that the Big Five constructs are measured, they might well change over time; however, the personality theory guiding this work posits the notion of genetic traits that do not develop or change.

This conception of personality becomes tautological when the measure of agreeableness includes items that are lexically very close to the antisocial behavior that it supposedly causes and predicts. It is no surprise, then, that the measure predicts itself; that is, agreeableness predicts agreeable behavior. It means little, though, that agreeableness might "cause" agreeable behavior. Distressingly, the theory offers little in the way of a process explanation for behavior, little insight into how behaviors develop, and even less in the way of guidance for the design of an intervention program. More dynamic personality concepts that are consistent with the premises of intervention are skills, competencies, schemas, scripts, and styles of acting on the world.

A Process Model of Personality

A process approach to personality starts with the online mental operations that occur during a social interaction that eventuate in an antisocial act such as assault, vandalism, or burglary. Certain operations, such as perceiving threat from others or judging that the benefits of engaging in a crime outweigh the costs, are associated with antisocial behaviors. Further, it is hypothesized that habitual patterns in these operations are acquired through experience and come to act as personality characteristics that guide future behavior. This constructivist approach to personality has origins in the work of Mischel (1999), follows from the information-processing model of competence by Nobel Laureate Simon (1957), and is carried today by models of social cognition (Cervone and Shoda 1999) and information processing (Dodge 2003; Huesmann 1988).

In response to a challenging social stimulus, such as being teased, "dissed," or provoked, or in response to an opportunity for personal gain, such as observing an unguarded cash register or unoccupied home, an individual responds in a time-sequential series of mental operations that lead to a behavioral response. The first step is to encode the cues in working memory. Individual differences in encoding patterns, such as hypervigilance to hostile cues or inattention to external controls, may increase the likelihood of antisocial behavior. The second step is to interpret the encoded cues and give them meaning. A person who regularly attributes hostile intent to another becomes likely to engage in retaliatory aggression.

The third step is the experience and regulation of emotion that leads to goal-setting. Emotions motivate action, just as goals do. Regulating anger is crucial to prevention of aggression. Self-defensive goals are relatively likely to lead to retaliatory assault, and self-centered instrumental goals lead to violations of others' property. Relationship goals lead to restraint. The next step is to access from memory one or more possible behavioral responses to the interpreted social cue. A person who has ready access to numerous antisocial responses and little access to nonaggressive competent responses may be likely to engage in antisocial behavior. Merely generating antisocial responses from memory does not inevitably lead to behaving aggressively, however, and so the next step is a response evaluation step that is as familiar to economists as behavioral decision making. The consequences of behaving in a particular way are contemplated, particularly the evaluation of the positive and negative outcomes of a behavior and the valuation of those consequences in costs and benefits. Some problems of criminal behavior occur because the individual fails to engage in response evaluation altogether and simply acts impulsively. Other problems occur when an individual disengages morally from consideration of others' consequences (Bandura 1999).

Habitual styles of decision making, such as overvaluing immediate outcomes and undervaluing deferred outcomes, are likely to be associated with criminal behaviors. Finally, a behavioral decision is made and enacted.

Several theoretical assertions of this approach make it differ from a static trait approach. First, specific mental operations (such as hypervigilance to hostile cues, making a hostile attribution about another's intent, adopting a self-defensive goal, and evaluating the consequences of aggressing favorably) are hypothesized as the brain actions that lead to antisocial behaviors, whereas a trait approach does not articulate how the trait causes the behavior. Second, these mental operations are hypothesized as becoming habitual; that is, consistent across time within a person. They may be thought of as acquired personality characteristics because they explain how individuals differ in behavioral propensities. Some of these characteristics are skills, such as accurately interpreting others' intentions, being able to generate many solutions to challenging interpersonal problems, and patiently and accurately anticipating the outcomes of one's actions before responding. Some of these characteristics are biases or patterns in responding, such as a habitual pattern of overinterpreting hostile intent in others and a bias to anticipate that others will evaluate one negatively. Third, these habitual patterns are hypothesized as being acquired through experience. They are learned mental operations. The impact of parent, peer, and cultural influence on a person's development occurs through these mental operations. In fact, it is asserted that those exogenous influences exert their effect on behavior by influencing habitual styles of processing social information. Finally, because these patterns are learned, they might be changed through intervention.

This approach to personality has been embraced by diverse streams of research, and these mental operations are known variously as social-cognitive skills (Dodge et al. 1986), social cognitions (Cantor and Kihlstrom 1982), executive functions, heuristics (Kahneman and Tversky 1982), self-regulation, stereotypes, and internal working models of how the world operates (Bretherton 1999). A large body of empirical research supports the assertions of this model (see reviews by Orobio de Castro et al. 2002; Dodge, Coie, and Lynam 2006; Huesmann 1988).

An Ecological Model of Factors in the Development of Antisocial Behavior

Unlike the trait approach to personality, the processing model of personality posits that family, school and peer, and cultural factors influence the development of processing patterns that mediate behavior (see figure 8C.1). The trait approach asserts the sole role of genetic factors in traits, whereas the processing approach asserts environmental effects, genetic effects, and gene-environment interaction effects (e.g., Caspi et al. 2002).

The processing model also asserts that life experiences influence antisocial behavior through their impact on the acquisition of social-cognitive skills and processing patterns. For example, early mother-infant attachment security has a distal effect on later behavioral development by influencing

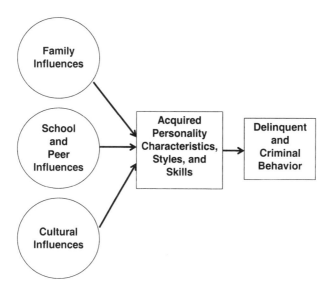

Fig. 8C.1 A schematic model of influences (and potential intervention loci) on anti-social behavior

the internal working models that a child develops about whether the world is a safe or threatening place (Bowlby 1980). Internal working models provide the basis for hostile versus benign attributions during social exchanges. Parents' management of a young child's misbehavior through rewards and punishments influence the child's acquisition of contingent probabilities about the consequences of aggressing and misbehaving (Dodge and Pettit 2003). Teachers influence a child's development of delinquent behavior by teaching the child about the consequences of acting in particular ways, exposing the child to alternate behavioral response options, and teaching the child to solve social problems and resolve conflicts systematically. Classroom peers influence a child's behavioral development by modeling values, teaching a child contingencies about consequences, and exposing a child to new behaviors that become part of a child's repertoire of response alternatives (Dodge and Pettit 2003). Culture broadly influences a child's goals and valuation of outcomes. A thorough literature review of these influences is not necessary to assert that opportunities for intervention abound by considering the various environmental influences on social-cognitive development across the life course.

Reinterpreting a Review of Interventions to Decrease Delinquency

The model described here provides a framework for reorganizing the Hill et al. review of interventions to prevent delinquency and crime. Some interventions target mental operations directly, such as social-cognitive skills training programs and cognitive behavior therapy. Other interventions target the environmental factors that presumably have an indirect effect on delinquent behavior by influencing social cognitions and mental operations.

This organizational scheme can be applied to the myriad interventions that are reviewed by Hill et al. They review interventions that they classify as school-based, social skills, family system, and nutrition.

School-based interventions are given high marks by Hill et al., who conclude that school-based "conflict resolution programs are generally quite effective in reducing antisocial behavior among youth." They also applaud after-school programs (and they conclude that academically-oriented programs are less effective than programs that emphasize social skills and character development) and peer relations enhancement programs. It would enhance the contribution of their review to classify these interventions as either directly targeting skills training or targeting teachers or peers as socializing agents. Those interventions that target teachers and classroom policies fit here, whereas those interventions that directly target social cognitive skills probably belong in the next section. The most well-known classroom-based approach is not mentioned, the Good Behavior Game (GBG), which alters disruptive behavior by manipulating group-level contingencies. Randomized controlled trials in first-grade classrooms have yielded positive effects on both proximal (Ialongo et al. 1999) and distal (Ialongo et al. 2001) time points.

Social skills interventions overlap with school-based interventions because many of these programs are delivered in school settings. These interventions fall squarely in the proximal mediator of acquired personality characteristics in figure 8C.1. Hill et al. conclude that some of these interventions are effective, but they are less enthusiastic about this type of intervention. In fact, they conclude that it is the intervention "most in need of future work" among all interventions reviewed, and they make reference to "the lack of efficacy for social cognitive interventions" even though meta-analyses by Landenberger and Lipsey (2005) indicate that interventions that address social-cognitive factors through cognitive-behavioral means are the most effective of all programs reviewed.

Hill et al.'s concept of social skills intervention is very narrow, as evident in their statement that social skills training "is intended to help those individuals lacking in even the most basic interaction abilities, such as making small talk and maintaining eye contact." Their distinction between social skills and social-cognitive skills interventions seems baseless. A broader concept would incorporate both types and would include interventions that target the array of mental operations just described as patterns of social information processing. As a consequence, the Hill et al. review of this category of interventions is cursory and fails to include many interventions that have been tested through randomized controlled trials and found to be efficacious in improving targeted skills and in preventing longer-term delinquency and crime.

For example, Greenberg and Kusche (1993) have developed an elementary classroom curriculum designed to teach the social cognitive skills described above, including accurate recognition of emotions in others and the self, accurate interpretation of others' intentions, and social problem solving. Their PATHS Program (Providing Alternative Thinking Strategies) has been found in randomized controlled trials to be effective in reducing aggressive behavior and promoting prosocial behavior (Conduct Problems Prevention Research Group 1999).

Hudley and Graham (1993) developed an intervention targeted toward reducing hostile attributional biases in African American children, with demonstrated success in reducing aggressive behavior through a randomized trial. Lochman's Coping Power Program, which is designed to enhance an array of social-cognitive skills in aggressive fourth- and fifth-grade boys, has yielded positive effects on reducing aggressive behaviors that persist a year later (Lochman and Wells 2004). Ross and Ross (1998) found that a cognitive program aimed at helping youth to stop and think about social problems, consider alternative strategies, and consider consequences of their actions had positive effects on reducing reoffending in a delinquent sample. Kazdin (2003) developed a variant of this approach called Problem-Solving Skills Training (PSST). He has found success in reducing aggressive behavior in both home and school settings, that is sustained for at least twelve months, in five replicated randomized controlled trials. Landerberg and Lipsey's (2005) meta-analysis of the array of cognitive-behavior programs for offenders reveals a positive mean effect size from randomized trials, with the strongest positive effects for interventions that address anger control and social problem-solving skills.

One comprehensive social skills intervention program that is reviewed favorably by Hill and colleagues is Botvin's Life Skills Training. However, Hill et al. do not classify this program as addressing social skills, even though it addresses the components of social information processing described earlier; specifically, self-management skills, goal-setting, problem-solving, and evaluation of consequences. Furthermore, Botvin and Griffin (2004) have found that the impact of this intervention on antisocial behavior outcomes is mediated by its effect on social-cognitive patterns such as decision making and perceptions of norms and consequences.

Family interventions consistently yield positive impact according to Hill et al. The basis for many of these interventions is Patterson, Reid, and Dishion's (1992) coercion theory. For example, the primary goal of Parent Management Training (PMT) is to alter the pattern of exchanges between parent and child during discipline events so that coercive behavior by each party is extinguished in favor of contingent, consistent, and clear rules that lead to compliance. The meta-analysis of forty studies by Farrington and Welsh (2003) yielded a mean effect size of .32 in preventing delinquency outcomes. Hill et al. appropriately emphasize three of the most thoroughly-studied programs: Functional Family Therapy, Multisystemic Therapy, and Multidimensional Treatment Foster Care. All of these programs help the parent to teach the child to understand contingencies for misbehavior and to solve problems more effectively.

Nutrition interventions reviewed by Hill et al. come out of the blue. The only intervention reviewed in this section is one that provides children with essential fatty acids found in fish oil. Here, Hill et al. abandon their reliance on rigorous randomized controlled trials to herald the promise of this intervention. Although the theory behind this intervention is that fish oil affects serotonergic functioning related to impulsive cognitions, the evidence is simply not conclusive yet because of the lack of randomized controlled trials. Most of the evidence is anecdotal or case study. Furthermore, their assertion that nutrition-based interventions require "little or no labor" completely ignores the major challenge in this intervention of getting high-risk, antisocial participants to comply with a treatment protocol in perpetuity.

Cultural interventions are not labeled as such by Hill et al., but they do review the Olweus Bullying Program (Olweus 1995), which is an attempt to change school, peer, and community cultural norms about aggressing and bullying. This program has been implemented widely in Scandinavia, with apparent positive effects. However, this conclusion is based on weak evidence of pre- to post-changes and dose-to-outcome correlations, but no randomized controlled trials.

Conclusion

The review by Hill and colleagues provides a contribution by focusing scholars' attention on the mediating processes that account for intervention effectiveness. However, they may be pointing researchers in the wrong direction with their terminology. They conclude, "noncognitive interventions can have as strong, if not stronger, effects than programs targeting IQ or the environment." Ironically, the interventions that they find to be most effective *do* target both cognitions and the environment. To call these interventions noncognitive is to create a false dichotomy. After all, all social behavior is brain-mediated. Certainly, the day of targeting IQ is long past, but effective interventions are those that target important mental operations in aggressive behavior, either through direct skill-building or indirectly through changing family, school and peer, and cultural environments that in turn affect a child's mental patterns of operating on the world.

References

Bandura, Albert. 1999. "Moral Disengagement in the Perpetration of Inhumanities." *Personality and Social Psychology Review* 3 (3): 193–209.
Botvin, Gilbert J., and Kenneth W. Griffin. 2004. "Life Skills Training: Empirical Findings and Future Directions." *The Journal of Primary Prevention* 25 (2): 211–32.

Bowlby, John. 1980. *Attachment and Loss, Volume 3: Loss*. New York: Basic Books.

Bretherton, Inge. 1999. "Updating the 'Internal Working Model' Construct: Some Reflections." *Attachment and Human Development* 1 (3): 343–57.

Cantor, Nancy, and John F. Kihlstrom. 1982. "Cognitive and Social Processes in Personality." In *Contemporary Behavior Therapy*, edited by G. T. Wilson and C. Franks, 142–201. New York: Guilford.

Caspi, Avshalom, Joseph McClay, Terrie E. Moffitt, Jonathan Mill, Judy Martin, Ian W. Craig, Alan Taylor, and Richie Poulton. 2002. "Role of Genotype in the Cycle of Violence in Maltreated Children." *Science* 297 (5582): 851–54.

Cervone, Daniel, and Yoishi Shoda. 1999. *The Coherence of Personality: Social-Cognitive Bases of Consistency, Variability, and Organization*. New York: Guilford.

Conduct Problems Prevention Research Group. 1999. "Initial Impact of the Fast Track Prevention Trial for Conduct Problems: I. The High-Risk Sample." *Journal of Consulting and Clinical Psychology* 67:631–47.

Cunha, Flavia, and James J. Heckman. 2008. "Formulating, Identifying, and Estimating the Technology of Cognitive and Noncognitive Skill Formation." *Journal of Human Resources* 43 (4): 738–82.

Dodge, Kenneth A. 2003. "Do Social Information Processing Patterns Mediate Aggressive Behavior?" In *Causes of Conduct Disorder and Juvenile Delinquency*, edited by Benjamin B. Lahey, Terrie E. Moffitt, and Avshalom Caspi, 254–74. New York: Guilford Press.

Dodge, Kenneth A., John E. Bates, and Gregory S. Pettit. 1990. "Mechanisms in the Cycle of Violence." *Science* 250 (4988): 1678–83.

Dodge, Kenneth A., John D. Coie, and Donald Lynam. 2006. "Aggression and Antisocial Behavior in Youth." In *Handbook of Child Psychology: Volume 3, Social, Emotional, and Personality Development*, 6th ed., series editor W. Damon, and volume editor N. Eisenberg, 720–71. New York: Wiley.

Dodge, Kenneth A., and Gregory S. Petit. 2003. "A Biopsychosocial Model of the Development of Chronic Conduct Problems in Adolescence." *Developmental Psychology* 39 (2): 349–71.

Dodge, Kenneth A., Gregory S. Pettit, Cynthia L. McClaskey, and Melissa M. Brown. 1986. "Social Competence in Children." Serial no. 213. *Monographs of the Society for Research in Child Development* 51 (2): 1–85.

Farrington, D. P., and B. C. Welsh. 2003. "Family-Based Prevention of Offending: A Meta-Analysis. *Australian and New Zealand Journal of Criminology* 36: 127–51.

Greenberg, Mark T., and Carol A. Kusche. 1993. *Promoting Social and Emotional Development in Deaf Children: The PATHS Project*. Seattle, WA: University of Washington Press.

Heckman, J. J. 2008. "Schools, Skills, and Synapses." *Economic Inquiry* 46 (3): 289–324.

Heckman, J. J., S. H. Moon, R. Pinto, P. A. Savelyev, and A. Q. Yavitz. 2010. "The Rate of Return to the HighScope Perry Preschool Program. *Journal of Public Economics* 94 (1-2): 114–28.

Heckman, James J., Jora Stixrud, and Sergio Urzua. 2006. "The Effects of Cognitive and Noncognitive Abilities on Labor Market Outcomes and Social Behavior." *Journal of Labor Economics* 24 (3): 411–82.

Hudley, Cynthia A., and Sandra Graham. 1993. "An Attributional Intervention to Reduce Peer-Directed Aggression among African-American Boys." *Child Development* 64 (1): 124–38.

Huesmann, L. Rowell. 1988. "An Information-Processing Model for the Development of Aggression." *Aggressive Behavior* 14 (1): 13–24.

Ialongo, Nicholas, Jeanne Poduska, Lisa Werthamer, and Sheppard G. Kellam. 2001. "The Distal Impact of Two First-Grade Preventive Interventions on Conduct Problems and Disorder in Early Adolescence." *Journal of Emotional and Behavioral Disorders* 9 (3): 146–60.

Ialongo, Nicholas S., Lisa Werthamer, Sheppard G. Kellam, C. Hendricks Brown, Songbai Wang, and Yuhua Lin. 1999. "Proximal Impact of Two First-Grade Preventive Interventions on the Early Risk Behaviors for Later Substance Abuse, Depression, and Antisocial Behavior." *American Journal of Community Psychology* 27 (5): 599–641.

Kahneman, Daniel, and Amos Tversky. 1982. "The Simulation Heuristic." In *Judgment under Uncertainty: Heuristics and Biases,* edited by Daniel Kahneman, Paul Slovic, and Amos Tversky, 201–09. New York: Cambridge University Press.

Kazdin, Alan E. 2003. "Problem-Solving Skills Training and Parent Management Training for Conduct Disorder." In *Evidence-Based Psychotherapies for Children and Adolescents,* edited by Alan E. Kazdin and John R. Weisz, 241–62. New York: Guilford Press.

Landenberger, Nana A., and Mark W. Lipsey. 2005. "The Positive Effects of Cognitive-Behavioral Programs for Offenders: A Meta-Analysis of Factors Associated with Effective Treatment." *Journal of Experimental Criminology* 1 (4): 451–76.

Lochman, John E., and Karen C. Wells. 2004. "The Coping Power Program for Preadolescent Aggressive Boys and Their Parents: Outcome Effects at the 1-Year Follow-up." *Journal of Consulting and Clinical Psychology* 72 (4): 571–78.

McCrae, Robert R., and Paul T Costa Jr. 1997. "Personality Trait Structure as a Human Universal." *American Psychologist* 52 (5): 509–16.

Miller, Joshua D., Donald Lynam, and Carl Leukefeld. 2003. "Examining Antisocial Behavior through the Lens of the Five Factor Model of Personality." *Aggressive Behavior* 29 (6): 497–514.

Mischel, Walter. 1999. "Personality Coherence and Dispositions in a Cognitive-Affective Personality System (CAPS) Approach." In *The Coherence of Personality: Social-Cognitive Bases of Consistency, Variability, and Organization,* edited by Daniel Cervone and Yuichi Shoda, 37–60. New York: Guilford.

Olweus, D. 2005. "A Useful Evaluation Design, and Effects of the Olweus Bullying Prevention Program." *Psychology, Crime & Law* 11 (4): 389–402.

Orobio de Castro, Bram, Jan W. Veerman, Willem Koops, Joop D. Bosch, and Heidi J. Monshouwer. 2002. "Hostile Attribution of Intent and Aggressive Behavior: A Meta-Analysis." *Child Development* 73 (3): 916–34.

Patterson, G. R., J. B. Reid, and T. J. Dishion. 1992. *A Social Learning Approach: Volume 4, Antisocial Boys.* Eugene, OR: Castalia.

Ross, Robert R., and Bambi D. Ross. 1998. "Delinquency Prevention through Cognitive Training." *New Education* 10:70–5.

Simon, Herbert A. 1957. *Models of Man.* New York: Wiley.

Welsh, B. C., C. J. Sullivan, and D. L. Olds. 2010. "When Early Crime Prevention Goes to Scale: A New Look at the Evidence." *Prevention Science* 11:115–25.

Family Income, Neighborhood Poverty, and Crime

Sara B. Heller, Brian A. Jacob, and Jens Ludwig

9.1 Introduction

Criminal offending and victimization are disproportionately concentrated among disadvantaged people living in economically distressed areas. This cross-sectional correlation between poverty and crime, together with growing concerns about the social costs of America's system of mass incarceration, have led many to wonder whether shifting resources from prisons to social programs would control crime at a lower cost. This is not a new idea. For example, distress in 1820s Paris about the "apparent failure of French penal strategies" prompted calls to focus more attention on the "root causes" of crime, such as individual poverty and income inequality (Beirne 1987, 1143). The idea that the geographic concentration of poverty itself might contribute to crime as another key root cause dates back at least to the "Chicago School" of Sociology in the 1930s (Shaw and McKay 1942). A Gallup poll taken in 2006 suggests that two-thirds of the American public favor reducing crime through increased social spending, while just one-third

Sara B. Heller is a PhD student in the Harris School of Public Policy at the University of Chicago and a US Department of Education Institute for Education Sciences predoctoral fellow in the Committee on Education. Brian A. Jacob is the Walter H. Annenberg Professor of Education Policy; professor of economics; and director of the Center on Local, State, and Urban Policy (CLOSUP) at the Gerald R. Ford School of Public Policy, University of Michigan; and a research associate of the National Bureau of Economic Research. Jens Ludwig is the McCormick Foundation Professor of Social Service Administration, Law, and Public Policy at the University of Chicago, director of the University of Chicago Crime lab, a research associate of the NBER, and a codirector of the NBER Working Group on the Economics of Crime.

Thanks to Philip Cook, Lance Lochner, John MacDonald, Justin McCrary, Lawrence Katz; participants in the 2009 National Bureau of Economic Research (NBER) Summer Institute preconference and January 2010 NBER research conference in Berkeley; two anonymous referees for helpful comments; and Laura Brinkman for research assistance. All opinions and any errors are, of course, our own.

favors additional spending on enforcement activities.[1] A different poll found that the public believes the most effective ways to prevent crime are, after teaching young people moral values and providing them with recreational opportunities, efforts to "increase business/economic development in poor neighborhoods to create living-wage jobs."[2]

On the other hand, there remains great skepticism in some quarters about the ability of government social programs to reduce crime, based in part on time series patterns about what happens to crime following implementation of new antipoverty initiatives. For example, crime was a major problem in New York City throughout the 1970s despite the city's various new social policy efforts, leading David Brooks to argue in the *New York Times* that the city's "crime wave made it hard to think that social problems would be solved strictly by changing material circumstances" (Brooks 2010, A27). John Podhoretz (2010, 28) has argued that "every effort to cure [social pathologies] through large-scale government action only made matters worse, in one of the most potent demonstrations of the law of unintended consequences." The perceived futility (or worse) of government antipoverty efforts is not limited to the experiences of America's largest urban areas. A recent widely cited article in the *Atlantic Monthly* argues that government efforts to deconcentrate poverty in low-income neighborhoods contributed to large *increases* in crime in America's midsized cities (Rosin 2008).

In this chapter, we review the existing theory and evidence about how and why government efforts to reduce family- or neighborhood-level poverty might influence aggregate crime rates. We come down somewhere in the middle of the debate. In our view, the skeptics about government social programs are probably too pessimistic. The best available empirical evidence suggests that government efforts to increase the incomes of poor families, or to help them move out of the highest-poverty urban areas, can reduce criminal involvement. One plausible mechanism is the link between family or neighborhood environments and children's developmental outcomes.

An important caution, however, is that most of this evidence comes from the study of small-scale policy initiatives; the effects of large-scale policy changes could be different. In fact, little is known about how to deconcentrate poverty on a large scale because only families living in public housing, who represent a small share of all poor households, appear to be amenable to moving out of high-poverty areas in response to government housing interventions. Moreover, given the plausibly central role of human capital, even small-scale policy efforts to reduce poverty may not be as cost-effective as policies that directly seek to increase human capital, discussed in the chapters in this volume by Lance Lochner (chapter 10), Seth G. Sanders

1. See http://www.albany.edu/sourcebook/pdf/t2282006.pdf.
2. See http://www.soros.org/initiatives/usprograms/focus/justice/articles_publications/publications/hartpoll_20020201/Hart-Poll.pdf.

(chapter 12), Richard G. Frank and Thomas G. McGuire (chapter 4), and Patrick L. Hill and colleagues (chapter 8).

The next section of our chapter lays out some basic facts that help motivate our analysis. We document the strong cross-sectional relationship between poverty and crime within countries, which has for centuries led people to hypothesize that social policy could be an important lever for reducing crime. We note that the strong within-country cross-sectional correlation between poverty and crime does not seem to be as evident in cross-sectional comparisons *across* different countries in the developed world or in trends of poverty and crime within the United States over time. While these types of comparisons are often referenced in public debates about crime policy, none of these analyses is capable of providing reliable evidence about the causal link between poverty and crime. The fact that family- or neighborhood-level poverty is correlated with criminal involvement does not necessarily imply that crime rates need decline as a result of social policies designed to mitigate poverty. Observed correlations between criminal behavior and either individual- or community-level disadvantage may simply reflect the influences of other family attributes that directly affect both youth crime and how much income families have or where families decide to live (see Jencks and Mayer 1990; Mayer 1997). Time series comparisons are complicated by the fact that many determinants of crime are changing over time, not just poverty levels.

In section 9.3, we present a conceptual framework that lays out how additional income might affect crime. Our focus is on juvenile crime, in large part because the available micro-level evidence provides the best information on this age group. The costs of this focus in terms of generalizability may be at least partially justified by the fact that rates of criminal offending peak between late adolescence and early adulthood, depending on the specific type of crime (see, for example, Blumstein and Cohen 1987; Cook and Laub 2002). The basic insight from this simple framework is that the expected effect on crime of antipoverty programs is theoretically ambiguous—declines in economically motivated crime or improvements in children's developmental environments may be offset by increased consumption of goods that are closely linked to crime (like drugs and alcohol) or exposure to more lucrative opportunities for theft.

Of course, at extreme levels, poverty itself must surely matter. No one can believe that starvation, disease, and homelessness can be anything but harmful for children's developmental and criminal outcomes as well as catalysts for desperate acts by adolescents and adults. At the same time, the behavioral effects of additional family income presumably decline as family income increases—that is, that the behavioral consequences of a $1,000 transfer are larger for poor families than for very rich ones. The relevant question for public policy, then, is whether incremental changes in transfer programs that affect either the level or concentration of poverty within the ranges that we observe in modern America will reduce crime. Similarly, it is critical to know whether this approach could achieve large-scale crime reductions and how the benefits and costs of this approach compare to those of other strategies.

The fourth section of our chapter reviews the available empirical evidence about the relationship between family or neighborhood poverty and crime, particularly how policies designed to change these social conditions affect crime. Our review is selective, focusing primarily on recent policy experiments with clear sources of identifying variation that help overcome the selection bias problems that plague much of the previous empirical literature. The desire to overcome selection concerns leads us to focus disproportionately (though certainly not exclusively) on means-tested housing subsidies, which represent a fairly large part of the American social safety net and, importantly, are not an entitlement.[3] The excess demand for housing subsidies provides an unusually good opportunity for the identification of causal relationships between criminal activity and both family- and neighborhood-level poverty.

Our reading of the available research suggests there is reason to believe that both family- and neighborhood-level disadvantage are causally related to criminal behavior. More precisely, the specific types of policies that have been examined in the literature to date—either transferring resources to poor families or helping poor families move into less disadvantaged social settings—seem capable of reducing arrest rates, particularly for adolescents. It is harder to draw confident conclusions from the available data about the key behavioral mechanisms that underlie these relationships.

The lack of good evidence about mechanisms limits our ability to refine policy design, especially because the specific effects of social programs on crime are likely to depend on how the design details shape consumption patterns and work effort. For example, both money and parental time are important inputs into a child's development. There is some evidence that antipoverty programs that create relatively larger work incentives may lead to relatively more antisocial behavior by adolescents within these families, presumably due to some decline in parental monitoring and supports.

The final section of our paper discusses what is known about how these

---

3. Federal spending on housing assistance for the poor was around $40 billion in 2006, substantially more than the $28 billion spent on Temporary Assistance for Needy Families (TANF). These figures are derived as follows: the U.S. House of Representatives Ways and Means Committee "Green Book" for 2008 reports that a total of $42.2 billion was spent on housing programs by the U.S. Department of Housing and Urban Development (HUD) although part of the $7 billion spent on block grant programs by HUD may go to nonhousing activities such as crime prevention or child care under the Community Development Block Grant program. The U.S. Department of Education also spends around a half-billion dollars per year on rental assistance to rural families in the Section 521 program; see http://www.obpa .usda.gov/budsum/FY10budsum.pdf. Some low-income homeowners may also receive a tax subsidy through the mortgage interest deduction if they itemize.

interventions would operate at a large scale as well as the difficulties that would arise from trying to substantially expand the scope of these types of programs. We also discuss what is known about how the benefits and costs of these types of interventions compare to alternative crime-control efforts, including mass incarceration and human capital interventions.

9.2   Descriptive Patterns for Poverty and Crime

Within the United States, criminal offending and victimization rates tend to be disproportionately concentrated among low-income people living in high-poverty communities. For example, the 2004 homicide rate in Hyde Park—the racially and economically mixed neighborhood that is home to the University of Chicago—was 13 per 100,000. The homicide rate in the directly adjacent neighborhood of Washington Park, where nearly three-quarters of children live below the poverty line and 98 percent of residents are African American, was nearly five times as high (64 per 100,000). For many people, this pattern provides prima facie evidence for the causal effects of individual- or neighborhood-level poverty on criminal involvement. But this correlation may be misleading if the underlying determinants of why some families wind up living in poverty (or in high-poverty areas) are themselves also directly relevant for criminal involvement.

Cross-country comparisons are also frequently used to draw inferences about the underlying determinants of criminal behavior, an approach that shares the same methodological limitations of within-country cross-section comparisons but, interestingly, does not seem to provide the same support for a strong poverty-crime link: countries that either spend relatively more on social programs or have lower poverty rates or both do not consistently have lower crime rates.

The United States serves as a particularly interesting case study. Compared to most other developed nations, we spend a much lower share of our gross domestic product (GDP) on social programs for the nonelderly poor, and we have a much larger proportion of the population with incomes below 50 percent of the median.[4] While there are some differences across countries in how crimes are defined and the willingness of citizens to report crime to the police or to survey interviews, data assembled by the United Nations suggest that crime rates in the United States are not substantially different from those found in other developed nations. For example, in 1999, the over-

---

4. Data from the Luxembourg Income Study (LIS) shows the proportion with incomes below 50 percent of median for selected countries are the United States, 17 percent; Mexico, 20 percent; Ireland, 16.5 percent; Australia, 13 percent; Italy, 13 percent; United Kingdom, 12 percent; Canada, 11 percent; Germany, 8 percent; France, 7 percent; and Sweden, 6.5 percent. The overall average across the LIS is 10.8% (Burtless and Smeeding 2007). Three percent of U.S. GDP goes to nonelderly social programs, compared to 6 percent in other Anglo Saxon countries and 12+ percent in Northern European or Scandinavian countries (Burtless and Smeeding 2007).

all rate of crimes reported in official police statistics was 8,517 per 100,000 inhabitants in the United States compared to 10,061 in England and Wales. The total number of recorded assaults in 1999 per 100,000 inhabitants was 805 in the United States compared to 833 in England and Wales.[5] The one crime for which the United States is clearly an outlier compared to most other developed nations is homicide, which is probably due to the relatively greater involvement of guns in violent crime in the United States compared to other places (see Zimring and Hawkins 1997).

A third common—but flawed—way to assess the poverty-crime relationship is to compare trends in both poverty and crime to see if the two are related. Figure 9.1 shows that the official poverty rate has held fairly steady at around 13 percent between 1967 and 2008. Figure 9.1 also shows that over this same time period, income inequality, measured as the ratio of incomes for households at the 90th percentile of the distribution divided by the income of households at the 10th percentile of the distribution (the "90/10 ratio"), has increased substantially (see also Autor, Katz, and Kearney 2008).

Income segregation across neighborhoods has also been increasing steadily since the 1970s. This can be seen in figure 9.2, which shows a steady increase in what Watson (2009) terms the Centile Gap Index (CGI). The CGI measures how far the average family income within a neighborhood (Census tract) deviates in percentile terms from the median tract family income, compared to how far it would deviate under perfect integration. Figure 9.2 also shows some increase over time in a different measure of isolation, the exposure of the bottom quintile of the income distribution to itself, which is the fraction of bottom quintile families in a typical bottom quintile family's Census tract.[6]

One potential exception to these generally gloomy trends is the indication

---

5. See United Nations Seventh Survey on Crime Trends and the Operations of Criminal Justice Systems, 1998–2000; http://www.unodc.org/pdf/crime/seventh_survey/7pv.pdf.

6. One might think that steady poverty rates and increasing inequality reflect constant or falling levels of social spending. On the contrary, over this same time period, total spending on social programs increased substantially, from $59 billion in 1968 (in constant 2002 dollars) to $373 billion by 2002 (figure 9.3). Spending on medical benefits increased most sharply over this time period, but spending on cash aid has also increased considerably. While spending on means-tested housing programs has stagnated since the mid-1970s, the total number of homeowners and renters receiving housing assistance has increased. Nevertheless, even now only around 28 percent of income-eligible households receive means-tested housing assistance (Olsen 2003). Also relevant for present purposes is the fact that the mix of means-tested housing programs has changed over time (Quigley 2000; Olsen 2003). Over the past several decades, an increasingly large share of housing assistance is delivered in the form of housing vouchers, which provide households with a subsidy to lease a unit of their own choosing in the private-housing market, rather than public housing or other forms of project-based housing. Given long wait-lists for housing assistance in most cities, unit-based subsidy programs like public housing essentially offer families a "take-it-or-leave-it" offer to live in a given housing unit in a given location, whereas vouchers rely more on family decisions about where (and whether) to move. As we discuss further in the following, families with housing vouchers live in lower-poverty areas compared to those in public or project-based housing (see also Olsen 2003).

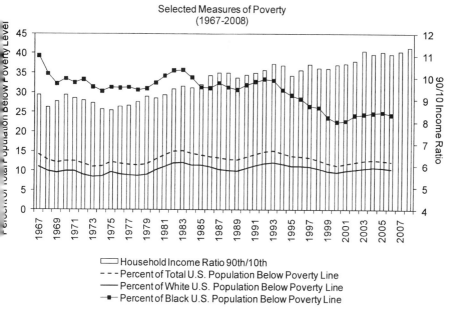

Fig. 9.1 Trends in poverty and income inequality

Sources: U.S. Census Bureau, Historical Income Inequality Tables; U.S. Census Bureau, Historical Poverty Tables.

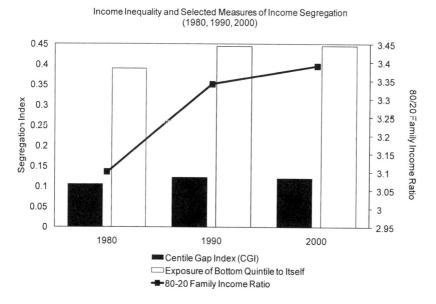

Fig. 9.2 Trends in measures of income segregation from Watson (2009)

Source: Watson 2009.

of some improvement in well-being for African Americans over the past several decades, at least on selected measures, which may be quite important given the disproportionate involvement of blacks in crime as both victims and offenders. Figure 9.1 shows that since the early 1990s, the poverty rate among blacks has declined by nearly a third (from 33 to 24 percent). Figure 9.3 shows that since 1970, the amount of neighborhood racial segregation in America has declined in U.S. metropolitan areas. This figure, taken from Glaeser and Vigdor (2003), shows the dissimilarity index, defined as the proportion of blacks who would need to change Census tracts in order to achieve perfect integration (where the share of blacks in each Census tract would equal the share of blacks in the overall metropolitan area so that if a metropolitan area was 40 percent black, each tract would also be 40 percent black).

Crime rates do not appear to be systematically related to the trends in any of the previously mentioned measures of family- or neighborhood-level disadvantage (see also Cook 2009). Crime rates have been much more cyclical over the past several decades (figure 9.4) than either the overall share of Americans living in poverty or the different measures of neighborhood segregation shown in the preceding. The data on crime trends shown in figure 9.4 come from the FBI's (Federal Bureau of Investigation 2008) Uniform Crime Report (UCR) system for homicides, all serious (Part 1) violent crimes (homicide, rape, robbery, aggravated assault), and all serious

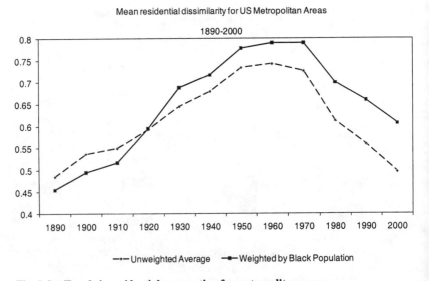

Fig. 9.3   Trends in residential segregation for metropolitan areas
Sources: Authors' calculations from Cutler and Glaeser (1997) and Cutler, Glaeser, and Vigdor (1999).

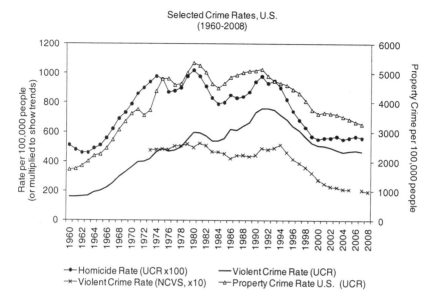

Fig. 9.4   Crime trends in the United States

Source: Bureau of Justice Statistics, National Crime Victimization Survey, and own calcu
lations.

property crimes (motor vehicle theft, burglary, and larceny), as well as self-
reports about crime victimizations from the National Crime Victimization
Survey (NCVS).

To the extent that there is any visible evidence of an association between
changes in social conditions and crime, it is limited to the concurrent drop
over the 1990s in both crime rates and the poverty rate for blacks. This
pattern falls far short of definitive proof of a causal relationship, however,
because both measures could be declining over this period for a variety of
other reasons. This highlights the general problem in comparing trends in
aggregate time series data: many things are changing over time, which makes
it extremely difficult to isolate the effects of a single causal factor. For example, during the 1990s, the black poverty rate was falling—but over the
same period, spending on police and prisons increased substantially, the
crack epidemic of the late 1980s began to ebb, and the first birth cohorts
exposed to legalized abortion in the early 1970s started to reach adolescence
(Levitt 2004).

In the end, neither aggregate trends nor cross-country comparisons reveal
the strong connection between disadvantage and crime that is suggested
by cross-sectional, within-country comparisons of the crime experiences
across more versus less disadvantaged citizens. But despite being commonly
invoked in public debates, none of these comparisons is capable of isolating

the causal effects of poverty on crime. Adjudicating whether there is indeed a causal connection between poverty and crime requires stronger research designs.

9.3   Conceptual Framework

Social policies that are designed to increase families' income or reduce the level of disadvantage in their neighborhoods may influence criminal behavior through a variety of different mechanisms. The relevant mechanisms likely depend on the specific policy lever employed. In this section, we lay out a conceptual framework that helps clarify the key mechanisms through which different antipoverty policies might affect criminal behavior. Our intent is to highlight which potentially relevant mechanisms have complementary versus offsetting effects and how the design of a social program may influence its net impact on crime.

We focus on understanding criminal behavior by juveniles because, as noted in the preceding, this is the population for which the best empirical evidence is available. Late adolescence and early adulthood are the peak ages of criminal offending. Juveniles are also in a formative stage of human capital development (in terms of academic, socioemotional, and behavioral skills; decisions about schooling attainment; and health). Because this kind of human capital formation appears to be strongly predictive of criminal behavior (see, for example, Lochner and Moretti [2004] and Lance Lochner's chapter in this volume [chapter 10]), we consider it to be a potentially important mechanism.

To put our framework in a larger context, we begin with the canonical model from Gary Becker for the "supply of criminal offenses." The number of offenses, O, that an individual commits during any particular period is determined by:

$$O = O(p,f,u),$$

where p is the probability of conviction per offense, f is the punishment per offense, and u is a "portmanteau variable" that captures other relevant factors like the income available to the individual through the legal labor market and his or her willingness to engage in illegal activities (Becker 1968, 177).[7] Becker's focus is on the optimal amounts of p and f—how society can most efficiently minimize the social costs of crime by manipulating the likelihood of being caught and the punishment for a given crime. While this focus is important for criminal justice policy, our analysis here shifts attention to the u term. In fact, we might consider the question of whether resources should be transferred from mass incarceration to social programs to effectively be

---

7. We assume this last variable is scaled to have a positive relation to the number of offenses, so anything that increases u will increase crime and vice versa.

a question of the relative impacts of p, f, and u on O as well as the relative costs to society of achieving changes in these three "inputs" to crime.

To help us think through how various antipoverty policies might affect criminal behavior, we view u—an individual's inclination toward criminal behavior—as shaped by five interacting factors: parental wealth, parental time investment, a youth's level of human capital, the wealth of all other families in an individual's neighborhood, and local neighborhood resources like schools or police. These factors are clearly not independent. For example, human capital will be a function of both parental time and wealth and potentially neighborhood wealth and resources as well. Parent time and wealth are jointly determined by parents' labor supply decisions but are two distinct resources that might independently affect their children's criminal behavior. Because the determinants of u are likely to depend on previous as well as current investments and experience, changes in the potentially relevant factors that influence offending behavior might have varying effects on crime by age. We return to this idea briefly when we discuss the empirical evidence.

9.3.1   Effects of Resource Transfer Programs

Thinking about the role of these five factors helps us trace through the potential effects on criminal behavior from an increase in family income. We begin by analyzing the simplest case: how crime may change in response to a simple cash transfer. The direct effect of increased income, holding other factors constant, is likely but not certain to decrease crime. All else equal, a youth should have less incentive to steal something desirable if his or her parents can afford to buy it. More income may also change a family's routine activities in a way that reduces the likelihood that potential victims and offenders interact (Cohen and Felson 1979). For example, buying a car could reduce the risk that a child is victimized by a gang on the walk to school every day or even feels the need to join a gang for protection along that walk. On the other hand, additional income could lead to increased consumption by household members (potentially by youth as well as parents) of goods like alcohol and drugs, which contribute to crime through diminished inhibitions, capacity for planning, or increased levels of aggression. The partial effect of increasing income while holding other inputs constant is, therefore, ambiguous.

Even a simple cash transfer that increases family income, however, is not likely to have just this ceteris paribus effect; it will also create changes in other relevant inputs. Most clearly, more income may increase children's human capital. There is a large research literature suggesting that more human capital would reduce crime in a variety of ways—by providing better labor market options so that crime is relatively more costly or by decreasing the appeal of illegal activity. Empirically, human capital measures like intelligence quotient (IQ) scores are one-half to two-thirds of a standard deviation lower for criminal offenders compared to the general population (for some reason, these disparities tend to be somewhat larger for verbal than for nonverbal intelligence); more serious offenders have yet lower IQ scores still (Herrnstein 1995, 49–50). People with relatively higher human capital may also better appreciate the consequences of their actions or have higher levels of what psychologists and neuroscientists call executive functioning, which is related to self-regulation skills such as "inhibitory control, strategies of problem solving, memory, and self-monitoring" (Posner and Rothbart 2007, 80). Previous research has shown that a range of socioemotional and behavioral skills related to aggression, self-control, self-efficacy, moral reasoning, attribution of blame, and emotional coping, in some cases even when measured fairly early in life, are predictive of crime and related behaviors (see Agnew 1992; Herrnstein 1995; Heckman, Stixrud, and Urzua 2006; and chapter 8 by Patrick L. Hill and his colleagues in this volume).

However, as human capital theory makes clear, the size of the effect of income depends on how much of the increased wealth parents spend on investments in their children. Even parents who care deeply about their children's developmental outcomes do not care *exclusively* about those outcomes. So parents who receive additional income are likely to spend at least part of this extra money on normal goods that are not necessarily developmentally productive. In this case, only some fraction of each dollar transferred would be expected to improve child outcomes. Mayer (1997) confirms this idea empirically, finding that when low-income parents get additional income, they tend to spend it largely on additional housing expenditures, transportation, and food consumed away from home—not the physical inputs that seem most related to children's human capital development, such as books or developmentally enriching activities like museum visits.

Another possibility is that increased family income could change the productivity of parents' human capital investments in their children even if it does not change the absolute amount of investment. For example, previous research suggests that poverty status is positively correlated with the likelihood of suffering from depression and other mental health disorders, which could interfere with parents' ability to produce children's human capital or to successfully supervise them.[8] In this case, increased income could reduce

8. Moore et al. (2006) find that 10.4 percent of children in families under 200 percent of the poverty line have mothers with depressive symptoms; for families over 400 percent of the poverty line, the proportion drops to 2.3 percent. Data from the National Comorbidity Survey-Replication (NCS-R) suggests that minorities and people with fewer years of schooling attainment are, if anything, somewhat less likely than others to have had a mental health disorder over their lifetime but are somewhat more likely to have a disorder in the past twelve months (Kessler et al. 2003, 2005). One explanation for this pattern is that more disadvantaged populations seem less likely than others to either receive mental health treatment or to receive treatment from a mental health specialist (Wang et al. 2005). Frank and Meara (2009) use data from the National Longitudinal Survey of Youth 1979 (NLSY79) and find that maternal mental health is strongly correlated with negative child outcomes, even when analyses are done that compare siblings within the same families.

stress and mental health problems among parents, potentially reducing crime by improving the quality of parenting and supervision that children experience (i.e., increasing the productivity of the inputs in the human capital production function).

Increased income may also change the amount of time parents spend with their children. Economic theory suggests that an increase in income from a cash transfer is likely to decrease the amount of time parents spend at work—more money creates an income effect that reduces work and increases leisure. If parents spend some or all of this extra time with their children, we might expect a decrease in crime because of increased parental supervision (Aizer 2004; Dwyer et al. 1990) or increased human capital development, assuming that time children spend interacting with parents is more developmentally productive than the most likely alternative activities.[9]

These changes in parental time use become particularly important when we recognize that antipoverty programs are often structured in ways that intentionally or unintentionally change the incentives for parental work. For example, many programs reduce benefit payments as family earnings increase, which effectively increases the marginal tax rate on earnings. Working in the other direction, many programs have rules that require a variety of behaviors in exchange for funding, from spending on a particular kind of good (as with food stamps or public housing) to meeting work requirements (as with Temporary Assistance for Needy Families, or TANF, and the Earned Income Tax Credit, or EITC). The way these rules shape work incentives varies considerably by program, and the details are likely to be important factors in how social spending changes u. We expect policies that increase parental work along with family income may have smaller crime-reducing effects than policies that are work neutral or reduce work effort. Policies that raise income and parental work could in principle even increase youth crime despite the gain to families in income.[10] This is not intended to reflect a value judgment about the merits of incentivizing work as part of antipoverty programs, because society has many different objectives for such programs—we are only noting the potential consequence for this one important behavioral outcome.

So far, we have implicitly assumed an intervention that increases income for just a small subset of families, leaving the income of everyone else unaffected. Such a policy change would reduce both the relative and absolute

9. One important potential exception is the case in which compensatory early childhood programs like Head Start substitute for parent time with very young children; for more on that literature, see Lochner (chapter 10 in this volume).
10. In reality, any particular policy's effects on work effort are likely to be heterogeneous. For example, at low income levels, the EITC increases the marginal returns to legal work, suggesting more work income and less time at home. Over the phase-out income range, however, the EITC effectively increases marginal tax rates for certain workers, potentially creating the reverse effect. Such design details are likely to be important in considering the net impact of poverty policies on crime.

level of poverty experienced by program participants although the only sort of policy that would affect just a small share of families would be one that either limited eligibility to a narrow population or else conditioned receipt on behavioral requirements that only a relatively small subset of families could meet. In such cases, declines in *relative* poverty could be a relevant mechanism in affecting criminal behavior above and beyond the results of changing the family's absolute material condition. For example, if income boosts human capital, and people are competing on the basis of their skills for prosocial rewards like grades or jobs (Jencks and Mayer 1990), changes in relative poverty may matter independently of the increase in income or human capital on its own. In other words, the ratio of own wealth to everyone else's wealth may be important. Relative poverty also features prominently in sociological ideas like "strain theory" and its variants, which suggest that crime results from frustration when people are unable to achieve goals like wealth and status and that this frustration may be particularly acute when people are observing others who are more successful (Merton 1938; Agnew 1992).

Larger-scale antipoverty policies, on the other hand, would change the income of most others in the community as well, not just individual families. This possibility further complicates our prediction of the net effect of a transfer policy on criminal behavior. Large scale antipoverty programs would change the absolute poverty status of program recipients, but not their relative economic status—or at least not relative to other families in the bottom part of the income distribution. Large-scale transfer programs could generate some beneficial impacts for youth if, for example, having more affluent neighbors increases the ability of poor families to borrow from friends in response to unexpected negative income shocks. However, such policies would also increase the value of the "loot" (televisions, cars, etc.) that is available to steal in a community and increase aggregate consumption levels of goods like alcohol and drugs that augment the risk of involvement with crime as either offender or victim (that is, "criminogenic" and "victimogenic" goods).

9.3.2 The Theoretical Effects of Policies that Reduce Neighborhood Poverty

Also of interest are policies designed to reduce the exposure of poor families to high-poverty neighborhood environments, which often takes the form of subsidizing poor families' moves to wealthier neighborhoods.[11] The net

---

11. A few policies, like the Harlem Children's Zone, focus on improving existing neighborhoods rather than moving families out of poor neighborhoods. In general, such programs should have a similar positive effect on neighborhood wealth as voucher-type programs. They may also increase family income by improving the local economy (thus minimizing any negative effects of increased relative poverty) but decrease parental time at home (if parental employment increases). We discuss such policies briefly in the concluding section but focus on the theoretical effects of mobility policies because they are both more prevalent and better researched.

effect on criminal behavior from this type of change depends on the magnitude of the effects from changing relative poverty, changes in the availability of loot, and other spillovers that come from living near more affluent adults such as increased exposure to middle-class adults who serve as role models to signal the value of schooling and work (Wilson 1987).

Moving to a less disadvantaged neighborhood might also change other attributes of one's neighbors or neighborhood. For example, neighborhoods might vary in the norms that local adults have about various behaviors, including parenting, which could affect the quantity or quality of time parents spend with children and, hence, their human capital. For example, Annette Lareau (2002, 2003) finds that the middle-class families she studies tend to view parenting as an effort in "concerted cultivation," while many poor and working-class families in her sample view child development as the "accomplishment of natural growth," something that just happens. The contrast in parenting practices across class is particularly stark in the realm of language use. Hart and Risley (1995) find that by age three, children in professional families speak more per hour and have larger vocabularies than the *parents* of children in families on welfare. Social norms regarding the value of schooling and work could potentially also vary across neighborhood wealth levels, as in the "culture of poverty" arguments from Oscar Lewis (1959, 1966). Wealthier neighborhoods may also affect youths' penchant to engage in crime through informal social control or the willingness of local adults to help enforce shared prosocial norms (Sampson, Raudenbush, and Earls 1997).

Moving to a less disadvantaged neighborhood could also improve the quality of the local institutions that families experience. Improved local institutions could reduce crime directly. For example, if policing in some neighborhoods is better than in others, p or f might be higher in more economically affluent areas, thus reducing crime by increasing its costs. More affluent neighborhoods may also have higher-quality schools, thus increasing human capital, in part because higher-quality teachers seem to prefer teaching more affluent and higher-achieving children (Hanushek, Kain, and Rivkin 2004). On the other hand, it is possible that increasing neighborhood wealth could have adverse effects on criminality as well. In schools, the competition for grades or other prosocial rewards may be more intense in affluent areas and thus harm human capital, as under relative deprivation or competition models (Jencks and Mayer 1990). New job opportunities for parents may also decrease the time they have available to spend with their children, resulting in increased crime, but augment family income, which may create an offsetting effect.

In sum, theory yields ambiguous predictions about the sign, much less the magnitude, of the crime effects resulting from increasing family or neighborhood income. The five factors we consider—family income, parental time with children, children's human capital, neighborhood income, and neighborhood resources—are likely to have varied and interacting effects.

Still, some predictions do come out of our conceptual framework. Although income transfers may or may not reduce crime on net, those that reduce (or at least do not change) parental labor supply seem likely to generate larger declines in criminal behavior than those that push parents to work more. Neighborhood mobility programs also have theoretically ambiguous effects on criminal behavior but may generate the largest changes in criminal behavior in cities where there is relatively more variation across neighborhoods in social environments and the quality of local institutions.

In addition to highlighting the interactions between human capital development, parental time use, and neighborhood resources, our framework also suggests that the effects of smaller-scale income-transfer programs differ from those of large-scale programs. This is both because decisions to participate in crime might be affected by relative as well as absolute poverty status and because large-scale income-transfer programs may increase community-level consumption of criminogenic and victimogenic goods like drugs and alcohol. In our review of the evidence, we will discuss what is known about these candidate mechanisms.

9.4   Empirical Evidence

We have seen that the crime effects of policies designed to mitigate family or neighborhood poverty are hard to predict on the basis of theory alone. Raising incomes may push in different directions on different determinants of crime, making the overall impact dependent on whether the changes in factors increasing crime are more or less important than the ones decreasing it. Given the theoretical uncertainty about the size, or even direction, of the effect of additional income on crime, we now turn to a consideration of the empirical evidence.

Table 9.1 summarizes the results of the studies discussed in more detail in the following, listing both intent-to-treat (ITT) and treatment-on-the-treated (TOT) estimates. Our discussion focuses on the latter because we aim to compare program benefits to costs, and program costs are usually calculated on a per-participant basis. As table 9.1 reports, Jacob and Ludwig (2010) find that a transfer program providing a 50 percent average increase in family income (for families averaging around $14,000 in annual income) reduces violent and total arrests by 20 percent for males. In terms of potential mechanisms, there is some evidence that changes in human capital and time with parents may underlie their findings. A variety of welfare-to-work programs that increase parental labor supply confirm that parents' time at home may be an important determinant of adolescent outcomes. Although few direct crime measures are available in these studies, parental work incentives decrease adolescent test scores by .06 standard deviations, while grade repetition and special education services increase. For older adolescents, suspensions, expulsions, and school dropout also increase.

Table 9.1   Summary of key findings from research literature

Policy change	Effect on inputs	Effect on crime
Income transfer (housing voucher to families in private-market housing; change in consumption of housing and nonhousing, no change in neighborhood; Jacob and Ludwig 2010)	CHAC, private housing market baseline: *Family income → increase:* average of 50% additional income. *Human capital → increase:* ~10% increase in graduation, no change in test scores. *Time with parents → increase:* 10% decline in parental work. *Neighborhood income and resources → flat:* no change in observable neighborhood characteristics.	TOT: ~20% decrease in both violent and total arrests, driven largely by males. ITT: ~12% decrease in violent and total arrests.
Earnings supplements (Bloom and Michalopoulos 2001; Gennetian et al. 2002; Hamilton et al. 2001; Morris, Duncan, and Rodriguez 2007; Morris, Gennetian, and Duncan 2005)	MDRC welfare-to-work experiments: *Family income → increase:* 14% additional income in earnings supplement programs, no change in work-incentive only programs. *Human capital → decrease:* test scores down ~.06 SD (though increases for young children), increased grade repetition (12%) and special education (12%). For older adolescents, more dropout (46%) and suspensions/expulsions (28%). *Time with parents → decrease:* typically 10–30% increase in parental work. *Neighborhood income and resources → flat:* Some indication of increased moving. Few measures of neighborhood quality, no change in those available.	No direct measures, some indications of increased behavioral problems.
Mobility program (housing voucher to families in public housing at baseline; change in neighborhoods; Kling, Ludwig, and Katz 2005; Kling, Liebman and Katz 2007; Ludwig et al. 2008, 2010)	Moving to Opportunity: *Family income → flat:* no change in employment or earnings. *Human capital → increase* (females): Increase education outcomes for females only. *Time with parents → possible increase, no direct measures:* .08 SD (ITT) increase in parent mental health. *Neighborhood income and resources → increase:* ~40% decrease in neighborhood poverty rate (20% for ITT), plus changes in other attributes. <u>CHAC, public housing at baseline:</u> *Family income → not yet analyzed.* *Human capital → increase:* early results suggest .05 SD (ITT) reading score increase, .08 for math. *Time with parents → not yet analyzed.* *Neighborhood income and resources → increase:* ~40% decrease in neighborhood poverty rate, plus changes in other attributes.	<u>Moving to Opportunity:</u> TOT: 38% decrease in youth violent-crime arrests. Large decrease (85%) in arrests for property crimes for females, but large increase (77%) in property-crime arrests for male youth. ITT: 16% decrease in youth violent-crime arrests. 35% decrease in female property crime arrests; 32% increase for males. <u>CHAC, public housing at baseline:</u> TOT: 43% decrease in total arrests and 50% decrease in violent arrests, driven largely by males. ITT: 18% decrease in total arrests and 24% decrease in violent arrests.

Notes: CHAC = Chicago Housing Authority Corporation, Inc.; TOT = treatment-on-the-treated; ITT = intent-to-treat; MDRC = Manpower Demonstration Research Corporation; SD = standard deviation.

In terms of mobility programs, a 40 percent decrease in neighborhood poverty rates (off of a base of around 40 percent tract poverty rate) leads to about a 40 percent decline in arrests for violent crime (Kling, Ludwig, and Katz 2005; Ludwig et al. 2010). Male property crime, however, may increase, although the two mobility studies we discuss provide conflicting evidence on this possibility. In terms of mechanisms, moves to lower-poverty areas seem to increase educational outcomes of girls and the mental health of parents but not parental income or employment (Kling, Leibman, and Katz 2007). The following section discusses these findings in greater detail. We begin with evidence on the effects of additional family income and then turn to the effects of mobility policies designed to deconcentrate neighborhood poverty.

9.4.1   The Effects of Family Poverty on Crime

Our review of the literature focuses on the question of greatest relevance for policy: would reducing poverty also reduce crime, and, if so, how can we maximize the cost-effectiveness of each dollar spent? The first step in answering this question is to establish whether there really is a causal relationship between income and crime.

A large body of observational evidence has clearly established that individual income levels are negatively correlated with crime and positively correlated with a variety of human capital measures (e.g., cognitive, socio-emotional, and behavioral skills) that are predictive of less criminal behavior (Bjerk 2007; Duncan and Brooks-Gunn 1997; Duncan, Ziol-Guest, and Kalil 2010). Yet the fact that family income is correlated with crime, even after conditioning on a wide range of observable attributes, is not conclusive evidence for a causal relationship with criminal behavior. It may be that other omitted variables actually drive both poverty and crime. Distinguishing between the causal effects of poverty and other factors is crucial for public policy purposes. If poverty is a by-product of some other individual- or family-level characteristics that also lead to criminal behavior, providing additional income may not have much impact on crime. In our review of the evidence, we focus on studies that attempt to overcome the selection bias problem by exploiting variation in family income that is unrelated to individual or family choices.

A subset of the literature uses naturally occurring variation in income to overcome omitted variable concerns and estimate the effect of income on young children's human capital. Some studies compare the outcomes of siblings who experienced different levels of family incomes as they were growing up. These types of studies generally provide supportive evidence for a strong protective association between family income and various developmental outcomes of children that seem to be predictive of future criminality (Duncan et al. 1998; Levy and Duncan 1999; Blau 1999). Other studies rely on policy- or event-induced variation in family income, like changes caused by local plant closings or variation in the generosity of social program benefits across family structure, time, or region (Dahl and Lochner 2005; Milligan and Stabile 2008; Oreopolous, Page, and Stevens 2005). Most of these studies find that increased income improves a range of child and family human capital indicators, from test scores to aggression to maternal depression, although several important studies have also found contrary evidence (see Mayer 1997; Smolensky and Gootman 2003).

For our purposes, there are two main limitations to these types of studies. The first is that in most cases, there is still concern about omitted variables that may confound the apparent causal link between income and human capital. In the sibling comparisons, for example, one must necessarily wonder whether whatever underlying factors are generating changes in family incomes over time might also have independent effects on children's outcomes. If so, the results of these studies would not isolate the causal effects of income per se. Similarly for plant closings, it is possible that the nonmonetary effects of parental job loss (family stress, disruptive moves) in addition to the income changes themselves might be affecting children's outcomes. The studies of policy variation are often similarly problematic. For example, Dahl and Lochner (2005) take advantage of the fact that the EITC became substantially more generous over the 1990s and that these EITC expansions generated larger changes in family income for some families than others as defined by baseline characteristics like mother's age, race, and educational attainment. Their study, however, assumes that the only reason children in families with different observable characteristics like mother's age, race, and education experience different trends over the 1990s in test scores is because some families gain more from the EITC expansions than others. One might worry about confounding from other changes in policy or social factors that are disproportionately relevant for lower-socioeconomic status (SES) families.[12] In other words, few of these studies provide convincing evidence that increased income actually caused improved child outcomes, which is a problem for policymakers who want to know about the causal effects of providing additional income.

The second limitation of these kinds of studies is that none of them measures crime. Even if we did believe that these studies identify income's causal role, they provide information on how income affects test scores, earnings later in life, social and motor skills, and child or parent mental

---

12. For example, families who would have benefited most from increases in the EITC over the 1990s may also have benefited more from the tripling over this period in federal Head Start spending (see Head Start Program Fact Sheet at http://eclKc.ohs.acf.hhs.gov/hslc/Head%20 Start%20Program/Head%20Start%20Program%20Factsheets/HeadStartProgra.htm) or from the fact that the violent crime rate declined by nearly 30 percent and the homicide rate declined by nearly 40 percent (U.S. Statistical Abstracts 2001). Additionally, the fraction of American children covered by Medicaid increased by perhaps as much as two-thirds during that period (Mann, Rowland, and Garfield 2003), and the welfare caseload declined by around one-half (Sawhill et al. 2002).

438   Sara B. Heller, Brian A. Jacob, and Jens Ludwig

health. Although estimates of how money affects these kinds of human capital measures are undoubtedly important, they are necessarily only part of the story. What we are missing is both a sense of how much an increase in human capital measures like achievement test scores actually decrease crime as well as whether an income increase affects other inputs like parental time or neighborhood quality in important ways.[13]

Jacob and Ludwig (2010) try to overcome these problems by taking advantage of a housing-voucher wait-list lottery that was carried out in the city of Chicago. In 1997, the firm running the city's voucher program, the Chicago Housing Authority Corporation, Inc. (CHAC), opened the program's waiting list for the first time in a dozen years. Because more than 82,000 income-eligible families applied, far more families than there were vouchers available, CHAC randomly assigned applicants to the program wait-list. More than 90 percent of the voucher applicants were living in private-market housing at baseline. These families receive a voucher subsidy (on average, around $8,265 per year per family), of which they take around half in the form of reductions in out-of-pocket spending on housing (i.e., increased spending on all other goods), while the rest of the subsidy is consumed in the form of more housing. The equivalent variation of the voucher is around $6,860 per year, compared to an average baseline income of around $14,000. The equivalent variation of the voucher is not so dramatically different from the government cost of the voucher because low-income families would devote a sizable share of additional cash to extra housing anyway.

Interestingly, families living in private-market housing devote almost all of the extra housing consumption to increasing the quality of the housing unit rather than neighborhood—vouchers generate almost no detectable changes in neighborhood environments for these families. This finding is not unique to the Chicago sample—a similar pattern was found in the Experimental Housing Allowance Program of the 1970s (Struyk and Bendick 1981).[14] The key observation for present purposes is that for these previously

---

13. Lochner and Moretti (2004) supply an estimate of the effect of a particular measure of human capital—increased schooling due to changes in compulsory schooling laws—on crime. It is tempting to use this finding to supply the missing estimate of human capital's effect on crime. It is not clear, however, how to translate this effect into an estimate of other human capital measures' impacts on crime, nor does the estimate capture the other changes we might expect from an income transfer program like changes in parental income or time use. We will use Lochner and Moretti's estimates in the following in discussing policy-induced changes in high school graduation and years of schooling in particular.

14. This pattern seems unlikely to be due simply (or at least exclusively) to discrimination in the housing market or the reluctance of private-market landlords to accept housing vouchers because there is variation across voucher recipients in their baseline neighborhood poverty rates and other characteristics. The variation across families in baseline neighborhood conditions, combined with the fact that voucher receipt has little detectable impact on the average neighborhood environments of families that receive vouchers, means that even voucher families in relatively less economically disadvantaged baseline neighborhoods are able to find and lease up rental units in either their baseline neighborhood or one with similar attributes. Presumably, part of the explanation for why families who are already living in private-market housing do

unsubsidized families who were already living in the private housing market, the voucher "treatment" is essentially a large resource transfer rather than a neighborhood mobility intervention (that is, a change in family income rather than neighborhood wealth or resources). The vouchers generate large increases in nonhousing consumption as well as housing consumption.

The large increase in income caused by housing voucher receipt results in an almost 20 percent decline in both violent and overall arrests, which is driven largely by crime reductions among males. To the extent that arrests change proportionally to the number of offenses committed, this study provides us with the total effect of wealth on offenses: on average, when families receive a housing voucher with an equivalent variation of around 50 percent of baseline income, crime decreases by around 20 percent (which implies an income elasticity of something like –0.4).

While this is a very useful estimate in and of itself, the CHAC study also provides some insight into the mechanisms underlying this change. A closer look at the relevant mechanisms may be particularly important to policymakers as it can help to uncover what actually changed when incomes increased, which should inform decisions on how to most cost-effectively target government spending. For example, the Chicago study finds that voucher receipt increased high school graduation rates by 2.5 percentage points (about 10 percent of the control mean), which, like the effect on criminal behavior, is driven largely by males. This suggests that the additional income served to increase the human capital of program youths (as measured by educational attainment; there was no change in test scores).[15] Lochner and Moretti's (2004) study suggests a 10 percentage point increase in high school graduation decreases violent crime by 20 percent, which implies that the 2.5 percentage point increase in the CHAC sample's graduation rate may be responsible for about a 5 percent decrease in violent crime. In other words, the increase in schooling attainment caused by the 50 percent increase in income may account for perhaps one-quarter of the decrease in crime resulting from that income change.

So what accounts for the other three-quarters of the voucher (income change) effect on crime? One possibility is that graduation only captures part of human capital's influence on crime so that other, unmeasured aspects of human capital also put downward pressure on crime rates. Our model also suggests two other possibilities, both of which find some support within the CHAC evidence. One is the direct effect of family income on crime.

---

not use vouchers to move into substantially different types of neighborhoods is that the presence of family and friends (social networks) in the baseline neighborhoods creates a source of path-dependence in residential locations.

15. Given the study's large sample, the zero impacts on achievement test scores are fairly precisely estimated: the 95 percent confidence intervals around these point estimates suggest the effect of a subsidy with equivalent variation of $6,860 on Iowa Test of Basic Skills (ITBS) reading and math scores is no larger than .04 and .07 of a standard deviation, respectively.

Although the evidence is imprecise, unemployment insurance records provide some support by indicating that the CHAC youth may have reduced their formal-sector work (Jacob and Ludwig 2010). Decreased work may be an indication that the direct effect of money matters, either through an income effect that decreases the desire for money-producing work (legal or illegal) or through changes in routine activities (fewer late-night work shifts that increase the chances that youth are out at high-risk times). Given the imprecision of the estimates, however, it is difficult to say with confidence how important this mechanism is likely to be.

The second possibility, which is accompanied by more precise evidence, is the effect of the amount of time parents spend with their children. Data from quarterly unemployment insurance (UI) earnings records show that receipt of a housing voucher reduces the quarterly earnings (and, hence, presumably the total hours worked) for the mothers of CHAC youth by around 10 percent (Jacob and Ludwig 2011). If less time at work means more time at home, this evidence tentatively suggests that the amount of adult supervision youth receive (or adult help in human capital development) may be an important determinant of criminal behavior.

The possibility that parental time at home with children is an important determinant of crime should be of interest to policymakers given the policy push to encourage single women with children to join the workforce (via TANF work requirements and EITC earnings supplements). Some additional direct evidence on this point comes from a set of thirteen different welfare-to-work experiments run by the Manpower Demonstration Research Corporation (MDRC) that tested different work-incentive "treatments." All treatments increased parental employment, generally between 10 and 30 percent. Some treatment groups experienced little change in total family income because increased earnings were offset by reductions in welfare payments, while in other experiments the treatment groups received additional income from earnings supplements. Analysis of the pooled set of experiments provides evidence that increased maternal work leads to increased rates of academic problems for adolescents and that any increases in income that families may have experienced were not enough to offset the harmful human capital effects of the declines in parental time that families experienced.[16] Although reduced human capital is predictive of increased criminal behavior, it is not a direct measure of the programs' effects on crime.

16. Across all program types, treatment-group mothers were less likely than controls to report that their adolescents were performing above average in school (−15 percent), and more likely to report they had repeated a grade (+12 percent) or had received special education services (+12 percent). In the studies that tracked older adolescents, mothers of those aged fourteen to sixteen at baseline reported increased suspensions and expulsions (+28 percent) as well as school dropout (+46 percent) (Gennetian et al. 2002). Importantly, these negative effects on adolescents were generally not statistically different between the programs that increased income and those that did not although they did tend to cluster among programs that did not (Gennetian et al. 2002). This suggests that changes in maternal employment, rather than

Evidence on changes in treatment youths' delinquent and criminal behavior is more limited.[17]

It is important to note that the effects of changes in maternal time and family income appear to be heterogeneous across age groups. In evaluating the same set of studies, Morris, Duncan, and Rodrigues (2007) show that each $1,000 increase in family income improved test scores for two- to five-year-olds by .06 standard deviations (and had a deleterious effect of similar magnitude for ten- to fifteen-year-olds). Work-only programs had no effect on cognitive skills, which would seem to provide evidence against William Julius Wilson's argument that parental work itself may improve child outcomes by imposing discipline and regularity (Wilson 1996). Much of the beneficial impact of family income on young children seems to come from increased utilization of center-based care among families that experience higher income (Gennetian et al. 2007).

The implications of the finding on young children are twofold. First, it may be that work-based income supplements could have long-term crime reduction potential, as young children experience human capital gains that may reduce their future levels of crime. This may or may not offset the harm to adolescents' human capital (and, hence, crime), depending on the magnitude of the long-term effects. Second, the reasons for this differential impact across ages are worth exploration. If it is simply that young children are still supervised at daycare when their parents are at work, while older children are left alone, one policy solution might be an increase in after-school activities that provide supervision for older children. If it is that youths' human capital is differentially responsive to the same change in inputs (as in Cuhna and Heckman 2008), policymakers may want to think more carefully about the ages of children in families targeted by work incentive programs.

The apparent role of parents' time with children raises the possibility that parenting interventions could achieve similar results at a lower cost by targeting one of the relevant mechanisms. A focus on increasing the time parents invest in their children or improving the quality of that time is appealing, particularly given the vast literature connecting high-quality parenting to positive child outcomes. Parenting does seem to respond to intervention—both home-based programs and center-based programs that include

---

changes in income itself, may be driving the behavioral impacts. The findings also suggest that whatever increases in income some of the treatment groups experienced did not provide enough of a protective effect on adolescents to offset the harmful effects of reductions in mother time at home, and, in fact, the increased income within the context of less maternal supervision could even have exacerbated the socially harmful changes in adolescent behavior.

17. Of the thirteen welfare-to-work studies evaluated, only one measured delinquent behaviors directly. It showed increases in truancy and alcohol use but not drug or weapons use (Gennetian et al. 2002). Of the three programs with data on police contact, one showed increased involvement with law enforcement. However, the fact that these outcome measures are limited to a small number of programs, some of which had attrition problems at follow-up, means that the crime results should be interpreted with some caution.

a parenting component have been shown to change adult behavior, including nurturance toward children, disciplinary actions, and, in some cases, the amount of developmentally productive material in the home (Brooks-Gunn and Markman 2005). These changes do translate into improved child outcomes although to varying degrees. Center-based programs with parenting components appear to be more successful than just home visitation at improving school readiness and academic outcomes, but classroom-based parent training programs have also reduced behavioral problems in young children (Brooks-Gunn and Markman 2005). The malleability of parenting behavior raises the possibility that even something as simple as tasking social service caseworkers with encouraging more positive parenting styles among clients might reduce juvenile crime.

Returning to our main topic, taken together the CHAC and MDRC evidence suggests that the design of income-transfer programs may matter a great deal in shaping their effects on juvenile crime. Programs that increase income and reduce parental work effort may reduce juvenile criminal involvement through some combination of increased human capital, a standard income effect that reduces "work effort" by youth in the illegal sector and increased parental time available for monitoring and supporting youth. But programs that push parents to work more may have more complicated effects that differ across the ages of the children in the home.

Several limitations of the available evidence about antipoverty programs are important to mention. First, the data are not rich enough to determine whether there are nonlinear effects of income, which would be important for targeting income transfers in the most efficient way possible. A second limitation is that our discussion thus far focuses on partial equilibrium effects—what happens when we give a specific family additional income. It is possible that any large-scale policy designed to raise family income would also increase the level of wealth in neighborhoods more generally. Although we will see that the evidence on general equilibrium effects is limited, we can, at a minimum, learn something about the effects of changing neighborhood wealth and resources from the empirical literature about "neighborhood effects" on crime.

9.4.2   The Empirical Effects of Changing the Concentration of Poverty on Crime

Observational evidence makes clear that crime is concentrated in poor neighborhoods. This raises the possibility of reducing crime through policies aimed at deconcentrating poverty—either by moving poor families to richer neighborhoods or by improving the economic well-being and general social conditions of neighborhoods as a whole. Drawing causal conclusions from the observed correlations between the concentration of poverty and crime is complicated by selection concerns. Most families have at least some degree of choice about where they live. Observational studies might confound the causal effects of neighborhood environments with those of hard-to-measure individual and family characteristics associated with neighborhood selection.

Perhaps the best observational study of "neighborhood effects" is the Project on Human Development in Chicago Neighborhoods (PHDCN), which is a longitudinal study of approximately 3,000 children ages zero to eighteen in 1997. The PHDCN includes a great deal of information about child and parent outcomes as well as the neighborhood, school, and family context that these children experience over a seven-year study period. The rich set of covariate information available for the PHDCN study sample, together with the data set's longitudinal structure, help control for many potential confounders.

Sampson, Raudenbush, and Earls (1997) find that the willingness and capacity of local adults to work together to enforce shared prosocial norms, what they called "collective efficacy," is one of the strongest neighborhood-level predictors of violent crime. Sampson, Morenoff, and Raudenbush (2005) find that differences between blacks and whites in neighborhood attributes, particularly the share of the neighborhood that is immigrant and the proportion that works in professional or managerial jobs, may explain a large portion of the black-white difference in self-reported violent behavior.[18] Both findings suggest that the types of adults in a neighborhood may reduce crime in a number of ways: by shaping the probability of being caught or, potentially, human capital more generally (e.g., through the expectations children have about the returns from education). The PHDCN data also suggest that children who witness gun violence are more likely to be involved in violent crime later on (Bingenheimer, Brennan, and Earls 2005), which, if taken at face value, suggests that the specific crime events occurring in poor neighborhoods might contribute importantly to criminal behavior.

Given concerns about identification in the observational literature, a great deal of policy attention has been devoted to the quasi-experimental Gautreaux mobility program in Chicago, which resulted from a 1966 racial discrimination lawsuit against the Chicago Housing Authority (CHA) filed by a public housing resident named Dorothy Gautreaux. As a result of a U.S. Supreme Court decision, the CHA began providing public housing families with housing vouchers that could be used only in neighborhoods in the city or suburbs that were less than 30 percent black. Most families are thought to have accepted the first available apartment (Kaufman and Rosenbaum

---

18. Although we might worry that PHDCN data are self-reported, the findings are corroborated by more reliable data. After linking the PHDCN youth data to official arrest records, Kirk (2008) also finds that neighborhood characteristics have a significant impact on the probability of arrest. In this case, concentrated disadvantage is the only significant neighborhood-level predictor, both before and after controlling for self-reported offending (Kirk 2008). Unlike Sampson, Morenoff, and Raudenbush (2005), however, Kirk does not control for the concentration of professionals; it is unclear if measures of disadvantage would still significantly predict arrests if he had.

1992). Gautreaux families who wound up moving to the suburbs experienced dramatically different neighborhood environments from those moving to other parts of the city, both with respect to sociodemographic characteristics like racial composition (an average of 96 percent white versus 99 percent black) and neighborhood safety. Relative to city movers, Gautreaux suburban movers were much less likely to consider their neighborhood dangerous at night (31 versus 71 percent, respectively), and only 2 percent of suburban movers reported that their new neighborhood was unsafe during the day, compared to 44 percent of city movers (Rubinowitz and Rosenbaum 2000).

Although reports of safety are not synonymous with crime outcomes (which have not been directly examined for the Gautreaux sample), the differences in human capital are suggestive. A comparison of a survey sample of 342 families found that suburban movers were 75 percent less likely than city movers to have dropped out of school (20 percent versus 5 percent), more likely to be in a college track in high school (24 versus 40 percent), twice as likely to attend any college (21 percent versus 54 percent), and almost seven times as likely to attend a four-year college (4 percent versus 27 percent). The only educational attainment measure for which the suburban students did not appear to be doing significantly better than the city students was their grade point average, which could simply reflect higher grading standards in suburban schools (Rubinowitz and Rosenbaum 2000, 134–36).

Given evidence that human capital generally, and educational attainment specifically, have a negative effect on crime, we can reasonably assume that if moving to a wealthier suburban neighborhoods increases human capital, it would also exert downward pressure on individual crime, holding all else equal. If we use Lochner and Moretti's (2004) estimates for the effects of schooling on crime, these suburban-city differences in schooling outcomes in Gautreaux would suggest that arrest rates should be around 7 to 10 percent lower for suburban movers for all crimes and up to 20 or 30 percent lower for violent crimes. This is necessarily only a partial effect, however, because we do not have direct crime measures that would also capture the effects of any changes in parent income or time use from new employment opportunities and community influences or the new availability and protection of loot. An additional limitation of this evidence is that the Gautreaux study was not a true randomized experiment. Families did have some choice in whether they accepted the first apartment offered, and there is some evidence that families who ended up in the suburbs were different at baseline from those who ended up in the city (Votruba and Kling 2009).

Fortunately, the Gautreaux results helped motivate the U.S. Department of Housing and Urban Development (HUD) to carry out a large-scale randomized mobility experiment known as Moving to Opportunity (MTO). Since 1994, a total of 4600 low-income families with young children living in public housing in five cities (Baltimore, Boston, Chicago, Los Angeles, and New York) were randomly assigned into three different groups: the experimental group (offered housing vouchers to move that could only be used in Census tracts with 1990 poverty rates below 10 percent), Section 8-only group (unrestricted vouchers), and a control group that did not receive any additional services under MTO but did not lose access to other social services to which they were otherwise entitled. Around 41 percent of families assigned to the experimental group relocated through the program, as did 55 percent of those assigned to the Section 8-only group.

Five years after baseline, experimental families who moved with an MTO voucher lived in Census tracts with 2000 poverty rates 17 percentage points lower than control families (who lived in tracts with 39 percent poor, on average), with smaller impacts on share minority (nearly 10 percentage points compared to a control mean of around 88 percent) (Ludwig et al. 2008). In other words, the vouchers clearly created changes in neighborhood quality, in terms of both poverty and other observable neighborhood characteristics, which are convincingly independent of any individual or family factors that might confound a causal story in nonexperimental data. As such, they can help us identify whether neighborhood quality affects crime overall, while MTO follow-up data can potentially provide some insight into mechanisms.

The moves induced by the MTO vouchers did have a significant effect on criminal involvement. Follow-up data measured around five years after baseline finds that parents and children who move through MTO feel safer than controls and experience household victimization rates around 20 percent lower than the control group's victimization rate (Orr et al. 2003). Through the first two years after random assignment, the offer of a housing voucher creates a net reduction in youth criminal behavior: both male and female youth in the experimental group experience fewer violent-crime arrests compared with those in the control group, with treatment-on-the-treated effects on the order of 40 percent of the control mean. Females are also arrested less often for other crimes as well.

However, by three or four years after random assignment, the treatment effects for male and female youth diverge. Although the beneficial effects on most crime types persist for female youth, property crime arrests and self-reported rates of other antisocial or risky behaviors become more common for experimental than control group males (Kling, Ludwig, and Katz 2005; Kling, Liebman, and Katz 2007).[19]

Kling, Liebman, and Katz (2007) use variation in poverty rates across and within MTO cities to explore whether the effects of the voucher vary by neighborhood poverty. They find that changes in risky behavior (they do

19. Because social harm is much greater for violent than property crime, the net effect of MTO moves is to substantially reduce the social costs of criminal behavior by MTO youth.

not analyze crime directly) vary fairly linearly with neighborhood poverty rate although in opposite directions for boys and girls (girls engage in less risky behavior as neighborhood poverty decreases, whereas boys engage in more). This evidence is useful in establishing that it is not the move, per se, that drives the effects of the voucher, but rather the characteristics of the new neighborhood. It does not, however, identify which aspects of neighborhood quality captured in a poverty rate actually shape criminal behavior.

For policymakers who are considering mobility policies as a crime reduction tool, it is important to understand which aspects of the neighborhood environment matter most in determining criminal behavior. Ludwig and Kling (2007) find that the largest treatment effects on violent-crime arrests are evident in the cities in which the MTO experimental group experiences the largest decline in percent minority. Based on the postmove survey of MTO participants, Ludwig and Kling hypothesize that this is due to the increased presence of drug markets in racially segregated neighborhoods. The MTO experimental group families also wound up moving into neighborhoods with higher-quality policing services compared to controls, and so an increased deterrent threat of punishment could also play some role in explaining MTO's role in reducing violent behavior. (Note that if the likelihood of arrest is higher in low-poverty areas, the MTO analysis may overstate any adverse crime impacts of MTO moves by increasing property-crime arrests among male youth even if actual criminal behavior was constant or decreased, and the MTO effect on female youth might be even more beneficial than the arrest data reveal.) The MTO families also experienced pronounced improvements in parents' mental health (Kling, Leibman, and Katz 2007), raising the possibility that the improved neighborhood conditions served to increase the time parents spent with their children or the productivity of that time. As explained in the preceding, such changes may have direct effects on crime in terms of supervision as well as indirect effects through human capital improvements.

In terms of the overall, reduced form estimate of the effect of improved neighborhood quality on crime, some corroborating evidence comes from the study of the Chicago CHAC housing voucher lottery described in the preceding (Ludwig et al. 2010). Unlike with families who are living in private-market housing at baseline for whom voucher receipt generates a large change in household consumption but almost no change in neighborhood environments, voucher receipt for families who live in public housing at baseline generates changes in Census tract characteristics of a similar magnitude to MTO. The change in neighborhood poverty rates in both cases is about 40 percent of the control mean, with relatively little effect in either study of voucher use on neighborhood racial segregation (Ludwig et al. 2008, 2010). In other words, providing vouchers to those in public housing turns out to be a mobility intervention rather than simply a large income transfer.

For youth who were ages twelve to eighteen at baseline, the intent-to-treat effect from being offered a CHAC voucher is a reduction in violent-crime arrests by around 24 percent, while the effect of actually leasing up with a voucher (the effects of treatment on the treated) is a 50 percent arrest reduction from the control complier mean. In the Chicago CHAC voucher study, the results are driven by males, and there is no sign that these results dissipate over time. Importantly, there is no evidence of any increase in property-crime arrests for males at any point during the postlottery period. The evidence of declines in criminal behavior is clear among those who were adolescents at the time their families received vouchers and somewhat less clear for children who were younger when their families were offered vouchers (though the number of such children in the study sample is not very large).

The CHAC study also provides some additional insight into potential mechanisms. Although the results for schooling outcomes are preliminary, they suggest that the test scores of children in public-housing families who were offered a voucher increased (ITT of about .05 standard deviations in reading and .08 in math). This result suggests that increased school quality and schooling attainment may play a role in reducing juvenile crime—a finding consistent with studies of randomized lotteries for public school choice that suggest moving to lower poverty schools with higher achieving peers and better quality teachers reduces arrests, particularly for high-risk groups (Cullen, Jacob, and Levitt 2006; Deming 2009a).

However, academic improvement cannot be the only mechanism through which neighborhood change affects criminal behavior: in the CHAC study, voucher receipt leads to reduced rates of violent-crime arrest among young household heads (eighteen to thirty at baseline) as well as juveniles. These household heads are obviously not directly affected by any changes in school quality that result from changing neighborhoods but would be affected by other aspects of the neighborhood environment.[20] So while improved schools and increased test scores may be relevant to the impact of neighborhoods on criminal behavior, the CHAC evidence suggests that they are not the only driving mechanism. Early results also tentatively suggest that there is little change in parental labor supply for families in public housing at baseline. Stronger conclusions will have to await further analysis of the CHAC data.

---

20. Jacob (2004) uses variation in neighborhood environments among Chicago public housing families generated by plausibly random variation in the timing of when their housing projects were demolished by the Chicago Housing Authority. Jacob's study finds no statistically significant impact on achievement test scores although this finding may not be inconsistent with the studies reported in the preceding because Jacob did not directly examine criminal behavior. After all, the randomized MTO study found declines in violent-crime arrests for male and female youth, as well as declines in all other types of offenses for female youth, without detectable changes in children's achievement test scores. Note also that the studies described in the preceding all focus on examining "neighborhood effects" on families who volunteered to move, which stands in contrast to Jacob's sample of families who were all compelled to move when their housing project was demolished.

Why we see an increase in property arrests among male youth who move into lower-poverty areas in MTO but not in the Chicago CHAC voucher study is unclear. Because the CHAC study did not collect survey data, it is impossible to know if changes in collective efficacy or maternal depression differed across the two studies in a way that affected boys differently. Alternatively, it may be that moving out of a poor neighborhood in Chicago is substantively different from moving out of a poor neighborhood in the other MTO cities. While MTO seemed to have more pronounced beneficial impacts on achievement test scores in Chicago than in most of the other demonstration sites (Burdick-Will et al., forthcoming), Chicago does not seem to be very different from the other MTO sites in terms of the effect on overall youth outcomes (Kling, Liebman, and Katz 2007, 97) and if anything had more adverse impacts on violent-crime arrests than in the other MTO sites (Ludwig and Kling 2007).

Taken together, the MTO and CHAC findings provide evidence that increases in neighborhood quality can have a sizable negative effect on crime rates, with the possible exception of property crime. The evidence is less clear in terms of the mechanisms at work. We have seen some tentative indications that maternal depression (and presumably the accompanying changes in time use and parenting quality) could be at work, as could changes in adult social norms, the probability of being caught, and the availability of things to steal.

9.5   Policy Implications

We began our review of the evidence with two key questions: whether policies intended to reduce either individual poverty or its geographic concentration could reduce crime on net, and, if so, how to maximize the cost-effectiveness of such policies by targeting the mechanisms that matter. We believe that the empirical evidence now available, particularly studies that rely on policy-induced variation in social conditions, supports the conclusion that both kinds of poverty policies can, in fact, reduce crime. The clearest crime reductions are among adolescent boys, perhaps not surprising given that males commit the bulk of crimes and that many other policy interventions appear to effect boys and girls differently (Almond and Currie 2010). The magnitudes of the policies' effects are potentially large: a 50 percent increase in income reduces male arrests by 20 percent, and a 40 percent reduction in neighborhood tract-level poverty reduces violent crime by almost 40 percent for both genders. (The latter may increase male property crime as well, though the total social costs of criminal behavior by youth who relocate still declines; see Kling, Ludwig, and Katz 2005.) Our confidence that moving to a less disadvantaged neighborhood reduces criminal involvement is strengthened by similar findings from studies of public school choice lotteries (Cullen, Jacob, and Levitt 2006; Deming 2009a).

Although the evidence on mechanisms is much less clear, there is some suggestion that the quality and quantity of the time parents spend with adolescents may be quite important. This finding is particularly relevant given the current set of poverty policies like TANF and the EITC that incentivize work, and it deserves further research attention. Additionally, while school quality and improved cognitive skills may be part of the story, neither seem to be the sole drivers of observed reductions in criminal behavior from policies that seek to either increase family income or help families move to less distressed neighborhoods.

The conclusion that both income transfer and mobility programs can reduce crime is important in and of itself. But the fact that the small-scale interventions reviewed here are capable of decreasing criminal offending does not mean that large-scale versions of these interventions would necessarily be capable of achieving similar effects. A second question worth considering is how the benefit-cost ratios of these interventions compare to alternative uses of government resources.

In the case of mobility programs like MTO, the cost to the government of providing low-income families with housing vouchers rather than public housing may be very low, and, in fact, many housing economists claim that the cost per housing unit is lower for vouchers than public housing (Olsen 2003; Shroder and Reiger 2000). The more important types of costs with mobility programs are nonmonetary. Large-scale efforts to relocate poor families out of high-poverty areas could lead to more reconcentration of poverty than what is observed with the smaller-scale mobility programs that have been studied to date. The "tipping" literature in economics suggests that even small changes in neighborhood composition can generate large mobility responses by other residents (Schelling 1971; Becker and Murphy 2000; Card, Mas, and Rothstein 2008). Perhaps more important, most existing studies only consider the effects of mobility programs on the movers. There may also be broader impacts on both originating and destination neighborhoods caused by changing neighborhood composition. While there are a few studies that suggest policy efforts to resort disadvantaged families across schools or neighborhoods might lead to overall declines in the aggregate crime rate (Weiner, Lutz, and Ludwig 2009) or related outcomes like educational attainment and income (Cutler and Glaeser 1997), identification is more challenging with aggregate-level studies.

In any case, the scope for public policy to resort poor people to less disadvantaged or distressed social settings seems quite limited. As discussed in the preceding, giving housing vouchers to families who are already living in private-market housing enables them to move into rental units that have dramatically higher rents. Yet families spend almost all of this rent increase on higher unit quality rather than improved "neighborhood quality." One candidate explanation is path dependence in residential locations due to social network ties, which could suggest the potential value of housing policies that enable groups of families to move together. This type of "buddy voucher" has, to our knowledge, never been tried. While providing housing vouchers to public housing families does lead them to move into less distressed neighborhoods and might even save the government money (Olsen 2003), only 1 percent of all people living in metropolitan areas are in public housing (Quillian 2005). Public school choice plans could serve as an alternative way to resort children across one particularly important social setting, but the scope for substantial changes in economic or racial segregation will be limited by the massive amounts of persistent residential segregation in American schools. For example, consider that Cook County, Illinois residents are 67 percent white, compared to just 9 percent in the Chicago Public Schools.

An alternative to moving families out of disadvantaged neighborhoods is to try to directly change those aspects of the neighborhood that produce crime through community-level interventions. Perhaps the most famous example is the Harlem Children's Zone, which tries to improve the well-being of poor families in high-poverty areas through expanded educational and social services. While there is some debate about the effects of Harlem Children's Zone on children's academic outcomes (for example Dobbie and Fryer [2010] versus Whitehurst and Croft [2010]), perhaps most relevant for present purposes is that to the best of our knowledge, no study has yet examined the effect of this intervention on criminal behavior by neighborhood residents. A related community-level strategy is to try to change the social norms surrounding violence that may mediate the link between neighborhood poverty and crime, which is one of the strategies employed by the Ceasefire program in Chicago. This strategy is motivated in part by the belief within the public health community that efforts to change social norms have contributed to long-term declines in smoking and increased use of seat belts. One observational study of Chicago Ceasefire by Skogan et al. (2008) seems encouraging although this is an area where additional research activity would seem to have high payoffs.

In terms of the other social policy strategy we consider here—income transfer programs—the data reviewed in this chapter suggest that providing some families with large changes in income, but leaving the incomes of most everyone else in the community unchanged, can reduce criminal behavior among youth. In principle, larger-scale resource transfer programs could generate less beneficial impacts if relative as well as absolute poverty status matters because a large across-the-board change in incomes for everyone at the bottom of the income distribution will, unlike a small-scale program, create little change in the relative income standing of program recipients (at least relative to other people in the bottom part of the distribution). Moreover, large-scale resource transfers may increase the "loot" available in the community to steal and increase community-level consumption of criminogenic and victimogenic goods like drugs and alcohol. It is interesting to note, for example, that aggregate-level studies find that improved macroeconomic conditions yield mixed impacts on rates of different types of crime (Cook and Zarkin 1985; Ruhm 1995, 2000; Raphael and Winter-Ebmer 2001; Ruhm and Black 2002; Evans and Moore 2009).[21]

In addition to the question of whether transfer programs could successfully be taken to scale, it is also important to consider whether doing so would be more cost-effective than alternative uses of government resources. While we do not know of any good benefit-cost analysis of programs that simply provide cash to poor families, a reasonable guess for the benefit-cost ratio for the effects of providing housing vouchers to previously unsubsidized families (i.e., those living in private-market housing already for whom voucher receipt is "near cash") is about 1.5 (Carlson et al. 2009).[22] As is standard in benefit-cost analyses, this calculation assumes that the monetary benefit to the recipients offsets the monetary cost to taxpayers and, thus, counts the amount of the voucher itself as a transfer rather than a "cost" of the program. It does, however, include the following as true costs of the program: administrative costs not passed onto recipients (e.g., the cost of the employees used to process the voucher claims, etc.) and the deadweight loss associated with raising tax revenue and providing in-kind rather than cash benefits (e.g., distortion of labor supply). The benefits include welfare increases from all sources, not just changes in criminal behavior.

21. In addition, Evans and Topoleski (2002) find that rates of violent crime, motor vehicle theft, and larceny increase after casinos open up on Indian reservations although we note that this is not a pure test of the effects of across-the-board resource transfers because casinos also change the composition of who spends time on these reservations. Other quasi-experimental studies have found that plant closings and the opening of Indian gaming facilities are associated with improvements in adult mental health or children's externalizing disorders (Costello et al. 2003; Dew, Bromet, and Schulberg 1987; Kessler, House, and Turner 1987).

22. The Carlson et al. (2009) benefit-cost estimate is not perfect because the study mixes together the behavioral effects of giving vouchers to people in public housing (for whom voucher receipt is essentially a neighborhood mobility treatment) with the behavioral effects of giving vouchers to families already in private-market housing (for whom voucher receipt is more like a near-cash transfer). But the Chicago study is, nonetheless, not out of line with the ballpark estimate from Carlson et al.; giving vouchers to private-market households reduces the social cost of crime committed by youth by around $400 to $3,300 per year, while the impact of vouchers on high school graduation rates (increase of around 10 percent) might add another $10,000 or $12,500 in lifetime benefits per child per voucher-receiving household as well. This last figure is derived as follows: data from the fifty largest school districts in the United States suggest an average four-year high school graduation rate of about 50 percent (Swanson 2009), while estimates by Henry Levin and his colleagues suggest that the present value of the benefits to society from having a child graduate from high school rather than drop out may be on the order of $200,000 to $300,000 per year. Levin et al. (2007) report public savings on the order of $209,000 per high school graduate. Their calculation is conservative in only counting increased tax payments as a benefit from improved labor market prospects; if we also include the increased earnings to the high school graduate him- or herself, the benefits may be closer to $300,000 although Levin's calculation also includes around $30,000 in benefits from crime reductions, so if we subtract that off to avoid double counting, the right figure might be more toward the midpoint of this range. Our estimate for the savings per child is then equal to 10 percent of a 50 percent baseline high school graduation rate (so change in graduation likelihood of 5 percentage points) times $250,000.

The 1.5 ratio suggests that the total benefits of this type of "near cash" transfer to poor families may outweigh the costs. Our conceptual framework and review of the literature suggests that transfer programs that increase parental work effort (thus decreasing time at home) may have smaller beneficial impacts on crime in the short term or even adverse effects. In comparison, programs that target direct improvements in the developmental environments of young children (including but not limited to parenting) do appear to have quite high benefit-cost ratios, even if one were to focus exclusively on the crime-related benefits (Belfield et al. 2006; Campbell et al. 2002; Deming 2009b; Garces, Thomas, and Currie 2002; Karoly et al. 1998; Ludwig and Miller 2007; Ludwig and Phillips 2007; Schweinhart et al. 2005). Previous research also provides at least suggestive evidence for high benefit-cost ratios for interventions that seek to develop socioemotional and behavioral skills among high-risk adolescents and young adults (see for example Lipsey, Landenberger, and Wilson 2007; Pearson et al. 2002; Wilson, Bouffard, and MacKenzie 2005; Drake, Aos, and Miller 2009; and Hill et al. chapter 8 in this volume). Both transfer programs and human capital interventions may have larger benefit-cost ratios than incarceration although there is considerable uncertainty about the benefits and costs to society of imprisoning the marginal offender (Donohue 2009).

It is important to note that policies designed to reduce family or neighborhood poverty are likely to have a range of other, noncrime benefits that we do not discuss here. They may also have social costs, as evidenced by the public's disagreement about the role of government in providing financial or in-kind assistance to poor families. Our argument is not about the worth of these types of social programs as a whole. Our point is more limited but nonetheless relevant to broader policy decisions: even though efforts to improve social conditions may reduce crime, there are important limits to the scope of these policies (in the case of mobility interventions) and important questions about whether income transfers would be the most cost-effective way to reduce crime, if that is the key objective of interest.

References

Agnew, Robert. 1992. "Foundation for a General Strain Theory of Crime and Delinquency." *Criminology* 30 (1): 47–87.
Aizer, Anna. 2004. "Home Alone: Supervision after School and Child Behavior." *Journal of Public Economics* 88 (9–10): 1835–48.
Almond, Douglas, and Janet Currie. 2010. "Human Capital Development before Age Five." NBER Working Paper no. 15827. Cambridge, MA: National Bureau of Economic Research.
Autor, David, Lawrence F. Katz, and Melissa S. Kearney. 2008. "Trends in U.S. Wage Inequality: Revising the Revisionists." *Review of Economics and Statistics* 90 (2): 300–23.

Becker, Gary S. 1968. "Crime and Punishment: An Economic Approach." *Journal of Political Economy* 76 (2): 169–217.

Becker, Gary, and Kevin M. Murphy. 2000. *Social Economics: Market Behavior in a Social Environment.* Cambridge, MA: Harvard University Press/Belknap.

Beirne, Piers. 1987. "Adolphe Quetelt and the Origins of Positivist Criminology." *American Journal of Sociology* 92 (5): 1140–69.

Belfield, Clive R., Milagros Nores, Steve Barnett, and Lawrence Schweinhart. 2006. "The High/Scope Perry Preschool Program: Cost-Benefit Analysis Using Data from the Age-40 Followup." *Journal of Human Resources* 41 (1): 162–90.

Bingenheimer, Jeffrey B., Robert T. Brennan, and Felton J. Earls. 2005. "Firearm Violence Exposure and Serious Violent Behavior." *Science* 308 (5726): 1323–26.

Bjerk, David. 2007. "Measuring the Relationship between Youth Criminal Participation and Household Economic Resources." *Journal of Quantitative Criminology* 23 (1): 23–39.

Blau, David. 1999. "The Effect of Income on Child Development." *Review of Economics and Statistics* 81 (2): 261–76.

Bloom, Dan, and Charles Michalopoulos. 2001. "How Welfare and Work Policies Affect Employment and Income." MDRC Monograph. New York: Manpower Demonstration Research Corporation.

Blumstein, Alfred, and Jacqueline Cohen. 1987. "Characterizing Criminal Careers." *Science* 237 (4818): 985–91.

Brooks, David. 2010. "Children of the '70s." *New York Times,* May 17, A27.

Brooks-Gunn, Jeanne, and Lisa B. Markman. 2005. "The Contribution of Parenting to Ethnic and Racial Gaps in School Readiness." *The Future of Children* 15 (1): 139–68.

Burdick-Will, Julia, Jens Ludwig, Stephen Raudenbush, Robert Sampson, Lisa Sanbonmatsu, and Patrick Sharkey. Forthcoming. "Converging Evidence for Neighborhood Effects on Children's Test Scores: An Experimental, Quasi-Experimental, and Observational Comparison." In *Whither Opportunity? Rising Inequality and the Uncertain Life Chances of Low-Income Children,* edited by Greg J. Duncan and Richard Murnane. New York: Russell Sage Foundation.

Burtless, Gary, and Timothy M. Smeeding. 2007. *Poverty, Work and Policy: The United States in Comparative Perspective, Before the Subcommittee on Income Security and Family Support, House Committee on Ways and Means.* http://www.brookings.edu/~media/Files/rc/testimonies/2007/0213poverty-burtless/20070213.pdf.

Campbell, Frances A., Craig T. Ramey, E. P. Pungello, S. Miller-Johnson, and J. J. Sparling. 2002. "Early Childhood Education: Young Adult Outcomes from the Abecedarian Project." *Applied Developmental Science* 6 (1): 42–57.

Card, David, Alexandre Mas, and Jesse Rothstein. 2008. "Tipping and the Dynamics of Segregation." *Quarterly Journal of Economics* 123 (1): 177–218.

Carlson, Deven, Robert Haveman, Thomas Kaplan, and Barbara Wolfe. 2009. "The Benefits and Costs of the Section 8 Housing Subsidy Program: A Framework and First-Year Estimates." La Follette School Working Paper no. 2009-025. Madison, WI: La Follette School of Public Affairs, University of Wisconsin-Madison.

Cohen, Lawrence E., and Marcus Felson. 1979. "Social Change and Crime Rate Trends: A Routine Activity Approach." *American Sociological Review* 44 (4): 588–608.

Cook, Philip J. 2009. "Crime Control in the City: A Research-Based Briefing on Public and Private Measures." *Cityscape: A Journal of Policy Development and Research* 11 (1): 53–80.

Cook, Philip J., and John H. Laub. 2002. "After the Epidemic: Recent Trends in Youth Violence in the United States." *Crime and Justice* 29 (1): 1–37.

Cook, Philip J., and Gary A. Zarkin. 1985. "Crime and the Business Cycle." *Journal of Legal Studies* 14 (1): 115–28.

Costello, E. Jane, Scott N. Compton, Gordon Keeler, and Adrian Angold. 2003. "Relationships between Poverty and Psychopathology: A Natural Experiment." *Journal of the American Medical Association* 290 (15): 2023–29.

Cullen, Julie Berry, Brian A. Jacob, and Steven Levitt. 2006. "The Effect of School Choice on Participants: Evidence from Randomized Lotteries." *Econometrica* 74 (5): 1191–1230.

Cunha, Flavio, and James J. Heckman. 2008. "Formulating, Identifying and Estimating the Technology of Cognitive and Noncognitive Skill Formation." *Journal of Human Resources* 43 (4): 738–82.

Cutler, David M., and Edward L. Glaeser. 1997. "Are Ghettos Good or Bad?" *Quarterly Journal of Economics* 112 (3): 827–72.

Cutler, David M., Edward L. Glaeser, and Jacob L. Vigdor. 1999. "The Rise and Decline of the American Ghetto." *Journal of Political Economy* 107 (3): 455–506.

Dahl, Gordon B., and Lance Lochner. 2005. "The Impact of Family Income on Child Achievement." NBER Working Paper no. 11279. Cambridge, MA: National Bureau of Economic Research.

Deming, David. 2009a. "Better Schools, Less Crime?" Unpublished Working Paper, Harvard University, Kennedy School of Government.

———. 2009b. "Early Childhood Intervention and Life-Cycle Skill Development: Evidence from Head Start." *American Economic Journal: Applied Economics* 1 (3): 111–34.

Dew, M. A., E. J. Bromet, and H. C. Schulberg. 1987. "A Comparative Analysis of Two Community Stressors' Long-Term Mental Health Effects." *American Journal of Community Psychology* 15 (2): 167–84.

Dobbie, Will, and Roland G. Fryer, Jr. 2010. "Are High-Quality Schools Enough to Close the Achievement Gap? Evidence from a Social Experiment in Harlem." NBER Working Paper no. 15473. Cambridge, MA: National Bureau of Economic Research.

Donohue, John. 2009. "Assessing the Relative Benefits of Incarceration: The Overall Change over the Previous Decades and the Benefits on the Margin." In *Do Prisons Make Us Safer? The Benefits and Costs of the Prison Boom,* edited by Steven Raphael and Michael Stoll, 269. New York: Russell Sage Foundation.

Drake, Elizabeth K., Steve Aos, and Marna G. Miller. 2009. "Evidence-Based Public Policy Options to Reduce Crime and Criminal Justice Costs: Implications in Washington State." *Victims and Offenders* 4 (2): 170–96.

Duncan, Greg J., and Jeanne Brooks-Gunn. 1997. *Consequences of Growing Up Poor.* New York: Russell Sage Foundation.

Duncan, Greg J., W. Yeung, Jeanne Brooks-Gunn, and J. Smith. 1998. "How Much Does Childhood Poverty Affect the Life Chances of Children?" *American Sociological Review* 63 (3): 406–23.

Duncan, Greg J., Kathleen M. Ziol-Guest, and Ariel Kalil. 2010. "Early-Childhood Poverty and Adult Attainment, Behavior, and Health." *Child Development* 81 (1): 306–25.

Dwyer, Kathleen M., Jean L. Richardson, Kathleen L. Danley, William B. Hansen, Steven Y. Sussman, Bonnie Brannon, Clyde W. Dent, C. Anderson Johnson, and Brian R. Flay. 1990. "Characteristics of Eighth-Grade Students Who Initiate Self-Care in Elementary and Junior High School." *Pediatrics* 86 (3): 448–54.

Evans, William N., and Timothy J. Moore. 2009. "The Short-Term Mortality Consequences of Income Receipt." Working Paper, Department of Economics and Econometrics, University of Notre Dame.

Evans, William N., and Julie H. Topoleski. 2002. "The Social and Economic Impact of Native American Casinos." NBER Working Paper no. 9198. Cambridge, MA: National Bureau of Economic Research.

Federal Bureau of Investigation. 2008. *Uniform Crime Report.* Washington, DC: U.S. Department of Justice. http://www.fbi.gov/ucr/cius2008/data/table_38.html.

Frank, Richard G., and Ellen Meara. 2009. "The Effect of Maternal Depression and Substance Abuse on Child Human Capital Development." NBER Working Paper no. 15314. Cambridge, MA: National Bureau of Economic Research.

Garces, Eliana, Duncan Thomas, and Janet Currie. 2002. "Longer-Term Effects of Head Start." *American Economic Review* 92 (4): 999–1012.

Gennetian, Lisa A., Danielle Crosby, Chantelle Dowsett, and Aletha Huston. 2007. "Maternal Employment, Early Care Settings, and the Achievement of Low-Income Children." Next Generation Working Paper no. 30. New York: Manpower Demonstration Research Corporation.

Gennetian, Lisa A., Greg J. Duncan, Virginia W. Knox, Wanda G. Vargas, Elizabeth Clark-Kauffman, and Andrew S. London. 2002. "How Welfare and Work Policies for Parents Affect Adolescents: A Synthesis of Research." MDRC Report. New York: Manpower Demonstration Research Corporation.

Glaeser, Edward L., and Jacob Vigdor. 2003. "Racial Segregation: Promising News." In *Redefining Urban and Suburban America: Evidence from Census 2000.* Vol. 1, edited by Bruce Katz and Robert E. Lang, 211–34. Washington, DC: Brookings Institution.

Hamilton, Gayle, Stephen Freedman, Lisa Gennetian, Charles Michalopoulos, Johanna Walter, Diana Adams-Ciardullo, Anna Gassman-Pines, et al. 2001. "How Effective Are Different Welfare-to-Work Approaches? Five-Year Adult and Child Impacts for Eleven Programs." MDRC Monograph. New York: Manpower Demonstration Research Corporation. http://www.mdrc.org/publications/64/overview.html.

Hanushek, Eric A., John F. Kain, and Steven G. Rivkin. 2004. "Why Public Schools Lose Teachers." *Journal of Human Resources* 39 (2): 326–54.

Hart, Betty, and Todd Risley. 1995. *Meaningful Differences in the Everyday Experience of Young American Children.* Baltimore, MD: Paul Brooks.

Heckman, James J., Jora Stixrud, and Sergio Urzua. 2006. "The Effects of Cognitive and Noncognitive Abilities on Labor Market Outcomes and Social Behavior." *Journal of Labor Economics* 24 (3): 411–82.

Hernstein, Richard J. 1995. "Criminogenic Traits." In *Crime,* edited by James Q. Wilson and Joan Petersilia, 39–64. San Francisco, CA: Institute for Contemporary Studies Press.

Jacob, Brian A. 2004. "Public Housing, Housing Vouchers, and Student Achievement: Evidence from Public Housing Demolitions in Chicago." *American Economic Review* 94 (1): 233–58.

Jacob, Brian A., and Jens Ludwig. 2011. "The Effects of Housing Assistance on Labor Supply: Evidence from a Voucher Lottery." *American Economic Review* (forthcoming).

———. 2010. "The Effects of Family Resources on Children's Outcomes." Working Paper, University of Michigan.

Jencks, Christopher, and Susan E. Mayer. 1990. "The Social Consequences of Growing Up in a Poor Neighborhood." In *Inner-City Poverty in the United States,* edited by L. E. Lynn, Jr. and M. G. H. McGeary, 111–86. Washington, DC: National Academies Press.

Karoly, Lynn A., Peter W. Greenwood, Susan S. Everingham, Jill Hoube, M. Rebecca Kilburn, C. Peter Rydell, Matthew Sanders, and James Chiesa. 1998. *Investing in*

Our Children: What We Know and Don't Know about the Costs and Benefits of Early Childhood Interventions. RAND Corporation Monograph. Santa Monica, CA: RAND Corporation.

Kaufman, Julie E., and James E. Rosenbaum. 1992. "The Education and Employment of Low-Income Black Youth in White Suburbs." *Educational Evaluation and Policy Analysis* 14 (3): 229–40.

Kelly, Morgan. 2000. "Inequality and Crime." *Review of Economics and Statistics* 82 (4): 530–39.

Kessler, Ronald C., Patricia Berglund, Olga Demler, Robert Jin, Doreen Koretz, Kathleen R. Merikangas, A. John Rush, Ellen E. Walters, and Philip S. Wang. 2003. "The Epidemiology of Major Depressive Disorder: Results from the National Comorbidity Survey Replication (NCS-R)." *Journal of the American Medical Association* 289 (23): 3095–3105.

Kessler, Ronald C., Patricia Berglund, Olga Demler, Robert Jin, Kathleen R. Merikangas, and Ellen E. Walters. 2005. "Lifetime Prevalence and Age-of-Onset Distributions of *DSM-IV* Disorders in the National Comorbidity Survey Replication." *Archives of General Psychiatry* 62 (6): 593–602.

Kessler, R. C., J. S. House, and J. B. Turner. 1987. "Unemployment and Health in a Community Sample." *Journal of Health and Social Behavior* 28 (1): 51–9.

Kirk, David S. 2008. "The Neighborhood Context of Racial and Ethnic Disparities in Arrest." *Demography* 45 (1): 55–77.

Kling, Jeffrey R., Jeffrey Liebman, and Lawrence Katz. 2007. "Experimental Analysis of Neighborhood Effects." *Econometrica* 75 (1): 83–119.

Kling, Jeffrey R., Jens Ludwig, and Lawrence F. Katz. 2005. "Neighborhood Effects on Crime for Female and Male Youth: Evidence from a Randomized Housing Voucher Experiment." *Quarterly Journal of Economics* 120 (1): 87–130.

Lareau, Annette. 2002. "Social Class and Child Rearing in Black Families and White Families." *American Sociological Review* 67 (5): 747–76.

———. 2003. *Unequal Childhoods: Class, Race, and Family Life.* Berkeley, CA: University of California Press.

Levin, Henry, Clive Belfield, Peter Muennig, and Cecilia Rouse. 2007. "The Costs and Benefits of an Excellent Education for All of America's Children." Report. New York: Center for Cost-Benefit Studies of Education, Teachers College, Columbia University. http://www.cbcse.org/media/download_gallery/Leeds_Report_Final_Jan2007.pdf.

Levitt, Steven D. 2004. "Understanding Why Crime Fell in the 1990s: Four Factors that Explain the Decline and Six that Do Not." *Journal of Economic Perspectives* 18 (1): 163–90.

Levy, Dan, and Greg J. Duncan. 1999. "Using Sibling Samples to Assess the Effect of Childhood Family Income on Completed Schooling." Working Paper. Evanston, IL: Northwestern University.

Lewis, Oscar. 1959. *Five Families: Mexican Case Studies in the Culture of Poverty.* New York: New American Library.

———. 1966. *La Vida: A Puerto Rican Family in the Culture of Poverty.* New York: Random House.

Lipsey, Mark W., Nana A. Landenberger, and Sandra J. Wilson. 2007. "Effects of Cognitive-Behavioral Programs for Criminal Offenders." The Campbell Collaboration Library. Oslo: The Campbell Collaboration. http://www.campbellcollaboration.org/doc-pdf/lipsey_CBT_finalreview.pdf.

Lochner, Lance, and Enrico Moretti. 2004. "The Effect of Education on Crime: Evidence from Prison Inmates, Arrests, and Self-Reports." *American Economic Review* 94 (1): 155–89.

Ludwig, Jens, Brian A. Jacob, Greg J. Duncan, James E. Rosenbaum, and Michael Johnson. 2010. "Neighborhood Effects on Crime: Evidence from a Randomized Housing Voucher Lottery." Working Paper, University of Chicago.

Ludwig, Jens, and Jeffrey Kling. 2007. "Is Crime Contagious?" *Journal of Law and Economics* 50 (3): 491–518.

Ludwig, Jens, Jeffrey Liebman, Jeffrey Kling, Greg J. Duncan, Lawrence F. Katz, Ronald C. Kessler, and Lisa Sanbonmatsu. 2008. "What Can We Learn about Neighborhood Effects from the Moving to Opportunity Experiment? A Comment on Clampet-Lundquist and Massey." *American Journal of Sociology* 114 (1): 144–88.

Ludwig, Jens, and Douglas L. Miller. 2007. "Does Head Start Improve Children's Life Chances? Evidence from a Regression Discontinuity Approach." *Quarterly Journal of Economics* 122 (1): 159–208.

Ludwig, Jens, and Deborah A. Phillips. 2007. "The Benefits and Costs of Head Start." NBER Working Paper no. 12973. Cambridge, MA: National Bureau of Economic Research.

Mann, Cindy, Diane Rowland, and Rachel Garfield. 2003. "Historical Overview of Children's Health Care Coverage." *The Future of Children* 13 (1): 31–53.

Mayer, Susan E. 1997. *What Money Can't Buy: Family Income and Children's Life Chances.* Cambridge, MA: Harvard University Press.

Merton, Robert K. 1938. "Social Structure and Anomie." *American Sociological Review* 3 (5): 672–82.

Milligan, Kevin, and Mark Stabile. 2008. "Do Child Tax Benefits Affect the Well-being of Children? Evidence from Canadian Child Benefit Expansions." NBER Working Paper no. 14624. Cambridge, MA: National Bureau of Economic Research.

Moore, Kristin Anderson, Elizabeth C. Hair, Sharon Vandivere, Cameron B. McPhee, Michelle McNamara, and Thomson Ling. 2006. "Depression among Moms: Prevalence, Predictors, and Acting Out among Third Grade Children." *Child Trends Research Brief,* Publication no. 2006-19. Washington, DC: Child Trends.

Morris, Pamela, Greg J. Duncan, and Christopher Rodrigues. 2007. "Does Money Really Matter? Estimating Impacts of Family Income on Young Children's Achievement with Data from Random-Assignment Experiments." Next Generation Working Paper no. 27. New York: Manpower Demonstration Research Corporation.

Morris, Pamela A., Lisa A. Gennetian, and Greg J. Duncan. 2005. "Effects of Welfare and Employment Policies on Young Children: New Findings on Policy Experiments Conducted in the Early 1990s." *Social Policy Report* 19 (2). New York: Manpower Demonstration Research Corporation.

Olsen, Edgar O. 2003. "Housing Programs for Low-Income Households." In *Means-Tested Transfer Programs in the United States,* edited by Robert A. Moffit, 365–442. Chicago: University of Chicago Press.

Oreopolous, Philip, Marianne Page, and Ann Huff Stevens. 2005. "The Intergenerational Effects of Worker Displacement." NBER Working Paper no. 11587. Cambridge, MA: National Bureau of Economic Research.

Orr, Larry, Judith D. Feins, Robin Jacob, Erik Beecroft, Lisa Sanbonmatsu, Lawrence F. Katz, Jeffrey B. Liebman, and Jeffrey R. Kling. 2003. *Moving to Opportunity: Interim Impacts Evaluation.* Washington, DC: U.S. Department of Housing and Urban Development.

Pearson, Frank S., Douglas S. Lipton, Charles M. Cleland, and Dorline S. Yee. 2002. "The Effects of Behavioral/Cognitive-Behavioral Programs on Recidivism." *Crime and Delinquency* 48 (3): 476–96.

Podhoretz, John. 2010. "The Upper West Side, Then and Now." *Commentary,* May, 27–31.

Quigley, John M. 2000. "A Decent Home: Housing Policy in Perspective." In Brookings Papers on Urban Affairs, Issue no. 1: 53–99. Washington, DC: Brookings Institution.

Quillian, Lincoln. "Public Housing and the Spatial Concentration of Poverty." Paper presented at the Population Association of America Meeting, Philadelphia, PA, March 31–April 2, 2005.

Raphael, Steven, and Rudolf Winter-Ebmer. 2001. "Identifying the Effect of Unemployment on Crime." *Journal of Law and Economics* 44 (1): 259–83.

Rosin, Hanna. 2008. "American Murder Mystery." *Atlantic Monthly,* July/August. http://www.theatlantic.com/magazine/archive/2008/07/american-murder-mystery/6872/.

Rubinowitz, Leonard S., and James E. Rosenbaum. 2000. *Crossing the Class and Color Lines: From Public Housing to White Suburbia.* Chicago: University of Chicago Press.

Ruhm, Christopher J. 1995. "Economic Conditions and Alcohol Problems." *Journal of Health Economics* 14 (5): 583–603.

———. 2000. "Are Recessions Good for your Health?" *Quarterly Journal of Economics* 115 (2): 617–50.

Ruhm, Christopher J., and William E. Black. 2002. "Does Drinking Really Decrease in Bad Times?" *Journal of Health Economics* 21 (4): 659–78.

Sampson, Robert J., Jeffrey D. Morenoff, and Stephen Raudenbush. 2005. "Social Anatomy of Racial and Ethnic Disparities in Violence." *American Journal of Public Health* 95 (2): 224–32.

Sampson, Robert J., Stephen Raudenbush, and Felton Earls. 1997. "Neighborhoods and Violent Crime: A Multilevel Study of Collective Efficacy." *Science* 277 (5328): 918–24.

Sawhill, Isabel V., R. Kent Weaver, Ron Haskins, and Andrea Kane. 2002. *Welfare Reform and Beyond: The Future of the Safety Net.* Washington, DC: Brookings Institution.

Schelling, Thomas C. 1971. "Dynamic Models of Segregation." *Journal of Mathematical Sociology* 1 (2): 143–86.

Schweinhart, L. J., J. Montie, Z. Xiang, W. S. Barnett, C. R. Belfield, and M. Nores. 2005. *Lifetime Effects: The HighScope Perry Preschool Study through Age 40.* Monographs of the HighScope Educational Research Foundation. Ypsilanti, MI: HighScope Press.

Shaw, Clifford R., and Henry D. McKay. 1942. *Juvenile Delinquency and Urban Areas.* Chicago: University of Chicago Press.

Shroder, Mark, and Arthur Reiger. 2000. "Vouchers versus Production Revisited." *Journal of Housing Research* 11 (1): 91–107.

Skogan, Wesley G., Susan M. Hartnett, Natalie Bump, and Jill Dubois. 2008. *Evaluation of CeaseFire.* National Institute of Justice, Office of Justice Programs Report. Washington, DC: National Institute of Justice.

Smolensky, Eugene, and J. Appleton Gootman. 2003. *Working Families and Growing Kids: Caring for Children and Adolescents.* Washington, DC: National Academies Press.

Struyk, Raymond J., and Mark Bendick, Jr., eds. 1981. *Housing Vouchers for the Poor: Lessons from a National Experiment.* Washington, DC: Urban Institute Press.

Swanson, Christopher B. 2009. *Cities in Crisis 2009: Closing the Graduation Gap.* Editorial Projects in Education, Inc. Report. Bethesda, MD: Editorial Projects in Education, Inc.

Votruba, Mark, and Jeffrey Kling. 2009. "Effect of Neighborhood Characteristics on the Mortality of Male Black Youth: Evidence from Gautreaux." *Social Science and Medicine* 68 (5): 814–23.

Wang, Philip S., Michael Lane, Mark Olfson, Harold A. Pincus, Kenneth B. Wells, and Ronald C. Kessler. 2005. "Twelve-Month Use of Mental Health Services in the United States: Results from the National Comorbidity Survey Replication." *Archives of General Psychiatry* 62 (6): 629–40.

Watson, Tara. 2009. "Inequality and the Measurement of Residential Segregation by Income in American Neighborhoods." NBER Working Paper no. 14908. Cambridge, MA: National Bureau of Economic Research.

Weiner, David A., Byron F. Lutz, and Jens Ludwig. 2009. "The Effects of School Desegregation on Crime." NBER Working Paper no. 15380. Cambridge, MA: National Bureau of Economic Research.

Whitehurst, Grover J., and Michelle Croft. 2010. *The Harlem Children's Zone, Promise Neighborhoods, and the Broader, Bolder Approach to Education.* Brown Center on Education Policy at Brookings Report. Washington, DC: Brookings Institution.

Wilson, D. B., L. A. Bouffard, and D. L. MacKenzie. 2005. "A Quantitative Review of Structured, Group-Oriented, Cognitive-Behavioral Programs for Offenders." *Criminal Justice and Behavior* 32 (2): 172–204.

Wilson, William Julius. 1987. *The Truly Disadvantaged: The Inner City, the Underclass, and Public Policy.* Chicago: University of Chicago Press.

———. 1996. *When Work Disappears: The World of the New Urban Poor.* New York: Alfred A. Knopf.

Zimring, Franklin E., and Gordon Hawkins. 1997. *Crime Is Not the Problem.* New York: Oxford University Press.

Comment   Ilyana Kuziemko

This chapter deftly handles a wide variety of evidence on the relationship between family and neighborhood poverty and criminal activity, and this comment will not attempt to discuss all the points the authors make. Instead, it will focus on the relationship between parental labor supply and children's human capital formation. The authors highlight several studies that suggest that programs that incentivize low-income single parents to work might have negative and even criminogenic effects on children. As the authors note, this idea runs counter to much of the thinking behind U.S. poverty policy, which since at least the 1990s has been heavily influenced by the notion that parents of poor children—usually single mothers—should work outside the home.

In this comment, I first discuss the trade-offs parents make in deciding how to divide their time endowment between working outside the home and spending time at home with their children and how these trade-offs vary with

Ilyana Kuziemko is assistant professor of economics and public affairs at Princeton University, and a faculty research fellow of the National Bureau of Economic Research.

the earning potential of parents. I then describe the variation since 1940 in two key proxies for the quantity of time a child spends with a parent—family composition and parental labor supply—and consider whether it mirrors variation in proxies for criminal activity. I also briefly discuss cross-country comparisons.

Balancing Time in the Labor Market with Time at Home with Children

The idea that time spent with parents is an important input in child development is not particularly controversial. Obviously, children's well-being is not merely a function of the time they spend with parents but is also increasing in consumption (up to some point, at least), and, therefore, in most households, parents must balance time spent at home with children and time earning income in the labor market. While the substitution effect suggests that parents with higher human capital—and, thus, higher earning potential—would spend less time with their children (and more time at work) than parents with lower human capital, the income effect would make them have greater demand for time at home as well.

Indeed, the result that generally obtains is that children of parents with relatively low human capital receive less time with their parents and less consumption. Take as an example single versus married mothers. Figure 9C.1 shows the labor supply of these two groups since 1940, using U.S. Census data from 1940 to 2000 and the American Community Survey (ACS) in 2008. Single mothers have always worked more than married mothers, even though throughout the sample period the former group has had sub-

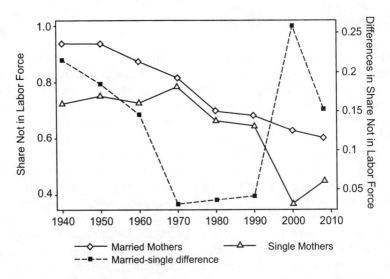

Fig. 9C.1   Share of single and married mothers not in the labor force, 1940–2008

Notes: Data taken from 1940–2000 decennial Census microdata and the 2008 American Community Survey microdata. All results use the provided person-level weights.

stantially lower educational attainment. Between 1970 and 1990, when the relationship between labor supply and income is weakest for single mothers as welfare payments were at their most generous level, the differences between the two groups narrow, only to fan out again after welfare reform in the 1990s.

That single mothers would work more is hardly surprising—they cannot depend on a partner for any economic support. However, in terms of child development, a single mother's decision to work may entail a higher cost; unlike her married counterpart, she cannot depend on another partner for help with child supervision, and she would have little income to purchase quality child or after-school care.

Family Composition and Parental Labor Supply in the United States

This section shows how family composition and parental labor supply has varied over time for different groups of children. I will often focus on black-white differences, both because young black men are generally overrepresented in arrest and prison data and because race can serve as a convenient, if crude, proxy for income.

Figure 9C.2 shows the share of children under age eighteen who live in the same household as their father, again using Census and ACS data. As is well documented, the share of black children living with their father plummeted during this period, from 70 percent in 1940 to 40 percent in 2008. Similarly, black children were 20 percentage points less likely to live with their fathers than were white children in 1940, whereas that difference is

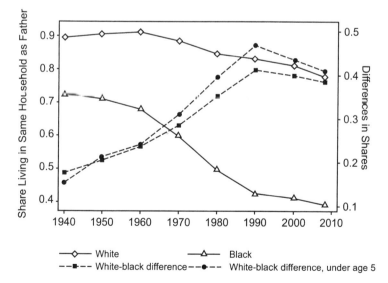

Fig. 9C.2   Share of children who live in the same household as their father
Notes: See figure 9C.1 notes.

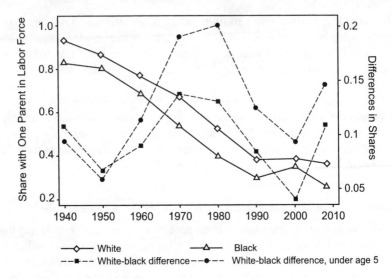

Fig. 9C.3   Share of children in two-parent households with at least one parent not working

Notes: See figure 9C.1 notes. "Not working" is defined as being out of the labor force, not merely unemployed.

roughly 40 percentage points today. The final series in figure 9C.2 shows that the white-black difference is slightly more pronounced for children under five—the age period during which Heckman (2006) and others argue investments in children are most crucial in fostering positive adolescent and adult outcomes.

Figure 9C.3 shows that even among families in which both parents are living together, black children have always been less likely to have a nonworking parent, and the white-black difference today is about the same as in 1940 though it has bounced around during the sample period. Again, the black-white difference is especially pronounced for younger children.

While it is interesting to consider how well these trends mirror the corresponding trends for measures of criminal behavior, it is essential to keep in mind the serious limitations of such an exercise. First, of course, correlation is not causation. Second, just as labor market supply is a rough proxy for the quality and quantity of parent-child time, criminal justice statistics such as the incarceration rate are rough proxies for actual criminal behavior.[1]

Keeping those caveats in mind, the rough correlation between these mea-

---

1. In particular, I certainly do not wish to dismiss the possibility that, relative to whites, blacks are treated more harshly by the criminal justice system conditional on the same behavior or that lawmakers intentionally increase punishment for behaviors that blacks are more likely to engage it (e.g., using crack instead of powder cocaine).

sures and criminal activity are encouraging. Incarceration rates throughout the second half of the twentieth century have been higher for blacks than for whites, with a sharp increase in relative black incarceration rates for cohorts born after, say, 1965, when the share of black children living with their father begins to plummet. As documented in Western (2006), 11 percent of black men born between 1945 and 1949 have been imprisoned at some point before their thirty-fifth birthday, compared to 1.4 percent of white men. For the cohort born between 1965 and 1969, that statistic rose by 9.5 percentage points for blacks and only 1.5 percentage points for whites. The potential explanatory power of family composition seems especially promising in light of the many factors the authors list—such as the decrease in residential segregation and the increase in blacks' relative income—that would have predicted lower rates of relative incarceration after 1965.

Family Composition and Parental Labor Supply across Countries

The cross-country comparisons presented in this section should probably be taken with even more caution than the previous analysis. I rely on data compiled by the Organization for Economic Cooperation and Development (OECD), and as these data are often drawn from different national data sets and thus variable definitions can differ across countries, we should take these cross-country differences as representing rather rough comparisons.[2]

Similar to the comparison between blacks and whites in the United States, American children are far more likely to live with only one parent than are their counterparts in other OECD countries. Among children under age fifteen, 25.8 percent live in single-parent families in the United States, compared to 13.3 percent in France, 10.7 percent in the Netherlands, and an OECD average (which includes the United States) of 15.9 percent.

Within household type, U.S. parents work more than other OECD parents. American children in two-parent households are much more likely to have both their parents work than are children in two-parent households in other OECD countries. Just over 72 percent of U.S. two-parent households with children under age fifteen have both parents working, compared to an OECD average of 60 percent. Similarly, 37 percent of single parents in the OECD stay home with their children, compared to only 23 percent in the United States.

As before, these comparisons roughly mirror those for adolescent and young adult outcomes between the United States and comparable countries. The incarceration rate, probability of committing or being a victim of homicide, and teenage pregnancy rates are all substantially higher in the United States.

2. All data in this section is from the OECD Family Database, located at http://www.oecd.org/document4/0,3343,en_2649_34819_37836996_1_1_1_1,00.html.

Concluding Thoughts

The evidence on the effects of parental labor supply on child outcomes that the authors present in this chapter spark many interesting research and policy questions.

First, it must be noted that the evidence on this question is still rather sparse, and, thus, future work from researchers on the question would be indeed welcome. There is varying evidence from welfare-to-work studies on how the labor supply of single mothers affects children and how this effect varies by the age of the child (see Grogger, Karoly, and Klerman 2002). Given that the greatest increase in the labor supply of low-income single mothers came in the late 1990s, researchers will soon have the opportunity to observe the children born during that period as they reach more criminogenic ages.

Second, research could also focus on whether effective substitutes for parental time at home exist. Do grandparents or after-school enrichment programs provide the same benefits? It may be difficult if not impossible to affect the trends underlying household composition or parental labor supply, but policy can affect the quality of the time children spend away from their parents. For example, per-child public expenditure on childcare is $794 in the United States, compared to an OECD average of $2,549 (and over $5,000 in Scandinavia).

Finally, both the chapter and this comment have generally focused on mothers' labor supply, given the high poverty rates of single-mother households. However, whether mothers work outside the home is only one component of the quantity and quality of time children spend with parents. Future work might consider how contact with fathers affects the development of children and adolescents from at-risk groups. This question presents greater data challenges—as fathers will often not be in the same household as the child, household survey data is often not helpful—and, thus, represents an understudied but perhaps essential factor in improving outcomes for low-income children.

References

Grogger, J., L. A. Karoly, and J. A. Klerman. 2002. "Consequences of Welfare Reform: A Research Synthesis." Discussion Paper. Santa Monica, CA: RAND.
Heckman, J. J. 2006. "Skill Formation and the Economics of Investing in Disadvantaged Children." *Science* 312 (5782): 1900–1902.
Western, B. 2006. *Punishment and Inequality in America.* New York: Russell Sage Foundation.

Education Policy and Crime

Lance Lochner

10.1 Introduction

In 1997, over two-thirds of all prison inmates in the United States were high school dropouts (Harlow 2003). Although education policy has not been a major factor driving trends in crime over the past twenty-five years—high school completion rates have remained relatively stable since the 1980s, while crime has both risen and fallen dramatically during that time—it is natural to ask what role education policy does and should play in affecting crime rates in the United States. Put another way, where is the marginal dollar best spent: on police, prisons, or schools? All three appear to reduce crime, but education and training have many benefits that prisons and police do not. In fact, Donohue and Siegelman (1998) argue that well-targeted preschool-type programs might be more cost-effective criminal deterrents than raising incarceration rates. Lochner and Moretti (2004) make a strong case for increasing high school graduation rates as an alternative to increasing the size of police forces.

Despite promising evidence that education-based policies and early childhood interventions can play an important role in helping reduce crime, evidence is still limited and sometimes mixed. The link between schooling and crime is more complicated than simple prison statistics suggest. This chapter

Lance Lochner is associate professor of economics and holds the CIBC Chair in Human Capital and Productivity and the Canada Research Chair in Human Capital and Productivity at the University of Western Ontario, and is a research associate of the National Bureau of Economic Research.

For their comments and suggestions, I thank David Card, Phil Cook, David Deming, Jens Ludwig, and participants at the National Bureau of Economic Research (NBER) Economics of Crime Control Conferences in Boston, Massachusetts, and Berkeley, California.

reviews evidence in this rapidly growing area and develops a human capital-based theory for interpreting much of this evidence.

We first discuss the relationship between education and crime from an economic perspective, developing a simple model that sheds light on key ways in which early childhood programs and policies that encourage schooling may affect both juvenile and adult crime. The model developed in section 10.2 is grounded in human capital theory and paints with a broad brush. It emphasizes the choice individuals face between legitimate work and criminal activity, with its associated punishments. By altering the relative rewards of work and crime, educational investments affect decisions to engage in crime. While the model does not incorporate all avenues through which education may affect crime, it serves as a useful point of reference.

In section 10.3, we discuss evidence on the impacts of educational attainment and school quality/choice on adult crime. The evidence from studies of educational attainment on crime is largely consistent with a human capital-based theory of crime, suggesting that increases in schooling reduce most types of adult crime (e.g., Lochner 2004; Lochner and Moretti 2004). Studies of school choice and increases in school quality paint a more nuanced picture: sizeable improvements in school quality produce minor (at best) improvements in student achievement and educational attainment, while they appear to substantially reduce crime during late adolescence and early adulthood (Cullen, Jacob, and Levitt 2006; Deming 2009a). It is unclear whether "better" schools largely improve social development or the peers and social networks of disadvantaged youth. We next discuss the contemporaneous relationship between school attendance and crime. Using exogenous policy changes and other events that effectively force students to stay in school or take extra days off (e.g., changes in compulsory schooling laws, teacher in-service days, and strikes), a few recent studies have shown that school attendance affects crime in rich and complex ways. Forcing some students to stay in school an extra year or two reduces both violent and property crime substantially (Anderson 2009), consistent with the time allocation human capital model developed in section 10.2. Yet day-to-day changes in school attendance have opposing effects on violent and property crime. An extra day of school appears to reduce property crime while *increasing* violent crime (Jacob and Lefgren 2003; Luallen 2006). The latter most likely reflects social interaction effects from bringing together hundreds of adolescents and letting them all loose at the same time.

Section 10.4 reviews a number of recent studies that examine the long-run impacts of early childhood, school-based, and young adult training interventions on juvenile and adult crime. While a few early preschool programs have produced sizeable long-run reductions in crime—most famously, Perry Preschool—other quite similar programs have not. School-based programs focused on improving social development among "risky" children have been shown to reduce crime through early adulthood. Finally, job training for young adults (e.g., Job Corps) appears to reduce self-reported arrests and convictions during the period of intensive training, but it yields negligible lasting effects on crime. Altogether, the evidence suggests that reductions in crime can be achieved by a wide range of human capital-based intervention strategies.

We discuss a number of policy issues related to education and its potential role as a crime-fighting strategy in section 10.5 and offer concluding thoughts in section 10.6.

10.2   The Economics of Education and Crime

Why might education reduce crime, and should its effects vary across different types of crimes? How might education and human capital policies help reduce crime? To answer these questions, we develop a simple economic model that formalizes a number of key channels through which education may affect crime. We then provide a brief discussion of other factors that may help determine the relationship between education and crime.

10.2.1   A Two-Period Model of School, Work, and Crime

To better understand the effects of early childhood programs and education policy on criminal behavior, we consider a simple two-period model of human capital investment, work, and crime. The model developed here abstracts from many things to focus attention on the effects of education and human capital-based policies on crime.[1] It emphasizes the role of education as a human capital investment that increases future legitimate work opportunities, which discourages participation in crime. This is consistent with numerous recent studies that show that higher wages reduce crime (e.g., Grogger 1998; Machin and Meghir 2004; Gould, Mustard, and Weinberg 2002) and decades of research in labor economics showing that education increases wage rates (see, e.g., Card 1999).

The two key assumptions of this human capital-based approach are (a) individual rationality and (b) the fact that crime requires time: in terms of planning, simply "hanging around" waiting for something to happen, carrying out the activity, avoiding arrest, or incarceration. Regarding the second, a number of studies discuss the implicit "wage rates" for time spent engaging in property crimes like drug dealing or burglary.[2] Yet for many other offenses, especially violent offenses, the criminal act itself may require little time; however, expected time in police stations, courtrooms, and prison cells may be substantial. The total time associated with most criminal acts may, in fact, be dominated by expected incarceration time. Taking this into

---

1. For a more detailed treatment of the life-cycle human capital investment problem and the age-crime profile, see Lochner (2004).
2. See Freeman (1999) for a survey of this literature.

account, the expected time associated with many violent offenses is likely to exceed that for most property crimes as seen in table 10.1 (from Lochner 2004), which reports probabilities of arrest, probabilities of conviction conditional on arrest, probabilities of incarceration conditional on conviction, estimated time served if incarcerated, and overall expected time served per crime committed for common violent and property crimes.

Now consider the choices faced by adolescents and adults. In the first period (adolescence), individuals are assumed to allocate their time to crime ($c_1 \geq 0$), work ($L_1 \geq 0$), and human capital investment ($I \geq 0$) subject to the time constraint $c_1 + L_1 + I = 1$. In the second period (adulthood), individuals decide only between crime ($c_2 \geq 0$) and work ($L_2 \geq 0$) subject to $c_2 + L_2 = 1$. In considering time spent committing crime, it is useful to think generally about the total expected time spent planning and committing crimes, avoiding arrest, "hanging around" waiting for an opportunity to arise, and in court or jail/prison.

While we do not explicitly model childhood, we assume that individuals enter adolescence with a set of endowments that affect subsequent behavior. These endowments may be shaped by early family and public investments. As a result, they may be manipulated by early childhood interventions as well as school-based policies (e.g., elementary school quality, preschool programs). We explicitly consider three types of adolescent "endowments" developed throughout childhood: "learning productivity" A, initial human capital levels H_1, and "criminal propensity" θ. It is useful to think of these three "endowments" quite generally, as parameters that embody individual characteristics as well as the environment faced by individuals. For example, A reflects anything that increases the productivity of adolescent human capital investments (either through formal schooling or more informal on-the-job training). This may include raw intelligence quotient (IQ), peers, or local middle or high school quality. Similarly, θ represents any factors that may affect the net expected returns to crime for an individual (e.g., criminal skill, preferences for risk, or a personal aversion to crime or prison).

Human capital investments through schooling and training improve adult skills H_2:

(1) $$H_2 = H_1 + h(I, H_1; A),$$

where $h(\cdot)$ is increasing in each of its arguments (i.e., $h_j > 0$ for $j = I, H_1, A$), and there are diminishing marginal returns to investment (i.e., $h_{II} < 0$). These conditions ensure that education and training increase human capital at a diminishing rate. We further assume that students with higher levels of human capital, H_1, and learning productivity, A, produce more human capital for any amount of investment ($h_{IA}, h_{IH} > 0$). Both ability and initial skill levels are, therefore, complementary with skill investment.

For each unit of time spent working, L_t, an individual earns H_t. Thus, H_t reflects an individual's potential earnings if he or she devotes all his time to

Table 10.1   Expected punishment associated with incarceration (Uniform Crime Reports)

Crime	Probability of arrest	Probability of conviction conditional on arrest	Probability of incarceration conditional on conviction	Unconditional probability of incarceration	Estimated months served if incarcerated	Expected days served per crime committed
Violent crimes	0.25	0.22	0.79	0.043	91	119.4
Murder and nonnegligent manslaughter	0.85	0.67	0.95	0.544	248	4,102.4
Forcible rape	0.15	0.39	0.90	0.051	136	212.2
Robbery	0.15	0.36	0.89	0.047	94	134.8
Aggravated assault	0.30	0.17	0.71	0.035	59	63.2
Property crimes	0.06	0.11	0.68	0.004	24	3.2
Burglary	0.07	0.27	0.76	0.015	29	13.2
Larceny-theft	0.05	0.08	0.61	0.002	20	1.4
Motor vehicle theft	0.10	0.08	0.73	0.006	17	3.1

Source: Lochner (2004).

Notes: Probability of arrest computed from crimes and arrests in the United States (Uniform Crime Reports, 2000) adjusted for nonreporting to the police (National Criminal Victimization Survey, 2000). It is assumed that all murders are reported to the police. Probability of conviction conditional on arrest divides total arrests in the United States by total state and federal convictions for 2000. Probability of incarceration conditional on conviction is based on reporting of state courts. Estimated months served if incarcerated applies to state prisoners and is estimated by the U.S. Department of Justice based on sentence lengths handed out that year and the average percent of sentences served by prisoners released that year. Unless otherwise noted, all criminal justice figures are for 2000 and are taken from Durose and Langan (2003).

work. Investment, I, has no immediate payoff; however, it may be subsidized by the government at rate s. These subsidies more generally represent any incentives the government may provide for schooling or training.

Assume that time spent committing crime each period, c_t, yields a net return of $N(c_t, H_t; \theta)$. where, for simplicity, we abstract from uncertainty about punishment.[3] As noted earlier, the parameter θ represents any factors that may affect the net returns to crime for an individual. As such, θ is a function of early childhood investments, family background, and neighborhoods, as well as law enforcement and incarceration policies. In general, the net expected returns to crime, as well as the marginal returns to crime N_c, may be positive or negative. However, we assume that $N_{c\theta} > 0$, so persons with a high θ have a greater total and marginal expected return from crime.

For criminals, the net marginal return to crime (N_c) must be positive, but this need not be the case for noncriminals. Many individuals commit crime while working or attending school. This suggests that $N_{cc} < 0$ whenever $N_c > 0$ (i.e., if net returns to crime increase with the amount of time spent committing crime, they do so at a diminishing rate).[4] We, therefore, make this assumption throughout.

On the one hand, individuals with more human capital are likely to be better criminals as well as better workers. (White collar crimes like fraud and embezzlement are perfect examples.) On the other hand, more highly skilled workers experience greater losses in earnings while imprisoned, and they may also have a greater aversion to crime (as emphasized by Usher 1997). The following analysis assumes that the positive effects of human capital on criminal returns weakly outweigh the negative effects on expected costs associated with punishment, so $N_H \geq 0$, $N_{cH} \geq 0$ and $N_{HH} \leq 0$. Of course, human capital is likely to have negligible effects on the returns to many property crimes (i.e., $N_H = 0$, a case not ruled out in our analysis).

The Individual's Decision

Taking (A, H_1, θ) and s as given, individuals choose investment and time spent in work and crime to maximize the present value of lifetime earnings. Assuming a gross interest rate $R \geq 1$, and substituting in the time constraints, individuals

(2) $\max_{I, c_1, c_2} [H_1(1 - I - c_1) + sI_1 + N(c_1, H_1; \theta)] + R^{-1}[H_2(1 - c_2) + N(c_2, H_2; \theta)],$

---

3. We implicitly assume that any expected punishments are incurred during the period the crime is committed. This is consistent with the fact that most juveniles caught committing crime face relatively short periods of incarceration. Dealing more explicitly with uncertainty and lags in punishment would not change the nature of most results discussed here. See Lochner (2004, 2010) for a life-cycle model that explicitly incorporates these features.

4. If net marginal returns were positive and increasing, individuals would specialize.

subject to the human accumulation equation (1) and the time constraints $I \geq 0$, $c_1 \geq 0$, $c_2 \geq 0$, and $I + c_1 \leq 1$.

While the individual decision problem is framed as an income maximization problem and directly applies to crimes with a financial motive, the framework can also be used to study violent crime. In the case of violent crime, the function $N(\cdot)$ reflects the monetary equivalent of any "psychic" or nonpecuniary benefits from violent crime.

We assume that $s < H_1$, so that investment subsidies are not large enough to make investment more lucrative than work unless there is some future return on investment. The problem yields the following interior first-order conditions for I, c_1, and c_2:

$$(3) \qquad H_1 - s = R^{-1}[(1 - c_2) + N_H(c_2, H_2; \theta)] \, h_I(I, H_1; A)$$

$$(4) \qquad H_1 = N_c(c_1, H_1; \theta)$$

$$(5) \qquad H_2 = N_c(c_2, H_2; \theta).$$

These conditions hold for individuals who allocate some time to each activity during adolescence and adulthood and are useful for studying investment, work, and crime at the intensive margin.[5] Individuals equate the marginal returns on investment and crime each period to their potential legitimate wage rate H_t (less any investment subsidies in the case of investment).[6] Because it is fixed at any point in time, this wage rate reflects the opportunity cost for individuals in choosing how much time to spend investing in new skills or on the commission of crime. Among adolescents who spend some time working, small increases in investment (e.g., due to an increase in its return) will come at the expense of adolescent work and not juvenile crime; juvenile crime will also trade off with work (at the margin) and not investment. This suggests that we might not expect significant "incapacitation" effects of school on crime among students who also participate heavily in the labor market.

Equation (3) shows that schooling provides returns in the form of higher future earnings from work and potentially from crime through increased human capital. If education does not raise the returns from crime, youth that plan to spend more time committing crime as an adult will benefit less from school and should, therefore, choose to invest less in their human capital. Thus, a negative relationship between schooling and adult crime may result

---

5. The second-order conditions are not particularly informative. They do require that $N_{cc} < 0$, as assumed. While the second-order conditions do not necessarily hold everywhere for all possible parameterizations, we assume that they hold at any given interior solution for the (local) comparative static results derived in the following.

6. Equations (4) and (5) and diminishing marginal returns to crime ($N_{cc} < 0$) are consistent with higher average "wage rates" for many property crimes (relative to typical legitimate opportunities) as discussed in Freeman (1999).

from individual heterogeneity in tastes for crime or from local differences in criminal opportunities, law enforcement, and punishment regimes.

The effect of educational attainment on adult crime is embodied in equation (5). Anything that increases investment in human capital raises H_2, which raises the returns from legitimate work and the opportunity cost of engaging in crime. Of course, human capital may also raise the return to crime, so the net effect of schooling on adult crime depends on the balance of these two effects. In general, we would expect education to provide greater returns in the labor market than for most types of crime, so education should reduce adult crime. Notice that individuals with a higher learning ability A will benefit more from school, so we might expect greater reductions in adult crime among smarter youth in response to school-based policies. Of course, there is little scope for school-based policies to reduce crime among those who would normally eschew crime as adults in the first place. As such, education-based initiatives aimed at adolescents are likely to achieve greater reductions in crime if they target relatively intelligent (high A) youth with low initial skill levels (H_1) and high returns to crime (i.e., high θ).

For youth with high enough returns to crime or investment such that they choose not to work at all during adolescence (i.e., $I^* + c_1^* = 1$), conditions (3) and (4) reduce to a single first-order condition equating the marginal returns on adolescent crime with the marginal returns on investment: $N_c(1 - I, H_1; \theta) - s = R^{-1}[(1 - c_2) + N_H(c_2, H_2; \theta)]h_I(I, H_1; A)$. Among these individuals, time spent investing and adolescent crime trade off one-for-one, so education-based policies may have sizeable impacts on crime among nonworking juvenile criminals.

Education and Early Childhood Policies

We consider the implications of policies which may alter incentives to invest in human capital (i.e., changes in s) as well as earlier childhood or school-age policies that impact adolescent "endowments" (A, H_1, θ).[7] Our results apply to individuals who spend some time in both school and on crime during adolescence and who spend some time committing crime and working during adulthood. In some cases, the effects of policies differ (as noted) between individuals who also spend some time working during adolescence and those who do not.

The following condition is useful for a number of results.

CONDITION 1. $N_{cH} \le 1$.

This condition implies that human capital does not raise the returns to crime more than it raises the returns to legitimate work. It may not hold in

---

7. Policies to improve high schools may also directly affect the productivity of time spent in school, A, and socialization, θ. In this sense, these parameters may be directly manipulated by policy; however, we assume that they are not freely chosen by adolescents. Of course, families may shape these parameters through earlier investments as discussed in the preceding.

the case of certain types of white-collar crimes, but it is likely to hold for most common "street" crimes like larceny, assault, or robbery.

We first discuss the effects of education subsidies, or policies that generally encourage schooling.[8]

RESULT 1. *A marginal increase in education subsidies, s (a) increases investment in human capital; (b) does not affect crime for working adolescents but reduces crime among nonworking adolescents; and (c) reduces adult crime if Condition 1 holds and increases adult crime otherwise.*

Education subsidies do not affect criminal behavior for adolescents who work because the amount of time spent committing crime is determined only by their potential wage rate. Time spent investing trades off one-for-one with time spent working.[9] Nonworking adolescents increase their investment and reduce their criminal activity in response to higher investment subsidies. For them, criminal activity necessarily trades off with investment. As long as the returns to human capital are higher in the legitimate sector than the criminal sector, education subsidies will reduce adult crime rates.

It is worth noting, however, that crimes with a higher return to skill than legitimate work will tend to increase (among adults) in response to education subsidies. Thus, it is possible that some forms of white-collar crime may increase following policies that promote skill investments.

Because parental inputs, family background, early childhood programs, and school quality operate on the "endowment" parameters (A, H_1, θ), understanding how these parameters affect individual decisions is important. We begin by studying the effects of changes in learning productivity, A.

RESULT 2. *A marginal increase in learning productivity,* A *(a) increases investment in human capital if* N_{HH} *is sufficiently close to zero; (b) does not affect crime for working adolescents but reduces crime among nonworking adolescents (if* $N_{HH} \approx 0$*); and (c) reduces adult crime if Condition 1 holds and increases adult crime otherwise.*

Policies that increase learning productivity or cognitive ability have qualitatively similar effects to an increase in education subsidies. Not surprisingly, an increase in the productivity of schooling (or learning ability) causes individuals to invest more in their skills. Adolescent criminal activity is unaffected by small changes in A for working adolescents. Because

---

8. All results are derived formally in the appendix.

9. The fact that wage rates are unaffected by hours worked but criminal earnings are declining in time spent committing crime is key to this result. If wage rates depend on the number of hours worked, time spent committing crime during adolescence will be affected by an investment subsidy even for those who are working. Additionally, if incarceration extends for many years into the future, an investment subsidy may reduce adolescent crime among workers because the expected costs from future incarceration are increasing in investment (Lochner 2004, 2010). Finally, large enough education subsidies could cause youth to stop working altogether, in which case they would also reduce their criminal activity.

initial potential wage rates are fixed, individuals simply substitute work for investment.[10] More investment means higher levels of human capital and higher wage rates during adulthood. As long as the criminal returns to human capital are not too high, this lowers adult crime and increases time spent working. Nonworking adolescents commit less crime in response to an increase in A because higher investment must trade off with time spent committing crime.

Policies that raise initial skill levels (H_1) can yield different implications, especially for adolescents.

RESULT 3. *Among working adolescents, an increase initial skill levels, H_1, reduces adolescent crime if Condition 1 holds; otherwise, it increases adolescent crime. Among nonworking adolescents, if human capital does not affect the net returns to crime (i.e., $N_H = 0$), then an increase in H_1 increases investment and reduces both adolescent and adult crime.*

As long as human capital is rewarded more in the labor market than the criminal sector, an increase in the skills of working youth reduces juvenile crime. However, it has ambiguous effects on investment because it raises both the opportunity cost of and return to education. This means that it is not possible to generally sign the effects of changes in H_1 on adult human capital and crime for working youth; however, we would typically expect adult crime to be decreasing in H_1. Among nonworking adolescents, increases in skill have no effect on the opportunity cost of investment. As such, an increase in H_1 unambiguously raises their investment and reduces their participation in crime at all ages (if human capital does not affect criminal returns).

Finally, we discuss the effects of policies that alter the expected returns to crime. These policies may have their effects through socialization or simply through increasing the probability of arrest or incarceration.

RESULT 4. *A reduction in criminal returns, θ, reduces adolescent crime for working adolescents. If Condition 1 holds and $N_{H\theta} \leq 0$, then a reduction in θ also (a) increases schooling investments; (b) reduces adolescent crime for nonworking adolescents; and (c) reduces adult crime.*

A lower criminal return directly encourages individuals to work more at all ages. By shifting time from crime to work during adulthood, a reduction in criminal returns raises the return to investment (assuming criminal returns to skill are low). Increased schooling investment increases adult wage rates, which causes individuals to further reallocate time from crime to work as

10. As with education subsidies, large increases in A may cause youth to stop working altogether and substitute away from crime as well. It is also likely that individuals with a higher learning ability also possess a higher initial skill level H_1 by the time they reach adolescence, in which case criminal activity during adolescence would be lower for those with high A and H_1. The effects of H_1 on crime are discussed further in the following.

adults. Thus, the endogeneity of schooling and work leads to larger reductions in adult crime than would be predicted if either were held fixed.

These results, particularly the last, highlight why cross-sectional comparisons of education and crime are difficult to interpret. On the one hand, youth who invest more through school should commit less crime as adults. On the other hand, youth planning to spend much of their adult lives on crime (and in jail) receive little return from school and will choose to invest little in school. Thus, a negative education–crime relationship can arise because education reduces crime or because a life of crime renders education useless.

10.2.2   Other Ways in Which Education May Affect Crime

Education may also teach individuals to be more patient (Becker and Mulligan 1997). This would discourage crime because forward-looking individuals place greater weight on any expected future punishment associated with their criminal activities. To the extent that time preferences are affected by schooling, crimes associated with long prison sentences (or other long-term consequences) should be most affected. Education may also affect preferences toward risk. If schooling makes individuals more risk averse, it should discourage crime with its greatest effects on offenses that entail considerable uncertainty in returns or punishment. Finally, schooling may affect the set of people individuals interact with on a daily basis in school, work, or their neighborhoods. Assuming more educated people interact more with other educated people who are less inclined to engage in crime, this is likely to compound any reductions in crime associated with schooling.[11] In most cases, mechanisms related to changes in preferences or social interactions suggest that educational attainment is likely to reduce most types of crime among adults.

10.2.3   School Attendance and Contemporaneous Crime

It is useful to distinguish between the effects of educational attainment on subsequent criminal activity and the way in which school attendance itself affects contemporaneous crime. The latter relationship is likely to be driven by three mechanisms. First, school may have an incapacitation effect—youth cannot be in two places at once, and many criminal opportunities are more limited in school than on the streets. Of course, school does not last all day, so this effect depends, in part, on the ease with which youth can engage in crime during nonschool hours. This mechanism is inherent in the time allocation problem in the preceding. Second, longer periods of school attendance should increase human capital levels and improve future employment prospects. This, in turn, may make juvenile arrests and long periods of detention more costly, reducing incentives to engage in crime while enrolled in

---

11. See Glaeser, Sacerdote, and Scheinkman (1996) for a model of crime where social interactions are important.

school.[12] Third, schools bring hundreds of adolescents together for the day and then let them all loose at the same time. The social interaction effects from doing this are far from obvious, but it is quite possible that this leads to altercations and more general group-based delinquency. The incapacitation and human capital effects are likely to imply negative effects of school attendance on crime, while the social interaction effect could be positive or negative.

10.3   Evidence on Education and Crime

We now discuss evidence on the effects of educational attainment and school quality and choice on subsequent criminal outcomes. We also review empirical studies that analyze the relationship between school attendance and contemporaneous crime.

10.3.1   Educational Attainment and Crime

We have discussed four primary reasons schooling might affect subsequent crime: (a) education raises wage rates, which raises the opportunity costs of crime; (b) education may directly affect the financial or "psychic" rewards from crime; (c) education may alter preferences for risk-taking or patience; and (d) schooling may affect the social networks or peers of individuals. For most crimes (except, possibly, white-collar crimes), one would expect these forces to induce a negative effect of schooling on adult crime.

Empirically, there is a strong negative correlation between educational attainment and various measures of crime. In 1997, 75 percent of state and 59 percent of federal prison inmates in the United States did not have a high school diploma (Harlow 2003).[13] After controlling for age, state of birth, state of residence, year of birth, and year effects, Lochner and Moretti (2004) still find significant effects of schooling (especially high school completion) on the probability of incarceration in the United States as reported in figure 10.1.[14] In 2001, more than 75 percent of convicted persons in Italy had not completed high school (Buonanno and Leonida 2006), while incarceration

---

12. The preceding model abstracts from this by implicitly assuming that punishments occur in the same period that crimes are committed and that there are no long-term effects of punishment on human capital or employment opportunities; however, it is straightforward to incorporate these effects in a life-cycle model with multiperiod punishments as in Lochner (2004, 2010).

13. These figures exclude those who received a General Educational Development (GED) diploma. As shown in Cameron and Heckman (2003) and Heckman and LaFontaine (2006), individuals with a GED perform like high school dropouts rather than graduates in the labor market. Roughly 35 percent of state inmates and 33 percent of federal inmates completed their GED with more than two-thirds of these inmates earning their GED while incarcerated. A small percentage of those who did not receive a high school diploma had participated in some vocational or postsecondary courses. See Harlow (2003).

14. These figures report the coefficients on indicators for different years of completed schooling from the 1960, 1970, and 1980 Censuses for white and black men ages twenty to sixty.

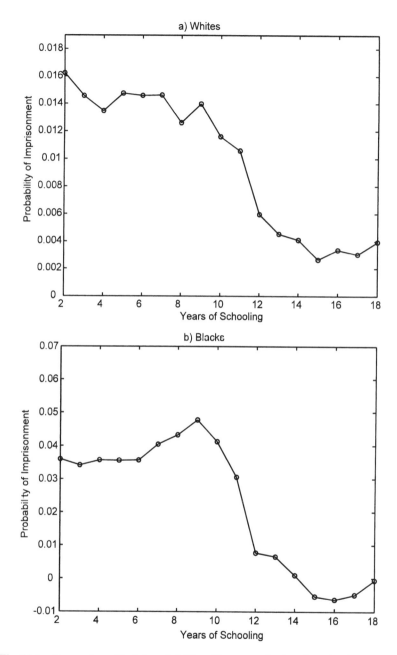

Fig. 10.1   Regression-adjusted probability of incarceration by education (men ages 20–60)

Source: Lochner and Moretti (2004).

Notes: From 1960, 1970, and 1980 U.S. Censuses. Regressions control for age, state of birth, state of residence, cohort of birth, state, and year effects.

rates among men ages twenty-one to twenty-five in the United Kingdom were more than eight times higher for those without an education qualification (i.e., dropouts), relative to those with a qualification (Machin, Marie, and Vujic 2010).

Differences by education are also apparent in self-reported survey measures of crime. For example, in the 1980 wave of the National Longitudinal Survey of Youth (NLSY), 34 percent of American men ages twenty to twenty-three with eleven or twelve years of completed schooling self-reported earning some income from crime, compared with 24 percent of those with twelve years of school, and only 17 percent of those with more than twelve years. The effect of education is magnified if we consider more active criminal engagement: 4.2 percent of twenty to twenty-three-year-old NLSY men completing ten or eleven years of school reported earning more than half their income from crime, compared with 1.4 percent of those with twelve years and 0.7% of those with at least some college education. Similar patterns are observed for violent crime in the NLSY. See Lochner (2004) for further details.

Early studies of the relationship between education and crime focused on their correlation conditional on measured individual and family characteristics using standard regression methods.[15] For example, Witte and Tauchen (1994) find no significant relationship between educational attainment and crime after controlling for a number of individual characteristics. Grogger (1998) estimates a significant negative effect of wages on crime, but he finds no relationship between years of completed schooling and crime after controlling for individual wage rates. Of course, increased wages and earnings are important consequences of schooling. Thus, this study suggests that education may indirectly reduce crime through increased wage rates.

These earlier studies must be interpreted with caution. A negative cross-sectional correlation between education and crime, even after controlling for measured family background and neighborhood characteristics, does not necessarily imply that education reduces crime. Standard regression studies are unlikely to estimate the causal effect of eduction on crime (i.e., the effect of increasing someone's schooling on his criminal activity) for a number of reasons. First, unobserved individual characteristics like patience or risk aversion are likely to directly affect both schooling and criminal decisions. Individuals who choose more schooling (even after conditioning on observable characteristics) might also choose less crime regardless of their education level, in which case regression-based estimates do not identify a causal effect. Second, using variation in crime and education across states or local communities may also produce biased estimates. Governments may face a

15. Ehrlich (1975) provides an early empirical exploration of predicted effects of education on crime from a human capital perspective. See Witte (1997) for a survey of the early empirical literature on education and crime.

choice between funding police or good public schools, which would tend to produce a spurious positive correlation between education and crime. Alternatively, unobserved characteristics about communities or their residents may directly affect the costs or benefits of both education and crime. For example, communities with few job opportunities that reward schooling may also be faced with severe gang problems. While it is often possible to account for permanent unobserved differences across communities by examining the relationship between changes in schooling and crime over time, this approach does not account for the effects of changing unobserved community characteristics. Third, reverse causality is another important concern, for reasons discussed in section 10.2. Individuals who plan to heavily engage in crime (e.g., because they are particularly good at it, enjoy it, or live in areas with plenty of illicit opportunities) are likely to choose to leave school at a young age. Arrests or incarceration associated with juvenile crime may also cause some youth to drop out of school early (Hjalmarsson 2008).

Recently, economists have attempted to address these difficult issues and to estimate the causal effects of schooling on crime using instrumental variable (IV) methods. In the context of estimating the effect of educational attainment on crime, an instrument is valid if it induces variation in schooling but is uncorrelated with other factors that directly affect criminal proclivity (e.g., individual preferences or abilities, local law enforcement). Intuitively, this approach exploits differences in educational attainment across individuals that arise in response to factors that have no direct impact on criminal decisions. An ideal instrument would randomly assign some youth to drop out of high school and others to finish. Then, comparing the differences in crime rates across these groups would identify the causal effect of high school completion on crime. In practice, we typically do not observe such perfect experiments, but researchers can sometimes come close.

Because crime itself is difficult to measure, researchers are often forced to use measures of arrest or incarceration rather than actual crimes committed. It is possible that education reduces the probability of arrest and incarceration or the sentence lengths administered by judges, in which case estimates based on measures of arrest or incarceration incorporate these effects in addition to any effects of education on actual crime. While there is little direct evidence on these issues, Mustard (2001) finds negligible effects of defendant education levels on the sentence lengths they receive. Furthermore, results using self-reported measures of crime in the NLSY support the case that education reduces actual violent and property crime and not just the probability of arrest or incarceration conditional on crime (Lochner 2004; Lochner and Moretti 2004).[16]

---

16. There has been considerable debate among criminologists on the merits of self-reported measures of crime versus official measures of arrest. Most studies find a reasonably high correlation between the two; however, it is generally agreed that the two measures offer distinct

Many recent empirical studies analyze crime aggregated at some geographic level, exploring the effects of average educational attainment on crime, arrest, conviction, or incarceration rates. In order to address concerns with endogeneity or unobserved heterogeneity, researchers have typically turned to IV estimation or a differences-in-differences strategy using changes in state or national rules that affect schooling decisions. An aggregate-level regression is often specified as follows:

$$(6) \qquad y_{calt} = \beta E_{alt} + \gamma X_{alt} + d_{lt} + d_{cl} + d_{al} + d_{ct} + d_{at} + d_{ca} + \varepsilon_{calt}$$

where y_{calt} is a measure of the crime, arrest, or incarceration rate for some offense type c, age group a, in location l, in year t. In some cases, only a single measure of crime is used (e.g., incarceration or total arrests), in which case the c subscript is extraneous. E_{alt} is an aggregate measure of educational attainment for age group a in location l at time t (e.g., average schooling attainment or high school completion rates). X_{alt} is a set of observable characteristics that may vary across age, location, and time (e.g., racial composition of an area). The ds represent indicator variables that account for unobserved differences by age/cohort, location, year, and criminal offense types. The term d_{lt} allows for location-specific time effects, which accounts for time varying unobserved location-specific differences that may reflect differences in local public spending, economic conditions, or law enforcement. The inclusion of d_{cl} allows the average distribution of crime or arrest types to differ across areas. For example, some states may focus arrests more heavily on one type of crime, while others focus on other types. Or some areas may be more amenable to certain crimes while others are not. Similarly, the age distribution of crime or arrests need not be the same across areas—some age groups may be more crime-prone in some areas or arrest policies with respect to age may differ across areas. The term d_{al} absorbs long-run differences in age-arrest patterns across locations. Crime-specific and age-specific time trends in arrest common to all areas are accounted for by d_{ct} and d_{at}, respectively. Finally, d_{ca} accounts for long-term differences in age-crime profiles across different types of criminal offenses. Given these fixed effects, identification of the effect of education on crime is achieved through time variation in cohort educational attainment levels across different locations. The absence of d_{alt} indicator variables in equation (6) is, therefore, central to identification.

Lochner and Moretti (2004) examine state-level male arrest rates by criminal offense and age (five-year age categories beginning at ages twenty

---

and complementary information about criminal activity. Comparisons of self-reported arrests versus official arrests tend to find a stronger correlation, with agreement increasing further for self-reported versus official measures of criminal convictions. A number of studies report greater underreporting of crimes and arrests by blacks; however, studies vary considerably on this. See the classic Hindelang, Hirschi, and Weis (1981) for comprehensive treatment of the issue or Thornberry and Krohn (2000) for a more recent survey of this literature.

to twenty-four through fifty-five to fifty-nine) from the Federal Bureau of Investigation's (FBI) Uniform Crime Reports (UCR) for the United States in 1960, 1970, 1980, and 1990. This data is linked to 1960 to 1990 decennial U.S. Census data on educational attainment and race to estimate equation (6), where y_{calt} represents log arrest rates for a specific offense, age category, state, and Census year. They specifically analyze arrest rates for murder, rape, assault, robbery, burglary, larceny, auto theft, and arson. In using log arrest rates, the effect of education is assumed to be the same in percentage terms for each type of crime included in the regression. They explore the effects of both average years of schooling and high school completion rates at the cohort level (cohorts are defined by year of birth given year t and age a) in state l as of time t (i.e., E_{alt}). In addition to including all the d fixed effects in equation (6), they also include the percent of males that are black in age group a living in state l at time t (i.e., X_{alt}).

The main methodological contribution of Lochner and Moretti (2004) is the use of changes in state-specific compulsory schooling laws over time as IVs for schooling.[17] Intuitively, this strategy measures the extent to which an increase in a state's compulsory schooling age leads to an immediate increase in educational attainment and reduction in subsequent crime rates for affected cohorts.[18] Lochner and Moretti's (2004) analysis suggests that changes in compulsory schooling laws are exogenous and not related to prior trends in schooling or state expenditures on law enforcement, so it appears to be a valid instrument. Other studies reach similar conclusions about the exogenous nature of changes in compulsory schooling laws in other contexts (e.g., Acemoglu and Angrist 2001; Lleras-Muney 2002).

Lochner and Moretti (2004) estimate equation (6) using both ordinary least squares (OLS) and IV estimation. Using OLS, they find that a one-year increase in average education levels in a state reduces state-level arrest rates by 11 percent. Instrumental variable estimates suggest slightly larger effects although they are not statistically different. These estimated effects are very similar to the predicted effects derived from multiplying the estimated increase in wages associated with an additional year of school by the estimated effects of higher wage rates on crime (from Gould, Mustard, and Weinberg 2002). This suggests that much of the effect of schooling on crime may come through increased wage rates and opportunity costs as emphasized in the model of section 10.2. Given the strong relationship between high school completion and incarceration apparent in figure 10.1, Lochner and Moretti (2004) also estimate specifications using the high school

17. The relevant compulsory schooling age is based on the state law that applied when a cohort was age fourteen.
18. It is worth noting that this strategy (i.e., using compulsory schooling ages to instrument for average attainment) identifies the effects of raising average educational attainment levels via increases in schooling among high school dropouts. Policies that largely increase average attainment by increasing college completion rates could have very different effects.

completion rate as a measure of schooling. Ordinary least squares estimates suggest that a 10 percentage point increase in high school graduation rates would reduce arrest rates by 7 percent, while IV estimates suggest a slightly larger impact of 9 percent.

Lochner and Moretti (2004) also estimate separate effects of education for different types of crime using OLS (including interactions of criminal offense type with education in equation [6]). These results suggest similar effects across the broad categories of violent (murder, rape, robbery, and assault) and property (burglary, larceny, motor vehicle theft, and arson) crime—a one year increase in average years of schooling reduces both property and violent crime by about 11 to 12 percent. However, the effects vary considerably within these categories. A one-year increase in average years of schooling reduces murder and assault by almost 30 percent, motor vehicle theft by 20 percent, arson by 13 percent, and burglary and larceny by about 6 percent. Estimated effects on robbery are negligible, while those for rape are significantly positive. Additional specifications suggest quantitatively similar effects for a 10 to 20 percentage point increase in high school graduation rates. Their results for rape are surprising and not easily explained by standard economic models of crime.[19]

Lochner (2004) follows a very similar approach using the same UCR data from 1960 to 1980; however, he also examines white-collar crime. Ordinary least squares estimation of equation (6) produces *positive,* though statistically insignificant, effects of schooling on arrest rates for white-collar crimes (forgery and counterfeiting, fraud, and embezzlement). Estimates for violent and property crime are negative and similar to those of Lochner and Moretti (2004).

Lochner and Moretti (2004) also use individual-level data on incarceration and schooling from the 1960, 1970, and 1980 U.S. Censuses to estimate the effects of educational attainment on the probability of imprisonment separately for black and white men (ages twenty to sixty). Their estimates control for age of the respondent (three-year age categories), state of birth, state of residence, cohort of birth, and state-specific year effects. Most important, controlling for state-specific year effects allows for the possibility that different states may have different time trends for law enforcement policies or may simply exhibit different trends in aggregate criminal activity. Analogous to their analysis of state-level arrest rates, they use state-level changes in compulsory schooling ages as an instrument for educational attainment. Although this analysis uses individual-based measures of incarceration and schooling, variation in schooling laws at the state-year level effectively identifies the effect of education on crime. As with the estimates

---

19. However, the results are consistent with some specifications in Gould, Mustard, and Weinberg (2002), which suggests that local wage rates are positively correlated with local crime rates for rape.

for aggregate arrest rates, identification comes from the fact that in any given state and year, different age cohorts faced different compulsory schooling laws during their high school years, causing them to acquire different levels of schooling and to commit crime at different rates. Again, both OLS and IV estimates are very similar and suggest that, on average, an extra year of education reduces the probability of imprisonment by slightly more than .1 percentage point for whites and by about .4 percentage points for blacks. In their sample, the probability of incarceration for male whites (blacks) without a high school degree averaged .83 percent (3.6 percent), which translates into a 10 to 15 percent reduction in incarceration rates for both white and black males associated with an extra year of completed schooling. These estimated effects are comparable to those for arrest rates described earlier. Ordinary least squares results suggest that completion of the twelfth grade causes the greatest drop in incarceration, while their is little effect of schooling beyond high school (see figure 10.1).

Oreopoulos and Salvanes (2009) reproduce the Lochner and Moretti (2004) IV results for black males using the same estimation strategy with a slightly different specification and an expanded sample that includes men ages twenty-five to sixty-four from the 1950 to 1980 U.S. Censuses.[20] Their estimate suggests that an additional year of completed schooling reduces incarceration rates among black men by about 20 percent.

Machin, Marie, and Vujic (2010) exploit a 1972 increase in the minimum schooling age (from age fifteen to sixteen) in England and Wales to estimate the effects of schooling on criminal convictions for property and violent crimes over the period 1972 to 1996. Using both IV and regression discontinuity methods, identification effectively comes from cohort-level changes in schooling attainment and crime for cohorts turning fifteen immediately before and after the law change.[21] Among men, they estimate that a one-year increase in average schooling levels reduces conviction rates for property crime by 20 to 30 percent and violent crime by roughly one-third to one-half as much.[22] Compared to estimates for the United States by Lochner and Moretti (2004), the impacts of education on property crime appear to be greater in the United Kingdom, while the effects on violent crime are weaker.

20. Most notably, they do not include state and state-specific year effects in their specification. They also remove individuals with greater than twelve years of schooling from their sample. Their measures of compulsory schooling ages differ as well, incorporating the fact that some states allow for exceptions to the dropout age under certain conditions.

21. They estimate models aggregated to the year-age level for individuals ages eighteen to forty from 1972 to 1996. To alleviate concerns that other important economic or social factors may have changed at the same time the compulsory schooling age increased, they include a rich set of covariates: year and age indicators, fraction British-born, fraction employed, fraction nonwhite, and fraction living in London.

22. Estimated effects on male property crime are statistically significant, while effects on male violent crime are not. Estimated effects for women are, unfortunately, very imprecise.

Buonanno and Leonida (2006) estimate the effects of educational attainment on crime rates in Italy using regional panel data from 1980 to 1995. Their unit of observation is a region year (they examine twenty Italian regions), and they estimate a restricted form of equation (6) using OLS. Specifically, they control for region and time fixed effects (d_l and d_t), along with region-specific quadratic time trends (assuming $d_{lt} = \delta_{1l}t + \delta_{2l}t^2$), and a rich set of time-varying region-specific covariates.[23] These estimates are identified from the relationship between changes in regional education levels and crime rates (around smooth regional time trends). Their estimates suggest that a 10 percentage point increase in high school graduation rates would reduce property crime rates by 4 percent and total crime rates by about 3 percent. (Effects on property crime are statistically significant, while effects on total crime are not.) They find no evidence to suggest that university completion reduces crime.[24]

Merlo and Wolpin (2009) take a very different approach to estimating the relationship between schooling and subsequent crime. Using individual-level panel data on black males ages thirteen to twenty-two from the NLSY, they estimate a discrete choice vector autoregression model in which individuals can choose to engage in crime, attend school, or work each year.[25] These decisions are allowed to depend on unobserved individual-specific returns to each activity as well as crime, schooling, and work choices the previous year. Using estimates for their model, Merlo and Wolpin simulate the effects of changing youth schooling status at age sixteen on subsequent outcomes. Their estimates suggest that, on average, attending school at age sixteen reduces the probability a black male ever commits a crime over ages nineteen to twenty-two by 13 percentage points and the probability of an arrest over those ages by 6 percentage points. These represent 42 percent and 23 percent reductions in self-reported crime and arrest rates, respectively, for black males not in school at age sixteen.

A final study worth mentioning examines the effects of an explicit education subsidy on youth burglary rates in England. Between 1999 and 2002, England piloted Educational Maintenance Allowances (EMA), which provided subsidies of up to £40 per week (plus bonuses for completion of coursework) for low-income sixteen to eighteen-year-old youth to attend

---

23. Covariates include employment rates, GDP per capita, GDP growth rates, average wage rates, the fraction of crimes without an arrest, police per capita, and the length of time in the judicial process.

24. Buonanno and Leonida (2006) also generalize their econometric specification to allow for an effect of lagged crime rates on current crime rates, estimating this using a generalized method of moments estimator to account for the endogeneity of lagged crime rates. This specification produces similar estimated effects of schooling on crime.

25. Crime, work, and school are not mutually exclusive activities in this framework—individuals can do any combination of these three activities in each year. An individuals is said to have engaged in crime in any year if they self-reported any of the following offenses: theft, other property crime, sold drugs, or assault.

school. The program was administered in fifteen local areas with low schooling participation rates. During the same time period, the Reducing Burglary Initiative (RBI) funded sixty-three different local burglary reduction schemes as a separate pilot project. Roughly half of all EMA pilot areas were also selected for the RBI. Sabates and Feinstein (2008) use a differences-in-differences strategy to identify the effects of each pilot program as well as the combination of the two on burglary. Specifically, they compare changes in burglary conviction rates before and after the introduction of RBI, EMA, or both against a set of comparison areas. While baseline burglary conviction rates were much higher in EMA and EMA-RBI combined areas relative to the comparison areas, annual growth rates in burglary conviction rates prior to the programs were quite similar across all three classifications. To reduce concerns about differences between the treated and untreated areas, Sabates and Feinstein control for a number of time varying area-specific factors likely to affect crime and limit their sample of comparison areas to those that best "match" the distribution of demographic characteristics in the pilot areas.[26] Their findings suggest that the combination of both the EMA and RBI significantly reduced burglary rates by 1.3 per 1,000 youth (about 5.5 percent), relative to the "matched" comparison areas. Effects of the EMA alone were slightly lower but still significant. While there are obvious concerns about the extent to which time varying determinants of burglary are the same for treated and comparison areas, Sabates and Feinstein (2008) show that estimated effects on burglary rates for nineteen to twenty-one-year-olds (who were not offered the education subsidy) were much lower and statistically insignificant.

10.3.2   School Quality and Crime

If human capital acquisition, socialization, or preference modification are important mechanisms determining the impacts of educational attainment on crime, then it is likely that school quality and the type of schools students attend also affect criminal behavior. While there are no studies that directly estimate the effects of measured school quality on crime, three recent studies on school choice and desegregation provide some useful insights.

Cullen, Jacob, and Levitt (2006) and Deming (2009a) examine the importance of school choice in large urban U.S. school districts (Chicago and Charlotte-Mecklenburg, respectively) on a variety of student outcomes, including delinquency and crime. Both studies examine the effects "winning" a randomized lottery for admission to schools children selectively

---

26. Their regressions control for unemployment rates for individuals under twenty-five, proportion of students eligible for free school meals, number of qualified teachers, pupil-teacher ratios, and the number of supplementary staff for ethnic minorities, percent of youth with no schooling qualifications as of age sixteen (i.e., dropouts), and the percent of unauthorized half-days missed in secondary school. We discuss results based on the "matched" sample of comparison areas.

apply to.[27] By comparing the outcomes for youth who win versus lose a particular school admission lottery, they estimate the effects of being offered admission to that school, relative to the preferred alternative. This reflects the "intention to treat" (i.e., the effects of being offered the opportunity to attend better schools) and not necessarily the effects of actually attending that school because many students did not ultimately enroll in schools for which they were admitted by lottery. However, both studies find that "winning" a lottery does significantly increase enrollment in that school. Because many students applying outside their assigned local school are from disadvantaged backgrounds and neighborhoods, on average, lottery winners end up attending better quality schools, as measured by such things as student achievement scores, value added (i.e., growth in achievement), student behavioral problems, or teacher quality. In this sense, these studies offer an opportunity to examine the effects of school quality, broadly defined, on delinquency and crime.

Cullen, Jacob, and Levitt (2006) find that winning a high school lottery in Chicago significantly raises peer graduation rates by 6 percent and the share of peers who test above national norms by about 14 percent; however, lottery winners appear to be placed in lower tracked classes within the better schools. Interestingly, they find no evidence that lottery winners perform better on a wide range of academic measures (e.g., math and reading tests, enrollment, days absent) and some evidence that they are more likely to drop out of high school. The latter may be due to a mismatch between student ability and school demands. Despite the disappointing findings regarding academic outcomes, students who won lotteries to high achievement Chicago public schools reported nearly 60 percent fewer arrests on a ninth grade student survey. These winners also reported getting into less trouble at school, and school administrative data suggest that they had lower incarceration rates during school ages. Of course, it is possible that schools themselves affect student arrest and incarceration rates through differential disciplinary policies (or criminal opportunities), so it is important to study whether these reductions in arrests/incarceration persist beyond high school.

To this end, Deming (2009a) examines the impacts of open enrollment lotteries (for middle and high schools) on adult criminal outcomes seven years after random assignment.[28] Given his interest in the effects of school choice

27. In both cases, students could always choose to attend their neighborhood school. If any additional positions were available in a school, an open enrollment lottery was run based on all other students who applied to that school/program. Lotteries were random within population subgroups (e.g., by race or family income).

28. He merges Charlotte-Mecklenburg school district data with data on adult (ages sixteen+) arrests and incarceration from Mecklenburg County and the North Carolina Department of Corrections.

on crime, he categorizes males based on their likelihood of arrest, which he estimates as a function of demographic characteristics, earlier math and reading test scores, and other school-related behaviors at young ages. For his entire sample of middle and high school lottery participants, "high-risk" youth (defined as those in the top quintile of predicted arrest probability) have seven times more felony arrests (seven years after random assignment) than the average student from the bottom four quintiles combined.

Like Cullen, Jacob, and Levitt (2006), Deming (2009a) estimates significant effects of winning a school lottery on the quality of school attended, especially among high-risk youth, but no effects on achievement tests. There appears to be some effect on student enrollment during high school years, but there is no evidence that high-risk lottery winners are more likely to graduate from high school.[29] Among high school lottery winners in the high-risk category, Deming (2009a) estimates a significant 0.35 (roughly 45 percent) reduction in the number of adult felony arrests (cumulative as of seven years after the lottery) with an associated savings in victimization costs of $4,600 to $16,600.[30] Because many crimes do not lead to an arrest, the total benefits to potential victims and society are likely to be much larger. His estimates suggest that winning middle school lotteries also reduces crime among high-risk youth with most effects of a similar order of magnitude.

Court-ordered school desegregation policies enacted since *Brown vs. Board of Education of Topeka* in 1954 dramatically altered the types of schools blacks attended in many American districts. In most cases, the resources and average student achievement of schools attended by blacks would have improved markedly.[31] Guryan (2004) estimates that these desegregation efforts significantly increased high school graduation rates among blacks by 2 to 3 percentage points but had no effect on white graduation rates. Weiner, Lutz, and Ludwig (2009) examine whether these changes affected county-level homicide rates.[32] Their estimates suggest that homicide deaths among blacks ages fifteen to nineteen declined by 17 percent in the first five years after court-ordered desegregation, while homicide deaths among white fifteen to nineteen-year-olds declined by about 23 percent. Homicide deaths among slightly older whites and blacks also declined. In looking at

29. There is more evidence of effects on high school graduation and college attendance among the lower-risk quintiles.

30. These victimization costs (in year 2009 dollars) assign costs based on the type of offense using cost estimates from Miller, Cohen, and Wiersema (1996). They do not include justice system or enforcement costs. The larger figure uses a cost of $4.3 million for murder, while the smaller uses a value of $125,000 (twice the cost of rape).

31. For example, Reber (2007) shows that integration efforts in Louisiana from 1965 to 1970 were accompanied by large increases in per-pupil funding for black students.

32. They use data on homicide death by year and county over the period 1958 to 1988 from vital statistics and data on homicide victims and arrestees from the Supplemental Homicide Report from 1976 to 2003.

offenders, they find that arrest rates for homicide declined by one-third for blacks ages fifteen to nineteen, while there was no decline for young whites. Combining Guryan's (2004) estimated effect on high school graduation rates with the estimated effects of schooling on crime from Lochner and Moretti (2004), they argue that much of the effect may be coming from the increased schooling among blacks associated with desegregation.

For some perspective, it is interesting to compare these findings with those from the Moving-to-Opportunity (MTO) experiment, which provided housing vouchers to low-income families to move out of high poverty neighborhoods. Evaluations of MTO report that families receiving the housing vouchers moved into neighborhoods with about 25 percent lower poverty rates; however, these moves only led to modest improvements in the quality of schools youth attended and no improvements in their cognitive achievement (Sanbonmatsu et al. 2006). Kling, Ludwig, and Katz (2005) report that the MTO housing vouchers led to lasting reductions in arrests for both violent and property offenses among young females, short-term reductions in violent crime arrests for males, and delayed *increases* in property crime arrests for males. Overall, any reductions in crime were modest at best.

Taken together, these studies suggest that simply improving the schools attended by disadvantaged youth appears to be much more successful in reducing criminal activity (though not necessarily in improving academic outcomes) than changing neighborhoods. Given the mixed findings on educational attainment levels (with modest positive effects at best), the impacts of better schools on crime appear to be driven largely by school quality and not "quantity." Whether it is the quality of teachers and instruction or of student peers is less obvious. The fact that test scores did not improve among lottery winners suggests that the main effects of attending "better" schools on delinquency and crime are likely to be attributed to better socialization, better peer interactions, improvements in noncognitive skills, or changes in preferences. It is, therefore, interesting that substantial improvements in "neighborhood peers" do not yield the same benefits in terms of crime reduction.

10.3.3   Contemporaneous Schooling and Crime

We now consider the relationship between contemporaneous schooling and crime. As noted earlier, there are three main ways in which altering youth's schooling attendance is likely to affect their contemporaneous engagement in crime: (a) incapacitation, (b) raising the costs of future punishment through human capital accumulation, and (c) social interactions facilitated by bringing youth together. The incapacitation and human capital effects of schooling on crime are likely to be negative, while the sign of the social interaction effect is theoretically ambiguous.

Three relatively recent studies shed light on these effects by estimating the impacts of different "interventions" that directly affect youth schooling attendance.[33] Anderson (2009) examines the effects of increasing state compulsory schooling ages on crime among affected youth (i.e., forcing some youth to stay in school), while Jacob and Lefgren (2003) and Luallen (2006) estimate the effects of extra days off from school due to teacher in-service days or teacher strikes (i.e., keeping youth out of school). The policies analyzed by these studies differ in two important respects. First, increases in compulsory schooling ages typically "require" students to stay in school at least one additional year and sometimes more, whereas teacher in-service days and strikes are of very short duration. Second, while teacher strikes and in-service days release all students from school, changes in compulsory schooling laws typically affect a small set of marginal students. All three potential effects of school attendance on crime are likely to be relevant to changes in compulsory schooling, while the effects of in-service days and teacher strikes are likely to be limited to incapacitation and social interactions. Any social interaction effects are likely to be magnified in the latter cases due to the universal nature of the policy.

Rather than use changes in compulsory schooling laws as instruments for educational attainment, Anderson (2009) estimates the direct effect of these laws on contemporaneous county-level arrest rates (from the UCR) from 1980 to 2006 among affected youth ages sixteen to eighteen. Specifically, his estimates are identified from within-county fluctuations in arrests (around county-specific trends) for sixteen to eighteen-year-olds (relative to thirteen to fifteen-year-olds) over time as state compulsory schooling ages change.

Anderson's estimates for total arrest rates imply that a compulsory schooling age of seventeen significantly reduces age seventeen arrests by about 8 percent (5.4 arrests per 1,000 youth) compared to a compulsory schooling age of sixteen or less. Similarly, an age eighteen compulsory schooling age significantly reduces arrests by 9.7 to 11.5 percent at ages sixteen to eighteen. Separating arrests by type of offense, he estimates that compulsory schooling laws significantly reduce both property and violent arrests for sixteen to eighteen-year-olds. Although estimated effects of schooling age laws on drug-related crimes are sizeable, the effects are typically not statistically significant. Overall, the estimates generally suggest that forcing youth to spend an extra year or two in high school significantly reduces their arrest rates over that period.

Jacob and Lefgren (2003) examine the effects of single-day changes in school wide attendance on juvenile crime and arrest rates in twenty-nine large American cities from 1995 to 1999. Exploiting teacher in-service days

33. Using individual-level data, earlier studies by Gottfredson (1985), Farrington et al. (1986), and Witte and Tauchen (1994) explore the cross-sectional relationship between time spent in school and contemporaneous crime, concluding that time spent in school significantly "reduces" criminal activity. Unfortunately, these findings are difficult to interpret given the simultaneous nature of the crime and schooling choices.

across jurisdictions over time as an exogenous source of variation in school days, they essentially compare local juvenile crime rates on days when school is not in session to those when it is.[34] Their findings suggest that an additional day of school reduces serious juvenile property crime by about 14 percent that day while it *increases* serious juvenile violent crime by 28 percent. These results are consistent with an "incapacitation effect" of school that limits participation in property crime. However, the increased level of interaction among adolescents facilitated through schools may raise the likelihood of violent conflicts (and other minor delinquency) after school. Interestingly, they find no evidence to suggest that school days simply shift crime to other days without changing overall crime rates.

Luallen (2006) follows a similar approach, using teacher strikes (typically lasting about five days) rather than in-service days as an exogenous source of school days. Using data from the state of Washington for 1980 to 2001, Luallen (2006) estimates that an extra day of school reduces arrests for property crimes by about 29 percent, while increasing arrests for violent crimes by about 32 percent in urban areas. The effect on property crime is roughly double the effect estimated in Jacob and Lefgren (2003), while the effect on violent crime is quite similar. In rural and suburban areas, Luallen finds insignificant effects on both violent and property crime arrests. Thus, the incapacitation and social interaction effects appear to be particularly strong in urban areas and negligible elsewhere.

10.4   Evidence on Human Capital-Based Interventions from Birth to Young Adulthood

A growing body of evidence suggests that early childhood and school-age interventions can reduce adult crime rates. Most famously, the High/Scope Perry Preschool Program substantially lowered arrest rates through age forty for a sample of low-income minority children in Ypsilanti, Michigan. Several other early childhood interventions have produced similar effects on delinquency; however, others have not. We briefly review studies of early childhood and school-age interventions that have analyzed educational and criminal/delinquency outcomes during late adolescence or adulthood.[35] We then discuss a few programs aimed at improving school participation among adolescents or that directly provide training to adolescents and young adults.

Table 10.2 summarizes four small-scale early childhood interventions (Abecedarian Project, Chicago Child Parent Center [CPC], High/Scope Perry

---

34. Their main specification includes controls to account for the possibility that crime may be higher on certain days of the week or that different cities may experience different monthly crime cycles.

35. See Karoly et al. (1998) or Blau and Currie (2006) for more comprehensive surveys of early childhood programs.

Table 10.2   Effects of selected early childhood programs on educational attainment and adult crime

Program	Program description	Program population	Methodology	Education effects	Crime effects
Abecedarian Project	Full-time full-year preschool from infancy to kindergarten	Developmentally at-risk children; Chapel Hill, NC	Random assignment	Increased high school graduation rate by 0.03 (0.70 vs. 0.67) and enrollment in 4-year college by 0.22** (0.36 vs. 0.14)	No significant effects by age 21
Chicago Child Parent Center	Half-day preschool (school year) ages 3 and 4	Low-income minority children; Chicago, IL	Matched sample	Increased high school completion rate by 0.09 (0.57 vs. 0.48) for females and 0.14** (0.43 vs. 0.29) for males	By age 18, reduced fraction arrested by 0.08** (0.17 vs. 0.25)
High/Scope Perry Preschool	Half-day preschool (school year) ages 3 and 4, biweekly home visits	Low-income black children at risk of school failure; Ypsilanti, MI	Random assignment	Increased high school graduation rates by 0.52** (0.84 vs. 0.32) for females and reduced graduation rates by 0.04 (0.50 vs. 0.54) for males	By age 40, reduced fraction arrested 5 or more times by 0.10** (0.24 vs. 0.34) for females and 0.24** (0.45 vs. 0.69) for males
Infant Health & Development Program	Weekly/biweekly home visits from 0–36 months, full-time full-year pre-school 12–36 months	Low birth weight preterm infants, 8 sites	Random assignment	No significant effect on high school dropout (approximately 10% dropout rate)	No significant effects on arrests by age 18

Sources: Effects for Abecedarian Project taken from Campbell et al. (2002) and Clarke and Campbell (1998). Effects for Chicago Child Parent Center taken from Reynolds et al. (2001). Effects for Perry Preschool taken from Schweinhart et al. (2005). Effects for Infant Health & Development Program taken from McCormick et al. (2006).

**Significant at the 5 percent level.

Preschool, and Infant Health and Development Program [IHDP]), their target populations, study methodology, and estimated effects on educational attainment and crime at ages eighteen or older. All of the programs included a preschool component, ranging from full-time, full-year care from birth to kindergarten (Abecedarian) to half-day preschool at ages three and four (Chicago CPC and Perry Preschool). Perry Preschool and IHDP also included regular home visits at preschool ages as part of their curriculums.[36] All of the programs targeted youth facing some form of disadvantage. Abecedarian and Perry Preschool specifically targeted children at-risk of having problems developing normally in school. Children enrolling in the Chicago CPC were all minorities selected from families with low socioeconomic status (SES). The IHDP drew from a more heterogeneous population, targeting preterm children born of low birth weight (less than 2,500g). Overall, these studies cover a reasonably broad range of potential preschool-based interventions and target populations. (We discuss findings for Head Start in the following.)

Youth from all four of these programs were followed until at least age eighteen, enough time to determine whether the programs have medium-term effects on the education and criminal behavior of participants. Only the Chicago CPC was not evaluated using randomized trials; however, Reynolds et al. (2001) use a strong design of matching treated children with other comparison children based on age of kindergarten entry, eligibility for and participation in government-funded programs, and neighborhood and family poverty. Children from the matched comparison sample would also have been eligible for the program had they lived in a neighborhood with a center. Sample sizes range from around 100 children for Perry Preschool to 1,300 for Chicago CPC.

Both Chicago CPC and Perry Preschool significantly increased high school completion rates overall; however, the Chicago CPC had more sizeable effects on male graduation rates, while Perry Preschool only raised female graduation rates (Reynolds et al. 2001; Schweinhart et al. 2005). The IHDP had no effect on high school dropout rates by age eighteen, while Abecedarian increased college attendance but not high school completion (McCormick et al. 2006; Campbell et al. 2002). These programs typically produced short-term gains in achievement scores and sometimes generated lasting gains.

The final column of table 10.2 reports estimated effects of these programs on late juvenile and adult crime. As alluded to in the preceding, Perry Preschool had significant effects on lifetime crime measured as of age forty

---

36. All of the programs typically provided other additional services to families and children (e.g., nutritional and health services). While a subsample of the Abecedarian participants received an extended school-age intervention for the first few years of school, we focus on the preschool component of the program. The additional school-age services did not substantially impact the educational attainment or crime outcomes discussed here.

(Schweinhart et al. 2005). Reductions in the fraction arrested five or more times were substantial for both males and females. Both showed reductions of about one-third; however, the size of the effect in absolute terms is much larger for males given their higher baseline crime rate. Reductions in crime for Perry Preschool students were observed across a broad range of crimes (e.g., drug, property, and violent crimes) and were apparent even at younger ages. The Chicago CPC also reduced arrest rates (by age eighteen) by about one-third (Reynolds et al. 2001). Another widely cited family support and preschool program, the Syracuse University Family Development Research Program, showed significant reductions in juvenile delinquency measured at a slightly earlier age: 6 percent of preschool participants had been placed under probation services by age fifteen compared to 22 percent of controls (Lally, Mangione, and Honig 1988).[37] The estimated savings in reduced criminal justice expenditures and victimization costs resulting from the crime reductions of Perry Preschool and Chicago CPC are sizeable. Using a 3 percent discount rate, Belfield et al. (2006) estimate that the Perry Preschool produced a social benefit of over $150,000 (year 2000 dollars) per child from crime reduction alone.[38] Reynolds et al. (2001) estimate that reductions in juvenile crime through age eighteen associated with the Chicago CPC saved society roughly $8,000. Findings like these, especially those for Perry Preschool, led Donohue and Siegelman (1998) to conclude that small, rigorous early intervention programs may pay for themselves through reduced crime rates alone if they can be targeted to high-crime groups.

Not all early childhood programs in table 10.2 yield reductions in crime. While modest reductions in self-reported convictions and incarceration through age twenty-one were observed for Abecedarian, none of these effects are statistically significant (Campbell et al. 2002). Based on administrative records of adult criminal charges in North Carolina, Clarke and Campbell (1998) report nearly identical rates of arrests and criminal charges (as of age twenty-one, on average) for treatment and control children in the Abecedarian study. Similarly, IHDP produced no significant effects on crime through age eighteen (McCormick et al. 2006).

What is different about Abecedarian and IHDP that these programs did not produce the same reductions in crime? It is difficult to point to any

37. The Elmira Nurse Home Visitation Program provided home visits by nurses to first-time mothers who were young, unmarried, or of low SES. Nurses visited homes for randomly assigned mothers during pregnancy and for the first two years of the child's life. Olds et al. (1998) report mixed but encouraging effects of the program on delinquency at age fifteen: treated youth were more likely to self-report being stopped by the police but had fewer incidences of arrests and convictions.

38. This figure is for benefits through age forty. Using a 7 percent discount rate produces a social benefit from crime of about $67,000 (Belfield et al. 2006). Heckman et al. (2009) report that savings from crime reduction account for about 40 to 65 percent of the benefit-cost ratio for Perry Preschool, depending on assumptions about discount rates (0 to 7 percent) and the cost of murder.

particular curriculum difference although not all preschools are alike. Abecedarian began preschool at infancy and continued through kindergarten—the longest of any program. It was also full-day, year-round, unlike Perry Preschool or Chicago CPC. Like Perry Preschool, it showed sizeable gains in achievement and IQ, so it is difficult to attribute its lack of effects on crime to inadequate intervention. The only obvious program difference between Abecedarian and Perry Preschool or Chicago CPC that might explain the absence of any impact on crime is its lack of a "home visit" component, but IHDP included home visits by nurses from birth through three years of age. The IHDP began early but also ended when Perry Preschool and Chicago CPC began (age three), so it is possible that the early home visit combined with later preschool care is a key combination of services necessary for long-term impacts on delinquency and crime.

An alternative hypothesis is that the environments more than the specifics of the programs were important in determining impacts on crime. Chapel Hill is a midsized, mostly white and relatively affluent university city in the South, while Ypsilanti is a smaller industrial city with a sizeable minority population. Chicago CPC sites were in low-income neighborhoods in a large urban midwestern city. (The IHDP had sites throughout the United States.) It seems quite possible that the same program might have different effects in each city. As noted by Barnett and Masse (2007), crime rates were 70 percent higher in Ypsilanti than Chapel Hill when the respective program participants would have been age fifteen. They speculate that there may have been little crime to prevent among the Abecedarian sample; however, Clarke and Campbell (1998) report that the two control samples (Perry and Abecedarian) had very similar arrest rates (around 40 percent) by their early twenties. McCormick et al. (2006) report that juvenile arrest rates among controls were similar for the IHDP and Chicago CPC as well. So, among the target populations for these programs, crime rates were fairly similar even if local crime rates were quite different. Of course, it is possible that the long-term effects of early childhood programs depend as much on the environment in which participants grow up as on individual and family characteristics of the participants themselves. If so, it is important to exercise caution in extrapolating benefits from any single program or community to the wider population.

Despite the fact that children targeted by all programs were disadvantaged, there is a sizeable difference in baseline educational attainment levels between Abecedarian and IHDP on the one hand and Chicago CPC and Perry Preschool on the other. High school graduation rates were 70 percent among Abecedarian controls; dropout rates (as of age eighteen) were only 10 percent among the IHDP controls. These both compare quite favorably with Chicago CPC and Perry Preschool controls who had high school completion rates ranging from 30 to 50 percent. Neither IHDP nor Abecedarian increased high school graduation rates. While Abecedarian improved college attendance rates, this does not appear to be an important margin for crime (see figure 10.1). Given the tight link between high school dropout and crime discussed earlier, it may not be particularly surprising that Abecedarian and IHDP did not reduce crime given their negligible effects on high school completion. Yet Perry Preschool substantially reduced male crime rates without raising educational attainment among males. Clearly, early interventions may reduce delinquency and criminal behavior without significantly improving final schooling outcomes.

In the end, there is no easy explanation for the different findings across studies. While the results from these studies are individually powerful given their research designs (most are based on random assignment), it is difficult to draw strong conclusions overall about the efficacy of early childhood interventions as a national crime-fighting strategy. The fact that sample sizes are quite modest and that program populations are not necessarily representative of the United States raises additional questions. This itself may explain some of the variation in findings across studies. It is natural to ask how these programs would affect other populations. Questions about scalability have also been raised: can these programs and their effects be reproduced at a larger scale? These issues have led a number of researchers to analyze the largest early childhood program in the United States: Head Start. This program targets children from low-income families usually living in low-income communities and has served hundreds of thousands of children throughout the United States since its inception in 1967.

Because no large-scale long-term random assignment studies of Head Start are available, researchers have employed nonexperimental methods. These studies generally examine impacts on national samples of individuals served by Head Start, using data from the Panel Survey of Income and Dynamics (PSID) or Children of the National Longitudinal Survey of Youth (CNLSY). We next discuss those studies that examine the impacts of Head Start on behavioral problems, delinquency, or measures of adult crime.

Garces, Thomas, and Currie (2002) and Deming (2009b) use a family fixed effects approach to estimate the effects of Head Start on a variety of long-term outcomes. By comparing siblings who did and did not attend a Head Start program at ages three to five, they address important concerns about permanent or long-run differences across families that may affect decisions about preschool or Head Start enrollment.[39] Garces, Thomas, and Currie (2002) use data from the PSID, examining adult outcomes for individuals born between 1964 and 1977, while Deming (2009b) uses data from the CNLSY and examines outcomes for individuals born in the late 1970s and

39. Of course, they leave unanswered the question as to why some siblings enroll in Head Start, while others from the same family do not and, more important, whether different enrollment decisions are related to underlying differences in child abilities or other factors that may affect outcomes later in life.

early 1980s. Despite using the same empirical approach, the two studies find quite different patterns for Head Start impacts on educational attainment and criminal behavior. Garces, Thomas, and Currie (2002) estimate significant increases in high school completion (by 20 percentage points) and college attendance (by 28 percentage points) for whites only, while Deming (2009b) estimates an 11 percentage point increase in high school completion rates and a 14 percentage point increase in college attendance for blacks only. Excluding GED recipients, Deming (2009b) estimates a smaller (7 percentage points) and statistically insignificant effect on high school completion for blacks, suggesting that much of their apparent improvement in high school completion is due to increases in the GED.[40] Regarding crime, estimates by Garces, Thomas, and Currie (2002) suggest that Head Start reduces the probability of being booked or charged with a crime by about 12 percentage points among blacks, with no effect on whites. Deming (2009b) finds no significant effects of Head Start on crime for blacks or whites.[41]

Carneiro and Ginja (2008) use a regression discontinuity design to estimate the effects of Head Start on adolescent outcomes, including the probability that someone is sentenced for a crime. Their approach exploits the fact that Head Start imposes strict eligibility criteria related to family income and structure: children ages three to five are eligible if family income is below the federal poverty guidelines or if the family is eligible for public assistance. Because these criteria vary across states and time, the income thresholds vary across these dimensions as well. They exploit this exogenous variation in eligibility, assuming the effects of family income (when children are ages three to five) on subsequent outcomes are continuous. Using data from the CNLSY on youth who would have enrolled in Head Start during the 1980s and 1990s, they estimate that participation in Head Start at ages three to five significantly reduces the probability (by 31 percentage points) a sixteen to seventeen-year-old male is sentenced for a crime (based on self-reports). They estimate similar effects for a sample of blacks only. These estimates measure the effect of Head Start on children who were at the margin of eligibility for the program and, therefore, represent the effects we might expect with modest expansions of the program.

Altogether, the nonexperimental evidence on Head Start appears to suggest some long-term effects on education and crime, but findings vary in important ways across studies.[42] The strongest effects on crime appear to

40. The substitution between high school degrees and GED receipt is less relevant for the earlier cohort studied by Garces, Thomas, and Currie (2002) because the GED was much less common in the 1980s relative to more recent years.
41. His measure of crime is an indicator equal to one if the respondent reports having been convicted of a crime, been on probation, sentenced by a judge, or is in prison at the time of the interview.
42. While Head Start may affect juvenile and adult crime even if it has no effect on educational attainment (as with males in the Perry Preschool program), one might speculate that any increases in schooling (especially high school years) associated with Head Start should

exist for blacks although Deming (2009b) finds no effect on crime for either blacks or whites. Combined with the evidence from smaller-scale programs evaluated by randomized trials, there is limited but important evidence that early childhood interventions can reduce crime later in life for youth from disadvantaged backgrounds.

A recent program, Fast Track, introduced in four sites around the United States, provides group- and individual-based services to children from grades one through ten. The program specifically targets children from high crime and poverty neighborhoods who exhibit conduct problems in kindergarten, with the primary aim of preventing antisocial behavior and psychiatric disorders. The program focuses on three elements of development: social and cognitive skills, peer relationships, and parenting. During early grades, parents were offered training and home visits to help improve parenting skills, while children were engaged in group activities to foster friendships and tutoring sessions in reading. As children aged, more individualized services were provided, along with group sessions aimed at dealing with the transition to middle school, resistance to drugs, and so on. The program also incorporated a classroom intervention during grades one to five at schools with program children. Teachers implemented two to three sessions per week designed to promote social and emotional competence and to reduce aggression. Experimental estimates based on random assignment suggest that the program produced sustained improvements in conduct disorders and antisocial behavior over grades three to nine (Conduct Problems Prevention Research Group [CPPRG] 2007). As of grade nine, high risk youth (those from the top 3 percent of conduct problems in kindergarten) receiving the Fast Track program showed significant reductions in self-reported delinquency and criminal behavior; however, no significant effects on antisocial behavior were found for other youth.[43] Two recent follow-up studies (CPPRG, forthcoming, 2010) suggest that the reductions in crime and conduct problems extend at least two years beyond the conclusion of the program (last measured at grade twelve/age nineteen) and continue to be focused on youth that were initially "high risk." Effects on juvenile conduct

---

lead to reductions in crime as estimated by Lochner and Moretti (2004). Under this assumption, estimates from Ludwig and Miller (2007), which suggest that roughly doubling Head Start spending (per capita) increases high school completion rates by as much as 4 percentage points, imply that this policy should also reduce arrest rates by up to 3 to 4 percent. Of course, multiplying the Garces, Thomas, and Currie (2002) estimated effects of Head Start on schooling attainment among whites by Lochner and Moretti's (2004) estimated effects of education on crime suggests that Head Start attendance should significantly reduce incarceration rates among whites, while analogous estimates from Deming (2009b) suggest that Head Start should reduce crime among blacks. Yet these studies estimated no effect of Head Start attendance on self-reported measures of arrest, conviction, or incarceration rates for these populations.

43. Results for antisocial behavior are based on an index created from self-reports of serious delinquent/criminal actions like stealing something worth more than $100, assault, selling heroin or lysergic acid diethylamide (LSD), and sexual assault.

disorders did not appear to decline after the program, while effects on crime showed some fade-out.

Experimental evaluations of two earlier, more limited elementary school-age interventions are worth commenting on because they also focused largely on social development among high-risk children. The Montreal Longitudinal Experimental Study provided social skills training to first and second grade children, along with teacher and parent training over those same years. Boisjoli et al. (2007) report that by age twenty-four, children receiving the intervention (compared to control children) were twice as likely to have completed high school and only half as likely to have a criminal record. The Seattle Social Development Project intervened over a longer period (grades one to six); however, it only provided teacher and parent training (aimed at improving child social and emotional skill development). As of age twenty-one, Hawkins et al. (2005) estimate that the six-year intervention had increased high school graduation rates from 81 to 91 percent and significantly reduced self-reported crime and official lifetime court charges (from 53 to 42 percent).

Altogether, the evidence from Fast Track, the Montreal Longitudinal Experimental Study, and the Seattle Social Development Project suggests that comprehensive school-age programs designed to improve social development can produce lasting impacts on educational attainment, conduct disorders, and criminal behavior. In many ways, these programs emphasized social over cognitive development, relative to the preschool programs summarized in table 10.2. Of course, both sets of programs were broad-based and yielded improvements in both domains.[44]

Programs targeted to older adolescents and young adults have shown mixed results. The Quantum Opportunity Program provided entering high school students with a mentor/tutor that aided them in schoolwork and community activities for four years. Financial incentives designed to encourage high school graduation and college enrollment were provided for educational, service, and developmental activities. A recent random assignment evaluation of the program reported no significant improvements in schooling or reductions in crime six years after scheduled high school graduation (Schirm, Stuart, and McKie 2006). In part, this may be due to the relatively low participation by youth in program activities.[45]

The Job Corps provides intensive basic educational and vocational training for economically disadvantaged youth and young adults ages sixteen to twenty-four throughout the United States. The program also offers a wide range of other services (e.g., counseling, social skills training, health educa-

44. This is largely consistent with recent estimates of skill production functions for both cognitive and "noncognitive" skills (e.g., see Cunha and Heckman 2008).
45. On average, youth spent only 177 hours per year on educational, community, and developmental activities. Roughly one in four spent no time at all in these activities by the fourth year of the program.

tion, job placement services). The average participant is enrolled for about eight months, with most living in residence at training sites. The program's primary goal is to improve employment and earnings prospects. Based on a recent random assignment evaluation, Schochet, Burghardt, and Glazerman (2001) conclude that the program produced modest positive impacts on postprogram employment and earnings. The program also reduced self-reported arrest rates by about 30 percent during the first year after random assignment, when most youth would have been enrolled. Reductions in subsequent years were smaller and statistically insignificant. The program also significantly reduced conviction rates by about 17 percent during the four years following random assignment.[46] Conclusions from the less-expensive and nonresidential JOBSTART program are largely consistent with these findings (Cave et al. 1993).[47]

Collectively, these studies indicate that human capital-based interventions from early childhood to early adulthood can reduce juvenile and adult crime, at least for some populations. To understand why, it is useful to briefly return to the model laid out in section 10.2 to aid in interpreting these findings. The model suggests that effective interventions may reduce juvenile and adult crime by improving child learning productivity, A, increasing adolescent human capital levels, H_1, or by socializing children (i.e., lowering θ). While preschool programs highlighted in table 10.2 may raise learning abilities, achievement gains are generally short-lived and limited to primary school ages. Evidence of reduced criminal activity among adolescents attributed to early intervention programs, suggests that these programs raise initial market skills (H_1) or reduce criminal returns (θ) through socialization. School-based programs for high-risk youth like Fast Track emphasized social development (i.e., lowering θ) over cognitive achievement; yet they also likely improved adolescent human capital levels H_1. Despite the difference in emphasis between the two types of programs, both have shown the ability to significantly reduce juvenile and adult crime. Job training programs for adolescents and young adults directly operate on the incentives to invest in human capital (analogous to an increase in the subsidy rate s in our model)

46. An earlier study by Long, Mallar, and Thornton (1981) estimated that the social benefits from reduced criminal activity among Job Corps participants amounted to over $7,000 (in 2008 dollars) per participant—almost 30 percent of the total social benefit of the program.

47. JOBSTART offered many of the same basic components of the Job Corps to a similar population. Cave et al. (1993) find modest (and statistically insignificant) positive effects on earnings three to four years after random assignment for the full sample; however, earnings increased roughly 25 percent (in years three and four) for male participants with a prior arrest (i.e., had an arrest since age sixteen but prior to random assignment). Among male participants with no prior arrest, the program significantly reduced self-reports of an arrest (6.4 percentage points or 36 percent) during the first year after random assignment (i.e., the training year) but did not reduce the fraction arrested in subsequent years. Among males with a prior arrest, the program (insignificantly) reduced the fraction reporting an arrest over the first four years after random assignment by about 8 percent and had negligible effects on arrests during the first year. There were no significant effects on arrests for female participants.

and have led to modest reductions in crime during periods of heavy training. These programs have produced only modest increases in earnings and negligible long-run effects on crime, however, suggesting that simply training low-skilled adolescents does not provide the same promise as earlier interventions that act on individual endowments.

10.5   Policy Lessons

In this section, we discuss a number of important policy lessons regarding human capital policies and crime. First, we summarize evidence on the social savings from crime reduction that we might expect from policies that increase educational attainment or enrollment, improve school choice and quality, or expand access to early childhood interventions. Second, we highlight a few subpopulations and schooling margins that are likely to yield the greatest social gain from crime reduction. Finally, we discuss a few other lessons based on the evidence.

10.5.1   Valuing the Social Benefits from Crime Reduction

Lochner and Moretti (2004) estimate that increasing educational attainment levels in the population yields sizeable social benefits. Specifically, they calculate the social savings from crime reduction that would result from a 1 percentage point increase in high school graduation rates in the United States. Table 10.3 summarizes their exercise, translating all dollar values into 2008 dollars using the Consumer Price Index for All Urban Consumers (CPI-U). Column (1) reports total costs per crime associated with murder, rape, robbery, assault, burglary, larceny/theft, motor vehicle theft, and arson.[48] Column (2) reports the predicted change in total U.S. arrests based on the Lochner and Moretti (2004) offense-specific arrest estimates discussed earlier and the total number of arrests in the 1990 UCRs. Column (3) adjusts the arrest effect in column (2) by the number of crimes per arrest. In total, nearly 100,000 fewer crimes would have taken place in 1990 if high school graduation rates had been 1 percentage point higher. The implied social savings from reduced crime are shown in column (4). Savings from murder alone are as high as $1.7 billion. Savings from reduced assaults amount to nearly $550 million. Because the estimates suggest that schooling increases rape and robbery offenses, increased costs associated with these crimes partially offset the benefits from reductions in other crimes.

The final row reports the total savings from reductions in all eight types of crime. Because these figures only include a partial list of crimes (e.g., nearly 25 percent of all prisoners in 1991 were incarcerated for drug offenses according to the U.S. Department of Justice [1994]) and do not include all

---

48. These costs include incarceration and victim costs. See notes to table 10.3 or Lochner and Moretti (2004) for details.

Table 10.3   Social benefits of increasing high school completion rates by 1 percent

	Total cost per crime	Estimated change in arrests	Estimated change in crimes	Social benefit
Violent crimes				
Murder	4,506,253	−373	−373	1,683,083,243
Rape	132,938	347	1,559	−207,270,899
Robbery	13,984	134	918	−12,839,495
Assault	14,776	−7,798	−37,135	548,690,721
Property crimes				
Burglary	1,471	−653	−9,467	13,920,409
Larceny/theft	295	−1,983	−35,105	10,347,853
Motor vehicle theft	1,855	−1,355	−14,238	26,414,558
Arson	58,171	−69	−469	27,302,131
Total		−11,750	−94,310	2,089,648,519

Source: Lochner and Moretti (2004).

Notes: These costs reflect incarceration and victim costs. Victim costs are taken from Miller, Cohen, and Wiersema (1996). Incarceration costs per crime equal the incarceration cost per inmate multiplied by the incarceration rate for that crime (approximately $25,000). Incarceration rates by offense type are calculated as the total number of individuals in jail or prison (from U.S. Department of Justice 1994) divided by the total number of offenses that year (where the number of offenses are adjusted for nonreporting to the police). Incarceration costs per inmate are taken from U.S. Department of Justice (1999). All dollar figures are translated into 2008 dollars using the CPI-U.

costs associated with each crime (e.g., private security measures are omitted), these amounts are likely to underestimate the true social benefit associated with increasing high school graduation rates. Still, the savings are substantial: the social benefits of a 1 percentage point increase in male U.S. high school graduation rates (from reduced crime alone) in 1990 would have amounted to more than $2 billion. This represents more than $3,000 in annual savings *per additional male graduate.*

Open school enrollment lotteries and desegregation efforts also appear to reduce crime rates by improving school quality. Deming (2009a) estimates that reductions in arrests associated with offering better quality school options to a high-risk youth produces a roughly $16,000 social savings to victims over the next seven years. Because better schools are also likely to have reduced crimes that never led to an arrest, total victimization savings are likely to be even greater. Total social savings should be still larger once savings on prisons and other crime prevention costs are factored in.

The effects of school attendance on contemporaneous juvenile crime rates are more complicated. Studies estimating the effects of day-to-day changes in attendance suggest that in urban communities additional school days reduce property crime while increasing violent crime (Jacob and Lefgren 2003; Luallen 2006). Overall, the social costs associated with increased violence are likely to dominate the benefits from reduced property crime. On the other hand, Anderson (2009) estimates reductions in both violent and property juvenile crime associated with increases in compulsory schooling ages. Thus, his findings suggest an overall social savings from juvenile crime reduction although he does not attempt to put a dollar value on the effects.

Evidence on the effects of early childhood and school-age interventions are mixed. Long-run impacts on juvenile delinquency and adult crime can be substantial for disadvantaged youth. For example, estimates suggest that Perry Preschool produced a social benefit from crime reduction of roughly $150,000 per child (through age forty). On the other hand, Abecedarian produced no significant impacts on crime. In choosing between programs or policies, it is, of course, important to incorporate the wide-ranging benefits of early childhood programs (e.g., higher earnings, better health, etc.). Even if early interventions are not more cost-effective in reducing crime when compared against more traditional law enforcement or justice system policies, they may provide greater total social value once all benefits are considered.

10.5.2   Where Are the Big Returns?

Given the most sizeable reductions in crime appear to result from the final years of high school, policies that encourage high school completion would seem to be most promising in terms of their impacts on crime.[49] Because crime rates are already quite low among high school graduates, policies that only encourage college attendance or completion are likely to yield much smaller social benefits from crime reduction although they may be desirable on other grounds.[50] To the extent that postsecondary education policies (e.g., lowering college costs) reduce crime, much of their effect may actually come through encouraging disaffected high school students to graduate rather than drop out.

In general, policies designed to encourage schooling among more crime-prone groups are likely to produce the greatest benefits from crime reduction. Consistent with this, the school-age Fast Track program appears to have reduced juvenile crime only among very high-risk children, showing little impact on even moderately high-risk children (CPPRG 2007, 2010). Similarly, Deming (2009a) estimates that improved school choice for middle and high school students leads to significant reductions in arrests for high-risk youth but not for others. As Donohue and Siegelman (1998) conclude, the overall efficiency of early childhood programs as a crime-fighting strat-

49. See Hanushek and Lindseth (2009), Jacob and Ludwig (2008), or Murnane (2008) for recent discussions of policies to improve schooling outcomes in the United States.

50. The fact that crime declines substantially with high school completion but not college attendance suggests that net expected returns from crime for most individuals lie somewhere between the wages of high school dropouts and graduates. See Freeman (1999) for a summary of evidence regarding criminal wages and earnings.

egy is likely to depend heavily on the ability to target high-risk children at very young ages. The same is likely to be true for school-age interventions.

Social benefits from crime reduction also vary across gender and race. Men commit much less crime than women, on average. Thus, it is not surprising that crime-related benefits from education policies and interventions are typically much smaller for females than males (e.g., Perry Preschool, Job Corps). This is true even though programs sometimes reduce female and male crime rates by similar amounts in percentage terms. While there are no studies to date comparing the impacts of educational attainment on female versus male crime rates, there would have to be a substantially larger proportional effect on female crime rates to produce overall crime reductions to rival those estimated for men. Among men, Lochner and Moretti (2004) estimate much larger effects of additional schooling on incarceration rates among blacks relative to whites. Garces, Thomas, and Currie (2002) estimate that Head Start significantly reduces crime for blacks but not whites; however, Deming (2009b) estimates no effect on crime for either group, while Carneiro and Ginja (2008) estimate similar large effects on both. Because crime rates are much higher among blacks than whites, on average, policies would generally need to produce much larger proportional reductions in white crime rates to achieve similar absolute reductions in crime. None of the evidence surveyed here suggests that this is the case.

10.5.3   Additional Policy Lessons

A few other useful lessons can be drawn from the studies surveyed here.

First, education policies can reduce property crime as well as violent crime. In the United States, the estimated effects of educational attainment or school enrollment on property and violent offenses appear to be quite similar in percentage terms (Lochner and Moretti 2004; Anderson 2009).[51] Even murder appears to be quite responsive to changes in educational attainment and school quality (Lochner and Moretti 2004; Weiner, Lutz, and Ludwig 2009).

Second, higher wages increase the opportunity costs (including work foregone while incarcerated) of both property and violent crime. Lochner and Moretti (2004) show that the estimated effects of educational attainment on crime can largely be accounted for by the effects of schooling on wages and the effects of wages on crime. This is important because it suggests that policymakers can reduce crime simply by increasing labor market skills; they need not alter individual preferences or otherwise socialize youth. Of course, as evidence from the Job Corps and other training programs suggests, this is not necessarily an easy task. Training programs targeted at low-skill adolescents and young adults have modest (at best) effects on earnings and crime.

---

51. Estimates from Machin, Marie, and Vujic (2010) suggest that education reduces property crime more than violent crime in the United Kingdom.

On the other hand, encouraging youth to finish high school (e.g., through compulsory schooling laws) appears to substantially increase earnings and reduce crime. Preventing early school dropout is likely to be more successful than trying to compensate for dropout a few years later.

Third, education-based policies need not increase educational attainment to reduce crime. Studies on school choice lotteries (Cullen, Jacob, and Levitt 2006; Deming 2009a) suggest that providing disadvantaged urban youth with better schools can substantially reduce juvenile and adult crime, even if it has small effects on educational outcomes. Perry Preschool had no effect on male schooling levels but substantially reduced male crime rates through age forty (Schweinhart et al. 2005).

Fourth, evidence that violent crime is higher on school days than nonschool days in urban districts suggests that social interaction effects are particularly important for juvenile violent crime (Jacob and Lefgren 2003; Luallen 2006). Smart policing efforts may be able to help address some of the problems associated with schools releasing lots of adolescents at the same time. For example, an increased police presence immediately after school or other major adolescent congregations let out may be warranted. Or, on nonschool days, it may be wise for police to focus more on targets or areas of juvenile property crime, worrying less about violent crime. The "hot spot" or "problem-oriented policing" literature in criminology suggests that informed targeting of police efforts to high crime areas (and, by extension, times) can be effective at reducing overall crime rates.[52] Alternatively, it may be useful to consider ways of designing after-school youth programs or other weekend activities to minimize violent behavior afterward.

10.6   Conclusions

There is growing evidence that improvements in school quality and increases in educational attainment, especially high school completion, reduce adult violent and property crime rates. Policies that induce students to spend an extra year or more attending school also appear to reduce juvenile crime. These findings are broadly consistent with a human capital-based model of crime and work. For most types of crime, additional schooling is likely to raise legitimate wage rates much more than the returns to crime, thereby discouraging the latter. Lochner and Moretti (2004) argue that the reductions in violent and property crime associated with increased schooling is roughly equivalent to the effect of education on wages multiplied by the effect of increased wages on crime. Thus, most of the effect of education on violent and property crime may come from increased wages. By contrast, education may increase the returns to white-collar crime more than the returns to work.

52. For a recent survey of this literature, see Braga (2005).

Consistent with this, Lochner (2004) finds that arrest rates for white-collar crime increase when education levels rise.

Education-based programs may also socialize youth, reducing personal or psychic rewards from crime. Emphasizing social and emotional development, school-age programs like Fast Track have shown the ability to significantly reduce later conduct disorders and crime (among high-risk children). These programs also improved educational outcomes, which may explain some of their impacts on crime. Perry Preschool reduced male (and female) crime rates without affecting male schooling outcomes. Thus, the program appears to have improved social development or increased early skill levels (without noticeably affecting subsequent schooling investments). Evidence from school choice lotteries suggests that improvements in school and peer quality can lead to reductions in crime without raising student achievement or educational attainment. The most likely explanation for the reduction in crime is that higher quality schools better socialize youth or provide them with a better set of peers. Yet evidence from the MTO experiment suggests that moving families to lower poverty neighborhoods does not produce the same reductions in crime, complicating any explanation related to peer effects or social networks.

Education may also increase patience or alter preferences for risk; however, neither seems to be central to the estimated impacts on crime. Property crimes are generally associated with less than one month of expected time in jail or prison conditional on being sentenced (see table 10.1), hardly enough time for modest changes in patience to play much of a role. Property crimes also have very low expected probabilities of arrest (typically less than 10 percent chance) and even lower probabilities of incarceration (typically less than 1 percent), so there is little actual uncertainty in outcomes associated with these crimes (see table 10.1). Yet estimated impacts of schooling on property crime are similar to those for violent crime, which entails much longer and more uncertain prison sentences.

Altogether, the evidence suggests that while efforts to socialize youth can be effective, simply providing them with valuable market skills can discourage them from choosing a life of crime. In terms of crime reduction, human capital-based policies that target the most disadvantaged (and crime-prone) are likely to be the most efficient, while also promoting a more equitable society. To that end, increasing high school graduation rates and improving our nation's worst inner-city schools are likely to yield the greatest social return.

Although policies that increase school attendance for a year or more (e.g., increased compulsory schooling ages) appear to reduce both violent and property crime (Anderson 2009), a few extra days off from school may actually lead to reductions in violent crime, especially in urban areas (Jacob and Lefgren 2003; Luallen 2006). From a human capital perspective, the increased opportunities that open up for youth attending an additional year of schooling should raise the future costs of incarceration associated with juvenile crime. This may serve as an important additional criminal deterrent that does not exist for day-to-day changes in the school calendar. In general, the effects of longer periods of attendance on contemporaneous juvenile crime are consistent with the subsequent effects of additional schooling on adult crime. The evidence on day-to-day changes in the school calendar highlights the possibility that by bringing many adolescents together, schools may foster negative interactions that lead to violence after school is out. Schools may also bring youth together who then look for trouble once they leave school grounds. Policies that find ways to address these problems may be effective at reducing juvenile violence after school. For example, after-school programs may help keep youth busy long enough to prevent some after-school violence, or they may simply delay the problems. Police might be deployed differently on school days and nonschool days, focusing on violent juvenile activity on school days and juvenile property crime on nonschool days.

There are many ways by which early childhood interventions may affect juvenile and adult crime. The human capital approach favored in this chapter highlights the potential effects of these programs on learning abilities, adolescent skill levels, and socialization or tastes for crime. These programs may also affect childhood preferences, including risk aversion, patience, or self-control. While a few early childhood programs have produced sizeable reductions in both juvenile and adult crime—most famously, Perry Preschool—other quite similar programs have not. School-age interventions focused on developing social and emotional skills have proven successful at reducing later conduct disorders and crime, especially among very high-risk children. The benefits from reduced crime associated with successful programs certainly warrant the attention they have received, yet we still need to know much more about why other programs have not produced the same effects. Is it the curriculum, the population served, or the later school and postschool environment faced by program participants? Two things are clear. First, preschool and school-age programs have substantially reduced crime for some disadvantaged high-risk populations. Even if these gains cannot be expected in all cases, they are large enough to warrant careful consideration on a broader scale. Second, successful programs did not always increase educational attainment, even when they significantly reduced juvenile and adult crime rates. Thus, disappointing achievement or educational outcomes need not imply the absence of benefits from crime reduction.

Given current evidence, it is difficult to draw strong conclusions about the relative benefits of trying to target and "treat" children at very young ages versus intervening at later ages to keep adolescents from dropping out of high school. Of course, we need not choose one or the other. Indeed, both are likely to be important components of a broad-based national crime-fighting agenda. Calculations by Lochner and Moretti (2004) and Donohue and Seigelman (1998) suggest that both human capital-oriented policies are competitive with more traditional law enforcement and incarceration efforts when all benefits are considered.

Appendix
Comparative Statics Results

In this appendix, we derive comparative static results for the model discussed in the chapter. We first derive results for the "fully interior" case where optimal investment and crime decisions satisfy $0 < I, c_1, I + c_1, c_2 < 1$. Then we derive results for the case when adolescents choose not to work, so optimal investment and crime satisfies $I + c_1 = 1$ and $0 < I, c_1, c_2 < 1$.

Following the text, assume that $N(\cdot)$ and $h(\cdot)$ are twice continuously differentiable in all arguments and that $N_c > 0$, $N_{cc} < 0$, $N_{c\theta} > 0$, $N_H \geq 0$, $N_{HH} \leq 0$, $N_{cH} \geq 0$, $h_I > 0$, $h_{II} < 0$, $h_{IH} > 0$, $h_{IA} > 0$, $h_H > 0$, and $h_A \geq 0$.

Case 1: Working Adolescents

Define the individual objective function to be maximized with respect to I, c_1, c_2:

$$F(I, c_1, c_2; A, H_1, \theta, s) \equiv [H_1(1 - I - c_1) + sI_1 + N(c_1, H_1; \theta)]$$
$$+ R^{-1}[H_2(1 - c_2) + N(c_2, H_2; \theta)].$$

At an interior optimum (i.e., optimal investment and crime satisfy $0 < I, c_1, I + c_1, c_2 < 1$):

$$F_I = -H_1 + s + R^{-1}[(1 - c_2) + N_H(c_2, H_2; \theta)]h_I(I, H_1; A) = 0$$
$$F_{c_1} = -H_1 + N_c(c_1, H_1; \theta) = 0$$
$$F_{c_2} = R^{-1}[-H_2 + N_c(c_2, H_2; \theta)] = 0.$$

Assuming $s < H_1$ combined with $F_I = 0$ implies that $1 - c_2 + N_{H_2} > 0$ at an optimum. Given $N_H \geq 0$, this is necessary for optimal $c_2 \in (0,1)$ as required for an interior solution. We use the fact that $1 - c_2 + N_{H_2} > 0$ at an interior optimum repeatedly throughout this appendix without further reference.

Second-order conditions for a maximum require a negative definite hessian matrix of second derivatives for F:

$$H = \begin{pmatrix} F_{II} & F_{Ic_1} & F_{Ic_2} \\ F_{Ic_1} & F_{c_1 c_1} & F_{c_1 c_2} \\ F_{Ic_2} & F_{c_1 c_2} & F_{c_2 c_2} \end{pmatrix},$$

where $F_{Ic_1} = F_{c_1c_2} = 0$ and

$$F_{II} = R^{-1}[(1 - c_2 + N_{H_2}) h_{II} + N_{H_2H_2}h_I^2] < 0$$

$$F_{c_1c_1} = N_{c_1c_1} < 0$$

$$F_{c_2c_2} = R^{-1}N_{c_2c_2} < 0$$

$$F_{Ic_2} = R^{-1}h_I(N_{H_2c_2} - 1).$$

Condition 1 implies that $F_{Ic_2} \leq 0$; otherwise, $F_{Ic_2} > 0$ when Condition 1 does not hold.

Result 1: Effects of s

Using Cramer's rule, observe that $\partial I/\partial s = -F_{c_1c_1}F_{c_2c_2}/|H| > 0$, because $F_{Is} = 1, F_{c_1s} = F_{c_2s} = 0$, and $|H| < 0$ at an optimum (second-order condition [SOC] for a maximum). We obtain $\partial c_1/\partial s = 0$ and $\partial c_2/\partial s = F_{c_1c_1}F_{Ic_2}/|H|$. If Condition 1 holds, then $\partial c_2/\partial s \leq 0$; otherwise, $\partial c_2/\partial s > 0$.

Result 2: Effects of A

Notice $F_{c_1A} = 0$:

$$F_{IA} = R^{-1}h_{IA}(1 - c_2 + N_{H_2}) + R^{-1}h_Ih_AN_{H_2H_2}$$

$$F_{c_2A} = R^{-1}h_A(N_{c_2H_2} - 1).$$

The first term in F_{IA} is greater than zero at an optimum; however, the second term is generally negative. Yet for $h_I < \infty$ and $h_A < \infty$, there exists some small $\varepsilon > 0$ for which $F_{IA} > 0$ if $N_{HH} > -\varepsilon$ by continuity. $F_{c_2A} \leq 0$ if Condition 1 holds; otherwise, it is strictly greater than zero.

Applying Cramer's rule, we obtain $\partial I/\partial A = -F_{c_1c_1}(F_{IA}F_{c_2c_2} - F_{c_2A}F_{Ic_2})/|H|$. Thus, $\partial I/\partial A > 0$ if $N_{HH} > -\varepsilon$. We also obtain $\partial c_1/\partial s = 0$ and $\partial c_2/\partial A = -F_{c_1c_1}(F_{II}F_{c_2A} - F_{Ic_2}F_{IA})/|H|$. If Condition 1 holds, then $\partial c_2/\partial A \leq 0$; otherwise, $\partial c_2/\partial A > 0$.

Result 3: Effects of H_1

Notice:

$$F_{IH_1} = -1 + R^{-1}[h_{IH_1}(1 - c_2 + N_{H_2}) + h_IN_{H_2H_2}(1 + h_{H_1})]$$

$$F_{c_1H_1} = N_{H_1c_1} - 1$$

$$F_{c_2H_1} = R^{-1}(1 + h_{H_1})(N_{c_2H_2} - 1).$$

While $F_{c_1H_1} \leq 0$ and $F_{c_2H_1} \leq 0$ if Condition 1 holds (otherwise, both are positive), it is not possible to generally sign F_{IH_1}. As such, it is not possible to sign $\partial I/\partial H_1$ and $\partial c_2/\partial H_2$. Using Cramer's rule, one can show that $\partial c_1/\partial H_1 = -F_{c_1H_1}(F_{II}F_{c_2c_2} - F_{Ic_2}^2)/|H|$. Because $F_{II}F_{c_2c_2} - F_{Ic_2}^2 > 0$ at a maximum, $\partial c_1/\partial H_1 \leq 0$ if Condition 1 holds; otherwise, $\partial c_1/\partial H_1 > 0$.

Result 4: Effects of θ

Notice:

$$F_{I\theta} = R^{-1}h_I N_{\theta H_2}$$

$$F_{c_1\theta} = N_{c_1\theta} > 0$$

$$F_{c_2\theta} = R^{-1}N_{c_2\theta} > 0.$$

Cramer's rule implies that $\partial c_1/\partial\theta = -F_{c_1\theta}(F_{II}F_{c_2c_2} - F_{Ic_2}^2)/|H| > 0$ because $F_{II}F_{c_2c_2} - F_{Ic_2}^2 > 0$ at a maximum. Furthermore, $\partial I/\partial\theta = -F_{c_1c_1}(F_{I\theta}F_{c_2c_2} - F_{Ic_2}F_{c_2\theta})/|H|$ and $\partial c_2/\partial\theta = -F_{c_1c_1}(F_{II}F_{c_2\theta} - F_{I\theta}F_{Ic_2})/|H|$. If Condition 1 holds and $N_{H\theta} \leq 0$, then $\partial I/\partial\theta \leq 0$ and $\partial c_2/\partial\theta > 0$. If Condition 1 does not hold and $N_{H\theta} > 0$, then $\partial I/\partial\theta > 0$ and $\partial c_2/\partial\theta > 0$.

Case 2: Nonworking Adolescents

We now consider the problem when optimal investment and first-period crime satisfy $I + c_1 = 1$. Imposing $c_1 = 1 - I$, the individual objective function to be maximized with respect to I and c_2 is

$$G(I,c_2;A,H_1,\theta,s) \equiv [sI + N(1 - I,H_1;\theta)]$$

$$+ R^{-1}[H_2(1 - c_2) + N(c_2,H_2;\theta)].$$

At an interior optimum (i.e., optimal investment and crime satisfy $0 < I, c_2 < 1$)

$$G_I = s - N_c(1 - I,H_1;\theta) + R^{-1}[(1 - c_2) + N_H(c_2,H_2;\theta)] h_I(I,H_1;A) = 0$$

$$G_{c_2} = R^{-1}[-H_2 + N_c(c_2,H_2;\theta)] = 0.$$

For optimal $c_2 \in (0,1)$, it must be the case that $1 - c_2 + N_{H_2} > 0$. This implies that $s < N_c(1 - I,H_1,\theta)$ at an optimum because $G_I = 0$. We use the fact that $1 - c_2 + N_{H_2} > 0$ (at an optimum) repeatedly in the following.

Second order conditions for a maximum require negative definite

$$\tilde{H} = \begin{pmatrix} G_{II} & G_{Ic_2} \\ G_{Ic_2} & G_{c_2c_2} \end{pmatrix}$$

with $|\tilde{H}| > 0$, where

$$G_{II} = N_{c_1c_1} + R^{-1}[(1 - c_2 + N_{H_2}) h_{II} + N_{H_2H_2}h_I^2] < 0$$

$$G_{c_2c_2} = R^{-1}N_{c_2c_2} < 0$$

$$G_{Ic_2} = R^{-1}h_I(N_{H_2c_2} - 1).$$

Condition 1 implies that $G_{Ic_2} \leq 0$; otherwise, $G_{Ic_2} > 0$.

We derive comparative statics results for I and c_2 in the following. Because $c_1 = 1 - I$, $\partial c_1/\partial x = -\partial I/\partial x$ for any variable x.

Result 1: Effects of s

Clearly, $G_{Is} = 1$ and $G_{c_2s} = 0$, so Cramer's rule implies that $\partial I/\partial s = -G_{c_2c_2}/|\tilde{H}|$ > 0 and $\partial c_2/\partial s = G_{Ic_2}/|\tilde{H}|$. If Condition 1 holds, then $\partial c_2/\partial s \leq 0$; otherwise, $\partial c_2/\partial s > 0$.

Result 2: Effects of A

Notice:

$$G_{IA} = R^{-1}h_{IA}(1 - c_2 + N_{H_2}) + R^{-1}h_I h_A N_{H_2 H_2}$$
$$G_{c_2A} = R^{-1}h_A(N_{c_2H_2} - 1).$$

As was the previous case, for $h_I < \infty$ and $h_A < \infty$, there exists some small $\varepsilon > 0$ for which $G_{IA} > 0$ if $N_{HH} > -\varepsilon$ by continuity. $G_{c_2A} \leq 0$ if Condition 1 holds; otherwise, $G_{c_2A} > 0$.

Applying Cramer's rule, we obtain $\partial I/\partial A = -(G_{IA}G_{c_2c_2} - G_{c_2A}G_{Ic_2})/|\tilde{H}|$. Thus, $\partial I/\partial A > 0$ if $N_{HH} > -\varepsilon$. We also obtain $\partial c_2/\partial A = -(G_{II}G_{c_2A} - G_{Ic_2}G_{IA})/|\tilde{H}|$. If Condition 1 holds, then $\partial c_2/\partial A \leq 0$; otherwise, $\partial c_2/\partial A > 0$.

Result 3: Effects of H_1

Notice:

$$G_{IH_1} = -N_{c_2H_1} + R^{-1}[h_{IH_1}(1 - c_2 + N_{H_2}) + h_I N_{H_2H_2}(1 + h_{H_1})]$$
$$G_{c_2H_1} = R^{-1}(1 + h_{H_1})(N_{c_2H_2} - 1).$$

While $G_{c_2H_1} \leq 0$ if Condition 1 holds (otherwise, it is positive), it is not possible to generally sign G_{IH_1}. If $N_H = 0$, then $G_{Ic_2} < 0$, $G_{IH_1} > 0$, and $G_{c_2H_1} < 0$. In this case, applying Cramer's rule yields $\partial I/\partial H_1 > 0$ and $\partial c_2/\partial H_2 < 0$.

Result 4: Effects of θ

Notice:

$$G_{I\theta} = -N_{c_2\theta} + R^{-1}h_I N_{\theta H_2}$$
$$G_{c_2\theta} = R^{-1}N_{c_2\theta} > 0.$$

Clearly, $G_{I\theta} < 0$ if $N_{H\theta} \leq 0$; otherwise, it cannot generally be signed. If Condition 1 holds and $N_{H\theta} \leq 0$, then applying Cramer's rule yields $\partial I/\partial \theta \leq 0$ and $\partial c_2/\partial \theta > 0$.

References

Acemoglu, Daron, and Joshua Angrist. 2001. "How Large are Human Capital Externalities? Evidence from Compulsory Schooling Laws." In *NBER Macroeco-*

nomics Annual 2000, edited by Ben S. Bernanke and Kenneth Rogoff, 9–74. Cambridge, MA: MIT Press.

Anderson, Mark. 2009. "In School and Out of Trouble? The Minimum Dropout Age and Juvenile Crime." Working Paper, University of Washington.

Barnett, W. Steven, and Leonard N. Masse. 2007. "Comparative Benefit-Cost Analysis of the Abecedarian Program and Its Policy Implications." *Economics of Education Review* 26 (1): 113–25.

Becker, Gary S., and Casey B. Mulligan. 1997. "The Endogenous Determination of Time Preference." *Quarterly Journal of Economics* 112 (3): 729–58.

Belfield, Clive R., Milagros Nores, W. Steven Barnett, and Lawrence Schweinhart. 2006. "The High/Scope Perry Preschool Program: Cost-Benefit Analysis Using Data from the Age-40 Followup." *Journal of Human Resources* 41 (1): 162–90.

Blau, David, and Janet Currie. 2006. "Pre-School, Day Care, and After-School Care: Who's Minding the Kids." In *Handbook of the Economics of Education.* Vol. 2, edited by Eric Hanushek and Finis Welch, 1163–1278. Amsterdam: Elsevier Science B.V.

Boisjoli, Rachel, Frank Vitaro, Eric Lacourse, Edward D. Barker, and Richard E. Tremblay. 2007. "Impact and Clinical Significance of a Preventive Intervention for Disruptive Boys." *British Journal of Psychiatry* 191 (5): 415–19.

Braga, Anthony. 2005. "Hot Spots Policing and Crime Prevention: A Systematic Review of Randomized Controlled Trials." *Journal of Experimental Criminology* 1 (3): 317–42.

Buonanno, Paolo, and Leone Leonida. 2006. "Education and Crime: Evidence from Italian Regions." *Applied Economics Letters* 13 (11): 709–13.

Cameron, Stephen V., and James J. Heckman. 1993. "The Nonequivalence of High School Equivalents." *Journal of Labor Economics* 11 (1, part 1): 1–47.

Campbell, Frances A., Craig T. Ramey, Elizabeth Pungello, Joseph Sparling, and Shari Miller-Johnson. 2002. "Early Childhood Education: Young Adult Outcomes from the Abecedarian Project." *Applied Developmental Science* 6 (1): 42–57.

Card, David E. 1999. "The Causal Effect of Education on Earnings." In *Handbook of Labor Economics.* Vol. 3A, edited by Orley Ashenfelter and David E. Card, 1801–63. Amsterdam: Elsevier Science B.V.

Carneiro, Pedro, and Rita Ginja. 2008. "Preventing Behavior Problems in Childhood and Adolescence: Evidence from Head Start." Working Paper, University College London.

Cave, George, Hans Bos, Fred Doolittle, and Cyril Toussaint. 1993. *Jobstart: Final Report on a Program for School Dropouts.* New York: Manpower Demonstration Research Corporation.

Clarke, Stevens H., and Frances A. Campbell. 1998. "Can Intervention Early Prevent Crime Later? The Abecedarian Project Compared with Other Programs." *Early Childhood Research Quarterly* 13 (2): 319–43.

Conduct Problems Prevention Research Group (CPPRG). 2007. "Fast Track Randomized Controlled Trial to Prevent Externalizing Psychiatric Disorders: Findings from Grades 3 to 9." *Journal of the American Academy of Child and Adolescent Psychiatry* 46 (10): 1250–62.

————. 2010. "Fast Track Intervention Effects on Youth Arrests and Delinquency." *Journal of Experimental Criminology* 6 (2): 131–57.

————. Forthcoming. "The Effects of the Fast Track Preventive Intervention on the Development of Conduct Disorder across Childhood." *Child Trends.*

Cullen, Julie, Brian Jacob, and Steven Levitt. 2006. "The Effect of School Choice on Participants: Evidence from Randomized Lotteries." *Econometrica* 74 (5): 1191–1230.

Cunha, Flavio, and James J. Heckman. 2008. "Formulating, Identifying and Estimating the Technology of Cognitive and Noncognitive Skill Formation." *Journal of Human Resources* 43 (4): 738–82.

Deming, David. 2009a. "Better Schools, Less Crime?" Working Paper, Harvard University.

———. 2009b. "Early Childhood Intervention and Life-Cycle Skill Development: Evidence from Head Start." *American Economic Journal: Applied Economics* 1 (3): 111–34.

Donohue, John J., III, and Peter Siegelman. 1998. "Allocating Resources among Prisons and Social Programs in the Battle against Crime." *Journal of Legal Studies* 27 (1): 1–44.

Durose, Matthew R., and Patrick A. Langan. 2003. *Felony Sentences in State Courts, 2000.* Bulletin no. NCJ 198821. Washington, DC: United States Department of Justice, Bureau of Justice Statistics.

Ehrlich, Isaac. 1975. "On the Relation between Education and Crime." In *Education, Income, and Human Behavior,* edited by F. Thomas Juster, 313–38. New York: McGraw-Hill.

Farrington, David P., Bernard Gallagher, Lynda Morley, Raymond J. St. Ledger, and Donald J. West. 1986. "Unemployment, School Leaving and Crime." *British Journal of Criminology* 26 (4): 335–56.

Freeman, Richard. 1999. "The Economics of Crime." In *Handbook of Labor Economics.* Vol. 3C, edited by Orley Ashenfelter and David Card, 3529–71. Amsterdam: Elsevier Science B.V.

Garces, Eliana, Duncan Thomas, and Janet Currie. 2002. "Longer-Term Effects of Head Start." *American Economic Review* 92 (4): 999–1012.

Glaeser, Edward, Bruce Sacerdote, and Jose Scheinkman. 1996. "Crime and Social Interactions." *Quarterly Journal of Economics* 111 (2): 507–48.

Gottfredson, Denise C. 1985. "Youth Employment, Crime, and Schooling: A Longitudinal Study of a National Sample." *Developmental Psychology* 21 (3): 419–32.

Gould, Eric, David Mustard, and Bruce Weinberg. 2002. "Crime Rates and Local Labor Market Opportunities in the United States: 1979–1997." *Review of Economics and Statistics* 84 (1): 45–61.

Grogger, Jeffrey. 1998. "Market Wages and Youth Crime." *Journal of Labor Economics* 16 (4): 756–91.

Guryan, Jonathan. 2004. "Desegregation and Black Dropout Rates." *American Economic Review* 94 (4): 919–43.

Hanushek, Eric A., and Alfred A. Lindseth. 2009. *Schoolhouses, Courthouses, and Statehouses: Solving the Funding-Achievement Puzzle in America's Public Schools.* Princeton, NJ: Princeton University Press.

Harlow, Caroline W. 2003. *Education and Correctional Populations.* Washington, DC: U.S. Department of Justice, Bureau of Justice Statistics.

Hawkins, J. David, Richard F. Catalano, Rick Kosterman, Robert Abbott, and Karl G. Hill. 2005. "Promoting Positive Adult Functioning through Social Development Intervention in Childhood. Long-Term Effects from the Seattle Social Development Project." *Archives of Pediatrics and Adolescent Medicine* 159 (1): 25–31.

Heckman, James J., and Paul LaFontaine. 2006. "Bias-Corrected Estimates of GED Returns." *Journal of Labor Economics* 24 (3): 661–700.

Heckman, James J., Seong H. Moon, Rodrigo Pinto, Peter Savelyev, and Adam Yavitz. 2009. "The Rate of Return to the High/Scope Perry Preschool Program." NBER Working Paper no. 15471. Cambridge, MA: National Bureau of Economic Research.

Hindelang, Michael J., Travis Hirschi, and Joseph G. Weis. 1981. *Measuring Delinquency.* Thousand Oaks, CA: Sage.

Hjalmarsson, Randi. 2008. "Criminal Justice Involvement and High School Completion." *Journal of Urban Economics* 63 (2): 613–30.

Jacob, Brian, and Lars Lefgren. 2003. "Are Idle Hands the Devil's Workshop? Incapacitation, Concentration, and Juvenile Crime." *American Economic Review* 93 (5): 1560–77.

Jacob, Brian, and Jens Ludwig. 2008. "Improving Educational Outcomes for Poor Children." NBER Working Paper no. 14550. Cambridge, MA: National Bureau of Economic Research.

Karoly, Lynn A., Peter W. Greenwood, Susan S. Everingham, Jill Hoube, M. Rebecca Kilburn, C. Peter Rydell, Matthew Sanders, and James Chiesa. 1998. *Investing in Our Children: What We Know and Don't Know about the Costs and Benefits of Early Childhood Interventions.* Santa Monica, CA: RAND.

Kling, Jeffrey, Jens Ludwig, and Lawrence Katz. 2005. "Neighborhood Effects on Crime for Female and Male Youth: Evidence from a Randomized Housing Voucher Experiment." *Quarterly Journal of Economics* 120 (1): 87–130.

Lally, J. Ronald, Peter Mangione, and Alice Honig. 1988. "The Syracuse University Family Development Research Program: Long-Range Impact of an Early Intervention with Low-Income Children and Their Families." In *Parent Education as Early Childhood Intervention: Emerging Directions in Theory, Research, and Practice,* edited by Douglas R. Powell, 79–104. Norwood, NJ: Ablex.

Lleras-Muney, Adriana. 2002. "Were Compulsory Attenance and Child Labor Laws Effective? An Analysis from 1915 to 1939." *Journal of Law and Economics* 45 (2): 401–36.

Lochner, Lance. 2004. "Education, Work, and Crime: A Human Capital Approach." *International Economic Review* 45 (3): 811–43.

———. 2010. "Non-Production Benefits of Education: Crime, Health, and Good Citizenship." Working Paper, University of Western Ontario.

Lochner, Lance, and Enrico Moretti. 2004. "The Effect of Education on Crime: Evidence from Prison Inmates, Arrests, and Self-Reports." *American Economic Review* 94 (1): 155–89.

Long, David, Charles Mallar, and Craig Thornton. 1981. "Evaluating the Benefits and Costs of the Job Corps." *Journal of Policy Analysis and Management* 1 (1): 55–76.

Luallen, Jeremy. 2006. "School's Out . . . Forever: A Study of Juvenile Crime, At-Risk Youths and Teacher Strikes." *Journal of Urban Economics* 59 (1). 75–103.

Ludwig, Jens, and Douglas L. Miller. 2007. "Does Head Start Improve Children's Life Chances? Evidence from a Regression Discontinuity Design." *Quarterly Journal of Economics* 122 (1): 159–208.

Machin, Stephen, Olivier Marie, and Suncica Vujic. 2010. "The Crime Reducing Effect of Education." Working Paper, University College London, August.

Machin, Stephen, and Costas Meghir. 2004. "Crime and Economic Incentives." *Journal of Human Resources* 39 (4): 958–79.

McCormick, Marie C., Jeanne Brooks-Gunn, Stephen L. Buka, Julie Goldman, Jennifer Yu, Mikhail Salganik, David T. Scott, et al. 2006. "Early Intervention in Low Birth Weight Premature Infants: Results at 18 Years of Age for the Infant Health and Development Program." *Pediatrics* 117 (3): 771–80.

Merlo, Antonio, and Kenneth Wolpin. 2009. "The Transition from School to Jail: Youth Crime and High School Completion among Black Males." Penn Institute for Economic Research Working Paper no. 09-002. Philadelphia: University of Pennsylvania.

Miller, Ted, Mark Cohen, and Brian Wiersema. 1996. *Victim Costs and Consequences: A New Look.* Final summary report to the National Institute of Justice, February. Washington, DC: National Institute of Justice.

Murnane, Richard J. 2008. "Educating Urban Children." NBER Working Paper no. 13791. Cambridge, MA: National Bureau of Economic Research.

Mustard, David. 2001. "Racial, Ethnic and Gender Disparities in Sentencing: Evidence from the U.S. Federal Courts." *Journal of Law and Economics* 44 (1): 285–314.

Olds, David L., Charles R. Henderson, Jr., Robert Cole, John Eckenrode, Harriet Kitzman, Dennis Luckey, Lisa Pettitt, Kimberly Sidora, Pamela Morris, and Jane Powers. 1998. "Long-Term Effects of Nurse Home Visitation on Children's Criminal and Antisocial Behavior: 15-Year Follow-Up of a Randomized Controlled Trial." *Journal of the American Medical Association* 280 (14): 1238–44.

Oreopoulos, Philip, and Kjell G. Salvanes. 2009. "How Large are Returns to Schooling? Hint: Money Isn't Everything." NBER Working Paper no. 15339. Cambridge, MA: National Bureau of Economic Research.

Reber, Sarah. 2007. "School Desegregation and Educational Attainment for Blacks." NBER Working Paper no. 13193. Cambridge, MA: National Bureau of Economic Research.

Reynolds, Arthur J., Judy A. Temple, Dylan L. Robertson, and Emily A. Mann. 2001. "Long-Term Effects of an Early Childhood Intervention on Education Achievement and Juvenile Arrest: A 15-Year Follow-Up of Low-Income Children in Public Schools." *Journal of the American Medical Association* 285 (18): 2339–46.

Sabates, Ricardo, and Leon Feinstein. 2008. "Effects of Government Initiatives on Youth Crime." *Oxford Economic Papers* 60 (3): 462–83.

Sanbonmatsu, Lisa, Jeffrey R. Kling, Greg J. Duncan, and Jeanne Brooks-Gunn. 2006. "Neighborhoods and Academic Achievement: Results from the Moving to Opportunity Experiment." *Journal of Human Resources* 41 (4): 649–91.

Schirm, Allen, Elizabeth Stuart, and Allison McKie. 2006. *The Quantum Opportunity Program Demonstration: Final Impacts.* Washington, DC: Mathematica Policy Research.

Schochet, Peter, John Burghardt, and Steven Glazerman. 2001. *National Job Corps Study: The Impacts of Job Corps on Participants' Employment and Related Outcomes.* Princeton, NJ: Mathematica Policy Research.

Schweinhart, Lawrence J., Jeanne Montie, Zongping Xiang, W. Steven Barnett, Clive R. Belfield, and Milagros Nores. 2005. *Lifetime Effects: The High/Scope Perry Preschool Study through Age 40.* Ypsilanti, MI: High/Scope Press.

Thornberry, Terence, and Marvin Krohn. 2000. "The Self-Report Method for Measuring Delinquency and Crime." In *Criminal Justice 2000: Innovations in Measurement and Analysis,* edited by David Duffee, Robert D. Crutchfield, Steven Mastrofski, Lorraine Mazerolle, and David McDowalll, 33–83. Washington, DC: National Institute of Justice.

U.S. Department of Justice. 1994. *Profile of Inmates in the United States and in England and Wales, 1991.* Washington, DC: U.S. Department of Justice.

———. 1999. *State Prison Expenditures, 1996.* Washington, DC: U.S. Department of Justice.

Usher, Dan. 1997. "Education as a Deterrent to Crime." *Canadian Journal of Economics* 30 (2): 367–84.

Weiner, David, Byron Lutz, and Jens Ludwig. 2009. "The Effects of School Desegregation on Crime." NBER Working Paper no. 15380. Cambridge, MA: National Bureau of Economic Research.

Witte, Ann D. 1997. "Crime." In *The Social Benefits of Education,* edited by J. Behrman and N. Stacey, chapter 7. Ann Arbor, MI: University of Michigan Press.

Witte, Ann D., and Helen Tauchen. 1994. "Work and Crime: An Exploration Using Panel Data." NBER Working Paper no. 4794. Cambridge, MA: National Bureau of Economic Research.

Comment   Justin McCrary

Lochner's chapter provides theoretical and empirical support for the idea that education reduces crime. On the theoretical side, section 10.2 presents a two-period model emphasizing the trade-offs between work, school, crime, and leisure. A more detailed analysis along these lines may be found in Lochner (2004), but the two-period version nicely summarizes key trade-offs. On the empirical side, section 10.3 reviews the recent empirical literature on the relationship between education and crime. Section 10.3 is primarily, though not exclusively, focused on contributions utilizing quasi-experimental approaches such as instrumental variables. The articles reviewed cover a broad set of research questions:

1. What is the effect of an additional year of schooling on the future criminality of an individual?
2. What is the effect of attending a higher quality school on the future criminality of an individual?
3. What is the effect of an additional day of schooling on the contemporaneous criminality of an individual?
4. What is the effect of early childhood interventions on crime?

My comments cannot hope to address the breadth of topics covered in the chapter. Instead, I focus on two major points. First, I ask what might be meant, conceptually, by question (1) outlined in the preceding. I conclude that is notably more complicated than, for example, the second and third questions. Second, I consider the implications of short time horizons for the effect of education on crime.

What Is Meant by the Effect of Education on Crime?

Researchers often dispute the appropriate interpretation of estimated quantities, even when the estimates are based on randomized variation. When they can be defined in such a way as to avoid competing interpretations, counterfactual outcomes are a core device for clarifying meanings. Fix s at a reference level of schooling. Let $Y_i(0)$ denote the outcome that individual i would obtain under schooling level $S_i = s$, and let $Y_i(1)$ denote the outcome that the same individual would obtain under schooling level

Justin McCrary is professor of law at the University of California, Berkeley, a faculty research fellow of the NBER, and a codirector of the NBER Working Group on the Economics of Crime.

$S_i = s + 1$. With random assignment of a factor affecting schooling, we can usually estimate a quantity such as $E[Y_i(1) - Y_i(0)|D_i = 1]$ or the average of the causal effects $Y_i(1) - Y_i(0)$ for a subpopulation defined by $D_i = 1$.

In fortuitous situations, researchers agree on the meaning of the counterfactual outcome pair $[Y_i(0), Y_i(1)]$ and the subpopulation defined by $D_i = 1$ is of interest. Suppose that half of one group is randomly assigned to complete twelve years of education and the other half is randomly assigned to complete eleven years of education, and suppose there are no compliance problems (so that assigned schooling was equal to actual schooling). Then the difference in means for the two subgroups identifies $E[Y_i(1) - Y_i(0)]$. If researchers agree on the meaning of $[Y_i(0), Y_i(1)]$, then this is a meaningful quantity capturing the central tendency of the causal effect of schooling level $s + 1$, as compared to schooling level s. In this setting, all units have $D_i = 1$, and the subpopulation for which causal effects are measured is under the control of the researcher (who, I assume, determines the original subpopulation subject to random assignment). In settings where compliance with treatment assignments is not guaranteed, the researcher does not entirely control the subpopulation over whom causal effects are estimated. Suppose that because of the compliance problem, those randomly assigned to complete twelve years of education do not necessarily actually complete twelve years of education. For example, the researcher might be using an encouragement design, and encouragement may not be very effective. Then instrumental variables estimates $E[Y_i(1) - Y_i(0)|D_i = 1]$ under the auxiliary assumption of monotonicity, where now D_i indicates whether the individual completed more schooling than he or she otherwise would have, by virtue of treatment assignment (Imbens and Angrist 1994). This subpopulation is defined both by the researcher's initial sampling choices as well as individual choice subsequent to random assignment. In many contexts, but not all, this type of subpopulation is of interest.

However, even if the subpopulation over whom causal effects are estimated is of interest, it may be hard to define the pair $[Y_i(0), Y_i(1)]$ in such a way that different researchers agree on the meaning. That this should occur is not surprising. After all, counterfactual outcomes are conceptual. Let us turn to a specific example.

A useful device for clarifying meanings of counterfactual outcomes is the description of hypothetical experiments. This approach, championed by the statisticians Paul W. Holland and Donald Rubin, even has a slogan: "no causation without manipulation" (Holland 1986; Rubin 1986).[1] Let us

---

1. Within economics, this approach to defining causality is sometimes met with derision. I interpret this approach somewhat more forgivingly. I view this approach not as much as being about *defining* causality and instead as being about *communicating* what parameter is under discussion. When researcher *a* can describe an experimental manipulation that would recover the effect researcher *a* is trying to measure, researchers *b*, *c*, and *d* cannot possibly be confused about what researcher *a* means. Researchers *b*, *c*, and *d* may disagree about whether the causal

use the device of the hypothetical experiment to clarify what might be meant by "the effect of an extra year of education on crime."

Suppose we randomly assigned half of a group of high school sophomores to an additional compulsory year of schooling. Suppose further that there are no compliance problems so that the difference in sample means between the two groups is a measure of the central tendency of the causal effects of an additional year of schooling for high school sophomores. Next, we define $Y_i(1)$ and $Y_i(0)$ as the level of crime that would obtain with and without the additional year of schooling, respectively. This begs the question: what aspect of crime is to be measured and at what date? Suppose we obtain agreement that the interesting feature of criminality is number of arrests in the last calendar year, and suppose moreover that we either have access to administrative or self-report arrest data that we trust (or perhaps we are simply willing to hold our nose). Even having reached consensus on what aspect of criminal involvement is to be measured, we still face the issue of the appropriate date of measurement.

Measuring crime at school exit is plainly undesirable: the age profile of criminal involvement rises extraordinarily rapidly between fifteen and nineteen. Such a measurement protocol would conflate the effects of the schooling intervention with the age profile. This is precisely the type of omitted variables bias that randomization seeks to overcome.

Measuring crime at the same date eliminates problems of noncomparability in terms of the age profile. In particular, this ensures that time because random assignment is balanced between the treatment and control groups. This simple, but powerful, consideration indicates that it is desirable to measure criminality as of the same date, regardless of how much schooling was obtained.

So let us choose a specific example of such a measurement protocol. Suppose that the outcome measured is the number of arrests in the last 365 days, as of May 1 of the year after randomization. By assumption, those in the treatment group are still attending school, and those in the control group are no longer in school. With this definition of counterfactual outcomes, the individual specific causal effect $Y_i(1) - Y_i(0)$ measures—indeed, may primarily measure—the incapacitation effect of schooling. By this, I mean simply that by its nature, crime is hard to commit while in school because much of schooling is spent sitting at a desk. Alternatively, the fact that school lets out at the same time and that youth may be engaged in similar transportation routes home, perhaps preceded by a period of "hanging out," could lead to *more* crime, by virtue of the prevalence of victims. In any event, the

---

effects in question are of interest, but all four researchers will be talking about the same concepts. Relatedly, when researcher *a* seeks to describe the effect of interest, yet finds it difficult to describe an experiment that would recover an estimate of that effect, researchers *b*, *c*, and *d* may be confused about what researcher *a* means. This is particularly true when researchers are working from different disciplinary traditions.

environments of the treatment and control groups differ—but in ways that have nothing to do with the accumulation of human capital (the putative mechanism for the schooling-crime causal connection).

Suppose that instead we seek to measure the number of arrests in the last 2×365 days, measured as of May 1 the year subsequent to randomization. Then, acknowledging that those in the treatment group had less criminal involvement in the first 365 days, we confront the reality that this fact has implications for all future levels of criminal involvement. It is widely understood that involvement in crime exhibits complex serial correlations. On the one hand, involvement in crime in one period leads to information networks that may aid in subsequent criminal involvement. This might lead the number of arrests in the last 2×365 days to exhibit a *larger* gap between treatment and control than the number of arrests in the first 365 days. On the other hand, involvement in crime in one period increases the probability of incarceration in jail or prison. This then leads to an offsetting mechanical shift in crime; those assigned to treatment may have a level of crime that is mechanically lower at first (because they are in school), but if pretrial detention or imprisonment is sufficiently prevalent, then this may in fact lead to a mechanically relatively *higher* level of crime in the medium term (because those in the control group are more likely to be detained or imprisoned). This is offset by the presumptively positive serial correlation in activity that would result were the criminal justice system to use fines— which do not take offenders out of circulation—in place of imprisonment.

These problems would seem to continue as the length of follow-up increases. Indeed, interpretation may even become more difficult with a longer follow-up. Economists tend to emphasize an offender psychology where individuals engaged in crime understand ex ante the consequences of such a choice; criminologists tend to emphasize an offender psychology where it is only after imprisonment that a potential offender will take seriously the idea that punishment is the logical consequence of repeated criminal behavior. For an economist, it is thus plausible that prison increases human capital and leads to a net increase in criminal activity upon release. Criminologists tend not to discount such a possibility but also are willing to think of an individual who, after an imprisonment spell, desists because of the realization that the system will, in fact, punish. Thus, in addition to the earlier difficulties of determining whether individuals are systematically incapacitated and for how long, we now additionally are forced to take a stand on the effects on subsequent criminality of having experienced punishment.

To me, this complicated mixture of mechanisms renders question (1) hopelessly confusing. The only thing I find myself able to make sense of is the narrow policy evaluation: "we spent X dollars encouraging students to attend an additional year of school, and at a five-year follow-up, those in the treatment group seem to have Y fewer arrests than those in the control group. In light of the rate of apprehension, p, believed to prevail for these types of crimes, this suggests that the program achieved an annual crime reduction per dollar spent of 0.2 ($Y/p)/X$." This kind of analysis is not necessarily connected to behavioral concepts but may, nonetheless, be practical and useful.

However, I find questions (2) and (3) to be quite easy to make sense of. Question (4) is confusing to me for the types of reasons outlined in the preceding, but the policy evaluation associated with question (4) is of obvious interest.

The Effect of Education on Crime When Offenders Have a Taste for the Present

> Johnny Weeks: "It'll be better tomorrow, Bubbs."
> Reginald Cousins: (derisively) "Dope fiend talking about tomorrow . . . tomorrow ain't shit. Today, Johnny—today."
> —*The Wire,* Season 3

Short time horizons may well characterize the bulk of the offender population. Punishments for crime are experienced in the future, and the benefits are experienced largely in the present. Thus, the process of self-selection in the marketplace implies that those doing crime must be selected on a taste for the present. A majority of arrestees test positive for one or more serious drugs at the time of arrest; drug use is presumably both cause and consequence of a foreshortening of the planning horizon. Indeed, the dominant modern view within criminology is that crime is the result of self-control problems on the part of the potential offender (Gottfredson and Hirschi 1990). These considerations suggest that it is reasonable to model the potential offender as having a taste for the present and perhaps even dynamically inconsistent preferences (Strotz 1955).

If potential offenders have short time horizons, then it is implausible that education could exert large influences on criminal behavior through the types of channels emphasized in the human capital framework emphasized in section 10.2 of the chapter. In particular, the mechanisms emphasized in the chapter are as follows: (a) schooling leads to increased wage rates in the near term as well as in the future, and (b) crime becomes less attractive as the wage rate increases. I do not dispute mechanism (a). Several decades of careful research supports the idea that an increase of even one year of education results in a noticeable increase (e.g., 10 percent) in wage rates (Card 1999). However, I am not confident in mechanism (b). In particular, if potential offenders have short time horizons, then it would be surprising to find that the prospect for an increase in wages over the life cycle would affect decisions in the present.

Lee and McCrary (2009) present evidence that youth in Florida largely fail to respond to the prospect of adult sanctions and continue to participate in crime at the same rate after the transition to adulthood as they did prior to adulthood. There are two obvious interpretations of this finding: (a) individual offenders have short time horizons, or (b) individual offenders do not believe they will be caught. Under either interpretation, there should be little effect of education on crime as long as "the effect of education on crime" is understood to be about human capital. Of course, there is an important distinction between potential offenders and actual offenders. It could well be that potential offenders have relatively long time horizons and actual offenders have quite short time horizons, on average, and similar beliefs regarding the probability of apprehension.

A feature of this chapter is that it underscores throughout that education may affect crime through information networks. This may well be true. Indeed, my own sense is that this type of mechanism, while not the focus of current economic modeling, may well be the most important connection between education and crime. This likely has little to do with time preferences. If such a connection is important, then education could exert a powerful influence on crime even if schooling leads to scant human capital accumulation.

References

Card, David E. 1999. "The Causal Effect of Education on Earnings." In *Handbook of Labor Economics*. Vol. 3A, edited by Orley Ashenfelter and David E. Card, 1801–63. Amsterdam: Elsevier Science B.V.

Gottfredson, Michael R., and Travis Hirschi. 1990. *A General Theory of Crime*. Stanford: Stanford University Press.

Holland, Paul W. 1986. "Statistics and Causal Inference." *Journal of the American Statistical Association* 81 (396): 945–60.

Imbens, Guido W., and Joshua D. Angrist. 1994. "Identification and Estimation of Local Average Treatment Effects." *Econometrica* 62 (2): 467–75.

Lee, David S., and Justin McCrary. 2009. "The Deterrence Effect of Prison: Dynamic Theory and Evidence." Unpublished manuscript, University of California, Berkeley.

Lochner, Lance. 2004. "Education, Work, and Crime: A Human Capital Approach." *International Economic Review* 45 (3): 811–43.

Rubin, Donald B. 1986. "Statistics and Causal Inference: Which Ifs Have Causal Answers." *Journal of the American Statistical Association* 81 (396): 961–62.

Strotz, R. H. 1955. "Myopia and Inconsistency in Dynamic Utility Maximization." *Review of Economic Studies* 23 (3): 165–80.

11

Improving Employment Prospects for Former Prison Inmates
Challenges and Policy

Steven Raphael

11.1 Introduction

In 2007, over 725,000 inmates were released from either state or federal prison. Many of these individuals have served multiple terms in prison, cycling into and out of correctional institutions for much of their adult lives. Many have very low levels of education and little work experience, are disproportionately male and minority, and return to social networks with weak connections to the formal labor market. Not surprisingly, a high proportion of former inmates reoffends or violates the provisions of their conditional release, with the majority serving subsequent prison terms.

Stable employment is often characterized as being of central importance to the successful reentry of former inmates into noninstitutionalized society. Most released inmates are in the age range when labor force attachment is the strongest and where conventional norms regarding responsible adult behavior center around steady work and support of dependents. Formal work may provide daily structure and routine that help keep former inmates from further run-ins with the law. Finally, steady employment (or the making of concerted efforts toward procuring steady employment) is often a provision of an inmate's conditional release, compliance with which is monitored by parole officers.

Former inmates face a number of challenges in searching for work. First, the relatively low human capital endowment of most former inmates limits their employment prospects. Second, stigma associated with felony convic-

Steven Raphael is professor of public policy at the Goldman School of Public Policy, University of California, Berkeley.

This paper has benefited greatly from the input of Phil Cook, Jens Ludwig, Justin McCrary, and Jeffrey Smith.

tions as well as outright employment bans further limits the available set of employment opportunities. Moreover, racial prejudice interacts in a complex manner with one's criminal history records in the screening and hiring practices of employers, further handicapping the employment prospects of prison releases.

In this chapter, I analyze the employment prospects of former prison inmates and review recent programmatic evaluations of reentry programs that either aim to improve employment among the formerly incarcerated or aim to reduce recidivism through treatment interventions centered on employment. I begin by presenting an empirical portrait of the U.S. prison population. Using nationally representative survey data, I characterize the personal traits of state and federal prison inmates, including their level of educational attainment and age as well as the prevalence of physical and mental health problems. I then turn to those who are released in any given year. To be sure, releases differ from the stock of inmates at a particular point in time, in that those with shorter sentences are disproportionately represented. Nonetheless, there is surprising consistency between the average characteristics of the stock and flow. Thus, the more detailed information available with regard to health, mental health, and substance abuse problems is likely revelatory with regard to those released from prison in any given year.

Having described the supply side, I turn to the demand side of this particular segment of the U.S. labor market. Using a 2003 survey of California establishments, I characterize employers' preferences with regard to hiring convicted felons into nonmanagerial, nonprofessional jobs. The data reveal a strong reluctance to hire such workers and the widespread use by employers of criminal background checks through for-profit security firms. In fact, the pervasiveness of the use of criminal background checks is such that it is unlikely that someone with a felony conviction can successfully conceal this information from employers. The employer responses also reveal that roughly one-quarter of the employers of nonmanagerial workers are legally prohibited from hiring convicted felons. These employers are less likely to hire men; more likely to hire African American applicants; and less likely to hire Hispanics, especially Hispanic men. I conduct multivariate analyses of the impact of checking criminal backgrounds on the likelihood of hiring workers of difference race/gender combinations, using legal prohibition against hiring felons as an instrument for checking. The results for most groups are unstable across specification. However, the data strongly indicate that establishments that check are consistently more likely to hire African American males, suggesting that the information revealed through background checks may be counteracting a high propensity among employers to assume all black applicants have criminal backgrounds.

With a solid characterization of the supply and demand sides of the labor market, I turn to a discussion of the research evidence evaluating efforts to improve employment prospects and reduce recidivism among former prison inmates. The volume of nonexperimental studies of such efforts is great, and the central tendencies of the findings of this research tend to depart from the findings of experimental evaluations. While I present some discussion of meta-analyses of these nonexperimental findings and discussion of why the conclusions from this research differ from the experimental analyses, I devote the bulk of my discussion to the handful of experimental evaluations that have occurred in the United States.

Characterizing the experimental research overall is difficult as the interventions are all quite distinct, and the outcome variables analyzed differ considerably from program to program. Moreover, in the face of heterogeneity in the impact of such interventions and the availability of substitute programs for individuals randomized into the control group, it is difficult to decisively draw conclusions regarding the patchwork of efforts made across the country to aid the reintegration of former prison inmates. There is some evidence that providing transitional employment reduces recidivism among former prison inmates, with one particularly promising model being reproduced and evaluated experimentally at five locations across the country. There is conflicting evidence with regard to the impact of income support on criminal activity, with two separate experiments yielding conflicting results. These latter two studies illustrate the sensitivity of programmatic effects to contextual aspects of the intervention in terms of the manner in which support is delivered and the social services that are coupled with these efforts. There is also evidence that early interventions for at-risk youth that focus on basic education and workforce development appear to reduce arrest rates by significant and substantial amounts.

In general, the experimental research does provide reasons for optimism in that many of these efforts do yield significant impacts. However, the knowledge frontier regarding effective interventions is quite porous, as such experimental evaluations are few and far between. Given the large social costs associated with failed reentry, additional rigorous research on the effectiveness of such efforts is sorely needed.

11.2 Characterizing Prison Inmates and Prison Releases

Former inmates reentering noninstitutionalized society face a number of challenges in procuring and maintaining stable employment. Of first-order importance, former inmates tend to have low levels of educational attainment, little formal work experience, and have other characteristics associated with poor employment prospects. Those who serve time in U.S. prisons are hardly a random sample of the U.S. population. Individuals who pass through the nation's prisons tend to come from poverty, suffer disproportionately from physical and mental health problems as well as substance abuse problems, and come from minority groups with historically poor relative outcomes in the U.S. labor market.

Table 11.1 presents tabulations from the 2004 Survey of Inmates in State and Federal Corrections Facilities (SISFCF). The SISFCF is a nationally representative survey of prison inmates carried out by the U.S. Census Bureau. I use these data to describe the average characteristics of state and federal prisoners. While the majority of inmates are in one of the fifty state systems (90.4 percent), the federal prison system is quite large, with the number of federal prisoners in 2007 (199,000) exceeding the prison populations of the largest states (for example, California with 174,000 and Texas with 171,000). The table reveals several stark patterns. First, the prison population is overwhelmingly male (roughly 93 percent in both the state and federal systems), a pattern that describes U.S. prison populations throughout most of the twentieth century (Raphael and Stoll 2009). Educational attainment prior to prison admission is quite low. Among state prison inmates, fully two-thirds had less than a high school education prior to admission on the current prison term. The comparable figure for federal inmates is 56 percent. Racial and ethnic minorities are heavily overrepresented among the incarcerated. Approximately one-fifth of state prison inmates are Hispanic as are one-quarter of federal prisoners. Slightly less than half of both state and federal prisoners are African American.

Prison inmates tend to be older than one might expect given the age trajectory of criminal offending. In particular, numerous researchers have demonstrated a sharp drop-off in offending after eighteen years of age, with greater proportions of those who are criminally active as youth desisting as a cohort ages through its twenties (Grogger 1998; Sampson and Laub 2003). Table 11.1 reveals that the median inmate is in his mid thirties, suggesting that for many, prison is the lasting result of crime committed in one's earlier years. The SISFCF data do indeed reveal relatively early criminal initiation among those serving time. The median state inmate is arrested for the first time at the age of seventeen, while the comparable median for federal prison inmates is eighteen. Moreover, when asked about when one commenced engaging in various criminal activities, the median inmate indicates fourteen years of age. Fully 75 percent indicate that they were criminally active by age sixteen.

I am able to characterize the physical and mental health of prison inmates using the 2004 survey. The SISFCF asks whether one has ever been diagnosed with a series of physical and mental health conditions. It is difficult to assess whether prison inmates are more likely to suffer from the health conditions listed in the table, as the question inquires whether one has ever been diagnosed but does not measure the annual incidence or prevalence of the condition in question. Moreover, one would want to age-adjust in drawing comparisons to the general population. Nonetheless, there are some conditions for which the lifetime cumulative risk for inmates appears to be particularly high. For example, 9.5 percent of state inmates indicate that

Table 11.1	Characteristics of state and federal prisoners in 2004	
	State prisoners	Federal prisoners
Proportion of prison population	0.904	0.096
Proportion male	0.932	0.929
Education attainment prior to admissions		
Elementary school	0.029	0.040
Middle school	0.165	0.143
Some high school, no degree	0.472	0.374
High school graduate	0.195	0.214
More than high school	0.139	0.227
Proportion Hispanic	0.182	0.251
Race		
White	0.487	0.433
Black	0.430	0.460
Other	0.083	0.107
Age distribution		
25th percentile	27	29
50th percentile	34	35
75th percentile	42	44
Age at first arrest		
25th percentile	15	16
50th percentile	17	18
75th percentile	21	23
Age first engaged in criminal activity		
25th percentile	12	12
50th percentile	14	14
75th percentile	16	16
Health conditions		
Diabetes	0.047	0.061
Heart problems	0.093	0.086
Kidney problems	0.061	0.057
Asthma	0.144	0.115
Hepatitis	0.095	0.076
Indicators of mental health/substance abuse		
Participated in alcohol/drug treatment program	0.605	0.649
Manic depression, bipolar	0.097	0.041
Schizophrenia	0.046	0.019
Posttraumatic stress	0.057	0.031
Anxiety disorder	0.071	0.046
Personality disorder	0.059	0.032
Other mental health problem	0.019	0.008
Any diagnosed mental health problem	0.248	0.144
Ever attempted suicide	0.129	0.059
Program participation while incarcerated		
Vocational education/job training	0.273	0.314
Education program	0.312	0.454
Religious studies	0.302	0.312
Have a definite date of release	0.660	0.842
		(*continued*)

Table 11.1   (continued)

	State prisoners	Federal prisoners
Year of expected release		
2003/2004	0.459	0.266
2005	0.159	0.147
2006	0.091	0.111
2007	0.061	0.084
2008 or later	0.190	0.323
Expect to eventually be released conditional on not having a definite release date	0.872	0.863
Earliest year of expected release		
2003/2004	0.353	0.182
2005	0.134	0.121
2006	0.074	0.102
2007	0.041	0.082
2008 or later	0.359	0.470

Sources: Figures in the table are tabulated from the 2004 Survey of Inmates in State and Federal Corrections Facilities.

they have been diagnosed with hepatitis at some point in time. The combined annual incidence of hepatitis A, B, and C in 2006 among the U.S. population is approximately 3.1 per 100,000.[1] Thus, the lifetime risk for state inmates is over 3,000 times the annual incidence of the disease. For other conditions, such as diabetes, for example, where ever being diagnosed is likely to be quite close to the prevalence rate, the proportion of inmates indicating that they are diabetic does not appear to be particularly high (4.7 percent of state inmates and 6.1 percent of federal inmates, compared with 11.2 percent for all U.S. men twenty or over).

It is perhaps easier to compare the prevalence of chronic mental health conditions to those of the adult population. For example, the inmate survey indicates that 9.7 percent of state inmates report that they have been diagnosed with manic depression, bipolar disorder. The comparable figure for all U.S. adults is roughly 2.6 percent. While 4.6 percent of state prison inmates and 1.9 percent of federal prison inmates indicate that they have been diagnosed with schizophrenia, the comparable figure for U.S. adults is 1.1 percent.[2] Prison inmates certainly have high rates of current and prior substance abuse issues. Over 60 percent of both state and federal prison inmates indicate that they have participated in an alcohol/drug treatment program while incarcerated.

One might think that an incarceration spell would present an ideal opportunity to intervene and augment the job skills and educational attainment

1. See http://www.cdc.gov/mmwr/preview/mmwrhtml/ss5702a1.htm, accessed on November 8, 2009.
2. See http://www.nimh.nih.gov/health/publications/the-numbers-count-mental-disorders-in-america/index.shtml#Bipolar, accessed on November 8, 2009.

of prison inmates. As the tabulations at the bottom of table 11.1 indicate, nearly 90 percent of inmates indicate that they will eventually be released from prison with well over half anticipating that they will be released within the next three years. When queried, however, few inmates indicate that they have participated in education or vocational training programming. For example, in state prisons, only 27 percent indicate participation in a vocational/job training program, while 31 percent say they have participated in an education program. This low rate is consistent with the finding in Wolf-Harlow (2003) that only 26 percent of state inmates indicate that they complete a general educational development (GED) diploma while incarcerated (equal to approximately 40 percent of inmates who had less than a GED upon admission). Participation rates in federal prisons are somewhat higher, though federal prisoners only constitute 9 percent of the prison population.

To be sure, the reentry challenge in any given year is faced by those who leave prison and not necessarily the population of current inmates. In fact, for a sizable minority of the prison population (at least 10 percent), release from prison is not a foreseeable possibility. Nonetheless, the characteristics of those released from prison do not differ appreciably from the average characteristics of the stock of inmates. Table 11.2 presents tabulations from the releases file of the 2003 National Corrections Reporting Program (NCRP) data. These data present micro-level information on all inmates leaving state prisons during the 2003 calendar year for participating states. In 2003, thirty-five states participated in the NCRP, with the prison populations of the participating states accounting for 85 percent of the national total. I provide tabulations for all reentering inmates as well as inmates by race/ethnicity.

Similar to the stock of inmates, prison releases are overwhelmingly male (0.897) and are disproportionately minority (52 percent black and 20 percent Hispanic). Roughly 54 percent of returning inmates have not completed a high school degree, with a slightly higher figure for black and Hispanic releases and a slightly lower figure for white releases. The higher educational attainment among releases may reflect either positive selection along this dimensions or the completion of GED coursework while incarcerated.

The median reentering inmate is thirty-two years of age (two years younger than the median prisoner) and is finishing a twenty-one-month spell in prison. However, many of these inmates have served prior time, with fully 33 percent indicating that they have a prior felony incarceration (prior to the current spell). Certainly, many have also served time in local jails awaiting the adjudication of the charges leading to the current spell. These extensive histories inside correctional institutions are likely to further diminish the skills of former inmates relative to otherwise similar individuals who have not done time. In particular, cycling in and out of prison is likely to severely limit the accumulation of employment experience that is generally rewarded

Table 11.2   Characteristics of state prisoners released in 2003

	All inmates	White	Black	Hispanic
Demographics				
Male	0.897	0.876	0.907	0.934
White	0.464	1.000	0.000	0.888
Black	0.519	0.000	1.000	0.097
Hispanic	0.202	0.069	0.007	1.000
Educational attainment				
8th grade or less	0.114	0.124	0.085	0.261
9th grade	0.114	0.111	0.112	0.146
10th grade	0.151	0.130	0.175	0.126
11th grade	0.157	0.116	0.203	0.106
12th/GED	0.386	0.432	0.351	0.328
Some college	0.060	0.065	0.061	0.024
College graduate	0.009	0.011	0.010	0.005
Special Education	0.007	0.010	0.005	0.004
Age percentiles				
25th	24.7	25.3	24.3	24.3
50th	32.0	33.0	31.7	30.1
75th	39.9	40.5	39.9	37.8
Time served percentiles[a] (months)				
25th	11.3	10.6	10.9	14.9
50th	20.8	19.6	21.3	24.0
75th	39.9	36.1	42.0	43.5
Conditionally released	0.739	0.732	0.702	0.856
Prior felony incarceration	0.327	0.292	0.410	0.203
Offense				
Murder/homicide	0.025	0.022	0.026	0.029
Rape/sex assault	0.043	0.058	0.028	0.046
Robbery	0.073	0.046	0.097	0.074
Assault	0.081	0.075	0.078	0.105
Other violent	0.022	0.027	0.017	0.027
Burglary	0.116	0.142	0.097	0.105
Larceny	0.128	0.150	0.120	0.079
Motor vehicle theft	0.024	0.025	0.016	0.041
Other property	0.037	0.046	0.030	0.030
Drugs	0.321	0.249	0.391	0.343
Other	0.128	0.159	0.100	0.121

Source: Tabulated from the 2003 NCRP data base.
[a]Refers to time served for release offense.

in the labor market. In prior longitudinal research on young offenders entering the California state prison system, I found that over a ten-year period, the median inmate of a given cohort of prisoners spends nearly six years cycling in and out prison (Raphael 2005). Finally, nearly three-quarters of released inmates are conditionally released, meaning that they are under the active supervision of the state's community corrections system.

The observable human capital characteristics of prison releases can be used to characterize where in the earnings distribution these individuals are likely to fall. While there is no information in the NCRP regarding employment and earnings prior to incarceration, one can use data from the census to impute likely earnings based on observable characteristics and compare prison releases to all adult labor force participants.

To make this comparison, I first use data from the 2003 American Community Survey (ACS) to estimate the relationships between observable demographic and human capital characteristics and annual earnings. Specifically, using all adults eighteen to sixty-five years of age with positive labor earnings during the course of 2003, I calculate average annual log earnings as well as the variance in log earnings by gender, age, race, and education level.[3] I then assign annual earnings to each prisoner released in 2003 observed in the 2003 NCRP data using the earnings and variance estimate for each inmate's gender/age/race/education cell to draw an observation at random from the estimated distribution.[4] Next, I estimate the vigintiles (5th, 10th, 15th, etc. percentiles) of the national annual log earnings distribution for all adults with positive earnings and for males only. I then calculate the cumulative distribution of prison releases across the vigintiles of each national distribution using the simulated earnings distribution for recent releases.

Figure 11.1 presents the results of this exercise. The simulated earnings distribution of inmates based on observable traits is heavily concentrated in the bottom of the national earnings distribution. Using the earnings distribution for all adults with positive income, approximately 46 percent of inmates are within the bottom quartile, while 70 percent lie below the median. Relative to the national earnings distribution for men, the simulation suggests that 56 percent of inmates lie within the bottom quartile, while 75 percent have below-median earnings.

Certainly, former prison inmates are likely to be negatively selected from the earnings distributions within these gender/race/age/education cells. Our description of the inmate population in table 11.1 found a substantial prevalence of substance abuse and mental health problems and evidence that many of these men and women have been criminally active since very early ages. Such characteristics certainly would not increase labor productivity. Moreover, the tabulations from the NCRP data in table 11.2 indicate that many of these inmates have served substantial amounts of time in prison. That is to say, within specific age cells, these inmates are likely to have less

---

3. For age, I define the brackets eighteen to twenty, twenty-one to twenty-five, twenty-six to thirty, thirty-one to thirty-five, thirty-six to forty, forty-one to forty-five, forty-six to fifty, fifty-one to fifty-five, fifty-six to sixty, and sixty-one to sixty-five. For race, I define the three categories white, black, and other. For education, I define seven categories corresponding to the education groups defined in table 11.2. Those who indicate special education are lumped into the category eighth grade or less.

4. I drop inmates that are less than eighteen and over sixty-five years of age. This eliminates very few observations. In drawing random earnings observations, I assume that the earnings distribution within cells is log-normal.

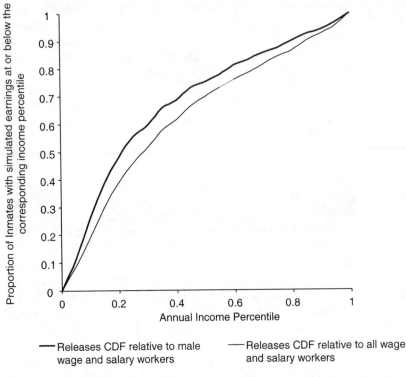

Fig. 11.1   Cumulative density functions of prison releases by their simulated position in the annual earnings distribution for all wage and salary workers and male wage and salary workers

formal labor market experience relative to otherwise similar individuals who have not served time.

Thus, the stock of current prison inmates as well as those released from prison in recent years are described by very low levels of education; low levels of work experience conditional on age; high proportion minority; and a high prevalence of substance abuse, health, and mental health problems. Based on observable education, age, and race alone, it is likely that most of these individuals would be concentrated in the bottom quartile and the overwhelming majority below of the median of the nation annual wage and salary income distribution.

11.3   The Demand Side of the Labor Market for Former Prisoners

The characterization of former prison inmates strongly suggests that low human capital is one of their principal obstacles to securing and maintaining employment postrelease.[5] Beyond the impact of low skills endowments, there is reason to believe that employer hiring preferences and, in some instances, public policy may be further handicapping job seekers with criminal records. Employers may actively screen out those with prior convictions and prior time served for a number of reasons. First, employers may consider prior criminality a predictor of important unobservable traits, such as honesty or dependability. This may be particularly important to employers filling positions where monitoring by management is imperfect and where it may be difficult or costly to readily observe worker productivity.

Second, employers may fear being held liable for any criminal actions committed by their employees on the company's time. In negligent hiring/ negligent retention cases, an employer may be sued for monetary damages caused by the criminal actions of any employee who the employer either knew or should have known had committed prior crimes, rendering the employee unsuitable for the position in question. Not surprisingly, past research analyzing employer stated preference with regard to hiring those with criminal histories consistently finds that employers filling positions requiring substantial contact with customers are among the most reluctant to hire former prison inmates (Holzer, Raphael, and Stoll 2006, 2007).

Finally, employers may be prohibited under local ordinances, state law, and sometimes federal law from hiring convicted felons into specific occupations. According to Bushway and Sweeten (2007), ex-felons are barred from employment in roughly 800 occupations across the country, with the composition of these bans varying across states and, in some instance, localities. Occupations covered by such bans range from barber shop owners to emergency medical technicians to cosmetologists.

An additional factor that may further exacerbate the weak employment prospects of former inmates is the lack of regulatory guidance with regard to how and in what circumstances an employer should consider criminal history records. The Legal Action Center (2004) finds that in nearly all states there is no standard governing the consideration of prior criminal history records by employers and occupational licensing agencies. In many states, employers can fire anyone who is found to have a criminal history record

---

5. One might contend that low human capital should not impact the likelihood that one is employed due to difficulty in securing a job. Specifically, wages should drop to clear the market for the least-skilled workers, suggesting that wages should be lower for former inmates, yet they should not suffer disproportionately from involuntary unemployment. Once we introduce search frictions, however, the low human capital endowments of former inmates as well as the stigma experienced in the formal labor market may lower the rate at which employment offers arrive. While endogenous adjustment of one's reservation wage may offset the impact on unemployment duration, it is still likely that such less-desired job seekers will experience more unemployment as a result. Such reasoning is consistent with the strong empirical association between observable human capital and employment. It is also consistent with the noted large decrease in the exit rate from nonemployment among black males that cooccurs with the notable declines in employment among black men (Juhn 1992).

regardless of the gravity of the offense, the time since conviction, or the relevance of the past behavior to one's current job responsibilities. In addition, employers are generally free to consider and discriminate based upon one's criminal history in hiring, with many states allowing employers to consider arrests not leading to conviction.

Whether reluctance among a subset of employers to hire former prison inmates or those with felony convictions results in market level impacts on employment rates, unemployment rates, or wages is an important question that parallels related theoretical and empirical debates in the economics of labor market discrimination. Specifically, discrimination against a specific group in the labor market by a subset of employers need not result in market-level wage differentials or greater difficulty in procuring employment. For example, the growing body of audit studies revealing lower call-back rates for black workers (Turner, Fix, and Struyk 1991; Fix, Galster, and Struyk 1993; Pager 2003) or workers with traditionally black names (Bertrand and Mullainathan 2004) certainly identify employers who exhibit bias in terms of their hiring choices. However, black workers may respond by concentrating their search efforts on firms with reputations for fair treatment, resulting in segregation across establishments. If black job searchers are a small group relative to availability of employment opportunities at firms that do not discriminate, the existence of discriminating firms will not lead to a racial wage disparity (Heckman and Siegelman 1993).[6]

In the current context, however, the proportion of employers expressing reluctance to hire convicted felons is quite high (as we will soon see). Moreover, there are theoretical arguments based in the theory of search that indeed link the presence of employers that discriminate to market-level differences in employment and earnings through search frictions. Black (1995) presents a model whereby the existence of discriminating employers reduces the job-offer arrival rate experienced by black job searchers relative to white job searchers. Consequently, black job searchers lower their reservation wages and, in equilibrium, experience a wage penalty unrelated to productivity. The key aspect of this model is that even employers who do not bear animus against black workers have the incentive to offer black workers less as they are more likely to accept the low wage offer.

In a recent working paper, Lanning (2010) has extended Black's model in several important directions and has developed a methodology for using search theory to simulate the impact of the differential call-back rates on market outcomes. Lanning uses the reduced-form equations from a discrimination search model to estimate the reservation wages of youth in the National Longitudinal Survey of Youth 1979 (NSLY79). These reservation

---

6. Heckman and Siegelman (1993) also argue that the matching on observables common in audit studies may not sufficiently account for differences in unobservable characteristics by group correlated with observable signals or variance in these characteristics.

wage distributions are then used to simulate the impact of differences in hiring rates of an order of magnitude equal to those estimated in the extant auditing literature on unemployment duration and market wages by group. A key finding of this analysis is that modest differences in hiring rates can result in notable differences in outcomes between groups. As we will soon see, the stated reluctance to hire convicted felons is quite widespread. In the context of the models offered by Black (1995) and Lanning, such preferences may translate into wage penalties and lower employment for former inmates.

Interestingly, in a mid-1970s review of the employment problems of former inmates, Phil Cook (1975) reviews several studies that generally find little evidence that former inmates have great difficulty finding employment although the jobs they found tended to be low paying with little room for advancement. A dual labor market interpretation of these earlier studies would be that a criminal conviction and prison history do not impact the ability to find work but may shut some former inmates out of the market for good jobs. However, this review was written at a time when the incarceration rate was roughly one-fifth today's rate, and prior prison sentences may have been less salient as an issue to employers. Moreover, it is certainly more difficult to conceal a criminal history record today than in the past, a key factor cited in several of the papers reviewed in Cook (1975) explaining why a criminal record did not pose particular problems at the time.

How important is prior criminal history to the screening and hiring practices of employers? Can and do employers actually check the criminal pasts of their applicants? Does such screening impact the likelihood of hiring workers from specific demographic groups? In this section, I explore these questions using the 2003 Survey of California Establishments. The survey was conducted by the Survey Research Center at the University of California, Berkeley. The sample frame includes business and nonprofit establishments with at least five employees, excluding government agencies; public schools or universities; and establishments in either the agricultural, forestry, or fisheries industries. Establishments were first stratified by size group, with each stratum sampled in proportion to the proportion of employment accounted for by the size category. Within strata, establishments are sampled at random. The intention behind the specific sampling frame is to generate estimates that are likely representative either for the average worker in these establishments or the average job seeker looking for employment in these establishments (assuming that hiring occurs in proportion to the stock of employees). A total of 2,806 establishments were sampled, 2,200 of which met the eligibility criteria (private sector, more than five employees). Interviews were completed with 1,080 establishments.[7]

7. The response rate for this survey (0.49) is roughly in line with comparable establishment surveys (see, for example, Holzer 1995; Holzer, Raphael, and Stoll 2006). The documentation

11.3.1   Descriptive Analysis

Table 11.3 presents tabulations regarding employer responses to queries about the acceptability of certain types of applicants for the most recently filled nonmanagerial, nonprofessional position. Employers are asked to think of the most recent position filled that meets these criteria. They are then asked whether they would definitely, probably, probably not, or definitely not accept a specific type of applicant. The survey inquires about three applicant traits: an applicant with a criminal record, an applicant who has been unemployed for a year or more, and an applicant with minimal work experience.[8]

Fully 71 percent of employers indicate that they would probably not or definitely not hire a worker with a criminal record (with definitely not being the modal response of 37 percent of establishments). The comparable figure for a worker who has been unemployed for a year is 38.6 percent, while the comparable figure for a worker with minimal experience is 59.1 percent. In prior research with Harry Holzer and Michael Stoll (Holzer, Raphael, and Stoll 2006) using data from an older establishment survey, we found a comparable reluctance to hire those with criminal records and much less reluctance to hire workers who have been unemployed, current welfare recipients, and workers with little experience. The one category of applicants for whom employers exhibit comparable (yet still less severe) reluctance to hire was applicants with gaps in their employment histories. Certainly, prior criminal history and unaccounted-for gaps in one's resume may be related in reality and in the minds of employers. In all, the California data and prior research clearly indicate a particular reluctance to hire workers with criminal pasts.

Whether and how employers act on the preferences evident in table 11.3 will depend on the information they have regarding criminal histories. With direct information on criminal history records (either through a direct query of the applicant or through a formal information search), employers can screen directly on the information at hand. In the absence of such information, however, employers may use signals of prior criminality, such as race,

---

for this survey does not provide detailed comparisons of the characteristics of responding and nonresponding establishments although it does note that the response rate was slightly lower for larger firms. The survey includes weights that adjust for differences in nonresponse rates across size categories as well as weights that adjust for differences in sampling rates across categories. The results presented in this section are not sensitive to whether one adjusts for differences in nonresponse rates across categories. All results presented here use the provided survey weights.

8. The exact wording of the question is "Next, think about the most recently hired, non-managerial, non-professional position in your establishment. Please tell me if you would have definitely accepted, probably accepted, probably not accepted, or definitely not accepted each type for that position." They are then queried about several type of applicants one of which is ". . . an applicant who had a criminal record." The survey does not specify whether this means someone who has been convicted of felony, convicted of misdemeanor, or has an arrest record with no convictions (all of which may turn up in a background check).

Table 11.3   Indicators of employer willingness to hire workers with specific characteristics into nonprofessional, nonmanagerial jobs

Degree of acceptability for the most recently filled position	Has a criminal record	Unemployed for a year or more	Minimal work experience
Definitely accept	0.018	0.077	0.090
Probably accept	0.271	0.538	0.318
Probably not accept	0.339	0.368	0.454
Definitely not accept	0.371	0.018	0.137

Source: All figures are tabulated from the 2003 Survey of California Establishments.

Table 11.4   Frequency with which employers check the criminal backgrounds of job applicants for nonmanagerial, nonprofessional jobs

	Always	Sometimes	Never
All establishments	0.598	0.122	0.280
By stated acceptability of applicants with criminal records			
Definitely accept	0.333	0.072	0.595
Probably accept	0.576	0.141	0.283
Probably not accept	0.504	0.157	0.339
Definitely not accept	0.702	0.063	0.235
By whether they are legally prohibited from hiring a convicted felon into the position			
Felons prohibited	0.854	0.066	0.080
Felons permitted	0.522	0.132	0.347

Source: All figures are tabulated from the 2003 Survey of California Establishments.

gender, education, neighborhood of residence, or gaps in one's employment history, to probabilistically screen out workers with high likelihood (actual or perceived) of prior criminal activity.

Table 11.4 presents tabulations of employer responses to a question asking how frequently they check the criminal backgrounds of applicants for nonprofessional, nonmanagerial jobs. Nearly 60 percent of employers indicate that they always check criminal history records, while 12 percent indicate that they sometimes check. This figure is considerably higher than that observed in prior surveys. For example, in a mid-1990s survey of establishments in four metropolitan areas spread across the country, Holzer, Raphael, and Stoll (2006) found that only 32 percent of employers indicated that they always check. A comparable 2001 survey of Los Angeles employers showed that roughly 46 percent of employers always check. While the differences in table 11.4 relative to these earlier results may reflect the differing sample frames and locations, the higher propensity to check may reflect in part a decline in the cost of checking associated with increasing computer power, the computerization of criminal history records, and an increasing degree of openness of state criminal history repositories to public information requests.

Table 11.4 also presents these distributions by the employer's stated willingness to hire those with criminal histories and by whether the employer is legally prohibited from hiring a convicted felon into the job in question. There is a very strong relationship between checking and whether the employer indicates that a convicted felon is an acceptable applicant. While only 33 percent of employers who indicate that they would definitely accept a worker with a criminal history indicate that they always check criminal backgrounds, the comparable figure for those who would definitely not hire such a worker is roughly 70 percent. Regarding employers who are legally prohibited from hiring convicted felons (roughly 25 percent of the sample), 85 percent indicate they always check criminal backgrounds. The comparable figure for establishments not subject to such a legal prohibition is 52 percent.

Figure 11.2 presents tabulations of the methods used by employers to check criminal history records. Note, the proportions in the figure sum to more than 1 as employers can indicate that they use multiple methods to screen applicants on this dimension. A relatively small proportion of employers indicate that they simply ask the applicants (0.112), and an even smaller proportion indicates that they initiate their own query of the state attorney general. Nearly 80 percent indicate that they outsource the screening to a security establishment, such as Pinkerton.

Given the strong stated reluctance of many employers to hire convicted felons along with the apparent ubiquity of criminal history information, one might wonder which establishments are the most likely to hire former prison inmates and what impact, if any, do these preferences, legal prohibitions,

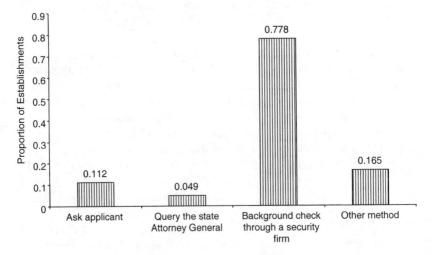

Fig. 11.2   Methods used to acquire information on applicant criminal history records among establishments that check

and hiring practices have on employment outcomes. To explore these questions, tables 11.5, 11.6, and 11.7 present the average characteristics of establishments after stratifying along a number of dimensions. Table 11.5 splits establishments into two groups: those unwilling to hire those with criminal history records (those indicating that they would definitely not or probably

Table 11.5   **Comparison of establishments that are wiling and unwilling to hire applicants with criminal records**

	Unwilling to hire	Willing to hire	P-value, test for significant difference in means
Distribution across industries			
Construction	0.034	0.084	0.001
Manufacturing	0.173	0.168	0.843
Transportation, utility, and communications	0.034	0.046	0.374
Wholesale trade	0.060	0.045	0.346
Retail trade	0.168	0.142	0.307
FIRE	0.101	0.044	0.004
Hotel/lodging	0.013	0.024	0.239
Health service	0.096	0.208	0.000
Other services	0.321	0.239	0.011
Establishment size			
5–9	0.106	0.145	0.082
10–19	0.221	0.216	0.865
20–49	0.174	0.100	0.003
50–99	0.110	0.233	0.000
100–249	0.230	0.179	0.076
250–999	0.111	0.083	0.178
1,000+	0.047	0.044	0.826
Perceived future hiring plans			
Expand	0.305	0.384	0.016
Stay the same	0.534	0.486	0.172
Contract	0.161	0.129	0.208
Characteristics of most recent hire			
Female	0.570	0.583	0.551
Black	0.047	0.071	0.119
Black male	0.018	0.050	0.005
Hispanic	0.374	0.435	0.035
Hispanic male	0.132	0.146	0.567
Median age	30	30	
Level of educational attainment			
No high school degree	0.020	0.182	0.000
High school graduate	0.347	0.493	0.001
Some college	0.401	0.246	0.000
College graduate	0.231	0.078	0.000
Average hourly wage	14.17	11.18	0.000

Notes: Employers indicating that they would either definitely or probably accept an applicant with a criminal record are categorized as willing, while those indicating that they would probably or definitely not hire such an applicant are categorized as unwilling.

not accept such an applicant) and those that are willing (those indicating that they definitely would or probably would accept such an applicant). Table 11.6 stratifies employers into those legally prohibited from hiring a convicted felon into the most recently filled, nonprofessional, nonmanagerial job and those that are not. Finally, table 11.7 stratifies establishments into those that

Table 11.6   **Comparison of establishment that are prohibited from hiring convicted felons to establishments that are not legally prohibited**

	Not prohibited from hiring convicted felons	Prohibited from hiring felons	P-value, test for significant difference in means
Distribution across industries			
Construction	0.055	0.030	0.130
Manufacturing	0.214	0.067	0.000
Transportation, utility, and communications	0.041	0.035	0.706
Wholesale trade	0.062	0.017	0.007
Retail trade	0.182	0.060	0.000
FIRE	0.081	0.108	0.215
Hotel/lodging	0.019	0.012	0.541
Health service	0.113	0.206	0.000
Other services	0.234	0.464	0.000
Establishment size			
5–9	0.124	0.065	0.013
10–19	0.189	0.297	0.000
20–49	0.148	0.118	0.247
50–99	0.149	0.121	0.285
100–249	0.245	0.215	0.352
250–999	0.103	0.114	0.643
1,000+	0.043	0.071	0.082
Perceived future hiring plans			
Expand	0.344	0.278	0.060
Stay the same	0.476	0.659	0.000
Contract	0.180	0.062	0.000
Characteristics of most recent hire			
Female	0.572	0.724	0.000
Black	0.023	0.081	0.000
Black male	0.011	0.041	0.002
Hispanic	0.389	0.367	0.549
Hispanic male	0.151	0.081	0.007
Median age	30	30	
Level of educational attainment			
No high school degree	0.080	0.017	0.001
High school graduate	0.417	0.282	0.002
Some college	0.293	0.510	0.000
College graduate	0.211	0.192	0.646
Average hourly wage	13.10	14.54	0.011

Note: Stratification based on employer response to the question "Are convicted felons prohibited by law from holding this job?"

Table 11.7   **Comparison of establishments that do not check the criminal history of applicants to those that do**

	Don't check criminal histories	Check criminal histories	P-value, test for significant difference in means
Distribution across industries			
Construction	0.073	0.034	0.006
Manufacturing	0.153	0.211	0.032
Transportation, utility, and communications	0.021	0.049	0.036
Wholesale trade	0.104	0.036	0.000
Retail trade	0.267	0.121	0.000
FIRE	0.084	0.083	0.968
Hotel/lodging	0.018	0.016	0.797
Health service	0.051	0.153	0.000
Other services	0.229	0.298	0.027
Establishment size			
5–9	0.161	0.091	0.001
10–19	0.257	0.199	0.038
20–49	0.230	0.109	0.000
50–99	0.119	0.158	0.110
100–249	0.171	0.246	0.009
250–999	0.056	0.135	0.000
1,000+	0.006	0.063	0.000
Perceived future hiring plans			
Expand	0.347	0.328	0.565
Stay the same	0.511	0.508	0.934
Contract	0.143	0.164	0.391
Characteristics of most recent hire			
Female	0.519	0.603	0.103
Black	0.018	0.063	0.005
Black male	0.007	0.032	0.018
Hispanic	0.356	0.412	0.096
Hispanic male	0.109	0.139	0.203
Median age	28	30	
Level of educational attainment			
No high school degree	0.046	0.067	0.201
High school graduate	0.452	0.351	0.023
Some college	0.387	0.342	0.418
College graduate	0.116	0.241	0.000
Average hourly wage	11.52	14.09	0.000

check criminal history records (either always or sometimes) and those that do not. In each table, we present the industrial distribution, the distribution across size categories, the survey respondents perceived future hiring plans, and average characteristics of the recently hired nonexempt employee for each stratum.

Beginning with table 11.5, there are a number of notable differences between establishments that are willing and unwilling to hire those with criminal history records. Construction and health services establishments are relatively overrepresented among establishments willing to hire. The latter finding is somewhat of a surprise because health services establishments are often subject to bans on hiring convicted felons. Retail trade and other service establishments are somewhat underrepresented among those willing to hire. Unfortunately, the current survey does not contain information on the degree of customer contact that each employee will have. However, prior research using similar establishment surveys reveals a strong negative association between willingness to hire and the degree of contact between customers and the potential employee (Holzer, Raphael, and Stoll 2006). With regard to size, larger establishments are generally overrepresented among employers who are unwilling to hire those with criminal history records.

Given the strong-stated aversion to hiring applicants with criminal records and the fact that this aversion is stronger than that observed for other applicants with problematic signals, one might hypothesize that an applicant with a criminal history record will be at the end of the hiring queue. In other words, employers may only hire such workers when unmet labor needs are great or during times of expansion. While I cannot assess how differences in labor market conditions impact employer attitudes toward such workers (the survey is of establishments in one state at roughly the same point in time), I can explore whether these attitudes depend on the employer's anticipated future hiring plans. Indeed, establishments that indicate that they plan to expand hiring are overrepresented among employers that are willing to hire applicants with criminal histories. The opposite is the case for establishments that indicate that they are planning to contract in the future. To the extent that this patterns holds up to controlling for other firm characteristics, this may provide guidance to labor market intermediaries serving former inmates regarding how to target the employment search.

Establishments that are willing to hire convicted felons tend to be filling positions with less-educated people relative to establishments that are unwilling. Nearly 20 percent of recent hires are at establishments that are willing have less than a high school degree, while roughly 70 percent have no more than a high school diploma. The comparable figures for establishments that are unwilling to hire is 2 percent and 37 percent, respectively. In addition, the establishments that are unwilling to hire pay considerably higher wages.

While there are no differences in the proportion female or the median age of recent employees at these establishments, establishments that indicate a willingness to hire applicants with criminal histories are more likely to hire black applicants, with a fairly large difference for black male applicants (3.2 percentage points). While at first one might expect that a strong aversion to hiring convicted felons should lower the probability of hiring black applicants, upon further reflection it becomes clear that the relationship between such preference and racial hiring outcomes is complex and may induce offsetting effects. Certainly, African Americans, and African American men in particular, are more likely to have criminal history records (Raphael 2005). As a consequence, one might expect that those employers that are the least willing to hire those with criminal histories should be the least likely to hire blacks. However, an aversion to hiring felons may interact with screening practices in a manner that might actually increase the likelihood of hiring a black applicant. Those who are unwilling to hire criminal applicants are also more likely to conduct formal criminal background reviews. If employers overestimate the relationship between race and criminality, checking criminal backgrounds may actually improve the prospect of black applicants with clean histories. Holzer, Raphael, and Stoll (2006) find some evidence of such an impact, noting that those employers who are unwilling to hire yet don't check criminal backgrounds are the least likely to hire black applicants even after controlling for the relative supply of black applicants to the establishment.

There is additional research suggestive of the ambiguous impact of formal screening on the hiring of minority applicants. Autor and Scarborough (2008) find that formal screening devices do not reduce the hiring of blacks, despite the relatively poor performance of black applicants on standardized assessments. While this work does not address criminal background checks, the results parallel the argument made here. The authors analyze hiring outcomes at a large national retail chain that introduced formal test-based applicant assessment procedures. The relatively low black test scores coupled with the strong effect of scores on the likelihood of being hired yield the prediction that introducing the formal screening would reduce black hiring rates by nearly 20 percent. However, the authors find no such reduction, suggesting that the subjective assessments of black applicants by interviewers prior to testing negatively impacted black hiring rates.

While not directly addressed toward the issues of statistical discrimination, a recent audit study by Pager (2003) provides further evidence that employer perception of the relationship between race and criminality may interact in a complicated manner. Pager conducted an audit study in Milwaukee, whereby pairs of auditors of the same race were sent to apply for the same jobs, one with a spell in prison listed on his resume and one with no such signal. Among the white auditors, 34 percent of the nonoffenders received a call-back in contrast to 17 percent of ex-offenders. The comparable figures for blacks were 14 and 5 percent. Consequently, Pager draws two conclusions. First, the ex-offender stigma effect is larger for blacks (based on the 65 percent reduction in the call-back rates for black ex-offenders relative to the 50 percent reduction for whites).[9] Second, that animus based

___

9. However, the percentage point decline in the call-back rate for white offenders (17 points) exceeds the percentage point decline for black offenders (9 points).

racial discrimination against blacks is more important in explaining the inferior employment outcomes of black men (based on the finding that black nonoffenders receive fewer call-backs than white ex-offenders).

However, statistical discrimination provides an alternative interpretation of the low call-back rate for black nonoffenders. In Pager's (2003) study, the auditor marked as an ex-offender explicitly signals having been in prison by including in-prison work experience on his resume. The nonoffending auditor does not reveal a criminal past. If employers believe that all young black are criminally active, the low call-back rate for black nonoffenders may reflect statistical discrimination.[10] Moreover, as noted by Bushway (2004), the audited sample of job openings explicitly excludes job openings where a background check is likely (for example, jobs that are legally closed to ex-offenders and job advertisements with explicit mentions of background checks). Moreover, the majority of employers audited care enough about the criminal backgrounds of the applicants to inquire about it on their application forms.

While employer apprehensions about hiring applicants with criminal histories are unlikely to aid the employment search of reentering former inmates, legal prohibitions against hiring felons most certainly close many doors. Nearly one-quarter of the employers in the California survey indicate that they are legally prohibited from staffing their most recently filled exempt job with a convicted felon. Moreover, as the survey excludes public schools and universities and government agencies, this may be a lower-bound estimate of the proportion of recent hires bound by such prohibitions.

Table 11.6 presents comparisons of establishment characteristics for those indicating that they are legally prohibited from hiring a convicted felon into their most recently filled nonmanagerial, nonprofessional position and those indicating no such restriction. Beginning with industry, establishments in the financial services; insurance; and real estate, health services, and personal services industries are overrepresented among establishments that cannot hire felons. To explore these patterns by industry in greater detail, appendix table 11A.1 presents the proportion of establishments that are subject to the legal prohibition by two-digit industry code. As the data becomes quite thin when spread across so many groups, the table also presents standard errors as well as the observation count for each industry. There are several notable patterns in these tabulations. We observe fairly high proportions of establishments subject to such legal prohibition in specific transportation, utility,

---

10. One possible test of this hypothesis would be to assess whether there is an order effect on the likelihood that the black nonoffender auditor received a call-back. Specifically, in instances when the ex-offender applies first, the appearance of the prison information on the auditor's resume may prime a cognitive association between race and crime in the mind of the employer. To the extent that this triggers the subjective assessment of the employer, one should observe a lower call-back rate for the nonoffender black auditor in audits when he is the second to apply.

and communications industries, including local passenger transportation. A similar pattern is observed for nearly all subcategories of the financial service industries. Over 35 percent of establishments in the health services industries are prohibited from hiring convicted felons, while 90 percent of social services establishments are subject to such prohibitions.

Returning to table 11.6, there is little evidence of a systematic relationship between legal prohibitions and establishment size. Establishments that plan to expand in the future are somewhat underrepresented among those prohibited from hiring felons, however, so are establishments that plan to contract. There are some notable differences in the average personal characteristics of recent hires. Establishments that are legally prohibited from hiring felons are more likely to hire women, more likely to hire African American applicants, and less likely to hire Hispanics (Hispanic males in particular). The impact on gender may reflect the fact that convicted felons and released inmates are overwhelmingly male. The impact on the likelihood that the most recent hire is black is somewhat counterintuitive given the higher likelihood that African Americans have criminal history records. However, statistical discrimination against blacks coupled with an impact of the prohibition on the likelihood that establishments check criminal history records may explain this pattern (we explore this issue in greater detail in the following).

Finally, establishments that are prohibited from hiring felons tend to hire more educated workers, with over 70 percent of recent hires having more than a high school degree. The comparable figure for establishments that are not prohibited is approximately 50 percent. Hourly wages at prohibited establishments exceed those at nonprohibited establishments by nearly 10 percent.

The final comparison in table 11.7 contrasts the characteristics of establishments that check criminal history records (either always or sometimes) in the process of screening job applicants to those that do not. As one might expect, establishments in industries where the proportion subject to legal hiring prohibitions is high are overrepresented among establishments that check (e.g., health services, other services, transportation, communications, and utilities). Establishments that check are disproportionately larger, perhaps due in part to the fact that in these data larger establishments tend to be more likely to have formal human resource departments. There is no apparent relationship between whether an establishment checks and future hiring plans. We do, however, see a positive relationship between checking and proportion of recent hires that are female and that are black. Finally, establishments that check hire more educated workers and pay substantially higher wages (a nearly 20 percent wage difference).

The large wage premiums associated with checking criminal backgrounds, being unwilling to hire convicted felons, and being prohibited from hiring former prison inmates suggest that former inmates that do find jobs are overly concentrated in the very low-wage labor market (consistent with Cook's [1975] characterization of the labor market faced by formers inmates in the mid-1970s). These pay differentials may be interpreted as either reflecting productivity differentials between convicted felons and others (a traditional human capital interpretation) or, perhaps, convicted felons being relegated to low-wage secondary-sector jobs (an interpretation more in line with dual labor market theory). Under the latter interpretation, acquiring secondary-sector employment may be less of a problem for former inmates relative to the problem of acquiring a job with decent pay and benefits. Indeed the patterns evident in tables 11.5, 11.6, and 11.7 suggest that the employment opportunities available to convicted felons are generally inferior.

However, the recent audit evidence presented in Pager (2003) does show considerable penalties in terms of call-back rates associated with a criminal history record. As was discussed in the review of the search models presented by Black (1995) and Lanning (2010), there are plausible and intuitively appealing theoretically arguments that link these lower call-back rates to both more unemployment (as well as nonemployment) and lower wages.

11.3.2   Multivariate Analysis

The descriptive statistics thus far reveal several patterns suggesting that employers consider criminal history records when screening job applicants and that such consideration may impact the demography of who employers hire. Moreover, the peculiar patterns regarding race suggest that the desire to screen out those with criminal histories may interact with employer perceptions of the likely past criminal behavior of applicants from different racial groups and, consequently, impact hiring outcomes through a number of channels. In this section, I explore these patterns in greater detail. In particular, I assess whether the relationship between employer expansion plans and employer willingness to hire applicants with criminal histories survives, controlling for observable establishment characteristics. I also model the impact of checking criminal history records on hiring outcomes using legal prohibitions against hiring felons as an instrument.

Table 11.8 presents the results from a series of linear probability regressions of a dummy variable indicating willingness to hire someone with a criminal history record (using the definition from the stratification in table 11.5) on indicators for the establishment's future hiring plans as well as a host of control variables. The first specification only includes indicator variables for whether the establishment plans to stay the same size or contract in the near future (with planned expansion being the omitted category) as control variables. The second specification adds a complete set of dummy variables for the two-digit industry codes listed in appendix table 11A.1 and seven size categories. Specification (3) adds a full set of interaction terms between the industry and size dummies, while specification (4) adds a dummy for being

Table 11.8   Multivariate analysis of the relationship between the establishment's future expansion plans and willingness to hire applicants with a criminal history record

	(1)	(2)	(3)	(4)
Stay the same	−0.068	−0.057	−0.049	−0.040
	(0.032)	(0.033)	(0.036)	(0.039)
Contract	−0.093	−0.093	−0.028	−0.045
	(0.044)	(0.046)	(0.054)	(0.060)
F-statistic[a]	3.100	2.480	0.790	0.600
P-value	(0.046)	(0.084)	(0.452)	(0.549)
Industry and size dummies	No	Yes	Yes	Yes
Industry/size interaction terms	No	No	Yes	Yes
Control for prohibition against hiring felons, whether the establishment checks backgrounds, and dummies for education attainment of most recent hire	No	No	No	Yes

Notes: Dependent variable = willingness to hire a convicted felon.
Standard errors are in parentheses. Establishments that plan to expand are the omitted category. All models are estimated using a linear probability regression.
[a]This is a test statistic and p-value from a test of the null hypothesis that the coefficients on the two variables measuring the establishment's future hiring plans equal zero.

subject to prohibition against hiring felons, a dummy for whether the establishment checks criminal history records, and dummies for the educational attainment of the most recent hire.

Absent controls variables, there are indeed statistically significant differences in stated willingness to hire across establishments defined by their future hiring plans. Those who plan to stay the same size are roughly 7 percentage points less likely to indicate that they are willing to hire such workers relative to expanding establishments. For establishments that plan to contract, the comparable differential is 9 percentage points. The F-test of the joint significance of these two coefficients indicates that the difference in means across these three categories is statistically significant at the 5 percent level of confidence.

Adding industry and size dummies to the specification does not appreciably alter this result although the addition of these two sets of control variables attenuates the coefficients slightly. Permitting interaction terms between industry and size category, however, yields insignificant coefficients on the variables measuring future hiring plans in both specifications (3) and (4). This is in part due to the relatively large standard errors in these more complete specifications (relative to effect sizes estimated in model [1] with no controls). Thus, while there is some support for the hypothesis that expanding establishments are more likely to hire convicted felons, this result is somewhat sensitive to controlling for observable characteristics.

A legal prohibition against hiring convicted felons can impact hiring outcomes through two channels. First, through reviews of criminal history records or through deterring applications from job seekers with felony convictions, such a prohibition will directly exclude convicted felons from employment, a factor that will disproportionately impact demographic groups with high felony conviction rates. Second, the additional screening prompted by the legal prohibition may counteract erroneous subjective beliefs, revealing clean criminal histories where employers might assume otherwise. Such a salutary effect should also have a disproportionate impact on the hiring of applicants of groups with high felony conviction rates as these are, perhaps, the applicants that employers are more likely to assume have criminal records.

Table 11.9 presents results from a series of multivariate regressions of specific hiring outcomes on a dummy variable indicating that the establishment was legally prohibited from hiring a convicted felon into the most recently filled position. As all of the dependent variables analyzed are binary, all models are linear probability models. The table presents only the coefficient on the prohibition dummy to conserve space. Specification (1) includes only the prohibition dummy. Specification (2) adds a complete set of two-digit

Table 11.9   Multivariate regression estimates of the impact of a legal prohibition against hiring convicted felons on the likelihood that the most recent hire into a nonmanagerial, nonprofessional job is male, black, or Hispanic

Outcome variable	Specification (1)	Specification (2)	Specification (3)
Male	−0.152[a]	−0.004	0.049
	(0.036)	(0.039)	(0.045)
Black	0.058[a]	0.065[a]	0.086[a]
	(0.014)	(0.017)	(0.020)
Black male	0.030[a]	0.046[a]	0.063[a]
	(0.010)	(0.012)	(0.015)
Black female	0.027[a]	0.018	0.023
	(0.010)	(0.012)	(0.014)
Hispanic	−0.022	−0.139[a]	−0.106[b]
	(0.037)	(0.038)	(0.043)
Hispanic male	−0.070[a]	−0.034	−0.007
	(0.026)	(0.028)	(0.033)
Hispanic female	0.048	−0.105[a]	−0.099[a]
	(0.033)	(0.033)	(0.035)

Notes: Standard errors are in parentheses. The coefficients in the table come from multivariate regressions of the outcomes on a dummy indicating whether the employer checks criminal backgrounds. The specifications are as follows: specification (1) includes no control variables; specification (2) includes sixty dummies for two-digit industry codes and dummies for the seven establishment size categories listed in tables 11.5 through 11.7; specification (3) adds a complete set of interaction terms between the sixty industry dummies and the seven size dummies.

[a]Parameter estimate statistically significant at the 1 percent level of confidence.
[b]Parameter estimate statistically significant at the 5 percent level of confidence.

industry and size dummies, while specification (3) adds interaction terms between industry and size.

The negative impact of prohibitions on the hiring of male applicants disappears after adding controls for industry and establishment size as do the initially significant effects for black women and Hispanic men. For Hispanics overall and Hispanic women, the specifications beyond the bivaraite model in column (1) show significant negative impacts of the prohibition.

For black males, the table reveals a consistently significant (at the 1 percent level of confidence) positive impact of felony prohibitions on their likelihood of being hired. The probability that the most recent hire is a black male increases from 3 to 6.8 percentage points (depending on the specification) when the establishment is prohibited from hiring felons. To be sure, it may be the case that jobs that are legally off limits to convicted felons draw disproportionately from the pool of African American male workers. Unfortunately, the data do not include any variable gauging the racial composition of the applicant pool although one might believe that black job applicants would also be drawn toward firms where they feel the likelihood of being treated fairly is high. It is notable that we do not see a positive significant effect of the prohibition on the likelihood that black women are hired beyond the estimate from the bivaraite specification in the first column.

Finally, table 11.10 presents the instrumental variables models relating checking to hiring outcomes. For each model, the prohibition against hiring felons is used as an instrument for whether the establishment checks criminal backgrounds. The identifying assumption here is that the prohibition impacts hiring outcomes only through an impact on the use of this particular screening tool. This assumption would be violated if past problems with felon employees usher in the hiring prohibitions and if the incidence of such problems is correlated with the gender or racial composition of workers at the firm. The first-stage coefficient on the legal prohibition dummy is presented in the last row of the table. The instrument exhibits a strong and significant impact on the likelihood of checking in all specifications.

There is little evidence of an impact of checking that is consistently significant and stable across specifications for males overall, for black females, and for Hispanic males. We do observe a consistent positive effect of checking backgrounds on the likelihood that the most recent hire is an African American male. While the standard errors are quite large on these estimates, the estimates are significant at the 1 percent level in all specifications. To be sure, these local average treatment effect estimates are likely too large to represent what would happen, on average, if all employers were subjected to such a restriction. Nonetheless, the consistent positive impact suggests a more complex relationship between this screening tool and the demographics of recent hires than one would expect based on exclusion alone.

Table 11.10   Instrumental variables estimates of the impact of employers using criminal background checks on the likelihood that the most recent hire into a nonmanagerial, nonprofessional job is male, black, or Hispanic

Outcome variable	Specification (1)	Specification (2)	Specification (3)
Male	−0.571[a]	−0.017	0.266
	(0.154)	(0.229)	(0.243)
Black	0.217[a]	0.376[a]	0.457[a]
	(0.033)	(0.121)	(0.151)
Black male	0.114[a]	0.267[a]	0.336[a]
	(0.039)	(0.087)	(0.104)
Black female	0.103[a]	0.109	0.121
	(0.039)	(0.073)	(0.081)
Hispanic	−0.078	−0.796[a]	−0.556[b]
	(0.139)	(0.282)	(0.264)
Hispanic male	−0.258[a]	−0.190	−0.029
	(0.104)	(0.172)	(0.180)
Hispanic female	0.180	−0.607[a]	−0.527[a]
	(0.124)	(0.225)	(0.210)
First stage coefficient on prohibition against hiring felons	0.266[a]	0.173[a]	0.188[a]
	(0.033)	(0.035)	(0.038)
F-statistic,[c] first-stage (P-value)	64.97	24.43	24.47
	(0.001)	(0.001)	(0.001)

Notes: Standard errors are in parentheses. The coefficients in the table come from instrumental variables regressions of the outcomes on a dummy indicating whether the employer checks criminal backgrounds. A legal prohibition against hiring felons into the particular job is used as an instrument for checking. The specifications are as follows: specification (1) includes no control variables; specification (2) includes sixty dummies for two-digit industry codes and dummies for the seven establishment size categories listed in tables 11.5 through 11.7; specification (3) adds a complete set of interaction terms between the sixty industry dummies and the seven size dummies.

[a]Parameter estimate statistically significant at the 1 percent level of confidence.

[b]Parameter estimate statistically significant at the 5 percent level of confidence.

[c]Test-statistics from a test of the null hypothesis that the coefficient on the prohibition against hiring felons in the first-stage equation is equal to zero.

11.4   Employment-Based Prisoner Reentry Programs: Do We Know What Works?

With the tremendous increase in U.S. incarceration rates and the consequent increase in the annual outflow of prison inmates, reentry services are receiving increasing attention from researchers and policymakers. An increasing minority of U.S. men (and for some demographic subgroups, the majority) will at some point face the challenge of reintegrating into noninstitutional society after a spell in prison. Identifying effective practices for fostering success in reentry is of paramount importance.

Much of the growth in the U.S. incarceration rate since the mid-1970s is attributable to an increased propensity to use incarceration as punish-

Table 11.11   Comparison of three-state transition probability matrix for 1980
                   and 2005

	Destination state		
Origin State	Not Incarcerated, not on parole	Incarcerated	Parole
A: 1980			
Not incarcerated, not on parole	0.99937	0.00063	0
Incarcerated	0.08211	0.52830	0.38958
Parole	0.40390	0.13073	0.46538
B: 2005			
Not incarcerated, not on parole	0.99826	0.00174	0
Incarcerated	0.12697	0.50629	0.36674
Parole	0.29738	0.29335	0.40927

Source: Author tabulations from National Prisoner Statistics data for various years.

ment as well as an increase in the typical amount of time one can expect
to serve conditional on the crime committed and on being sent to prison
(Raphael and Stoll 2009). However, an increase in the rate at which those
conditionally released from prison fail and are returned to custody has also
played a fairly large role. To illustrate this fact, table 11.11 presents estimates
of annual transition probabilities between three possible states of being:
(a) not incarcerated and not on parole, (b) incarcerated, and (c) on parole.
I use data from the National Prisoner Statistics data base measuring beginning year prison population as well as parole population counts and aggregate annual releases and admissions to estimate these transition probabilities
for 1980 and for 2005.

A comparison across the two panels in table 11.11 reveals two large
changes. First, the transition probability from not incarcerated/not on parole to incarcerated increases nearly 2.8 times, from 0.00063 to 0.00174.
This probability corresponds to the admissions rate into prison out of the
general population not under the supervision of the criminal justice system.
Second, the annual rate at which those on parole fail and are returned to
custody increases by a factor of 2.2, from 0.13 to 0.29.[11] This latter transi-

11. Note, the figures in table 11.11 do not reveal a large decrease in the transition probability out of prison, what one would expect if the average amount of time served were to have
increased. In fact, if we sum the two transition probabilities out of incarceration (either due
to unconditional release or conditional release), the annual release rate increased from 0.47 to
0.49, suggesting that the typical term served in prison actually declines over this period. Such
an inference, however, fails to account for the change in the composition of prisoners. Over
this time period, the composition of the incarcerated shifts markedly away from violent and
property offenders to those convicted of drug crimes and those serving additional time on
parole violations. These latter two groups generally serve shorter sentences than the former
two groups. If one conditions on crime committed, the release probability does indeed decline
over this time period. In all, an increase in the expected value of time served conditional on
crime committed and conditional on being sent to prison likely explains a third of the increase
in incarceration over the past few decades (Raphael and Stoll 2009).

tion probability is one stark indicator of an increasing likelihood of failed prisoner reentry.

The transition matrices in table 11.11 can be used to illustrate the importance of failed reentry as a contributor to growth in incarceration. Specifically, the probability matrices can be used to solve for steady-state values of the proportion of the population in each possible state. Multiplying the proportion in prison by 100,000 yields the steady-state incarceration rate (as conventionally measured by researchers and by the U.S. Bureau of Justice Statistics) consistent with the transition probabilities of each matrix.[12] Figure 11.3 displays these steady-state values for 1980 and 2005. The steady-state incarceration rate increases over this time period from 167 per 100,000 to 553 per 100,000. This predicted increase of 386 inmates per 100,000 exceeds the actual increase observed over this period (an actual change of 351 per 100,000). The two figures, however, are of similar magnitude.[13]

For the purposes of benefit-cost analysis, one might be interested in assessing how the increase in the parole failure rate has impacted the national incarceration rate. Alternatively, one might be interested in simulating how an intervention that would reduce the parole failure rate by a given amount would impact the national incarceration rate (and by extension, expenditures on corrections). Figure 11.3 presents alternative steady-state calculations for 2005 substituting various counterfactual parole failure rates. First, I substitute the transition probabilities from parole for 1980 into the 2005 matrix. Doing so yields a counterfactual steady-state incarceration rate of 427, nearly 30 percent lower than the actual rate for 2005.

I also calculate the steady-state rates under two alternative counterfactuals: (a) a reduction in the parole failure rate of 5 percentage points, and (b) a reduction in the parole failure rate of 10 percentage points. For both

12. I calculate the steady-state incarceration rates in the following manner. To begin, define the column vector P_t as the three-by-one vector with elements equal to the population shares in each possible state for year t. The sum of all three elements must equal 1 for any given year. Define the matrix T as the transition probability matrix, where each element, T^{ij}, gives the probability of transitioning from state i to state j over a given time period (in this case, a year). The proportional distribution of the U.S. population across the three states in any given year can be rewritten as a linear function of the state distribution in the previous year and the transition probability matrix, or $P_{t+1} = T'P_t$. Assuming a stable T, the system reaches the steady state when applying the transition matrix to the population-share vector at the beginning of the year yields the same population distribution at the beginning of the subsequent year. That is to say, in steady state, it must be the case that $P_t = P_{t+1} = P$, where we drop the time subscript to indicate the steady-state value. When combined with T, this gives the steady-state condition $P = TP$. This latter equation in conjunction with the condition that all elements of P must sum to 1 can be used to derive the steady-state shares for all elements in P.

13. In both years, the steady-state values exceed the actual values. In 1980, the steady-state value of 167 exceeds the actual incarceration of 140 by roughly 17 percent, while in 2005 the steady-state value of 553 exceeds the actual value of 491 by 11 percent. The fact that the steady-state value exceeds the actual value yields the prediction that the national incarceration rate in each year is in the midst of a dynamic adjustment process toward the higher steady-state rate. Johnson and Raphael model this dynamic adjustment process and the likely implications for crime rates (Johnson and Raphael 2008).

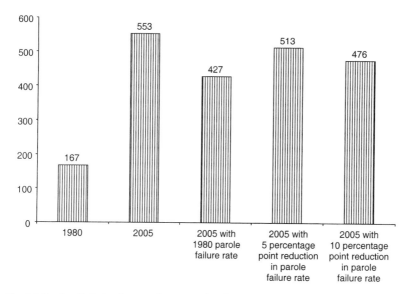

Fig. 11.3   **Implied steady-state incarceration for 1980, 2005, and several counter-factual values for 2005**

scenarios, I assume equal size increases in the probability of successfully transitioning off parole and the probability of remaining on parole into the next year.[14] These simulations suggest that interventions that have even modest impacts on the parole failure rate could lead to substantial reductions in the prison population. The 5 percentage point reduction leads to decline in the steady-state incarceration rate of 40 per 100,000 (7 percent relative to the original 2005 value). A 10 percentage point reduction yields a decline in the steady-state incarceration of 77 per 100,000 (a 14 percent decline).

The impact of successful reentry programs on the incarceration rate and corrections expenditures along with the social cost-savings associated with consequent reductions in victimization costs suggest that the payoffs to effective reentry programs are potentially quite high. What does existing research tell us about reentry efforts to date? Are there identifiable best-practices that can be replicated on a large scale to aid reentry and reduce the U.S. incarceration rate through postrelease programming? In this section, I address these questions.

11.4.1   Empirical Evaluations of Prisoner Reentry Programs:
Results from Nonexperimental Evaluations

Given the fractious nature of corrections in the United States (there are fifty-one independent corrections systems), there are a multitude of pro-

14. Note the rows of the transition probability matrices must sum to 1.

grams designed to aid reentry of released prison inmates or minimize criminal activity through the delivery of various services. In many instances, these programs are sanctioned and funded by state governments and coordinate service delivery with state parole and local probation departments. Many such programs also receive funding from various federal government agencies and, in some instances, private foundations.

As there is no standard set of reentry services delivered across the country, there are literally hundreds of alternative programs and approaches, ranging from cognitive behavioral therapy, to family reunification services, to employment services of all forms for released inmates and high-risk individuals. Consequently, there are also hundreds of empirical evaluations of these efforts.

Nearly all of these evaluations make use of nonexperimental techniques. In their exhaustive meta-analysis of all English-language evaluations of prisoner reentry and crime-abatement programs, Drake, Aos, and Miller (2009) identify 545 such program evaluations. Less than 5 percent of these evaluations utilize a randomized-control research design. Not surprisingly, the central tendencies of large meta-analyses based on nonexperimental studies tend to find much larger impacts of program interventions on criminal offending than do the experimental evaluations (contrasting the results in Drake, Aos, and Miller [2009]; Aos, Miller, and Drake [2006]; and Wilson, Gallagher, and MacKenzie [2000]) with the experimental studies reviewed in the following). This difference may certainly be due in part to the inability of the nonexperimental research to adequately address selection bias due to unobserved differences between program participants and nonparticipants. However, heterogeneity in the impact such programs have on participants coupled with substitution among randomized control group members toward other available interventions may also explain these disparities (Heckman and Smith 1995).

Clearly, those who stand to benefit the most from receiving reentry services following release from prison should be the most likely to seek out such services. Whether one is randomized into the treatment group of a specific program does not preclude those with potentially large gains from seeking out services elsewhere, especially when there are many small competing service providers. In practice, most existing programs are more likely to serve individuals who wish to participate. Those who are induced to participate through random assignment into a treatment group are likely to be compositionally different from those who seek out services on their own. In other words, the program effect for the participant on the margin may be considerably smaller than the impact for the inframarginal participant, a fact that is also consistent with the disparity between experimental and nonexperimental research findings. Many of the experimental studies do not estimate the impact of the intervention on incremental service delivery and generally do not attempt to estimate the distribution-of-effects sizes beyond the average impact.[15]

Drake, Aos, and Miller (2009) provide the most up to date and complete meta-analysis of anticrime programs that operate through service delivery to either former inmates or high-risk individuals such as disadvantaged youth. The authors searched for all English-language evaluations conducted since the 1970s that met three broad criteria: (a) each evaluation had to make use of a comparison sample with reasonable balance on observable covariates between the treatment and comparison groups, (b) evaluations had to include program dropouts as well as program completers in the tabulation of effect sizes, and (c) the evaluation must contain estimates for an impact of some indicator of criminal activity, be it self-reported, arrest, conviction, and so on. Using all available evaluations that meet these criteria coupled with a standardization of effect size that attenuates effect estimates for studies with relatively less rigorous methodological design, the authors estimate the average impact on the criminal outcome for over fifty prototypical in-prison and postprison interventions.[16]

The meta-analysis yields fairly large average effects of in-prison vocational and basic education programs (on the order of 9 percent reductions in criminal activity among the treated).[17] The authors also find an impact of roughly 7 percent of in-prison cognitive behavioral therapy. Such therapy focuses on the thoughts, assumptions, and beliefs of the criminally active, with the aim of identifying thought patterns leading to negative behaviors and imparting participants with the tools for correcting these thought processes (National

15. Heckman, Smith and Clements (1997) evaluate alternative methods for uncovering heterogeneity in the program effects of experimental interventions. In addition to using probability theory to bound the distribution of program effects (discussed as well in Heckman and Smith 1995), the authors present a model for incorporating information on the program participation decision with the aim of extrapolating the distribution of program effects in an environment when such impacts are likely to be heterogeneous. Djebbari and Smith (2008) apply these methods to a reevaluation of the Mexican conditional-cash-transfer program, Progressa, and find strong evidence of systematic heterogeneity.

16. The authors developed a five-point scale with higher values indicating a stronger methodological design. A score of five was assigned to randomized-control studies. Studies employing quasi-experimental research designs with good balance on covariates between the treatment and control samples that adjust for observable differences between treatment and comparison observations were assigned a score of four. The authors note that convincing instrumental variables studies, regression-discontinuity studies, as well as natural experiments fall into this grouping. Other rigorous quasi-experimental studies with less convincing identification strategies were assigned a value of three. A two was assigned when pretreatment values for covariates and outcomes are imbalance between the comparison and treatment groups, while a value of one was assigned to studies that did not employ a comparison group. The authors only include studies with a value of three or higher. In the meta-analysis, effect sizes for group-three studies are discounted by 50 percent, while effect sizes for group-four studies are discounted by 25 percent. Group-five effect sizes are not discounted.

17. The estimates of criminal activity vary considerably across the studies included in this meta-analysis although most are based on posttreatment arrests and convictions. The studies also vary according to the follow-up time periods of analysis. The authors include the estimated impact on the longest follow-up period reported in each study.

Research Council [NRC] 2008). Postrelease workforce development efforts are also found to reduce criminal offending by roughly 5 percent.

11.4.2   Results from Experimental Evaluations of Employment-Based Programs

Over the past three decades, there have been a handful of experimental evaluations of programs that are intended to reduce criminal activity and foster employment among either former inmates or high-risk groups. The meta-analysis by Visher, Winterfield, and Coggeshall (2005) identify all such experimental evaluations occurring in the United States through the late 1990s. Here I review the results of this research along with findings from a few recent experimental studies of prisoner reentry efforts.

There have been several evaluations aimed at assessing whether income support for released inmates reduces recidivism rates. The Living Insurance for Ex-Prisoners (LIFE) program was carried out in Baltimore between 1972 and 1974 and evaluated by Mallar and Thornton (1978) and discussed in detail in Rossi, Berk and Lenihan (1980). The target population was former inmates with a very high likelihood of future arrest for a property crime and no history of drug or alcohol dependence returning from prison to the Baltimore area. The program defined four treatment groups. The first group received a $60 check once a week for thirteen weeks along with job placement assistance. In theory, benefits were supposed to be reduced with increases in labor income at a benefit reduction rates less than one, but in practice all men received the full amount of their grant within thirteen weeks or shortly thereafter. Any unused allocation at the end of the thirteenth week could be collected within the period of a year postrelease. The second group received financial assistance but no job placement services. The third group received unlimited job placement services only. The final group provided the controls.

Among those receiving financial assistance, arrests for property crimes were 8.3 percentage points lower (significant at 5 percent) and the proportion not arrested over the subsequent year was 7.4 percentage points higher. There was no statistically significant effect of treatment on employment, where the presumption was that the program created very large negative incentives against working (see the discussion in chapter 2 of Rossi, Berk, and Lenihan 1980). There were also no measurable benefits from receiving job placement assistance.[18]

Based on these findings, the Temporary Aid Research Project (TARP) implemented an income-support program on a larger scale (Rossi, Berk, and Lenihan 1980). A key difference relative to the LIFE program, however,

---

18. In a linear probability model of posttreatment arrest, Mallar and Thorton (1978) estimate a marginal effect of job placement assistance of 0.053 with a standard error of 0.0418 in a model controlling for being assigned to receive financial assistance, a quadratic in age, having at least a high school degree, and a dummy indicating white.

was that the program was administered through the state agencies handling unemployment insurance claims. This was meant to mimic how such a program would actually operate if institutionalized by a specific state. In addition, treatment groups were defined to create variation in benefits length as well as benefit reduction rates, and the programs were implemented in different states (Georgia and Texas). The TARP program contained five randomized treatment groups. Three of the groups received financial assistance (one for twenty-six weeks with 100 percent benefit reduction rate, one for thirteen weeks with a 100 percent benefit reduction rate, and one for thirteen weeks with a 25 percent benefit reduction rate) with the provision that unused allotment at the end of the specified period could be used for a period of up to a year. A fourth group was offered employment services only. A fifth group was offered nothing but payment for the interviews. Finally, a sixth group was also identified that was not interviewed but for whom administrative records were analyzed.

The evaluators found no effect of the intervention on arrests, either overall or for specific crimes, in either state. However, there were substantial negative impacts of the program on employment. The authors speculate that the lack of an impact on arrests reflects offsetting impact on criminal activity of (a) the decline in employment (leading to more criminal activity) and (b) the transition aid leading to less criminal activity.

A number of studies have evaluated the impact of providing transitional jobs on the employment and criminal activity of high-risk populations. The National Supported Work (NSW) intervention, implemented during the 1970s, targeted four hard-to-employ groups: long-term welfare recipients, ex-offenders defined as those convicted and incarcerated for a crime in the last six months, drug-addicts defined as those currently enrolled in a drug treatment program, and high school dropouts. The original evaluation was carried out by the Manpower Demonstration Research Corporation (MDRC 1980). While the original evaluation distinguishes drug addicts from ex-offenders, it is likely the case that there was a fair degree of overlap among these groups. Ninety percent of the ex-addicts had prior arrests, with the average participants having served nontrivial amounts time. The selection criteria were chosen to ensure selection of the most disadvantaged in terms of labor market prospects. Regarding ex-offenders, the eligibility criteria were "age 18 or older; incarcerated within the last 6 months as the results of a conviction." For ex-addicts, the criteria were "age 18 or older; enrolled in a drug treatment program currently or within the preceding 6 months."

The program provided transitional jobs in work crews with "graduated stress" in terms of productivity and punctuality requirements as time on the program increased. Participants were time limited in terms of how long they could remain employed in the transitional job, with the limits varying across sites from twelve to eighteen months. The impacts differ substantially by participant type. The long-term Aid to Families with Dependent Children (AFDC) recipients experienced significant increases in employment after leaving their supported-work jobs. To be specific, by the last quarter of the follow-up period (twenty-five to twenty-seven months after enrollment), quarterly employment rates for AFDC treatment members exceeded that of the control group by 7.1 percentage points. By this point, none of the treatment group members were employed in a transitional supported-work job. They also experience significant increases in earnings and wages and significant decreases in welfare benefits receipt.

For former addicts, there was a delayed impact on posttransitional-jobs employment, with significant and substantial increases (on the order of 10 percentage points) in employment up to two years after leaving the program. In a series of comparisons of cumulative arrests and convictions post-random assignment, the researchers find significant impacts on the amount of criminal activity committed by former addicts, with much of the program impact appearing to coincide with being employed. Finally, there was very little evidence of any impact in any domain for the ex-offender group.

Uggen (2000) reanalyzes the data from the NSW demonstration with an explicit focus on heterogeneity in effect size by age. Unlike the initial evaluation, Uggen pools all respondents with a prior criminal history and analyzes the impact of being assigned to placement in a transitional job on the arrest hazard and the likelihood of earning illegal income. After stratifying the treatment groups into those twenty-six and under and those twenty-seven and over, Uggen finds no treatment effect for the younger group but quite large effects on arrests for the older group (on the order of 10 percentage points on the cumulative arrest probability by the end of three years).

A more recent effort to provide transitional employment to former inmates is the Center for Employment Opportunities (CEO) program based in New York City. Researchers at MDRC are in the process of conducting a multiyear evaluation of this program. The CEO program provides transitional employment to former inmates coupled with basic educational services (when needed) as well as other forms of social support. Participants work in crews and perform services for various public- and private-sector clients. Participation among those assigned to the treatment group is high (roughly 70 percent), and the typical participant remains in a transitional job for about eighteen weeks. Once a participant demonstrates stability and solid work skills, a CEO staff member facilitates the transition to a regular employer.

The evaluations of this program show large impacts on employment for the first three quarters post-random assignment (Bloom et al. 2007). These effects are due entirely to a high propensity to be employed in CEO-provided transitional jobs in the treatment group. By the fourth quarter following assignment, the difference in employment rates between the treatment and control groups disappears.

Regarding recidivism, the one-year evaluation found little impact for most participants but did find a substantial effect for participants receiving services within three months of release (Bloom et al. 2007). This pattern is consistent with the time-profile of the postrelease failure hazard. One aspect of the evaluation's design that bears mentioning is that program participants were drawn from individuals who had been referred to CEO by their parole officer. Many of these individuals arrived at CEO many months after being released from prison. It is a well-known fact that the return-to-custody hazard among released inmates spikes within a few months of release and declines quite sharply thereafter (NRC 2008). Thus, a program targeted at individuals who have survived the high hazard period may not yield as large an impact as an intervention targeted at those who have just been released.

The evaluation of second-year results yielded a more broad-based impact of the intervention on criminal activity. Redcross et al. (2009) find that in the second year after randomization, treatment group members were 7.7 percentage points less likely to be convicted of a crime (with most of the difference due to misdemeanor offenses) and 7 percent less likely to have experienced a postrelease incarceration in either prison or jail. The MDRC is currently evaluating similar transitional jobs programs at five other sites across the country.

A number of programs have been targeted at what one might consider high-risk individuals that may have already offended and done time or who have a high likelihood of offending. Some of these efforts were not specifically designed to reduce recidivism or the likelihood of participation in criminal activity yet treated many individuals who would be the target recipients of such efforts. For example, among the groups targeted by the national Job Training Partnership Act (JTPA) evaluation were out-of-school youth (Bloom et al. 1994).

The evaluation used a randomized-control design to evaluate the labor market impacts of the workforce development services offered under JTPA. The evaluation randomized eligible program applicants to either a treatment or control group at a nonrandom set of sixteen service delivery areas between 1987 and 1989. For all participants, the impact of treatment on earnings and employment were estimated for the two and a half years following randomization.[19] The study looked specifically at four target groups: adult men, adult women, and out-of-school youth of each gender. For out-of-school youth, the evaluation also assessed the impact of the program on self-reported arrest.

One useful aspect of this evaluation was the collection of data on the receipt of alternative services by control group members. Accounting for

19. The then General Accounting Office (GAO) produced a long-term follow-up study in 1996 that estimated program impacts on earnings and employment for five years posttreatment. Much of the positive effects on earnings and employment for adult men and women were found to disappear over this longer term period (see GAO 1996).

control group substitution toward other services as well as incomplete take-up among those assigned to treatment are taken into account allows estimation of the incremental services delivered as a result of assignment to the treatment group. Heckman et al. (2000) show that a fair proportion of the control group received workforce development service elsewhere, while nearly a third of the treatment group did not take-up. While, assignment to the treatment group did indeed significantly increase services delivered, the modest impact of the program on earnings and arrests should be considered against the modest incremental service delivery caused by the treatment.

The JTPA program involves what one might consider traditional workforce development programs: on-the-job training, job-search assistance, remedial classroom instruction, occupational training. The program significantly increased GED completion among high school dropouts (over 10 percentage point effects for adult high school dropouts). The program also had substantial effects on earnings for adult males and females (intent-to-treat effects of around 8 to 10 percent and treatment-on-the-treated effects on the order of 15 percent). There were no effects of the intervention on the earnings and employment of disadvantaged youth of either gender.

The analysis of arrest outcomes for youth was based on self-reports. Among those youth with prior arrests, there was no measurable impact of treatment on arrest. Among male youth who had never been arrested, there was a significant *increase* in arrests observed for treatment group members (on the order of 5 to 7 percentage points). The authors speculate that this might be the result of the fact that the JTPA program encouraged participants to be forthright about their involvement with the criminal justice system with employers.

The Job Corps provided a much more intensive intervention targeted at high-risk youth (evaluated by Schochet, Burghardt, and Glazerman 2001). The Job Corps program is targeted toward disadvantaged youth sixteen to twenty-four years of age. Most participants in the program reside at a Job Corps center (usually over 80 percent), with the average participant staying eight months. Treatment involves a heavy dose of academics, vocational training, and life skills courses. The evaluation randomized a subset of the 80,000 plus Job Corps applicants from 1994 to 1996 to either a control group (that was prohibited from enrolling in Job Corps for four years) or a treatment group that was offered a spot. Roughly 73 percent of the treatment took-up. A small portion (around 3 percent) of the control group crossed over (mostly three years postrandomization).

The program had substantial effects on educational attainment and vocational training. Treatment group members completely the equivalent of an additional year of schooling relative to control group members. Given the relationship between educational attainment and offending documented in Lochner and Moretti (2004), this particular aspect of the Job Corp program may explain the factors behind the observed treatment effect on offending.

The program also had sizable effects on employment (on the order of 5 percentage points) and earnings for the period starting roughly one year after randomization (most participants left the program within a year of starting). During the first four quarters after randomization, the arrest rate for the treatment group was roughly 1 percentage point lower relative to the control group (relative to control base of 3 to 5 percent). These arrest effects are highly significant. The treatment-on-the-treated estimates of the percent ever arrested or charged is 5.2 percentage points, with 4.2 percentage points occurring in the first year. These are significant at the 1 percent level. There was a 3 percentage point difference in the proportion convicted over the forty-eight postrandomization months and a 2 percentage point difference in the percent incarcerated. These effect sizes are relative to control baselines of 25.2 and 17.9 percent, respectively. Estimated impacts were substantially larger for men. The arrest treatment effect was 5 percentage points, the convicted treatment effect was 4 percentage points, while the incarcerated treatment effect was 3.1 percentage points, all significant at the 5 percent level. There were no significant effects for females or for male nonresidents.

It is noteworthy that in contrast to the JTPA evaluation, Job Corps delivered significant impacts on both employment as well as criminal offending for youth. The large impact on educational attainment may have been one important mediating factor. Clearly, the residential component of the program is likely to have been important as well as this aspect of the program likely removed youth from social networks that may have enhanced the likelihood of poor outcomes. Despite the high costs associated with this program, it is notable that cost-benefit analysis accompanying the official evaluation concludes that Job Corps passes the cost-benefit test. Most of the benefits occur in the form of the value of increased productivity as well as a reduction in service use among program participants (McConnell and Glazerman 2001).

The JOBSTART program is largely patterned after the Job Corps program (Cave et al. 1993), the key differences being that JOBSTART does not provide a stipend, and JOBSTART is a nonresidential program. The program targets seventeen- to twenty-one-year-old school dropouts and delivers academic services, occupational and vocational training, and job placement services. The randomized-control evaluation of this program was principally concerned with the domains of educational attainment and employment outcomes, though the report also includes information on welfare receipts, fertility, and criminal activity (based on whether one is ever arrested). There is no information on incarceration.

Similar to the results for Job Corps, the program had a large treatment effect on the likelihood of completing a GED or a high school diploma (on the order of 13 percentage points). Treatment group members experienced small declines in employment and earnings in the first postrandomization year (most likely due to the time demands of participation in the program) and slightly higher earnings and employment in all other years. With regard to arrests, the treatment had a fairly large impact on the likelihood of being arrested in the first year for male participants (over 6 percentage points) but no impact on the arrest likelihood at the end of the four-year evaluation.

To summarize the experimental research, there is some evidence that income support, transitional employment, and human capital investments in former and potential future inmates may reduce criminal behavior and recidivism. The results, however, are not entirely consistent across studies. Perhaps the weakest evidence is observed for income support. There is reason to believe that the small scale intervention under the LIFE program involved very intensive case work among program implementers on behalf of the formers inmates, while delivery of income support through the TARP program occurred at arm's length and involved much more rigorous enforcement of the benefit reductions with labor income. Any large-scale implementation of such assistance is perhaps more likely to take the form of the TARP evaluation than the LIFE program, calling into question this approach. Nonetheless, these are the only two experimental studies exploring the effects of income support. Such efforts combined with different sets of services or alternative rules regarding interactions with labor income may yield different outcomes.

Transitional employment appears to have particular promise. Moreover, several programs providing transitional employment are being evaluated with a randomized-control design at different locations across the country; thus, we are likely to learn much more about such interventions. Both the NSW and CEO evaluations find substantial evidence of heterogeneity in program effect, suggesting that perhaps the hardest to serve are the least likely to benefit. It is somewhat surprising that despite large impacts on employment in the first few quarters postassignment, there is little overall impact on measures of criminal offending in the CEO evaluation. While this may be due to the sampling frame used to generate experimental subjects, this basic pattern for year one is sobering.

Perhaps the brightest prospects are observed for at-risk youth. All of the programs reviewed (JTPA, Job Corps, JOBSTART) have substantial impacts on the educational attainment of participants, with Job Corps adding nearly a full year of instructional time. The more extensive measures of criminal behavior in Job Corps and JOBSTART both yielded evidence of substantial impacts of these programs on criminal participation.

11.5   Conclusion

Successfully connecting reentering prison inmates to suitable employment opportunities is a formidable task. Those who end up in U.S. prisons are perhaps among the lowest skilled adults in society and have a number of personal problems (health and behavioral) that render many of them difficult to employ. Employers exhibit a strong reluctance to hire such workers, are increasingly reviewing the official criminal backgrounds of applicants through formal record searches, and are often prohibited by law from hiring convicted felons.

To the extent that difficulty finding a job contributes to parole failure, effective reentry policy may result in substantial social benefits. I have shown that modest declines in parole failure rates can lead to notable declines in incarceration. Given the relatively high variable cost of incarcerating additional felons (as well as the capital costs associated with new prison construction that many states with overcrowded systems are currently facing) and the potential reduction in victimization costs associated with lower offending, the benefits of such interventions clearly extend beyond the benefits accrued by the former inmate himself. What we know about such efforts from experimental evaluations is rather porous and context specific. One does walk away with the impression that such interventions matter and do work, yet the interventions differ considerably across demonstrations (both in program design and implementation). Thus, it is difficult to draw general lessons that would be useful in designing larger-scale interventions intended to address the enormity of the current policy challenge.

Appendix

Table 11A.1   **Proportion of establishments legally prohibited from hiring a convicted felon into the last filled nonmanagerial, nonprofessional job by two-digit standard industrial classification codes**

Industry	Proportion prohibited	Standard error	N
General building contractors	0.148	0.095	15
Heavy construction contractors	0.000	0.000	4
Special trade contractors	0.190	0.073	30
Food and kindred products	0.028	0.040	18
Textile mill products	0.000	0.000	3
Apparel and related products	0.000	0.000	5
Lumber and wood products	0.000	0.000	7
Furniture and fixtures	0.000	0.000	6
Paper, allied products	0.382	0.217	6
Printing and publishing	0.032	0.051	13
Chemicals, allied products	0.174	0.114	12
Petroleum refining and related industries	0.416	0.285	4
Rubber and plastics	0.000	0.000	4
Leather and leather products	0.000		1
Stone, clay, and glass products	0.000	0.000	8
Primary metal industries	0.000	0.000	8

(continued)

Table 11A.1   (continued)

Industry	Proportion prohibited	Standard error	N
Fabricated metal products	0.034	0.061	10
Machinery except electrical	0.060	0.052	22
Electrical equipment	0.055	0.038	36
Transportation equipment	0.308	0.109	19
Instrument-related products	0.239	0.114	15
Miscellaneous manufacturing	0.123	0.134	7
Railroad transportation	0.000	0.000	3
Local passenger transportation	0.487	0.204	7
Trucking and warehousing	0.163	0.095	16
Transportation by air	0.295	0.456	2
Transportation services	0.067	0.251	2
Communication	0.365	0.139	13
Electric, gas, sanitary services	0.000	0.000	6
Wholesale trade	0.051	0.037	36
Wholesale trade nondurable goods	0.121	0.062	29
Building materials, hardware, and garden supply	0.154	0.147	7
General merchandise	0.137	0.069	26
Food stores	0.000	0.000	17
Auto dealers and service stations	0.087	0.075	15
Apparel accessories stores	0.000	0.000	8
Furniture and home furnishings	0.132	0.169	5
Eating and drinking places	0.084	0.034	67
Miscellaneous retail stores	0.147	0.091	16
Banking	0.353	0.123	16
Credit agencies, except banks	0.226	0.132	11
Securities, commodity brokers, services	0.595	0.174	9
Insurance carriers	0.645	0.144	12
Insurance agents, brokers, and services	0.214	0.130	11
Real estate	0.205	0.090	21
Holdings, real estate, and investment companies	0.000	0.000	2
Hotels, recreation lodging places	0.168	0.071	29
Personal services	0.303	0.188	7
Miscellaneous business services	0.207	0.046	77
Auto repair, services, and garages	0.039	0.052	15
Miscellaneous repair services	0.000	0.000	6
Motion pictures	0.069	0.090	9
Amusement recreation services	0.253	0.105	18
Health services	0.359	0.044	118
Legal services	0.124	0.147	6
Social services	0.895	0.065	23
Museums, botanical gardens, zoos, and gardens	0.285	0.226	5
Membership organizations	0.093	0.075	16
Engineering and management services	0.475	0.078	42

References

Aos, Steve, Marna G. Miller, and Elizabeth K. Drake. 2006. *Evidence-Based Public Policy Options to Reduce Future Prison Construction, Criminal Justice Costs, and Crime Rates.* Olympia, WA: Washington State Institute for Public Policy.

Autor, David H., and David Scarborough. 2008. "Does Job Testing Harm Minority Workers? Evidence from Retail Establishments." *Quarterly Journal of Economics* 123 (1): 219–77.

Bertrand, Marianne, and Sendhil Mullainathan. 2004. "Are Emily and Greg More Employable than Lakisha and Jamal?" *American Economic Review* 94 (4): 991–1013.

Black, Dan. 1995. "Discrimination in an Equilibrium Search Model." *Journal of Labor Economics* 13 (2): 309–33.

Bloom, Dan, Cindy Redcross, Janine Zweig, and Gilda Azurdia. 2007. "Transitional Jobs for Ex-Prisoners: Early Impacts from a Random Assignment Evaluation of the Center for Employment Opportunities Prisoner Reentry Program." MDRC Working Paper. New York: Manpower Demonstration Research Corporation.

Bloom, Howard S., Larry L. Orr, George Cave, Stephen H. Bell, Fred Doolittle, and Winston Lin. 1994. *The National JTPA Study, Overview: Impacts, Benefits, and Costs of Title II-A.* Bethesda, MD: Abt Associates.

Bushway, Shawn D. 2004. "Labor Market Effects of Permitting Employer Access to Criminal History Records." *Journal of Contemporary Criminal Justice* 20 (3): 276–91.

Bushway, Shawn D., and Gary Sweeten. 2007. "Abolish Lifetime Bans for Ex-Felons." *Criminology and Public Policy* 6 (4): 697–706.

Cave, George, Hans Bos, Fred Doolittle, and Cyril Toussaint. 1993. *JOBSTART: Final Report on a Program for School Dropouts.* New York: Manpower Demonstration Research Corporation.

Cook, Philip J. 1975. "The Correctional Carrot: Better Jobs for Parolees." *Policy Analysis* 1 (1): 11–54.

Djebbari, Habiba, and Jeffrey Smith. 2008. "Heterogeneous Impacts in PROGRESA." IZA Discussion Paper no. 3362. Bonn, Germany: Institute for the Study of Labor.

Drake, Elizabeth K., Steve Aos, and Marna G. Miller. 2009. "Evidence-Based Public Policy Options to Reduce Crime and Criminal Justice Costs: Implications in Washington State." *Victims and Offenders* 4 (2): 170–96.

Fix, Michael, George C. Galster, and Raymond J. Struyk. 1993. "An Overview of Auditing for Discrimination." In *Clear and Convincing Evidence: Measurement of Discrimination in America,* edited by Michael Fix and Raymund J Struyk, 1–68. Washington, DC: Urban Institute Press.

General Accounting Office (GAO). 1996. *Job Training Partnership ACT: Long-Term Earnings and Employment Outcomes.* CAO/HEHS-96-40. Washington, DC: General Accounting Office.

Grogger, Jeff. 1998. "Market Wages and Youth Crime." *Journal of Labor Economics* 16 (4): 756–91.

Heckman, James, Neil Hohmann, Jeffrey Smith, and Michael Khoo. 2000. "Substitution and Dropout Bias in Social Experiments: A Study of an Influential Social Experiment." *Quarterly Journal of Economics* 115 (2): 651–94.

Heckman, James, and Peter Siegelman. 1993. "The Urban Institute Audit Studies: Their Methods and Findings." In *Clear and Convincing Evidence: Measurement of Discrimination in America,* edited by Michael Fix and Raymund J Struyk, 187–258. Washington, DC: Urban Institute Press.

Heckman, James, and Jeffrey Smith. 1995. "Assessing the Case for Social Experiments." *Journal of Economic Perspectives* 9 (2): 85–110.

Heckman, James, Jeffrey Smith, and Nancy Clements. 1997. "Making the Most Out of Programme Evaluations and Social Experiments: Accounting for Heterogeneity in Programme Impacts." *Review of Economic Studies* 64 (4): 487–535.

Holzer, Harry J. 1996. *What Employers Want: Job Prospects for Less-Educated Workers.* New York: Russell Sage Foundation.

Holzer, Harry J., Steven Raphael, and Michael A. Stoll. 2006. "Perceived Criminality, Criminal Background Checks and the Racial Hiring Practices of Employers." *Journal of Law and Economics* 49 (2): 451–80.

————. 2007. "The Effect of an Applicant's Criminal History on Employer Hiring Decisions and Screening Practices: Evidence from Los Angeles." In *Barriers to Reentry? The Labor Market for Released Prisoners in Post-Industrial America,* edited by Shawn Bushway, Michael Stoll, and David Weiman, 117–49. New York: Russell Sage Foundation.

Johnson, Rucker, and Steven Raphael. 2008. "How Much Crime Reduction Does the Marginal Prisoner Buy?" Goldman School of Public Policy Working Paper. Berkeley, CA: University of California, Berkeley.

Juhn, Chinhui. 1992. "Decline of Male Labor Market Participation: The Role of Declining Market Opportunities." *Quarterly Journal of Economics* 107 (1): 79–121.

Lanning, Jonathan A. 2010. "Opportunities Denied, Wages Diminished: Using Search Theory to Translate Audit Pair Study Findings into Wage Differentials." Working Paper, Albion College.

Legal Action Center. 2004. *After Prison: Roadblocks to Reentry, a Report on State Legal Barriers Facing People with Criminal Records.* New York: Legal Action Center.

Lochner, Lance, and Enrico Moretti. 2004. "The Effect of Education on Criminal Activity: Evidence from Prison Inmates, Arrest, and Self-Reports." *American Economic Review* 94 (1): 155–89.

Mallar, Charles D., and Craig V. D. Thornton. 1978. "Transitional Aid for Released Prisoners: Evidence from the Life Experiment." *Journal of Human Resources* 13 (2): 208–36.

McConnell, Sheena, and Steven Glazerman. 2001. *National Job Corps Study: The Benefits and Costs of Job Corps.* Princeton, NJ: Mathematica Policy Research.

Manpower Demonstration Research Corporation (MDRC). 1980. *Summary Findings of the National Supported Work Demonstration.* Cambridge, MA: Ballinger.

National Research Council (NRC). 2008. *Parole Desistance from Crime and Community Integration.* Washington, DC: National Academies Press.

Pager, Devah. 2003. "The Mark of a Criminal Record." *American Journal of Sociology* 108 (5): 937–75.

Raphael, Steven. 2005. "The Socioeconomic Status of Black Males: The Increasing Importance of Incarceration." In *Poverty, the Distribution of Income, and Public Policy,* edited by Alan Auerbach, David Card, and John Quigley, 319–57. New York: Russell Sage Foundation.

Raphael, Steven, and Michael A. Stoll. 2009. "Why Are So Many Americans in Prison?" In *Do Prisons Make Us Safer? The Benefits and Costs of the Prison Boom,* edited by Steven Raphael and Michael Stoll, 27–71. New York: Russell Sage Foundation.

Redcross, Cindy, Dan Bloom, Gilda Azurdia, Janine Zweig, and Nancy Pindus. 2009. *Transitional Jobs for Ex-Prisoners: Implementation, Two-Year Impacts, and Costs of the Center for Employment Opportunities (CEO) Prisoner Reentry Program.* New York: Manpower Demonstration Research Corporation.

Rossi, Peter, Richard A. Berk, and Kenneth J. Lenihan. 1980. *Money, Work, and Crime: Experimental Evidence.* New York: Academic Press.

Sampson, Robert J., and John H. Laub. 2003. "Life-Course Desisters? Trajectories of Crime among Delinquent Boys Followed to Age 70*" *Criminology* 41 (3): 555–92.

Schochet, Peter Z., John Burghardt, and Steven Glazerman. 2001. *National Job Corps Study: The Impact of Job Corps on Participants' Employment and Related Outcomes.* Princeton, NJ: Mathematica Policy Research.

Turner, Margery Austin, Michael Fix, and Raymund J. Struyk. 1991. *Opportunities Denied, Opportunities Diminished.* Washington DC: Urban Institute Press.

Uggen, Christopher. 2000. "Work as a Turning Point in the Life Course of Criminals: A Duration Model of Age, Employment, and Recidivism." *American Sociological Review* 65 (4): 529–46.

Visher, Christy A., Laura Winterfield, and Mark B. Coggeshall. 2005. "Ex-Offender Employment Programs and Recidivism: A Meta-Analysis." *Journal of Experimental Criminology* 1 (3): 295–315.

Wilson, David B., Catherine A. Gallagher, and Doris L. MacKenzie. 2000. "A Meta-Analysis of Corrections-Based Education, Vocation, and Work Programs for Adult Offenders." *Journal of Research in Crime and Delinquency* 37 (4): 347–68.

Wolf-Harlow, Caroline. 2003. *Education and Correctional Populations.* NCJ 195670. Washington, DC: Bureau of Justice Statistics, Office of Justice Programs, U.S. Department of Justice.

Comment   Jeffrey Smith

Introduction

Raphael's chapter contains three separate but related analyses. The first part of the chapter presents descriptive evidence on the characteristics of current convicts and recently released ex-convicts. The second part considers the demand side of the labor market for ex-convicts. It presents descriptive univariate and multivariate evidence on the characteristics of firms that report a willingness to hire individuals with criminal records. It also provides evidence on which employers collect information on the criminal histories of applicants and how they do so and on the role of occupational prohibitions on the hiring of ex-felons in firms' decisions regarding the collection of criminal background information as well as other hiring outcomes. The final part of the chapter surveys the available evidence on the effectiveness of programs that aim to improve the labor market outcomes of ex-convicts. In what follows, I review each part of the paper in turn, highlighting key results as well as limitations or alternative interpretations of the findings. I conclude by offering some suggestions for additional research and, not unrelated, for

Jeffrey Smith is professor of economics at the University of Michigan, and a research associate of the National Bureau of Economic Research.

alternative policy responses to the very real employment problems faced by ex-convicts even in the best of labor markets.

The Supply Side: Characteristics of Criminals

Raphael does a very nice job of clearly presenting a great deal of information in a relatively small space. Two findings stood out to me as warranting some further discussion. First, the fraction of prisoners who report participating in education and training programs is surprisingly low. Prison represents an ideal time for investment in skills because opportunity costs cannot get much lower. To the extent that supply rather than demand drives this figure, it suggests a failure of policy; treating people after they get out of prison, at least with skill investment treatments, makes much less sense than treating them in prison, both due to the higher opportunity costs and because credit constraints will likely kick in for many ex-convicts once they end their spell of incarceration and reenter the outside world.

Second, I found the results on the age of first criminal activity stunning. These patterns have important implications for thinking about potential interventions to reduce both initial crime and criminal recidivism and also for thinking about the evaluation of interventions aimed at disadvantaged students in middle school and high school.

In terms of limitations, I missed two things in the data presented in this analysis. First, I would have liked to have seen a clear differentiation between regular high school completion and receipt of a general educational development (GED) diploma. We know from the literature, for example, Heckman, Humphries, and Mader (2011), that these represent quite different credentials. That a GED does not really equal a high school diploma does not mean that policy should not promote GED acquisition, but it does mean that we should collect data on the two credentials separately and discuss them separately rather than lumping them together. When the available data do not distinguish between the two (as is apparently the case here), that should affect our interpretation of the observed patterns.

Second, in addition to the conventional human capital measures such as years of schooling and work experience, it would be of great interest to know how current convicts and ex-convicts compare to the general population on measures of noncognitive skills and other noncognitive features, such as appearance, valued by employers in the labor market. I suspect that ex-convicts do worse than average on these characteristics even conditional on years of schooling and work experience. Of course, having measures of "ability" in the form of test scores would be nice too. More broadly, the more we know about the characteristics that ex-convicts bring to the labor market, the easier it is to sort out why they have trouble securing and persisting in employment and the easier it is to come up with potential interventions to improve outcomes. All these omissions reflect limitations of the underlying survey instruments rather than omissions from the analysis, but highlighting these limitations in the data provides encouragement for improved data collection in the future and also enriches our understanding of the variables presently available in the data.

The Demand Side: Who Will Hire Ex-Convicts?

I found the evidence on employer willingness to hire and on the empirical importance of prohibitions on hiring ex-felons in this section clear and convincing but have a couple of interpretational comments.

First, in regard to the labor market impact of having a criminal record, it pays to think about some simple models of the labor market. As shown in Becker's (1971) classic work on labor market discrimination, the existence of some employers who will hire individuals from a particular group matters more than the existence of some employers who will not. In the simplest labor market of neoclassical economics, as long as enough employers will hire individuals from a particular group (albeit possibly at a lower wage), the entire effect of being in the disliked group manifests in terms of reduced wages, rather than employment. In this simple model, the existence and extent of a wage penalty depends on the number of employers willing to hire the ex-convicts and on the wage discount required by the marginal firm that does so. The data reassure the reader that some employers express a willingness to hire ex-convicts but provide no information about the wage differential required, a wage differential that may manifest itself not necessarily in differences in money wages within firms (which are legally constrained) but in terms of ex-convicts sorting into low-wage firms within industries. More broadly, the high rate of nonemployment among ex-convicts presents a puzzle for this model, unless it is augmented with a minimum wage. If many ex-convicts lack the skills, hard and soft, required for the value of their marginal product to exceed the minimum wage (and other hiring and firing costs), then persistently high levels of nonemployment can arise. This line of reasoning suggests the value of examining policies such a subminimum wage for ex-convicts or wage subsidies above and beyond those implicit in the existing Earned Income Tax Credit (EITC).

Search models of the labor market of the sort developed by the winners of this year's Nobel Prize add frictions to the standard model and so allow for unemployment even in good times as workers spend time and effort looking for a job and firms spend time and effort on looking for workers. The audit pair study by Pager (2003) cited in the chapter implicitly operates within the search framework. It estimates differences in requests for interviews in response to applications between (ideally) otherwise identical individuals with and without a criminal record. Putting aside issues about what counterfactual to use for the time the ex-convict spends incarcerated, the key problem with this study is that it does not provide information on an outcome we really care about. If applications do not cost much in terms of time and money, even quite large differences in the probabilities of getting an interview, and of hiring conditional on getting an interview, are consistent with a fairly small difference in the amount of time employed. To take an extreme example, suppose that ex-convicts get an interview 10 percent of the time and that they get hired conditional on an interview only 10 percent of the time. If each application takes an hour inclusive of travel time and such and each interview takes two hours, then the expected cost of getting an offer for an ex-convict is 100 applications (= 100 hours) and 10 interviews (= 20 hours) or 120 hours or three weeks of full-time job search. This cost is much too small to generate the differences in employment rates observed in the data. Of course, to the extent ex-convicts can predict which employers prefer not to hire ex-convicts, they can do better by avoiding those employers. This all suggests either that the real issue relates to the value of what many ex-convicts can produce relative to the costs associated with hiring them or that we need a better understanding of what goes wrong in the job search process than is provided by the audit pair studies.

The multivariate analysis toward the end of this part of the chapter raises some issues both substantive and econometric. First, I am not quite sure what to make of the regressions that have an indicator for employer willingness to hire as the dependent variable and an indicator for performing a background check as an independent variable. Absent some evidence that employers make these choices in sequence, these strike me as two jointly determined outcomes, both of which should be on the left-hand side of different models. Second, I think Raphael makes too little of the fact that his estimates of the effects of employer background checks on the demographic characteristics of the most recent hire represent a Local Average Treatment Effect (LATE); see, for example, Imbens and Angrist (1994) or Angrist and Pischke (2009) for formal discussions of the economics and econometrics of LATEs. In the present context, what matters is that, as the name suggests, these estimates capture the change in outcomes for firms that do not undertake a background check if not required to do so but do undertake one when prohibited from hiring ex-felons for a given job. Put differently, it measures the effect of a background check for employers whose behavior regarding background checks is changed by the requirement not to hire ex-felons for a particular job. This parameter certainly has substantive and policy interest, but it may or may not provide much information about the effects of background checks on employment at firms that always do them, whether or not they are hiring for a position prohibited to ex-felons.

Policy Responses: Evaluating Programs Aimed at Increasing Ex-Convict Employment

Effectively summarizing the large literature on programs aimed at improving the employment chances of ex-convicts (with some additional programs aimed at at-risk youth added in) represents a daunting task. Raphael takes the not unreasonable approach of relying on published meta-analyses of the nonexperimental literature combined with more detailed examination of some particularly interesting experimental evaluations.

I have three sets of comments on this discussion. First, I want to throw a little bit of cold water on the implicit endorsement of the "hierarchy of evidence" notion that experiments always and everywhere dominate non-experimental evaluations. Yes, to be sure, nonexperimental studies often seem to follow Sturgeon's Law (named after science fiction writer Theodore Sturgeon) that "95 percent of everything is crap." But his law is too strong, even in a relatively weak evaluation literature like this one. My point is that random assignment evaluations solve one very important problem, namely that of nonrandom selection into treatment. As discussed in Heckman and Smith (1995, 2000) and Heckman et al. (2000), many other potential problems remain, including partial compliance with treatment assignment, selective attrition from the data, low power, and low treatment fidelity. In some experimental evaluations, one or more of these problems can do enough damage to make the experiment of lower value than a high quality nonexperimental evaluation. Thus, it pays to take studies on an individual basis, rather than judging them solely on the basis of the identification strategy they employ.

Second, I think Raphael overemphasizes the positive in reviewing the experimental evaluations. For example, the Job Corps, though notable among active labor market programs for youth in actually producing positive impacts not just on GED receipt but on actual labor market outcomes, looks less impressive in the long-term follow-up results presented in Schochet, Burghardt and McConnell (2006) and ultimately fails to pass a cost-benefit test for most participants. Along the same lines, the Job Training Partnership Act (JTPA) evaluation found no effect on youth, that is, not just no statistically significant effect but (essentially) zero or negative point estimates. More generally, increasing GED receipt without increasing earnings accomplishes little and should perhaps induce pessimism about the value of the GED rather than optimism about the value of the programs that promote them. We have much more to learn about how to make these programs effective.

Third, Raphael neglects the implications of his literature review for evaluation policy in this area. One implication of the evidence he reviews is that the social resources devoted to the evaluation of programs for ex-convicts (or future ex-convicts) might yield a larger amount of policy-relevant knowledge per dollar with a smaller number of high quality evaluations. I have in mind here the sort of research program undertaken in recent years by the Institute for Education Sciences (IES). They have lifted the quality of the entire literature that evaluates primary and secondary school programs by funding and monitoring a series of thoughtful, well-designed evaluations of important educational treatments. Almost all of these studies use either random assignment or regression discontinuity designs. They have, usually, sample sizes adequate to pick up effects of reasonable size. The Institute of Education Sciences (2008) describes the IES strategy in greater detail; it merits consideration and replication in this policy context.

Conclusions and Extensions

As documented here and in, for example, Western (2007), the United States has a large number of current and future ex-convicts. This chapter and the broader literature make clear that the characteristics of ex-convicts suggest troubles in the labor market. Adding to these supply-side concerns, many employers face legal prohibitions on hiring ex-felons for particular occupations or face uncertainty regarding legal liability for the workplace actions of any ex-convicts they hire. These realities of the supply and demand sides of the labor market, combined with the remarkably weak evaluation record of programs aimed at improving the employability of adult ex-convicts, suggest the value of exploring some alternative lines of research and policy experimentation beyond those already mentioned.

First, much work remains to imprint on the literatures on poverty, demography, education, and low-skill labor markets the importance of considering how crime and, most particularly, incarceration, matter. The large number of Americans currently enmeshed one way or another with the criminal justice system has important implications for analyses in all of these areas but too often remains in the background or even unmentioned in otherwise high quality studies.

Second, early interventions likely have a role to play, particularly given the early age at which children initiate criminal activity according to the evidence in the first part of the chapter. James Heckman has led a recent burst of research on such programs within economics. The evidence in Heckman et al.'s (2010) careful and systematic reconsideration of the data from the famous Perry Preschool intervention shows that reductions in adult crime represent an important component of its overall impact. While further research on the very long-term impacts of such programs would add great value, so would shorter-term evaluations of programs aimed at children around the age when they are first at risk of engaging in criminal activity. Also, adding criminal outcomes to evaluations of educational interventions more generally (particularly interventions targeted at schools in disadvantaged areas) would provide the foundation for a broader understanding of how aspects of schooling affect criminal behavior and also enhance the breadth and meaningfulness of the cost-benefit analyses of such interventions. Making criminal records routinely available for such purposes with appropriate privacy protections (in the same way that earnings records from the Unemployment Insurance system now get used routinely in evaluations of active labor market programs) would speed the progress of knowledge accumulation in this area.

Third, one way to reduce the number of ex-convicts is to reduce the number of convicts, and one way to reduce the number of convicts is to reduce the number of individuals who commit crimes. One neglected strategy for reducing the number of individuals who commit crimes consists of the simple and direct expedient of reducing the number of crimes. For example, legalizing activities such as prostitution and the use and sale of recreational drugs seems promising in this regard. The United States got along just fine for much of its history prior to banning these activities and, at least in the case of prostitution, the activity remains legal in most other developed countries. Indeed, one compelling and underappreciated justification for ending the so-called War on Drugs, or at least shutting down the marijuana front in that war, is that doing so would substantially reduce the number of young men from disadvantaged backgrounds caught up in the criminal justice system at a relatively early age.

Finally, research on trial programs that expunge the criminal records of individuals thought to have clearly demonstrated integration into the labor market and a cessation of criminal activity, at least for the purposes of reporting to employers and employer liability, would illuminate their potential to improve the labor market success of ex-convicts. Such programs could improve outcomes both directly by removing some ex-convicts from among those prohibited to work in certain occupations or who show up as ex-convicts in employer background checks, and indirectly, by adding an additional incentive for good behavior during the time period over which reintegration is measured. A related treatment worth evaluating would remove arrests (as opposed to convictions) from the criminal records made available to employers on the grounds that people should be treated as innocent until proven guilty in a court of law. It seems odd to this observer that any police officer who gets it into his or her head to arrest someone can thereby reduce their labor market prospects for life.

References

Angrist, Joshua, and Jörn-Steffen Pischke. 2009. *Mostly Harmless Econometrics: An Empiricist's Handbook.* Princeton, NJ: Princeton University Press.

Becker, Gary. 1971. *The Economics of Discrimination.* Chicago: University of Chicago Press.

Heckman, James, Neil Hohmann, Jeffrey Smith, with the assistance of Michael Khoo. 2000. "Substitution and Drop Out Bias in Social Experiments: A Study of an Influential Social Experiment." *Quarterly Journal of Economics* 115 (2): 651–94.

Heckman, James, John Eric Humphries, and Nicholas Mader. 2011. "The GED." In *Handbook of the Economics of Education.* Vol. 3, edited by Erik Hanushek, Stephen Machin, and Ludger Wössman, 423–84. Amsterdam: North-Holland.

Heckman, James, Seong Moon, Rodrigo Pinto, Peter Savelyev, and Adam Yavitz. 2010. "Analyzing Social Experiments as Implemented: A Reexamination of the Evidence from the HighScope Perry Preschool Program." *Quantitative Economics* 1 (1): 1–46.

Heckman, James, and Jeffrey Smith. 1995. "Assessing the Case for Social Experiments." *Journal of Economic Perspectives* 9 (2): 85–110.

———. 2000. "The Sensitivity of Experimental Impact Estimates: Evidence from the National JTPA Study." In *Youth Employment and Joblessness in Advanced Countries,* edited by David Blanchflower and Richard Freeman, 331–56. Chicago: University of Chicago Press.

Imbens, Guido, and Joshua Angrist. 1994. "Identification and Estimation of Local Average Treatment Effects." *Econometrica* 62 (4): 467–76.

Institute of Education Sciences. 2008. *Rigor and Relevance Redux: Director's Biennial Report to Congress.* IES 2009-6010. Washington, DC: U.S. Department of Education.

Pager, Devah. 2003. "The Mark of a Criminal Record." *American Journal of Sociology* 108 (5): 937–75.

Schochet, Peter, John Burghardt, and Sheena McConnell. 2006. *National Job Corps Study and Longer-Term Follow-Up Study: Impact and Benefit-Cost Findings Using Survey and Summary Earnings Records Data, Final Report.* Princeton, NJ: Mathematica Policy Research.

Western, Bruce. 2007. *Punishment and Inequality in America.* New York: Russell Sage Foundation.

Crime and the Family
Lessons from
Teenage Childbearing

Seth G. Sanders

12.1 Introduction

In an influential summary paper, Loeber and Stouthamer-Loeber (1986) conduct a meta-analysis on the literature on family factors and their correlation with conduct problems and delinquency. After careful review of both longitudinal studies and concurrent studies that compare delinquents with nondelinquents, they conclude that lack of parental supervision, parental rejection, and parent-child involvement are among the most powerful predictors of juvenile conduct problems and delinquency. Contained within this review there is an important and overlooked finding—the effect of these factors seems to be about the same for boys and girls. That this finding has gotten considerably less attention than the main finding of the role of family factors on delinquency most likely stems from a simple fact—crime is mostly a male activity.

Teen childbearing is, of course, an entirely female activity. Like crime in boys, teenage childbearing is consistently correlated positively with family background factors that measure disadvantage. These include being from a single-parent family, being on Aid to Families with Dependent Children/ Temporary Assistance for Needy Families (AFDC/TANF) as a young adolescent, and having parents with lower education. It is hard to identify an aspect of family disadvantage that is not correlated the same way for crime in boys and teenage childbearing in girls. The central argument of the chapter is that much is to be gained by considering teenage childbearing for girls and crime for boys as two variants of antisocial behavior, perhaps even stemming from the same developmental process. We argue that the same developmental

Seth G. Sanders is professor of economics and public policy at Duke University, and director of the Duke Population Research Institute.

process that led boys to grow up willing to violate the social norms necessary to commit crime led girls to violate the social norms in their own domain.

There are both empirical and theoretical reasons to believe this view. Figure 12.1 presents a five-year moving average of the annual percentage change in teenage childbearing. We begin the time series in 1975 because, while teenage childbearing was substantially higher in the 1950s and 1960s, it was largely within marriage. Theoretically, it is teenage childbearing outside of marriage that does not accord with social norms. Figure 12.1 also presents a five-year moving average of the annual percentage change in violent crime and property crime. What is clear from figure 12.1 is that these two patterns are remarkably coincident. All three series fall through the 1970s reaching a trough in 1983, rise steeply between 1983 and 1988, and then fall until 1998 and rise again thereafter.

Theories in developmental psychology link the "production of children" to the development of criminal behavior and teenage childbearing. These theories were developed to explain regularities between early childhood conditions, childhood aggression, conduct disorder, juvenile delinquency, and, finally, criminal behavior in adolescence and beyond. While there are

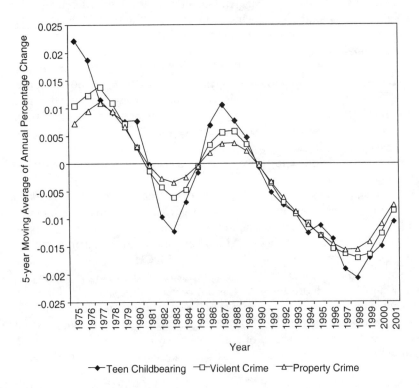

Fig. 12.1   Teen childbearing and crime

many theories that make a link between biology, childhood conditions, and personality outcomes, Moffitt (1993) lays out an elegant one that has had a major impact on psychology and criminology. Moffitt classifies individuals into two groups. These groups differ in the continuity of antisocial behavior across age and in their responsiveness to life events in adolescence. Life-course-persistent (LCP) individuals display antisocial behavior at a young age, and antisocial behavior remains a stable personality trait over the life course and over all kinds of conditions and situations. According to Moffitt, the source of this personality type may originate as biological; then in childhood, it is enforced or dampened by interactions between the parents and the child. Adolescence-limited (AL) individuals are involved in crime only through their adolescent years and display low levels of antisocial behavior both before and after adolescence. Moffitt speculates that in modern society, where adult responsibilities begin well after physical maturation, adolescents display this form of antisocial behavior as rebellion. During adolescence, the two groups are indistinguishable, both displaying serious delinquency. But ALs have well-developed empathy, are generally of higher intelligent quotient (IQ), and are able to weigh the costs and benefits of criminal activity, especially after adolescence.

Another underappreciated advantage of the developmental perspective, and the one emphasized here, is that by concentrating on the origins of antisocial behavior in general rather than crime specifically it is a theory that applies equally to males as it does to females. According to Moffitt (1993), while adolescent antisocial behavior may express itself differently in teenage boys and girls, the basic taxonomy and the origins of groups remains the same. This is different than other gendered theories, especially in sociology, that, for example, emphasize the absence of a male role model affecting boys more than girls (Anderson 2000; Parker and Reckdenwald 2008).

A reasonable question is why might policymakers care about this developmental theory and about the theory being applicable to both boys and girls? Most of the policy manipulations in this volume attempt to change incentives or opportunities to commit crime in order to limit it. Policies such as increased policing or imprisonment work by trying to influence the behavior of crime-prone individuals. Policies explored here, such as supporting good parenting practices, operate by trying to change the fraction of the population that will become crime-prone. The ultimate policy question is, could shifting dollars from policing and imprisonment toward family support, especially supporting parenting aimed at building self-regulation in children, be effective in lowering crime? While we do not answer this important question here, we do address its plausibility. We also suggest that it is impossible to answer the cost-effectiveness of such a shift without taking into account the possible efficacy of lowering teen childbearing and its associated costs through the same shift in resources.

Section 12.2 of the chapter discusses in more detail how family structure may affect antisocial behavior in boys and girls. This section argues that that by thinking about teenage childbearing and crime as two versions of antisocial behavior, there is a clear intergenerational link—mothers displaying the female version of antisocial behavior (teenage childbearing) would have boys that display the male version (crime). We review the literature on the link between teenage childbearing and crime and conclude that it is among the most robust findings on family structure and crime. In section 12.3 we review the empirical evidence in economics of the link between two family policies and the rise of crime in the late 1980s and then its subsequent decline—abortion laws and divorce laws—and touch on the role of changing welfare policy. We conclude that the evidence here is fragile, and the fragility stems from extremely limited time series and spatial variation in policy. Section 12.4 then takes a brief look at randomized controlled trials (RCTs) that try to manipulate directly aspects of parent-child interactions. As a whole, the RCTs that intervene to provide support in childrearing seem positive, but the impacts on crime and teenage childbearing remain inconclusive. Section 12.5 concludes.

12.2   Teen Childbearing and Crime

We have argued that teenage childbearing and crime stem from the same source, family upbringing that increases the propensity to develop antisocial behavior. The most extreme forms of bad parenting are neglect and abuse, which is consistently shown to increase the rate of externalizing behavior when children enter their adolescent years. One recent study by Jonson-Reid et al. (2010) used official report data on child maltreatment from the Missouri Division of Social Services (DSS) with behavioral data from 4,432 epidemiologically ascertained Missouri twins from the Missouri Twin Registry (MOTWIN). The rates of childhood abuse for a child was examined when his or her cotwin was in one of four groups: monozygotic (MZ) with the cotwin displaying externalizing behavior, dizygotic (DZ) with the cotwin affected, DZ with the cotwin unaffected, and MZ with the cotwin unaffected. Given the assumption of equal environment, the difference in the rate of externalizing behavior between MZ and DZ twin outcomes for a given cotwin status can be interpreted unequivocally as effects of gradations in inherited liability. The analysis showed strong effects of child maltreatment on externalizing behavior; it also showed that the effects were strongest when a MZ cotwin displayed externalizing behavior. This suggests that there is an additional role for inherited factors but does not mitigate the large role of childhood maltreatment.

There is now ample evidence that young mothers are much more likely to be reported for physical and sexual child abuse or child neglect. Lee and George (1999) examine child maltreatment among the 1982 to 1988 birth cohorts in Illinois. They use administrative data for the entire population of abuse and neglect cases and match this to birth certificate data so that the incidence rate of child maltreatment can be estimated and correlated with risk factors. Even after controlling for other sociodemographic factors, maternal age and poverty were each strong predictors of a substantiated report of all types of child maltreatment. The results indicate that the two factors combined compound the risk of being a victim of substantiated child maltreatment.

How child maltreatment is linked to antisocial behavior in adolescents is not entirely clear, but one theory revolves around the known link between the neurotransmitter serotonin and impulsive and aggressive behavior. Both the temporal lobes and the prefrontal cortex help regulate mood and behavior. One theory is that impulsive or poorly controlled behavior stems from a functional abnormality in serotonin levels or in these brain regions. Much of the work on gene-environment interactions revolves around genes that regulate neurotransmitters, especially serotonin and dopamine.

Given the close link between antisocial behavior in adolescents and criminal behavior in adults, it is perhaps not surprising that one factor that has been found to be robust in both the economics and psychology literature is the link between the age of a mother when she first gave birth and the criminal propensity of all of her children. This literature draws an interesting distinction between the age of the mother when the study child was born and her age when she first gave birth. Two excellent studies, one by Nagin, Pogarsky, and Farrington (1997) and another by Grogger (1997) find similar results using data from different sources. Nagin, Pogarsky, and Farrington (1997) use data from the Cambridge Study in Delinquent Development, a prospective longitudinal study of 411 males from working class London born in 1952 or 1953. Grogger uses data from the National Longitudinal Survey of Youth, 1979 (NLSY79), a prospective longitudinal nationally representative sample of more than 6,000 men in the United States born in 1958 to 1965. Despite differences in the focus, country, and time period, both studies find strong evidence that the age of a woman when she first gives birth is strongly negatively correlated with criminality of all of her children.

One difference between the two studies is whether there is any role for the age of the mother at the study child's birth; Nagin, Pogarsky, and Farrington (1997) find no role at all; Grogger (1997) presents mixed results. When a categorical variable reflecting a study child's mother being less than eighteen when the study child was born is entered into the regression model, this variable is uncorrelated with the study child's criminal outcome. However, when the age of the mother at the study child's birth is entered linearly and regressed against the study child's criminal outcome, there does appear to be evidence that being born when your mother is older reduces criminal propensity. Much of the variation that identifies the linear effect of the age of the mother at the study child's birth comes from comparing outcomes of women having children in their early twenties versus later twenties because most childbearing in the sample occurs when women are in their twenties. Grogger uses this linear effect to predict the effects of delaying teenage child-bearing from age sixteen to older adult ages, but it is clear that this prediction relies on a strong functional form assumption.

One enormous advantage of Nagin, Pogarsky, and Farrington (1997) is the rich data that allow them to begin studying the *mechanism* behind the correlation between age of a child's mother when the child is born and criminality. They lay out three potential mechanisms: (a) life course-immaturity; (b) persistent poor parenting/poor parental role models; and (c) diminished resources. The life course-immaturity mechanism is that teenagers lack the development and maturity to raise a child properly. One version of the persistent poor parenting mechanism is that women become teenage mothers because they lack self-control, are impulsive, self-centered, quick-tempered, inconsistent, and avoid difficult tasks with delayed benefits. These same factors make them poor parents and lead to the intergenerational transmission of antisocial behavior (see, for example, Gottfredson and Hirschi 1990). The diminished resources mechanism focuses on the classic mechanism emphasized in sociology between impoverishment and antisocial behavior.

Nagin, Pogarsky, and Farrington (1997) find bivariate evidence that both being born to a mother whose first child was born when she was a teenager and being born to a young mother per se increases criminality; however, once they control for family size, only the former effect remains. Having more children clearly means resources are spread across more family members, and this they take as evidence against mechanism (a) because there is no direct effect mother's age at the study child's birth and for mechanism (b) because larger family size entirely explains the direct effect of a mother's age at the study child's birth. In order to explain the effect of being born to a mother whose first child was born when she was a teenager, Nagin, Pogarsky, and Farrington use the extremely detailed data that document persistent poor parenting and other measures of diminished resources. Once controlling for these factors, the mother's age at her first child's birth also no longer affects the criminal outcomes of her children. Besides family size, which remains strongly significant, the most significant factors that mediate the effect of mother's age at first birth on her children's criminality are the child's father's criminality and whether the father separated from the mother by age ten. Nagin, Pogarsky, and Farrington conclude then that it is most likely a combination of persistent poor parenting and diminished resources that explains the link between teenage childbearing and the criminal outcomes of those children.

One issue worth discussing is how to interpret the strong role that family size plays on explaining all of the effect of being born to a teenage mother and half of the effect of being born to a mother whose first birth was as a teen. Nagin, Pogarsky, and Farrington (1997) prefer the interpretation of larger families being more resource constrained, which is clearly true. But from a host of work, we believe that the timing of fertility is closely linked to a number of person-specific factors. Moreover it is likely that teen mothers that end up having very large families are different in these factors from teen mothers who are able to better space the interval between children and, perhaps, even to have the next child within marriage. This raises the possibility that "family size" might also be picking up the kinds of unobserved factors described by Gottfredson and Hirschi (1990) that make teen mothers poor parents. While not interpreted in this way, Nagin, Pogarsky, and Farrington present evidence that family size is not likely to be just reflecting "diminished resources." If a teenage mother with a child has a second child, her family size goes from two people to three people. If we put aside for a moment any correlation between family size and economic resources, resources per person would be reduced by 33 percent by this one-child increase. If a teenage mother with four children has a fifth child, her family size goes from five people to six people. Resources per person are reduced by 17 percent. If increased family size was only affecting "diminished resources," then we would expect the criminality of children to rise much more when a mother with one child had an additional child than when a mother with four children had an additional child. In fact, among teenage mothers, criminality of children is the same when a woman has one or two children, but the criminality of children from families with five children is 50 percent higher than families with four children. One interpretation for this pattern is that teenage mothers who have no more children or one more child are both displaying a large degree of "self-control." But very large family sizes might also be correlated with very low levels of self-control.[1]

Pogarsky, Lizotte, and Thornberry (2003) contribute additional evidence using the same basic strategy of Nagin, Pogarsky, and Farrington (1997) but use contemporary data from the United States—the Rochester Youth Development Study (RYDS). The RYDS sampled 1,000 seventh-grade and eighth-grade students enrolled in public school in Rochester, New York in the 1987 to 1988 school year. Students and their parents were reinterviewed semiannually from 1988 to 1992 and annually from 1994 to 1997. In 1997, the average age of the respondent was twenty-two. Like Nagin, Pogarsky, and Farrington, Pogarsky, Lizotte, and Thornberry find no role for the age of the mother at the study child's birth, and they also find a strong role for the age of the child's mother at her first birth. Unfortunately, because the RYDS does not include completed family size, which was found to play a major mediating role in Nagin, Pogarsky, and Farrington, Pogarsky, Lizotte, and Thornberry cannot control for it. Pogarsky, Lizotte, and Thornberry do find that one variable does mediate the effect of being born

1. Another plausible interpretation is that women's total resources might fall with the number of children. If so, women with five or more children may be especially poor, lending credence to the "diminished resource" interpretation.

to a mom whose first birth was as a teen—the number of changes in family structure during the first two and a half years of the survey. Because children almost always live with their biological mothers, this variable measures the short-term changes in the mother's relationships with the child's father, child's stepfather, and mother's boyfriends. While Pogarsky, Lizotte, and Thornberry find that changing family structure mediates the effect of being born to a mom whose first birth was as a teen, the effect remains strong and significant even after controlling for measures of parenting and diminished resources.

In summary, there is strong evidence of a link between age at a mother's first birth and criminality of sons; there is weaker evidence of link between a mother's age at the study child's birth and criminality of her sons. Nagin, Pogarsky, and Farrington (1997) suggest that early childbearing is correlated with poor parenting and role modeling and with reduced access to resources, and these are the principal mechanisms through which the association between early childbearing and criminality of sons operates. If one believes that a series of short-term relationships could detract from parenting, then the poor parent/role model mechanism is also suggested by Pogarsky, Lizotte, and Thornberry (2003). Confirmation of reduced access to resources is not as consistently confirmed as it plays a limited role in Pogarsky, Lizotte, and Thornberry (2003) and no role in the studies that model current criminality against state welfare benefits when the young adult was a child.

12.3   Evidence on Family Policy and Crime

While figure 12.1 presents the strong comovement of teenage childbearing and crime, it is not clear what might have changed in families or what would have caused such a change. A worsening situation for children with regard to their upbringing in the early to mid-1970s would twenty years later lead to increased antisocial behavior. During this time period, there were at least three large social changes affecting the family: changes in abortion laws, divorce laws, and the size of the welfare system.

In January 1973, *Roe v. Wade* established that the right to privacy allowed women to seek abortions up until the point when the fetus became viable, which the court defined as twenty-four weeks. In the companion case, *Doe v. Boulton,* it also allowed abortion at later gestational ages when needed to protect a women's health. These decisions affected abortion laws in forty-five states. California, New York, Washington, Hawaii, and Alaska had liberalized abortion in 1970.

There is considerably more variation in divorce laws across states than abortion laws. There are many state laws governing various aspects of divorce, including whether one party can unilaterally seek it, the needed length of time separated before seeking divorce, laws governing division of property, and whether fault is used as a criterion for the division of property.

The right to seek a divorce unilaterally has been the focus of much of the literature on divorce and its effects. The early to mid-1970s was a time of enormous change in divorce laws, just as it was for abortion. Between 1970 and 1975, twenty-eight states moved from divorce requiring mutual consent to divorce being available unilaterally. California, Washington, and Hawaii all adopted unilateral divorce during this period; Alaska has had the longest history of unilateral divorce (1935), and New York has still not adopted unilateral divorce.

Finally, beginning in the late 1960s, there was a considerable expansion in cash and in-kind transfers to poor families. Prior to the Food Stamp Act of 1964, transfers to the poor through federal programs was largely limited to cash transfers from the AFDC program. Beginning in the late 1960s, there was a great expansion of both the food stamp program and Medicaid, the primary program that provides medical care to poor people under age sixty-five. The Food Stamp program expanded by about 1 million people per year from 1965 to 1970, reaching 6 million recipients in May of 1970. Then by February 1971, the program reached 10 million recipients, and by October 1975 reached 15 million recipients. Geographic expansion accounts for a large part of the growth. Similarly, Medicaid was established in 1965 through title XIX of the Social Security Act and expanded geographically through 1982. With health care costs rising faster than other prices, Medicare comprises a rising fraction of transfers to poor families.

Figure 12.2 graphs the monthly welfare transfer to a family of four in New York. Figure 12.2 graphs both the dollar value of AFDC benefit (in US$1982) and an estimate of the total dollar value of transfers that include AFDC, food stamps, and the value of Medicaid. The early 1970s saw an expansion in the real value of cash transfers. But the big expansion in welfare benefits came from benefits from the newer food stamp and Medicare program. Support to poor families expanded precipitously between the late 1960s and mid-1970s and have been in a long-term decline since. Policy changes in the Reagan administration (Omnibus Budget Reconciliation Act [OBRA]) account for the first steep fall in welfare benefits; an even more important policy change during the Clinton administration (Personal Responsibility and Work Opportunity Reconciliation Act [PRWORA]) fundamentally changed the cash transfer system instituting work requirements and, importantly, time limits on the receipt of benefits (not pictured).

All of these policy changes may have affected parent-child interactions. Abortion gave women greater choice on the timing of birth. This may have caused a change in the composition of births, with women not in a position to raise children terminating their pregnancies. It also may have reduced the number of unwanted births in other ways. With the expansion of unilateral divorce, there was rapid rise in the number of divorces and the number of children being raised without two parents in their home. And the rapid rise in welfare benefits, while potentially mitigating poverty for children,

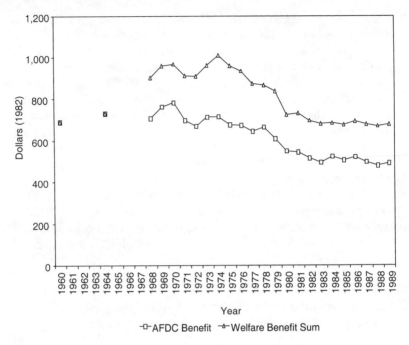

Fig. 12.2   Monthly welfare benefits for family of four, New York

often occurred in a context of these benefits being directed to unmarried mothers. As emphasized by Becker (2000), it also may have instituted a devaluation of work and a rise in the "welfare culture."

While all of these factors may be potential explanations for the coincident rise in teen childbearing and crime, what is also clear is that sorting across these will be difficult. The early to mid-1970s was a time of great change in family policy, and these policies tended to move together both over time and within states. We review the following literature on the link between abortion policy and crime and divorce policy and crime. We note here that no work to date attempts to simultaneously distinguish the effect of these multiple policy changes; it is an empirical issue whether there is enough independent variation to do so.

12.3.1   Abortion Law Changes and Crime

In an influential paper, Donohue and Levitt (2001) investigate the effects of abortion liberalization on crime. They offer evidence that legalized abortion has contributed significantly to crime reductions in the 1990s. The evidence that is most compellingly exogenous is that crime rates began to fall roughly eighteen years after abortion legalization. The very states that allowed abortion in 1970 experienced declines earlier than the rest of the nation. They also offer evidence that states with high abortion rates in the

1970s and 1980s experienced greater crime reductions in the 1990s. Their controversial claim is that legalized abortion accounted for as much as 50 percent of the drop in crime over the 1990s.

Donohue and Levitt (2001) have been criticized on a number of grounds, and a full critique is beyond the scope of this chapter (see Joyce 2004; Foote and Goetz 2005; Ananat et al. 2009; and Joyce 2009). The one critique relevant here raised both by Joyce (2004) and Foote and Goetz (2005) is that results are substantially weaker if we adopt the practice of clustering residuals at the state level (rather than the state-by-year-of-birth level as in Donohue and Levitt's original paper). The difference is important if, for example, there is a correlation between the error for, say, seventeen-year-olds in one year and other age groups (besides eighteen-year-olds) in the following year within a state.[2] The essential issue is that because only five states liberalized abortion prior to 1973, at its core, evidence revolves around patterns of crime in these five states relative to other states. No matter how many people are observed across states, it may be that most of the information is contained in the average crime level in these five states versus the other forty-five states.[3] The lack of power for detecting effects is endemic to the empirical design because there is very little independent variation in the policy of interest. That Donohue and Levitt (2001) are able to make progress at all is because their measure of historic abortion rates combines whether abortion was legal in a state when a young adult was in utero with the abortion level in that state in that year. This part of the variation is more easily criticized because states vary a good deal in the level of abortion even after legalization in predictable ways (for example, abortion rates per capita are low in Utah and high in California, New York, and Washington, DC). Adding fixed effects to the model takes out fixed state-level characteristics, which is helpful but does not account for changes over time such as the composition of the population. However, it is notable that a recent paper by Donohue, Grogger, and Levitt (2009) finds that historic abortion rates are negatively correlated with contemporaneous teen childbearing rates.

Criminologists and increasingly some economists dismiss the Donohue and Levitt (2001) results because simple plots of age-specific crime rates are inconsistent with a large cohort effect following the legalization of abortion. Because Donohue and Levitt's analysis does not use age-specific crime rates, this time series pattern was not assessed in their work. In states affected by *Roe v. Wade*, it should be that crime rates for sixteen-year-olds should peak

2. This point became much more appreciated in the empirical microeconomics literature after Bertrand, Duflo, and Mullainathan (2004) showed its numerical importance in a number of applications.

3. This statement is more precisely true the more correlated are observations within states. It is somewhat unclear in Donohue and Levitt (2001) exactly what variation is empirically important, variation in effective abortion rates driven by the adoption of abortion reforms or the growth in the number of abortions within a state after reforms.

in 1989, sixteen years after the 1973 legislation; for seventeen-year-olds, it should peak in 1990; for eighteen-year-olds in 1991, and so on. Similarly for the five states that liberalized in 1970, the peak for sixteen-year-olds should occur in 1986; for seventeen-year-olds in 1987, and so on. Joyce (2009) displays these simple plots, and there is no evidence of this pattern. For the states that liberalized in 1970, the peak for all ages is between sixteen and twenty in 1992, suggesting no presence of a cohort pattern. Donohue and Levitt criticize this evidence as they believe that the crack epidemic clouds the cohort effect they uncover. But Joyce (2009) argues that the same cohort argument should hold at older ages if Donohue and Levitt are correct and the crack epidemic largely did not affect older men and women. If Donohue and Levitt are right, twenty-seven-year-olds in the early liberalizing states should show peak crime rates in 1997, twenty-eight-year-olds in 1998, and so on. Time series plots show no discontinuity at any age between twenty-seven and thirty in either *Roe v. Wade* states or early liberalizing states.

The bottom line is that it is asking a great deal of aggregate data to reveal a pattern where cause and effect are separated by sixteen or more years, especially when the main variable of interest has limited temporal variation across states. It is little wonder that the relationship between abortion and crime remains controversial. Having said this, the link between the "wantedness" of children or how parents treat children and criminality is entirely justified on theoretical grounds. For this reason, it may be fruitful to examine other aspects that affect how children were raised that display more variation across time and space.

12.3.2   Divorce Law Changes and Crime

Divorce laws display substantially more variation across time and states. Unilateral divorce states allow either the husband or wife to sue for divorce without the consent of the other party. Friedberg (1998) classifies states into unilateral versus mutual consent states. Unlike legal abortion, which became the law in all states in 1973, there are still five states where divorce is by mutual consent; in addition, while a great number of states changed from mutual consent to unilateral divorce between 1968 and 1973, nine states adopted unilateral divorce prior to 1968, and ten states adopted unilateral divorce after 1973. This gives considerably more variation over time in when state policy may have affected families relative to abortion policy.[4]

Many studies have established bivariate correlation between being raised in a single-parent home and increased risk of involvement in crime as boys become young adults (Rebellon [2002] among others). Similarly, the bivariate relationship between being raised in a single-parent home and increased

---

4. However, in both cases, no state has reverted back to its original policy of mutual consent after adopting unilateral divorce. In this sense, the experimental design is similar to abortion laws in that we have not had the opportunity of observing the effects of removing the policy as would be done in a "cross-over" design.

risk of teenage childbearing in girls is also well established (Manlove [1997], among others). In many of these studies, this relationship holds after controlling for a number of observed factors. What is more controversial is whether single parenthood per se is responsible for these outcomes or if other omitted factors contribute to both single parenthood and antisocial behavior.

Changes in divorce laws possibly could help us answer this question as it is now generally agreed that these changes in divorce laws did, in fact, lead to a short-term increase in divorce (Wolfers 2006). Caceres-Delpiano and Giolito (2011) use these changes in divorce laws to investigate the effects of family structure on crime. Specifically, they investigate whether it is true that there is consistently a rise in crime thirteen to sixteen years following the liberalization of divorce laws. They find an impact of around a 15 percent increase in the murder rate and the rate of aggravated assault thirteen to sixteen years after unilateral divorce laws were passed. Two other patterns are notable. First, there is little evidence that divorce laws affect crime in the first ten years after the laws are enacted; second, in companion work, they find that the probability of living in an institution increase 35 percent fifteen years or more after the divorce reform was passed (Caceres-Delpiano and Giolito 2011). This paper also established that the reform decreased family income and increased the fraction of mothers below the poverty line. For children, they find that just after the reform, the probability that a child goes to a private school decreased and the likelihood that a child was held back in school increased, and Gruber (2001) confirms that their completed level of schooling is reduced.[5]

Finally, changing resources available through the welfare system might affect the rate of crime and teen childbearing when children become young adults. Lack of financial resources available to young children have been implicated in many studies as a source leading to antisocial development. Importantly, there is a great deal of both time series and spatial variation in AFDC payments even prior to the 1996 welfare reform act PRWORA. Both Donohue and Levitt (2001) and Caceres-Delpiano and Giolito include measures of historic resources available through the AFDC system. Donohue and Levitt and Caceres-Delpiano and Giolito (2011) find that these are largely uncorrelated with the rate of crime eighteen years later.[6] This lack

5. A second indication that the lack of variation in abortion laws limits their usefulness in understanding crime patterns is that any negative correlation between abortion laws and crime rates are eliminated when divorce laws are also included in the analysis.

6. Donohue and Levitt (2001) find that the state AFDC maximum payment fifteen years prior to crime in the current year is uncorrelated with any crime category. Caceres-Delpiano and Giolito (2011) estimate the effect of being in a state that historically had an Assistance to Families with Dependent Children-Unemployment Parent (AFDC-UP) program (results not reported in the paper but reported in personal communication, December 25, 2009). AFDC UP states had considerably higher welfare benefit levels. For example, in 1975, non-AFDC-UP states had an average value of welfare benefits (Medicaid, AFDC, and food stamps) of $515

of correlation between state historic AFDC payments and crime is itself interesting; many studies suggest that material deprivation of individuals as children raise the rate of physical aggression in children and crime in young adults. But parental income involves parental choice (unlike state AFDC payments). One interpretation that parental resources are correlated with aggression and crime of children where state AFDC payments are not correlated is that unobserved factors that lead to bad parental choices in the labor market are correlated with bad parental choices in child rearing.

It is worth drawing attention to a previous debate on cause of the rise in out-of-wedlock childbearing over the 1970s and 1980s. Three main hypotheses have been put forward: (a) the decline in the manufacturing sector that provided good jobs to low-skilled men, making low-skilled men less "marriageable" (Neckerman and Wilson 1987); (b) the rise in the welfare state and the "return" to single motherhood (Murray 1984); and (c) the spread of the pill and abortion and its equilibrium effect on out-of-wedlock sexual behavior (Akerlof, Yellen, and Katz 1996). All three of these events began in the mid-1960s and continued into the early 1970s, and the spread of the pill had little spatial variation. But an area's reliance on the manufacturing industry and state welfare policy have a good degree of variation. Careful work by Brien (1997) shows that the decline in the number of marriageable men did affect out-of-wedlock childbearing, but only a modest amount, and it does not explain the black-white difference in out-of-wedlock childbearing. And careful work by Moffitt (1990) suggests only a modest effect of increased welfare payments on out-of-wedlock childbearing. While the Akerlof, Yellen, and Katz model remains difficult to test, we have made progress in this debate by at least eliminating (a) and (b) as major causes. I suspect we may be in much the same situation in explaining the rise and fall in crime rates over the 1980s and 1990s.

In my view, the Caceres-Delpiano and Giolito (2011) paper is the most compelling to date to link family policy to crime, but it, as well as Donohue and Levitt (2001), fail in one important way—they do little to elucidate the mechanism. As they show, changes in divorce laws raised the rate of single-parent households and also changed a host of other circumstances for children including their access to resources and their level of human capital. In general, it remains difficult to separate the many factors that link childhood conditions and antisocial behavior, but some intervention studies (discussed in the following) are beginning to do this.

---

per month in 1989 dollars; AFDC-UP states had a benefit sum of over $700. Julio Caseres-Delpiano also supplied additional analysis of the fifteen-year lagged state AFDC maximum benefit level on property crime, violent crime, murder, rape, robbery, and aggravated assault. With the exception of property crime, which was small in magnitude and marginally significant, fifteen-year lagged ADFC was not statistically related to any criminal outcome (personal communication, December 27, 2009).

12.4   Evidence from Intervention Studies

There are now a number of intervention studies that look to see how various interventions affect antisocial behavior of children and adolescents and criminal outcomes as adolescents become adults. While there have been many programs implemented to curb antisocial behavior and young adult crime, there has been a shortage of rigorous evaluation of programs. In 2001, the surgeon general issued a report *Youth Violence: A Report of the Surgeon General* that suggested four criteria for what constitutes evidence of a model program (U.S. Department of Health and Human Services 2001). According to this report, a "model" program met the following criteria:

- Rigorous experimental design (experimental or quasi-experimental)
- Significant deterrent effects on:
  - Violence or serious delinquency
  - Any risk factor for violence with a large effect (.30 or greater)
- Replication with demonstrated effects
- Sustainability of effects

When looking across multiple interventions, only five programs met these criteria. These include (a) Functional Family Therapy (FFT); (b) Multidimensional Treatment Foster Care (MTFC); (c) Multisystemic Therapy (MST); (d) Seattle Social Development Project (SSDP); and (e) Prenatal and Infancy Home Visitation by Nurses, also known as the Nurse Family Partnership (NFP). What is particularly interesting about this list is that four of the five programs had a strong home-based family intervention component (all except SSDP). When the surgeon general reviewed programs that were "promising" but not conclusive or were shown not to work, many more of these programs did not have family intervention as a major component (including Perry Preschool and other school-based programs). The five programs varied in important ways, including the target population, the length of treatment, the intensity of treatment, and sample size. But these differences should be discussed in the context of all five programs having a component of parental training, especially parental management of difficult child behavior.

The largest study and the study that has received the most critical evaluation and replication is the NFP. The NFP was first implemented in 1977 and now serves 20,000 families in twenty states in the United States. Besides extensive research on the impacts of the NFP, there have also been excellent studies documenting its cost-effectiveness. In addition, President Obama has pledged that the highly successful NFP and similar home visiting programs will be expanded to reach all low-income, first-time mothers, and funding for expanding this program is included in the 2010 budget. Because intervention studies are reviewed in great detail in chapter 8 and its accompanying comment section, we discuss them here only as an example of the potential of family intervention. We do provide, however, the major elements of all five of these programs and their impacts on crime in table 12.2 so that a comparison to NFP may be made.

12.4.1   The Nurse Family Partnership

The NFP program's first evaluation began in Elmira, New York in 1977. The original study enrolled 400 mostly disadvantaged first-time mothers and their children; half were assigned to receive home visitation by nurses (HVN) and the rest assigned to a control group that receive transportation for prenatal and well-child care but no nurse visits. Elmira, New York was predominantly white, rural, and poor in 1977. The practical effect of recruiting first-time mothers from a poor area is that a large fraction (47 percent) were teenage mothers (age eighteen or below), and 62 percent were single parents. Visits began during pregnancy and continued until the child's second birthday. Olds et al. (1988) felt that each of these four elements was essential. Targeting *first-time parents* provided the best chance of promoting positive behavior in mothers before negative behaviors had become habituated; having the program *in the home* was essential because this is where most parenting occurs (and because it did not rely on parents to travel to a site); having *nurses* deliver the program was essential because mothers would trust them to know about pregnancy and the care of infants; and having *visits begin during pregnancy* would mitigate damaging effects in the prenatal environment and would build trust between mother and nurse, making mothers more receptive to parenting advice.[7]

Nurse visits had three goals: healthier prenatal care; more sensitive child care; and a better maternal life course. To help mothers, nurses helped women return to school, find work, and practice family planning. Nurses helped women improve their health-related behaviors, improve the quality of their infant care, and improve their personal development by setting achievable goals and to use problem-solving methods to gain control over the difficulties they encounter (Olds, Henderson, and Kitzman 1994). The NFP is a moderately intense intervention with about thirty visits of up to ninety minutes in length or forty-five hours over two and a half years.

The NFP experiment was repeated in Memphis in 1987 and Denver in 1994. Because the Elmira experimental positive results (discussed in the following) proved stronger for disadvantaged first-time mothers, the recruitment in these studies was limited to *disadvantaged* first-time mothers. Across studies, the NFP has been shown to be statistically significantly related to

---

7. This was tested in the 1994 Denver experimental implementation of the NFP. Here, both nurses and paraprofessionals delivered the NFP curriculum; Olds finds that nurse home visitors are more effective than paraprofessionals in delivering the NFP curriculum and that the positive effects of the program are larger with nurse home visits (Olds et al. 2004).

a host of positive outcomes for women and children. For example, by two years after the birth of their first child, Olds et al. (1986) and Kitzman et al. (2000) find the following:

- Among low-income unmarried teen mothers, the rate of child abuse or neglect was 4 percent for mothers receiving HNV; it was 19 percent in the control group (Elmira, New York).
- Women receiving HNV smoked 25 percent fewer cigarettes over the course of their pregnancy than the control group (Elmira, New York).
- Women receiving HNV had 23 percent fewer pregnancies, and when pregnancies occurred, there was longer spacing (Memphis, Tennessee; similar for Elmira, New York).
- Children whose mothers received HNV had 80 percent fewer days of hospitalization for injuries than the control group (Memphis, Tennessee).

A host of other positive outcomes have been observed in the two years following the mother's first birth, including higher rates of work and completing school for mothers and better language and executive functioning scores for children.

The central question for us is could the NFP prevent crime? Certainly the NFP lowers the factors that have been consistently shown to be correlated with crime, including family size, child abuse and neglect, and arrested neurological development due to in utero insults such as smoking. A 1997 study of mothers thirteen years after the Elmira intervention ended suggests that all of these benefits were sustained over time. In a 1998 study, Olds et al. (1998) follow up the children of the Elmira, New York sample when the child was fifteen years old. They find that children born to women who were unmarried and from households of low socioeconomic status (risk factors for antisocial behavior) and who received HNV reported that their adolescent child had fewer instances (incidence) of running away (0.24 versus 0.60; $P = .003$), fewer arrests (0.20 versus 0.45; $P = .03$), fewer convictions and violations of probation (0.09 versus 0.47; $P = .001$), fewer lifetime sex partners (0.92 versus 2.48; $P = .003$), fewer cigarettes smoked per day (1.50 versus 2.50; $P = .10$), and fewer days having consumed alcohol in the last six months (1.09 versus 2.49; $P = .03$). They also reported that their children had fewer behavioral problems related to use of alcohol and other drugs (0.15 versus 0.34; $P = .08$). Because of the high correlation between early onset of antisocial behavior and adult criminality, these results bode well for the chances of the NFP to reduce adult crime, but the analysis has not been done to date.

What is notable is the NFP benefits were not limited to the criminality. For example, in the NFP, at age fifteen, the children that received treatment had 0.92 sexual partners, on average; the children in the control group had

2.48 sexual partners, on average. That is, the NFP treatment reduced the number of sexual partners at age fifteen by 150 percent, a result that is highly statistically significant! Age fifteen is too early to know the effect on teenage childbearing, but an educated guess is that teenage childbearing will also be reduced.

In a recent working paper, Bartik (2009) estimates the average benefits of the NFP. He considers the reduced cost of emergency room visits; the savings for the child abuse and neglect system; the increased state and local tax payments of the mom due to increased employment and earnings; reduced welfare payments to the mom; decreased costs to the criminal justice system due to fewer arrests, less court time, and less jail and prison time, principally due to less criminal activity as the child ages; and state and local tax payments of the child due to increased employment and earnings when the child becomes an adult. Table 12.1 presents these estimates. What is clear is that the NFP potentially has great benefits to society. Of the benefits, the decreased cost to the criminal justice system for the children when they become adults comprises almost 40 percent of the total benefit. Bartik argues that given that the cost of each case is, on average, $8,000 to $10,000 (US$2007), it is likely that the NFP is a cost-effective program. He further argues that from a localities perspective, part of the costs are often paid by the Medicaid system, and additional federal funds will be available if President Obama's expansion of the NFP is funded. While this is true, Bartik warns:

> These NFP fiscal benefits are not immediate. Many of the most important fiscal benefits accrue over time, and may occur 5, 10, or more years after the NFP program begins delivering services in the prenatal period to a low-income first-time mother. However, the present value of these gross fiscal benefits does appear to significantly outweigh the costs of the program. How this affects state and local policy depends upon whether policymakers adopt a long-term perspective. (6)

While the program does appear cost-effective, it is important to recognize that the calculation of the cost savings through the criminal justice system is based on an important projection. There is empirical evidence on the NFP's effect on reduced arrests and jail time for the mother and on reduced arrests of the child up to age fifteen. The third and largest effect in this calculation, however, is the reduced arrest and jail time of NFP children in their adult years. Because this has not yet been observed, Bartik (2009) forecasts this based on the relationship between reduced arrests of the child prior to age fifteen on the odds of the child having an adult criminal career. However, a recent study follows the children of the NFP to age nineteen, linking in administrative arrest data from the criminal justice system. This study shows that while there is substantial evidence that criminal behavior of girls is significantly reduced, there is no impact on the arrest rate of boys at age

Table 12.1   Breakdown of present value of fiscal benefits from the Nurse Family
Partnership (NFP) program per NFP case

Category of fiscal benefit	Present value of fiscal benefits per case (2007$)
Reduced emergency room visits	156
Reduced child welfare system costs due to reduced child abuse and neglect	1,322
Increased state and local taxes from mom's added employment	1,898
Decrease in welfare system payments to mom	4,771
Decrease in criminal justice system costs (principally costs of child's adult criminal career)	5,894
Increased state and local taxes from increase in child's earnings as an adult	1,231
Total fiscal benefit	15,273

Source: From Bartik (2009). See Bartik (2009) for assumptions and methods.
Note: Dollar figures are rounded to nearest dollar. Present value is calculated using 3 percent real discount rate.

nineteen. It is unclear what this means over the life course, and it may be that as boys age, the positive impacts of the NFP will appear (as they have appeared for girls). But it will be some time before we know whether the size of the impact on crime used in Bartik's cost-benefit calculation will hold for the NFP children.

12.5 Conclusion

Overall, there are several lessons that we can draw from the literature linking the family to criminal outcomes. First, the evidence on the link between a woman being a teen mother and the subsequent criminal behavior of all of her children seems strong. These children are typically raised without two parents and no doubt in frustrating circumstances for their mothers. That increased ease of divorce increases the criminal behavior of children is also consistent with a link between family structure and crime. Interestingly, the NFP that directly intervenes to aid teenage mothers has shown effects at reducing criminal outcomes when their children become young adults, although it is not clear whether these effects will be sustained at older ages. Three other programs (in table 12.2), all with a major component of family therapy, show impacts of reducing crime or crime precursors among adolescents and young adults.

This chapter argues that developmental theory nicely ties together two lines of research that have to date preceded independently: crime in boys and childbearing in girls. From the perspective of developmental theory, these are simply two expressions of antisocial behavior where the domain of that behavior is sex-specific. Recognizing this possibility allows us to look at

Table 12.2   Five model youth antiviolence programs identified in surgeon general's report (2001)

	Nurse Family Partnership	Functional Family Therapy	Multidimensional Treatment Foster Care	Multisystemic Therapy	Seattle Social Development Project
Investigator/ organization	David L. Olds, University of Colorado	James F. Alexander, University of Utah	Patricia Chamberlain, Oregon Social Learning Center	Scott W. Hengeeler, Medical University of South Carolina	J. David Hawkins, University of Washington
Target population	First-time mothers (Elmira, NY); African American disadvantaged first-time mothers (Memphis, TN); disadvantaged first-time mothers (Denver, CO)	At-risk (often offending) youth 11–18 and their younger siblings	Adolescent youth with severe criminal behaviors	Violent and chronic juvenile offenders	1st graders and 5th graders, 18 public elementary schools (Seattle, WA)
Sample size	354, 189 NHV, and 165 C (Elmira, NY); 1139, 230 HNV (prenatal only), 228 HNV, 681 C (Memphis, TN); 735, 245 paraprofessional HV, 235 NHV, 255 C (Denver, CO)	40, 20T, 20C (1973 study); 86, 40 T, 46 C (1977 study); 750, 323 T, 427 C (2002 study)	79, 37 T, 42 C (1997 study)	84 (1992, study 5); 176 (1995, study 6); 155 (1997, study 7); 93 (2006, study 14)	643, 144 Full T, 256 Late T, 205 C
Method of recruitment/ assignment	Antepartum clinics	Random court referrals, random assignment	Random assignment from court referrals	Random assignment from court referrals	Nonrandom assignment by classroom
Length of treatment	6 months prenatal; 2 years postnatal; 45 hours	8–12 sessions over 3 months; up to 30 hours	Until restoration of parental custody (typically 3–6 months)	Approximately 4 months; approximately 50 hours	Teachers: 5 days of in-service training Parents: 4–7 sessions (voluntary, 53% of time fail to take up)
Place of treatment	In home	Conducted both in clinic settings as an outpatient therapy and as a home-based model	Foster care homes	Part in home, part in schools and community	Schools

Description of treatment	A nurse home visitor is assigned to the family and works with that family for the duration of the program. Nurses help parents address three areas: improvement of the mother's development; the care the parents provide their child; and the family's pregnancy planning, educational achievement, and participation in the workforce. Nurses provide a comprehensive educational program designed to help parents provide better care for their child. Nurses also help parents clarify goals, develop problem-solving skills, and develop support systems of family and friends who may be able to help them care for their child.	*Engagement phase:* alliance building, negativity reduction, blame reduction, developing shared family focus to present problem. *Behavioral change:* change skills of family members, increasing competency to perform tasks (e.g. communication, parental supervision, problem solving). *Generalization phase:* generalize, maintain, and support changes family has made. Focus turns from within family change to how family interacts with community (e.g., schools, extended family).	An individualized plan created by case manager and foster family that emphasizes behavioral management techniques and the foster home environment. The home environment to provide youth with structure, limits, and rules. Also behavioral skills training, such as interpersonal skills and prosocial behaviors, discipline techniques, role modeling, establishing rules and consequences for youth, eliminating exposure to negative peer influences, and providing youth with positive and productive relationships. Monitor and reward behavior and provide youth with daily feedback and structure.	Interventions improve caregiver discipline practices, enhance family affective relations, decrease youth association with deviant peers, increase youth association with prosocial peers, improve youth school or vocational performance, engage youth in prosocial recreational outlets, and develop an indigenous support network of extended family, neighbors, and friends to help caregivers achieve and maintain such changes. Family-based approach but also emphasizes social networks (removing child from deviant peers)	Teachers: proactive classroom management (e.g., consistent classroom expectations and routines, explicit instructions for behavior) interactive teaching (e.g., monitor student comprehension, reteach material when necessary), and cooperative learning (e.g., teams of students of different ability and background as learning partners). Parents: offered child behavior management skills and skills to reduce their children's risks for alcohol and drug use.
Length of follow-up	At age 15	Up to 5 years	1 year	Study 5: 5 years; study 6: 4 years, 13.7 years; study 7: 1.7 years; study 14: 1.5 years	At age 21
Effects on crime outcomes	At age 15: fewer arrests (0.20 vs. 0.45); fewer convictions and probation violations (0.09 vs. 0.47).	18 months after study: approximately 30% reduction in recidivism (2002 study); diffusion effects on siblings.	Boys had significantly fewer arrests, incarceration, were more likely to report no further arrests posttreatment. Boys reported significantly less criminal and delinquent behaviors.	Study 5: 43% decline in recidivism; study 6: 69% decline in recidivism (at 4 years), 54% decline in rearrest and 57% decline in days incarcerated (at 13.7 years); study 7: no significant decline in recidivism; study 14: 37% decline in rearrests.	No significant effects on arrests in last year or court charge in last year; significant 20% reduction in probability of every charged (0.53 C vs. 0.42 T).

Source: U.S. Department of Health and Human Services (2001).

the literature that links teen childbearing to criminal outcomes of the children in a new way—antisocial behavior may have a strong intergenerational correlation. And there are reasons to believe that this association may be hard to break because there is evidence that the combination of poverty and either immaturity or the personality traits of young mothers may limit their parenting ability, which may be a root cause of next generation's antisocial behavior. In the extreme, these factors have been linked to child abuse and neglect, but it is reasonable that less extreme forms of maltreatment could lead to negative outcomes as well.

Any policy designed to reduce the crime rate of boys that is targeted at the boy's family should start with an obvious fact—under the best of circumstances, raising children is difficult. When you layer on top of this financial strain that is emotionally taxing and self-control issues that many parents of these boys have either due to immaturity or personality traits that lead to early childbearing to begin with, you have a volatile mix that is not likely to lead to good parenting. To the degree that programs like NFP work, it may be because they address the central issue of helping young mothers learn to cope when parenting is difficult. While we do not yet know whether greater help with parent-child interaction skills could help, developmental theory would suggest that targeting mechanisms may help children.

While the intervention studies are encouraging, they remain small and have several limitations. The largest of the studies has less than 1,200 subjects and often multiple treatments are tried. By contrast, more than 20,000 adults and out-of-school youths who applied for the Job Training Partnership Act (JTPA) were randomly assigned to a "treatment group" or to a "control" group that was ineligible for JTPA-funded services. In addition, all family intervention evaluations were carried out in specific locations largely chosen for convenience (often close to the location of the PIs [Principal Investigator] University). Again, by contrast, the RCT for the JTPA trial was conducted in sixteen sites across the United States that were chosen in a systematic fashion. In general, consistent interviewing of study subjects as they develop is not conducted, making it difficult to understand the exact pathways through which these interventions work.

If, in fact, large-scale adoption of the NFP does occur as the Obama administration hopes, a research agenda that borrows from the experience of the JTPA is likely to be useful. We could make a great deal of progress if both experimental and nonexperimental data were collected on subjects. Nonexperimental data that follow very large samples that take up programs selectively can make an extremely valuable addition to RCTs, especially if pretreatment outcome factors are measured. Economists are exceptionally well positioned to help with analysis of both experimental as well as nonexperimental data and to help design creative evaluations that rely on variation that is other than random assignment. Economists may also be best positioned to conduct important cost-benefit and cost-effectiveness analysis, which is rudimentary to date.[8] But unlike job training, exceptionally well-developed models and years of work in other fields are already established in this area and far exceed the current thinking in economics. The challenge will be to integrate the considerable skills that economists can bring to this area and for economists to be open to models that are quite foreign to economists as a rule. These include serious models on the development of what economists label "preferences," an area that economists have been reluctant to tackle until recently. Tackling this issue is highly relevant for public policy but is equally relevant for theory, economic and otherwise.

While we cannot yet answer the ultimate policy question of whether resources should be shifted from imprisonment and policing to early childhood intervention, there are several questions we can answer that inform this ultimate question. Both experimental evidence from programs such as the NFP and nonexperimental evidence from changes in divorce laws suggest that improved parenting may reduce criminality in offspring. Second, in assessing whether such a switch in resources would be cost-effective, the link between teen childbearing in girls and crime in boys is essential—assessing the cost-effectiveness with respect to crime would miss all of the cost-savings that would come from reducing teenage childbearing. While several studies, including some of my own, suggest that teen childbearing per se has little long-term costs to women or society, this statement is conditional on women arriving at the teen years having experienced enormous cumulative disadvantage relative to women who avoid teen pregnancy.[9] Women who become pregnant as teens have had such cumulative disadvantage prior to pregnancy (including, on average, bad parenting themselves) that much of the damage to life changes has already been done. Programs that focus on family support and parenting are aimed at mitigating this cumulative disadvantage at least in part. These factors almost certainly could lead to better life outcomes. While this chapter focuses on early childhood investment on antisocial behavior, in a series of papers, James Heckman has argued that through what he terms "socialization," these types of investment are also likely to improve schooling and labor market outcomes.[10] It is these factors that early child intervention programs are targeting, and their potential promise lies in the wide array of important outcomes that they may improve.

8. For example, even the best cost-benefit analyses rely on calculating the discounted present value of costs and benefits for a cohort over a lifetime. An alternative way of thinking about the problem is that we are in an equilibrium that reflects our current high levels of crime in society. A universal and permanent implementation of a program would move society to a new lower equilibrium level of crime. In the new equilibrium, we would be expending resources on the young but gaining benefits from the old that had been previously treated (like in a social security system). The question then is how much does it cost annually to maintain this new equilibrium? This analysis would avoid tricky questions like the appropriate discount rate.

9. See Hotz, McElroy, and Sanders (2005) as one example.

10. See Heckman, Stixrud, and Urzua (2006) as one example.

References

Akerlof, George A., Janet Yellen, and Lawrence F. Katz. 1996. "An Analysis on Out-of-Wedlock Childbearing in the United States." *Quarterly Journal of Economics* 111 (2): 277–317.
Ananat, Elizabeth O., Jonathan Gruber, Phillip B. Levine, and Douglas Staiger. 2009. "Abortion and Selection." *Review of Economics and Statistics* 91 (1): 124–36.
Anderson, Elijah. 2000. *Code of the Street: Decency, Violence, and the Moral Life of the Inner City.* New York: Norton.
Bartik, Timothy J. 2009. "Estimated State and Local Fiscal Effects of the Nurse Family Partnership Program." Upjohn Institute Staff Working Paper no. 09-152. Kalamazoo, MI: W. E. Upjohn Institute for Employment Research.
Becker, Gary S. 2000. "Guess What? Welfare Reform Works." *Hoover Digest* 1. Stanford, CA: Hoover Institution, Stanford University. http://www.hoover.org/publications/hoover-digest/article/7205.
Bertrand, Marianne, Esther Duflo, and Sendhil Mullainathan. 2004. "How Much Should We Trust Differences-in-Differences Estimates?" *The Quarterly Journal of Economics* 119 (1): 249–75.
Brien, Micheal J. 1997. "Racial Differences in Marriage and the Role of Marriage Markets." *Journal of Human Resources* 32 (4): 741–78.
Caceres-Delpiano, Julio F., and Eugenio Giolito. 2011. The Impact of Unilateral Divorce on Crime. *Journal of Labor Economics,* forthcoming.
Donohue, John J. III, Jeffrey Grogger, and Steven D. Levitt. 2009. "The Impact of Legalized Abortion on Teen Childbearing." *American Law and Economics Review* 11 (1): 24–46.
Donohue, John J. III, and Steven D. Levitt. 2001. "The Impact of Legalized Abortion on Crime." *Quarterly Journal of Economics* 116 (2): 379–420.
Foote, Christopher L., and Christopher F. Goetz. 2005. "Testing Economic Hypotheses with State-Level Data: A Comment on Donohue and Levitt (2001)." Federal Reserve Bank of Boston Working Paper no. 05-15. Boston, MA: Federal Reserve Bank of Boston.
Freidberg, Leora. 1998. "Did Unilateral Divorce Raise Divorce Rates? Evidence from Panel Data." *American Economic Review* 88 (3): 608–27.
Gottfredson, Michael R., and Travis Hirschi. 1990. *A General Theory of Crime.* Stanford, CA: Stanford University Press.
Grogger, Jeffrey. 1997. "Incarceration-Related Costs of Early Childbearing." In *Kids Having Kids: Economic Costs and Social Consequences of Teen Pregnancy,* edited by Rebecca A. Maynard, 231–56. Washington, DC: Urban Institute Press.
Gruber, Jonathan. 2001. *Risky Behavior among Youths: An Economic Analysis.* Chicago: University of Chicago Press.
Heckman, James J., Jora Stixrud, and Sergio Urzua. 2006. "The Effects of Cognitive and Noncognitive Abilities on Labor Market Outcomes and Social Behavior." *Journal of Labor Economics* 24 (3): 411–82.
Hotz, V. Joseph, Susan McElroy, and Seth Sanders. 2005. "Teenage Childbearing and Its Life Cycle Consequences: Exploiting a Natural Experiment." *Journal of Human Resources* 40 (3): 683–715.
Jonson-Reid, Melissa, Ned Presnall, Brett Drake, Louis Fox, Laura Bierut, Wendy Reich, Phyllis Kane, Richard D. Todd, and John N. Constantino. 2010. "Effects of Child Maltreatment and Inherited Liability on Antisocial Development: An Official Records Study." *Journal of the American Academy of Child and Adolescent Psychiatry* 49 (4): 321–32.

Joyce, Ted. 2004. "Did Legalized Abortion Lower Crime?" *Journal of Human Resources* 39 (1): 1–28.

———. 2009. "A Simple Test of Abortion and Crime." *Review of Economics and Statistics* 91 (1): 112–23.

Kitzman, Harriet, David L. Olds, Kimberly Sidora, Charles R. Henderson Jr., Carole Hanks, Robert Cole, Dennis W. Luckey, Jessica Bondy, Kimberly Cole, and Judith Glazner. 2000. "Enduring Effects of Nurse Home Visitation on Maternal Life Course: A 3-Year Follow-up of a Randomized Trial." *Journal of the American Medical Association* 283 (15): 1983–89.

Lee, Bong, and Robert George. 1999. "Poverty, Early Childbearing, and Child Maltreatment: A Multinomial Analysis." *Child and Youth Service Review* 21 (9/10): 755–80.

Loeber, R., and M. Stouthamer-Loeber. 1986. "Family Factors As Correlates and Predictors of Juvenile Conduct Problems and Delinquency." In *Crime and Justice: An Annual Review of Research*, vol. 7, edited N. Morris and M. Tonry, 29–149. Chicago: University of Chicago Press.

Manlove, Jennifer. 1997. "Early Motherhood in an Intergenerational Perspective: The Experiences of a British Cohort." *Journal of Marriage and Family* 59 (2): 263–79.

Moffitt, Robert. 1990. "The Effect of the U.S. Welfare System on Marital Status." *Journal of Public Economics* 41 (1): 101–24.

Moffitt, Terrie E. 1993. "Adolescence-Limited and Life-Course-Persistent Antisocial Behavior: A Developmental Taxonomy." *Psychological Review* 100 (4): 674–701.

Murray, Charles. 1984. *Losing Ground: American Social Policy, 1950–1980.* New York: Basic Books.

Nagin, Daniel S., Greg Pogarsky, and David P. Farrington. 1997. "Adolescent Mothers and the Criminal Behavior of Their Children." *Law and Society Review* 31 (1): 137–62.

Neckerman, Kathryn, and William J. Wilson. 1987. "Poverty and Family Structure: The Widening Gap between Evidence and Public Policy Issues." In *The Truly Disadvantaged: The Inner City, the Underclass, and Public Policy,* edited by William J. Wilson, 63–92. Chicago: University of Chicago Press.

Olds, David L., Charles R. Henderson Jr., R. Chamberlin, and R. Tatelbaum. 1986. "Preventing Child Abuse and Neglect: A Randomized Trial of Nurse Home Visitation." *Pediatrics* 78 (1): 65–78.

Olds, David L., Charles R. Henderson Jr., Robert Cole, John Eckenrode, Harriet Kitzman, Dennis Luckey, Lisa Pettitt, Kimberly Sidora, Pamela Morris, and Jane Powers. 1998. "Long-Term Effects of Nurse Home Visitation on Children's Criminal and Antisocial Behavior: Fifteen-Year Follow-Up of a Randomized Controlled Trial." *Journal of the American Medical Association* 280 (14): 1238–44.

Olds, David L., Charles R. Henderson, and Harriet Kitzman. 1994. "Does Prenatal and Infancy Nurse Home Visitation Have Enduring Effects on Qualities of Parental Caregiving and Child Health at 25 to 50 Months of Life?" *Pediatrics* 93 (1): 89–98.

Olds, David L., JoAnn Robinson, Lisa Pettitt, Dennis W. Luckey, John Holmberg, Rosanna K. Ng, Kathy Isacks, Karen Sheff, and Charles R. Henderson Jr. 2004. "Effects of Home Visits by Paraprofessionals and by Nurses: Age 4 Follow-up: Results of a Randomized Trial." *Pediatrics* 114:1560–68.

Parker, Karen F., and Amy Reckdenwald. 2008. "Concentrated Disadvantage, Traditional Male Role Models, and African-American Juvenile Violence." *Criminology* 46 (3): 711–35.

Pogarsky, Greg, Alan J. Lizotte, and Terence P. Thornberry. 2003. "The Delinquency of Children Born to Young Mothers: Results from the Rochester Youth Development Study." *Criminology* 41 (4): 1249–86.

Rebellon, Cesar J. 2002. "Reconsidering the Broken Homes/Delinquency Relationship and Exploring Its Mediating Mechanism(s)." *Criminology* 40 (1): 103–36.

U.S. Department of Health and Human Services. 2001. *Youth Violence: A Report of the Surgeon General.* Washington, DC: U.S. Department of Health and Human Services.

Wolfers, Justin. 2006. "Did Unilateral Divorce Laws Raise Divorce Rates? A Reconciliation and New Results." *American Economic Review* 96 (5): 1802–20.

Comment   Terrie E. Moffitt and Stephen A. Ross

Seth Sander's chapter concludes that policymakers are considering large-scale early-childhood education programs to promote children's self-control skills, with the aim of reducing the crime rate and improving citizens' health and wealth as well. Experiments and economic models suggest such programs could reap benefits. Yet evidence is needed that self-control is truly important for the health, wealth, and public safety of the population. By following a cohort of 1,000 children from birth to age thirty-two, we show here that childhood self-control predicts physical health, substance dependence, personal finances, and criminal offending outcomes, following a gradient of self-control. In another cohort of 500 sibling pairs, the sibling with lowest self-control had poorest outcomes, despite both siblings sharing their family background.

Economists, including the authors of chapters in this book, are drawing attention to individual differences in self-control as a key consideration for policymakers who seek to enhance the physical and financial health of the population and reduce the crime rate (Heckman 2007). The current emphasis on self-control skills of conscientiousness, self-discipline, and perseverance arises from the empirical observation that preschool programs that targeted poor children fifty years ago, although failing to achieve their stated goal of lasting improvement in children's intelligence quotient (IQ) scores, somehow produced by-product reductions in teen pregnancy, school

Terrie E. Moffitt is the Knut Schmidt Nielsen Professor in the departments of Psychology and Neuroscience, and Psychiatry and Behavioral sciences, and the Institute for Genome Sciences and Policy at Duke University, and is professor in the Social, Genetic and Developmental Psychiatry Centre at the Institute of Psychiatry, King's College London. Stephen A. Ross is a science assistant at the National Science Foundation.

This research received support from the U.S. National Institute for Aging (NIA; AG032282), the National Institute of Mental Health (NMIH; MH077874), the National Institute of Child Health and Development (NICHD; HD061298), the National Institute of Dental and Craniofacial Research (NICDR; DE015260), the National Institute of Drug Abuse (NIDA; DA023026), the U.K. Medical Research Council (MRC; G0100527, G0601483) and Economic and Social Research Council (ESRC; RES-177-25-0013), and the New Zealand Health Research Council.

dropout, delinquency, and work absenteeism (Carneiro and Heckman 2003; Doyle et al. 2009; Heckman 2006).

The Dunedin Study Design

In the context of this timely, ubiquitous and intense policy interest in self-control, we summarize findings from the Dunedin longitudinal study of a complete birth cohort of 1,037 children born in one city in one year, who we have followed from birth to age thirty-two years with minimal attrition. Our study design is observational and correlational; this is in contrast to experimental behavioral-economics experiments that yield compelling information about the consequences of low self-control. However, some economists have cautioned that "behavior in the lab might be a poor guide to real-world behavior" (Levitt and List 2008). The naturalistic Dunedin Study complements experimental research on self-control by providing badly needed information about how well children's self-control, as it is distributed in the population, predicts real-world outcomes after children reach adulthood. The Dunedin Study's birth-cohort members with low self-control and poor outcomes have not dropped out of the study (96 percent retention). This enabled us to study the full range of self-control and to estimate effect sizes of associations for the general population, information that is requisite for informed policy making (Moffitt et al. 2011).

We assessed the children's self-control during their first decade of life. Reports by parents, teachers, researcher-observers, and the children themselves gathered across ages three, five, seven, nine, and eleven years were combined into a single highly reliable composite measure. Mean levels of self-control were higher among girls than boys, but the health, wealth, and public-safety implications of childhood self-control were equally evident and similar among both males and females. Dunedin children with greater self-control were more likely to have been brought up in socioeconomically advantaged families and had higher IQs; we thus tested whether childhood self-control influenced adults' health, wealth, and crime independently of their social-class origins and IQ.

Predicting Crime

We obtained records of study members' court convictions at all courts in New Zealand and Australia by searching the central computer systems of the New Zealand police; 24 percent of the study members had been convicted of a crime by age thirty-two. Children with poor self-control were significantly more likely to be convicted of a criminal offense, even after accounting for social-class origins and IQ.

Predicting Health

When the children reached age thirty-two years, we assessed their cardiovascular, respiratory, dental, and sexual health, as well as their immune functioning by carrying out physical examinations to assess the metabolic syndrome, airflow limitation, periodontal disease, sexually-transmitted infection, and inflammation status, respectively. We summed these five clinical measures into a simple physical health index for each study member; 43 percent of study members had none of the biomarkers, 37 percent had one, and 20 percent had two or more. Childhood self-control predicted adult health problems, even after accounting for social-class origins and IQ.

Predicting Substance Dependence

We also conducted clinical interviews with the study members at age thirty-two to assess substance dependence (tobacco, alcohol, and cannabis dependence, as well as dependence on other street and prescription drugs), following *Diagnostic and Statistical Manual of Mental Disorders* 4th edition (*DSM-IV*) criteria (American Psychiatric Association 1994). As adults, children with poor self-control had elevated risk of substance dependence, even after accounting for social class and IQ. This longitudinal link between self-control and substance dependence was verified by people study members had nominated as informants who knew them well: as adults, children with poor self-control were rated by their informants as having alcohol and drug problems.

Predicting Wealth

Childhood self-control foreshadowed the study members' socioeconomic status and income in adulthood. At age thirty-two, children with poor self-control were also less financially planful. Compared to other thirty-two-year-olds, they were less likely to save money, and they had acquired fewer financial building blocks for the future (such as home ownership, investment funds, or retirement plans). Children with poor self-control reported more money-management difficulties and had accumulated more credit problems. This longitudinal link between self-control and adult financial problems was verified by informants who knew them well: as adults, children with poor self-control were rated by their informants as poor money managers. Poor self-control in childhood was a stronger predictor of these financial difficulties than study members' social-class origins and IQ.

Sibling Comparisons

Policymaking requires evidence that isolates self-control as the active ingredient affecting health, wealth, and crime, as opposed to other influences on children's futures. In the Dunedin Study, statistical controls revealed that self-control had its own associations with outcomes, apart from childhood social class and IQ. However, each Dunedin Study member grew up in a different family, and their families varied widely on many features that affect children's adult outcomes. A compelling quasi-experimental research design that can isolate the influence of self-control is to track and compare siblings.

To apply this design, we turned to a second sample, the Environmental-Risk Longitudinal Twin Study (E-risk), where we have been tracking a birth cohort of British twins since their birth in 1994 to 1995 with 96 percent retention. When the E-Risk twins were five years old, research staff rated each child on the same observational measure of self-control originally used with Dunedin children as preschoolers. Although the E-risk children have been followed only up to age twelve years, their self-control already forecast many of the adult outcomes we saw in the Dunedin Study. We applied sibling fixed effects models to the 504 same-sex dizygotic pairs because they are no more alike than ordinary siblings (with the added advantages of being the same age and sex). Models showed that the five-year-old sibling with poorer self-control, as compared to his or her sibling with better self-control, was significantly more likely as a twelve-year-old to begin smoking (a precursor of adult poor health), perform poorly in school (a precursor of adult wealth accumulation), and engage in antisocial conduct problems (a precursor of adult crime).

Comment

For all of these associations, we observed a self-control gradient in which boys and girls with less self-control had less health, less wealth, and more crime as adults than those with more self-control at every level of the distribution of self-control. Effects were marked at the extremes of the self-control gradient. For example, by adulthood, the highest and lowest fifths of the population on measured childhood self-control had respective rates of multiple health problems of 11 percent versus 27 percent; rates of polysubstance dependence of 3 percent versus 10 percent; rates of employment in low-status jobs of 24 percent versus 46 percent, and crime conviction rates of 13 percent versus 43 percent. Our findings were consistent with a universal approach to early intervention to enhance self-control at all levels. The observed gradient implies room for better outcomes even among the segment of the population whose childhood self-control skills were somewhat above average. Programs to enhance children's self-control have been developed and positively evaluated, and the challenge remains to improve them and scale them up for universal dissemination (Greenberg 2006; Layard and Dunn 2009; National Scientific Council on the Developing Child 2007). Innovative policies addressing self-control might reduce a panoply of societal costs, improve public safety, save taxpayers money, and promote prosperity.

References

American Psychiatric Association. 1994. *Diagnostic and Statistical Manual of Mental Disorders.* 4th ed. Washington, DC: American Psychiatric Association.
Carneiro, P., and J. J. Heckman. 2003. "Human Capital Policy." In *Inequality in*

America: What Role for Human Capital Policy?, edited by J. J. Heckman and A. Krueger, 77–240. Cambridge, MA: MIT Press.

Doyle, O., C. P. Harmon, J. J. Heckman, and R. E. Tremblay. 2009. "Investing in Early Human Development: Timing and Economic Efficiency." *Economics and Human Biology* 7 (1): 1–6.

Greenberg, M. T. 2006. "Promoting Resilience in Children and Youth: Preventive Interventions and Their Interface with Neuroscience." *Annals of the New York Academy of Sciences* 1094:139–50.

Heckman, J. J. 2006. "Skill Formation and the Economics of Investing in Disadvantaged Children." *Science* 312 (5782): 1900–1902.

———. 2007. "The Economics, Technology, and Neuroscience of Human Capability Formation." *Proceedings of the National Academy of Sciences* 104 (33): 13250–5.

Layard, R., and J. Dunn. 2009. *A Good Childhood: Searching for Values in a Competitive Age.* London: Penguin.

Levitt, S. D., and J. A. List. 2008. "*Homo economicus* Evolves." *Science* 319 (5865): 909–10.

Moffitt, T. E., L. Arseneault, D. Belsky, N. Dickson, R. J. Hancox, H. L. Harrington, R. Houts, et al. 2011. "A Gradient of Childhood Self-Control Predicts Health, Wealth, and Public Safety." *Proceedings of the National Academy of Sciences,* forthcoming. Available online at www.pnas.org.

National Scientific Council on the Developing Child. 2007. *The Science of Early Childhood Development.* http://www.developingchild.net.

Contributors

Christopher Carpenter
The Paul Merage School of Business
University of California, Irvine
Irvine, CA 92697-3125

Jonathan P. Caulkins
Heinz College
Carnegie Mellon University
5000 Forbes Avenue
Pittsburgh, PA 15213-3890

Philip J. Cook
Sanford School of Public Policy
Duke University
Durham, NC 27708-0245

Carlos Dobkin
Department of Economics
University of California, Santa Cruz
1156 High Street
Santa Cruz, CA 95064

Kenneth A. Dodge
Sanford School of Public Policy
Duke University
Durham, NC 27708

John J. Donohue III
Stanford Law School
Crown Quadrangle
559 Nathan Abbott Way
Stanford, CA 94305

Steven N. Durlauf
Department of Economics
University of Wisconsin
1180 Observatory Drive
Madison, WI 53706-1393

Benjamin Ewing
Yale Law School
127 Wall Street
New Haven, CT 06511

Richard G. Frank
Department of Health Care Policy
Harvard Medical School
180 Longwood Avenue
Boston, MA 02115

Jeffrey T. Grogger
Harris School of Public Policy
University of Chicago
1155 East 60th Street
Chicago, IL 60637

Jonathan Guryan
Institute for Policy Research
Northwestern University
2040 Sheridan Road
Evanston, IL 60208

Sara B. Heller
Harris School of Public Policy
University of Chicago
1155 East 60th Street
Chicago, IL 60637

Patrick L. Hill
Department of Psychology
University of Illinois, Urbana-
    Champaign
603 East Daniel Street
Champaign, IL 61820

Brian A. Jacob
Gerald R. Ford School of Public
    Policy
University of Michigan
735 South State Street
Ann Arbor, MI 48109

Ilyana Kuziemko
361 Wallace Hall
Princeton University
Princeton, NJ 08544

Lance Lochner
Department of Economics
University of Western Ontario
1151 Richmond Street, North
London, Ontario N6A 5C2 Canada

Jens Ludwig
Harris School of Public Policy
University of Chicago
1155 East 60th Street
Chicago, IL 60637

Robert J. MacCoun
Richard and Rhoda Goldman School
    of Public Policy
University of California, Berkeley
2607 Hearst Avenue
Berkeley, CA 94720-7320

John MacDonald
Department of Criminology
University of Pennsylvania
483 McNeil Building
3718 Locust Walk
Philadelphia, PA 19104-6286

Justin McCrary
School of Law
University of California, Berkeley
329 North Addition, Boalt Hall
Berkeley, CA 94720-7200

Thomas G. McGuire
Department of Health Care Policy
Harvard Medical School
180 Longwood Avenue
Boston, MA 02115

Terrie E. Moffitt
Department of Psychology and
    Neuroscience
Duke University
Box 104410
Durham, NC 27707

Daniel S. Nagin
H. John Heinz III College
Carnegie Mellon University
5000 Forbes Avenue
Pittsburgh, PA 15213-3890

David Peloquin
Yale Law School
127 Wall Street
New Haven, CT 06511

Anne Morrison Piehl
Department of Economics
Rutgers, The State University of
    New Jersey
75 Hamilton Street
New Brunswick, NJ 08901-1248

Harold Pollack
School of Social Service
    Administration
University of Chicago
969 East 60th Street
Chicago, IL 60637

Steven Raphael
Goldman School of Public Policy
University of California, Berkeley
2607 Hearst Avenue
Berkeley, CA 94720-7320

Peter Reuter
School of Public Policy
University of Maryland
College Park, MD 20742

Brent W. Roberts
Department of Psychology
University of Illinois, Urbana-
    Champaign
603 East Daniel Street
Champaign, IL 61820

Stephen A. Ross
National Science Foundation
4201 Wilson Boulevard
Arlington, VA 22230

Seth G. Sanders
Department of Economics
Campus Box 90097
Duke University
Durham, NC 27708

Eric Sevigny
Department of Criminology and
    Criminal Justice
University of South Carolina
1305 Greene Street
Columbia, SC 29208

Karen Sixkiller
Department of Psychology
University of Illinois, Urbana-
    Champaign
603 East Daniel Street
Champaign, IL 61820

David Alan Sklansky
School of Law
University of California, Berkeley
Berkeley, CA 94720-7200

Jeffrey Smith
Department of Economics
University of Michigan
611 Tappan Street
Ann Arbor, MI 48109-1220

Jeffrey Swanson
Department of Psychiatry and
    Behavioral Sciences
Duke University School of Medicine
Box 3071, Medical Center
Durham, NC 27710

Geoffrey Williams
Department of Economics
Rutgers, The State University of
    New Jersey
New Jersey Hall
75 Hamilton Street
New Brunswick, NJ 08901-1248

Author Index

Subject Index

Page numbers followed by "f" or "t" refer to figures or tables, respectively.